WORLD MOUNTAIN RANGES

THE PYRENEES

The High Pyrenees from the Cirque de Lescun to the Carlit Massif

by
Kev Reynolds

Morning sun on the north face of the Vignemale

WORLD MOUNTAIN RANGES

THE PYRENEES

The High Pyrenees from the Cirque de Lescun to the Carlit Massif

by
Kev Reynolds

2 POLICE SQUARE, MILNTHORPE, CUMBRIA, LA7 7PY
www.cicerone.co.uk

This book is dedicated to Jean and Pierre Ravier –
at the forefront of *Pyrénéisme* for over half a century –
in gratitude for their inspiration.

ACKNOWLEDGEMENTS

Sincere thanks to all Pyrenean enthusiasts at home and abroad who have kept me supplied with information on every aspect of these mountains; to those with whom I've shared a rope, trail or unmarked pass – especially Michael Adams, Nigel Fry, Alan Payne, Peter Smith, Keith Sweeting, Hugh Walton and my wife and daughters; to Rosemary Durose for numerous translations; and to Jonathan Williams at Cicerone for his patient understanding as deadlines have been missed whilst working on this guide. I am also indebted to my editor Hazel Clarke, to Vickie Hunter for her work on the layout, and to Barbara Linton, who drew the maps. All have added much to this guide. My thanks, too, to the staff at the Association Randonnées Pyrénéennes in Tarbes. But most of all I wish to acknowledge the decades of advice and encouragement received from Jean and Pierre Ravier of Bordeaux, whose knowledge and love of the Pyrenees is all-embracing and so willingly shared.

Kev Reynolds

OTHER CICERONE BOOKS BY KEV REYNOLDS

100 Hut Walks in the Alps

Alpine Pass Route

Alpine Points of View

Annapurna – a Trekker's Guide

Central Switzerland – a Walking Guide

Chamonix to Zermatt – the Walker's Haute Route

Écrins National Park

Everest – a Trekker's Guide

Kangchenjunga – a Trekker's Guide

Langtang, Helambu and Gosainkund – a Trekker's Guide

Manaslu – a Trekker's Guide

The Bernese Alps

The Cotswold Way

The Jura *(with R Brian Evans)*

The North Downs Way

The South Downs Way

The Wealdway and Vanguard Way

Tour of Mont Blanc

Tour of the Jungfrau Region

Tour of the Oisans

Tour of the Vanoise

Walking in Austria

Walking in Kent, vols. 1 and 2

Walking in Sussex

Walking in the Alps

Walking in the Valais

Walking in Ticino

Walks and Climbs in the Pyrenees

Walks in the Engadine

The lowest and largest of the Pessons Lakes

ISBN-13: 978 1 85284 420 2
ISBN-10: 1 85284 420 5
Reprinted 2010 (with updates)
A catalogue record for this book is available from the British Library.

Printed by KHL Printing, Singapore

Advice to Readers

Readers are advised that, while every effort is made by our authors to ensure the accuracy of guidebooks as they go to print, changes can occur during the lifetime of an edition. Please check Updates on this book's page on the Cicerone website (**www.cicerone.co.uk**) before planning your trip. We would also advise that you check information about such things as transport, accommodation and shops locally. Even rights of way can be altered over time. We are always grateful for information about any discrepancies between a guidebook and the facts on the ground, sent by email to info@cicerone.co.uk or by post to Cicerone, 2 Police Square, Milnthorpe LA7 7PY, United Kingdom.

Warning

Mountain walking can be a dangerous activity carrying a risk of personal injury or death. It should be undertaken only by those with a full understanding of the risks and with the training and experience to evaluate them. While every care and effort has been taken in the preparation of this guide, the user should be aware that conditions can be highly variable and can change quickly, materially affecting the seriousness of a mountain walk. Therefore, except for any liability which cannot be excluded by law, neither Cicerone nor the author accept liability for damage of any nature (including damage to property, personal injury or death) arising directly or indirectly from the information in this book.

To call out the Mountain Rescue, ring the international emergency number 112: this will connect you via any available network. Once connected to the emergency operator, ask for the police.

Front cover: Pic du Midi d'Ossau from the Lacs d'Ayous

CONTENTS

The Cirque de Barroude

Map Key

	ridge
	glacier
⌂	refuge
	road
■	habitation
	col/pass
▲	summit
	forest/woodland
	lake/tarn
	minor road
	national boundary
	railway
	national park boundary
	river
	tunnel
*	waterfall

Symbols Key

★ highlights walks Ⓒ climbs summits for all

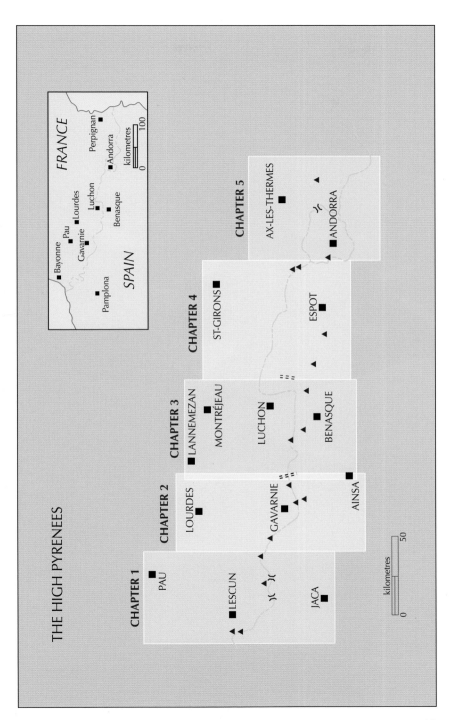

THE HIGH PYRENEES

CHAPTER 1
PAU
LESCUN
JACA

CHAPTER 2
LOURDES
GAVARNIE
AINSA

CHAPTER 3
LANNEMEZAN
MONTRÉJEAU
LUCHON
BENASQUE

CHAPTER 4
ST-GIRONS
ESPOT

CHAPTER 5
AX-LES-THERMES
ANDORRA

SUMMARY MAP

FRANCE
Bayonne
Pau
Gavarnie
Lourdes
Luchon
Benasque
Perpignan
Andorra
Pamplona
SPAIN
kilometres
0   100

kilometres
0   50

11

Pic Carlit rises above Étang de Lanoux

INTRODUCTION

The principal charm of the Pyrenees consists in the unrivalled scenery.
Charles Packe (1826–1896)

Between the Atlantic shores of the Côte Basque and the Mediterranean at Cape Cerbère, the Pyrenees form a natural frontier between France and Spain, throughout which walkers, trekkers and climbers have almost unlimited opportunities to exercise their sport among landscapes as diverse and appealing as any to be found in Europe.

This 400km-long range consists of lush meadows and glaciers, limestone pavements, rugged granite peaks and deep canyons, dense forests, turbulent rivers born among spectacular waterfalls, and hundreds upon hundreds of mountain lakes. And since the mountains form a geographical, as well as a political, divide, contrasts between the northern French slopes and those of the south are extreme. Crossing from one side to the other is not only to enter a new country, it is to exchange landform, vegetation and even climate. The terrain may be full of variety, but so too are the people who live there, a diverse population in terms of background, dialect and culture, with those living at extreme ends of the range being united only by a common disregard for political boundaries.

Comparison with other ranges is tempting but unwise; the mountains and valleys of the Pyrenees are uniquely Pyrenean. This uniqueness is perhaps best expressed in the way in which one can so easily experience a sense of remoteness and appreciate real solitude, if sought. The range has its tourist hot-spots, of course. There are popular valleys, notorious climbs, famed viewpoints. But the Pyrenees also have more than their fair share of secluded glens, remote and rarely trod peaks and corners of true wilderness. Some of the once pristine hidden places have been sacrificed to the hydro-engineer, but as yet comparatively little has been destroyed to make way for the bulldozed pistes and mechanical paraphernalia of the downhill ski industry. Anyone who wants to get away from it all can do so here with ease, and the wild camping is second to none.

With one or two misplaced spurs edging away from the main ridge crest to confuse its alignment, the Pyrenean chain runs almost unbroken from the Mediterranean Sea to Atlantic Ocean. Near the centre of the range a distortion occurs where the anomalous Vall d'Aran breaks this continuity with an overlap bridged by the 2070m Port de la Bonaigua. With a few notable exceptions the international frontier follows the watershed, but Vall d'Aran, though draining into France, has for centuries enjoyed Spanish sovereignty despite the fact that until the Viella road tunnel opened after the war, it was virtually inaccessible from Spain in winter.

Dawn light on Gavarnie, viewed from the edge of the Ossoue glacier

The mountains fall abruptly on the northern flank where the range is only 30–40km deep, while the southern side is much broader, presenting a rumpled landscape of ridges and strange, part-arid sierras folding one after another down to the Ebro basin. Glaciers are shrinking fast. Once the range was covered with ice, and glaciers pushed north as far as present-day Lourdes and Montréjeau, but there's only the Ossoue glacier on the Vignemale and a few smaller cirque glaciers left today, and these total less than 10km². But in the wake of this glacial recession lie more than a thousand glistening tarns in the High Pyrenees alone.

As for mountains, there are more than 270 summits above 3000m, many of which can be reached without need for much more than basic scrambling ability. However, there's no shortage of technical climbing routes among the highest grades too, as well as a variety of traditional mountaineering routes and plenty of scope for icefall climbing in winter.

Wildlife is abundant, yet many species remain elusive to all but the most dedicated of naturalists. Wild boar, deer, pine marten, wild cats and a few survivors of the European brown bear population restrict themselves largely to the forests and broadleaved woodlands. On the other hand isard – the native Pyrenean chamois – and marmot are both on the increase; the former, being as shy as its alpine cousin, is found in the more remote mountain heartlands, while the latter makes its presence known in practically every valley of the Central Pyrenees. Mouflon have been reintroduced, but the ibex is said now to have completely disappeared. The fire salamander, with its black and yellow patches, various lizards and the curious aquatic rodent known as the desman have their own specific habitats, while birds of prey are seen riding the thermals almost everywhere – including Europe's largest, the lammergeier, or bearded vulture.

Plantlife is incredibly rich, and it is not only the dedicated botanist but all who appreciate mountain flowers who will find the Pyrenees especially rewarding, for the range is known with some justification as the Flower Garden of Europe, with around 160 endemic species. While the range and diversity of species is largely associated with altitude and different climatic influences, four distinct groups of plants have a fairly wide distribution here: those of northwest Europe; others with a Mediterranean identity; typical alpine species; and those that have been marooned in the Pyrenees since the last Ice Age. Some, such as the Ramonda myconi, can be traced back to an era when the climate was subtropical.

There are three national parks – one in France, two in Spain – and several nature reserves. Not surprisingly they have their honeypot sites, but since these tend to concentrate the majority of visitors, that still leaves plenty of room for wildness, if not real wilderness, elsewhere. Although the parks have been created to protect some of the most dramatic or vulnerable locations, not all of the finest peaks and valleys are contained within their boundaries, and many truly spectacular features are located well beyond them.

ABOUT THIS BOOK

This book is an essential resource for the active walker, trekker and climber. It is packed with information on the wealth of opportunities that exist among some of Europe's finest mountains, and aims to enable the reader to make the most of those opportunities.

It serves as a guide to the best the region has to offer the outdoor enthusiast, and is intended to provide all the background information required when planning a trip there. Questions such as 'Where to walk?', 'What long treks are there?', 'Where and what to climb?' and 'What facilities exist for the skier in winter?' are all addressed. The focus is on activity, on creating a quality experience for those who are drawn to a wild and challenging landscape that just happens to be one of the finest in Europe.

The guide covers the High Pyrenees from the Cirque de Lescun on the edge of the Basque country in the west to the Carlit massif and flat-bottomed Cerdagne east of Andorra, and is divided into five regional chapters: the Western Valleys; Cirques and Canyons; the Central Pyrenees; Enchanted Mountains; and Andorra and the Eastern High Pyrenees. Although the main Pyrenean crest carries the frontier between France and Spain, the regional chapters cover both sides of the range, with sections following lines of communication between the foothills and the highest peaks, and crossing from one country to the other by accessible routes. Each of these chapters comprises sections devoted to individual valleys or groups of valleys which, together with their walling mountains, provide a comprehensive picture of the central and highest sections of this magnificent range.

Each chapter travels eastward describing the area valley by valley, as well as giving suggestions about suitable villages from which to make forays into the mountains and refuge details for climbers and trekkers 'living high'. At the start of each chapter is a list of the valleys described in that chapter, together with a note of specific highlights. There is a summary box at the end of each chapter with information on access and accommodation, as well as recommended topographical maps and guidebooks (where they exist) for the valleys and their summits.

Within each valley section the reader is directed to the finest walks, treks and climbs among the mountains under scrutiny. These are identified in the text by three symbols that distinguish walks ⬤, climbs ⓑ and summits accessible to all ⊗. In addition, the particular highlights of the area are indicated by a star symbol ★. Unlike a conventional walking book, detailed route descriptions are not included here; the guide does, however, provide an outline of specially selected routes, with a rough indication of the time such routes should take and of their severity, where applicable.

An extensive introduction to the guide gives all the practical advice and information you will need before leaving home. It tells you how to get to your destination, and what to expect once you get there. It offers a background to the mountains and their exploration, and provides a snapshot of the range with sections that help you focus on specific areas of activity, and suggests where best to exercise that activity. It also lists for the first time in an English-language guide all the Pyrenean 3000m summits and their location.

East of Pic Carlit lies a bewildering complex of tarns and pools

*The gentle
Bious valley makes
a partial moat round
Pic du
Midi d'Ossau*

The object of this book, then, is to inspire, entertain and inform, and to show those who have yet to make their first visit what a magical range of mountains this is. But since the Pyrenean environment is a fragile one, all who are tempted to go there should treat it with the respect and understanding that is its due, so that future generations will also be able to enjoy that which we treasure today.

Practicalities

WHEN TO GO

The independent traveller can visit the Pyrenees at any time of year, but the provision of services, and the level of activity possible upon arrival, will largely be dependent on factors such as public holidays, weather conditions, etc. Although walking, trekking, climbing and ski mountaineering can all be practised to some degree without reliance on external support, there are obvious closed seasons which affect the variety and availability of accommodation (hotels, *gîtes*, refuges and campsites). Most huts and *gîtes d'étape*, for example, are manned only from late May or June to late September, and at either end of this period some may be partially, or even completely, closed except at weekends, unless there is sufficient demand to extend the season.

From winter to mid-June a number of minor roads and high passes on the French slopes are likely to be snowbound, so approach journeys during this time should be planned to take any possible closure into account. Public transport services are also severely limited until the comparatively short summer season begins. This is generally in mid-June and lasts until early September.

In both France and Spain national holidays (see box for dates) can affect most shops, banks and other businesses, bringing possible inconvenience if you've not been forewarned, an almost certain increase in demand for those services which remain in operation, and greater numbers of visitors to the mountains. Note, too, that most shops and banks in villages and towns throughout the range close for at least 2 hours during the hottest part of the day – normally 1–3pm.

NATIONAL HOLIDAYS

France
January 1: New Year's Day
Easter Sunday
Easter Monday
Ascension Day (40 days after Easter)
Pentecost (7th Sunday after Easter + Monday)
May 1: May Day/Labour Day
May 8: VE Day
July 14: Bastille Day
August 15: Assumption of Virgin Mary
November 1: All Saints' Day
December 25: Christmas Day

Spain
January 1: New Year's Day
January 6: Epiphany
Good Friday
Easter Sunday
Easter Monday
May 1: May Day/Labour Day
Corpus Christi (early/mid June)
June 24: San Juan
July 25: Santiago
August 15: Assumption of Virgin Mary
October 12: National Day
November 1: All Saints' Day
December 6: Constitution Day
December 8: Immaculate Conception
December 25: Christmas Day

Estany de Monges, one of the many tarns on the northern edge of the Aigües Tortes national park

The **French and Spanish holiday period** (mid-July to mid/late August) is best avoided if your plans include any of the better-known sites, particularly within the national parks. Huts and campsites are then at their busiest, and solitude is hard to find – unless you know the 'secret' places, that is.

Low-level walks may be enjoyed in all seasons, depending on snowfall. However, many high mountain cols can be impassable until mid-June – or even later in exceptional years – so routes planned to tour the high country at this time should take account of the possibility of snow, ice or avalanche, especially on north-facing slopes. The period running from July to September is generally considered the optimum time for most mountain-based activities, but in a good year the second half of June can be idyllic, while September is probably the most settled month to tackle **long treks**; by then the more popular venues for **climbing** are also much less busy.

Snowfall is erratic and unpredictable, but the **ski season** usually takes off in February. Anyone with a passion for **ice climbing** – unless they live locally and can take advantage of conditions as they arise – will have to take pot-luck. The official winter season for climbing starts on 21 December and ends 20 March, but prime conditions can sometimes be enjoyed either side of these dates. Conditions that favour **ski mountaineering** or high-level touring may be expected in springtime, starting in March, but avalanche danger is ever present and extreme caution advised on unpisted slopes.

The Circ dels Pessons, after a summer snowstorm

WEATHER

Mountain weather is notoriously fickle, and in this the Pyrenees is no exception. However, on average the range enjoys 300 days of sunshine a year, which helps to raise expectations in advance of a visit.

To generalise, each season follows a rough formula: snow in winter, rain in spring, warm and sometimes humid summer days with frequent thunderstorms occurring, and cool, damp autumn periods; but one must look to different sections of the range to find specific patterns forming. Even then, micro-climates can and do affect individual massifs to a marked degree. At the western end, for example, the Atlantic is a major influence, pushing cool, moisture-laden airstreams far inland along the northern slopes, with around 200 days of rainfall a year in the Pays Basque. At the other extreme, the high-pressure systems of the Mediterranean rim influence the climate of the Catalonian mountain belt, giving long spells of rain-free weeks in summer, while the southern flanks of the High or Central Pyrenees lie in a rain shadow, and are affected by waves of hot, dry air drifting up from the Ebro basin.

Such extremes of precipitation are illustrated by the fact that the Basque country is one of the wettest regions in France, while the Eastern Pyrenees is the driest, with the Cerdagne holding the country's sunshine record.

High summer is a period of frequent, and sometimes violent, thunderstorms. These can occur with little advanced warning, especially south of the watershed, and climbers tackling high peaks or exposed ridges, as well as trekkers crossing remote country, should try to be well on their way down by early afternoon, which is when most Pyrenean storms erupt.

Storms notwithstanding, the weather tends to be better during the summer months at higher elevations on French mountains and border summits than it is in the valleys, where mist or low clouds frequently form over the low country – especially in the early morning. But thanks to the rain-shadow effect mentioned above, climbers south of the border often experience near perfect conditions, and relax on a warm, cloud-free summit while a short distance away to the north conditions are anything but settled.

Across the entire mountain range a rise in elevation of 100–200m can mean a fall in temperature of around 1°C, and almost everywhere (but especially on the north side of the border) temperature, cloud base and wind speed can change rapidly, so that what may start out as a reasonably fine morning can degenerate in a few hours to swirling mist and snowfall – even in summer. As a point of interest, the lowest summer temperature ever recorded on the summit of Pico de Aneto (3404m) was *minus* 15°C!

Autumn is well under way by October, after which the year starts to drift towards winter. Mountain huts are unmanned and solitude can be virtually guaranteed everywhere in the high valleys, except perhaps on fine weekends. Weather-wise these are often days of rain, and temperature inversion brings low cloud-seas with peaks jutting from them. This is the wettest time of year in the Western Pyrenees, where the annual rainfall is more than 150cm (60ins); the weather becomes unsettled over the Mediterranean, and the eastern mountains turn damp beneath grey skies. But on occasion an Indian summer spreads into early autumn, at which times October can be truly magical, with valley poplars and larchwoods shining their gold.

From November onward rain is a regular feature, with precipitation falling as snow on the mountains. The amount and frequency of winter snow varies from year to year, but the weather station on Pic du Midi de Bigorre reports an average of 118 days snowfall per annum.

WEATHER FORECASTS

France:
☎ 08 36 68 08 08
www.meteo.fr

Spain:
Western Pyrenees: ☎ 943 27 40 30
Central Pyrenees: ☎ 976 23 43 36
Eastern Pyrenees: ☎ 93 21 25 666 or 93 21 25 816

GETTING THERE

Travel from the UK is straightforward, with several options to consider, but which route to take and by which means largely depends on the specific location and type of activity planned upon arrival. There's not a lot of point in travelling by car if you plan to make a long and continuous trek across the range, but should you intend to walk or climb in a number of different massifs, then a private vehicle may be your best bet. If time is of the essence and you've no particular destination in mind, travel by air is the quickest and most convenient way to get there. The train journey, which takes less than 24 hours from London to the Pyrenean railhead via Paris, runs a good second best.

By Air

On the French side of the Pyrenees **Toulouse** and **Pau** are the most convenient airports for access to the mountains. British Airways have regular scheduled flights to **Toulouse** from Gatwick and Manchester, BMI flies there from Manchester, FlyBe from Birmingham and Easyjet from Gatwick and Bristol. No-frills Ryanair has flights to **Pau** from Stansted; the same airline also flies to **Biarritz**, **Carcassonne** and **Perpignan**.

British Airways and Iberia offer a range of scheduled flights to **Barcelona** and **Bilbao** from London airports. BA also fly to **Barcelona** from Birmingham and Manchester, while Iberia has direct flights from Manchester to **Barcelona**. easyJet fly to **Barcelona** from East Midlands, Bristol, Liverpool, Gatwick, Luton, Stansted and Newcastle, and to **Bilbao** from Stansted, Gatwick and Bristol. Ryanair fly to **Barcelona** from Stansted.

AIRLINE INFORMATION

Air France:
(www.airfrance.com)
bmi:
(www.flybmi.com)
British Airways:
(www.ba.com)
easyJet:
(www.easyjet.com)

FlyBE:
(www.flybe.com)
Iberia:
(www.iberia.com)
Ryanair:
(www.ryanair.com)

A limited number of charter flights are available, usually in the high summer or mid-winter ski seasons. **Tarbes-Lourdes** is one of the most conveniently situated airports, with easy access to such centres as Cauterets, Gavarnie and Barèges. It is sometimes possible to get a seat on a pilgrimage flight. Try Mancunia Travel (☎ 0161 228 2840). Although most charters are block-booked well in advance, spare seats are often sold at knock-down prices at the last minute. Fly/drive deals are also worth looking at.

By Rail

The standard journey by train from London Victoria to such destinations as **Lourdes, Luchon, Toulouse, Ax-les-Thermes** and **L'Hospitalet** (for Andorra) takes a little less than 24 hours, including transfer in Paris from Gare du Nord to Austerlitz. A night-sleeper 'couchette' is recommended. **Hendaye**, on the Atlantic coast, and **Perpignan** and **Cerbère** at the eastern end of the range, are likewise accessible in under 24 hours, although by travelling from London St Pancras to Paris via Eurostar can greatly reduce this time. By a combination of Eurostar and TGV, it is feasible to reach the Pyrenees from London in just 12 hours.

The fastest rail journey through France is by the **TGV Atlantique**, which has five daily services from Paris Montparnasse to Lourdes in around 6 hours. Other TGV destinations are: Bayonne, Biarritz, St-Jean-de-Luz, Hendaye, Pau, Toulouse and Perpignan. Costs are higher than on other SNCF services, and reservations are essential.

Alternative French rail destinations worth considering are **Oloron-Ste-Marie** (for the Aspe/Ossau region) and **Latour-de-Carol** in the Cerdagne (for the Carlit massif). Tickets for these, and other French rail services, are available through the usual agents in the UK, or via Rail Europe (see below). Ask for details of discount rates for students, over 60s and for family travel.

TRAIN INFORMATION

Eurostar:
(www.eurostar.com)

Rail Europe:
(www.raileurope.co.uk)

By Car

For two or more travelling together the journey by private car can be cost effective. A car is also useful if you have a lot of gear to take, and it allows greater flexibility than any alternative means of transportation. A variety of road routes head south through France, and unless you're determined to focus directly on the mountains and make a mad dash there, rather than use the journey down as part of the holiday, there's plenty to choose from. Remember that most autoroutes in France are toll roads. Beware of exceeding the speed limit on other roads, as radar traps operate everywhere and infringements usually carry an immediate fine. British and EU driving licences are valid, but an International Driver's Licence (IDL) could be more useful in the event of an accident as it contains information in nine languages. (IDLs are available in Britain from the AA or RAC.) Consider taking out breakdown insurance to cover the period of travel abroad before leaving home.

There are several cross-Channel options to consider between Dover/Folkestone and Calais/Boulogne: by ferry, or Le Shuttle through the Channel tunnel. Direct driving time from Calais or Boulogne to the Pyrenees is around 12–15 hours.

Portsmouth to Le Havre, Cherbourg or St Malo, and Plymouth to Roscoff, are alternatives worth considering by travellers from the southwest of England (allow 10–12 hours from St Malo/Le Havre/Cherbourg), while Plymouth to Santander and Portsmouth to Bilbao are both useful crossings for quick access to the Spanish side of the mountains (3–4 hours' driving time from Santander, less from Bilbao). Brittany Ferries operate the former service, P&O the latter.

CROSS-CHANNEL INFORMATION

Brittany Ferries: Portsmouth to Caen and St Malo; Plymouth to Roscoff and Santander; Poole to Cherbourg (www.brittanyferries.com)
Condor Ferries: Poole and Portsmouth to Cherbourg (www.condorferries.co.uk)
Norfolkline: Dover to Dunquerque (www.norfolkline.com)
P&O Ferries: Dover to Calais; Portsmouth to Bilbao (www.poferries.com)
SeaFrance: Dover to Calais (www.seafrance.com)
Transmanche: Newhaven to Dieppe (www.transmancheferries.com)

TRAVEL WITHIN THE PYRENEES

Visitors without their own vehicle who plan to move from one part of the range to another will find that reliance on public transport can consume a lot of holiday allocation. Rail networks in France and Spain edge into few valleys. Bus services operate to or from many roadhead villages, but journeys to east and west are invariably confused by the fact that most valleys – and bus routes – are channelled north or south.

In **France** the SNCF railway carries a line more or less from coast to coast parallel with, but at a distance from, the mountain chain. Fares are reasonable, services are frequent, and trains clean and fast. Leaflet timetables are available from stations, and regional railway maps can be bought from tobacconists. Tickets must be date stamped before boarding the train – orange-coloured machines for this are located at the entrance to station platforms. Note that on-the-spot fines are levied on anyone caught riding a train without a ticket.

On the western edge of the Aigües Tortes national park a granite plateau is dominated by the beautiful Estany Tort de Rius

Of especial interest to visitors to the Eastern Pyrenees is the Train Jaune, a single-track railway which travels 62km between Villefranche-de-Conflent and Latour-de-Carol in the Cerdagne, where it connects with the mainline Toulouse–Barcelona service.

SNCF buses with roadhead village destinations are usually found outside railway stations. However, services operated by private bus companies can be confusing and difficult to locate on a first visit, and valuable time can be spent searching for information.

In **Spain** railways operate at extreme ends of the mountain range. There's a service connecting San Sebastián and Pamplona via Alsasua, and another from Jaca to Canfranc-Estación below the Somport. South of the Aigües Tortes national park the nearest railway is at La Pobla de Segur (line from Lleida). East of this Puigcerdà is on the Toulouse– Barcelona line, while a rack-and-pinion railway, the Cremallera, runs between Ribes and Núria in the upper Freser valley.

Many Pyrenean villages in Spain are served by bus, most of which begin their journeys in the provincial capital, but note that very few services operate on Sundays and public holidays.

Andorra has neither airport nor railway, but there are daily buses to and from the capital, Andorra-la-Vella, connecting with L'Hospitalet (in France) via Pas de la Casa, and with La Seu d'Urgell and Barcelona (in Spain). Frequent bus services run within Andorra from the capital to Arinsal, El Serrat, Encamp, Soldeu and Pas de la Casa.

ACCOMMODATION

Except for the peak summer season (14 July – 15 August in France; 1–23 August in Spain), and perhaps all of February in ski resorts, it is usually possible to arrive in a Pyrenean town or village and find accommodation of some sort or another without difficulty – except for groups, that is. Mountain huts, on the other hand, can be full to capacity almost any time in July and August, and you should phone ahead wherever possible to be certain of getting a bed.

Hotels

On the French side of the Pyrenees these are graded up to three-star. Officially, hotels should not insist on guests taking meals, but half-board (*demi-pension*) invariably works out cheaper than just a room plus eating out. Single rooms are only marginally cheaper than doubles, while a third bed in a double room could be worth asking for, as it often provides good value for those travelling as a family or small group. The 'Logis de France' sign indicates a moderate-sized, often family-run, hotel with a good value-for-money reputation. For hotel details, enquire at the local tourist office on arrival or ask for accommodation lists in advance from the French Government Tourist Office – 178 Piccadilly, London W1V 0AL (☎ 09068 244 123 60p/min, e-mail: info.uk@franceguide.com, www.franceguide.com).

In Spain hotels are graded 1–5, with state-run *paradores* being near the top end of the scale. There are also *hostales*, which offer less elaborate accommodation, but note that *hostales-residencias* do not provide meals, except perhaps breakfast. *Pensiones* are merely cheaper hotels, while signs for *camas* or *habitaciones* indicate beds or rooms available in private houses or bars. *Camas y comidas* signifies that meals are also available.

Bed and Breakfast

Chambres d'hôte are found in increasing numbers in villages and small towns on the Pyrenean rim, and are a good way of meeting local people, if you speak their language. Note that prices quoted invariably refer to the room, not per person.

Self-catering

Self-catering accommodation on the French side of the mountains is easily arranged through the Fédération Nationale des Gîtes de France. In this context *gîtes* (as opposed to *gîtes d'étape* – see below) are usually apartments or private houses let during the holiday seasons. Write to: Gîtes de France, 59 rue St-Lazare, 75439 Paris cedex 09 (☎ 01 49 70 75 75, www.gites-de-france.fr). *Gîtes* are listed in the guide *Gîtes de France* published by Springfield Books.

Youth Hostels

There are a few youth hostels on both sides of the border, but these are sometimes block-booked by parties of schoolchildren or youth groups. Membership of the Youth Hostel Association is a requirement for staying overnight, so if it is your intention to use hostels during your visit, take out membership of your home association before leaving. In emergencies it is possible to join the association on arrival at a hostel, but that costs more than home membership. Details of all youth hostels in the Pyrenees can be found in Volume 1 of the International Youth Hostel Guide (which covers Europe and the Mediterranean).

YOUTH HOSTEL ASSOCIATIONS INFORMATION

An Oige, 61 Mountjoy Square, Dublin 1 (☎ 01 830 4555, www.irelandyha.org)

YHA (England and Wales), Trevelyan House, Dimple Road, Matlock DE4 3YH (☎ 0870 770 8868, e-mail: customerservices@yha.org.uk, www.yha.org.uk)

YHANI, 22 Donegal Road, Belfast BT12 5JN (☎ 028 9032 4733, www.hini.org.uk)

SYHA, 7 Glebe Crescent, Stirling, FK8 2JA (☎ 0870 155 3255, www.syha.org.uk)

International Youth Hostel Federation, e-mail: iyhf@iyhf.org.uk, www.hihostels.com

Gîtes d'étape

A chain of gîtes d'étape has been established by the Randonnées Pyrénéennes organisation right across the northern side of the range, most of which are located in roadhead villages and in trekking areas – especially on the route of the GR10. These are clearly marked on the 1:50,000 maps. Similar to private youth hostels, gîtes d'étape provide overnight accommodation in dormitories and, in many cases, separate bedrooms too – sheet sleeping bags should be used, as bedding is not normally provided. Self-catering facilities are available, hot meals are sometimes on offer, and showers are provided in the washrooms. For anyone planning a long tour of the French Pyrenees, they offer a good deal in terms of low-cost accommodation.

Campsites

There's no shortage of official campsites, mostly offering good facilities, with prices varying according to the standard certified, which is usually star rated. In France, where there's a choice, municipal sites are invariably the cheapest, while camping à la ferme (at a private farm) can be pretty basic as far as facilities are concerned. In the high season campsites on both sides of the border can be running at near capacity. Tourist offices can often supply a free Mapa de Campings, which lists practically all those on the Spanish side of the mountains. (In the UK try the Spanish National Tourist Office, 22–23 Manchester Square, London W1M 5AP, ☎ 020 7486 8077, fax: 020 7486 8034, www.tourspain.co.uk.)

Wild Camping

Some of Europe's finest wild camping (*camping sauvage*) is to be found in the Pyrenees. But while this is acceptable in many of the mountain regions, it is subject to certain restrictions and limitations in several places, and these restricted areas are spreading as tourist activity increases. In the French national park, for example, it is forbidden to pitch a tent within an hour's walk of a road or park boundary, and even in authorised areas camping is permitted for one night only. In the Ordesa and Aigües Tortes national parks of Spain, camping is not permitted except in designated areas. In Ordesa wild camping is officially banned below 2100m, while it is restricted to a minimum altitude of 2500m in the Pineta Cirque, and below 1800m in Añisclo and Escuaín. There are several other prohibited regions, as mentioned in the text. Outside these areas, however, the majority of high valleys make idyllic sites for wild camping. In Aragón wild camping is allowed anywhere above 1500m, as long as it's more than 2 hours from a road. Below 1500m you can camp freely more than 5km from an official site, and in excess of 1km from an urban area, but not within 100m of a road or river. Wherever you camp please be scrupulous with regard to the environment; leave no rubbish, do not pollute water supplies and be sensitive towards plants and wildlife. Faeces should be buried, and used toilet paper burned with care to avoid setting fire to vegetation.

Wild camping in the Pyrenees near the Refuge d'Arrémoulit

Mountain Huts

A chain of huts (*refuge* in French, *refugio* in Spanish, *refugi* in Catalan) has been established throughout the High Pyrenees. In France most are owned and maintained by either the Club Alpin Français (CAF) or the Parc National des Pyrénées (PNP), the national park authority; a few are privately run. In Spain the majority belong to various mountaineering clubs, but, as in France, others are privately owned. Those that are manned usually have a guardian resident only in the summer – roughly from late May/early June to late September, although dates vary. Only a handful are staffed at Easter or in the spring ski-touring season. For the remainder of the year a winter annexe with only basic amenities is available for use.

A few huts in the more popular areas are large enough to accommodate 100 or more. Most take half that number or less. Dormitory accommodation is the norm, with one or more large communal sleeping platforms being provided, with mattresses, blankets and pillows. There is no segregation of the sexes. Washroom facilities are sometimes extremely basic or non-existent, showers are rare, and the toilet is often a draughty lean-to. However, standards are improving and most manned huts are now equipped with solar-powered electricity.

Practically all Pyrenean refuges have special areas allocated for users to prepare their own meals, but such areas are not necessarily equipped with cooking facilities. Where a hut is staffed, hot meals and drinks are provided, with wine and beer usually for sale. Since most of these buildings are located far from any access road, expect prices charged to reflect the cost and difficulty of bringing in supplies by helicopter or mule. Members of mountaineering clubs or associations that have reciprocal arrangements with the owner-organisation of specific huts will benefit from a reduction in overnight fees (but not the cost of meals or drinks) on presentation of their membership card. In the UK contact the British Mountaineering Council (BMC) for up-to-date information on reciprocal rights (BMC, 177–179 Burton Road, Manchester M20 2BB, ☎ 0161 445 6111, email: office@thebmc.co.uk, www.thebmc.co.uk).

Most, if not all, manned refuges are equipped with telephones, and you should make every effort to phone ahead to book a place if you intend to stay overnight.

Unmanned huts vary in size, quality and facilities. Some are no more than stone shelters; others have a sleeping platform, fireplace and stove. A number are used by shepherds and may be inhabited when you arrive. The best have been well looked after by those who use them; they are built in idyllic locations – usually in remote country – and provide a rewarding night's lodging. But it's up to everyone who uses such huts to treat them with care and to leave them in good order for others to enjoy.

📖 Details of 800 or so refuges, gîtes and unmanned shelters in the Pyrenees can be found in Gîtes d'étape, Refuges: France et Frontières by Annick and Serge Mouraret (Rando Éditions). For internet listings of French refuges and gîtes see www.gites-refuges.com; Spanish huts are at www.refugiosyalbergues.com.

MAPS AND GUIDEBOOKS
French Maps
The Institut Géographique National (IGN) covers the French side of the frontier with sheets at 1:25,000 and 1:50,000 scale, which include spillage into Spain that varies from a few metres to several kilometres. The cartography is excellent, and on recent editions the majority of highlighted information – huts, *gîtes*, campsites, etc – is accurately marked. For most walking and trekking purposes the 1:50,000 **Carte de Randonnées** maps published by Rando Éditions in conjunction with IGN are more than adequate. The GR10, classic high-level route (HRP) and regional walking tours are all outlined for easy reference. Each map also carries a list of *gîtes d'étape*, refuges, tourist offices and telephone numbers for both mountain rescue and weather forecasts. Naturally the IGN's 1:25,000 **Top 25** sheets provide much greater detail than the 1:50,000 series, and will be of more use to climbers.

Spanish Maps
The traditional route of approach to the Maladeta region is through the Port de Venasque – out of the shadows of France into the sunlight of Spain

The quality of mapping south of the border does not match that of the French IGN series, but more recent editions show considerable improvement. The whole range within Spain is covered at a scale of 1:50,000 by **Servicio Geográfico del Ejército** (SGE) and the **Instituto Geográfico Nacional** (IGN). As with the French maps at the same scale mentioned above, these are suitable for walking and trekking purposes, although sheets published by **Editorial Alpina** (EA), accompanied by a slim guide in Castilian Spanish or Catalan, are easier to obtain in advance outside Spain and are therefore more often used. EA maps have been drawn either at 1:25,000 or 1:40,000 scales. Similar

to the Carte de Randonnées maps, Rando Éditions, in collaboration with the Institut Cartogràfic de Catalunya, publish a series covering the Central Pyrenees entitled **Mapa Excursionistas** at 1:50,000.

MAP AVAILABILITY

French IGN maps should be easy to find in towns and villages on the north side of the Pyrenees, but there's limited availability of Spanish maps south of the border – especially those of the Military Survey, which are almost impossible to obtain. It is better to order these well in advance of a visit. The largest map stockist in the UK is:

Edward Stanford Ltd, 12–14 Long Acre, London WC2E 9LP (☎ 020 7836 1321, e-mail: sales@stanfords.co.uk, www.stanfords.co.uk).

In the USA try:

Map Link Inc, 30 South Patera Lane, Unit #5, Santa Barbara, California 93117 (☎ 805 692 6777, e-mail: billhunt@maplinkinc.com, www.maplink.com).

For ordering maps on the internet – tap into:
Travellers World Bookshop (www.map-guides.com).

English-language Guidebooks
for Walkers, Trekkers and Climbers

The first English-language guide to the range – 'especially intended for mountaineers' is how its subtitle reads – appeared in 1862. This was Charles Packe's *Guide to the Pyrenees*, a rare gem, with nothing comparable being published for another 100 years. Recently, however, several guidebooks have come onto the market to meet an explosion of interest in these mountains.

In the UK Cicerone Press, publishers of this guide, have produced a series of guidebooks for walkers, trekkers and climbers, as follows.

- *Walks and Climbs in the Pyrenees* (Cicerone Press, 5th edn, 2008) by Kev Reynolds describes 170 routes on both sides of the frontier, including ascents of many of the highest peaks, plus the HRP between Lescun and Andorra. Regularly updated.
- *The Pyrenean Haute Route* (2009) by Ton Joosten describes the complete route from the Atlantic to the Mediterranean, broken into five sections.
- *The GR10 Trail* (2010) by Paul Lucia is a guide to the classic lowland traverse of the range from Hendaye to Banyuls-sur-Mer on the French side.
- *Through the Spanish Pyrenees* – GR11 (Cicerone Press, 4th edn, 2008) by Paul Lucia covers Spain's answer to the GR10, describing the traverse in 44 day stages.
- *Rock Climbs in the Pyrenees* (1990) by Derek L. Walker is the only English-language guide dedicated to the rock climber, with routes in six separate districts.

- *The Way of St James* (Cicerone Press, 2008) by Alison Raju, in two volumes (Le Puy to the Pyrenees and Pyrenees – Santiago – Finisterre), is a walkers' guide to the pilgrim route from Le Puy to Santiago which crosses the Pyrenees.

For low-key ascents of selected peaks, a three-volume series of guides was published in the 1970s/80s (2nd edn, 1988/89) by Gastons-West Col. Written by Arthur Battagel, they are:
- *Pyrenees West: Larrau to Gavarnie*; *Pyrenees Central: Gèdre to the Garonne Gap* and
- *Pyrenees East* (formerly *Pyrenees Andorra Cerdagne*) which covers Ariège, Andorra, Cerdagne, Roussillon, and Sierra del Cadí.

Other English-language guides are as follows.
- *Pyrenees 1, 2 and 3* by Roger Büdeler (Rother) cover much of the Central Pyrenees in a 3-volume series translated from the original German.
- *Trekking in the Pyrenees* by Douglas Streatfeild-James (Trailblazer Publications, 3rd edn, 2005) follows the route of GR10 but also strays into Spain to explore some of the more popular regions.
- *Trekking in Spain* by Marc Dubin (Lonely Planet, 1990) includes the Pyrenees, especially sections of GR11.
- *Landscapes of the Pyrenees* by Paul Jenner and Christine Smith (Sunflower Books, 1990) offers a selection of modest day-walks and car tours.
- *Walking in Spain* by Miles Roddis, Nancy Frey, Jose Placer, Matthew Fletcher and John Noble (Lonely Planet, 2nd edn, 1999) covers much of the mainland and islands, with the Pyrenees claiming a large share.
- *100 Walks in the French Pyrenees* by Terry Marsh (Hodder & Stoughton, 1992) is mostly confined to the PNP and adjacent Néouvielle regions; it is now out of print, but available on loan from some libraries.
- *Walking the Pyrenees* (Robertson McCarta, 1989) is, in effect, an English translation of the French topoguide to the GR10, with IGN mapping. Now out of print, some of the route and accommodation details are no longer applicable. Best avoided, except as a primer.
- *The Mountains of Andorra* by Alf Robertson and Jane Meadowcroft (Cicerone Press, 2005) is a well-researched guide to walks, treks, scrambles and via ferratas in this tiny Pyrenean country.

See also:
- *Long Distance Walks in the Pyrenees* by Chris Townsend (Crowood Press, 1991)
- *Classic Walks in the Pyrenees* by Kev Reynolds (Oxford Illustrated Press, 1989).

Both are now out of print, but can sometimes be found in libraries. Plenty of background reading of use for route planning.

- *Rough Guide to the Pyrenees* by Marc Dubin (Rough Guides, 6th edn, 2007) contains a number of useful walks ideas, but is of primary use to touring visitors.

French-language Walking/Trekking Guides

Guides published by Rando Éditions, 4 rue Maye Lane, BP 24, 65421 Ibos cedex (www.rando-editions.com) cover almost every Pyrenean region, including the more obscure, lesser-known valleys. The following list is a selection of guides dealing with regions within the area covered by the present book. Most were published during the 1990s.

- *Les 50 Plus Belles Randonnées dans les Parc National des Pyrénées*
- *Le Tour du Mont Perdu*
- *Le Guide Rando – Aspe-Ossau*
- *Le Guide Rando – Vignemale-Balaïtous*
- *Le Guide Rando – Gavarnie-Luz*
- *Le Guide Rando – Néouvielle*
- *Le Guide Rando – Luchon*
- *Le Guide Rando – Couserans*
- *Le Guide Rando – Haute Ariège*
- *Le Guide Rando – Cerdagne et Capcir*
- *100 Randonnées dans les Pyrénée-Atlantiques*
- *100 Randonnées dans les Hautes-Pyrénées*
- *100 Randonnées dans les Pyrénées Ariègeoises*
- *100 Randonnées dans les Pyrénées Orientales*
- *100 Randonnées en Aragon*
- *100 Randonnées en Catalogne*

See also:

- *50 Randonnées – Aure, Louron, Luchonnais* by Louis Audoubert (Éditions Milan).

A series of four topoguides to the GR10 have been published by the Fédération Française de la Randonnée Pédestre (FFRP).

French-language Climbing Guides

- *Passages Pyrénéens* by Rainier Munsch, Christian Ravier and Rémi Thivel (Éditions du Pin à Crochets, 1999) describes a selection of 284 routes between the Cirque de Lescun and Néouvielle massif. Excellent value and attractively produced.
- *Pyrénées: Courses Mixtes, Neige et Glace* by Francis Mousel (Éditions Franck Mercier, 1997) describes 156 winter routes on both sides of the frontier between Pic d'Aspe in the west and Canigou in the east. Illustrated with more than 150 photographs.

See also:
- *Les Pyrénées – Les 100 Plus Belles Courses et Randonnées* by Patrice de Bellefon (Denoël, 1976), a hardback tempter with many colour photographs, route diagrams, etc – part of a well-known series of books instigated by Gaston Rébuffat
- *100 Sommets des Pyrénées* by Georges Véron (Rando Editions, 2001) describes moderate, *voie-normale* type ascents.

Spanish Guides
- *GR11: Senderos de Gran Recorrido/Senda Pirenaica* (PRAMES, Zaragoza) – a three-volume guide to the GR11 covering Navarra/Gipuzkoa, Aragón and Andorra/Catalunya. The same work is also published as a two-package set in ring-binders.
- *Navarra Paso a Paso* (Sua Edizioak) – a topoguide for all the GR trails in Navarra.
- *GR11: Pirineo Vasco* (Sua Edizioak) – a topoguide to this long-distance traverse.

French and Spanish Magazines/Journals
The following selection of publications is mostly devoted to the Pyrenees, and sometimes includes new route details. Copies may be studied in the Alpine Club Library in London.
- *Pyrénées* – published quarterly in Toulouse by Éditions Milan
- *Revue Pyrénéenne* – published quarterly in Tarbes for the CAF du Grand Sud-Ouest
- *La Muntanya* – journal of the Centre Excursionista de Catalunya (CEC), published in Barcelona
- *Pyrenaica* – published by the Euskal Mendizale Federakundea in Bilbao.

HEALTH CONSIDERATIONS
Any health concern of visitors to the Pyrenees is likely to be limited, and related to their particular form of activity practised in the mountains. Walkers and trekkers may suffer blisters, muscle strain, heatstroke and/or heat exhaustion due to dehydration. Climbers may be affected by stonefall or other accident. But anyone taking part in a mountain-based pursuit should be aware of the risk of hypothermia, which can occur even in summer on wet and windy days, as well as in winter.

Insect bites and stings can cause severe discomfort, so apply repellent if you're susceptible. Stomach upsets are common, and often occur as a result of drinking contaminated water, so precautions should be taken when filling bottles from lakes or streams in case animals are grazing above. Use a filtration system or purification tablets, or heat your water to a rolling boil for 5 minutes or more in order to destroy impurities.

EU citizens are entitled to receive the same standard of medical treatment afforded to residents of the host country through the health services of either France or Spain. To make sure you do, carry a European Health Insurance (EHI) card with you. Application forms are available at post offices throughout the UK. Whilst you may have to pay for treatment at the time of need (except in an emergency), theoretically you should be able to claim most of this back once you arrive home. But be warned that such claims are notoriously slow to process, and your EHI card is no substitute for decent medical cover through a travel insurance policy. When considering travel insurance it would be wise to include cover for mountain rescue.

One of the finest valleys is that of Marcadau, easily reached from Cauterets, and with tremendous scope for walks, treks and modest climbs

The Mountains

THE PYRENEES – COAST TO COAST

The Basque country in the west consists of patchwork meadows, pastures and forests that are well watered by mists and rainclouds drifting in from the Atlantic. It is in essence a pastoral land whose shepherds wander from one side of the border to the other with complete disregard for political convention. The mountains are neither high nor rugged, yet the scenery has an attractive quality not to be lightly dismissed, and wandering through on trans-Pyrenean trails GR10 or GR11, for example, is to discover that altitude is not everything.

These **Western Pyrenees** of Pays Basque and Béarn on the French slopes, and of Navarre and a small portion of Alto Aragón on the Spanish, have a confused topographical layout. Instead of a single range of mountains, a series of hills spreads in various directions, and in the sometimes featureless terrain the frontier can be confusing to the walker. While the general picture is one of a fertile landscape dotted with attractive villages, there's also some astonishing karst country up on the border near the region's eastern limit where, on a barren, elevated plateau, there is practically no semblance of vegetation, the limestone having been washed clean and riven by deep fissures, holes and underground caverns, making the going treacherous for walkers in misty conditions. Elsewhere one looks upon a gentle hill country, unsurprising in the neat outline of modest heights, yet in the folds of some of these wooded hills lies a series of impressive ravines: the

The frontier ridge southeast of Pica d'Estats with a typical cloud-sea lapping the French slopes

gorges of Kakouetta and Ehujarré, Holzarté and Olhadybia, the last two visited by a *variante* of GR10.

Rising gradually eastward the Basque hills give way to more distinctive summits beyond the Col de la Pierre-St-Martin, where the grey imposing lump of Pic d'Anie, first of the 2500m peaks, marks the start of the so-called **High Pyrenees**, the region on which this book concentrates. This is limestone country, with delicate aiguilles to attract the climber, but as you progress towards the heart of the range, so limestone makes way for granite, then returns to limestone again. The highest mountains stand astride the frontier or close to it, and become alpine in both stature and appeal. Summits reach 3000m on the Balaïtous, and attain their maximum elevation of 3404m on Pico de Aneto (Néthou to the French) in the Maladeta massif. Aneto is virtually the pivot of the range, located almost at its central point, a slender summit crest above a sheet of ice.

East of Aneto most of the higher mountains gather south of the frontier in rugged massifs of tremendous appeal, while the northern ranges of Ariège are among the least visited of all, a complex area whose valleys tend to be deep and narrow and heavily wooded – although their upper limits are often spectacularly dotted with postglacial tarns.

The region of the High Pyrenees is without question the most scenically dramatic, and is where the three national parks, the last remaining glaciers, more than 1000 lakes and all the highest summits are found. Here too are the great cirques of Gavarnie, Estaubé, Troumouse, Barroude, Barrosa and Cagateille; the beautiful canyons of Ordesa, Añisclo and the little-known Escuaín; and some of the wildest and most remote valleys of all. It is among the High Pyrenees that the walker, trekker and climber will discover at its best both the true nature of the range and its dramatic qualities.

To the south a succession of pre-Pyrenean massifs, or sierras, reveal a few spectacular sites of interest to climbers, especially the conglomerate towers of the Mallos de Riglos, and the limestone walls and gullies of the Sierra del Cadí south of Andorra. Northeast of Andorra and forming a wall to the broad, flat-bottomed Cerdagne, the jutting granite peaks of the Carlit massif signal the last of the High Pyrenees. In their place the **Eastern Pyrenees** gradually subside towards the Mediterranean, Pic du Canigou (2784m) being the last mountain of note and a symbolic focus of attention for inhabitants of the low country to north and south. These final eastern hills have their own appeal, and seldom appear more attractive than when dusted with snow above the orchards and vineyards they shelter. In summer the mountains and sun-baked plateaux shimmer in the Mediterranean heat, and aromatic plants leave an unforgettable impression on all who travel there.

Formation and Structure

Around 250 million years ago the site of the present Pyrenean range was occupied by a Hercynian mountain mass. This was

Accessible from Cauterets, the Vallée du Marcadau is one of the most tranquil in all the Pyrenees

later submerged and covered by Secondary Era deposits beneath a continental sea, until being pushed up again by the same earth movements that created the Alps approximately 30–50 million years ago. During this mountain-building era, the comparatively pliable sedimentary beds folded, whereas the much older and more rigid platform broke up, with hot springs bursting through the fracture lines. As all this occurred, so forces of erosion were at work.

The true spine of the range, the Axial Zone, is characterised by sharply defined ridges and bold peaks where a number of granitic extrusions have thrust through the more easily eroded primary sediments – Balaïtous, Maladeta, Besiberri and so on. However, limestone and schist of a particularly resistant type is also found among some of the highest summits – Monte Perdido (Mont Perdu) is a good example, being Western Europe's highest limestone mountain. Nearby, the Cirque de Gavarnie (also limestone) reveals huge platforms of horizontal strata stacked one upon the other. Pic du Midi d'Ossau owes its distinctive shape to an extrusion of volcanic rock; the mountains of Ariège and Andorra have been carved from an especially hard gneiss, while the high valleys of the Cerdagne and Capcir, first cut from the Eastern Pyrenees by erosion, have been filled with an accumulation of clay, marl and gravel.

Glaciers of the Quaternary Ice Age (10,000 years ago) did much to give the range some of its most dramatic and appealing features. Although this glacial cover has almost completely disappeared today, there remain countless hanging valleys, more than 1000 tarns, dramatic cirques, sharp peaks and ragged crests – not to mention large tracts of glacial pavement being colonised now by the first plants – that reveal the work of these ancient ice sheets and add character to the landscape.

No less than the glaciers, water has helped shape the Pyrenees, and in many of the limestone massifs it is rainwater and snowmelt that have eroded the rock into a network of cracks and fissures, some of which penetrate to great depths and produce subterranean galleries and caverns – for example, those of Pierre-St-Martin. Other fissures become ravines and gorges, like those of the Basque country, or impressive canyons such as Añisclo and Escuaín.

NATIONAL PARKS

France

The **Parc National des Pyrénées** (PNP) follows an irregular line eastward from Col de Laraille on the frontier ridge south of Lescun to the edge of the Néouvielle massif – a distance of about 110km, with an area of 45,700 hectares under full protection. A larger peripheral

Sunrise over Pic du Midi d'Ossau

zone of more than 206,000 hectares allows limited development, including cableways for downhill skiing, right to the edge of the protected area, which sometimes leads to a conflict of interests. Designated in 1967, the park contains more than 100 mountain lakes and some of the finest peaks north of the border, including Pic du Midi d'Ossau, Balaïtous, Vignemale, Marboré and the cirques of Gavarnie, Estaubé, Troumouse and Barroude. The scenery is spectacular in almost every valley. Centres such as Laruns, Cauterets and Gavarnie provide easy access, while south of the Cirque de Gavarnie the park's boundary coincides with that of Spain's national park of Ordesa for a distance of just 15km. There's a wealth of well-maintained trails, a number of huts and limitless opportunities for walkers, trekkers and climbers. Flora and fauna is abundant, with a large number of outstanding birds of prey breeding there. Isard are numerous, as is the marmot population, and the brown bear is said to inhabit some of the forests. Mountain biking is banned from the park, and dogs are not allowed – even on a lead. The six principal valleys are, from west to east, those of Aspe, Ossau, Azun, Cauterets, Gavarnie and Aure.

Parc National des Pyrénées, 59 route de Pau, 65000 Tarbes (☎ 05 62 44 36 60, www. parc-pyrenees.com). PNP information offices are located in Argelès-Gazost, Cauterets, Gavarnie, Laruns, Luz-St-Sauveur and St-Lary-Soulan.

📖 *Parcs Nationaux des Pyrénées* by Bernard Clos (Éditions Jean-Marc de Faucompret/ Parc National des Pyrénées, 1991) is a sumptuous volume of colour photographs from the PNP and Ordesa national parks, with introductory text (in French) by Liliane Birman. See also *Le Parc National des Pyrénées* by Jean-François Labourie (Rando Éditions), a slim portrait of the park's six valleys.

Two important nature reserves have also been created. The **Réserve Naturelle de Néouvielle** forms an adjunct to the Parc National des Pyrénées, carrying protected-area status eastward. A region of granite mountains, lakes and forests, it was created in 1935 as the first such reserve in France, and is now under the same management as that of the national park. The only access road branches off the D929 near Aragnouet, southwest of St-Lary-Soulan, with a *navette* operating a service between Lac d'Orédon (just outside the reserve) and Lac d'Aubert. There are no huts within the reserve, and camping is limited to a single site near Lac d'Aubert, below and to the east of Pic de Néouvielle.

The **Réserve National d'Orlu** was formed in 1981 south of the Vallée d'Orlu near Ax-les-Thermes in Ariège. This comparatively small area of narrow forested glens lies to the north of the Carlit massif, with breeding herds of isard and roe deer. Access is by road from Ax-les-Thermes through Orlu (camping and *gîte*) and past Les Forges d'Orlu to a picnic area, beyond which private vehicles are banned.

Spain

South of the Cirque de Gavarnie lies the **Parque Nacional de Ordesa y Monte Perdido**, the oldest and smallest in the Pyrenees, having been created as long ago as 1918 in order to protect the Ordesa canyon. The original boundaries were extended in 1982 to a total of 15,600 hectares (more than five times its former size), and now include the nearby Valles de Añisclo and Escuaín, Circo de Pineta and Monte Perdido (Mont Perdu to the French). The scenery here is among the most dramatic in the Pyrenees, with soaring limestone walls, ice-crowned peaks, waterfalls, lush forests and barren uplands, and with the three magnificent canyons providing the main attraction. The park has a wide altitude range with a difference of around 2600m between the lowest and the highest points, which gives a huge variety of plants – some 1500 species being listed within the protected area. Wildlife, too, is abundant and varied, with 171 species of bird, 32 mammals, 8 reptiles and 6 species of amphibia, including a Pyrenean frog discovered as new to science in 1990. Climbing on the multi-coloured walls of Ordesa's canyon is spectacular, with plenty of vertical or overhanging pitches. Walks range from gentle valley-bed strolls to airy balcony paths with lots of exposure; from hour-long rambles to multi-day tours. Ordesa itself is one of the busiest tourist sites in the Pyrenees, although it's not difficult to escape the crowds if you've the energy and will to do so. Camping is restricted to specified areas, which include the immediate vicinity of the only manned hut in the park (Refugio de Góriz). Access to the Valle de Ordesa by private vehicle is no longer allowed during the busiest summer months, although buses run a shuttle service from a car park below Torla.

Campanula cochlearifolia – *found growing on the Aiguilles d'Ansabère*

NATIONAL PARKS OF THE HIGH PYRENEES

A Parc National des Pyrénées
B Parque Nacional de Ordesa y Monte Perdido
C Parc Nacional d'Aigües Tortes i Estany de Sant Maurici

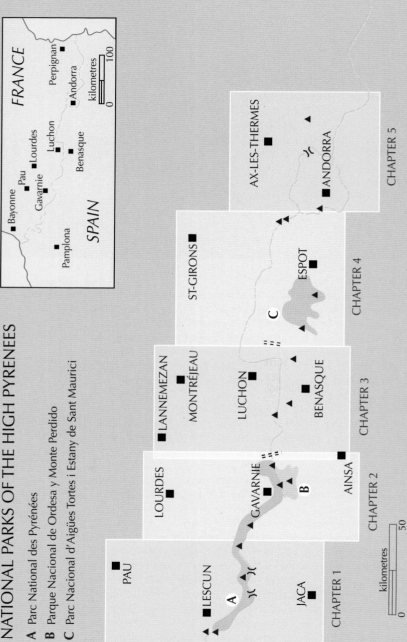

Parque Nacional de Ordesa y Monte Perdido, Plaza de Cervantes 5, 22071 Huesca (☎ 974 24 33 61, www.ordesa.net)

South of the Port de la Bonaigua, which links the Vall d'Aran with the rest of Catalonia, the **Parc Nacional d'Aigües Tortes i Estany de Sant Maurici** dates from 1955, but this too has been extended westward to include the headwaters of the Noguera de Tor above Caldes de Boí. The original core of the park, spreading out from the Sant Maurici lake above Espot, has suffered at the hands of the hydro-engineer, with regard not only to dam-building but also to the construction of jeep tracks that have to some extent devalued its wild nature. That being said, there are many utterly charming corners where a true sense of wilderness can still be found. The eastern sector has innumerable rocky peaklets on which to climb, while the western fringe carries a high granite ridge to over 3000m on Besiberri Nord. Countless lakes and small tarns adorn the high country and there are several manned huts that enable multi-day treks to be achieved without the need to carry heavy loads. Wild camping is officially forbidden within the national park, but there are campsites in Espot in the east and below Caldes de Boí in the west. Access for private vehicles is banned, but 4x4 taxis ferry visitors from Espot to the Sant Maurici lake, and eastwards into the national park from the La Farga car park just inside the Sant Nicolau valley between Boí and Caldes de Boí.

Parc Nacional d'Aigües Tortes i Estany de Sant Maurici, C/ Camp de Mart 35, 25004 Lleida (☎ 973 24 66 50, www.catalunya.net/aiguestortes) – national park offices are also situated in Espot and Boí.

📖 *El Parque Nacional de Aigües Tortes y Lago San Mauricio* (Editorial Everest)

Le Parc National d'Aïguestortes-massif des Encantats by Georges Véron and A. Jolis (Éditions Randonnées Pyrénéennes)

In addition to the two national parks outlined above, there are three *parques natural* in the Spanish Pyrenees, listed below from west to east.

Parque Natural Pirenaico Larra-Belagoa is located in the Western Pyrenees at the head of the Valle de Belagoa, through which the C137 road twists up to the frontier, which is crossed above Pierre-St-Martin. It is claimed that the European brown bear survives within the park, and there's a hut, manned throughout the year and accessible by bus from Pamplona, which makes a good base.

Parque Natural Posets-Maladeta extends either side of the two highest Pyrenean peaks, from the Valle de Gistaín on the west to the valley of the Noguera Ribagorçana on the east, while the Ésera valley, which divides the two massifs, is excluded below the Baños de Benasque (see 3:8, 3:9, 3:10). There's a Visitor Centre in Benasque and information office in Plan (Parque Natural Posets-Maladeta, Avda de la Paz, bajo, Huesca, ☎ 974 230 635).

Parc Natural del Cadí-Moixeró lies southwest of the Cerdagne, and the 2497m limestone Pedraforca provides special interest. The western half of the reserve contains the lovely massif of the Sierra del Cadí, whose north-facing walls hold a number of respected climbs. Inaugurated in 1983 the *parc natural* covers an area in excess of 400km^2, and protects Spain's largest herd of isard (see 5:7).

MOUNTAIN ACTIVITIES
WALKING

The Pyrenees contain some of Europe's finest and most challenging walking country, and there's enough variety and scope to fill a lifetime of holidays. Waymarked trails are mostly clear in or near inhabited country and around roadheads, while sparsely cairned routes lead across the more remote regions. Long-distance walks such as the *sentiers de grande randonnée* (*GR*), of which GR10 and GR11 are the longest example within the range, are guided by distinctive red-and-white paint flashes on rocks, buildings or trees, while the Pyrenean High Route (HRP) is irregularly marked – well in places, non-existent in others. In some of the more popular areas outside national parks, selected trails are waymarked – in France, yellow and red, and in Spain, yellow and white. These, known as *sentiers de petit randonnée* (France) or *pequeño recorrido* (Spain), are shorter routes devised to give novice mountain walkers outings that may be completed within a single day.

The Portillone crest is just visible above the Maladeta glacier

Equipment for Walkers

Whatever the level of walking envisaged, anyone heading into the mountains should be adequately shod, with boots that fit well, give good ankle support and have sturdy soles providing plenty of grip. For summer walks light clothing (shorts, tee shirt, sun hat) will be sufficient, but with back-up such as a fleece or pullover. A waterproof is essential if the holiday is to be spent on the French side of the mountains – particularly in the west. And even though hot, dry weather may be predicted on the Spanish slopes, be alert to the possibility of sudden storms that are by no means rare – native Pyrenean activists generally opt for a waterproof poncho or cape that also covers the rucksack. It is advisable to anticipate wet conditions throughout the Pyrenees, so make sure any clothing kept in your rucksack is contained within polythene bags or protected by a rucksack liner.

A pair of trekking poles will relieve a lot of knee and leg strain, especially for those carrying a full rucksack. Suncream and dark glasses are essential, as are first aid, a whistle for summoning help in an emergency, a detailed map of the area and a compass. A headtorch and spare battery, a minimum one-litre capacity water bottle and some emergency food ought to be carried at all times, and if you plan to use *gîtes d'étape* or mountain huts for accommodation, take a sheet sleeping bag as well.

Where to Walk

Looking at the range from west to east, the main walking centres/ areas may be summarised as follows.

France

Where the Basque country gives way to the High Pyrenees the small village of **Lescun**, west of the Aspe valley, is well provided with footpaths and tracks that lead over rolling pasture and through forest, as well as giving popular walks to the Cirque de Lescun and onto the frontier ridge. The ascent of Pic d'Anie is another option (1:2). Overlooking the Vallée d'Aspe, **Borce** has limited accommodation and a campsite, with good walking country close by, while **Etsaut**, in the valley below, also has a few beds and, like Borce and Lescun, is on the route of GR10 (1:3).

In the Vallée d'Ossau **Laruns**, and to a certain extent **Gabas**, make useful centres on which to base an exploration of valleys that surround Pic du Midi d'Ossau, including the classic tour of Pic du Midi and a circuit of the Ayous lakes. This is some of the most renowned walking country within the Parc National des Pyrénées, and solitude should not be expected, but there are quieter trails to be found on the east side of the valley (1:9).

On the way from Laruns to Col d'Aubisque the ski resort of **Gourette** enables walkers to enjoy some very pleasant hill country to the southeast, where there are tarns, green ridge crests and opportunities to make tours of two or three days' duration (1:8). On the eastern

The Refuge de la Brèche is one of the busiest of all Pyrenean huts

side of Col de Soulor, **Arrens-Marsous** is conveniently placed for exploration of valleys at the foot of Balaïtous and, for the motorist, the Vallée and Lac d'Estaing (2:2, 2:3).

Cauterets is one of the best centres on which to base a walking holiday, for several very fine valleys drain down to it: Lutour, de Gaube and Marcadau among them. Each one abounds with opportunities for walkers of all standards, and in each there's a mountain hut to extend the scope for long tours and explorations (2:4–2:7).

Without question the best-known feature of the Pyrenees is the Cirque de Gavarnie. At its base lies **Gavarnie**, a village of little appeal by day, but when the trippers have gone it's good enough for overnight accommodation – and the walking potential is vast (2:11). Nearby **Gèdre**, a short way downvalley, is the place to stay if you're interested in visiting the cirques of Estaubé and Troumouse (2:10), while just out of the main high mountain region, yet still close enough for visitors with their own transport, the little town of **Luz-St-Sauveur** offers a low-key alternative (2:7).

Barèges is regularly used as a base for commercial walking holidays, having access to country both north and south of the Tourmalet road. It also serves as a useful centre for walks to the outer rim of the Néouvielle massif (2:8, 2:9), although **St-Lary-Soulan** in the Vallée d'Aure is the nearest major centre for the Néouvielle region, albeit the standard approach involves a 20km journey by road. Other valleys worth looking at from a base at St-Lary are those of Rioumajou and Moudang, below the Spanish frontier ridge, but as with the approach to Néouvielle, to get to the entrance of these you'll need your own transport (3:1).

The next major valley east of St-Lary is the Louron, with a linking road across Col d'Azet coming down to the lovely Lac de Génos-Loudenvielle. The valley south of the lake narrows towards the road-head at Pont du Prat, from which point walkers can get up into some rugged little cirques, while the main valley itself offers more gentle, undemanding landscapes and walks to match. The neighbouring villages of **Loudenvielle** and **Génos** could serve as rewarding centres for a week's holiday (3:2).

Traditionally the spa town of **Luchon** (or to be precise, Bagnères de Luchon) was an important base for exploration of the Central Pyrenees, and today the number of walks accessible from it are sufficient to keep most activists happy through many a summer day. From the roadhead at the Hospice de France a centuries-old classic leads steeply to the Port de Venasque for a view into Spain and the Maladeta massif. Other walks project into the Vallée du Lys, to the Cirque de la Glère, or via the Granges d'Astau and Lac d'Oô for some remote mountain tarns below the frontier ridge. There's something to meet every taste (3:3, 3:4).

Southeast of St-Girons the sleepy spa of **Aulus-les-Bains** in the upper reaches of the Vallée du Garbet offers walks to the spectacular Cascade d'Ars, Étang de Guzet and the seemingly remote collection of tarns lying below Refuge de Bassiès on the route of GR10 (4:6). Mountains of Haute-Ariège mark the southern horizon. **Vicdessos** and nearby **Auzat**, though modest and somewhat limited in accommodation and facilities, provide access to a range of outings within the Vallée du Vicdessos, whose upper reaches nudge against the borders of both Spain and Andorra (5:1).

Farther east another spa town, **Ax-les-Thermes**, makes a good base from which to explore the Vallée d'Orlu (the Oriège) and outer reaches of the Carlit massif (5:4). Ax is on a mainline railway, and is the nearest major resort town north of Andorra. The road to Andorra forks below Pas de la Casa, with the southeast branch crossing Col de Puymorens, with **Porté** below providing an easy way into the Carlit region from the west (5:5), while further south the villages of **Saillagouse** and **Eyne** are well situated for an exploration of valleys on the south side of the Cerdagne, some of which are noted for their alpine flowers and bird migrations (5:6).

ACCOMPAGNATEURS

A number of valley resorts in the French Pyrenees have their own Bureau des Guides, whose members are not solely concerned with climbing or more general mountaineering routes. Most employ certified *accompagnateurs en moyenne montagne*, who may be hired by groups or individuals to lead mountain walks, often on a specific theme such as geology or flora and fauna. In winter *accompagnateurs* may also guide snowshoe excursions among the mountains. With an *accompagnateur* language should not be a significant barrier, since a condition of qualification is a working knowledge of English and one or two other European languages. If there is not a Bureau des Guides advertised in your valley base, enquire at the local tourist office, as there are also many licensed guides operating independently. Alternatively contact the Associations Départementales des Accompagnateurs en Montagne (ADPAM):

Pyrénées Atlantiques
ADPAM, Eric Corno, 64490 Etsaut (☎ 05 59 34 86 15)

Hautes Pyrénées
ADPAM, 2 pl. Lafayette, 65200 Bagnères de Bigorre (☎ 05 62 95 19 19)

Haute Garonne
ADPAM, Jean Pierre Daffos, Henne Morte, 31160 Aspet (☎ 05 61 88 84 12)

Ariège
ADPAM, Ouilié Daniel, 1 route de la Prade, 09220 Vicdessos (☎ 05 61 64 83 96)

Aude
ADPAM, Michel Sagnol, 5 rue des Merisiers, 11340 Belcaire (☎ 04 68 20 77 38)

Pyrénées Orientales
ADPAM Secrétariat, Les Enfants de la Planète, Le Balcon de Cerdagne, Bât 7, Font-Romeu (☎ 04 68 30 62 02)

The UK equivalent of *accompagnateurs* are registered members of the British Association of International Mountain Leaders (BAIML), several of whom lead walking holidays in the Pyrenees. For information visit their website on www.baiml.org.

For information on rock climbing and mountaineering guides, contact the Compagnie des guides des Pyrénées at 28 rue du Barège, 65120 Esquièze-Sere (☎ 06 07 86 31 61).

Spain

Just over the border on the south side of Col du Somport, at the head of the Rio Aragón, the ski resort of **Candanchú** (1550m) may not be the most aesthetically pleasing of places to stay – especially when the snow has gone – but, being on the route of GR11, it has one or two *albergues* that are open throughout the year and are well spoken of, and for walkers with their own transport there's plenty to explore in various side-valleys heading downstream. An alternative base in the Valle del Aragón (otherwise known as the Valle de Canfranc) is **Canfranc-Estación** at the current railhead, with its huge international station and one-street line of buildings astride the Somport road. Tributary valleys feed in from east and west, and at the northern end of the main valley there are modest summits to reach and cross-border walkers' passes to enjoy (1:4).

For a more lively and atmospheric base, the town of **Jaca**, just out of the mountains where the Aragón spills into an open plain, suggests a mix of lowland indulgence with a sudden burst of activity when the mountains call from the north. Local guides and *accompagnateurs* (*guia acompañante* in Spanish) operate from Mountain Travel on Av. Rgto Galicia (☎ 974 35 57 70), which organises courses and adventure holidays (1:4).

The next cross-border road-pass east of the Aragón is the Pourtalet, giving a tremendous view of Pic du Midi d'Ossau just over the frontier in France. The Rio Gallégo flows down through the Valle de Tena, and immediately north of the Embalse de Lanuza a spur cuts off the main road to **Sallent de Gállego**, a convenient base for the exploration of the upper valley of the Aguas Limpias, whose headwaters gather below the Balaïtous. This is very fine country indeed, with a whole host of walking expeditions to tackle (1:10).

Further south along the Rio Gallégo, near the top end of the Embalse de Búbal, both **Panticosa** and the neighbouring spa of **Balneario de Panticosa**, 10km away, also provide accommodation for walkers, with trails, modest ascents and sections of GR11 to follow (1:10).

In the next major valley system to the east of Panticosa **Torla**, situated on the edge of the Ordesa national park, is understandably popular. There's no shortage of walking opportunities here, not only in Ordesa's canyon but also in the adjacent Ara valley too. It is, however, inordinately busy during the high summer. The wonderful Añisclo canyon can also be reached from Torla by strong walkers, although two or three days should be set aside for a proper tour through the surrounding countryside (2:12–2:14).

Bielsa, which is 13km from the road tunnel linking Spain with France, sits at the mouth of the Valle de Pineta, a charming valley flanked by big mountain walls and with Monte Perdido at its head. There are some good, if tough, walks to be made from the valley head, but as with most of these Spanish resorts, you'll need your own transport to get there. Either that, or spend your money on taxis – where they're available (2:16).

Plan and, to a limited extent, **San Juan de Plan**, in the Valle de Gistaín, whose upper reaches lie below the West Face of the Posets

West of the Renclusa refugio, Pico de Paderna overlooks a small tarn in the Maladeta massif

massif, are modest in size and facilities, but they give access to some splendid walking country, although the best base is the *refugio* at the summer hamlet of **Viadós**, with a wonderland on its doorstep (3:5).

Benasque is one of the prime centres of activity in the Spanish Pyrenees, being situated in the Ésera valley, which flows between the Maladeta and Posets massifs, whose surrounding glens provide almost unlimited scope for both walkers and climbers. As the mountains here are topped by the highest summits in the range, and the scenery is so appealing, Benasque attracts plenty of visitors, but there's no shortage of accommodation, and several authorised campsites are scattered along the Ésera on the edge of the *parque natural* (3:7–3:10).

The Vall d'Aran is an anomaly, lying on the northern side of the mountains yet being Spanish throughout. **Salardú** is without question the best walking base, with side glens to explore both north and south of the main valley. The Pyrenean High Route passes through the village, which boasts a distant view of the Maladeta massif. As with most of the neighbouring villages, Salardú has a splendid Romanesque church, and despite new development retains a pleasing architectural style based on tradition (4:7).

Boí (also spelt Bohi) is located in the valley of the Noguera de Tor, which projects into the western end of the Aigües Tortes national park. A range of one-day and multi-day hikes lies just to the north, while **Espot** serves as the main base for walking and/or climbing activity in the park's eastern sector. Unfortunately there's no obvious valley base on the south side of the park, although visitors with their own transport could stay in **Capdella** (30km north of Pobla de Segur) or one of the campsites further downstream in Vall Fosca and face a drive up to the Sallente dam, where paths climb to a bounty of tarns, accessible summits and walkers' passes. To make the most of countless opportunities within the Aigües Tortes region, one should consider using the *refugis* that have been built in and on the edge of the national park (4:9–4:11).

On the eastern side of the Noguera Pallaresa, **Tavascan** enables the little-known country of the upper Vall de Cardós to be enjoyed, while the hamlet of **Àreu** is the last habitation in the Vall Ferrera. Both these valleys are headed by attractive country worth exploring on foot (4:13, 4:14).

Finally, at the head of a precipitous gorge above the Rio Freser, and served by a rack-and-pinion railway from Ribes de Freser via Queralbs, **Núria** is overlooked by the Puigmal, a high point on the frontier ridge walling the Cerdagne. Roadless Núria is neither resort nor mountain village, but a complex of religious sanctuary, hotel, restaurant and railway station set in an open basin of pasture, and with a youth hostel offering budget accommodation. As a base Núria provides opportunities for ascents of some of the highest local mountains, which give fairly long but non-technical outings, plus walks along the GR11, and several opportunities for straying across the border into tributary glens that flow down to the French Cerdagne (5:7).

Andorra

Within Andorra's mountain rim **Arinsal** is useful for walkers planning to make the ascent of its highest mountain, Pic de Coma Pedrosa, as well as a selection of walks in the neighbourhood. **El Serrat**, near the head of the Valira del Nord, offers walks to the Tristaina lakes and northeast into the Rialp valley. Then there is **Canillo**, roughly situated in the centre of Andorra, which, with good public transport, also enjoys plenty of walking opportunities nearby. Towards the eastern end of the country, **Soldeu** is located near the idyllic Vall d'Incles, one of the least exploited of Andorra's glens (5:3).

GUIDEBOOKS FOR WALKERS

📖 *Walks and Climbs in the Pyrenees* by Kev Reynolds (Cicerone Press, 5th edn, 2008)

100 Walks in the French Pyrenees by Terry Marsh (Hodder & Stoughton, 1992, o/p)

Landscapes of the Pyrenees by Paul Jenner and Christine Smith (Sunflower Books, 1990)

The Mountains of Andorra by Alf Robertson and Jane Meadowcroft (Cicerone Press, 2005)

See also list of walking guides in French under 'Maps and Guidebooks' above.

WALKING HOLIDAYS

Several UK companies, and companies based in the mountains but run by ex-patriot Britons, offer walking holidays in the Pyrenees, among them:

- Borderline Holidays (☎ 05 62 92 68 95, www.borderlinehols.com) – based in Luz-St Saveur, Peter Derbyshire and Jude Lock offer guided walking and wild-life holidays in summer, and ski packages in winter, with accommodation in Barèges or Luz

- Exodus, Grange Mills, Weir Road, London SW12 0NE (☎ 0870 240 5550 www.exodus.co.uk)) – offer a choice of walking and trekking holidays on both sides of the border

- Headwater Holidays, The Old School House, Chester Road, Castle, Northwich CW8 1LE (☎ 01606 720099 www.headwater-holidays.co.uk) – walking holidays in the Central Pyrenees

- HF Holidays, Imperial House, Edgeware Road, London NW9 5AL (☎ 020 8905 9388, e-mail: info@hfholidays.co.uk, www.hfholidays.co.uk) – guided walks from St Lary

- Inghams (brochures and bookings through high street travel agents) organise holidays in selected Andorran resorts, with guided walks available

- Pyrenean Mountain Tours, c/o 2 Rectory Cottages, Wolverton, Tadley, Hants RG26 5RS (☎ 01635 297209, e-mail: pmtuk@aol.com, www.pyrenees.co.uk) – year-round holidays based in Luz-St-Sauveur. This company also offers self-guided walks and can assist with airport transfers, maps and route advice

- Ramblers Holidays, Box 43, Welwyn Garden City, Herts AL8 6PQ (☎ 01707 331133, www.ramblersholidays.co.uk) – walking holidays in the Cerdagne

- Thomson Lakes and Mountains (brochures and bookings through high street travel agents, www.thomsonlakesandmountains.com) offer centre-based walking holidays in Arinsal and Soldeu, Andorra.

TREKKING

If we take trekking to mean walking multi-day routes across rugged landscapes, then arguably the finest trekking in all Europe is to be found in the Pyrenees. Dozens of *grande randonnée* trails have been established throughout France, many of which explore sections of these mountains, and the Spanish are following suit with their *gran recorrido* routes. With three ultra-long-distance treks (GR10, GR11 and the HRP) making a coast-to-coast traverse, and many shorter, but no less varied, waymarked GR trails – not to mention a host of unofficial tours – the trekker is clearly spoilt for choice. The following section summarises some of the options, but it is by no means a comprehensive list of possibilities, for there's great pleasure to be had in devising your own treks by linking existing trails or, for the truly adventurous – and those with advanced map-reading and mountain-walking skills – tackling pathless terrain and crossing remote passes. Publications mentioned against some of the routes are noted in more detail under 'Maps and Guidebooks' above, while topoguides for French GR routes are produced by the Fédération Française de la Randonnée Pédestre (FFRP, 64 rue de Gergovie, 75014 Paris), and are generally available in the UK at Stanfords in London.

Trekking near Refuge de Larribet en route to Balaïtous

GR10 – Sentier des Pyrénées

Between Hendaye on the Atlantic coast and Banyuls-sur-Mer on the Mediterranean, the GR10 can rightly claim to be one of the great walks of France, not simply for its length, but also for the scenic quality of the route and its cultural diversity. This 800km-long trek travels mostly along the north flank of the mountains (but occasionally touches the Franco-Spanish border) at around mid-height, and

📖 *The GR10 Trail* by Paul Lucia (Cicerone Press, 2003)

Trekking in the Pyrenees by Douglas Streatfeild-James (Trailblazer, 3rd edn, 2005)

The complete route is marked on a series of maps published under the generic title of Carte de Randonnées at a scale of 1:50,000, but beware old editions which may not accurately portray the route's upgrading.

is broken into something like 50 day-stages. Overnight accommodation in the form of *gîtes d'étape* or mountain huts, but sometimes hotels, is available on almost every stage, and the route is waymarked throughout as it links a succession of footpaths, tracks and minor roads on its journey from one coast to the other. Despite this waymarking, navigational skills are still called for on the crossing of remote areas, such as are found in parts of Haute-Ariège, and the demand for a good level of fitness may be gauged by the fact that more than 47,500m of ascent and descent will have been achieved by the time the Mediterranean comes in sight.

GR11 – La Senda Pirenaica

This Spanish equivalent of GR10 tackles the wilder and more sparsely populated country on the south side of the international frontier. Though not quite as challenging as the Pyrenean High Route (see below), it is a tougher proposition than its counterpart on the French side of the border on account of the necessity to carry food and a cooker, plus tent or bivouac equipment, for those occasions on which there's an absence of more conventional lodging at the end of a day. Navigation is often more problematical than on GR10, thanks to a superabundance of trails or cairns in some areas and their virtual non-existence in others, and the extension of jeep tracks (*pistas*) in a few places that has not been marked even on the latest edition maps, while some maps incorrectly show the route in a few specific districts. Waymarking is by red-and-white paint flashes, except where the route goes through the national parks of Ordesa and Aigües Tortes. GR11 involves less overall height gain and loss than does GR10, thanks to several west–east oriented valleys which carry it onward. These points being duly noted, GR11 affords the wild-country trekker and backpacker an opportunity to explore some of the most attractive mountains and valleys south of the watershed.

📖 *Through the Spanish Pyrenees: GR11* by Paul Lucia (Cicerone Press, 4th edn, 2008) is the only English-language guide to the route.

GR11 Senderos de Gran Recorrido, in Spanish, is published by Prames S.A. This loose-leaved book is useful for the maps at 1:50,000 scale which are included.

Maps covering the whole route at 1:50,000 are those of the Servicio Geografico del Ejercito.

Pyrenean High Route

The coast-to-coast journey of the **Haute Randonnée Pyrénéenne** (HRP) makes a demanding high-level traverse of the range, often along the frontier crest, and descends into valleys only where necessary. This classic route, which is one of Europe's longest and most challenging mountain treks, should be attempted only by strong, experienced walkers with proven navigational skills, scrambling ability and a good head for heights. There is no one definitive route, but a number of *variante* stages working steadily eastward that are regularly reviewed and refined. Waymarking is sporadic and non-existent in places, and although there are many refuges along the way, accommodation is by no means available at the end of every one of its 45 or so stages, so camping or bivouac gear should be carried. As long periods are spent away from habitation, food supplies also need to be taken. Trekkers should start each stage early in the morning, shortly after dawn for preference, to take advantage of cooler conditions; and keep away from ridges if a storm threatens. Because of the likelihood of snow and/or ice remaining in some of the high gullies, on cols and sections of ridge in the central part of the range, it is prudent to carry an ice axe and plan the route so as not to reach the High Pyrenees before about the beginning of July. The weeks of high summer can lead to difficulties locating water sources, but days of heavy rain and even snow are not unknown. Anyone setting out to walk the complete HRP should allow lots of extra days to cover all eventualities.

Other GR Trails in the Pyrenees

*   **GR7** – this epic route through France begins in the Vosges and reaches the Pyrenees near Andorra.

A high-route trekker stands on the frontier crest east of the Aiguilles d'Ansabère. French valleys are hidden beneath a cloud-sea

📖 See *The Pyrenean Haute Route* by Ton Joosten (Cicerone Press, 2nd edition 2009) for an up-to-date route description. The route is marked on the Carte de Randonnées series of 10 maps published by Rando Éditions at a scale of 1:50,000.

- **GR12** – much of this trail through Navarre follows the course of GR11.
- **GR15** – known as the Sendero Prepirenaico, it traces a route similar to, but much lower than, the GR11 along the Spanish flanks.
- **GR19** – is another Spanish waymarked route that remains within the boundaries of Alto Aragón.
- **GR36/GR4** – crosses the mountains of the Eastern Pyrenees, including Pic du Canigou, on a north–south traverse.
- **GR65** – the pilgrims' route to Santiago, the Sentier de St Jacques de Compostelle, which crosses the Pyrenees via the Ibañeta pass (📖 *The Way of St James:* vol. 1: *Le Puy to the Pyrenees* and vol. 2: *Pyrenees – Santiago – Finisterre* by Alison Raju (Cicerone Press)).
- **GR65/3** – is a variation of the classic GR65 itinerary, crossing by way of the Col du Somport to Jaca before heading west to join the main route.
- **GR107** – is based on a route taken by Cathars fleeing persecution in the 13th century from Montségur to the Sierra del Cadí. Also known as the Chemin des Bonhommes.
- **Le Sentiere Cathare** – trekking between Foix and the Mediterranean, linking ruined Cathar fortresses. See *The Cathar Way* by Alan Mattingly (Cicerone Press, 2006).

In addition to the linear GR routes there are numerous circuits and modest tours of specific regions on the French side of the range, known as **Grandes Randonnées** (or **Tours**) **de Pays**, outlined on the 1:50,000 maps. These tours vary in length from one to seven days, with accommodation usually available in *gîtes d'étape*, and were created by the Association Randonnées Pyrénéennes in order to bring benefits to local people.

CIMES-PYRÉNÉES (Centre d'Informations Montagne et Sentiers), 1 rue Maye Lane, BP 2, 65421 Ibos cedex, France (☎ 05 62 90 67 60, e-mail: cimes@randopyrenees.com, www.cimes-pyrenees.com)

The following is a sample selection of these Tours de Pays. Sections of some of the trails are described under specific valley sections of this guide.

Western High Pyrenees
- Tour de la Soule – in six stages
- Tour de la Vallée de Barétous – a short tour lasting three days
- Tour de la Haute Vallée d'Aspe – tackled in five day-stages

- Tour de la Haute Vallée d'Ossau – another five-day circuit
- Tour du Val d'Azun – a four-day tour
- Tour de la Vallée de Campan – a five-stage tour, with a three-day shorter option

Central Pyrenees
- Tour des Baronnies – basically a three-stage tour with optional one-day extension
- Tour de la Vallée d'Aure – a four-day circuit
- Tour des Vallées d'Oueil and du Larboust – a moderate three-day tour
- Tour du Cagire-Burat – takes six days to complete
- Tour du Biros – a five-day route
- Tour de le Massif des Tres Seigneurs – in five stages

Eastern Pyrenees
- Tour des Montagnes d'Ax – a full six-stage circuit
- Tour du Carlit – three to four days among the granite highlands of the Carlit
- Tour du Capcir – another four-day circuit
- Tour de le Pays de Sault – a five-day tour of the eastern Pays de Sault
- Tour des Fenouillèdes – this week-long tour explores the foothill country
- Tour des Tres Esteles – in two or three stages in the Têt valley

As an example of how a rewarding short trek can be created simply by linking a series of existing trails, the following outline tour describes a cross-border route which explores some of the most dramatic country within the adjacent national parks of the PNP and Ordesa. Other suggestions for treks of varying lengths can be found within the main body of this book.

The Two Parks Trek
This four- to five-day circuit can be tackled without the need to carry camping equipment, as there's accommodation available at the end of each stage. It could also be extended, shortened or varied by use of alternative trails. Study of the appropriate maps will reveal the options available.

From Gavarnie at the roadhead in the Vallée du Gave de Pau, the first stage leads to the Refuge des Sarradets (Refuge de la Brèche) just below the Brèche de Roland, which enjoys a grandstand view of the Cirque de Gavarnie. There are three ways by which to reach the hut:
- through the Vallée des Espécières to the Port de Boucharo, then along an easy path below Le Taillon heading east;

- via a scenic hillside path into the Vallée des Pouey Aspé, where a steep trail rises south to join the route from Port de Boucharo; or
- the recommended route, which climbs from the base of the cirque by way of the Échelle des Sarradets.

This last-named route is the more demanding, but it also offers the most dramatic views of the great cirque walls.

The next stage is short, but it gives an opportunity to visit the summit of Le Taillon and to explore the head of the Ordesa canyon. Out of the Sarradets refuge the way immediately ascends a short stretch of crevasse-free glacier to gain the Spanish frontier at the fabled Brèche de Roland. On the south side a path cuts round to the right and leads to the summit of Le Taillon, reckoned to be the easiest Pyrenean 3000m mountain. Back at the Brèche the way descends across a desolate patch of country whose few streams drain to unseen cascades that pour into the Ordesa canyon via one of its tributary glens, and eventually comes to the Góriz refuge on the lower western slopes of Monte Perdido.

Day Three leads into the Ordesa canyon. Trekkers can either take the direct route straight down the Soaso Cirque and follow the much-trodden GR11 trail past a series of impressive waterfalls or choose the alternative balcony path (the Faja de Pelay), which edges along the southern wall of the canyon, then joins the lower route near the roadhead car park via the knee-crunching Senda de los Cazadores. From the foot of the Senda follow GR11 downvalley to the confluence of the Rio Arazas and Rio Ara, then break away to the northwest, still on GR11 as it heads upstream through the narrows of the Rio Ara to Bujaruelo (San Nicolás de Bujaruelo), where an old hospice has been renovated and turned into a private refuge.

The next stage forges up the Ara, on the east bank of the river most of the way, to its headwall below the Vignemale. The Pyrenean High Route, which makes a traverse of this headwall, is gained in order to cross the Col des Mulets (2591m) on the Franco-Spanish border, giving access to the upper reaches of the Vallée de Gaube. There, with a direct view of the great North Face of the Vignemale, a night is spent in Refuge des Oulettes de Gaube.

The final stage of the trek climbs from the refuge over the 2734m Hourquette d'Ossoue, then descends past another hut, Refuge de Bayssellance, passes below the tongue of the Ossoue glacier and continues downvalley along the route of GR10 back to Gavarnie.

📖 Individual sections of this trek are described in *Walks and Climbs in the Pyrenees* by Kev Reynolds (Cicerone Press, 5th edn, 2008). Much of the route can be followed on the Carte de Randonnées map No. 4 *Bigorre* at 1:50,000. For the Ordesa canyon section use either *Ordesa and Monte Perdido National Park* (English version) published by Editorial Pirineo at 1:40,000 or the Editorial Alpina sheet *Ordesa y Monte Perdido*, also at 1:40,000. Editorial Alpina sheet *Vignemale Bujaruelo* at 1:30,000 covers the Ara valley section of the trek.

The Pyrenean environment is a fragile one, and all who walk, trek or climb there have a duty to help preserve it. None of the following guidelines will detract from your enjoyment of the mountain experience, but they will go some way towards preserving the unique qualities of the landscape.

- **Protect water supplies** – when off-site camping use a billy or other container for bathing or washing clothes, and dispose of the soapy residue well away from streams or lakes. Don't defecate within 50m of any water source, and completely bury faeces.

- **Burn used toilet paper** – if you get taken short on the trail please don't discard used toilet paper, which is not only unsightly but can also be a health hazard. Carry a cigarette lighter with you and burn soiled paper, taking care not to set fire to vegetation.

- **Leave no litter** – decomposition of foodstuffs can take up to six months, while food and drinks cans may remain intact for as long as 85 years. Mountain huts should not be treated as garbage centres; instead, take all rubbish out of the mountains for proper disposal in villages or towns.

- **Don't pick the flowers** – a number of plants are protected by law, but even those that are not should be left for others to enjoy.

- **Make no fires** – campers should take their own cooking fuel with them and not use local wood. Campfires are unnecessary, wasteful and a potential risk to vegetation.

- **Don't take short-cuts** – to avoid spreading trail erosion, please don't take short-cuts on winding paths.

A **Country Code** has been adopted in both France and Spain, as follows:

- Love and respect nature
- Avoid making unnecessary noise
- Destroy nothing
- Do not leave litter
- Do not pick flowers or plants
- Do not disturb wildlife
- Close gates behind you
- Protect and preserve the habitat
- Do not smoke or light fires in the forests
- Respect and understand the country way of life and its people
- Think of others as you think of yourself.

Among UK companies offering **trekking holidays** in the Pyrenees try:
Exodus, 9 Weir Road, London SW12 0LT (☎ 020 8675 5550, fax: 020 8673 0779, e-mail: sales@exodus.co.uk, www.exodus.co.uk)
Sherpa Expeditions, 131a Heston Road, Hounslow, Middx TW5 0RF (☎ 020 8577 2717, e-mail: sales@sherpaexpeditions.com,www.sherpaexpeditions.com).
See also Hilary Sharp, Trekking in the Alps, Chemin des Biolles, F-74660 Vallorcine, France (☎ 0033 450 54 62 09, e-mail: hilaryalp@aol.com, www.trekkinginthealps.com).

CLIMBING

The nature of climbing in the Pyrenees defies easy definition since it is as diverse as the rock itself. Whilst the majority of summits may be reached by modest routes requiring little more than a steep walk with a few scrambling sections, the range is not short of serious climbing venues. There are limestone aiguilles, impressive granite walls, sun-warmed sandstone features, flawless andesite and amazing phallic towers of conglomerate. There are outcrops of modest size, and buttresses and couloirs in big mountain settings that give climbs in excess of 800m. Although the more notorious routes grow year by year in popularity, it is common to have your chosen line – and sometimes the whole mountain face – to yourself. Bolt-protected sport routes have also become well established in a number of areas, although these rather fly in the face of traditions of *Pyrénéisme*, of which more below. To summarise, both sides of the frontier offer a wealth of climbing opportunities at assorted grades, with unlimited scope for those at the sharp end of the sport to develop virtually unexplored crags.

The grading of climbs is by the standard adjectival system in regard to the overall route (as below), with the internationally accepted numerical system denoting the difficulty of individual pitches.

	French	*Spanish*	*English*
F	facile	fácil	easy
PD	peu difficile	poco difícil	moderately difficult
AD	assez difficile	algo difícil	fairly difficult
TD/MD	très difficile	muy difícil	very difficult
ED	extrêmement difficile	extremadamente difícil	extremely difficult

The run-down of major climbing sites below provides a glimpse of the range's potential, while other possibilities are mentioned elsewhere in the main text.

France

Located in the Cirque de Lescun high above the west bank of the Aspe valley, the spectacular limestone pinnacles of the **Aiguilles d'Ansabère** rise against the Franco-Spanish border 3 hours' walk from Lescun. The Grande Aiguille (2377m) and Petite Aiguille (2271m) both give quality climbs on generally good rock, with several established classics dating from the 1950s, while the neighbouring Pic d'Ansabère, which has an easy scrambler's way to the summit, offers at least three TD routes of 150–250m in length. In the same district, but further north and easily accessible from Refuge de Labérouat above Lescun, the 300m high walls of the **Orgues de Camplong** flank the valley; the test-piece here is *Voie de l'Y* (270m, TD, V+/6a). Lescun is overlooked by the **Pics Billare**, and the East Face of both the Grand and Petit Pics offer exacting climbs worthy of attention (1:2).

On the east wall of the Aspe valley above Etsaut, but also approached from Les Eaux-Chaudes in the upper Vallée d'Ossau, the 2410m aiguille of **Capéran de Sesques** offers free climbing on the South Face *voie normale* (IV+), as well as artificial routes on the 130m North Face, first climbed in 1935 by Cazalet and Mailly (TD) (1:3, 1:9).

Pic du Midi d'Ossau is very much the symbol of the Pyrenees, despite its comparatively modest height of 2885m. This twin-summited granite monolith stands alone above lush pastures west of the Vallée d'Ossau, and from certain viewpoints resembles Mount Kenya. The Grand and Petit Pics are its most conspicuous features, the two separated by the deep cleft of La Fourche. With probably more hard climbing routes to offer than any other Pyrenean mountain, Pic du Midi is understandably popular in summer and winter. Rising above Refuge de Pombie, the Southeast Face is both large

The summit of Pic d'Ansabère provides a grandstand from which to study the Petite Aiguille

and complex; the North Face overlooks steep forests but is partially hidden from general view; the West Face falls to the lovely Bious meadows and holds the least climbing interest; while the East Face contains the *voie normale* (1:9).

On the far side of the Ossau valley Refuge d'Arrémoulit makes a good base for climbs on several nearby granite peaks, notably **Pic Palas**, **Pic de la Lie** and **Pic d'Arriel**, which has a fine route on its Northeast Face, *Nuit d'Insomnie* (1:9). The most westerly, and certainly one of the more remote 3000m peaks, the 3144m **Balaïtous**, carries the international border southeast of Pic Palas, and is noted for its long bristling ridges of coarse granite which give some of the finest traverses in all the Pyrenees. In general the faces of this big mountain are rather short (around 250m) with a variety of middle-grade climbs, although the Southeast Face boasts a 400m TD route, the *Eperon Elegante* (Gomez/Zapata, 1993) (2:3).

Due north of Balaïtous, but south of the Col d'Aubisque, the limestone **Massif de Gourette** has a group of summits of modest height (2000–2600m) that reward with many short rock problems and lots of potential for winter climbs. One of the smaller peaks, the **Pène Sarrière** (1936m), has a jaunty fin of an arête and an impressive East Face line included in *Les Pyrénées – Les 100 Plus Belles Courses* (see box below), while the 2614m **Pic de Ger** has routes of 500–600m in length (1:8).

Back on the frontier crest, and accessible from Cauterets and Gavarnie, the **Vignemale** is one of the great Pyrenean mountains, with four main summits crowning a group of north faces at the head of the Vallée de Gaube. Most of the climbing interest is concentrated on these, of which the Refuge des Oulettes de Gaube has an outstanding direct view. The rock is limestone, but of sometimes dubious quality, yet the surroundings are second to none, and there's a wonderful big-mountain atmosphere in its setting. The faces and buttresses have undeniable appeal, while the Couloir de Gaube between Piton Carré and Pique Longue has the most famous mixed route in the whole chain. First climbed in 1889 by Brulle, Bazillac, de Monts, Passet and Salles, it remains a serious outing more than a century later. Most of the established routes are climbed in a single day, except under winter conditions, when a bivouac is often necessary. But the length of some of the routes (800m) and difficulties of escape make bad weather especially unwelcome (2:6).

The Glacier d'Ossoue flows down the Vignemale's east flank and empties into the Ossoue valley. This in turn leads to the Gave de Pau just north of the renowned **Cirque de Gavarnie**, whose three rock bands, divided by two snow terraces, afford numerous climbing opportunities at assorted grades. The North Face of the 3009m Tour du Marboré is one of the popular classics. It was first climbed via the upper rock band in 1956 by Dufourmantelle and Jean Ravier and is now graded TD+. That route is 400m long, while a direct ascent of the whole cirque wall from base to summit is a 1200m

The Southeast Face, or Pombie Wall, of Pic du Midi d'Ossau has more routes than any comparable rock face in the Pyrenees

epic achieved as long ago as 1945 by Adagas and Malus. As a venue for winter climbing, of which more below, Gavarnie takes a lot of beating (2:11).

North of the big frontier mountains and west of the road to Lourdes, the valley crags below **Pic de Pibeste** abound with short (15–35m) rock problems, mostly with protection *in situ*. When the frontier peaks are storm-bound, often these crags are just far enough out of range to provide a dry alternative (2:1).

Both sides of the **Cirque de Troumouse** are worthy of attention. Troumouse itself has a variety of outings in the middle grades and some interesting North Face routes (2:10). The eastern side of the cirque wall overlooks the Barroude lakes and refuge, a splendid high pasture accessible only by a long walk. The **Barroude Wall** makes an impressive backdrop and gives middle-grade routes of around 400–450m (3:1).

The granite block of the **Néouvielle massif** lies to the north of Troumouse and is accessible from the Tourmalet road or, from the east, by way of St-Lary-Soulan. Although this is mainly a region for walkers, the climber has an outstanding array of short rock problems to choose from. The Crête d'Espade, which pushes north of Pic de Néouvielle, bristles with bolted sport routes, while the 400m North Face of Pic Long has a classic line first climbed by Robert Ollivier and Roger Mailly in 1933 (2:9).

A cluster of fine granite peaks at the head of the Vallée d'Oô, southwest of Luchon, concentrates climbing activity near the Spanish border, with the Espingo and Portillon refuges being particularly useful as an overnight base. The **Pics Lézat, Spijeoles** and **Quayrat** have a number of lines in the middle grades, as well as some more demanding routes of TD (3:3).

Still in France, but much further east in the Couserans district of Ariège, the 2838m **Mont Valier** presents a formidable-looking block with its East and Southeast faces soaring above the unguarded Refuge d'Aula, being separated by a prominent fin, the Southeast Spur. The classic route here is the 800m *Trou Noir* on the East Face, first climbed in 1971 by Louis Audoubert, Alain Blassier, Marc Galy and Monique Rouch, but there are TD routes also on the Southeast and North faces, while the *voie normale*, as is common among these mountains, is an uncomplicated ascent for unroped hill walkers usually made from Refuge des Estagnous (4:2).

East again, the **Dent d'Orlu** is a 2222m granite tooth which rises above the Vallée d'Orlu southeast of Ax-les-Thermes. Slab faces of 300–500m drop steeply on three sides, and some of the routes are bolted. Both the South and Southeast faces are accessible from the Orlu valley, but the East Face is reached by way of a walk from the Ax to Pailhères road (5:4).

Spain

If generalisations are to be accepted, climbing on the Spanish side of the mountains is a much warmer experience than activity on the northern peaks, with the need to avoid dehydration on some of the longer routes when fully exposed to the sun being a prime concern. **Los Mallos de Riglos**, about 40km northwest of Huesca off the road to Jaca and just outside the main Pyrenean block, are typically hot and dry in summer, with some unshaded routes adding a degree of seriousness beyond those difficulties created by the rock itself. The best time to climb here in order to avoid the fiercest temperatures is March–April and September–October, but if high summer cannot be avoided, it's essential to make an early start. The ruddy-brown towers of conglomerate create a remarkable backdrop to the medieval village of Riglos, as surreal as the Dolomites but in their own unique manner, and with vultures circling day by day. Routes are sensational, with lots of exposure and hairy abseil descents, climbs offering minimal fixed protection as well as multi-pitch bolted routes in the F6a–F7c range.

Derek L. Walker's *Rock Climbs in the Pyrenees* (see box below) provides a temptation (1:6).

Riglos is located on the east bank of the Rio Gállego, whose source is in the upper Valle de Tena near the Col du Pourtalet. A short distance south of this border crossing and west of the Gállego, the **Sierra de la Peña Telera** provides tremendous scope for climbers. The crest of this chain is over 10km long and dominates the west side of the upper valley. Despite the generally poor quality of the limestone a great number of routes have been achieved on the steep north-facing walls, some of which exceed 800m in height. A popular arena for winter climbing (see below), the valley also boasts a number of south-facing crags on which to climb when the mountains are out of condition (1:10).

In the same valley as the Peña Telera, but above the ski centre of Formigal, the **Peña Foratata** offers a more compact arena with 400–500m routes facing south, while in the tributary valley of the Rio Caldarés, the *escuela* of Las Foronias, beside the Panticosa to Balneario road, gives year-round crag climbing with effortless access. In his guide, Derek L. Walker comments that while climbing here 'it is not unusual to be in shirt sleeves at Christmas while surrounded by snow-capped peaks and ski aficionados' (1:10).

The south-facing sandstone walls of **Ordesa** strike every visitor entering from Torla with their multi-hued severity: Mondarruego, Tozal del Mallo, Punta Gallinero and the west-facing Fraucata hold an assortment of climbs overlooking one of the most scenically attractive of canyons. Most routes are long and steep, with overhanging sections (on the Tozal), but protection is usually good, although there are occasional loose areas that need extra care. Being in the national park, climbers are advised to note any restrictions that might affect their activities – especially with regard to an overnight bivouac prior to starting a climb (camping is forbidden here) (2:13).

Although not noted for quality rock routes, the **Maladeta massif** does in fact hold the highest area of difficult climbing in the Pyrenees. This is found on the steep north side of the crest which runs southeast from Aneto over the Espalda d'Aneto and Pico de Tempestades, culminating on Pico Margalida and remaining above 3200m throughout. Routes up to 350m high are tackled here in winter as well as summer, despite the long approach through the Ésera valley (3:10).

East of the Noguera Ribagorçana, which has the Viella road tunnel at its head, the granite **Besiberri massif** consists of a north–south ridge with six summits over 3000m. A traverse of this ridge makes a good day out, while rock climbs are mostly short but demand a long approach (4:9). However, northwest of Besiberri Nord, the 2786m **Tuc de Contessa**, which guards the entrance to both the Valls de Besiberri and Conangles, has several difficult routes on its North Face developed in the late 1990s by Eduardo Requeña (4:8).

The Besiberri Ridge forms the western limit of the Aigües Tortes national park. Climbing activity within the park mostly consists

The southerly pinnacle of the Agulles d'Amitges, seen from its twin

of short routes on a variety of peaklets that rise above the region's numerous lakes. The twin **Encantats** (Encantados) backing the Sant Maurici lake provide a good introduction with a 600m AD route via the long gash which divides the two summits, while the southwest (lower) of the **Agulles d'Amitges** in view above the *refugi* of the same name has a range of climbs up to TD grade on its South Face (4:11). Southwest of the Portarró d'Espot the **Agulles de Dellui** offer routes of III/3+ M5+ on the big slab North Face (4:9).

East again, but a little south of the main chain in the pre-Pyrenees, the **Sierra del Cadí** has a number of 300–400m climbs in the gullies that streak the north-facing walls, while the popular 2497m Pedraforca on the south side of the massif has lines of around 600m on its impressive North Face which rises above the Refugi Lluís Estasén (5:7).

The above is just a selection of highlights. Elsewhere within the main body of this guide more climbing possibilities are outlined, but the climber with an eye for a route will no doubt see opportunities beyond those mentioned in this book.

📖 *Rock Climbs in the Pyrenees* by Derek L. Walker (Cicerone Press, 1990)

Les Pyrénées: Les 100 Plus Belles Course et Randonnées by Patrice de Bellefon (Denoël, 1976)

Passages Pyrénéens by Rainier Munsch, Christian Ravier and Rémi Thivel (Editions du Pin à Crochets, 1999)

Escalade en Haute Vallée de l'Ariège by Thierry and Colette Pouxviel

Escaladas en Riglos by Felipe Guinda Polo

Escalades al Parque Natural del Cadí by Jaume Matas

MOUNTAIN RESCUE

In the more popular areas of the Pyreneees a helicopter may be used in mountain rescue attempts, but as all services have to be paid for by the person rescued, they should only be called upon in a real emergency. In the event of an accident help can be summoned via mobile phone, or by way of the nearest manned hut, village or public telephone. The number to call depends on location, as below.

Western Pyrenees

France   Oloron-Ste-Marie (☎ 05 59 10 02 50)

Spain   Navarra (☎ 112)

Central Pyrenees

France   Hautes-Pyrénées (☎ 05 62 92 41 41)

Haute-Garonne – PGHM Luchon (☎ 05 61 79 28 36)

CRS Luchon (☎ 05 61 79 83 79)

Ariège – PGHM Savignac (☎ 05 61 64 22 58)

Spain   Aragón (☎ 112)
           Jaca (☎ 974 31 13 50)
           Catalonia (☎ 085)

Eastern Pyrenees
France   PGHM Osséja (☎ 04 68 04 51 03)
           CRS Perpignan (☎ 04 68 61 79 20)

Spain   Catalonia (☎ 085)
Andorra (☎ 112)

Essential information to be conveyed to the rescuer/medical authority is:
- identity, age and number of casualties
- precise location of accident
- nature of injury – is the casualty conscious? bleeding?
- weather conditions at the accident site.

The international distress signal is six blasts on a whistle per minute – or six flashes by torch after dark – followed by a minute's pause; then repeat until a reply is received. The reply is three blasts or torch flashes, followed by a minute's pause.

The following signals are used to communicate with a rescue helicopter.

Help required: raise both arms above head to form a 'V'

Help not required: raise one arm above head, extend other arm downward

WINTER CLIMBING

Despite the range's southerly latitude and maritime climate, the high mountains have enormous potential for winter climbing and, access permitting, there's boundless scope for the creation of new routes on remote mountains as well as modern icefalls in established locations, many of which were pioneered by Rainier Münsch and Dominique Julien in the 1970s. However, conditions can and do change more rapidly than in the Alps, so that often the best routes are climbable for only limited periods, which favours local French and Spanish activists who are able to snatch opportunities as and when they arise. Skis or snowshoes are often useful for approaching the base of a chosen route.

All the main massifs from **Pic du Midi d'Ossau** eastward receive attention, although some are notoriously difficult of access in winter, the remote **Balaïtous** being a prime example, turning what in summer would be a fairly long approach into a serious expedition even before the climbing begins (2:3). Among the more popular venues the 2764m **Peña Telera**, located about 8km south of Pic du Midi on the Spanish side of the border, is now recognised as a major winter playground, with routes of 800m or more on its broad North Face which is riven by some magnificent gullies. As noted above, the rock is generally considered poor, but some 50 or so routes have been achieved here, the great classic being the *Dièdre Central* (Abajo/ Forn, 1970; 800m, TD+, V+/6a), first climbed under winter conditions in 1983 (1:10).

The north-facing **Vignemale** is regularly visited by *Pyrénéistes* in winter, when ice provides a useful adhesive in couloirs that are often threatened by stonefall in summer. The first major winter climb in the Pyrenees was achieved here in 1949 when Bernard Clos and Marcel Jolly repeated the original Barrio/Belloc route on the North Face of Pique Longue, and since then Piton Carré, Pointe Chausenque and the Petit Vignemale have all enjoyed the attention of winter specialists (2:6).

The nearby **Cirque de Gavarnie** provides some of Europe's best icefall climbing – there are up to a dozen icefalls of 200–300m – but following heavy snowfall the two shallow-angled terraces which separate the steep rock bands pose serious threat of avalanche. The collapse of cornices from the frontier crest have caused fatalities, as have windslab avalanches. That having been said, Gavarnie has become the unchallenged Mecca for winter climbing in the Pyrenees (2:11).

The **Cirque de Troumouse**, reached via Gèdre and Héas, is another popular ice-climbing venue, and there are about six icefalls (100–180m) on the north side of the Vallée de Héas accessible from the Gedre–Troumouse road (2:10). Another useful collection of icefalls can be found east of the Troumouse Cirque on both sides of the border and easily linked via the **Bielsa tunnel**. Whilst those on the Spanish side need to be tackled in the morning before the sun catches them, there's excellent climbing to be had in the medium grades, and a number of good three-pitch icefalls on the French side that make a first-rate introduction (3:1). South of the Spanish border post, the *Cascade Ordiceto* is a six-pitch climb with several 90° sections, and there are more 200m icefalls nearby with grade IV routes.

Still on the Spanish side of the Pyrenees, **Pico de Posets** and the neighbouring **Maladeta massif**, both approached from Benasque, are less busy than might be expected, but the Vallhiverna, which flows along the south side of the latter, gives access to the vast Northwest Face of the 3067m **Picos de Vallhiverna**, where *Arcadia* is a respected 500m route (45°–60°, but with a 70° section) pioneered in December 1993 by Jordi Agusti and Miguel Roca (3:9).

Northeast of the Vallhiverna, **Tuc del Mig de la Tellada** (2791m) walls the Vall de Molières (Mulleres) which drains down to the Noguera Ribagorçana near the Viella tunnel. The North and Northwest faces overlooking an unmanned bivouac hut have been developed with a variety of ice routes, some up to 500m long. The approach from the Ribagorçana appears to be free from avalanche danger under normal winter conditions (3:10).

On the eastern side of the Ribagorçana in summer the **Vall de Conangles** carries the Pyrenean High Route into the Besiberri massif, but in winter it supports a number of icefalls worth tackling, including the 300m *Escaleta Gorge* (D-, with one section of 85°) on the north flank of the valley. Both Tuc de Contessa and Tossal del Estanyets have couloirs that draw climbers from a base at the Sant Nicolau *refugi* by the Viella road tunnel (4:8).

In Ariège, winter sport can be found in the *Couloir de Tartereau* on **Pic de Maubermé**, the Northeast Couloir of **Pic de Crabère**, and the *Couloir Faustin* and Southeast Spur of **Mont Valier**, among others, while **Andorra** and as far east as the **Sierra del Cadí**, **Cerdagne** and the **Carlit massif** can all be rewarding following snowfall and a snap of good cold weather.

📖 *The Alpine Journal* usually gives a résumé of the most significant routes, but the following publications are highly recommended:

Pyrénées – Courses Mixtes, Neige et Glace by Francis Mousel (Éditions Franck Mercier, 1997)

Gavarnie Cascades de Glace by J. Paredes (Desnivel, 1995)

Pirineos, Hielo y Nieve by Joan Quintana (Editions Pleniluni, 1990)

Escalando en hielo y nieve por el Pirineo Aragonés by J. Javier Lasala (Editions Prames, 1995)

PYRÉNÉISME

The term *Pyrénéisme* is not restricted to climbing in the Pyrenees, but has a much broader connotation, for it represents an ethos – an attitude of mind best described as a holistic approach to mountain activity paralleled by an all-embracing appreciation of the upland environment.

During the earliest years of mountaineering, in the Pyrenees as in the Alps, a smokescreen of scientific enquiry was used to conceal a spirit of adventure pure and simple. Apart from a few notable exceptions, it was not until the 19th century had come of age that a more romantic attitude towards mountains was openly admitted. In turn this was largely overtaken in the Alps by a hard-nosed pragmatism fuelled by competition, while what may be called 'the romance of mountaineering' was allowed to mature in the Pyrenees, where climbing could, and did, develop its own momentum away from the spotlight of publicity.

That momentum, outlined in the 'Potted History' below, largely mirrored progress in the Alps, but *Pyrénéisme* possessed its own defining passion that implied an aesthetic and moral attitude towards mountains in general and mountaineering in particular. The 19th-century explorer/cartographer Franz Schrader (1844–1924), a Frenchman despite his Prussian-sounding name, expressed this when he wrote: 'When the mountain has taken possession of your heart, everything comes from it, and everything leads you back to it.' Packe, too, spoke of the pioneers' general disdain for 'the doctrine which transforms the mountains into enemies to be conquered, instead of friends, worthy of affection'.

Although an element of competition has often stretched the frontiers of Alpinisme, the much smaller world of *Pyrénéisme* has advanced more in a spirit of conviviality, played out by gifted amateurs unconcerned for recognition or glory. For the *Pyrénéiste* the mountain represents an arena for personal adventure to be experienced with humility. The very act of climbing demands *l'engagement* – a 'right way of doing things' – exemplified by the Ravier twins, Jean and Pierre (see box, 1:2), whose passion for all things Pyrenean would lead to the same expression of euphoria on coming upon a plant flowering in a hostile environment as in creating an advanced new route on an overhanging wall.

No one has done more to advance climbing standards in these mountains than the Raviers. Yet it is the manner by which standards are raised that counts, for *Pyrénéisme* demands that each climb be undertaken in an attitude of a moral, spiritual and aesthetic quest. It is an attitude alive as much in the early years of the 21st century as it was in the middle of the 19th, despite the creation of multi-bolted sport routes that threaten to devalue not only the cliffs upon which they are made, but the achievements of the climbers themselves.

Pyrénéisme celebrates the union of human endeavour with the world of nature without any attempt to conquer it.

See *Petit Précis de Pyrénéisme* by Joseph Ribas (Loubatières, 1998).

A POTTED HISTORY OF PYRÉNÉISME

With one or two isolated exceptions, the early climbing history of the Pyrenees belongs to the few geographers and military map-makers of both France and Spain who ventured onto the wild and remote uplands in the course of their duties. Notable among these were Roussel and La Blottière, who in 1719 published the first map of the range showing the principal cols, and Flamichon and Palassau, whose 1780 map gave the height of a number of peaks. Then came Reboul and Vidal from the Academy of Toulouse who, either together or separately, climbed the Turon de Néouvielle and Pic des Trois Conseillers in 1787, and Pic (or Grand) Quayrat the following year. They also encouraged an unnamed shepherd from the Aspe valley to make the first ascent of Pic du Midi d'Ossau in the 1780s 'in order to construct a triangulation turret on the summit'.

It was in 1787 that Baron Louis-Francois Ramond de Carbonnières, secretary to Cardinal Rohan, made his first visit to the Pyrenees as the

French Revolution was rumbling in Paris. Having met Reboul and Vidal on the Pic du Midi de Bigorre, he then set off on a journey of exploration which culminated in an attempt on the Maladeta. At a time when science was the one justification for climbing, Ramond's writings show that romantic adventure was his prime motive, and it is therefore not surprising that he is generally regarded as the father of *Pyrénéisme*. Although he failed to climb either the Maladeta or Pic de Néouvielle (both of which are comparatively straightforward under present-day conditions), Ramond's fame rests on his success on Monte Perdido in 1802, after having twice failed in 1797. Although his is sometimes claimed as the first ascent of this, the third highest Pyrenean summit, in truth that achievement went to his guides, Laurens and Rondau, who were sent ahead to recce the route with a local Spanish shepherd. Ramond made his ascent three days later.

From the Besiberri crest, the Maladeta massif can be seen across the depths of the Noguera Ribagorçana

Between 1825 and 1827 survey officers Peytier and Hossard, at work on the *Carte de France*, achieved first ascents of the difficult Balaïtous and somewhat easier Pic de Troumouse above Héas, and Pic du Maupas near Luchon, while further east the Pica d'Estats and neighbouring Montcalm were won by Coraboeuf and Testu of the same survey team.

Although in 1822 Chausenque had climbed the peak which now bears his name, the highest of the Vignemale's summits, Pique Longue, had to wait another 15 years before it received its first ascent despite, or perhaps because of, Chausenque's proclamation that it was impossible from France. In 1837 two guides from Gèdre, Henri Cazaux and Bernard Guillembet, succeeded by way of the Ossoue glacier (the present *voie normale*), but managed to fall into a major crevasse on the way. Rather than descend by the same route, they found an alternative way down into the Ara valley in Spain via the Cerbillona couloirs. It was by this rather circuitous route that Cazaux guided the single-minded Englishwoman Miss Anne Lister (who had climbed Perdido in 1830) to the top the following year on what was to prove a controversial ascent which nearly provoked litigation.

Aneto's supremacy having been established in 1817, it naturally became the focus of attention for climbers wishing to be the first on the crown of the Pyrenees. In the summer of 1842 Count Albert de Franqueville, a keen botanist and hunter of isard, met the young Russian officer Platon de Tchihatcheff in Luchon. Franqueville had ambitions to climb Aneto, but on learning that Tchihatcheff was in town organising an expedition with the same goal, the two decided to pool their resources and tackle the mountain together. With Jean Argarot and Pierre Sanio as their guides, they took along two local isard hunters, Bernard Ursule and Pierre Redonnet, and the party left Luchon on 18 July bound for Spain. In those days glaciers were considered fearful places, more so since the death of Barrau, so it is perhaps not surprising that Franqueville and Tchihatcheff should choose a somewhat devious route in an attempt to avoid what glaciers they could. (The mountain is defended on both north and south sides by icefields, which were far more profound in the 19th century than they are today.) Their route took them first to the site of the present-day Renclusa hut, where they spent a night of storm. Next day they went via Collado de Alba into the Cregueña glen, then crossed Collado de Cregueña to descend into the Vallhiverna to sleep in a squalid *cabana*. Leaving at daybreak they explored the mountain from the south, and although unable to avoid all the glaciers, emerged at Collado de Coronas to face the steep snow slope which leads to the rocks of the Puente de Mahoma (Pont de Mohammed). At 9am on 20 July 1842, the party crossed this short, exposed ridge, and gained the summit of Pico de Aneto for the first time. Four days later the jubilant Tchihatcheff made a second ascent, this time by the much more direct route via the Aneto glacier, which has since become the accepted *voie normale*.

The pace of mountaineering quickened after this, with first ascents being made of Pic Long (1846), Pic de Néouvielle (1847) and Pic de Perdiguère by Toussaint Lézat in 1850. The second highest Pyrenean summit, Pico de Posets, was claimed in 1856 by Halkett, Redonnet and Barrau, while in 1858 the young poet Alfred Tonnelle, making a tour of the Pyrenees, entered the Ésera valley, made the 34th ascent of Aneto, climbed the neighbouring frontier peaks of Sacroux and Sauvegarde, and with Pierre Redonnet as his guide on 1 August made the first ascent of the fine twin-pronged Forcanada (2872m), which rises at the head of the Valleta de la Escaleta. Two months later he had returned home to die of typhoid.

It was in the 1850s that the Leicestershire squire Charles Packe began what was to become a lifetime's devotion to the range. A keen botanist and mountain explorer, his travels were made with the detailed observation of a scientist, and in 1862 he published the first

English-language guidebook to the Pyrenees 'especially intended for the use of mountaineers'. This was subsequently revised and enlarged as his experience of the range grew; a number of his Pyrenean climbs and explorations were made with his friend, the great eccentric Henry Russell (see box, 2:11), whom he had first met on the shores of Lac Bleu. Though both Packe and Russell enjoyed the solitude to be found among mountains, they were also 'clubable' men, happy to share experiences and publicise the attractions of the Pyrenees to a growing band of enthusiasts.

Founded in London in 1857, the Alpine Club was the first to be devoted to the sport. This was followed by clubs founded in Austria (1862), then in Italy and Switzerland in 1863. At a meeting in Gavarnie between Russell, Packe, Frossard and Maxwell in 1864 the Société Ramond, a specifically Pyrenean club, was established. The French Alpine Club (CAF) came into being in Paris in

Charles Packe (1826–1896), Leicestershire squire and author of the first English-language guide to the Pyrenees

1874, the Pyrenees being represented at its inauguration by Russell (again), with Gourdon, Saint-Saud, Schrader and Wallon. Two years later, the Centre Excursionista de Catalunya (CEC) was founded in Barcelona, with a specific mountaineering section set up in 1908.

Such clubs did much to stimulate a healthy active interest in the Pyrenees at a time when all the highest summits had been taken, and a 'silver age' then began which led to some innovative routes being achieved. At the same time new efforts were being made in the field of mapping – in 1874, for example, Carlos Ibañez began to chart the Spanish side of the range at a scale of 1:50,000, and the following year Franz Schrader published his splendid map of Monte Perdido.

With the advent of more difficult routes being tackled, the name of Henri Brulle crops up time after time. In 1879 this lawyer from Libourne, near Bordeaux, teamed up with Jean Bazillac and, with the guides Sarrettes and Bordenave, climbed the 300m Clot de la Hount Couloir on the Vignemale, which overlooks the head of the Ara valley. Ten years later Brulle and Bazillac, with Roger de Monts, together with Francois Bernard Salles and the great Célestin Passet as guides, forged a route up the Couloir de Gaube on the Vignemale's North Face. This tremendous climb set a standard that was hard to follow, for it was so far ahead of its time that the route was not repeated in its entirety for another 44 years.

Other north-facing routes were attempted and won, including those on Monte Perdido (1878), Pic d'Astazou (1892) and Pic du Midi d'Ossau (1896). Brulle and de Monts were active in winter too, both separately and together. The walls of the Cirque de Gavarnie received

The magnificent western ridge of the Maladeta, the so-called Cresta de la Maladeta

a number of winter ascents, as did Aneto (1879), Posets, the Picos de Vallhiverna and Perdido, this last named being achieved by Roger de Monts, Célestin Passet and F.B. Salles in 1888.

In the early years of the 20th century the first tentative journeys on skis were pioneered. In 1901 Prosper Auriol led a group from the Canigou section of the CAF on a ski tour in the Eastern Pyrenees, while Henri Sallenave was active at the western end of the range, and Ledormeur, Robach and Marcel Parant were penetrating the high valleys of the Central Pyrenees. Ski ascents were made of Pico de Aneto by Falisse, Heid, Robach and Aubry in 1904, and the same year Falisse took his skis to the summit of the Vignemale with Donnay, Cintrat and Bourdil.

The new century saw a Franco-Spanish team consisting of Fontan de Négrin, Isidre Romeu, Raphael Angusto, F.B. Salles and Bartholomé Ciffre climb the higher of the twin Encantat peaks above the Sant Maurici lake. The following summer (1902) Henri Brulle was active on the more difficult Petit Encantat, making the first ascent with René d'Astorg and Germain Castagné, son-in-law of his favourite guide, Célestin Passet. It was Castagné who helped Jean d'Ussel achieve the Vignemale's Arête de Gaube in 1908, and the impressive Tempestades crest on Aneto four years later.

Around this time the five brothers Cadier emerged from the sleepy village of Osse in the Aspe valley and revelled in a number of exploits which brought them a long-lasting reputation. 'Five brothers with but one spirit', they had no need of guides but, with an aptitude for rock matched by a keen sense of adventure, took a particular delight in lengthy ridge tours. On one such tour they worked a way west from Aneto to Pic de la Munia in the Troumouse Cirque (1903), and on another occasion travelled from Pic Long to the Balaïtous, bivouacking throughout. Various of the brothers created new routes on the Encantats, on the Grand Bachimala, Crabioules and Marboré. On the ridges of Balaïtous, George and Edouard climbed the Tour de Costerillou, while Charles and Edouard tried on three occasions without success to force a new route on Pic du Midi d'Ossau from the northeast.

In 1911 Henri Brulle embarked on a three-year campaign of exploration in the Posets massif; five years later, on the north slopes of the neighbouring Maladeta, the CEC constructed the Renclusa *refugio* a short distance from the overhanging rocks that formed the original shelter of the pioneers.

Although still active, by the 1920s Brulle was in his late sixties and other climbers were snatching routes that, had he been younger, he may well have enjoyed creating for himself. But until Jean Arlaud came along there had been no single climber capable of wearing Brulle's crown. In 1920 Arlaud was 24. A Savoyard by birth, he had come to Toulouse to study medicine and at once was drawn to the Pyrenees. A natural climber with a flair for the unconventional approach, he began his career by repeating the routes of past masters, in particular those of Brulle, and then led the development of hard climbing in the heart of the range.

On 18 March 1920 Arlaud founded the Groupe des Jeunes (GDJ), whose members included Charles Laffont, Gaston Fosset and Pierre Abadie, each of whom was to help raise climbing standards and open up new routes from a series of GDJ camps. Between 1922 and 1935 Arlaud organised a number of these camps beside the lake of Sant Maurici in the Encantados region, but other areas were not excluded. Arlaud and Laffont turned to the Crabioules-Lézat arête in 1921, explored the firm granite of the Salenques Ridge in the Maladeta massif in 1922, and in 1925 tackled the thumb-like Capéran de Sesques between the Aspe and Ossau valleys, which had received its first ascent, free, only three years before by local-born Pierre Bourdieu. During 1925 he journeyed south of the Pic du Midi into the Valle de Tena, where he climbed the east gully of Pico de Anayet, and returned two years later to win the elegant Northwest Buttress of Peña Telera. In 1926 Arlaud opened up the Agulles de Travessani and created a route on the North Face of the Pic de Peguera, and, as one of a rope of six, he made the first north–south traverse of the classic Besiberri Ridge. The following year, with Abadie and Frossard, he climbed the East Arête of the Forcanada, and on the same day (4 August) other members of the GDJ – Marceillac, Saint-Jacques and Vecher – attacked the NNW Arête. Also in the summer of 1927, Arlaud and Laffont tried to make the second ascent of the Couloir de Gaube, but they were defeated at the very head of the gully at the noted crux section, where an overhanging 5m boulder had given Brulle's party (in 1889) more than two hours of extreme effort to overcome.

The GDJ camp of 1930 was set beside Lago (or Ibon) de Cregüeña under the Maladeta's western precipices. From there Arlaud, Barrué and Escudier traversed the Cresta de Alba – the so-called 'crest of the fifteen gendarmes'. In 1936 Arlaud went to Hidden Peak as doctor on the first French Himalayan expedition, and two years later had a fall on the Gourgs Blancs, from which he subsequently died. As for the *Groupe des Jeunes*, this continued until 1964, and from 1938 until 1963 published a regular report on its activities entitled *De Sac et de Corde*.

In 1933 a corps of enterprising French climbers formed the Groupe Pyrénéiste de Haute Montagne (GPHM). Founder members Henri Lamathe, Henri Le Breton, Jean Senmartin and Robert Ollivier were ambitious, thrusting and talented – the first three having the year before made the first ascent of the Northwest Arête of the Balaïtous – but there were others, too, who were ready to push back a few boundaries. On 13 July 1933 Barrio, Aussat and Loustaunau at last made the coveted second ascent of the Vignemale's *Couloir de Gaube* – Brulle's classic route of 1889. Just two days later Cazalet, Lamathe, Ollivier and Senmartin followed with the third ascent. The jinx of the Couloir was now well and truly defeated.

Less than a month after success on the Couloir de Gaube, Barrio and Bellocq turned their attention to the neighbouring 850m wall of

the Vignemale's North Face, which has since come to be regarded as one of the great climbs of the Pyrenees. In July 1934 Cazalet, Mailly and Ollivier pushed the first route on the Petit Pic du Midi d'Ossau from the west, and a year later Mailly and Ollivier created the fine Northwest Face of the same Petit Pic. Also in 1935 Roger Mailly and François Cazalet achieved the difficult North Face of the Capéran de Sesques, and in 1936, some 20 years after three attempts by the Cadier brothers had failed, Mailly and Ollivier won the respected Northeast Face of the Petit Pic du Midi.

Following the enterprise of members of the GPHM, active climbers began to look at more serious routes in winter. As if to underline this approach, two major climbs were carried out on the same day, 12 February 1939. While Aussat and Cazenave were forcing a way up the South Cirque of Pic du Midi d'Ossau, a few kilometres further east Cazalet, Mailly and Henri Sarthou were making the first winter traverse of the Costerillou Ridge on the Balaïtous.

Whilst climbing never actually ceased during the 1939–45 war, it was seriously curtailed. But towards the end of hostilities camps of the Jeunesse et Montagne, based on Cauterets and Gavarnie, encouraged the resumption of enterprising expeditions. First among these was the Northwest Buttress of Pointe Chausenque in 1945 by Simpson and Boyrie. Then, on the last day of August 1946, Marcel Jolly, with Paul Limargues and Marc and Jean Arnatou, created an exciting new route (now TD-) on Pointe Jean-Santé, a minor rock finger (in terms of height) but a major challenge that protrudes above Pic du Midi's South Cirque.

In 1948 two climbs in particular, set in the Gourgs Blanc/Clarabide group of frontier summits, underlined a return to routes of technical

Flowing down the east flank of the Vignemale, the Ossoue glacier is the longest in the Pyrenees

difficulty. On the Northeast Face of Pic Oriental des Crabioules, Jean Couzy and Lucien Georges created a 350m direct route (*Voie Couzy*: TD, V/A1) on poor rock in 11 hours of sustained effort, while a short distance further to the east, on the North Face of Pic de Maupas, a meandering line (*Voie Céréza*) was established by G. Barrère and F. Céréza on mostly excellent rock. Then, on 28 February 1949, Marcel Jolly and Bernard Clos turned to the North Face of the Vignemale and succeeded in making the first winter ascent of that impressive wall in a single day. More demanding winter routes followed, among them minor classics on Pointe Chausenque, the North Face of Piton Carré, a traverse of the Balaïtous's three arêtes and the North Face of the Tour du Marboré.

In the early 1950s the Ravier twins from Bordeaux, Jean and Pierre (see box, 1:2), quickly established themselves as the most adventurous and talented climbers yet seen in the Pyrenees by either leading or taking part in a number of the most difficult climbs attempted at that time outside the Alps. The first hint of this came on 8 May 1953 when Jean Ravier and André Armangaud drew an airy 500m line on the Southeast Face of Pointe Jean-Santé, but it was in 1954 that a brace of hard climbs effectively underscored their reputation. In July of that year, with Jacques Teillard, the brothers pushed a route up the North Face of Piton Carré in 9 hours, and on 12 and 13 August worked their way up the exposed NE Dièdre of the Grande Aiguille d'Ansabère with Guy Santamaria, using something like 50 pitons. This highly respected 300m route is now graded TD+ (V+/6a/6b+). The East Face of the same aiguille was revisited by Jean in the autumn of 1957 when, with Claude Dufourmantelle, Patrice de Bellefon and Raymond Despiau, a two-day siege resulted in a classic 300m line. Earlier, in the spring of

Early summer view from the edge of the Aneto glacier

that same year, Jean Ravier was with Dufourmantelle, Marcel Kahn, Noël Blotti and Claude Jaccoux to create what has become one of the most sought-after climbs in the Ordesa canyon, the original South Face route on the Tozal del Mallo.

It was also 1957 that saw the emergence of the Spanish pair J.-A. Bescos and R Montaner, who claimed the Northeast Face of the Cilindro de Marboré. The same duo went on to make the first winter traverse (in 1960) of the four main summits of Pic du Midi d'Ossau. In 1961 the celebrated Aragonese pair Alberto Rabadá and Ernesto Navarro (who were workmates in Zaragoza, but who tragically died together on the Eigerwand in 1963) took to the East Buttress of Punta Gallinero which looms over the entrance to the Cotatuero Cirque, and over a three-day period produced an exacting and somewhat complicated route graded TD+ (V/6a/6b); another eight years were to pass before it was repeated. Two months after their Gallinero success, Rabadá and Navarro spent no less than six days on Mallo Fire in the Riglos massif, making a free ascent of the 385m Southeast Buttress route which now takes their name. Also in 1961 a major step was taken with regard to long winter routes, when Patrice de Bellefon and Sylvain Sarthou entered the Cirque de Gavarnie and tackled Pic du Marboré by the Mur de la Cascade, Crête des Druides and Arête Passet, thus creating the longest winter climb in the Pyrenees (1500m).

One of the major climbs of the 1960s took place on the Embarradère Pillar, which buttresses the north side of the deep scoop separating the Grand Pic du Midi d'Ossau from the Petit Pic. In a two-day sortie on 17 and 18 July 1965, Jean and Pierre Ravier with Paul Bouchet created a sustained, semi-direct and somewhat athletic route (the *Voie Ravier*) of 350m in length, graded ED (V+/6b/6c), which is sometimes compared in difficulty with the Bonatti Pillar on the Drus. Other ED routes that flank it have since been made by a new generation of *Pyrénéistes*.

Climbing has never been the only expression of *Pyrénéisme*, for multi-day journeys of exploration across the mountains have long been a feature, going back to the first visit by Ramond de Carbonnières in the late 18th century, and magnificently illustrated by Dr Friedrich Parrot in 1817. Grandes Randonnées routes bring such journeys up to date at a mid-height level, but in 1968 Georges Véron of Tarbes created what is rightly seen as a true 'high route' along the mountains from the Atlantic to the Mediterranean. His Haute Randonnée Pyrénéenne is now justly acclaimed as one of Europe's finest and most challenging mountain treks. Then in 1986, Louis Audoubert and Guy Panozzo carried the high-route concept to the limit (or nearly so), when they made a complete traverse of the range along the watershed, in a journey of 700km, crossing 930 summits, with 49 bivouacs!

The Valle de Tena, which drains south from the Col du Pourtalet, was visited by Arlaud in the 1920s and then largely forgotten until,

Aneto, highest Pyrenean summit, is seen to advantage from Pico de la Maladeta

during the 1960s and 1970s, a new wave of climbers began to make serious incursions onto its crags, faces and buttresses. One of the foremost protagonists here was Ursi Abajo, who created a number of fine routes, including the 800m *Dièdre Central* (Gran Diedro) on the North Face of the Peña Telera. By the 1990s the 10km chain of the Telera had become a major scene of climbing activity, especially in winter.

Winter climbing, when conditions occur, has enjoyed a major renaissance in the past three decades and, not surprisingly, Gavarnie has borne the brunt of activity. But then there's so much scope – not only on the walls of the cirque, but on the Pics d'Astazou, for example. At the end of December 1977, a rope comprising Dominique Julien, Rainier Munsch, Henri Santan and Tony Bedel enjoyed a 600m route on the WNW Face of the Petit Pic d'Astazou, to the right of the 1885 classic Couloir Swan (Francis Swan and Henri Passet). Next to the Grand Astazou, the Northwest Couloir that runs down the cliffs of Pic Rouge de Pailla was treated to a TD+ ascent over two days in January 1979 by Bedel (again), this time sharing a rope with Bruno Prat, while at the other extreme end of the Gavarnie horseshoe, the Northwest Face of Pic Occidental des Gabiétous was attacked in January 1978 by Santan, Rodriguez, Sebie, Tomas and Uzabiaga.

The appeal of the old Vignemale classics, such as the Couloir de Gaube and Clot de la Hount Couloir, remain, but so do 'modern classics' like the 'Y' Couloir on Piton Carré (Jean and Pierre Ravier, 1965), each of which attracts winter ascents. But the quest for new routes both winter and summer remains a driving force that has carried *Pyrénéisme* into the 21st century. There may be no untrod summits left, but there is no shortage of new ways to reach them. What began so modestly in the late 18th century is renewed by successive generations. Three centuries on, *Pyrénéisme* has not yet lost its momentum.

SKIING

When snow conditions are at their best the Pyrenees can offer magnificent sport for on-piste skiing, although it has to be pointed out that runs rarely match those of the better-known alpine resorts. However, beginners and those at intermediate level are well catered for, and there's some fine cross-country terrain and plenty of scope for learning techniques for ski mountaineering. These are undoubted pluses. The other side of the coin is the environmental damage caused by insensitive development and associated road building on both sides of the international frontier. On the north side, in particular, France's attitude to purpose-built resorts is notorious, and the most hideous constructions have appeared on what once were sublime locations. Architectural anarchy has been given free reign in too many instances – and not only on the French slopes. Happily some of the older resorts that also cater for downhill skiing retain traditional values, but in truth it is the activist who can shun mechanical aids and other intrusive tourist infrastructure – the cross-country and experienced ski-mountaineering enthusiast – who will properly enjoy the *real* Pyrenees in winter.

Solitude in a snowbound landscape rewards with its own special magic, and non-skiers can also experience that magic by **snowshoeing** – a popular activity with local French enthusiasts, but only slowly taking off among visitors from Britain. There are several professional guides in Gavarnie, Cauterets and Barèges who will teach the basic techniques as well as those required for off-piste skiing, and a variety of tours ranging from two days to a week or more in length are organised most winters.

Pyrenean Mountain Tours arrange snowshoeing holidays/courses from a base in Luz-St-Sauveur: write c/o 2 Rectory Cottages, Wolverton, Tadley, Hants RG26 5RS (☎ 01635 297209, e-mail: pmtuk@aol.com). Try also **Borderline Holidays** (☎ 05 62 92 68 95, www.borderlinehols.com) or visit the website of the **British Association of International Mountain Leaders** (www.baiml.org), among whose members are several who lead snowshoe courses in the Pyrenees.

Cross-country skiing (*ski de fond*) was first practised as a sport in the Pyrenees in 1910, the most suitable terrain being found on the French side of the border. Listing from west to east these sites are at: Iraty, Somport, the upper Val d'Azun, Marcadau, the Plateau de Beille west of Ax-les-Thermes, and almost everywhere in the Cerdagne and Capcir regions. In the last mentioned, a network of cross-country tracks links all the villages.

Ariège Pyrénées ski de fond, Hôtel du Département, 09000 Foix (☎ 05 61 02 09 70)
Information for the Cerdagne/Capcir regions:
Maison du Capcir, 66210 Matemale (☎ 04 68 04 49 86)
Pyrénées catalanes ski de fond, 66210 Matemale (☎ 04 68 04 32 75)

Off-piste

The first ski traverse of the High Pyrenees, from Pic du Canigou to Pierre-St-Martin, was achieved in 1968 by Charles Laporte, taking 35 days in all. During the winter of 1994–5 Benoît Dandonneau, Francine Magrou and Rémi Thivel pioneered a complete traverse of the entire range from the Mediterranean to the Atlantic – a journey of some 700km, with a grand total of 63,000m of ascent, and 60 or more summits gained. The traverse took 51 days overall and, despite generally unfavourable conditions, the trio lost only four days through either heavy snowfall or the need to rest.

Other activists before and since have tackled major winter expeditions with varying degrees of success, for conditions that favour lengthy ski tours are notoriously difficult to predict in advance, but when they do arrive a wealth of opportunities is presented. In the Pyrenees **ski touring** is akin to mountaineering on skis, and all who embark on this activity should be aware of the sometimes acute risk of avalanche in off-piste areas. For although glaciers are somewhat sparse, variable temperatures added to heavy snowfall constitute a very real hazard to the ski mountaineer, especially on the steep French side of the mountains where experience counts for much. Avalanche beacons should be carried by all members of an off-piste ski party. In bad weather retreat to a valley is often achieved in the face of extreme danger, the ground is invariably very steep, and route-finding can be exacerbated by sudden mists giving white-out conditions or by the early loss of daylight. Half-buried huts can be difficult to locate, and heavy packs are unavoidable on multi-day trips. Since only a few huts are manned in the ski-touring season, self-sufficiency is essential. But perhaps the most important lesson to learn is – never attempt to push a route in bad weather.

📖 *Pyrenean High Route* by John Harding (Tiercel Publishing, 2000) describes a ski traverse of the range in nine stages between Pic d'Anie and Pic du Canigou, in which the hazards associated with the sport are clearly spelled out. The same traverse is described by Harding, a noted authority on ski mountaineering, on pp142–53 of *The Alpine Journal* for 1989/90. See also: *Guide des Raids à Skis* by Pierre Merlin (Denoël) – a French-language guide to the ski traverse of the Pyrenees.

Anyone going off-piste, especially on a lengthy tour in remote country, should be aware of potential avalanche risk and understand safety techniques – learnt first-hand either on a course or from an experienced fellow skier or mountaineer (□ *Avalanche Safety for Climbers and Skiers* by Tony Daffern, The Mountaineers, 1999). Learn to recognise particularly hazardous terrain and the climatic conditions that can set an avalanche in motion, and never stray off-piste alone. Be aware that 90% of avalanches involving skiers, climbers and walkers are triggered by the victims themselves. Skiers are especially vulnerable, since the lateral cutting action of skis can so easily disturb an unstable snow surface. Avalanche transceivers should be carried by all off-piste skiers, and before setting out they should be switched on. (Digital avalanche 'tracker' beacons may be hired from the Alpine Ski Club – hire@alpineskiclub.org.uk, www. alpineskiclub.org.uk.)

The four main types of avalanche are:

- *dry-snow avalanches* – most likely following heavy snowfall and before the sun reaches the slope

- *wet-snow avalanches* – can occur on recent snow, as well as when old snow melts in the sun's heat

- *windslab avalanches* – occur when layers of powder snow fail to consolidate on the underlying hard snow or ice; these often occur on slopes of between 25 and 45°

- *cornice, sérac or ice-cliff avalanches* – the result of collapsing unstable masses of snow or ice.

Generally speaking the safest routes to follow are:

- those through fairly dense tree cover

- those which traverse valleys and lower slopes beyond reach of expected avalanche run-out

- those that travel along broad ridges keeping well away from any edges that might be corniced.

Serious attention to advanced route planning is essential, and unless you have good local knowledge you should seek advice from someone who has – a mountain guide, member of a mountain rescue team or a local farmer or shepherd who should be able to point out which slopes are prone to avalanche so they can be avoided altogether. In French resorts and at the start of popular cross-country routes a Bulletin Neige et Avalanche (BNA) is often posted with an assessment of avalanche risk on a scale of 1–5. Call 08 36 63 10 20 (or 08 36 68 08 08) for information in French. For avalanche information in the Spanish Pyrenees call (Navarre) 906 365 331, (Huesca) 906 365 322 and Eastern Pyrenees/Catalonia 935 67 15 77 or 935 67 15 76.

Heavy snowfall accompanied by strong winds, or followed by a sudden rise in temperature, can make a lethal combination when avalanche risk is at its highest. In such conditions keep clear of the following terrain:

- slopes beneath cornices

- slopes in the lee of the wind

- convex slopes under stress

- south-facing slopes in direct sunlight
- open treeless slopes
- mountain basins
- gullies.

All the above should be avoided completely. However, should you face a situation where no alternative is available, close all pockets, tighten zips and hoods, release ski-retaining straps and take your hands out of the loops on your ski sticks. Then cross the slope one at a time and at a minimum of 100m intervals. In the unfortunate event of being caught in an avalanche:

- shout a warning to others so they can plot your course should you become buried
- discard rucksack, skis and sticks
- attempt to stay on the surface by making a swimming motion, or roll like a log off the avalanche debris
- if the above is impossible, cover your face to keep mouth and nostrils free of snow
- try not to panic – self-control is essential for survival
- in soft snow it may be possible to dig yourself free – but make sure you dig upwards
- if you cannot escape, try to hollow space for breathing in front of your face.

Surviving members of the ski/climbing party must recognise that time is of the essence if anyone caught by the avalanche is to be found alive, and the following procedures should be adhered to.

- Check for further avalanche danger, and note a safe escape route in case another slide follows.
- By use of ice axe, rucksack or item of clothing, mark the last point where the victim was seen in the path of the avalanche in order to focus the search area.
- Make a quick but careful search of the avalanche area, looking for signs of the victim, listening for sounds and probing the most likely places.
- If possible send one (two at most) survivor(s) for help, leaving all remaining members of the party to continue the search.
- If you are the sole survivor it is important that you make a thorough search before going for help – remember that victims can suffocate if not recovered soon.
- If the initial search is fruitless, probe with your ice axe.
- Concentrate on the surface area below the last point where the victim was seen – and mark the position of any pieces of equipment found.
- When the victim is found, treat immediately for shock; free the nose and mouth of snow and give mouth-to-mouth resuscitation where necessary; clear snow from clothing and place the victim in a sleeping bag, head downhill; administer other first aid as required.

See 'Mountain Rescue' box above for emergency telephone numbers.

Piste Skiing

Despite the unpredictability of skiable snow, almost 60 resorts have been established in the Pyrenees, of which 40 are on the French side, where the best piste skiing is likely to be found at **Barèges/La Mongie** – two resorts on opposite sides of the Col du Tourmalet with a combined tally of 69 pistes (highest lift at 2440m). Nearby **St-Lary-Soulan** in the Vallée d'Aure challenges La Mongie's supremacy with the **Pla d'Adet/Espiaube** complex boasting 33 runs from 30 lifts, the highest being 2400m, while the futuristic resort of **Piau-Engaly** has 21 lifts – the topmost at 2500m having a good snow record.

In **Andorra** the main ski areas are based at **Pas de la Casa** near the Port d'Envalira. This has consistently good snow, its lifts, linked with **Grau Roig**, giving a total of nearly 100km of pistes. It is, however, a grim and soulless place, like much of this tiny country's overblown development that shows little regard for the natural environment. Several other small resorts cater for the ski crowd (**Arinsal, Pal, Soldeu-El Tarter**), with **Ordino-Arcalis** at the head of the Valira del Nord offering perhaps the most agreeable backdrop.

The classic winter experience in Andorra, however, ignores the crowds and ugly resort development by making a **ski-mountaineering circuit** along the border ridges. This is ski touring of some quality which demands an understanding of snow conditions, an eye for potentially dangerous slopes, and the ability to ski for several days with a fairly cumbersome rucksack. A good sleeping bag, stove, food, ice axe, rope and snow-saw should be carried, and accommodation is taken in unmanned refuges and the occasional village.

Ski Andorra, avenue Tarragona 58–70, Despatx 14, AD500, Andorra la Vella, Andorra (☎ 376 805 200, www.skiandorra.ad)

Ski resorts in **Spain** suffer the dual problems of strong, direct sunlight and low precipitation, so snow conditions suitable for good pisted runs are unreliable and invariably short-lived. **La Molina** and nearby resorts south of Puigcerdà have lifts to nearly 2500m, and 137 snow cannons for those times when natural snow is in short supply. **El Formigal**, on the south side of the Col du Pourtalet, is one of the best, with north-facing runs on more than 50km of pistes, although its highest lift reaches only 2250m.

THE 3000m SUMMITS

Defining separate peaks and summits is no easy matter, and the criteria for establishing a Pyrenean 3000m mountain have for decades been open to debate which goes beyond simple altitude measurement. In 1935 a list of just 41 summits was published in the journal of the Unio Excursionista de Catalonia. In 1968 that number was increased by 16; in 1977 the total was given as 97, then amended to 122. In 1990

Lago de Cregüeña cradled below the Maladeta

a fresh inventory was agreed by *Pyrénéistes* from both sides of the border, giving a total of no less than 278 points of 3000m or more. So, according to definition (and for the time being), the Pyrenees can claim 129 principal 3000m summits and 67 secondary summits, with a further 82 ridge projections. Listing from west to east, these summits are divided into the geographical groups below.

Note 1: Maps: IGN refers to the Top 25 series at 1:25,000; CR to the Cartes de Randonnées; EA to Editorial Alpina
Note 2: Abbreviations: Fr = France, Sp = Spain; these refer to the location of principal summits.
Note 3: Not all maps agree on names, spellings or altitude measurements.

GROUP 1: BALAÏTOUS/MARCADAU

Maps: IGN 1647 OT *Vignemale, Ossau, Arrens*; CR 3: *Béarn*; EA *Panticosa Formigal*
Huts: Larribet, Ledormeur and Wallon (France), Respomuso (Spain)
See: Chapter 2

This westernmost group of 3000m summits is located along the frontier ridge east of the Vallée d'Ossau, with the Frondella Spur pushing SSW into Spain above the Respomuso lake. Approach routes from the north are via either the Vallées d'Arrens or Marcadau, and from the south along the valley of the Aguas Limpias from Sallent de Gállego.

1: Balaïtous (3144m)
Tour de Costerillou (3049m)
Aiguille d'Ussel (3020m)
Aiguille Cadier (Pico Anonimo) (3022m) (Sp)

2: Frondella Occidental (3069m) (Sp)
Frondella Central (3055m) (Sp)

3: Frondella Oriental (3001m) (Sp)

4: Grande Fache (3005m) (frontier)

GROUP 2: INFIERNO/ARGUALAS

Map: EA *Panticosa Formigal*
Hut: Respomuso. Balneario de Panticosa is a useful base.
See: Chapter 2

Gathered in two small groups southeast of the Balaïtous in Spain, these peaks form the upper western wall of the Rio Caldarés valley headed by the spa of Balneario de Panticosa. The Infierno peaks are known to the French as the Pics d'Enfer.

5:    Pico del Infierno Norte/Occidental (3073m)

6:    Pico del Infierno Central (3083m)

7:    Pico del Infierno Sur/Oriental (3076m)

8:    Pico d'os Arnales (3006m)
      Aiguille de Pondiellos (3011m)

9:    Pico de Garmo Negro (3051m)
      Algas Norte (Antecime N du Pic d'Algas) (3032m)

10:   Pico d'Algas (3036m)

11:   Pico de Argualas (3046m)

GROUP 3: VIGNEMALE

Maps: IGN 1647 OT *Vignemale, Ossau, Arrens*; CR 4: *Bigorre*
Huts: Oulettes de Gaube and Bayssellance
See: Chapter 2

Forming the Franco-Spanish frontier ridge between the valleys of Gaube and Ossoue to the north and the Ara to the south, this compact group contains the highest frontier summit in Pique Longue and the largest Pyrenean icefield, the Glacier d'Ossoue. Most activity is concentrated on peaks at the head of the Vallée de Gaube. Nearest centres are Cauterets and Gavarnie.

12:   Pique Longue (3298m)

13:   Piton Carré (3197m) (Fr)

14:   Pointe Chausenque (3204m) (Fr)
      Epaule de Chausenque (3154m) (Fr)

15:   Petit Vignemale (3032m) (Fr)

16:   Pic du Clot de la Hount (3289m)

17:   Cerbillona (3247m)
      Aiguille SW de Cerbillona (3051m) (Sp)

18:   Pic Central (3235m)

19:   Montferrat (3219m)

20:   Grand Pic de Tapou (3150m)

21:   Pic du Milieu (3130m)

GROUP 4: GAVARNIE/PERDIDO

Maps: IGN 1748 OT *Gavarnie*; CR 4: *Bigorre*; EA *Ordesa*; Editorial Pirineo *Ordesa-Monte Perdido*
Huts: Sarradets, Espuguettes, Tuquerouye (France), Góriz and Pineta (Spain)
See: Chapter 2

Forming the border rim of the Cirque de Gavarnie, or running in a line southeast of Pic du Marboré, this group contains some of the least demanding of the 3000m peaks, while Monte Perdido (Mont Perdu) is said to be Europe's highest limestone summit.

22: Pic Occidental de Gabiétou (3034m)
23: Pic Oriental de Gabiétou (3031m)
24: Le Taillon (3144m)
25: Casque du Marboré (3006m)
26: Tour du Marboré (3009m)
27: Epaule du Marboré (3073m)
28: Pic Occidental de la Cascade (3095m)
29: Pic Central de la Cascade (Pic Brulle) (3106m)
30: Pic Oriental de la Cascade (3161m)
31: Pic du Marboré (3248m)
32: Petit Pic d'Astazou (3012m)
33: Grand Pic d'Astazou (3071m)
34: Cilindro de Marboré (Le Cylindre) (3328m) (Sp)
    Dedo (Doigt) de Monte Perdido (3188m)
35: Monte Perdido (Mont Perdu) (3355m) (Sp)
    Punta Escaleras (3027m)
    Espolón (Epaule) de los Esparrets (3077m)
36: Soum de Ramond (Pico de Añisclo) (3254m) (Sp)
37: Los Esparrets (Baudrimont NW) (3045m) (Sp)
38: Pico de Baudrimont (3026m) (Sp)
39: Punta de la Olas (3002m) (Sp)

GROUP 5: MUNIA/TROUMOUSE

Maps: IGN 1748 OT *Gavarnie*; CR 4: *Bigorre*
Hut: Barroude. But note that Héas has limited accommodation, and Auberge le Maillet is especially well situated at the entrance to the Cirque de Troumouse.
See: Chapter 2

This compact group is gathered along the rim of the Cirque de Troumouse, mostly along the frontier ridge, but with Robiñera being set on a southerly spur off Pic de la Munia, and Pic Heid on the crest dividing the Troumouse Cirque from that of Barroude.

40: Pico Robiñera (Pic de la Louseras) (3003m) (Sp)

41: Pic de la Munia (3133m)
    Petite Munia (3096m)
42: Pic de Serre Mourène (3090m)
43: Pic de Troumouse (3085m)
    Pointe des Aires (3028m) (Fr)
44: Pic Heid (3022m) (Fr)

GROUP 6: NÉOUVIELLE

Maps: IGN 1748 ET *Néouvielle, Vallée d'Aure*; CR 4: *Bigorre*
Huts: La Glère and Packe
See: Chapter 2

The Néouvielle region is located some way north of the frontier ridge. Access is by road from Aragnouet-Fabian in Vallée d'Aure to the dammed lakes of Cap de Long and Aubert. Hut approaches are from Barèges in the north.

45: Pic de Campbieil (3173m)
    Campbieil SSW (3157m)
46: Pic d'Estaragne (3006m)
47: Pic Maou (3074m)
48: Pic Badet (3160m)
49: Pic Long (3192m)
50: Dent d'Estibère-Male (3017m)
51: Pic de Bugarret (3031m)
52: Pale Crabounouse (3021m)
53: Pic Maubic (3058m)
    Pointe Reboul-Vidal (3007m)
54: Turon de Néouvielle (3035m)
55: Pic des Trois Conseillers (3039m)
56: Pic de Néouvielle (3091m)
57: Pointe de Ramougn (3011m)

GROUP 7: BATOUA/BACHIMALA

Maps: IGN 1848 OT *Bagneres de Luchon, Lac d'Oô*; CR 5: *Luchon*; EA *Bachimala* and *Posets*
Huts: La Soula and Viadós for the eastern end of the group only
See: Chapter 3

Apart from Pic de Lustou, which sits on a ridge just to the north, and Pic de la Pez and Punta del Sabre briefly jutting to the south, all these summits mark the Franco-Spanish frontier on either side of Port de la Pez, the link between the Valle de Gistaín and Vallée du Louron. The most westerly summits overlook the Vallée de Rioumajou. Otherwise the shortest route of access is from Pont du Prat at the head of the Louron valley.

58: Pic de Batoua (Batoua SW) (3034m)
   Pic Central de Batoua (3028m)
   Pic NE de Batoua (3032m)
59: Pic de Lustou (3023m) (Fr)
60: Pic du Port de la Pez (3018m) (frontier)
61: Pic de la Pez (3024m) (Sp)
62: Pic de l'Abeillé (3029m) (frontier)
63: Pic Marcos Feliu (3067m)
   Petit Pic de Bachimala (3061m)
64: Pointe Ledormeur (3120m)
65: Grand Pic de Bachimala (Pic Schrader) (3177m)
66: Punta del Sabre (3136m) (Sp)

GROUP 8: POSETS

Map: EA *Posets*
Huts: Viadós, Estós and Angel Orús
See: Chapter 3

Containing the second highest Pyrenean summit (Pico Posets), this group is located south of the frontier ridge, from which it is separated by the Estós valley. Despite the proximity of the important Valle del Ésera to the south and southeast, climbing here gives a sense of remoteness. The massif lies within the Parque Natural Posets-Maladeta.

67: Bagüeñola S (Eriste S) (3045m)
68: Bagüeñola Central (Grand Eriste) (3053m)
69: Bagüeñola N (Eriste N or Beraldi) (3025m)
   La Forqueta SE (Turets SE) (3004m)
70: La Forqueta (Turets) (3007m)
   Diente Royo (3010m)
71: Pavots (Tucon Royo) (3121m)
   Tuca Forau de la Neu (3080m)
72: Diente de Llardana (3094m)
73: Las Espadas (3332m)
   Espadas N (3325m)
   Tuca de Llardaneta (3311m)
74: Pico Posets (Pico Llardana) (3375m)
   Posets N (3321m)
75: Pico de los Gemelos (Pic des Jumeaux Ravier) (3160m)
76: Pico de los Veteranos (3125m)
   Pico Inferior de la Paúl (3073m)
77: Pico de la Paúl (3078m)
78: Pico de Bardamina (3079m)

THE 3000m SUMMITS

Maps: IGN 1848 OT *Bagneres de Luchon, Lac d'Oô*; CR 5 *Luchon*; EA *Posets*
Huts: La Soula, Espingo, Portillon and Maupas in France; Estós in Spain
See: Chapter 3

Mostly ranged along the frontier ridge north of the Posets massif, this group also has a few summits rising from north-projecting ridge-spurs. The usual approach routes are via the Vallée du Louron (for the western end), Vallée d'Oô for the main central block, and Vallée du Lys for the easternmost peaks, although it's perfectly feasible to tackle some of the frontier summits from a base at the Estós refugio in Spain.

79: Pic de Gías (3011m) (Sp)

80: Pic de Clarabide (3020m)
    Clarabide Oriental (3012m)

81: Pic de Saint-Saud (3003m) (Fr)

82: Pic Camboué (3043m) (Fr)
    Pointe Lourde-Rocheblave (3104m)
    Tour Armengaud (3114m)
    Gourgs Blancs W (3122m)

83: Pic des Gourgs Blancs (3129m)

84: Pic Gourdon (3034m) (Fr)

85: Pic des Spijeoles (3065m) (Fr)
    Pic Belloc Sud (3007m)
    Pic Belloc Central (3006m)

86: Pic Belloc (3008m) (Fr)

87: Pic Jean Arlaud (3065m) (frontier)
    Pic Audoubert (3045m)
    Seil de la Baque W (3097m)
    Seil de la Baque E (3103m)

88: Cap du Seil de la Baque (3110m)
    Petit Pic du Portillon (3000m)

89: Pic du Portillon d'Oô (Pic Ollivier) (3050m)
    Perdiguère W (3176m)

90: Pic de Perdiguère (3222m)
    Hito del Perdiguère (3170m) (Sp)

91: Pic Royo (3121m)

92: Punta de Lliterola (3132m)
    Aguja de Lliterola (3028m)

93: Pic Occidental des Crabioules (3106m)

94: Pic Oriental des Crabioules (3116m)
    Pointe Mamy (3048m) (Fr)
    Pointe Lacq (3010m) (Fr)

95: Pic Lézat (3107m) (Fr)

96: Pic (or Grand) Quayrat (3060m) (Fr)
    Quayrat Nord (3046m) (Fr)

Aiguille Jean Garnier (3025m) (frontier)
Tusse de Remuñe (3041m)
Pic Rabadá (3045m)
Pic Navarro (3043m)
97: Pic de Maupas (3109m)
98: Pic de Boum (3006m)

GROUP 10: MALADETA/VALLHIVERNA

Map: EA *Maladeta Aneto*
Hut: Renclusa. The restored Hospital de Benasque (Llanos del Hospital) offers alternative accommodation at the northwest foot of the massif.
See: Chapter 3

At the head of the Ésera valley the Maladeta massif lies entirely on the south side of the frontier, moated on the north by the Rio Ésera and on the south by the Vallhiverna (Ballibierna). The massif contains several small glaciers and is notable for having the highest Pyrenean summit, Pico de Aneto (Néthou to the French), at 3404m. Three summits of 3000m are located on the large block of the Picos de Vallhiverna just south of the Maladeta, but Tuc de Molières (Mulleres) lies to the east on the ridge overlooking the deep valley of the Noguera Ribagorçana.

99: Pico de Alba (3107m)

100: Diente de Alba (3120m)
     Muela de Alba (3111m)
     Punta Delmás (3158m)

101: Pico Mir (3rd Pic Occidental Maladeta) (3184m)

102: Pico Sayó (2nd Pic Occidental Maladeta) (3211m)

103: Pico le Bondidier (3146m)

104: Pico Cordier (1st Pic Occidental Maladeta) (3263m)

105: Pico de la Maladeta (3308m)
     Pico Abadías (3271m)

106: Pico Maldito (Pic Maudit) (3350m)
     Aguja Haurillon (3075m)
     Aguja Cregüeña (3039m)
     Aguja Juncadella (3019m)

107: Pico de Aragüells (3030m)

108: Punta d'Astorg (3343m)

109: Pico del Medio (3340m)

110: Pico de Coronas (3294m)
     Punta Oliveras Arenas (3292m)

111: Pico de Aneto (3404m)
     Aguja Daviu (3350m)
     Aguja Escudier (3340m)
     Aguja Franqueville (3057m)

The Valle de Estós

Aguja Tchihatcheff (3042m)
Aguja Argarot (3031m)

112: Espalda (Epaule) de Aneto (3343m)
Punta Brecha de Tempestades (3267m)

113: Pico de Tempestades (Pic des Tempêtes) (3296m)

114: Pico Margalida (3244m)
Forca Estasen (Fourche du Vallon Bleu) (3028m)
Punta de la Brecha Russell (3195m)
Punta NW de Russell (3207m)

115: Pico de Russell (3205m)
Punta Russell Oriental (3035m)
Aguja SW Russell (3028m)
Anticima SE (3202m)

116: Tuca de les Culebras (3051m)

117: Picos de Vallhiverna (Tuca de Ballibierna) (3056m)
Vallhiverna E (3030m)

118: Tuc de Molières (Mulleres) (3010m)

GROUP 11: BESIBERRI

Map: EA *Vall de Boí*
Huts: Besiberri (bivouac shelter), Ventosa i Calvell
See: Chapter 4

Overlooking the western end of the upper Vall de Boí (the valley of the Noguera de Tor), and forming the east wall of the valley of the Noguera Ribagorçana, the granitic Besiberri group runs in a north–south line above a tarn-spangled landscape. Punta Alta, however, is separate from the main group, and is located east of the Cavallers lake. The shortest and easiest approach is from the roadhead above Caldes de Boí, where there are spaces for parking below the Cavallers dam. The whole area lies on the Spanish side of the mountains.

119: Besiberri Nord (3014m)

120: Besiberri del Mig N (Pic Simó) (3001m)

121: Besiberri del Mig S (Pic Jolis) (3003m)

122: Besiberri Sud (3030m)

123: Pic de Comaloforno (3033m)

124: Punta Passet (Pic Célestin Passet) (3001m)

125: Punta Alta (3014m)

Maps: IGN 2148 OT *Vicdessos, Pics d'Estats et de Montcalm*; CR 7 *Haute-Ariège Andorre* EA *Pica d'Estats Mont Roig*
Hut: Le Pinet (in France), Vall Ferrera (in Spain)
See: Chapter 4

Astride the Franco-Spanish border, this easternmost group of 3000ers is among the most remote of all. Haute-Ariège on the north and the high valleys of the Spanish province of Lérida are very sparsely populated, with only the roughest of roads (where they exist) forcing towards the inner regions. The nearest communities are no more than farming hamlets and approach routes are long. That is part of the area's appeal.

126: Pic de Sotllo (Pic du Port de Sullo) (3072m)

127: Montcalm (3077m) (Fr)

128: Punta NE (Pic Verdaguer) (3131m) (Fr)

129: Pica d'Estats (3143m)
Punta SE (Pointe Gabarró) (3115m)
Rodó de Canalbona (3004m)

📖 *Les 3000 des Pyrénées* by Juan Buyse (J&D Éditions, 1991) – first published in Spain as *Los tresmiles del Pirineo* (Ediciones Martínez Roca, 1990) – is a mine of information.

Pyrénées 3000 by Jacques Jolfre (Éditions Sud-Ouest, 1990) is a large-format collection of coloured photographs illustrating various 3000m peaks, together with a series of brief essays.

Pyrénées, Guide des 3000m by Luis Alejos (SUA Edizioak, 2003) – first published in Spain, this is a French translation (www.sua-ediciones.com)

See also pp139–44 of *The Alpine Journal* for 1995 for a descriptive summary.

Formalities

All foreign nationals visiting Andorra, France and Spain must be in possession of a current passport. Entry visas are not required for citizens of EU countries (including the UK), Canada, the USA and New Zealand, but visitors from Australia will need to obtain a visa before entering both France and Spain.

Health precautions

No essential inoculations are required. Take your European Health Insurance card to claim emergency medical treatment under the local health services. Medical insurance cover is also advised, even where reciprocal health agreements exist. Sufficient cover for search and rescue expenses should be included.

International dialling code

Andorra 00 376; France 00 33; Spain 00 34. When phoning to the UK from abroad the code is 00 44.

Languages

French, Castilian Spanish and Catalan. Catalan is the official language of Andorra, but both French and Castilian Spanish are widely spoken there.

Mountain Huts

Reciprocal rights cards (to obtain reduced overnight fees) are available to members of the British Mountaineering Council. Contact The BMC, 177–179 Burton Road, Manchester M20 2BB (☎ 0161 445 6111, e-mail: office@thebmc.co.uk)

National mountain/walking/trekking organisations

Andorra: FAM (Federació Andorrana de Muntanyisme), C Bra Riberaygua 39, 5è Andorra la Vella (☎ 867 444 www.fam.ad)

France: FFRP (Fédération Française de la Randonnée Pédestre), 14 rue Riquet, F-75019 Paris (☎ 01 44 89 93 93, www.ffrp.asso.fr)

Spain: FEDME (Spanish Federation of Mountain and Climbing Sports), Florida Blanca 75, Entio 2°, E-08015 Barcelona (☎ 934 26 42 67, www.fedme.es)

National Tourist Offices

Andorra Tourist Delegation, 63 Westover Road, London SW18 2RF (☎ 020 8874 4806, www.andorraonline.ad)

French Government Tourist Office, 178 Piccadilly, London W1J 9AL (☎ 09068 244 123, e-mail: info.uk@franceguide.com, www.franceguide.com)

Spanish National Tourist Office, 22–23 Manchester Square, London W1U 3PX (☎ 020 7486 8077, fax: 020 7486 8034, e-mail: londres@tourspain.es, www.tourspain.co.uk)

Pyrenean Tourist Information

Confédération Pyrénéenne du Tourisme, 54 boulevard de l'Embouchure, BP 2166-31022 Toulouse cedex 2 (☎ 05 61 13 55 88, e-mail: lespyrenees@wanadoo.fr)

CIMES (Centre d'Information Montagnes et Sentiers) www.cimes-pyrenees.net

Time: Andorra, France and Spain are all one hour ahead of GMT.

CHAPTER 1: The Western Valleys

The valleys of Aspe and Ossau in France; Aragón, Ansó, Echo and Tena in Spain; and their tributaries

THE WESTERN VALLEYS: CHAPTER SUMMARY

Location

South and southwest of Pau. The valleys of Aspe and Ossau are linked with their Spanish counterparts by way of the Cols du Somport and Pourtalet.

★ Highlights

◗ WALKS
- in and around the Cirque de Lescun (1:2)
- the Tour of Pic du Midi (1:9)
- exploring the valley head above Refugio Respomuso (1:10)
- sections of GR10, GR11 and the Pyrenean High Route (1:2, 1:3, 1:4, 1:9, 1:10)

❹ CLIMBS
- Aiguilles d'Ansabère (1:2)
- numerous routes on Pic du Midi (1:9)
- assorted routes on the Peña Telera (1:10)
- Mallos de Riglos (box, 1:6)

◈ SUMMITS FOR ALL
- Pic d'Anie (1:2)
- Pic d'Ansabère (1:2)
- Bisaurin (1:3–1:5)
- Pic du Midi d'Ossau (1:9)

Contents

CHAPTER 1
THE WESTERN VALLEYS

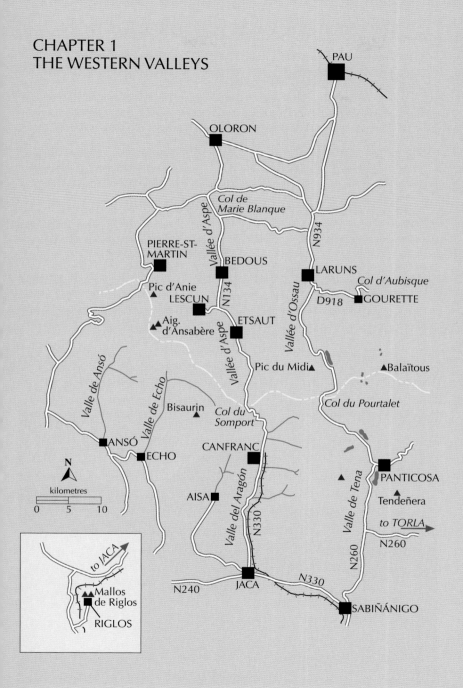

THE WESTERN VALLEYS: INTRODUCTION

With the lower Basque hills giving way on Pic d'Anie, the westernmost valleys of the High Pyrenees provide plenty of visual drama and scenic contrasts, and with two road passes crossing the watershed within a few kilometres of each other, it's easy to move from one country to the next without the need for lengthy detours. This can be particularly useful as a means of escape should bad weather be concentrated on the French valleys, for a comparatively short journey south can often reward with much improved conditions.

The Parc National des Pyrénées hugs the northern side of the border in a narrow strip spreading east from Col de Laraille where, typically, the French valleys are luxuriant with rich pastures and broad-leaved woodlands – habitat of some of the last remaining Pyrenean brown bears – while in summer the southern hillsides and valleys can be crisp and dry, the rivers shrivelled to meagre streams in wide beds of stones.

Limestone dominates at the western end; granite further east. The frontier crest around Pic d'Anie is noted for its astonishing karst landscape, especially south of the border. But of more immediate impact, the mountain view from Lescun is utterly serene as one gazes across a rolling green foreground to Pic d'Anie, the Pics Billare and the whole sweep of the Cirque de Lescun, with a tantalising hint of the Aiguilles d'Ansabère to the southwest. This is a tremendous region for walking and climbing, but so too is that of the Ossau-Tena section, where Pic du Midi d'Ossau is the undisputed monarch. There may be no 3000m summits until you move a little further east, but Pic du Midi and several other individual peaks display a grace of form that exceeds mere altitude measurement, and on their various walls those at the forefront of Pyrénéisme have created a number of classic lines.

The region has year-round appeal, for the Peña Telera – to name but one massif – is a winter climber's playground. Cross-country skiing is practised on both sides of the Col du Somport, while downhill skiing has developed on the Spanish slopes east and west of the col, and also below the Pourtalet at El Formigal.

Dawn light on Pic du Midi d'Ossau

1:1 VALLÉE D'ASPE

The Gave d'Aspe drains northward out of a limestone cirque crossed by the Col du Somport and bored through by a new and controversial road tunnel. In its upper reaches the valley has been shaped by a long-vanished glacier, but lower down the river has cut its way through rugged defiles before spilling out of the mountains to join the Gave d'Ossau at **OLORON-STE-MARIE**.

Lying about 30km southwest of Pau by road, Oloron is the natural gateway to the Vallée d'Aspe, for although the railway line currently

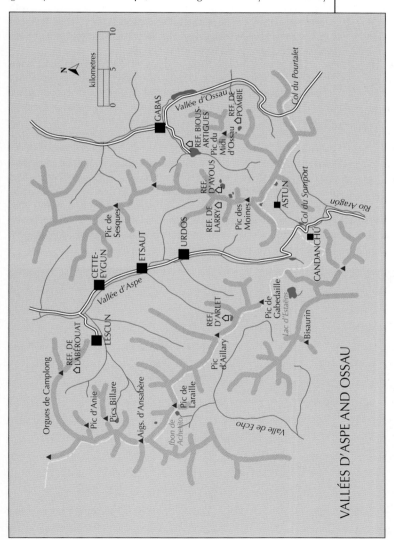

VALLÉES D'ASPE AND OSSAU

ends here the SNCF runs several buses each day up the valley to Urdos, with some continuing as far as Canfranc over the border.

Originally two separate towns, Oloron became a single entity in 1858. The site is an ancient one, and thought to have been an Iberian outpost. The Romans built their citadel on a hill just south of where the two rivers meet in the present-day quarter of Ste-Croix, and this was rebuilt as a military stronghold by the viscounts of Béarn at the end of the 11th century. Both Oloron and Ste-Marie were used as staging posts on the pilgrim route to Santiago de Compostela, which then travelled south along the Aspe and entered Spain by way of the Somport. Today a walk along the top of the old town ramparts west of the church gives a view up the Vallée d'Aspe along that pilgrim route towards the frontier mountains. The Office de Tourisme is found on Place de la Résistance (☎ 05 59 39 98 00).

Two parallel roads leave Oloron: N134 takes the west bank of the Gave d'Aspe, while D238/638 follows the east bank across farmland planted with wheat and maize divided by occasional wind-break lines of poplars. This latter road, the least travelled of the two, passes through the little spa of St-Christau, which lies at the foot of Pic Mail-Arrouy, and soon after comes to **ESCOT** on a terrace at the entrance to the Barescou valley. A diversion into this valley is worth making, for D294 climbs steadily among beechwoods heading east on a cross-country route to Bielle in the Vallée d'Ossau. After 10km it comes to **Col de Marie Blanque** (1035m), then eases down into the open grassland of the **Benou pastures**. Large herds of dairy cattle and horses graze unattended, several small tarns or pools adorn the pastureland, and a variety of undemanding ◐ walks are possible – although paths are not always clear on the ground.

The closely packed village of Sarrance in the Vallée d'Aspe

Just south of Escot D638 feeds into the main N134 where the latter crosses the Gave d'Aspe to its east bank, then enters the Escot gorge about 15km from Oloron. It is from here that the Vallée d'Aspe assumes its proper identity, and until it gains the Col du Somport the road journeys through a succession of defiles interspersed with more open and sunny breaks. Upstream beyond the gorge **SARRANCE** is bypassed. This attractive village consists of two parallel streets, one above the other, which lead to a focal point of an old monastic church with a splendid two-tier cloister. The village has a *fronton*, or outdoor *pelota* court, as if to underline its close proximity to the Basque country. (*Pelota* is the national game of the Basques.) From it a footpath climbs to a tree-shrouded calvary giving a good view of the village and the valley spreading beyond.

Though still only a village **BEDOUS** is much the largest so far met this side of Oloron, with a summer market on Thursdays, a tiny 18th-century château, an interesting church and a tourist office situated on Place Sarraillé dispensing plenty of useful brochures (☎ 05 59 34 71 48). The village also has an 11m climbing wall (☎ 05 59 34 79 03). For simple accommodation there are two *gîtes d'étape* and a municipal campsite, while a short distance west of the village **OSSE-EN-ASPE** also has a *gîte*. Out of Osse a minor road (D442) twists up to the cols de Houratate and Bouesou, providing good views of the limestone mountains to the south, and suggests an interesting, albeit tortuous, way of reaching Arette-la-Pierre-Saint-Martin. Another road east of Bedous climbs to **AYDIUS**, but footpaths also strike up the hillside and converge on that hamlet, where there's another *gîte d'étape*, before continuing across the mountains to Laruns in the Vallée d'Ossau.

- From Osse-en-Aspe the ascent of ⊗ **Le Layens** (1625m), which rises northwest of the village, is rewarding on account of the wide-ranging summit panorama which includes Pic du Midi de Bigorre in the east, a complex of Basque hills to the west, and Pic d'Anie to the south. Take the signed path of the Tour de la Vallée d'Aspe which loops up to cross the mountain's south ridge on a farm road. Here you break off to ascend the ridge to the top. Although only a modest peak, there's a difference in altitude of 1100m from valley to summit. Choose a clear day to make the most of the views.

A Tour of the Haute Vallée d'Aspe

Using Bedous as a starting point, a week-long ◯ walking tour of the upper valley could be devised, picking out some of the highlights of the Aspe–Ossau region. Such a tour is made possible thanks to a wealth of paths and tracks that criss-cross the flanking hillsides. Sections of GR10 and the Pyrenean High Route are adopted in the route outlined below.

Day 1: From **BEDOUS** cross the valley to Osse-en-Aspe, then head south to the village of Lees at the mouth of the little Lees–Athas valley. From here a trail, adopted by the longer Tour de la Vallée d'Aspe, carries the route on a rising traverse above the river, reaching **LESCUN** for overnight accommodation.

Day 2: Follow GR10 across the Plateau de Lhers and up to the wooded Col de Barrancq (1601m) – a short stroll southwest up the ridge rewards with views – then down to either **BORCE** or **ETSAUT**, both of which have *gîte d'étape* accommodation.

Day 3: Still following the route of GR10 head SSE from Etsaut before swinging east along the rock ledge of the Chemin de la Mâture. At the end of this the way curves right and rises to a narrowing of ridges, where Col d'Ayous gives a sudden surprise view of Pic du Midi d'Ossau. Immediately below stands the **REFUGE D'AYOUS**.

Day 4: Now leaving GR10 head south to Lac Bersau and continue up to Col des Moines (2168m) on the frontier ridge. This is on the route of the Haute Randonnée Pyrénéenne (HRP), which descends to Ibón del Escalar, slopes down into the Valle de Astún and goes along a minor road to the Col du Somport. Overnight at the ski resort of **CANDANCHÚ**.

Day 5: GR11 takes the route roughly westward, crossing and recrossing the frontier to Lac d'Estaëns (or Ibón d'Estanés) on the Spanish side. Crossing Pas de l'Echelle north of the lake the route of the HRP is regained – although this could have been followed from the Somport. The well-made path skirts below Pic de Gabedaille and brings this stage of the tour to a close at **REFUGE D'ARLET**.

Day 6: A short and easy walk heading northwest leads to Col de Saoubathou (1949m), a little north of the frontier ridge. By continuing along the HRP the ridge is gained at Col de la Cuarde. Follow this most of the way to Col de Pau before breaking away on a pleasant descent into rolling farmland and a series of narrow lanes heading for Lescun. Either overnight there or continue upvalley for another 1½hrs to **REFUGE DE LABÉROUAT**.

Day 7: This final stage uses waymarks of GR10 to gain the 1873m Pas d'Azuns, descends roughly northward to Col de Bouesou, then continues down to the Vallée d'Aspe, which is reached at Osse, a short stroll from **BEDOUS**.

About 3km south of Bedous **ACCOUS** rivals its neighbour for size and is, in fact, the valley capital. Standing a little east of the main road Accous boasts two hotels and a *gîte d'étape*, the Maison Despourrins (☎ 05 59 34 53 50), from which information may be had about walking tours in the Vallée d'Aspe. A recommended cross-country route ● for strong walkers heads southeast out of the village and tops the dividing ridge at the 1829m **Col d'Iseye**, then descends to the Vallée d'Ossau, which is reached midway between Laruns and Gabas in 6–7hrs. Another option is to go to Col d'Iseye, then work a way north (just to the right of the ridge) for an ascent of ● **Pic de la Marère** (2221m), whose summit enjoys an extensive panorama.

Near the head of the small valley leading to Col d'Iseye, but on the opposite side of the stream to the main path, stands the Cabane du Lapassa (1263m). Above it, on the south wall of the valley, the 2180m ⓑ **Ronglet** has two noted couloirs (the northwest and northeast) which often provide good winter climbing in the AD range – recommended period January to March.

1:2 THE CIRQUE DE LESCUN

Upstream from Accous the Vallée d'Aspe narrows once more, and at Pont de Lescun a secondary road breaks off to the right (west), signed to **LESCUN**. This is one of the nicest unspoilt villages in all the Pyrenees, made even more so by a justifiably celebrated panorama

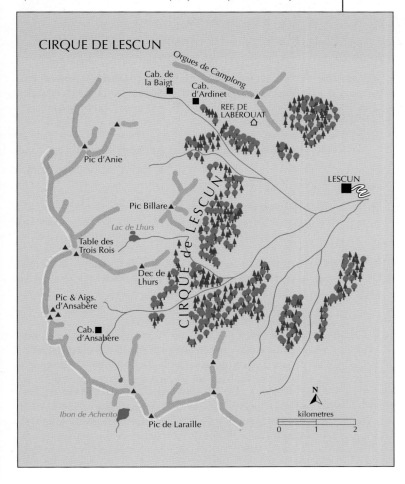

CIRQUE DE LESCUN

Orgues de Camplong

Cab. de la Baigt

Cab. d'Ardinet

REF. DE LABÉROUAT

Pic d'Anie

LESCUN

Pic Billare

Lac de Lhurs

Table des Trois Rois

Dec de Lhurs

Pic & Aigs. d'Ansabère

Cab. d'Ansabère

CIRQUE de LESCUN

N

kilometres

0   1   2

Ibon de Acherito

Pic de Laraille

Lescun,
westernmost village
on the French
slopes of the High
Pyrenees

of the Cirque de Lescun, whose mountains rise out of a pastoral foreground. There have been no overt attempts to prettify the stone houses of the village, which remains to all intents and purposes a community of mountain farmers. Their unadorned grey walls are topped by dark grey slate roofs, the houses clustered together on a sunny shelf of hillside overlooking a quilted landscape of drystone walls, fields and pastures backed by woods and impressive grey mountains. Lescun's situation is everything.

The classic, much photographed view is seen from a footpath which leaves the village at the end of a service road behind the church. This narrow path, used on the Tour de la Vallée d'Aspe, winds round the hillside as a charming belvedere and, looking back from it, Lescun provides the perfect foreground to a backdrop which includes most of the main peaks of the locality standing well spaced from one another. The Cirque de Lescun is quite unlike other well-known cirques in the Pyrenees. Instead of closing the head of a valley in a comparatively narrow horseshoe, the walling mountains here curve in a generous arc above beechwood and meadow. It is a tantalising view.

For accommodation within the village there's the two-star Hotel du Pic d'Anie, as well as dormitories in the 16-place Refuge du Pic d'Anie, a *gîte d'étape* opposite (☎ 05 59 34 71 54). There are also two other *gîtes* – the 20-place Maison de la Montagne (☎ 05 59 34 79 14) and the Gîte du Lauzart, which is annexed to the excellent campsite a little southwest of the village (☎ 05 59 34 51 77). Upvalley, 1½hrs on foot along a narrow service road, **Refuge de Labérouat** (☎ 05 59 34 50 43) is often taken over by youth groups or school parties. With 30 places, the refuge is manned from January to mid-October. Lescun has a post office and a small grocery store, and its only restaurant is located in the hotel. The Maison de la Montagne (see above) acts as the local Bureau des Guides, while M.A. Leclere (☎ 05 59 34 78 04) is a local *accompagnateur* (walking guide) who also leads cross-country ski trips and teaches snowshoe techniques.

★ WALKS FROM LESCUN

There's no shortage of walking opportunities here. With GR10 passing through the village, the HRP cutting across farmland just outside, and many other footpaths, farm tracks and minor lanes creating something of a grid through the district, a wide range of outings becomes possible – both day-walks and multi-day treks. For walkers using Lescun as a base, the following suggestions are among the local highlights.

- The valley head beyond ◌ **Refuge de Labérouat** makes a good day out. By following GR10 above the village along the edge of fields, crossing and recrossing a service road, the refuge is gained in about 1½hrs. Pic d'Anie and the Pics Billare look impressive nearby. From the refuge the way continues among beechwoods then out to rough, limestone-pocked pasture lined by the Orgues de Camplong. Just above the path stands the simple five-place Cabane d'Ardinet (1hr from Labérouat), from which Pic du Midi can be seen far off to the east. The GR10 trail pushes on a little further to another *cabane* used by shepherds (Cap de la Baigt), then breaks off to the right, climbing steeply to **Pas d'Azuns** (1873m; 3½hrs from Lescun) – from there to Arette-la-Pierre-Saint-Martin takes another 2–2½hrs. However, an alternative path continues to the head of the valley beneath Pic d'Anie, with the HRP crossing **Col des Anies** (2030m). From the col the ascent of ★◌ **Pic d'Anie** is uncomplicated in good weather, with way-marks and cairns directing the route across a limestone plateau, the final ascent being visible as a diagonal scar on the mountain-side. Allow 2hrs from Col des Anies – say 5hrs from Lescun – and 3hrs for the return.

- On the south side of Pic d'Anie lies the ◌ **Vallon d'Anaye**, with the Petit Billare acting as a gatepost, and some shattered rocks guarding its base. This little hanging valley is traversed by a *variante* of the HRP that enters by way of the 2086m Col d'Anaye at its head; the main HRP trail enters the lower reaches of the glen below the shepherd's huts of Cayolars d'Anaye. A good trail (the HRP) climbs into Vallon d'Anaye from one of the narrow farm roads that splay out from Lescun, and works its way up to the **Col d'Anaye** in 3hrs or so from Lescun. The col is on the Franco-Spanish border, and beyond it lies a karst landscape that can be exceedingly hazardous to wander over in poor visibility. The lower reaches of the *vallon* are very different to the slopes leading to the col, while the Spanish slope should be left to experienced mountain trekkers to explore.

- An ungraded route to the summit of the  **Grand Pic Billare** (2309m) can be made by experienced mountain walkers from the Vallon d'Anaye in about 3hrs. From the Cayolers d'Anaye it is necessary to head southwest, slanting up grass slopes to a saddle between Billare and the Pics de Peneblanque. At the crest bear left and follow it to the top.

- In a hollow formed by a horseshoe of ridges linking the Grand Pic Billare, Table des Trois Rois and the Dec de Lhurs WSW of Lescun, the little ⬤ **Lac de Lhurs** is another recommended destination for a day out. The way to it is quite steep, and for the first half views are restricted by dense woodland, but the upper half is particularly rewarding. The walk begins on a track (Parking Nabia, 1040m) reached by winding narrow lanes from the village. Tracks and footpaths climb through the Bois de Larrangus and, on emerging from the upper woodland, a short traverse below a steep rockface leads to a slope of scrub and an open avalanche runnel. Thereafter the path climbs the lip of a ravine to gain a high grassy shoulder with fine views, crosses the steep left-hand wall of the ravine and a tilted limestone pavement, and then comes to the Lac de Lhurs (1691m) about 3hrs from the start of the track (4hrs from Lescun). A small unmanned hut stands above the tarn's north shore, the steep walls of the Table des Trois Rois rise at the far end, while views out to the east from the outflow stream again show Pic du Midi in the distance.

Pic d'Anie, the most westerly of the High Pyrenees

- According to legend, the ⬳ **Table des Trois Rois** is where the kings of Aragón, Navarre and Béarn gathered to agree the frontiers of their respective territories. Overlooking the Lac de Lhurs it is a notable peak with a magnificent summit panorama. From the lake it may be climbed direct in 2hrs, while a more frequented route tackles the mountain along the northwest frontier ridge from Col des Ourtets (2150m) approached through the Vallon d'Anaye – 2½–3hrs from the Cayolars d'Anaye.

* Naturally enough most visitors to Lescun want to see the ◐ **Aiguilles d'Ansabère** at close hand. From the village a teasing hint shows only the stiletto-like tip of the Petite Aiguille, but there's so much more to admire. Climbers laden with gear usually drive as far as either Pont de Masousa or Pont Lamary (more parking space at the former) and walk from there. But note that the forest track between Masousa and Pont Lamary is not suitable for low-hung vehicles or those with dodgy springs. From the Lamary bridge (1½hrs walk from Lescun) a woodland path slants uphill and leads in 30mins to a grassy basin fringed with woods, with the twin Aiguilles d'Ansabère soaring above screes on the far side. The continuing path crosses a stream and climbs through the trees on the southwest side to gain the Cabanes d'Ansabère (basic, self-catering accommodation) about 1¼hrs from Pont Lamary. The astonishing finger of the Petite Aiguille bursts out of the screes nearby.

* Above the shepherds' huts a walker's route climbs up to **Col de Pétragème** (2082m), from where an easy scramble mounts the Spanish slope to the summit of ★ ◉ **Pic d'Ansabère** (2377m) in 2½hrs from the *cabanes*. The *pic* makes a wonderful viewpoint and a grandstand from which to study climbers at work on the nearby aiguilles, while southwest of Pic d'Ansabère **Mallo de Acherito** (Pic de la Cherito, 2358m) is another scrambler's summit gained from either Col de Pétragème or the pathless Col de la Chourique.

* Another option from the Cabanes d'Ansabère is to take the HRP path which climbs the hillside roughly southeast of the huts, and in 30mins reaches the little ◐ **Lac d'Ansabère** (1859m). The way continues up to the frontier ridge (2032m) and, after a brief traverse left, slopes down to the outflow of a much larger tarn on the Spanish side, **Ibón de Acherito** (1875m), in about 1¾hrs from the *cabanes*.

* These last two options could be used as part of a fairly demanding ◐ **circular walk** starting and ending at Pont Lamary. Instead of descending from the frontier ridge to the Ibón de Acherito's outflow, break away north of the lake and regain the ridge at Brèche de Hanas (2000m), which lies northeast of the lake between Pic du Lac de la Chourique and Pic de Laraille. Descend back into France aiming northeast over broken rocks until you join a path running from Pont Lamary to Col de Laraille (30mins from

The frontier ridge near Col de Pau

the Brèche). Follow this down to Pont Lamary in order to complete a 5–5½hr circuit. Yet another option is to take the **Col de Laraille** path from Pont Lamary up to the frontier ridge in 2½hrs, and while there you might as well make the ascent of ⊗ **Pic de Laraille** (2147m) more or less along the Spanish side of the ridge – allow 30mins or so from col to summit.

- • ◐ A second circuit, or rather a horseshoe of a walk, traces the frontier ridge southeast of Col de Laraille. If you have vehicle support with someone prepared to drive you to the start of the walk and meet you at the end (the two points being on opposite sides of a ridge), the route could be completed in 4½–5hrs. Begin at a parking place at 1112m about 4km south of Lescun in a little valley drained by the Ruisseau de Labranère. The path to **Col de Pau** continues south from the parking place, and in 30mins enters the national park (PNP) at Pont d'Itchaxe. From here to the col will take about 1½hrs. Col de Pau (1942m) is marked by a frontier stone, no. 276. Follow the crest round to the left, skirting Pic de Burcq on its French side, and continue to **Col de la Cuarde**, where the path leaves the crest and cuts across to a north-projecting ridge and the saddle of Col de Saoubathou. Before reaching this third col, however, join a descending path which slopes into the valley leading to Lhers. Halfway down this valley come to Parking d'Aumet (1140m) to complete the walk.

- Then there's the ◐ **Refuge and Lac d'Arlet**, just below the frontier crest on the French side of the mountains southeast of Col de Saoubathou. Used by walkers tackling the , the timber chalet-style building owned by the PNP can sleep 43 and is manned from mid-June to mid-September (☎ 05 59 36 00 99). The approach along the route of the **HRP** from the Cabanes d'Ansabère via Ibón de Acherito, Col de Burcq and Col de Saoubathou is a tough but rewarding 7½hr day. However, a shorter approach reverses the final stage of the horseshoe circuit described in the preceding paragraph; it begins at **Parking d'Aumet** and, heading south, rises towards the valley headwall, then joins the HRP to cut across Col de Saoubathou. Yet another option takes GR10 to **Col de Barrancq**, southeast of Lhers, and follows the ridge crest to the 2175m ⊗ **Pic de Labigouer** (a tremendous panorama), where the PNP boundary crosses, and on to Col de Souperet, where the path then leaves the crest, flanking Table de Souperet before joining the HRP at Col de Saoubathou. But a more direct hut approach comes from **BORCE** (see 1:3) through the Vallon de Belonce all the way.

- Perhaps the best way of returning to Lescun is by a two-day ◐ walk, leaving Refuge d'Arlet and heading southeast along the HRP across the Montagne de Banasse, then breaking off to descend north into the **Vallon de Baralet**, then via Col de Lagréou to **BORCE** (gîte d'étape). Next day take the GR10 back to Lescun.

Aiguilles d'Ansabère

CLIMBS FROM LESCUN

Although the ❶ Aiguilles d'Ansabère have naturally concentrated much of Lescun's climbing activity they do not hold a monopoly, for opportunities exist elsewhere – both within and on the edge of the Cirque de Lescun. Take, for example, the **Orgues de Camplong**, which spread in an orderly line northwest of Pic Oueillarisse above Refuge de Labérouat, and eventually direct the way to the neighbouring **Orgues d'Azun**. The Orgues are not individual peaks, but features on a longish crag wall offering routes of 250–300m in length. Although the rock is not always as sound as one would wish, the situation is light and open, and access straightforward. Three southwest-facing routes in close proximity above the beechwoods a short walk from the refuge illustrate what's available on the Orgues de Camplong.

The first is the 300m eight-pitch *Haine pour Aime* (ED, V/A1/6a+), climbed in 1993 by Benoît Dandonneau and Christian Ravier (son of Jean and a professional guide). Attacking the highest section of the Camplong wall, the route follows an elegant line which mounts by way of a series of slabs and cracks about 40m to the right of the classic test-piece the *Voie de l'Y* (Carrafancq & Cassou; 270m, TD, V+/6a). On this latter route, which dates from 1976, two pitches lead to an overhanging roof at the point where the two branches of the Y join. A short section of wall on the right (V+) then carries the route into a broad crack/chimney which points the way forward and closes the gap, so to speak, between this and the line of *Haine pour Aime*. Meanwhile, *Les Trentièmes Rugissants* takes off just 25m to the left of the Y. Here again Christian Ravier, but this time with Philippe Barthez, was instrumental in creating a 240m ED- route (V+/6a/6b+) that is rather more direct than either of its neighbours.

Further upvalley, on the southeast-facing **Orgues d'Azun** north of Pic d'Anie and west of the Pas d'Azun, Barthez and Christian Ravier have created *Jompi Keupon* (250m, TD, V+/6a). The standard approach to this is by way of the GR10 trail as far as the Cap de la Baigt *cabane* below Pas d'Azun, then west across scree to the base of the wall (1½hrs from the Labérouat refuge).

On the way to Refuge de Labérouat the bulky **Pics Billare** tend to dominate the southwest view. On both the **Grand Pic** (2309m) and the **Petit Pic** (2238m) routes of substance have been created. On the Petit Billare there are several fine lines, among them the original 700m *East Face* (J. & P. Ravier, Bouchet & Grenier, 1966), the 600m *Ataketo* (ED-, V+/6b), and the well-respected *Si Loin, Si Proche* (500m, ED/V+/6b) put up by Barthez, Cappicot and Christian Ravier in October 1996, while the *Couloir Oriental* on the **Grand Pic Billare** offers a 700m winter route (D+, V, 60°) which generally comes into condition between January and March.

Between the Pics Billare and the Ansabère Cirque the 2421m **Table des Trois Rois** offers a 300m *East Face* route (ED-, V+/6a/6c+) in full view of the little Lac de Lhurs.

A short distance further south along the frontier ridge the limestone pinnacles of the ★ **Aiguilles d'Ansabère** are among the most alluring in all the Pyrenees – the Grande Aiguille (Aig. Nord) measuring 2377m, and the Petite Aiguille (Aig. Sud) a slightly more modest 2271m. Both offer climbing of an airy and exhilerating nature in a lonely setting, and both share a tragic history.

On 23 June 1923 Lucien Carrive, a strong climber with several respectable routes behind him, partnered the young Armand Calame in an attempt by what is now the *Voie du Surplomb* on the short West Face of the Grande Aiguille which faces the Pic d'Ansabère. At the crux Carrive slipped, the rope broke and he fell to his death. Shaken, Calame continued to the summit, but on the descent, and using the shortened rope for an abseil, he too slipped and lost his life in the subsequent fall. Almost 50 years later the neighbouring Petite Aiguille was the scene of another tragedy when in March 1970 Baudéan and

Petite Aiguille d'Ansabère

Garrotté were caught by a winter storm after making a successful ascent. In the maelstrom Garrotté was killed in a fall, while his surviving partner was left hanging from their rope for nearly three days before being rescued.

Such tragedies underline the serious nature of climbing here, although the placement of bolts has inevitably increased both security and the number of ascents in recent years. The longest routes (300m+) are generally to be found on the East and Northeast faces, although the well-known south-facing *Spigolo Sud* of the **Petite Aiguille** is some 350m in all.

A number of attempts were made on the *Spigolo* in the decade before it was successfully climbed by Raymond Despiau and Patrice de Bellefon in August 1967. Siege tactics had been adopted by Despiau during the previous month: between 10–15 July with de Boysson, and from 18 to 21 July with J.C. Lucquet, he bolted and pegged his way towards the summit, returning to finish the route with de Bellefon on 22–23 August. On the same day that they reached the summit, the route was climbed in 14 hours by Jean Oscaby, Jean-Louis Perez and Toni Sarthou, who removed a number of pegs from it.

This *Spigolo Sud* is today graded ED (V+/7b). The lower section involves free climbing on moderate broken ground, but the upper 200m are vertical or outward leaning with bolts or pegs *in situ*, although these are widely and unevenly spaced. The situation is magnificently airy.

A variation of the original *Spigolo Sud* is the 300m *Zutopistes* (ED+, V+/6b+/7a), created in 1997 by Christian Ravier in partnership with J.L. Gontié, while other south-facing lines on the Petite Aiguille include *Zélus Vendus Zélus Pendus* (150m, ED+, V+/6a+/6c) and *Dernier Voyage* (200m, ED-, V/6c) – both claimed by Christian Ravier. Meanwhile, the classic *South Face*, put up by Montaner and Vicente from Aragón between 5 and 6 June 1956, is still highly thought of and graded TD- (V+/6a).

The **Petit Pic d'Ansabère** (2200m) provides a handful of challenging lines of 150–250m on the South and Southeast faces, while two very fine mixed winter routes exist on the 2377m **Pic d'Ansabère**. The 300m *Couloir Garroté* was first climbed as a pure rock route by Bouchet and the Ravier twins in 1970, then tackled in the winter of 1984 by Desbats, Grisu and Munsch (TD, V+/A1, 55–65°). More recently, in March 1999 Desbats and Christian Ravier created the imaginatively named *Théorème de la Peur* (Theorem of Fear) just to the right of the Garroté Couloir. *Théorème* is also around 300m in length and carries an overall ED- grade (50–90°, V/A2/6a).

The impressive **Grande Aiguille d'Ansabère** has several excellent routes to choose from on both its Northeast and East faces, as well as a 50m line on the West Face dating from 1928 (Cames and Sarthou, TD-, V) – the first major climb in the Pyrenees to use artificial aid. In the 1930s the Northeast Face attracted the attention of Henri Barrio, one of the leading members of the newly formed Groupe Pyrénéiste de Haute Montagne (GPHM), who made repeated attempts on the northeast *dièdre* – a superb route that was finally achieved in 1954 by Jean and Pierre Ravier with Guy Santamaria over 15 hours of sustained effort. This *NE Dièdre* was the first route on the face; it is fairly strenuous, about 300m long and graded TD+ (V+/6a/6b+). The rock is sound, except towards the top where a questionable ledge and a broken arête lead to the summit.

The East Face of this great pinnacle is noted for the smooth slabs which form the lower part and a great couloir that splits the upper wall and vanishes near the summit. The rock is mostly good, albeit with one or two notoriously crumbling sections, and over a two-day period in October 1957 (14hrs of climbing) it received the attention of a rope consisting of Patrice de Bellefon, Raymond Despiau, Claude Dufourmantelle and Jean Ravier. Their original *East Face* has long been recognised as a Pyrenean classic, which now carries a TD grade (300m, V+/6a+) – 4–5hrs. To the left of this is the 300m *Delit d'Opinion*, an eight-pitch, more or less direct line (6a/A2+) created by Pierre Puiseux and Christian Ravier using only nuts, pegs and a single skyhook for protection and aid.

Between the East Face original and the NE Dièdre, a third recommended route was established in 1965 by Hervé Butel and Jean Ollivier. The Dièdre Butolli is an elegant line which shares the initial approach used by its neighbours as far as the slabs which mark the junction of the East and Northeast faces. This is another 300m route with an ED grade (V+/6a/6b).

The Brothers Ravier

Throughout the second half of the 20th century the Ravier twins, Jean and Pierre, were at the forefront of Pyrénéisme, creating hundreds of new routes and gaining the admiration of fellow climbers both by their breadth of vision and their commitment to the range.

Born in Paris in 1933 they spent the war years (1940–45) in Tuzaguet, the small village in the *département* of Hautes-Pyrénées where their mother had grown up, and later used that as a base from which to explore the mountains nearby. But it was by repeating Henri Brulle's classic *Couloir de Gaube* on the Vignemale at the age of 17 that they announced their arrival on the scene, sampling one of the choicest of all early routes, which gave them a respect for the pioneers and their values.

In 1952 they put up a new route on the East Face of Pic de Gerbats on the Barroude Wall. For a couple of decades or so thereafter the name Ravier was attached to almost every new climb of note in the Pyrenees, often as a rope of two, but sometimes one or other would join a team of contemporaries with a similar vision – climbers such as Paul Bouchet, with whom they shared some 30 first ascents, Patrice de Bellefon, Claude Dufourmantelle and Bernard Grenier. With a natural aptitude for extreme rock and ice, and a keen eye for an untried line, their climbs were consistently bold as they pushed back the boundaries of possibility.

Their record of new ascents reads like a climber's wish-list, a selection of highlights being: Pointe Jean Santé, Southeast Face (1953); Grande Aiguille d'Ansabère, NE Dièdre (1954); Piton Carré, North Face (1954); Pic du Midi d'Ossau, Southwest Face (1955); Petit Pic du Midi, North Spur (1956); Tour du Marboré, North Face (1956); Tozal del Mallo, South Face original; and Grande Aiguille d'Ansabère, East Face (1957); Pic du Midi, South Pillar (1959); Vignemale, North Face – Dièdre Jaune (1964); Pic du Midi, Embarradère Pillar (1965) and the Grande Cheminée on the North Face (1967); Petit Billare, East Face (1966); Pene Blanque de Troumouse, North Face; and Pico Forcanada, North Face (1969). Long winter routes include the traverse of the three arêtes of the Balaïtous, and the four main points of Pic du Midi d'Ossau, and in the 1970s they ticked off the most difficult routes between the Aiguilles d'Ansabère and Gavarnie. Even as late as 1997 they were creating a new line on Monte Perdido.

The classic status of many of these climbs is assured, but it is the manner by which the ascents are made that underlines the Raviers' devotion to the spirit of Pyrénéisme. They climb as a means of expressing their oneness with the whole mountain environment; each ascent as a spiritual quest. That ethos is carried on by the guide Christian Ravier – Jean's son – whose extreme routes in the Cirque de Lescun and elsewhere show that he is a worthy successor to his father; by Philippe – son of Pierre – who is an accompagnateur; and by Pascal, a nephew, who shares the family's dedication to the Pyrenees.

Few, if any, amateur climbers have known these mountains in such an intimate way as the Ravier twins despite the fact that they live in Bordeaux, and their encyclopaedic knowledge has been put to good use when collaborating with Robert Ollivier in his route guides, as well as in the preparation of numerous articles, reports, technical notes and sketches for CAF journals and specific Pyrenean magazines such as Altitude and Pyrénées.

Further afield, Jean climbed in the Caucasus in 1959, and reached the summit of Jannu with Lionel Terray's expedition that made the first ascent of this 7710m Himalayan peak in 1962. The brothers have also made two expeditions to climb in the Sahara. See Prophets of Pyrénéism in The Alpine Journal, 2007.

1:3 UPPER VALLÉE D'ASPE

Back in the Vallée d'Aspe the N134 continues beyond Pont de Lescun towards the Somport, passes through the hamlet of **CETTE-EYGUN**, and about 3km later a minor side-road branches south, climbing to a terrace on which the attractive medieval village of **BORCE** is set. The single street is lined with stone-built houses, many of which have Gothic doors, mullioned windows and flowers set behind grilles. There are two gîtes d'étape that are open throughout the year: the 18-place Gîte Communal (☎ 05 59 34 86 40) and the smaller Gîte de groupe de l'Hôpital de St-Jacques (☎ 05 59 34 89 65). Above the village there's a campsite, Camping de Borce, which is usually

open from July to mid-September. Borce is visited by trekkers tackling the GR10; it also makes a useful base for walkers planning a trip to Refuge d'Arlet through the Vallon de Belonce. A short distance into this valley the left-hand (west) wall is guarded by the modest 1774m ⊗ **Pène d'Udapet**, whose summit provides a magnificent overview of the Cirque de Lescun, and on whose slabs ⑬ a variety of 300–350m sport climbs have been created.

Etsaut, in the Vallée d'Aspe, is an important staging post for trekkers on GR10

Lying below Borce in the main valley **ETSAUT** is a convenient staging post on GR10, having a small foodstore and a choice of accommodation. There are two *gîtes*: the Auberge La Garbure (☎ 05 59 34 88 98, www.garbure.net), and the Maison de l'Ours (☎ 05 59 34 86 38), with 20 beds – both open throughout the year. There's also the two-star Hôtel des Pyrénées, which houses the village's only restaurant, while a Maison du Parc National (☎ 05 59 34 88 30) in the disused railway station features exhibits relating to the Pyrenean brown bear. On the walling ridge east of Etsaut, but unseen from the village, the celebrated little aiguille of the ⑬ **Capéran de Sesques** (2410m) offers high-grade climbing, albeit only after a lengthy approach walk across the Col de Sesques. As the Capéran is usually approached from the Ossau valley, it is described more fully in 1:9. However, northwest of the Capéran the 2606m ⊗ **Pic de Sesques** (also known as l'Escarpu) is sometimes climbed by strong walkers prepared for a full day's exercise of about 6½–7hrs for the round trip from Etsaut. The route by the mountain's Northwest Ridge is not unduly difficult, but it involves more than 2000m of ascent and is quite steep.

Of more immediate interest to walkers visiting to Etsaut is the section of GR10 which goes along the celebrated **Chemin de la Mâture**. This spectacular path, which has been cut into a near-vertical cliff face, dates from 1772, when convicts were pressed into service on behalf of Louis XIV's navy at a time when timber from the Bois du Pacq was required for ships' masts. Huge tree trunks were dragged along the *chemin* before being floated down-river to the coast. Today the path, though perfectly wide and safe enough for laden backpackers, could unnerve anyone suffering from vertigo, but the only real hazard of which walkers should be wary is that caused by climbers whose abseil ropes are often fixed across the trail. (An alternative route crosses Col d'Arras above the cliffs and joins GR10 some way upvalley.)

• ● The GR10 trail is signed from the square in Etsaut and works a way roughly southward before turning east round a rocky spur, with the sturdy-looking Fort du Portalet seen perched on the opposite side of the ravine which slices the left-hand mountain wall. This privately owned 19th-century stronghold guards one of the narrowest sections of the Vallée d'Aspe and was used during World War II for the internment of anti-Nazis – a grim-looking building with an equally grim past.

• ● The Chemin de la Mâture begins as you turn the spur, with a sheer drop plunging to the Sescoué stream below. Beyond the cliff section, GR10 continues upvalley and in a little under an hour comes to the Borde de Passette (accommodation not yet available). After this the way curves south to gain Col de la Hourquette de Larry (2055m), and soon after turns to the east across Col d'Ayous (2185m) before dropping to **Refuge d'Ayous** (see 1:9) in full view of Pic du Midi d'Ossau, about 6–6½hrs from Etsaut. This is a splendid day's walk, but there are other options available. The first breaks away from GR10 at the Col de la Hourquette and mounts to the 2140m Col d'Aas de Bielle, beyond which a path descends to **Lac de Bious-Artigues** below Pic du Midi, where there's another refuge and access to a campsite a little over 1km down the road towards Gabas. A second option turns west between Col de la Hourquette and Col d'Ayous, and descends to the unmanned **Refuge de Larry**, where the path forks. One route leads down to Urdos, while the other swings round the mountainside towards Col du Somport – a path adopted as a *variante* of the HRP.

Site of a former customs post, **URDOS** is the southernmost village in the Vallée d'Aspe before N134 climbs to the Col du Somport. Making the most of cross-border traffic, the village has shops, a bank, petrol station and accommodation at the 12-bed Maison Férras and the two-star Hôtel des Voyageurs. There's also a campsite, Camping du Gave d'Aspe.

• About 7km south of Urdos the valley opens to the basin of ⊗ **Les Forges d'Abel**, where the Somport road tunnel begins. Here a small wooded tributary valley digs into the western hillside and leads to a cirque which carries the frontier ridge. A minor forestry road snakes into this Espélunguère tributary and provides access for strong walkers to reach the modest summit of **Pic de Gabedaille** (2258m) via the HRP trail and Col de la Contende (2½hrs from the roadhead). The summit panorama is vast, and includes the Balaïtous and unmistakable Pic du Midi d'Ossau in one direction, the full sweep of the Cirque d'Aspe to the south, and Pic d'Anie out to the northwest. Instead of returning by the same route, it's possible to make a circuit by continuing south on the Spanish side of the border as far as the col known as the Escalé d'Aigues Tortes (1635m), where you then descend back into the Espélunguère Cirque – a 4½hr circular walk.

- Another fine outing from the ◒ Espélunguère forest road strays across the border to **Lac d'Estaëns**, which is briefly visited by GR11. There are two route options for this: the more direct rises through beechwoods to a ladder by which you gain Pas de l'Echelle; the alternative crosses the Escalé d'Aigues Tortes and goes down to the damp water-meadows which give the col its name, then follows the waymarked path of GR11 heading southeast. By combining these two options a rewarding 3–4hr circuit can be achieved.

- Lac d'Estaëns is also on show to those making the ascent of the ★ ◉ **Bisaurin** (2669m), highest of the Aspe group summits. Although lying well within Spanish territory (see 1:5), this easy peak (under summer conditions) is regularly climbed from the northern side of the border. Whilst it could be tackled from the Espélunguère Cirque via the Pas de l'Echelle, it is perhaps more conveniently

The Cirque d'Aspe, where walkers' routes stray across the frontier

119

begun from the Sansanet basin, which lies a short distance south of Les Forges d'Abel. From the entrance to this basin a very fine view shows the backing wall of the Cirque d'Aspe rising out of the forest ahead, and closer acquaintance does not disappoint. Shortly before the N134 makes a hairpin a minor road descends obliquely to the right and leads to a parking area. The path used on this approach climbs westward through beechwoods, then over grass slopes to the Franco-Spanish border and on to a saddle with Lac d'Estaëns seen below. Instead of descending to it the way veers left into the lovely Valle de los Sarrios, rimmed by limestone crags of the Circo de Olibon. The path swings right to cross the Puerto de Bernera, with the Bisaurin seen ahead at the end of a valley flanked by the Sierra de Bernera. The ungraded *voie normale* tackles the mountain head-on from the east (5–6hrs from Sansanet). The same approach also makes a popular ascent on skis, while the North Face holds a selection of mixed routes (up to 80°), best tackled between January and April.

The final climb of N134 to the Col du Somport is achieved with a few hairpins above the Sansanet basin, passing the 12-place Gîte du Somport (☎ 05 59 34 79 03), then coming to the open vista of the col's summit at 1632m, with Spain's Aragón valley falling away in summer to a fold of shimmering sierras.

1:4 VALLE DEL ARAGÓN (VALLE DE CANFRANC)

The Rio Aragón begins its journey to the Ebro in the short Valle de Astún northeast of the Somport, and is soon joined by the Rio de Canal Roya and several other early tributaries as the main valley pushes south to Jaca, a little over 30km away. This is very different country to that of the Vallée d'Aspe, being much more open and less wooded – a bright and sunny landscape whose mountains demand close inspection before they reveal their true identity.

A road breaking south of the Col du Somport leads immediately to **CANDANCHÚ**, which, together with neighbouring Astún, claims to offer the best and most varied skiing in the Aragón Pyrenees. With the upper slopes at 2400m and a total of 55 pistes, more than half of which are either red or black runs, the long-established resort of Candanchú often retains skiable snow long after many other ski stations south of the border have given way to spring flowers (www.candanchu.com, ☎ 974 37 31 92). In addition to downhill sport, the ski ascent of **Pico de Aspe** (otherwise known as Pico de la Garganta, 2645m) provides a near certain method for adepts of avoiding the crowds – 2½–3hrs from the Tobazo lift.

Predictably, out of season the village holds little attraction, and the surrounding slopes are typically scarred and cluttered with hoists. But GR11 passes through, and trekkers seeking overnight accommodation may be greeted by what appears to be a place deserted. Hotels, bars and restaurants invariably close when the snow melts, although the two *albergues* can usually be relied upon to stay open throughout the year. Refugio-Albergue Valle del Aragón (☎ 974 37 32 22) has 68 places in small dormitories, offers guiding services and is used as a base for mountain-centred holidays for individuals and groups. The other *albergue*, the 60-place El Aguila (☎ 974 37 32 91), also enjoys a good reputation.

ASTÚN has been created in the valley of the same name only 4km from Candanchú, and in the ski season buses ply a service from one resort to the other. A more recent development than that of its neighbour, Astún claims 29 pistes, 7 of which are black and 13 red rated (www.astun.com, ☎ 974 37 30 34). Experienced off-piste skiers have the lure of an uncomplicated ascent of **Pic des Moines** (2349m), just over the border in 2½–3hrs from the car park, to win an unforgettable view of Pic du Midi, while there are possibilities for short cross-border tours too. A **circular ski tour** in the shadow of Pic du Midi could be made by crossing Col des Moines to the head of the Bious valley, then skiing southeast along a drainage course, which then curves southwest between Pène dou Lapassa and Pic de la Gradillère, where a return to Spain follows the crossing of Collado de Astún.

Spring's snowmelt reveals two lakes at the head of the Valle de Astún, with a 10 minute walk from one to the other. These are the Ibóns de Astún and Escalar. The first lies below and to the northwest of Collado de Astún, the second directly below Pic des Moines on one of the stages of the HRP, which then uses Col des Moines to access the French slopes. Pic des Moines itself is worth the 2hr ascent in summer as in winter, but otherwise the clutter of ski machinery has somewhat reduced the valley's appeal to walkers. Perhaps the best use of the Valle de Astún in summer is as a convenient route over the mountains to exploit the magnificent walking opportunities that exist around Pic du Midi d'Ossau (see 1:9).

• • •

After that brief diversion in the Valle de Astún, we descend Valle del Aragón and look into its other tributaries. Running alongside the Rio Aragón below the Somport the former arterial N330 road in effect extends the French route from Oloron-Ste-Marie, although the value of the ancient Somport crossing has been overtaken (or should this be *under*taken?) by the recently built EU-financed road tunnel between Les Forges d'Abel on the French side and Canfranc-Estación on the Spanish – part of a highly controversial road-building programme through the Vallée d'Aspe. The pilgrim route of the Camino de Santiago descends the Valle del Aragón on the east side of both road and river.

About 3km below the Col du Somport the road makes a hairpin to cross the Barranco de Rioseta which flows from the west. A short walk into this valley leads through flower meadows to the **Circo de Rioseta**, whose summit wall consists of ridge systems pushed out from Tuca Blanca, Pico de Aspe and Pico de Lecherín. On a mid-height terrace lies the Ibón de Tortiellas, and the map shows one or two paths that could be used to explore this visually attractive and comparatively little-known corner of the mountains.

THE CANAL ROYA TRIBUTARY

Virtually opposite the Rioseta, on the east side of the Valle del Aragón, lies the tributary valley of the ● **Canal Roya**, whose *pista* (rough track) and subsequent paths take the walker to the Anayet lakes below Pico de Anayet and to a choice of crossings leading to the Valle de Tena. Trekkers on GR11 head up this valley as part of the 6hr stage from Candanchú to Sallent de Gállego. There's a small official campsite near the entrance (the Canfranc, open April to mid-Sept) and an unmanned hut, Refugio de Lacuas, halfway through the valley that would do in an emergency, but otherwise no facilities exist here. A popular and highly recommended walk to the **Ibónes de Anayet** (2227m), east of the graceful Pico de Anayet, will take about 3hrs from the campsite following the route of GR11 all the way. From the lakes Pic du Midi is clearly seen to the north, while Pico de Anayet towers above to the west. Although the *voie normale* ascent of ●● **Pico de Anayet** (2545m) climbs easily from the southeast, the 500m North Face is a very different proposition, carrying a D grade (IV+) route which makes a fine mixed climb in winter (one pitch of 70°). It was first climbed in summer 1956 by Juan José Diaz and Julian Vicente, who followed with a winter ascent in February 1961. From the foot of the face to the summit, allow 3–4hrs. The same pair made the first ascent of the Northeast Arête (grade D) in April 1957. The 300m East Gully, known to the French as the *Couloir des Français*, is another winter challenge (an excellent mixed route of D- with one 75° section), originally climbed in summer by Jean Arlaud with Marceillac and Mobbe in 1925, while Rémi Thivel soloed the impressive *Fin de Siècle* (500m of ice and mixed climbing, 75°, and grade V rock) in February 1998. Meanwhile the nearby **Vértice de Anayet** (2559m) makes a medium-grade ski-mountaineering expedition.

From the ● Anayet lakes GR11 tops an old grass-covered moraine, then descends alongside the Barranco de Culivillas to another *pista* serving the new Formigal ski station, and continues eventually to Sallent de Gállego. An alternative crossing to Sallent via Formigal is used by a GR11 *variante* by way of the **Valle de Izas**, the next tributary of the Aragón flowing from the east. The entrance to this valley lies a little under 2km south of the Canal Roya, immediately behind the one-time prison fortress of Coll de Ladrones, which now serves as an interpretation centre with displays about the Somport road tunnel.

THE VALLE DE IZAS TRIBUTARY

The southern wall of the Valle de Izas has a variety of climbing options of particular interest in winter, when a series of gullies and ❶ **frozen waterfalls** come into condition, giving routes of 150–300m in length. Of particular note are the Cascade Notre-Dame and the celebrated *Histoire d'Ô* (grade III/4), climbed by Darrius and Julien in January 1980. At the far end of the valley's north wall **Pico Culivillas** (2528m) provides winter sport on its NNW Face, as well as an East Face Couloir (*Marchando una de Vermut*) graded AD with a magnificent panorama once the summit is reached.

At the centre of the Valle de Izas headwall stands Pico de las Tres Huegas, with cols on either side that are of more interest to walkers and trekkers in summer. Collado de Izas (2230m) on the northern ridge is favoured by the GR11 route, while the 2223m Collado de Escarra crosses further south. This last-named option takes walkers down to the dammed lakes of Escarra and Tramacastilla south of the Formigal ski grounds, and makes a very fine and more direct cross-country route for anyone planning to visit Panticosa and the Caldarés valley.

• • •

Just 8km down the road from the Somport pass N330 enters **CANFRANC-ESTACIÓN**, a one-street township notable for its astonishingly out-of-place international railway station built in a wave of misplaced optimism in 1928. Before 1973 the Jaca–Oloron railway passed through a tunnel beneath the Somport (the new road tunnel runs alongside it), but with the collapse of a bridge on the Aspe valley side and refusal by the French authorities to repair it, Canfranc's bold and impressive station – whose platforms are the second longest in Europe – became little more than an architectural white elephant. The station is still in operation, but at present serving just two trains a day to and from Jaca, although predictions are that international services could be resumed in due course.

As a place to stay, Canfranc is a little short on atmosphere; although, with a variety of good walking opportunities within reach, it could justifiably be used as a short-term base. There's a handful of hotels and an *albergue*, the Pepito Grillo (☎ 974 37 31 23), as well as several restaurants, shops and a bank. The tourist office can be contacted on ☎ 974 37 31 41 (note also: Asociación Turística Valle del Aragón, Plaza Ayuntamiento 1, Bajos, 22880 Canfranc-Estación, ☎ 974 37 21 84).

Between Canfranc-Estación and Canfranc-Pueblo – the neighbouring settlement that was almost completely destroyed by fire in 1944 – yet another tributary makes a knuckle indent of the Valle del Aragón's eastern wall. The **Valle de Ip** (or Val d'Yp) is a short, steep glen with a cirque headwall that towers above a dammed lake whose waters, and those of a smaller lake to the north of La Moleta, are used for hydropower. A basic, unmanned *cabaña* with 4 places is located northwest of Ibón de Ip at about 2020m. Blocking the south side of the valley above the *cabaña* is the massive **Peña Collarada** (2886m), whose ascent is usually made from Villanúa to the south; while the 2783m **Pala de Ip**, north of the lake, and 2760m **Pico Escarra**, which forms the valley's northeast cornerstone, are both climbed directly from the Valle de Ip. Some exciting ridge climbs are among the local attractions – Cuchiralles and Collarada giving airy situations with fine long views. From the Collado de Ip a 30m hole can be seen in the east ridge of the Peña Collarada – 'a prodigious hole which cuts through the mountain and whose base is filled with snow', according to Russell.

A short distance below the mouth of the Valle de Ip lies **CANFRANC-PUEBLO** which has a modest amount of facilities, including the 98-place **Refugio de Canfranc** (☎ 974 37 21 04) that is open all year. About 4km further south, and bypassed by the N330, lies **VILLANÚA**, whose grottoes are a well-known visitor attraction.

VALLE DE ARAGÜÉS

The Valle del Aragón continues southward, but just before coming to the picturesque Castiello de Jaca a minor route cuts northwest away from the Aragón on the way to Borau and Aisa, and continues across the hills to Jasa and Aragüés del Puerto in the **Valle de Aragüés**. This is the valley of the Rio Osia, whose source is on the southern slopes of the Bisaurin. In winter the Osia headwaters form part of the cross-country ski area of Lizara, but in summer walkers are drawn to the lovely open meadowlands. On the Llano Lizara meadows, at an altitude of 1540m, the former Refugio Lizara, base for ascents of the **Bisaurin** (2½–3hrs) and neighbouring summits as well as trekking routes across assorted passes, was unfortunately destroyed in 1999, but it is due to be reopened soon. Meanwhile Aragüés del Puerto downvalley has an *albergue-refugio* with 85 dormitory places (☎ 974 37 15 19).

• • •

Back in the Valle del Aragón, Castiella de Jaca, just 8km from Jaca, sits on the west bank of the valley opposite the Garcipollera tributary, a hunting reserve for deer and wild boar. But here the Rio Aragón bursts free of the main block of high mountains and spills out to a broad open plain running east–west commanded by **JACA**, the long-time capital of Aragón at an altitude of only 820m, backed by the Peña Oroel. With its massive star-shaped **citadel** and beautiful **Romanesque cathedral** to give it character, and standing at the junction of three major highways and with rail connections with Canfranc to the north and Huesca to the south, Jaca makes a useful base from which to explore this western end of the Spanish High Pyrenees.

A number of hotels provide a range of accommodation facilities. Sadly, the youth hostel has now closed, and there's only one campsite, the Victoria, which is open all year and located a little out of town on the way to Pamplona. The town has plenty of restaurants, bars, shops, banks and a hospital (☎ 974 35 82 00). The tourist office is situated on Avenida Regimento de Galicia just south of the citadel (☎ 974 36 00 98), close to the offices of Mountain Travel, a company which provides guiding services and runs an assortment of climbing, trekking and canyoning holidays in the Pyrenees (info@ mountaintravel.net ☎ 974 35 57 70).

1:5 VALLE DE ECHO

Northwest of Jaca, and running parallel to the Valle del Aragón, the valleys of Echo (or Hecho) and Ansó are the most westerly in Alto Aragón. Until recently they were little visited by tourists other than local Spanish families who hasten there at weekends, yet both valleys reward with splendid scenery and lots of walking potential at their head.

Valle de Echo is drained by the Río Aragón Subordán which rises under the frontier ridge north of the Bisaurín, at first easing through the water-meadows of Aguas Tuertas, then flowing a little north of west as the Guarrinza valley before making a sharp southerly curve to the pine and beech woodlands of Selva de Oza at 1140m. The valley now forges due south to the narrows of Boca del Infierno, where it kinks a little on the way to Siresa and Echo, the latter village being situated some 44km from Jaca.

Access by public transport is limited to a once-a-day bus from Jaca (not Sundays), which first serves Echo and Siresa before continuing west to Ansó. Overnight accommodation is available in each of these villages, but you'll probably need to make advance reservations for a summer or weekend stay.

Echo (or Hecho, pronounced with a silent 'h') is the birthplace of Alfonso I and an obvious base from which to explore the valley, although there's limited accommodation (including *refugios* and campsites) to be found further upstream. Echo having been destroyed during the Napoleonic wars, its local architecture is somewhat more recent than its historical heritage would suggest, but it's quite an imposing place for all that, with a curious and controversial set of 46 sculptures in stone and metal placed on the hillside outside the village. In terms of facilities, Echo boasts several *hostales*, a year-round campsite, Valle del Hecho, and a *Refugio-albergue* with 100 places (☎ 974 37 53 61). There are restaurants and bars and three banks.

Just 2km to the north **SIRESA** is a good, if smaller, alternative village base to that of Echo, although accommodation is severely limited here, with the only hotel being the Castillo d'Acher. The village proudly claims to have the oldest church in Aragón, the ninth-century San Pedro, which is said to have been central to a long-vanished monastery. Siresa huddles below the spur of the modest Sierra de los Cuellos de Lenito, which forms the eastern wall of a narrow tributary valley cutting into the mountains between the Valles de Echo and Ansó. Across the entrance to this valley to the west of Siresa ◉ a waymarked trail (then track) winds up the hillside to gain an easy saddle on the Sierra del Vedao overlooking Ansó. An hour's descent will take you to that village for an exploration of the lower Valle de Ansó (see 1:6 below).

The deeper you wander into the Valle de Echo the more imposing it becomes, with bare limestone crags rising from a luxury of forest and pasture. The valley's east wall is drained between Siresa and the Boca del Infierno gorge by the Barranco Agüerri. Near the confluence of the Agüerri with the Aragón Subordán, the latter river is crossed by the Puente de Santa Ana. From here a *pista* swings up the hillside to a grassy shelf and the **Refugio de Gabardito** (60 places, open all year, ☎ 974 37 53 87), from which ascents are made of the 2669m **Bisaurín** in 3½–4hrs via Collado del Foratón, and of **Agüerri** (2449m) and **Secús** (2341m) by a different route. In winter the surrounding area is used by cross-country ski enthusiasts.

Collado del Foratón (2032m) is a useful crossing point on the ridge which divides the Valle de Echo from that of the Rio Osia (see 1:4), and by linking these two valleys trekkers can conjure a variety of loop trips without the necessity of backpacking camping gear, thanks to well-situated *refugios* that have made this corner of the mountains so accessible.

Further north beyond the gorge, **Selva de Oza** (Selba d'Oza on some maps) at the end of the tarmac road some 14km from Echo, was formerly used as an overnight stop for GR11 trekkers, but the campsite closed several years ago, and the only facility open now is a rustic bar. Nonetheless, Selva makes a good starting point for a variety of walks and modest ascents. Among those recommended is the 4½hr ascent of the castle-like ◉ **Castillo de Acher** (2390m) to the east, a fine viewpoint from which to study the frontier peaks which here run in a great sweep of limestone across the upper valley. Bisaurín is also frequently climbed from Selva de Oza in 5–5½hrs.

• North of Selva a 3km *pista* leads to a car park at ◉ **La Mina**, which serves as a trailhead for a number of outings. The trans-Pyrenean GR11 crosses here, and may be adopted by day-visitors for walks up to the delightful **Aguas Tuertas** water-meadows above the Guarrinza valley (2–2½hrs) or beyond to the **Ibón d'Estanés** (Lac d'Estaëns – see 1:3) for a 5hr walk, plus time to return. Trekkers who have no need to return to La Mina could follow GR11 all the way to **Candanchú** (1:4) in a 6½hr walk. Yet another option would be to cut south from Ibón d'Estanés through the Valle de los Sarrios, crossing Puerto de Bernera and descending to the Refugio Lizara (assuming it has been rebuilt – otherwise camp in the meadows nearby). Next day head north-west over Collado del Foratón and descend back into the Valle de Echo.

Other options from La Mina include ascents of easy summits on the frontier ridge to gain contrasting views between the north and south sides of the border, among them ⊗ **Pic de Larraille** (Arraya de la Foyas, 2147m) in 2½–3hrs, **Pic Lariste** (Punta Christian, 2168m) in a similar time, or even **Pic d'Ansabère** (Petrechema, 2377m) in about 4hrs. Country spreading beyond this latter peak disappears into a bleached karst desert, while immediately to the east you gaze down the shafted flanks of the Aiguilles d'Ansabère to a jumble of scree and pasture. Southwest of Pic d'Ansabère, **Mallo de Acherito** (Pic de la Cherito, or Atxerito, 2358m) is another possibility, demanding 4hrs or so of effort, and each of the foregoing are approached – initially, at least – along the Acherito tributary.

Ibón de Acherito lies on the Spanish side of the frontier ridge east of the Aiguilles d'Ansabère (p109) at the head of Valle de Echo

- It is via this tributary that one of the more popular local outings is tackled – the trail to the ◐ **Ibón de Acherito**, a splendid little mountain lake trapped in a minor cirque below and to the west of Pic de Larraille and visited by trekkers on the HRP. To gain this tarn take the path on the north side of the Acherito stream for about 5mins, then break off to the right on an alternative trail which climbs steeply alongside another stream, the Las Foyas, which drains the frontier slopes. After crossing this near the unmanned, 12-place Refugio de la Solana de Buxe, continue to climb until joining the HRP, where you bear left on a gently rising traverse all the way to the Acherito lake.

Cross-border treks into France provide another possibility, including (from west to east):

127

- an unnamed crossing at **2032m** above Ibón de Acherito which leads down to the Cabanes d'Ansabère
- **Col de Pau** (Puerto del Palo, 1942m) for a direct route to Lescun
- **Col de la Cuarde** (Portillo La Cunarda, 1980m) for an approach to Lhers.

For details of the French side of these crossings, see 1:2 above.

Should your plan be to leave Valle de Echo heading west, GR11 provides one recommended 5–6hr option by way of a steepish 600m climb from La Mina to the **Collado de Petraficha** (1958m), then down to Zuriza in the Valle de Ansó (see 1:6). This is a splendid walk without difficulties of any kind, but among quality limestone scenery.

1:6 VALLE DE ANSÓ

Although **ANSÓ** is the main base for this most westerly valley of the Spanish High Pyrenees, it would be better to have your own transport to make the most of a visit, since by far the best and most interesting country is found some distance upstream near Zuriza, and there's no public transport in that direction. The once-daily bus from Jaca goes only as far as Ansó, which at least allows the independent traveller to get into the lower valley, and it may be possible to hitch a lift further north from there. Attractive to second-home owners Ansó village is currently enjoying the interest of tourists who have helped revive its fortunes. There are several hotels, restaurants and bars, and two banks. Camping is permitted (there is no official campsite) near the municipal swimming pool.

Some 14km north of Ansó through the gorge of the Rio Veral, the paved road reaches **ZURIZA** (1227m), then swings west into Navarre, leaving the High Pyrenees but with an option for motorists to cross into France by way of the Col de la Pierre-St-Martin. Zuriza is a lovely open basin at a junction of valleys and with mountains curving around it. Perhaps the most impressive of these is the 2049m **Peña Ezkaurre**, a bulky limestone bastion looming above the southwest corner, its summit – visited by trekkers on GR11– carrying the borders of Aragón and Navarre. As mentioned in 1:5 above, GR11 is a very fine walk which, east of Zuriza, follows the Barranco Petraficha nearly all the way to Collado Petraficha before dropping to La Mina in the Valle de Echo.

There is no village as such at Zuriza, but there's an excellent spacious campsite with an adjacent *albergue* open all year with 72 places and a restaurant service (☎ 974 37 01 96). There's also an unmanned hut nearby, while further north on the Plano de la Casa at 1320m the **Refugio de Linza** has 110 places and is manned throughout the year (☎ 974 37 01 12).

Plano de la Casa is the site of the Linza **cross-country ski** area and trailhead for an exploration of the karst plateau that spreads up against the French border around the **Pic des Trois Rois** (Mesa de los Tres Reyes, 2444m) and **Pic d'Anie**. Should you have plans to go up onto this plateau it's best to avoid it in poor visibility, for a compass needle can mislead here; the limestone is riven with deep fissures, and in many places the frontier culminates in a sharp drop to the head of a French valley.

Mallos de Riglos

In the pre-Pyrenean range of the Sierra de Loarre, some 30km or so southwest of **ⓑ** ★ Jaca, the compact massif of sandy-red conglomerate spires, turrets and buttresses of the Mallos de Riglos rises abruptly like remnants of a surreal medieval castle above the left bank of the Rio Gállego. Although outside any boundary of the High Pyrenees this is, unsurprisingly, an extremely popular climbing venue, with exposure of Dolomite proportions virtually guaranteed and the added interest of vultures sailing the thermals around and above the crags. Thanks to the peculiar nature of the rock, climbs are strenuous and open-handed, near vertical or overhanging, between 200m and 350m in length and with grades that range from 5a to 7b. Existing routes are mostly bolted, but a few mid-sized Friends and a bunch of wires could be useful, as could a couple of descendeurs for tackling some of the epic abseils that leave you hanging free from the cliff.

The best time to visit is either spring (March–April) or autumn (Sept–Oct), since many routes face south, and in summer climbing in the full sun can be debilitating. However, several walls do face north, so all is not lost if a summer visit cannot be avoided. An early start to a south-facing climb is recommended.

Climbing here began in 1929, but the first ascent of Mallo Pison, which dominates the village, was not achieved until 1946. Yet it was the Aragónese pair of Alberto Rabada and Ernesto Navarro who effectively put Riglos on the map with their ascent of Mallo Fire – the great thumb to the left of the Pison – over six days of hard free climbing in October 1961. The route remains a classic and is highly respected still, despite its present state of bolt protection. The third main area, Mallo Visera, marks the right-hand skyline above Riglos, its awesome overhanging face holding test-pieces such as *La Fiesta de los Biceps* (7a), *Moskitos* (6b), *Chinatown* (7a) and *El Zulu Demente* (7b).

The whitewashed village of Riglos that slumbers below the cliffs has a recently enlarged hut, **Refugio Gomez Laguna** (☎ 974 38 06 50), in which the route book is housed. Owned by the Montañeros de Aragón it has 80 places and meals provision, although many climbers choose to bivouac at the foot of the crags or use the campsite at Murillo in the valley about 20 minutes' drive away. The Spanish guidebook *Escaladas Riglos* by Felipe Guinda Polo has topos to help non-Spanish speakers, while Derek L. Walker's English-language guide, *Rock Climbs in the Pyrenees* (Cicerone Press), includes 16 of the best routes. A notice board just beyond the *refugio* gives information about walks in the area, one being a circuit of the massif. Editorial Pirineo publishes a map of the area at 1:40,000, *Reino de los Mallos*.

1:7 VALLÉE D'OSSAU

Flowing parallel to the Aspe on the north side of the frontier, the popular Vallée d'Ossau is the next district to the east (see map, section 1:3). Rising among the sheep-grazed pastures of the Cirque d'Anéou by the Col du Pourtalet, streams that form the Gave d'Ossau spill through a series of narrows before easing at Laruns and then pushing through the last of the mountain barriers to curve northwest to Oloron-Ste-Marie, while the road which has accompanied the river all the way from the Pourtalet now deserts it by heading for **PAU**, the elegant capital of the *département* of Pyrénées-Atlantique.

Birthplace of Henri IV (Henry of Navarre) in 1553, the town's defensive site on the north bank of the Gave de Pau was fortified in the 14th century by Gaston Fébus as part of a plan to create a unified Pyrenean kingdom. Over the centuries Pau's equable climate attracted many visitors, including a number of veterans of Wellington's army who settled there and built their villas around the town centre. By the middle of the 19th century the English community was around 2000 in number, introducing a taste of British culture with the steeplechase, fox hunting and golf, and it was only Queen Victoria's choice of coastal Biarritz for a month-long visit in 1889 that started Pau's decline as an all-year health resort. But it is the town's position in regard to the mountains which provides the main appeal so far as this guide is concerned. That, and its outlook and ease of access, for Pau has a TGV link with Paris, as well as train and SNCF buses to Oloron-Ste-Marie, from where other bus routes continue into the Aspe and Ossau valleys.

Accommodation in Pau is plentiful, including youth hostels and campsites. The tourist office (☎ 05 59 27 27 08) is found just north of the Boulevard des Pyrénées, opposite the Place Royale, while the town has its own Club Alpin Français (CAF) section located at 5 rue René Fournets (☎ 05 59 27 71 81).

From the celebrated **Boulevard des Pyrénées** it is claimed that on a clear day a 100km line of mountains may be seen stretched across the southern horizon. Whilst several individual peaks may be identified in that line, it is the unmistakable profile of Pic du Midi d'Ossau, 50km away, that captures one's attention. None with an interest in mountains could happily gaze on that scene without wanting to get to grips with at least one of those peaks – with Pic du Midi claiming preference. Even from this distance its appeal is obvious.

Crossing the Gave de Pau N134 strikes south as far as **GAN**, where it then forks. The west branch leads to Oloron and the Aspe valley, while D934 continues south towards the lower Vallée d'Ossau. A little further on remnants of the old frontal moraine that was responsible for deflecting the Gave d'Ossau from its intended course can be seen between **BUZY** and **ARUDY** on the road which links N134 and D934. In Arudy the Maison d'Ossau houses a display depicting prehistoric life in the Pyrenees, as well as an exhibition of local flora and fauna and the region's geology.

At **LOUVIE-JUZON** Pic du Midi comes into view framed by the valley walls, and from this angle it looks truly impressive, as though raised upon a mighty pedestal. However, east of the village, just north of the 1134m Pène Peyrou and surrounded by woodland, the ❻ **Rocher Blanc** has a number of 130m bolted routes for those occasions when the higher mountains are out of condition.

Here you enter the Ossau valley proper, and, travelling south, soon bypass the village of **BIELLE** which is seen to the right. This small but compact settlement was formerly the valley's capital, and it retains a certain dignity with several sturdy 16th-century houses, a 500-year-old church with a flamboyant Gothic porch, and an 18th-century château. Behind the village a minor road snakes up to the **Benou pastures** (gentle walks) and **Col de Marie Blanque** for one of the nicest of all cross-country road routes into the Aspe valley (see 1:1).

It's about 7km from Bielle to Laruns on a straight run through the valley on the west bank of the river. Roughly midway between the two, but on the east side of the valley, **ASTE-BÉON** is noted for the nesting site of a large colony of griffon vultures. **La Falaise aux Vautours** is the viewing centre (open daily April-Sept) which, in addition to a panoramic screen projecting the birds' behaviour patterns, also has exhibits of local Pyrenean interest.

On the hillside above Aste-Béon the *granges* (barns) of ❷ **Port d'Aste** make a focus for a pleasant if undemanding walk. The *granges* are set in a line facing west across the valley about 500m above the village, and there are several paths striking across the pastures above them. One of these provides an option of reaching the modest 1693m summit of **Le Toussau**, while others push further east across the hills via Col de Jaut to the heavily wooded valley of l'Ouzom – a winter challenge for **cross-country skiers**. A glance at the map reveals two or three possible circuits to be made there.

Just before coming to Laruns a secondary road cuts left to **BÉOST** and ◐ **LOUVIE-SOUBIRON**. From the first of these a walkers' route sets out for the **Col d'Aubisque** by way of **AAS**, which has accommodation at Auberge du Chemin de Pleysse, while from the latter a 6hr walk plunges into seldom visited country leading to **Col de Louvie** (1438m) in 3–3½hrs and **Ferrières** in the Vallée de l'Ouzom.

If you have your own transport **LARUNS** makes perhaps the most convenient base in the lower Vallée d'Ossau, otherwise its main purpose would be for restocking with supplies. The village has no less than seven campsites, five hotels and the Gîte/Refuge l'Embaradère at 13 Avenue de la Gare (☎ 05 59 05 41 88). There are adequate shopping facilities, restaurants and a post office, and the tourist office is located on the Place de la Mairie (☎ 05 59 05 31 41) in the same building that houses the Bureau des Guides (☎ 05 59 05 33 04).

Laruns sits at the confluence of the Gave d'Ossau and Le Valentin, the latter river being accompanied upstream as far as Gourette by D918 – part of the famed Route des Pyrénées, which here climbs to the 1709m Col d'Aubisque. Before continuing deeper into the Vallée d'Ossau it is proposed to divert along that road.

1:8 VALLÉE DU VALENTIN

A little over 4km from Laruns D918 sneaks through the gloomy spa of **EAUX-BONNES** (Office de Tourisme, ☎ 05 59 05 33 08), then continues for a further 10km to **GOURETTE**, a visually unappealing place in summer, but one which comes alive in winter as an intermediate ski resort with some 26 lifts serving about 30 pistes. The top lift is at almost 2380m. International ski and snowboard competitions have frequently been held here, while Col d'Aubisque, another 4km above Gourette, offers 20km of cross-country ski runs. Reached by bus from Pau via Laruns, Gourette has six hotels, some of which are only open in the ski season, and two manned refuges of particular interest to walkers, trekkers and climbers in summer: **Chalet-refuge du Club Alpin Français** (☎ 05 59 05 10 56) with 40 places, and the larger **Club Pyrénéa Sport** (☎ 05 59 05 12 42), which has 64 places. There's a tourist information office (☎ 05 59 05 12 17), a post office, one or two food shops, several café/restaurants and a cash dispenser.

Despite appearances Gourette is not the sole preserve in winter of the ski fraternity, for when conditions are suitable there are some challenging climbs to be made on those limestone peaks that form a southern backdrop to the resort. On the 2594m ⑬ **Pic d'Amoulat**, for example, the Northeast Face holds two renowned *goulottes* won by Rémi Thivel in January 1997 – the first of these, with Benoît Dandonneau, being the 320m *Mariage Blanc* (TD+, passages of 80/85°); the second, with Christian Ravier, being *Vive la Mariée* (300m, TD+, passages of 90°). The nearby **Pène Médaa** has a bevy of hard winter routes, including the 350m *Voie Julia* (Laurent/Pétuya, 1995; ED-, V, A2, 65°) which starts with a 70° wall and, higher up, has a vertical 10m section of water ice, while both the **Pic** and **Rognon de Ger** have their own test-pieces. Approach routes from Gourette are mostly straightforward.

Despite its lack of atmosphere and somewhat brutish apartment-block architecture Gourette has no shortage of interest when the snow has gone, for there are some good walking tours to be made from it and numerous rock climbs of all grades on those limestone peaks mentioned above, as well as on the well-known **Pène Sarrière**, where there are many shortish problems of 100–200m in length. There are plenty of modest summits to be reached by walkers too, including **Pic de Ger** (2613m), **Pène Blanque** (2550m) and the neighbouring **Pic Arre-Sourins** (2614m), and both the **Pic du Grand Gabizos** (the highest in the Eaux-Bonnes massif) and **Pic du Petit Gabizos** (2692m and 2639m) southeast of Gourette. Both these last-named summits require a degree of scrambling ability, which will naturally deter some walkers.

The view east from Col d'Uzious (2236m) in the Eaux-Bonnes massif

Once away from the pistes and ski tows there are some pleasant local walks available, notably to **Lac d'Anglas** and **Lac du Lavedan**, both of which take you below the East Face of Pène Sarrière. As the GR10 passes through Gourette, this important waymarked trail could be followed west for a full-day's back-country trek to Gabas, below Pic du Midi, or east to Arrens-Marsous.

- But perhaps the best option is to make a ☉ **two-day circular tour** by taking the path through the upper Valentin valley to Lac d'Uzious, then cross Col d'Uzious (2236m) above it to the southeast. From here you plunge down into a narrow hanging valley that empties eastward to Lac du Tech in the Vallée d'Arrens. Now wander downvalley to the outskirts of Arrens, where you join GR10 for the return to Gourette.

- Yet another option is to use Gourette as the starting point for a ☉ **lake-to-lake tour** in the granitelands of the Balaïtous massif. For this tour follow the previously mentioned route across Col d'Uzious, but some way above Lac du Tech find an alternative path that will take you up to Lac de Pouey Laun and on over Col d'Hospitalet to reach the *lac* and **Refuge de Migouélou**. There are continuing ways over the mountains to either **Refuge d'Arrémoulit** or **Refuge de Larribet**, and enough options to keep any wild-country trekker happy for a week or more.

1:9 THE UPPER VALLÉE D'OSSAU

The continuing D934 south of Laruns begins the climb to Col du Pourtalet in the wooded Hourat gorge, passing between neat box hedges before coming to the few buildings of **LES EAUX-CHAUDES**, a tiny 19th-century spa with an even less cheery aspect than Eaux-Bonnes. Accommodation is available here in the Chalet-Auberge la Caverne, which is open all year round. The road then crosses the river at the Pont d'Enfer and climbs on, passing the Miégebat power station near the entrance to the **Gorges du Bitet**, through which a walkers' route – initially on a forest track overlooking a series of cascades – pushes westward to **Col d'Iseye** and Accous in the Vallée d'Aspe. Two alternative routes break off before the col is reached in parallel glens cutting southwest. One leads to **Lac d'Isabe**, rimmed by cliffs in a cirque headed by Pic d'Isabe and Pic de Sesques, while the other makes for the celebrated thumb-like aiguille of ❶ **Capéran de Sesques**. Despite its long approach march (9km), the Capéran maintains a place of honour in local climbing history, thanks to its first ascent by Pierre Bordieu, rope free and solo, in June 1922. The classic North Face (130m, TD, IV/V+) was won by François Cazalet and Roger Mailly in 1935, and its status underlined 40 years later by inclusion in de Bellefon's *Les 100 Plus Belles Courses.*

The last hamlet in the Upper Vallée d'Ossau is **GABAS**, a string of buildings standing just below the opening of the tributary valley which leads to the Bious pastures and Pic du Midi d'Ossau. With the comparatively recent explosion of mountain activity in the Pyrenees, Gabas has assumed an importance far beyond its size. It boasts a Maison du Parc (☎ 05 59 05 32 13), with particular interest to walkers, and a mountain ecology centre with natural history displays. There's accommodation available in the 50-place, CAF-owned **Chalet-Refuge de Gabas** (☎ 05 59 05 33 14), manned from June to October and at weekends; and at the following hotels, the new Chalet des Pyrénées, the two-star Le Biscau and the Hotel-Restaurant Vignau. Trekkers tackling GR10 often spend the night here before embarking on the long but very fine trek to Gourette.

Breaking out of the Ossau valley at Gabas the narrow D231, which is used on the descent from the **Pic du Midi region** by GR10 trekkers, climbs steeply towards the southwest, running along the PNP boundary, and before reaching the dammed Lac de Bious-Artigues (4km from Gabas). Although situated almost 2km from the roadhead, this is the turning point for local buses. Currently there's a useful, once-a-day in each direction, bus service in summer linking Laruns with Bious-Artigues. The road actually ends at the lake, and the car park there is invariably overcrowded on every fine day in summer.

The southward view from the lake is magnificent, with ◖Pic du Midi rising abruptly out of woodland. But despite the towering presence of this Pyrenean symbol, it is by no means the best view of the

Refuge de Pombie, base for climbs on Pic du Midi's Southeast Face

mountain. For that you'll need to visit the Lacs d'Ayous, almost due west of Pic du Midi and reached by following the waymarked GR10 – at first into the lawn-like pastures south of Lac de Bious-Artigues, then as it forks right to climb among trees for a while before coming to the first of the Ayous lakes. **Refuge d'Ayous**, a PNP hut at 1982m, stands just above Lac Gentau (2hrs from the car park) and enjoys a stunning dawn view of the mountain reflected in the lake. The refuge has 50 places, and is manned from mid-June to mid-September with meals provided (☎ 05 59 05 37 00).

A third refuge serving Pic du Midi is set just above Lac de Pombie with a view onto the great Southeast Face of the mountain. ◖**Refuge de Pombie** is owned by the CAF and is largely used by climbers. With 50 places in summer, it is manned from June to the end of September (☎ 05 59 05 31 78). Although it's perfectly feasible to reach this refuge by way of a longish walk of 3–3½hrs from Lac de Bious-Artigues, two alternative routes are considerably shorter and of more value to laden climbers and backpackers. The first comes from a parking place by the *cabane* of Caillou de Soques in the deep valley to the east, by which a straightforward trail climbs to the hut in 2hrs. The other, and even shorter, approach of 1½hrs is made from the Cirque d'Anéou near Col du Pourtalet to the south. From here a well-trodden path leads over pastures to cross Col de Soum, with its sudden, breathtaking view of Pic du Midi's massive Pombie Wall ahead, followed by a gentle stroll down to the refuge.

No matter by which route one approaches the Pic du Midi d'Ossau, it never fails to impress.

Pic du Midi d'Ossau

Of all Pyrenean mountains ◖ ★ 136136 Pic du Midi is the most easily recognised. Whether seen from the foothills to the north, or from any number of vantage points to east or west, its profile is unmistakable. Although often described as the Matterhorn of the Pyrenees for the way it stands alone and unchallenged by neighbouring peaks, its shape is more akin to that of Mount Kenya, with two distinctive summits separated by the deep cleft of La Fourche.

Known affectionately as Jean-Pierre, it has neither glacier nor permanent snow-field, and at 2885m its altitude is modest even by local standards, yet the mountain is defended by great rock walls on which some of the most challenging climbs in the Pyrenees have been attempted and won. To the casual observer it has few weaknesses, so it comes as a surprise to discover that the first attempt to climb it was made as long ago as the 16th century.

It was in the spring of 1552 that François de Foix, the Count de Candale and Bishop of Aire, assembled an expedition with the principal aim of determining Pic du Midi's height. An account of this climb explains that: 'When the rock resisted their endeavours, they made use of ladders, grapnels, and climbing irons [and] by this means got as far as a place where they no longer saw any trace of wild beast or bird, though they saw birds flying about lower down; nevertheless, they were not yet at the top of the mountain, [but] in the end, he got to it, or within a little distance of it, with the aid of certain hooked sticks.'

Whether this early attempt was successful is not proven, but Jean-Pierre had definitely been climbed two centuries later, for Junker, a military surveyor, made an entry in his notebook for 20 March 1787 that he had seen a 'triangulation turret' upon the summit. This is thought to have been the work of an unnamed shepherd from the Aspe valley on behalf of the geographers Reboul and Vidal. A decade later, on 2 October 1797, Mathieu, another shepherd, took part in the first recorded ascent in the company of Guillaume Delfau. This was something of a landmark in mountaineering terms, for the climb was motivated purely by sporting instinct, rather than justified by the rationale of scientific endeavour that attended most ascents of the period.

The Petit Pic (2812m) had to wait until 1858 before receiving its first ascent from the Laruns guide Jean Biraben, accompanied by a local shepherd and a tourist-client, M. Smith, while the next notable event came in 1888 when Roger de Monts and his guide made the first winter ascent of the Grand Pic. Eight years later, in 1896, the highly talented team of Henri Brulle– and René d'Astorg, with the guides Célestin Passet and F.B. Salles, made the first ascent of the Grand Pic by way of the North Face and La Fourche. Their route is now graded AD, with one passage of IV.

Though Pic du Midi has two clearly identifiable peaks as its major features, two other summits are apparent only when viewed from the south – the towers of Pointe d'Aragon (2727m) and Pointe Jean Santé (2573m), each of which holds a number of serious climbing challenges. The first of these (Pointe d'Aragon) was climbed in 1907 by Jacques and Robert Blanchet with Jean-Pierre Esquerre, while Pointe Jean Santé was named after the man who made its first ascent, solo, by way of the Pombie-Suzon Couloir 20 years later.

The Southeast Face, or Pombie Wall, of Pic du Midi d'Ossau has more routes than any comparable rock face in the Pyrenees

In the decades between the two world wars, the next phase of climbing development centred mostly on secondary summits by what we may call 'sporting routes', many of which were put up by members of the Groupe Pyrénéiste de Haute Montagne (GPHM). In the 1930s the rope of Roger Mailly and Robert Ollivier saw a spate of hard new routes on the Petit Pic – on the West Face with François Cazalet in 1934, on the Northwest Face (TD+) in 1935 and on the Northeast Face (TD) in 1936; then on the Northwest Buttress of the Grand Pic (Pointe de France) in 1938.

On 9 August 1944 the first complete traverse of the four main peaks was achieved by Bernard and Jean Sanchette. Using the Pombie-Peyreget Couloir they first climbed Pointe Jean Santé, then from the Brèche Jean Santé to Pointe d'Aragon, along the arête of the Rein de Pombie to the Grand Pic, followed by descent into La Fourche. They then climbed the Petit Pic before descending the Arête de Peyreget. Today this major expedition, with something like 1400m of climbing, carries an overall D grade, with several passages of IV and one of V.

In the post-war years more technical routes were established on the walls, buttresses and towers of Pic du Midi, with some of the finest being won by the Ravier twins Jean and Pierre (see box, 1:2). In the 1950s they were active on the Southwest Face of the Grand Pic, the North Spur of the Petit Pic, East Spur of Pointe Jean Santé and South Face of the Doigt de Pombie. The *South Face Direct* on the impressive Pombie Wall was climbed by Jean Ravier and Bernard Grenier over the two days of 31 May and 1 June 1959, while in July that same year one of the ultimate routes of the period was the South Pillar of the Grand Pic (TD+), put up over two days by Patrice de Bellefon, Raymond Despiau, Bernard Grenier and Jean Ravier. The rock is first class, but with the final 150m of the pillar being either vertical or overhanging, much of the route was aided. Fifteen years after it was first climbed it still demanded a full day's effort, but in the summer of 1983 it was soloed in a little over an hour!

In May 1964 the Raviers joined up with Paul Bouchet for the 450m *SE Face Direct* on Pointe Jean Santé (ED-, V+, 6a/6b/6c), a route which took three days of sustained effort. The following year the same team created one of the epic routes of the decade with the two-day ascent of the 350m Embarradère Pillar below La Fourche (ED, V+, 6b/6c), heralded at the time as one of the hardest in the Pyrenees and compared with the Bonatti Pillar on the Drus.

The exploitation of Pic du Midi's many impressive features continues apace, with those in the vanguard of climbing development invariably finding yet new challenges there. Being the most easily accessible, the great Southeast Face which overlooks the Refuge de Pombie probably bears more lines than any other rock wall of comparable size in the Pyrenees, all in a big mountain setting of great charm. Most of the classic routes have now been soloed, and many regularly receive winter ascents too. The 1990s were especially rewarding for winter climbs, with some of the hardest being put up by Rémi Thivel, Benoît Dandonneau, Rainier Munsch and Christian Ravier.

But more than 200 years after its first ascent, Pic du Midi is far from being played out, and as long as there are climbers active in the Pyrenees, Jean-Pierre will be there to attract, seduce, challenge and reward.

⊘★ PIC DU MIDI'S *VOIE NORMALE*

The *voie normale* makes an entertaining ascent, and is recommended for walkers with a modicum of scrambling experience and a good head for heights. However, there is some danger from stonefall

(helmets advised), and two short passages of grade III climbing are involved. Summit views are far reaching and a just reward for the effort involved in getting there.

The route meanders up the broken East Face, which is accessed from Col de Suzon, north of the Pombie refuge. After an initial steep gully has been climbed you are faced with a slab in which a moveable peg or two aid the ascent – if not placed correctly these could cause problems on the descent. Above this slab a clear path works round to the right and leads up to an open chimney with a broken slab beside it. Climb either the slab or the chimney to a line of cairns. These eventually bring you to a long sloping groove (beware stonefall) in which one or two more pegs are found. At the top of the gully a large metal post (at 2657m) marks the correct route of descent, and this can be invaluable in poor visibility.

Continuing, the ascent winds half-left over the dome of the mountain known as the Rein de Pombie across a litter of broken rocks and scree as far as the very edge of the South Cirque. Here you work along the edge of the cirque to a saddle between two summits – the highest point is then reached by way of a short ridge broken by two steep gullies (3–3½hrs from Refuge de Pombie). Surprisingly the summit itself is flat and featureless, although the views are extensive. To the west far beyond the Lacs d'Ayous rise the Aiguilles d'Ansabère, while eastward the Balaïtous dominates a ragged skyline of peaks which includes the Vignemale.

Pic du Midi's South Cirque and four main summits. From left to right: Petit Pic, Grand Pic, Pointe d'Aragon and Pointe Jean Santé

WALKING TOURS OF PIC DU MIDI

There are two classic walking tours of Pic du Midi – the standard 5½hr circuit and an extended tour best spread over two days.

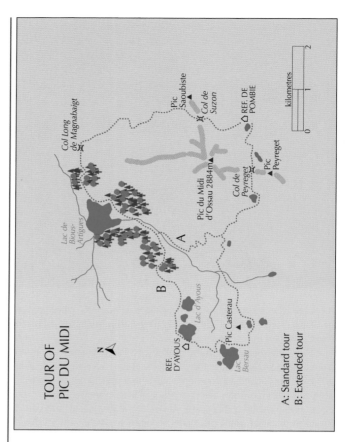

TOUR OF
PIC DU MIDI

Col Long
de Magnabaigt

Pic
Saoubiste

Col de
Suzon

REF. DE
POMBIE

Lac de
Bious-
Artigues

Pic du Midi
d'Ossau 2884m

Col de
Peyreget

Pic
Peyreget

A

B

Lac d'Ayous

REF.
D'AYOUS

Pic Casterau

Lac
Bersau

N

A: Standard tour
B: Extended tour

kilometres

0   1   2

- The ◐★ **standard tour of Pic du Midi d'Ossau** begins at Lac de Bious-Artigues and heads southwest counter-clockwise beyond the lake to gain the Bious pastures. About 40mins from the road-head ignore the GR10 path which breaks off to the right to Refuge d'Ayous and cross a footbridge (Pont de Bious) to enter the national park. The way then follows the Gave de Bious upstream as far as another trail junction, where a sign points left to Pombie by way of the Col de Peyreget. Climbing quite steeply, at first among trees, then opening to a view of a shepherd's *cabane* below to the right, in a little over 2hrs from the Bious-Artigues lake you come to Lac de Peyreget and another choice of trails. Head northeast over a chaotic region of rocks to gain Col de Peyreget (2300m), an obvious saddle between Pic Peyreget and the south-dipping ridge of Pic du Midi. From here you can see into the great rocky South Cirque of the mountain and ahead across the depths of the Ossau valley to the Balaïtous. (A magnificent view of Pic du Midi's four main peaks can be had by making a 25 minute diversion to the summit of Pic Peyreget.) East of the col an easy path used by the

HRP descends to the *lac* and Refuge de Pombie (3½hrs). From the hut wander north across the boulder tip of the Grande Raillère, cross Col de Suzon (2127m) and follow the path down through the lush Magnabaigt valley. At the far end the path veers left, eases over Col Long de Magnabaigt and descends through woodland to Lac de Bious-Artigues to conclude the tour.

• The ◑★ **extended tour of Pic du Midi** adds another 3hrs to the standard circuit, for it visits the PNP's Refuge d'Ayous and a collection of tarns west of the mountain. Although this hut can easily be reached in about 2hrs from Bious-Artigues, it is recommended to spend the night there in order to capture the magic of sunrise over Pic du Midi's shoulder – one of the great views of the Pyrenees and an unforgettable experience. The tour begins as for the standard circuit described above, but breaks away at the trail junction in the Bious pastures where GR10 veers right (a sign gives 1½hrs to Lac d'Ayous). Climbing at first through woodland you eventually emerge to the three Lacs d'Ayous, with Refuge d'Ayous overlooking Lac Gentau. From here the way veers roughly southward to Lac Bersau, skirts its eastern shore and crosses a minor col below Pic Casterau. Descending now to Lac Casterau, the way then drops more steeply to the Gave de Bious. A grassy gully is climbed above a shepherd's *cabane* to gain a pastureland, from where Pic du Midi towers overhead in dramatic fashion. Soon join a major path and bear right along it to reach Lac de Peyreget, which is on the route of the standard circuit.

OTHER WALKS IN THE OSSAU REGION

• A ◑ **variation of the Tour of Pic du Midi** leaves the main route at Lac de Peyreget and skirts the south side of Pic Peyreget to cross Col de l'Iou (2194m), then the grassy Col de Soum, before joining the standard tour at Refuge de Pombie.

• A 4½–5hr ◑ **circuit of the Ayous lakes** adopts a major part of the extended tour of Pic du Midi, and picks out the best paths and views west of the mountain. But after descending from Refuge d'Ayous to the Gave de Bious, instead of climbing to Lac de Peyreget the walk returns to Lac de Bious-Artigues through the idyllic Bious pastures.

• Above and to the north of Refuge d'Ayous, the ascent of the 2288m ◉ **Pic d'Ayous** can be made from the hut in 2–2½hrs via Col d'Ayous, which is crossed by GR10. From the col an undemanding scramble leads to the summit. Col d'Ayous is also the key to a cross-country route leading to **Etsaut** in the Vallée d'Aspe. This is best achieved by following GR10 all the way, passing along the famed Chemin de la Mâture (see 1:3) shortly before reaching the valley.

- West of Lac de Bious-Artigues lies the small hanging valley of the ◐ Aas de Bielle, with an accessible col at its head. Another recommended circular walk (4–5hrs) leads up to and across **Col d'Aas de Bielle** (very fine views to the Cirque de Lescun), then descends into the little Vallée de la Baigt de Sencours to meet GR10. Bear left and follow this popular trail as it climbs to Col d'Ayous then descends to Refuge d'Ayous. The return to Lac de Bious-Artigues simply traces the route of GR10 all the way.

- In view from ◐ Lac de Bious-Artigues looking northwest is another tributary valley, this one drained by the Arrec d'Aule, and with the little **Lac d'Aule** nestling in the cirque at its head at an altitude of 2042m. Above and to the northeast of the tarn stands **Pic d'Aule** (2392m). To reach the lake involves a steep walk of about 2½hrs from the roadhead, while Pic d'Aule is gained by way of Col de Héous in the ridge linking that summit with Pic Gaziès. The col is 30–45mins from the tarn, while Pic d'Aule is reached in a similar time from the col. Although non-technical, the ascent is over rough terrain, but there's a degree of solitude found here that is usually missing in country south of the Lac de Bious-Artigues.

• • •

Summit views from Pic du Midi include the Lacs d'Ayous and peaks of the Western Pyrenees

Returning to the Upper Vallée d'Ossau at Gabas, the D934 continues its climb towards Col du Pourtalet, and shortly after passing the turning for Lac de Bious-Artigues reaches the dammed, jade-coloured **Lac de Fabrèges**, with its large car park and *télépherique*

which serves the **Artouste-Fabrèges** ski complex in winter, and a railway operating a miniature tourist train in summer. Originally built to serve a hydro-electric project, the railway has been adapted as a tourist attraction, and the train now runs daily from early July to late September, weather permitting, for 9km at an altitude of 1950m high above the Vallée du Soussouéou almost as far as Lac d'Artouste. From the end of the line Refuge d'Arrémoulit, situated in boulder country above the southern end of the lake, may be gained by a walk of a little under an hour. From the northern end of Lac d'Artouste another trail plunges into a wild landscape; heading north initially, it crosses **Col d'Artouste** (2472m) and leads to the *lac* and Refuge de Migouélou. A third, more challenging route heads east from Lac d'Artouste and crosses **Col de la Lie** before descending to the upper reaches of the Vallée d'Arrens.

* ◐ Lac d'Artouste can also be gained by way of a demanding path that strikes up the steep mountainside from the east bank of Lac de Fabrèges. After rising through forest the way becomes more rugged as it follows the course of a stream draining from **Lac du Lurien** (2211m). The *lac*, which lies about 900m above the valley, is gained in about 3hrs. A little over 100m above it to the southeast, Col de Lurien makes a breach in a ridge pushed out from Le Lurien. Once across this ridge the way slopes down to Lac d'Artouste.

About 4km upstream of Lac de Fabrèges, with the contorted strata of Pic de Soques seen directly ahead on the Franco-Spanish border, the road makes a kink by some huge boulders opposite the basic shelter of **Caillou de Soques**. This is not only a regular starting point from which to approach Refuge de Pombie and Pic du Midi, but also a point from which to head east into the granitelands of the Balaïtous. Long-distance trekkers tackling the HRP cross the valley here on the way to Refuge d'Arrémoulit.

THE VALLON D'ARRIOUS TRIBUTARY

* The walk up the fairly steep and narrow ◐ **Vallon d'Arrious** provides tremendous views back to Pic du Midi as height is gained, especially from a grassy false col shortly before gaining Col d'Arrious. This is an idyllic spot with a levelling of turf, a clear stream chuntering over child-sized cascades, and the sort of views that demand a rest. On reaching Col d'Arrious (2259m), a little over 2hrs from Caillou de Soques, Pic Palas and Pic d'Artouste appear ahead, the cone-like Pic Palas directing the frontier ridge. At this col one has a choice of onward routes. The most obvious crosses the col heading northeast towards Lac d'Artouste, but after losing nearly 200m in height the path forks. The continuing descent leads to the lake, but the right-hand alternative resumes climbing on a steep trail to **Refuge d'Arrémoulit**

Refuge d'Arrémoulit, atmospheric base for climbs on the western edge of the Balaïtous massif

(2305m). Owned by the CAF the refuge has 30 places, a guardian from mid-June to late September and meals provision (☎ 05 59 05 31 79).

- The alternative path from ◒ Col d'Arrious also leads to Refuge d'Arrémoulit, but by a more direct route. At the col it breaks to the right and very soon arrives at the attractive, fjord-like Lac d'Arrious backed by Pic d'Arriel and a wash of screes. Now the path rises over a low ridge to a savage view of granite peaks, boulderscapes and glistening tarns, then takes a narrow ledge across the face of Pic du Lac d'Arrious. This ledge is the celebrated **Passage d'Orteig**, a dramatic, exposed traverse protected with a handrail, at the end of which cairns lead across a rough landscape of rocks and glacier-smoothed boulders before coming to the Arrémoulit refuge.

Set upon the north bank of Lac d'Arrémoulit, the refuge makes a very fine base for an exploration of this western edge of the Balaïtous region. It's a wild but immensely appealing country that will repay a few days of activity. For a start ◍ **Pic Palas**, at 2974m the dominating peak hereabouts, makes an obvious goal. Climbed by the military surveyors Peytier and Hossard in 1825, under the impression that they were tackling the Balaïtous, this handsome conical mountain provides an engaging outlook for a survey of the surrounding area and a first-rate viewpoint from which to study Balaïtous itself. Modest scramblers can reach the summit by the North Ridge (PD-), gained by the Brèche des Géodésians, which is thought to be the same route taken by Peytier and Hossard. On the Southwest Arête a more challenging route (AD+, passages of III and IV) was pioneered by the

The Balaïtous (centre), seen above Col du Palas, dominates the granite country east of Pic du Midi. Refuge d'Arrémoulit can just be seen left of the lake

German brothers Von Martin in 1913. This begins on Col du Palas and soon takes in the minor crown of Piton Von Martin (2785m), before striking up the ridge all the way to the summit. That leaves the Southeast Arête on which Robert Ollivier, with J. Arruyer and A. Petitjean, created a 300m AD route in 1937. On the Northeast Face overlooking the ⒷBatcrabère Cirque, a mixed route was climbed in March 1997 by Michel Bourdet and Alain Nadaud via the 250m Northeast Chimney. This comes into condition between January and March and is graded TD (V+/A1, 75–80°), but is approached from Refuge de Larribet, rather than Arrémoulit.

Further north, and gained by way of Lac d'Artouste and Col de la Lie, the Southeast Face of Ⓑ **Pic de la Lie** (2673m) holds several lines worth looking at. Of these, two which date from the early 1990s are especially recommended: *Allez les Petits* (250m, D+, IV+/V+) and the *Voie Franco-Argentine* (250m, TD, V+/6a).

To the south, and in full view of the Arrémoulit refuge, **Pic d'Arriel** (2824m) stands on the frontier ridge, a somewhat elegant peak whose summit makes another fine viewpoint. The *voie normale* here is via the Northwest Ridge, usually begun at Col de Sobe. However, the Northeast Arête has a PD route by way of a conspicuous diagonal gully system that leads onto the ridge, while on the ❶ Northeast Face a fine winter climb was created in March 1997 by Bruzy and Dupouy. *Nuit d'Insomnie* is about 400m long and carries an overall TD+ grade, but with passages of V+/A1, 80°. From hut to summit takes about 8hrs.

Not unnaturally it is the Balaïtous whose distant presence casts a metaphorical shadow over climbers based at the Arrémoulit refuge, and sooner or later they will no doubt be drawn to it. However, that mountain forms a major part of the following chapter, so for now we will resist its temptations and return to the upper reaches of the Ossau valley.

• • •

Above Caillou de Soques the road makes a long rising curve into the grassy **Cirque d'Anéou** for the final approach to Col du Pourtalet. In summer the grasslands here are grazed by large flocks of sheep to create a pastoral scene, with a backdrop of Pic du Midi teasing above an intervening ridge to the north. There's parking space just off the road, and a number of ◖ **walking routes** (not all of them clear on the ground) score across the pastures. The most heavily used is that which heads north to cross Col de Soum for the Refuge de Pombie (1½hrs), but another makes for the Col de Bious, which is found to the west between Pic Peyreget and Pic de la Gradillère. (Col de Bious is also known as Col d'Anéou, which is rather confusing since there's another col of that name on the frontier ridge.) From Col de Bious one could descend into the upper Bious pastures, or visit Lac Bersau and the Refuge and Lacs d'Ayous, or even divert south from close to Lac Bersau and cross Col des Moines on the frontier by an HRP *variante* into the head of the Valle de Astún – or maybe ascend Pic des Moines (2168m) above the col.

• But perhaps the best suggestion is to make a ◖ **full day's circuit** by crossing Col de Bious and descending to the upper Bious valley, then veering southwest under Pic Casterau until joining the HRP route towards Col des Moines. Instead of crossing the frontier remain on the French slopes and cut round below the crest before ascending the 2279m Pic d'Astu. Continue along the frontier ridge as far as a false summit just beyond Col d'Astu, where you then descend to the tiny Lac de Houer (2230m). Above this tarn traverse a saddle on the south side of Pic de la Gradillère, then complete the circuit by wandering over the Anéou pastures back to where you began.

Another option is to make the non-technical but rewarding ascent of ⊘ **Pic d'Anéou** (2364m), which rises from the frontier ridge southwest of Col du Pourtalet. The summit is gained via Col d'Anéou and the Spanish slopes, and views are very fine – north to Pic du Midi, south to Pico de Anayet, or west to the Bisaurin and a mass of Spanish sierras. It would be possible to continue northwest from here along the frontier on a circuit that would take in the summit of Pic de Canaourouye (2347m), then break away northeast to Pic de la Gradillère (2271m), and from there drop down to Col de Bious, where you then head east across the pastures of the Cirque d'Anéou.

Climbers in search of exercise on out-of-the-way rock will find that between Col d'Anéou and Col du Pourtalet the ❶ **Capéran d'Anéou** (Campana d'Anéou, 2212m) has a TD- route (V, A1) put up by Jean Oscaby and Gilbert Bergès in 1969.

Higher than the Somport by another 160m **Col du Pourtalet** (1794m) is often blocked by snow between November and early June. The hotel Col du Pourtalet offers seasonal accommodation. Beyond it the road sweeps into Spain and the Valle de Tena, the valley of the Rio Gállego.

1:10 VALLE DE TENA

Accompanied by the C136 to Biescas, and N260 lower down, the Rio Gállego drains southward from the Pourtalet through the Valle de Tena for something like 45km as far as industrial **SABIÑÁNIGO** (Asociacón Turistica del Valle de Tena, ☎ 974 49 01 96). Situated about 18km southeast of Jaca, Sabiñánigo is on the Zaragoza–Canfranc railway line, with infrequent bus links heading north into the valley to Biescas, Panticosa and Sallent de Gállego. The valley has mixed appeal. There's skiing at El Formigal and Panticosa; thermal baths at Balneario de Panticosa; climbing on Pico de Anayet, Peña Foratata, the vast walls of the Peña Telera and the Tendeñera; and walks of varying lengths and degrees of seriousness. There are hard snow and ice routes for the winter climber, and easy peak-bagging and a multitude of scrambles for the warmer months. There's windsurfing and sailing and paragliding too, and the valley has its own particular kind of beauty. Some, noting only the dams and hydro schemes, may dismiss it, but if at first glance the valley's appeal is not obvious, it should not be long before it is. A single visit is rarely sufficient to do the Valle de Tena justice.

Having entered across Col du Pourtalet the road descends a steady gradient, and in 3km a *pista* used by GR11 breaks off to the west into an open tributary valley, that of the Paco de Culivillas. By walking up this *pista* and eventually picking up the GR11 trail proper it is possible to reach a grassy plateau in which the **Ibones de Anayet** (2hrs) lie at the foot of Pico de Anayet, while Pic du Midi dominates the view north. (For climbs on **Pico de Anayet**, see 1:4 above.)

Above Sallent de Gállego, the valley of Aguas Limpias leads to the south side of Balaïtous

Just 2km beyond the Culivillas turning a side-road feeds into **EL FORMIGAL**, a modern, purpose-built ski resort of chalet-apartments stacked on the north side of the valley opposite the ski slopes. There are five hotels, four of which are either three- or four-star rated, but accommodation can be expensive and at a premium in the main winter season. The cheapest is the two-star Hotel Tirol. (For accommodation details try www.formigal.com or ☎ 974 49 00 00.) As for the skiing, this is on treeless north-facing slopes accessed by a cablecar, lifts and tows. The top lift is at 2250m and there are more than 50km of pistes, mostly red runs but with a few black rated. A regular ski bus ferries between El Formigal and Sallent de Gállego along the valley to the east.

El Formigal sits on the lower slopes of the rocky ❸ **Peña Foratata** (2341m), on which local climbers have worked out a number of routes, although there remains plenty of scope for further exploration. Derek L. Walker's English-language guidebook (see Western Valleys summary box) gives a selection of 400m climbs in the PD–TD range. On the flanks of the valley nearby winter often provides a number of fairly short icefalls giving three- or four-pitch climbs. Thanks to their situation these icefalls are frequently in good condition.

SALLENT DE GÁLLEGO also lies snug below the looming presence of the Peña Foratata at the confluence of the Rio Gállego and the Aguas Limpias – the latter a valley of great beauty which entices walkers into the heart of the mountains south of the Balaïtous. Sallent offers a blend of traditional mountain architecture and utilitarian tourist development. A neat little township, it has half a dozen hotels or *hostals*, several bars, restaurants and shops, a post office and two banks. The cheapest accommodation is likely to be found in the Albergue Foratata (☎ 974 48 81 12); otherwise try Hostal El Centro. (For tourist information, ☎ 974 48 80 05.)

ALONG THE AGUAS LIMPIAS

North of Sallent the mountains crowd either side of the ⬤ **Aguas Limpias valley**. Visitors without motorised transport should follow the GR11 along a track leaving the northern end of town and keeping to the left of the river, coming to the dam of the Embalse de la Sarra after about 40mins. Should you have your own transport you can drive this far on a narrow metalled road, then cross the dam and continue along the east side of the reservoir passing a hydro station. The road ends at the Puente de las Fajas at the far end of the lake, where there's limited parking space. Meanwhile, those who have walked all the way from Sallent should keep to the west side of the reservoir on a continuing trail.

Beyond the northern end of the lake the GR11 pushes into the valley on the west bank of the Aguas Limpias, passing between shrubs and neat meadows then rising to a footbridge above a series of cascades. The way enters a narrow wooded gorge – a dangerous region in late spring when avalanches threaten. As the gorge opens a little and begins to curve eastward a spectacular waterfall pours from the Laderas de Soba, then the valley narrows again, the path briefly hugging the left-hand wall before the gorge relaxes its grip with a meadow set beside the stream. Soon after this the path forks, with the left-hand option climbing for another 1½hrs to the Arriel lakes that lie in a wild and rocky amphitheatre below Pic Palas and the Balaïtous. The main trail, however, continues beside the Aguas Limpias, rising to a rugged upper valley of rocks, slabs and extensive screes, with the massive dam that blocks the Respomuso reservoir ahead. Above the dam wall the path zigzags left to gain more height before making a traverse to the large and comfortable **Refugio Respomuso** (2200m, manned all year, property of the FAM, 120 places, meals provision, ☎ 974 49 02 03), reached in about 2½hrs from the Embalse de la Sarra or 3½hrs from Sallent.

The Respomuso hut is a useful base for climbs on the Balaïtous and its attendant peaks, on the Picos de Frondella that rise above and behind it, and on a variety of summits that carry the frontier along the valley's headwall. There are also those peaks that rim the Circo de Piedrafita on the south side of the lake and the **Picos del Infierno** (Pics d'Enfer), a group of 3000m summits southeast of the hut which are usually climbed directly from the Cuello de Infierno. From the col, gained in about 2–2½hrs from the hut by way of the idyllic Ibón de Llena Cantal, the normal route (F) climbs south to reach the first summit, Pico del Infierno Norte (3073m), then continues along the ridge to Infierno Central (3082m) and finally Infierno Sur (3076m). An AD+ route (one passage of IV) was created in 1956 by P. Acuna and S. Rivas on the North Face, while an AD climb exists in the Couloir Nord (IV+).

In winter ◑★ **ski ascents** of many of these mountains are made possible from Respomuso when snow conditions allow, and

Campo Plano at the head of the Aguas Limpias, with frontier peaks east of Refugio Respomuso

in the cirque at the head of the valley lie numerous small tarns that attract walkers in summer. There are also two easy frontier crossings to be made: **Collado de la Piedra de San Martin** (Port de la Peyre-St-Martin, 2295m), which gives access to the north side of Balaïtous, and **Collado de la Facha** (Col de la Fache, 2668m), beyond which lies the Marcadau valley. And finally, there's the GR11 route which continues across the mountains to **Balneario de Panticosa** via two linked passes, Collado de Tebarray (2782m) and Cuello de Infierno (2721m). This crossing takes about 5hrs from Respomuso and makes a very fine trek.

• • •

Back in the main Valle de Tena below Sallent, the Lanuza reservoir stretches nearly 3km along the valley bed. On the east side the semi-submerged houses of the village that was sacrificed for its creation present a forlorn vision. A short distance beyond the southern limit of the reservoir the road passes through a tunnel and emerges at **ESCARRILLA**, which boasts a large and very busy campsite that is open all year. This growing village has two hotels and two restaurants.

Here the road forks. By taking the left-hand option one crosses the Rio Gállego on the Puente de Escarrilla and twists up to Panticosa, gaining wonderful backward views to the impressive limestone mass of the Sierra de la Peña Telera and south to the equally impressive Sierra de Tendeñera, a big wall of blue mountains running west to east with a summit crest that gently tilts from 2556m in the west to 2853m in the east.

PANTICOSA huddles 3km east of the main road on the north bank of the Rio Caldarés tributary. If you visit in summer it's hard to accept that this is an established ski resort with ambitions for growth. The lifts are on the south side of the glen serving 34km of pistes, mostly blue rated, but with 16 red runs and 4 black (for information, ☎ 974 48 71 12, www.panticosa-loslagos.com). In summer a *telecabina* operates for the benefit of walkers and climbers, who are then able to visit two mountain lakes and go up onto the crest of the Tendeñera. In summer Panticosa is the natural centre of climbing in the Valle de Tena, although walkers are probably best served by having a base in the spa at the end of the Caldarés valley. In Panticosa village there are two supermarkets, a post office, banks and plenty of accommodation, with seven one and two-star hotels, as well as the Pensión Peñablanca. For a full list of hotels and prices contact Panticosa Turistica SA (☎ 974 48 72 48).

The extensive limestone crest of the **Sierra de Tendeñera** south of the village holds a number of climbing routes, and the crest itself was soloed in the winter of 1993 in a three-day push by Javier Olivar, guardian of the Góriz refuge at the head of the Ordesa canyon. Beginning in the west on the Peña Blanca his traverse crossed all the main summits and finished in the valley of the Barranco del Turbón.

Winter offers plenty of opportunities on this massif, especially on the north side. The highest of its summits, the 2853m Ⓑ **Punta Tendeñera**, has a 300m AD route on the North Face put up in April 1982 by Javier Calvo and José Lalaguna, while the summer *voie normale* tackles the mountain by its Northeast Ridge from the Collado de Tendeñera and takes about 4hrs from Panticosa. On the North Face of the 2662m **Mallos de las Peñas** a 50–65° snow and ice route, *Ruta del Bakalao*, is just one of several lines that can be reached in little more than an hour from the lift system. Others include routes on the **Peña Blanca**, **Peña Roya** and the 2757m **Peña Sabocos**, where the 200m *Couloir Panticosa Ice* is a respected climb (D+ with several 70° pitches) dating from March 1990 (Armesto/Uriguen/Villasur). At the foot of the massif's western end, below Peña Blanca, lies the village of **HOZ DE JACA** overlooking the Embalse de Búbal. Accommodation is available here in the **Refugio de Montaña**, which has 40 places and meals provision (☎ 974 48 72 30).

A little over 1km from Panticosa on the way to Balneario, the south-facing crag known as Ⓑ **Las Foronias** (Peña d'Esforronias) has become a popular year-round playground, being easily accessible – only a few paces from the road. Locally based Julio Armesta was among the first to work out routes here in the early 1980s, along with Fernando Guzman and Enrique Villasur. The British pair Derek L. Walker and Stuart Smith discovered it in 1985, and Walker has been back several times since. His guidebook (Western Valleys summary box) gives no less than 21 topo routes. To summarise, the limestone here has agreeable friction and, being south facing, it dries quickly; there are a number of bolted routes, but also much that remains free up to 150m in length.

- Before moving upvalley to Balneario, it's worth pointing out that a ⬤ **cross-country trekking route** from Panticosa provides a direct way of reaching the Ordesa region in 1½–2 days. The route, which amounts to about 30km in length between Panticosa and Torla, was formerly adopted by GR11, but this major trail has since been rerouted further north from Balneario via the Cuello de Brazato. The 'old route', as it may be called, is on tracks or good quality paths virtually all the way, and from the outset follows the course of the Rio Bolática east of the village heading upstream, then curves southward alongside the Rio Ripera. Eventually this breaks away from the stream to climb roughly eastward to a small *cabane* that would do as an emergency shelter, then continues up to **Collado de Tendeñera** at 2327m, from where you gain a first view of the Mondarruego wall which guards Ordesa (see 2:13). The way descends now into the Valle de Otal, which eventually spills into the lovely Ara valley, but before doing so you cut off to cross Collado de Otal (1605m) and drop down to San Nicolás de Bujaruelo, and next day wander downstream to Torla near the mouth of the Ordesa canyon (see 2:13).

WALKS AND CLIMBS FROM BALNEARIO DE PANTICOSA

The Editorial Alpina map *Panticosa-Formigal* shows a pathway running along the hillside from above Panticosa eastwards before dropping to the road about 2km short of Balneario de Panticosa. This appears to offer a good alternative to road walking for visitors without their own transport, although there's a once-a-day bus service in July and August. At an altitude of 1636m the spa of **BALNEARIO DE PANTICOSA** (otherwise known as the Baños de Pandicosa) claims to be the highest permanent habitation in the Pyrenees. Set within a somewhat claustrophobic, steep-walled little amphitheatre at the head of the Caldarés valley, 8km northeast of Panticosa, the large, typical spa buildings line the roadhead near an attractive lake into which two cascading streams drain from a rim of high mountains. Balneario has no food shops other than a bakery, and some of the hotels will accept bookings only from users of the spa facilities, but more appropriate – and cheaper – accommodation for outdoor activists is available in the FAM-owned Casa de Piedra, which is open throughout the year, and has 108 places and meals provision (☎ 974 48 75 71).

In winter a 5.5km **cross-country ski circuit** is marked out here, but for most users of this guide it is as a summer base for walkers and climbers that the settlement appeals, for above the spa a glittering collection of mountain lakes trapped amid a crescent of high peaks, several of which exceed 3000m, entices activists out of the valley. The highest summits are found to the northwest, in the mountain block that separates the Valle de Caldarés from the Circo de Piedrafita and the Respomuso *refugio*. A cluster of seven 3000ers is accessible by a

The Picos del Infierno (Pics d'Enfer to the French), seen here from Pic de Cambalès on the frontier ridge, are usually climbed from Respomuso

choice of routes from Balneario. To attempt these perhaps the best option is to take a steep path climbing above the lake to Cuello de Pondiellos (2809m), reached in a little over 3hrs, followed by the Collado de Argualas (2860m), which enables you to tackle the southern group of peaks: ⊗ **Pico de Garmo Negro**, **Pico d'Algas** and **Pico de Argualas**. By heading north from the Pondiellos col it's possible to climb the three **Picos de Infierno** and the neighbouring **Pico d'os Arnales**. Alternatively the Infierno group can be approached from the 2721m Cuello de Infierno that is crossed by GR11. Each of these summits may be climbed by F-grade *voies normale*, but snow and ice routes appear in winter to give greater challenge. Among the winter pickings there's the ❿ *Couloir Franciso Granados* on Pico d'Argualas (200m, D, III, 70–80°), the *South Couloir* on Garmo Negro (AD-), and the 200m *North Couloir* (D-) on the highest of the Picos de Infierno.

Behind the spa church GR11 waymarks take a path north up to the ◕ **Bachimaña lakes** (1½hrs) under the frontier ridge, where one faces a range of options. The standard GR11 route breaks westward to the Lagos Azules, Cuello de Infierno and the Respomuso lake and *refugio*. Another keeps to the west bank of the upper Bachimaña lake (the east-bank route marked on the Editorial Alpina map should not be attempted), and from the northern end near the simple, unmanned Refugio Bachimaña Superior (8–10 places) it is possible to continue north on a recommended crossing of the frontier at the **Port du Marcadau** (Puerto de Panticosa) to reach the Refuge Wallon in 5–6hrs from Balneario. Yet another option is to skirt eastward from the Bachimaña *refugio* along the south shore of the lower **Bramatuero lake**, then climb to the upper lake in the Bramatuero Cirque – a 3hr walk in a wild landscape of lichened rock fringed with poor grass. Above this upper lake to the east lies the Collado de Letrero, by which the Ara valley can be reached by a fine trek, with the Vignemale seen almost directly ahead from the col.

- The eastbound GR11 route leaves Balneario de Panticosa bound for San Nicolás de Bujaruelo via the 2578m ◕ **Cuello de Brazato**, which is found about 200m above a trio of tarns nestling in a granite wilderness (2¼hrs to the lakes, another ½hr or so to the col). This stage of the long walk continues down to the Ara valley for a trekking day of around 7hrs, before heading into the Parque Nacional de Ordesa.

From the Cuello de Brazato the ascent of ⊗ **Pico de Bacias** (2760m), which rises southeast of the col, is recommended for the very fine summit panorama which is dominated by the Southwest Face of the Vignemale across the depths of the Ara, Ordesa to the east, the Picos de Infierno to the west, and the Sierra de Tendeñera to the south. Further south along the ridge from Pico de Bacias, and separated from it by another col, stand the twin **Picos de Brazato** (2719m and 2718m). These can be climbed easily from the Embalse de Brazato, with the 2702m **Pico Serrato** (otherwise known as Pico de Tablato) being added to the list while you're at it.

THE PEÑA TELERA

Back in the Valle de Tena the main C136 road runs along the west bank of the 6km-long Embalse de Búbal, but about 1km before its southern end a side-road cuts off to the right to **PIEDRAFITA DE JACA**, where there's the 40-place **Refugio Telera** (open and manned all year, with meals provision, ☎ 974 48 70 61), which serves climbers drawn to the chain of the **Sierra de la Peña Telera** that forms such a prominent and impressive wall above the village. This wall, officially named the **Sierra de la Partacúa**, but generally referred to as the Telera after its highest point, stretches for some 10km along the west flank of the Valle de Tena, although it is often obscured from roadside view by lesser intervening ridges and spurs.

The crest of this wall begins in the southeast with the 2307m **⑯ ★** Peña Blanca, and runs northwestward over a number of summits to the Pala de los Rayos (2590m). While the south side is rather gentle, folding as it does down to either the Rio Aurin or one of its tributaries, or to the valley of the Barranco del Puerto, the North Face is one long escarpment interrupted by a whole series of gullies and buttresses. The condition of the limestone is not good, but despite this scores of impressive lines have been climbed from 300m to 1000m in length. Where the Telera comes into its own is in the sheer volume of quality winter routes. When conditions are ripe, the massif abounds with perfect névé and amazing water- or snow-ice, and the scope for climbing is tremendous. But be warned, here as elsewhere in the Pyrenees, conditions for winter climbing are less stable than in the Alps, and can often be short-lived.

The North Face of the **Peña Telera** (2764m) itself looks truly appealing, the gently angled strata picked out in winter as bands of snow and ice. There are numerous well-respected lines here, the following selection being just a few of the plums. The 700m *Gran Diedro* is one of the classic routes. First climbed over two days in the summer of 1970 by Abajo and Forn, it received its first winter ascent over several days in 1983, but in February 1993 Mañuel de la Matta and Toni Casas completed it in a single day. Graded ED- (V/V+, 6a) the *Gran Diedro* is often wet, even in summer, and though essentially free, aid is used in the upper gully where large overhangs have to be avoided – there are short sections of V+ and A1. To the left of this major route, and sharing the same start, is the *Gran Diagonal*, another long classic which was climbed first in summer 1965 by Morandeira and Guttiérez, then repeated the following winter. The route, which carries an AD grade and is variously described as 600m, 700m and even 1000m in length (according to definition of the start), becomes progressively steeper and more narrow towards the top where it exits onto the Southeast Arête. A first-class itinerary.

To the right of the *Gran Diedro* a trio of pushy routes are found in close proximity. The first of these is the 550m *Couloir Maria José Aller* (D+), put up by J.M. Blanchard and Ricardo Martinena in February 1976, with *Chez Lulu* (Ballanger/Frédéric Chose, March 1994; 650m, TD) and *Super Lulu* (Zabalza/Beraza, January 1995; 650m, ED-, V+) just to the left, while to the right of the Maria José Aller Couloir lies *Couloir Maribel* on **Cima Capullo**. Dating from 1980 (Calvo/Laguna; 350m, D+, IV+) this is more sustained than *Maria José Aller* and steepens to 80° in one section. Also on Cima Capullo (2567m), the *Y Couloir* is a D-grade climb of about 250m, while a mixed buttress route on the *North Spur* is rated at D+.

Next along the wall beyond Cima Capullo is the 2612m **Cima sin Nombre**, with *Couloir Sin Na* (250m, D+); *Z Couloir*, a short snow gully graded AD; and a long mixed route on the *North Ridge*. **El Triptico** (2624m) has the 500m *Couloir Bu-bu* (AD), the *East Spur* (D+), *West Spur* (TD) and *Central Chimney* (TD).

After this comes **Punta Plana**, with the 400m couloir *Pacines* (PD) and the summer rock route *North Face Direct* (TD), first climbed in 1978. **El Pabillón** (2702m) climbs up a notch from Punta Plana and is graced by several TD routes, some of which received their first ascent from Javier Olivan and assorted partners in the 1980s: *Couloir Abraxas* (650m, 80–85°), the narrow *Couloir Maria Luisa* (500m, 80°) and *Goulotte du Croissant* (Chose/Péré; 700m, 70°). On the same North Face there's a 700m TD- route, *Voie Bochorno Glaciar*, and the *Couloir Moreras* (600m, D-).

This is just a sample to provide a flavour of what is available. Classics abound, but there remains vast scope for new routes and variations in summer as in winter.

A forestry *pista* twists roughly westward from Piedrafita de Jaca along the foot of the Telera massif, passing between the Ibón de Piedrafita and an unmanned *refugio* with places for about 15. After about 11km the track swings round to the northeast away from the rock wall to visit two lakes dammed for hydro purposes. The first of these is the **Ibón de Tramacastilla**, the second is the larger of the two, **Embalse de Escarra**. A 6–7hr circular walk which visits these lakes could be devised by adopting sections of the *pista* route and linking them with local paths, while a visit to the walkers' summit of **Pinindalluelo** (Tarmañones, 1974m) gives a splendid vantage point from which to study the Telera massif in one direction, the Sierra de Tendeñera in another, and Pic du Midi once more seen across the border to the north.

• • •

South of the Embalse de Búbal the C136 keeps to the west bank of the Rio Gállego, but after just 2km a *pista* cuts left into a minor tributary glen drained by the Barranco del Asieso, which makes a cleft in the flank of the Sierra de Tendeñera. Near the entrance stand the remains of a 13th-century hermitage, flanked by fortifications destroyed by

Napoleon's troops. A short distance inside this glen, on the south slope of the Peña de Hoz, the *escuala* of ⓑ **Santa Elena** offers a range of trackside climbs of 40–100m. According to Derek L. Walker's guide, 'friction moves abound, descent is by abseil [and] most routes have good natural protection'.

Another 4km down the road brings you to **BIESCAS**, a small township which gained instant notoriety in August 1996 when 87 people died as a result of a flash flood that devastated a campsite north of town. The present campsite, the Edelweiss, is on a different, and hopefully safer, site. The old part of town with typical Pyrenean architecture stands on the east side of the Gállego. There are several one- and two-star hotels, but the cheapest accommodation is likely to be at the Pensión Las Heras. The tourist office will provide details (☎ 974 48 50 02).

Biescas stands at the intersection of C136 from the Pourtalet and N260, the road which goes south for 14km to Sabiñánigo and east across country to Torla, the Parque Nacional de Ordesa and the Valle de Broto. A once-a-day, year-round bus service plies the route between Sabiñánigo and Torla via Biescas, which may be useful for activists planning to move on without their own transport. But with regard to the Valle de Tena, Biescas virtually marks its lower limit. From here on the Rio Gállego leaves the main block of mountains for more open spaces of the south.

ACCESS, BASES, MAPS AND GUIDES

Access

Vallée d'Aspe N134 from Pau. By train: Pau to Oloron-Ste-Marie. SNCF buses from Oloron to Bedous, Etsaut, Urdos and Canfranc.

Valle del Aragón N330 north from Jaca. Trains from Jaca to Canfranc-Estacíon. Buses from Jaca to Canfranc, Pau, Tarbes and Lourdes.

Valles de Echo and Ansó N240 west of Jaca, then north on minor roads. The lower valleys are served by once-daily bus from Jaca.

Vallée d'Ossau D934 south from Pau. By train: Pau to Oloron-Ste-Marie. SNCF and CIT-RAM bus services to Laruns. Buses from Laruns to Gabas, Lac de Fabrèges, Bious-Oumette and Col du Pourtalet.

Vallée du Valentin D918 southeast of Laruns. Bus from Pau via Laruns.

Valle de Tena N260 from Sabiñánigo or south from Col du Pourtalet on C136. By bus: Sabiñánigo to Biescas and Panticosa.

Valley Bases

Vallée d'Aspe Lescun, Borce and Etsaut

Valle del Aragón Jaca, Canfranc and Candanchú

Valle de Echo Echo and Siresa

Valle de Ansó Ansó

Vallée d'Ossau Laruns and GabasJ

Vallée du Valentin Gourette

Valle de Tena Panticosa, Balneario de Panticosa and Sallent de Gállego

Huts

A number of wardened and unmanned refuges (*refugios*) are located mostly in the higher regions. Details of huts are given in the text.

Maps

IGN Top 25 1547 OT *Ossau, Vallée d'Aspe*, 1:25,000

Carte de Randonnées 3 *Béarn*, 1:50,000

Editorial Alpina: *Ansó-Echo*, 1:40,000; *Candanchú Canfranc*; *Peña Telera*; *Sierra de Tendeñera* and *Panticosa Formigal* – each at 1:25,000

Walking and/or Trekking Guides

Walks and Climbs in the Pyrenees by Kev Reynolds (Cicerone Press, 5th edn, 2008)

100 Walks in the French Pyrenees by Terry Marsh (Hodder & Stoughton, 1992)

The Pyrenean Haute Route by Ton Joosten (Cicerone Press, 2nd edn, 2009)

The GR10 Trail by Paul Lucia (Cicerone Press, 2003)

Through the Spanish Pyrenees: GR11 by Paul Lucia (Cicerone Press, 4th edn, 2008)

Trekking in the Pyrenees by Douglas Streatfeild-Jones (Trailblazer, 3rd edn, 2005)

100 Randonnées dans les Pyrénées Atlantiques by Georges Véron (Rando Editions, 1991)

Walking in Spain by Miles Roddis *et al* (Lonely Planet, 2nd edn, 1999)

Climbing Guides

Rock Climbs in the Pyrenees by Derek L. Walker (Cicerone Press, 1990)

Escalades au Pic du Midi d'Ossau by Patrick Dupouey (Editions Denoël)

Passages Pyrénéens by Rainier Munsch, Christian Ravier and Rémi Thivel (Editions du Pin à Crochets, 1999)

Pyrénées – Courses Mixtes, Neige et Glace by Francis Mousel (Editions Franck Mercier, 1997)

See Also

Les Pyrénées: Les 100 Plus Belles Courses et Randonnées by Patrice de Bellefon (Editions Denoël, 1976)

100 Sommets des Pyrénées by Geroges Véron (Rando Editions, 2001)

CHAPTER 2: Cirques and Canyons

The Vallée du Gave de Pau and its tributaries in France, and valleys of the Parque Nacional de Ordesa in Spain

CIRQUES AND CANYONS: CHAPTER SUMMARY

Location

South of Lourdes, a series of valleys headed by the cirques of Gavarnie, Estaubé and Troumouse. The western boundary is Col d'Aubisque, the eastern limit extends southeast of Col du Tourmalet in the Réserve Naturelle de Néouvielle. On the Spanish side of the frontier the region is enclosed between the Rio Ara on the west and the Cinca on the east.

★ Highlights

◓ WALKS

- in the Vallées du Marcadau (2:5), Gaube (2:6) and Lutour (2:7) above Cauterets
- in and around the Cirque de Gavarnie (2:11)
- exploring the Néouvielle region (2:9)
- Ordesa (2:13) and Añisclo canyons (2:14)
- the Valle de Pineta (2:16)
- sections of the HRP (2:5, 2:6, 2:10, 2:11, 2:12, 2:17)

ⓒ CLIMBS

- assorted routes on Balaïtous (2:3)
- Vignemale North Faces (2:6)
- the walls of the Cirque de Gavarnie (2:11)
- Tozal del Mallo, Gallinero, etc, in Ordesa (2:13)

⛰ SUMMITS FOR ALL

- Grande Fache (2:5)
- Balaïtous (2:3)
- Vignemale (2:11)
- Pic du Taillon (2:11)
- Monte Perdido (2:13)

Contents

CHAPTER 2
CIRQUES AND CANYONS

CIRQUES AND CANYONS: INTRODUCTION

South of Lourdes some truly exceptional landscapes are to be found on either side of the frontier where two national parks share a common boundary – the Parc National des Pyrénées and the Parque Nacional de Ordesa y Monte Perdido which have now been added to the list of UNESCO World Heritage sites. This is cirque country, with valley heads bounded by huge curving rock walls and, on the Spanish slopes, mountains riven by deep canyons of impressive stature. Centres such as Cauterets, Gavarnie, Luz-St-Sauveur and Barèges in France, and Torla and Bielsa in Spain, are among the most popular in all the Pyrenees, and the range of walks and climbs is second to none.

Here are to be found the westernmost 3000m summits, the longest Pyrenean glacier and the biggest rock face. There are awesome ravines, 'lost' hamlets and a number of magnificent tarn-sprinkled valleys to wander in.

Apart from the Bielsa tunnel there are no cross-border roads within the area covered by this chapter, but several passes are accessible to walkers, most notably the fabled Brèche de Roland, that natural gateway in the high wall of the Cirque de Gavarnie from which the contrasting nature of the two sides of the range is best illustrated.

The renowned Cirque de Gavarnie, with its two gently angled snow terraces separating abrupt walls streaked with waterfalls in springtime

2:1 VALLÉE DU GAVE DE PAU

On the northern side of the watershed the natural way of approach to the mountains follows the Gave de Pau upstream from Lourdes as far as Gavarnie. At Argelès-Gazost the Col de Soulor road branches off into the valley of the Gave d'Azun (Vallée d'Arrens), where side-glens push deep into the mountains. At Pierrefitte-Nestalas a tributary valley breaks away south to Cauterets, while at Luz-St-Sauveur the D918 cuts off to the east into the Vallée de Bastan to Barèges and the Col du Tourmalet, bordering the Réserve Naturelle de Néouvielle. The last village before the Gavarnie roadhead is Gèdre, nestling just below the entrance to the Vallée de Héas, a tributary cutting southeast from the Gave de Pau, and through which one approaches the cirques of Estaubé and Troumouse, fitting neighbours to the better-known Cirque de Gavarnie.

LOURDES is the most important town, providing easy access to this section of the Pyrenees, for it stands at a junction of routes from Pau and Tarbes less than 50km from Gavarnie. Tarbes-Lourdes-Pyrenees airport is just 10km out of town, while the railway station has regular connections with Paris. SNCF buses serve Arrens, Cauterets, Luz-St-Sauveur, Gavarnie and Barèges. There's no shortage of accommodation, including campsites, but unless you're interested in religious pilgrimage there's little in Lourdes to detain the walker or climber. (Tourist information is found on Place Peyramale, ☎ 05 62 42 77 40.) However, if you've a few hours to idle away whilst waiting for a train on a wet day, the **Musée Pyrénéen** located in the château contains a number of exhibits of early mountaineering equipment, as well as books, documents, costumes, examples of Franz Schrader's maps, paintings and drawings dating from the 1870s, and the 99-year lease granted to Henry Russell (see box, 2:11) in 1889 in respect of the four summits of the Vignemale. For an outdoor time-killer, a funicular ride to the 948m **Pic du Jer**, southeast of town, rewards with a panoramic view and the option of descent by a marked path.

Heading south towards the mountains the N21 leaves Lourdes to parallel the Gave de Pau. After about 9km a minor road, D102, breaks off to the west and shortly reaches the village of **OUZOUS**, starting point for a popular tourist ascent of ⊗ **Pic de Pibeste** (1349m), a so-called *montagne enchantée* on which a large herd of mouflon is to be found. The trail is guided by yellow waymarks, gently at first, but above Col des Portes the way steepens to gain the summit in about 2½hrs. Located on the outer edge of the Pyrenees, a number of 3000m frontier peaks may be seen from the summit, including those of the Cirque de Gavarnie, Monte Perdido, the Vignemale and Balaïtous. Rather than descend by the same path, an alternative way down enables a circuit of about 4½hrs to be made. This alternative route descends to Ost near the junction of N21 and D102, then follows the latter road back to Ouzous.

Overlooking the Lourdes–Gavarnie road shortly before the Ouzous turning, the lower slopes of ➍ Pic de Pibeste hold a number of short, equipped climbing problems in the range 6a–7b. Luc Dusserm, who runs the Camping Soleil du Pibeste at **AGOS VIDALOS** (☎ 05 62 97 53 23), willingly shares his knowledge of these crags and keeps a topoguide for his guests.

Moving on through the Vallée du Gave de Pau, about 13km from Lourdes the N21 reaches **ARGELÈS-GAZOST**, a small-time spa resort with a choice of hotels, restaurants and campsites, situated in an open basin where the Gave d'Azun joins the Gave de Pau. The old town is medieval in aspect and quite the busiest part of Argelès, standing on a terrace above the thermal quarter where a viewing table on the Terrace des Étrangers near the tourist office overlooks the Gave d'Azun and its walling mountains. The Office de Tourisme is open daily in summer (☎ 05 62 97 00 25).

On the east side of the valley the ski station of **HAUTACAM** does not have the altitude for prolonged downhill runs, for the top station is only 1810m, although there's scope for cross-country skiing with about 12km of prepared trails, and in summer various walking possibilities exist. Of these, the cross-country route to **Lac Bleu** is recommended, as is the uncomplicated ascent of the 2463m **Pic de Léviste**, worth tackling for the panoramic view from the summit. The Hautacam road continues above the resort to Col de Tramassel on a ridge with views to Pic du Midi de Bigorre, and it is from here that several of these walks are possible.

2:2 VALLÉE D'ESTAING

Breaking away from the Gave de Pau, the D918 climbs out of Argelès-Gazost heading southwest on the way to Gourette and Laruns via the Cols de Soulor and Aubisque. The road follows the Gave d'Azun as far as Arrens-Marsous, but before this, just 4km from Argelès, a side-road leads into the Vallée d'Estaing, an enticing little valley drained by the Gave de Labat de Bun, whose upper reaches lie within the national park where the blocking mountains form a dividing wall between the Balaïtous massif and the Vallée du Marcadau. This minor road goes as far as the busy Lac d'Estaing, passing on the way the hamlet of **ESTAING** by a junction with a cross-country route from Arrens, and a little further south there's a *gîte d'étape*, Les Viellettes (☎ 05 62 97 14 37), used by GR10 trekkers and walkers tackling the four-day Tour du Val d'Azun (see 2:3).

Immediately before reaching **LAC D'ESTAING** the Hôtel-Restaurant du Lac on the left of the road has a reputation for good food, while at the southern end of the lake there's another restaurant and a campsite behind it. The lake itself makes an exceedingly popular outing for anglers and day-visiting tourists, and there's plenty

of excellent walking country nearby. Although there are no mountain refuges within the valley, **Refuge d'Ilhéou**, otherwise known as Refuge Raymond Ritter (32 places, manned mid-June to Sept, ☎ 05 62 92 52 38), is accessible in about 4hrs.

Lac d'Estaing, understandably popular with tourists, is the start of several fine long walks

• ◗★ GR10 draws alongside Lac d'Estaing on a long stage from Arrens to Cauterets. By taking that clear and well-marked trail southeast over **Col d'Ilhéou** (2242m), a morning's walk leads to Refuge d'Ilhéou (1985m), standing on the PNP border overlooking the mountain-girt tarn after which it is named. While GR10 continues to Cauterets by following the Gave d'Ilhéou down through the Vallée du Cambasque, another path picks a way along the lake's eastern shore before striking up the mountainside to cross the bounding ridge at **Col de la Haugade** (2311m) on an exhilarating route to Refuge Wallon in the Marcadau valley (4hrs from the Ilhéou refuge, 8hrs from Lac d'Estaing).

Some 400m or so above Lac d'Ilhéou to the southwest, a smaller tarn, **Lac du Hourat**, lies in a savage little cirque and is worth scrambling up to should you be staying overnight at the refuge. Above this tarn there's another possible crossing to the Vallée du Marcadau, while rising above the southern end of Lac d'Ilhéou **Pic de Courounalas** holds at least two serious challenges for rock climbers on its 300m North Face (see 2:4).

Between Lac d'Estaing and Col d'Ilhéou GR10 passes close to the Cabane du Barbat, with yet another tarn accessible from it. Lac du Barbat (2½hrs from Lac d'Estaing) lies below and to the northwest of the 2813m ⊘ **Grand Barbat**, a mountain whose summit may be gained without undue difficulty by its *voie normale* in about 2hrs from the tarn. The ascent is made by way of Brèche de Barbat and the mountain's southern ridge, and the view its summit affords is spectacular.

- A ◯ **two or three-day circuit** can be achieved by experienced mountain trekkers beginning at Lac d'Estaing, which includes a visit to the upper reaches of the Vallée du Marcadau, a real gem of a valley (see 2:5). At first the route heads upvalley beyond the lake keeping west of the Labat de Bun, before climbing through woodland, then entering the national park and a narrow shaft of valley. This narrow section opens as you come to a reedy tarn, Lac du Plaa de Prat (1656m), at the far end of which stands a small hut where the path forks. The left-hand option twists in numerous zigzags to Lacs Nère and Long in a high cirque, and provides an opportunity to make the ascent of the Grand Barbat from the south, while the route followed by our circuit climbs to other tarns set in an increasingly wild landscape. The route is not always easy to define, but a ridge is crossed northwest of Peyregnets de Cambalès to enter a stony basin where you join the trail of the Pyrenean High Route, then swing east to locate Col de Cambalès (2706m) – the key to entry into the upper Marcadau valley. It's a splendid walk which now continues down to Refuge Wallon (see 2:4), skirting numerous pools, tarns and waterfalls before treading pastures that lead directly to the hut. After spending a night there a good path tacks north to Lac Nère (a different Lac Nère to that mentioned above) and Lac du Pourtet. East of this last-named lake break away from the main path to cross Col de la Haugade on the way to Lac d'Ilhéou and

Lac d'Ilhéou and its refuge, midway between Cauterets and Lac d'Estaing

its refuge, and either enjoy the rest of the day there or continue to Lac d'Estaing by way of Col d'Ilhéou.

2:3 VALLÉE D'ARRENS

Beyond the Vallée d'Estaing turning, the D918 goes through **AUCUN** and in another 3km reaches **ARRENS-MARSOUS** at the foot of the Col de Soulor. Arrens is the main village of the district, with one hotel (Le Tech, ☎ 05 62 97 01 60) and a *gîte d'étape* (Auberge Camélat, ☎ 05 62 97 40 94), several private houses offering *chambres d'hôte*, a couple of campsites, post office, shops and tourist information in the Maison du Parc situated in the main square (☎ 05 62 97 49 49). There's a daily bus service except on Sundays to and from Lourdes, and from the village there's a hinted view through the upper reaches of the valley to the Balaïtous.

If you take the continuing D918 above Arrens, rising through avenues of trees towards Col de Soulor, the Balaïtous can again be seen to the south – an impressive sight, albeit a short-lived one – but when it disappears from view the great slab faces of the Gabizos peaks make up for that loss. At the 1474m col the road forks. The right branch twists down through green, moulded hillsides to **ARBÉOST** in the Vallée de la Ouzom, which furrows through the foothills, while the main route continues ahead, boldly engineered round the Cirque du Litor where several galleries highlight the danger from avalanche in winter and spring (snow usually closes this section between November and June). The Corniche des Pyrénées links Col de Soulor

Viewed from Pic de Cambalès to the southeast, Balaïtous appears to be an abrupt crown on a dome of rock, for its great ridge systems are mostly concealed

with Col d'Aubisque, after which the descent to Gourette and the Vallée d'Ossau begins. Meanwhile, Col de Soulor is traditionally used as the starting point for the **Tour du Val d'Azun**.

Tour du Val d'Azun

Outlined on sheet 3 of the Carte de Randonnées series, this ◐ three- or four-day walking tour remains some way from the high mountains, but ventures through charming green foothill country dotted with *granges* (stone-built barns), farms and small hamlets. Overnight accommodation is in *gîtes d'étape*.

Day 1: Initially sharing the route of GR101, from **COL DE SOULOR** the way heads north along a crest to the isolated 1654m summit of Cap d'Aout, then veers north-east to Col de Soum in a little over an hour. At Col de Bazès (1509m) a diversion onto Pic de Bazès is recommended, before descending to the Haugarou *gîte d'étape* in a little under 5hrs from Col de Soulor. The *gîte* has 16 places and is open all year except November (☎ 05 62 97 25 04). Without the Pic de Bazès diversion, this stage is only 3–3½hrs long, and it would be feasible for trekkers with only three days to spare to break away at Col de Bazès and go directly to Arcizans-Dessous (6½hrs), where Day 2 ends.

Day 2: This stage is also quite modest in length, requiring about 4½hrs of walking. At first descending alongside the Bergons stream, the route then heads east for a short distance before climbing south to gain Col de Couret (1351m) after about 1¼hrs. The way now veers left along a crest to mount the 1616m Soum de la Pène, after which it's downhill to Col de Liar, where you turn south and descend to **ARCIZANS-DESSOUS** in the Vallée d'Arrens. Overnight in the 15-place La Ribère *gîte* (☎ 05 62 97 09 11).

Day 3: Les Viellettes in the 1Vallée d'Estaingñ° is the destination for this third stage of the tour, which begins by cutting across to the small village of **BUN** and continues to **SIREIX** in the mouth of the Vallée d'Estaing. There are several options for the continuing walk. The shortest takes a path along the east flank of the valley, while another climbs to a very fine viewpoint at 1743m, and a third alternative makes the ascent of **Pic du Cabaliros** (2334m). Whichever option is chosen, overnight accommodation is in the *gîte* at **LES VIELLETTES** (details in 2:2 above).

Day 4: A 6-hour stage concludes the Tour du Val d'Azun. From Les Viellettes walk downvalley a short distance, then veer left and climb the western hillside to cross the ridge that divides the Vallées d'Estaing and Arrens, on the far side of which you cross the Gave d'Azun at **POUEY-LAUN**, a little west of 1Arrens-Marsous'±. Here you join 1GR10|√ and climb to the grassy Col de Saucède (1325m). Leaving GR10 at the col turn northeast and 30mins later reach **COL DE SOULOR**.

While D918 climbs out of Arrens for the ascent to Col de Soulor, a dead-end road pushes southwestward through the upper reaches of the Vallée d'Arrens to Lac du Tech, where there's a campsite, and continues for another 4km to a parking area at Porte d'Arrens.

From **LAC DU TECH** it's possible to make the ascent of the ⊗ **Grand Gabizos** (2692m), another of those secondary mountains that rewards with such fine views of the frontier peaks (4½hrs from the lake). The Gabizos massif consists of several summits from which bold ridges strike out like the wings of some giant bird. From the Soulor–Aubisque road the limestone **Petit** (or **Pic de**) **Gabizos** (2639m) appears almost symmetrical with three main ridges pushing roughly north, south and east above steep, impressive walls. The southernmost ridge, known as the ⓑ Crête des Taillades Blanques, is the link with the Grand Gabizos, and its traverse makes a very fine outing (AD+, 200m), which was pioneered in 1933 by Cazelet, Mailly and Ollivier. The Petit Gabizos in fact holds several worthwhile climbs, usually approached from the Soulor road. On the Northeast Face there's a 600m AD classic, while the West Face has a 200m TD+ line dating from 1960 (Bernard Grenier, J. & P. Ravier). Immediately north of Petit Gabizos, **Pic de Las Touergues** (2538m) has a 600m grade D route which follows through to Petit Gabizos itself, while a spur of the eastern ridge, the Crête de Bassiarey, has a 300m line, *No Smoking Couloir* (Férigo/Péré; TD-/TD+), first climbed in March 1999.

◖ Lac du Tech offers at least three long routes into neighbouring valley systems for experienced trekkers. The shortest of these crosses the eastern walling ridge at Col de Paloumère (2187m) to descend into the **Vallée d'Estaing**. Another heads west into remote country, passing round the outer rim of the Gourette massif, crosses the 2353m Col d'Ausseilla and picks a way down to the Vallée de Soussouéou, which spills out into the **Vallée d'Ossau** below Gabas. And a third option also begins by heading west, then branches north to tackle the grass saddle of Col d'Uzious (2236m), beyond which a very pleasant descent leads to **Gourette**. This last option is described in the opposite direction in 1:8.

The Vallée d'Arrens roadhead at **PORTE D'ARRENS** lies on the edge of a wonderland of high mountains and lakes, a region to delight the walker, trekker and climber. Three mountain huts are accessible from it: the PNP-owned **Refuge de Migouélou** (40 places, manned mid-June to mid-Sept, ☎ 05 62 97 44 92), **Refuge de Larribet** (45 places, manned at weekends from April to June, and daily June–September, ☎ 05 62 97 25 39) and the simple, unmanned **Refuge Ledormeur**, otherwise known as Refuge du Balaïtous, which has about 12 places.

A short distance north of the parking area, in the large meadow of Plaa d'Aste, a signposted path climbs steeply in countless zigzags up the western hillside, enters the national park and climbs again onto the lower slopes of Pic Arrouy before coming to a great glacial bowl containing **Lac de Migouélou**. On its eastern shore at 2278m stands the Refuge de Migouélou (2½–3hrs from Plaa d'Aste), and from here a scramble of less than 2hrs leads to the grandstand summit of ⊗ **Pic de Batbielh** (2651m) at the head of the small cirque of Les Lacarrats.

Two walkers' options present themselves from the refuge. One involves a return to the Vallée d'Arrens near Lac du Tech, the other makes a circular tour of the Balaïtous massif. Both routes are fairly demanding. The first, being considerably shorter than the other, could be completed in 6–6½hrs from Plaa d'Aste by fit walkers, while the Balaïtous circuit normally involves spending two nights in mountain huts and should be tackled only by experienced mountain trekkers.

The shorter route leaves the northern end of the Migouélou lake by its dam and twists up to ◯ **Col d'Hospitalet**, a 2548m dip in the connecting ridge between Pic des Tourettes and Pic Arrouy. On the far side of this the path descends to Lac de Pouey Laun and continues by way of the Pla d'Atigou and the little Vallon de la Lie, eventually coming to Lac du Tech near the campsite.

- The ◯ **Tour du Balaïtous** is a splendid itinerary linking numerous mountain tarns and crossing three major ridge systems, with one section that works its way round the Spanish side of the Balaïtous massif. A late afternoon ascent to Refuge de Migouélou is recommended for the first stage, while the following day involves crossing Col d'Artouste (2472m) at the southern end of the lake. This is achieved about an hour after leaving the refuge, but beware that snow often lies on the east side of the col until mid-July, in which eventuality extra care may be needed. The way then descends northwest to the Lacs de Carnau, before curving southwest to gain the barrage at Lac d'Artouste – invariably busy with tourists on clear-weather days in summer as it's reached by the Train Touristique d'Artouste from the Vallée d'Ossau. (A long descent to the Ossau valley is possible from the lake, with a path cutting

The FAM's Refugio Respomuso attracts walkers, trekkers and climbers to the Spanish side of Balaïtous, and is open all year

170

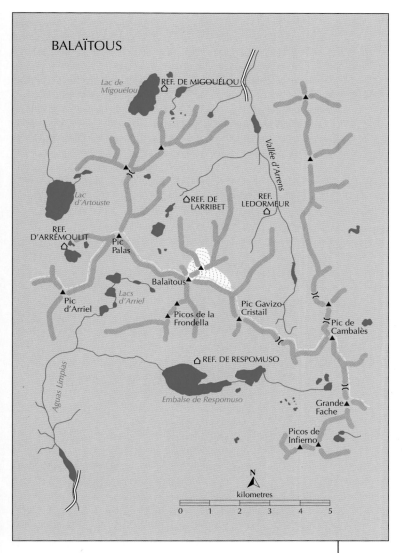

BALAÏTOUS

Lac de Migouélou

REF. DE MIGOUÉLOU

Vallée d'Arrens

Lac d'Artouste

REF. DE LARRIBET

REF. LEDORMEUR

REF. D'ARRÉMOULIT

Pic Palas

Balaïtous

Pic d'Arriel

Lacs d'Arriel

Picos de la Frondella

Pic Gavizo-Cristail

Pic de Cambalès

REF. DE RESPOMUSO

Aguas Limpias

Embalse de Respomuso

Grande Fache

Picos de Infierno

N

kilometres

0 1 2 3 4 5

through the Vallée de Soussouéou heading north.) The Tour du Balaïtous, however, goes along the west bank of Lac d'Artouste, then tackles a 300m climb to a sparkling granite boulderscape where Refuge d'Arrémoulit (2305m, see 1:9) overlooks yet more lakes and pools. The third stage is the longest of the tour, taking about 7hrs (walking time) to return to Porte d'Arrens. Following a section of the HRP a cairned route leads up to Col du Palas (2517m) in a little under an hour. This marks the Franco/Spanish border and rewards with a direct view across a stony basin to the Balaïtous in the east. Curving south the way descends to pass along the edge of the Lacs d'Arriel, then rounds a spur of the Picos de la Frondella before cutting southeast to the dammed Respomuso lake, near the eastern end of which stands the large and well-appointed Refugio Respomuso (2200m, see 1:10). More tarns lie beyond this, and just after passing Ibon de Campo Plano the route slants up to Port de la Peyre-St-Martin (2295m) to re-enter France. From here the route is straightforward, cutting down through a narrow glen to pass above the Lacs de Remoulis, below which the Gave d'Arrens leads the way to the car park at Porte d'Arrens.

With an abundance of climbing opportunities here, a walk of 2½hrs from Porte d'Arrens leads past the attractive Lac de Suyen, then cuts off to the right to gain Refuge de Larribet (2060m), the CAF-manned hut used as a base for climbs on the Balaïtous. Set in a small grassy

Balaïtous from the northwest, the view from Col du Palas. Dating from the early 1970s, the photograph shows the mountain's western defences, through which the voie normale *from Arrémoulit fights its way.*

basin due north of the mountain, the site was adopted in 1825 by the military surveyors Peytier and Hossard as they worked on a detailed survey of the region, during which they made the first ascent of Balaïtous itself. The hut lies just below the Crête de la Garenère, to the west of which a rough glacial hollow contains the Lacs de Batcrabère and a smaller cluster of tarns, the Lacs de Micoulaou – an extremely chaotic landscape that is not without its charm and with some appeal to rock climbers. The East Pillar of ⓑ **Pic d'Artouste** (2792m), which rises directly above the larger of the Batcrabère lakes, has a well-respected 250m route graded TD+ (IV+, 6a) that was climbed in 1998 by Desroussau, Massonier and Nicole. The East Face also has a splendid 400m TD- route, while in March 1997 another TD route (V+/A1) was put up on the Northeast Face of **Pic Palas**, as mentioned in 1:9.

Northeast of the Larribet refuge ⓑ **Pic Fachon** is a minor 2450m summit on whose Northwest Face some hard routes have been achieved, in both summer and winter. The 200m right-hand chimney climbed in the autumn of 1962 by Ronnet and Demoisy is graded TD- (IV+), while in January 1998 Daniel Lanne, a professional member of the mountain rescue team, pioneered two new routes: the first, with Jean Pierre Turon, is *Métamorphose* (TD+), a sustained 200m line up a narrow ice runnel; the second, with Michel Castillon, being *Excelsa* (ED1), which traces a mixed line to the left of *Métamorphose*, and is distinguished by two very narrow *goulottes*.

Balaïtous

At 3144m the granitic ⓑ ★ Balaïtous is the most westerly of the 3000m peaks, guarded by extensive ridge systems and little glaciers, standing astride the frontier south of the Vallée d'Arrens and east of the Vallée d'Ossau in one of the most remote sectors of the Pyrenees. Charles Packe, who made its second ascent, took so many days seeking a way to penetrate its defences in 1862 that he withdrew without discovering precisely which mountain to attack, and when he returned two years later he spent seven more days scrambling on and around the mountain before finally reaching the summit. It was only then, on finding a cairn left by his predecessors nearly 40 years earlier, that he realised his was not the first ascent.

Although the standard route is graded only F+ the massive Balaïtous deserves to be taken seriously. Known for its bristling, complicated ridges that give some long and magnificent traverses, it also has steep walls, aiguilles and several fine gullies, and approach routes are long enough to turn most climbs into a full day's effort. The immediate surroundings are savage, and summit views have been described as overlooking a 'vast chaos of bare ridges and mountain heights lying all silent and lifeless in the light of the sun' (Harold Spender, *Through the High Pyrenees*, A.D. Innes, 1898).

The ⊗ ★ *voie normale* is achieved by way of the West Ridge, usually approached not from Refuge de Larribet but from the Arrémoulit hut and the Gourg Glacé, a very fine, if devious, route of 4–5hrs. The easiest route from Larribet ascends the short but steep Glacier de las Néous, then tackles an obvious chimney (D+, III) on the North Face, which then opens to a gully leading almost directly onto the summit (4–4½hrs) – now a popular winter route. When Henry Russell climbed the Néous Chimney he wrote on emerging from it that he was 'half-mad with joy to see the [summit] cairn'.

At the head of the Pabat valley, which spreads south of the Larribet refuge, stands Cap Peytier-Hossard (2995m), a high point on the Northeast Ridge. Between the Cap and Balaïtous the ridge is split by the Brèche Peytier-Hossard, which gives access to the Vire Béraldi, a PD- route of about 5hrs.

On the Northwest Face the 400m *Grande Lezarde* is one of the harder routes (ED-), first climbed as a summer expedition in 1973, but made into a winter classic 20 years later by Michel Courtade, Michel Giboudeaux and Daniel Lanne (*Lézard Glacé*, IV+/V, 85/90°). The summer line is often climbed on wet rock, but this is transformed in winter as an interesting and very fine ice/mixed route.

Overlooking Ibon de Respomuso, the Southeast Face attracted a surge of activity in the 1990s with new climbs being created from a base near the dammed lake. In 1993 Gomez and Zapata claimed the *Eperon Elegante* (400m, TD, V+), followed the next summer with the *Dièdre Sud* (Abajo/Aldeguer/Gomez/Lopez; 250m, D+, V+), and in 1997 the 285m TD+ (V+) *Viva Zapata* by Ferrané and Pambrun.

But it is the ridges which provide Balaïtous with its identity and most of its appeal to rock climbers. The Northwest Arête, for example, first climbed in 1932 by Lamathe, Le Breton and Senmartin (500m, D, IV+), now has several variations, while the Crête de Costerillou, reaching eastward from the summit, is studded with towers, notably the Tour de Costerillou (3049m), on whose North Face Bertrand and Simpson made the original, very exposed, route in 1956 (250m, TD, V+), which has since become a classic test-piece on compact granite. As the *crête* reaches Pointe de la Defaite it curves south to Pic Soulano (2911m) and continues as the Crête du Diable, bristling with needles and turrets.

The ultimate expedition here is the traverse of the three ridges, a magnificent route more than 2.5km long first achieved in 1938 by the rope of Mailly and Barré, and one which usually takes around 10–12hrs from the foot of the Northwest Arête to the southern end of the Crête du Diable. The whole outing is now graded D+.

Despite its remoteness, the Balaïtous has become a major winter objective. In good conditions the approach on skis can be rewarding in itself, but any winter ascent has to be considered a serious and committing undertaking.

Due south of the Balaïtous stands the vast mass of the **Picos de la Frondella**, with a long crest running from the Brèche Latour to the lower of the Lacs d'Arriel. The highest summit is 3069m (Frondella Occidental), and there are numerous routes of assorted grades to be tackled on this and other sections of the massif, usually from a base at the Respomuso refuge (see 1:10). Frondella Central (3055m) makes for an interesting winter ascent on ski, and the slopes of the long crest stretching down to the southwest are said to provide excellent ski-runs in the spring.

The narrow glen which cuts down the eastern side of the Balaïtous holds prospects for a few moderate ascents on peaks that are still part of the massif, but are so positioned as to provide first-rate viewpoints from which to study the various ridges and

The steep little Néous glacier which leads to the North Face of Balaïtous

towers at close range. The first of these is the 2723m ⊗ **Pic des Cristayets**, which rises above the Lacs de Remoulis. While the ⑬ Northeast Buttress contains a 400m line graded TD, V+, 6a (Castella/ Ronnet, 1958), a pleasant scramble from the stone shelter of Toue de Casterie, south of the lakes, to the Brèche de las Néous leads onto the easy Southwest Ridge, just half an hour from the summit (3½hrs from Porte d'Arrens). Summit views of Balaïtous, the Crête de Costerillou and Néous glacier are outstanding and more than repay the time spent there. Note that the Brèche de las Néous can also be reached by a slightly more challenging route from the north – useful for climbers staying overnight in Refuge Ledormeur (1970m), the simple, unmanned hut which lies below the Crête Fachon.

Another easy summit to reach from the Toue de Casterie is ⊗ **Pic Soulano** (2911m), starting point for a traverse of the Crête du Diable. The *voie normale*, graded F+, shares the Cristayets route as far as the Brèche de las Néous on the linking ridge (2½–3hrs from Toue de Casterie to summit), while a harder route, graded D, IV+ (B. & P. Grenier, 1953), is found on the Spanish flank.

South of Pic des Cristayets, ⊗ **Pic Gavizo-Cristail** (2890m) adorns the frontier ridge as the southernmost peak of the massif. The view along the Crête du Diable towards Pic Soulano is most impressive, as is that of the Picos de la Frondella to the west. The *voie normale* here starts at Port de la Peyre-St-Martin, the crossing point for explorations of the south side of Balaïtous, from where the ascent is made via the Spanish slopes up a succession of uncomplicated rock terraces (3½–4hrs from Porte d'Arrens).

2:4 VALLÉE DE CAUTERETS

Continuing along the Gave de Pau upvalley from **ARGELÈS-GAZOST** the main road soon passes below **SAINT-SAVIN**, an attractive village with a fortified 12th-century Romanesque abbey worthy of a short detour. Then comes **PIERREFITTE-NESTALAS**, whose chemical plant emits clouds of pollution that hang over the valley. It is here that the 10km-long route to Cauterets (D920) leaves the Gave de Pau, heading southwest through wooded narrows.

CAUTERETS became fashionable in the 19th century when such notables as Louis Napoléon, George Sand, Flaubert and Victor Hugo spent time there. Today it is noted as both a spa and a ski resort, but is of interest primarily as a springboard from which to access a series of magnificent valleys for some rewarding walks and climbs. On a practical level, the town is served by SNCF bus from Lourdes, and up to six *navettes* a day carry passengers up the continuing Val de Jeret to Pont d'Espagne for the Vallées de Gaube and Marcadau. The wide selection of shops and atmospheric covered market are useful for stocking up on provisions for the mountains, including maps and French-language guidebooks. There are two *gîtes d'étape*, several campsites, a wide range of hotel accommodation and restaurants, banks, post office, a Bureau des Guides in the town centre near the **tourist office** (on place Maréchal-Foche, ☎ 05 62 92 50 50, www.cauterets.com) and a Maison du Parc by the defunct railway station.

For downhill ski enthusiasts the Télécabine du Lys serves the Cirque du Lys west of the town, from where several tows continue up to a maximum altitude of about 2400m. Although Cauterets has a good snow record, its winter valleys are perhaps better suited to cross-country skiing – the Vallée du Marcadau being of particular note. But it is the walker, trekker and climber who will gain most from the upper valleys and surrounding hillsides.

Above Cauterets there are five manned huts: **Refuge d'Ilhéou** (see 2:2), **Refuge Wallon** in the Marcadau valley (116 places, manned April and June–Oct, ☎ 05 62 92 64 28), **Refuge des Oulettes de Gaube** below the Vignemale (120 places, manned April and June–Sept, ☎ 05 62 92 62 97), **Refuge d'Estom** in the Vallée de Lutour (20 places, manned June–Sept, ☎ 05 62 92 74 86) and **Chalet-Refuge du Clot**, a short distance beyond Pont d'Espagne (45 places, manned all year except May, ☎ 05 62 92 61 27). There's also one unguarded hut, **Refuge Russell** (15 places, basic facilities only), located in the Vallée de Lutour northeast of Refuge d'Estom.

- East of Cauterets, the rounded ⊗ **Soum des Aulhères** (2168m) stands on the ridge dividing the Vallée de Cauterets from that of the Gave de Pau. The eastern slopes form part of the ski grounds of Luz-Ardiden, but in summer they are devoid of all but a few hardened walkers. While GR10 crosses the ridge north of Soum des Aulhères at Col de Riou (marked by the ruins of a former hotel), a 5–6hr circuit could be made via Col du Lisey and Col de Riou which takes in the summit. Anyone with sufficient time and energy could include a visit to **Pic de Viscos** (2141m), which rises north of Col de Riou and is gained without difficulty in about 1¼hrs.

- North of Cauterets the 2334m ⊗**Pic du Cabaliros** makes a popular ascent for fit walkers. Clearly marked on the IGN map of the area, the path climbs the western hillside to the edge of the Bois de la Peyre, then crosses a stream before twisting steeply to gain the ridge at Col de Contende, nearly 2km short of the summit. Below to the left lies the Vallée d'Estaing; to the right, the Vallée de Cauterets. Nearby stand the ruins of a one-time *hôtellerie*, beyond which the way dips to Col d'Anapéou, then rises easily along the crest to gain the summit in about 3½hrs from Cauterets.

- To the west of the town ⊗**Pic de Monne**, or Moun-Né (2724m), looming over the Cirque du Lys, is another popular mountain with Cauterets-based walkers, the summit being gained in about 4hrs, and it is interesting to note that in the 19th century local porters were often called upon to transport delicate ladies (and society gentlemen) to the top of the mountain by sedan chair.

- Also west of Cauterets GR10 wanders into the ◗ Vallée du Cambasque. A minor road, La Route du Cambasque, projects into the lower reaches of the glen with a large parking area at Le Courbet near the valley station of the Télécabin du Cambasque. From here GR10 waymarks push the way deeper into the valley before twisting up to Lac Noir and, shortly after, **Lac d'Ilhéou** and its refuge (about 2–2½hrs from Cauterets). Day-visitors invariably reject the valley route and choose instead to take the Télécabine du Lys and *télésiège* above that to the Crête du Lys, from where an hour's undemanding and mostly downhill walk reaches the same refuge.

To the south of Refuge d'Ilhéou **⑤ Pic de Courounalas** (2566m) offers one of the neighbourhood's toughest challenges for rock climbers, with the *North Face Direct* (300m, ED-, V+/6a) claimed by Béard and Rius in 1980, while a mixed route just to the right of that is a more recent discovery (January 1995) by Courtade, Gillet and Lanne named *Salade Mixte* (300m, TD+, V+/A1, 80°).

• Mention was made above (see 2:2) of a ◖ route across the ridge above Lac d'Ilhéou leading down into the Vallée du Marcadau. This ridge crossing can be adopted for a delightful **two-day circular walk**. Assuming one reaches the lake by way of the *téléphérique* and Crête du Lys, there will be sufficient time to cross Col de la Haugade and, curving below the Aiguilles de Castet Abarca, come to Lac du Pourtet. From here a good path heads south and, descending past Lac Nère, reaches Refuge Wallon in the Marcadau's pastureland. At least one night should be spent there to sample the tremendous range of walks and climbs nearby (see 2:5 below for details) before wandering downvalley to Val de Jeret, then past the waterfalls back to Cauterets.

2:5 VALLÉE DU MARCADAU

Without question the **VALLÉE DU MARCADAU** is one of the most beautiful in the Pyrenees, with lush pastures, stands of ancient twisted pine trees, attractive mountains, jagged aiguilles, wild little side-glens, and water lying almost everywhere. There are scores of tarns and tiny pools caught in hillside hollows or scoops of granite, while streams and cascades dazzle the light. Although none of the major peaks are located here, one summit, the Grande Fache on the frontier ridge, tops the 3000m mark, while several others provide challenging routes for rock climbers. Swathes of wild flowers colour the lower valley soon after winter snows recede, and pockets of alpines brighten the upper screes and high stony basins. Marmot and isard are common, and large birds of prey can often be seen drifting overhead. Prehistoric remains hint at the valley's early settlement, and although it has long been uninhabited (apart from the seasonal occupation of Refuge Wallon) the upper pastures were used as an open market by farmers from both sides of the frontier until the end of the 19th century. Grazing rights for these same pastures have traditionally belonged to French farmers until the end of July, when they would pass to their Spanish neighbours from the province of Panticosa.

Most visitors to the Marcadau make the initial journey through the Val de Jeret by car or *navette* as far as a large parking area at

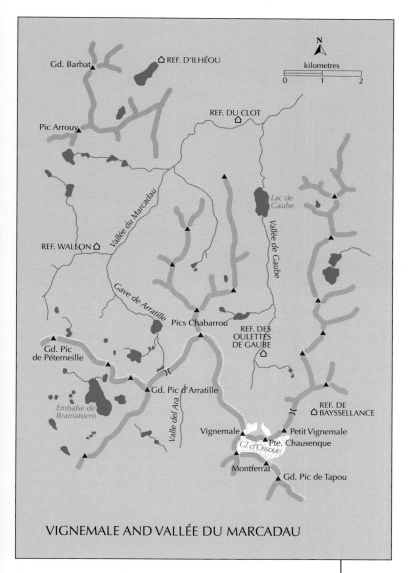

VIGNEMALE AND VALLÉE DU MARCADAU

Map labels:
Gd. Barbat · REF. D'ILHÉOU · REF. DU CLOT · Pic Arrouy · Lac de Gaube · Vallée du Marcadau · Vallée de Gaube · REF. WALLON · Gave de Arratille · Pics Chabarrou · REF. DES OULETTES DE GAUBE · Gd. Pic de Péterneille · Embalse de Bramatuero · Gd. Pic d'Arratille · Valle del Ara · REF. DE BAYSSELLANCE · Vignemale · Petit Vignemale · Pte. Chausenque · Gl. d'Ossoue · Montferrat · Gd. Pic de Tapou · kilometres 0 1 2 · N

Pont d'Espagne, but a very pleasant 2hr walk can be made along the Sentier des Cascades from the one-time spa of La Raillère, about 3km from Cauterets. The *sentier* keeps to the true left bank of the mountain torrent, which thunders over numerous waterfalls described by Tennyson in his 1861 poem 'In the valley of Cauterets'. It enters the national park and passes below the wooded flanks of ⊗ **Pic Péguère** (2316m), by which a very steep path leads to the summit in about 3½hrs, and from which a magnificent view is given to the North Face of the Vignemale.

Accessible from
Cauterets, the
Vallée du Marcadau
is one of the most
tranquil in all the
Pyrenees

Just beyond the bridge of Pont d'Espagne the privately owned Chalet-Refuge du Clot stands in the open Plateau du Clot, where two routes continue into the Vallée du Marcadau. (This is also where some 35km of cross-country ski pistes start out to explore the neighbourhood in winter.) The easier route continues as a private jeep road on the south side of the river, while the alternative cuts ahead through pastures on the opposite bank. The two are united where the road ends at **Pont du Cayan**, about 3km from Plateau du Clot.

At ◖ Pont du Cayan a trail climbs west to the Lacs d'Embarrat, while the main trail to Refuge Wallon continues upvalley on the left of the stream and soon reaches another junction, where the left-branching path climbs southeastward into the splendidly wild, remote and romantic **Vallon du Pouey Trénous**. A fairly demanding 7hr **circular trek** could be made by heading up into the Trénous glen, crossing the 2650m Brèche du Peyrot at its head (excellent view of the Vignemale's north wall), and descending south to Lac du Chabarrou. Edging the north shore of this tarn the way then drops steeply to the Vallée de Gaube, and follows a good path to Lac de Gaube and Pont d'Espagne.

From the path junction above Pont du Cayan, another pleasant hour's walk brings you to the **Refuge Wallon** (1866m), a rambling building staffed by the CAF. An older, much smaller and more basic refuge (permanently open) stands next door, and there's an attractive little chapel behind. Its situation is idyllic. From the hut terrace one looks southeast through the Arratille valley to catch sight of the Vignemale's Clot de la Hount Face over the dip of Col d'Arratille, and southwest to a group of peaks which carry the Spanish frontier along their summit crest. Two nearby cols offer straightforward routes over that frontier: Col de la Fache and Port du Marcadau – the first leading eventually to Sallent de Gállego via the Respomuso refuge, the second to Balneario de Panticosa. All that southern side of the watershed is described in 1:10, above.

◔ **Col de la Fache** is an easy 2664m saddle located midway between the Grande and Petite Fache west of the Wallon refuge. From it one gazes into Spain, to lakes and pools lying in a basin between the Picos de la Frondella and Circo de Piedrafita. A *variante* of the Pyrenean High Route (HRP) comes this way, and by reversing that route down to Ibon de Campo Plano trekkers interested in making a fairly tough one-day circular walk can pick up a trail at the eastern end of that tarn and head northeast up an undemanding slope to gain Port de la Peyre-St-Martin. On the French side of the pass, the main HRP trail works a way northeast to gain Col de Cambalès (2706m), by which the Marcadau is re-entered, followed by a wonderful pool-linked descent back to the Wallon refuge.

The 3005m ◔★ **Grande Fache** is the highest of the Marcadau's peaks, and is seen as a large pyramid south of Col de la Fache. Each year on 5 August a pilgrimage sets out from Refuge Wallon to climb to the summit as an act of remembrance in honour of those who have died among these mountains. By its *voie normale* there is nothing difficult in the ascent, which goes by way of the north ridge from the col (3–3½hrs from the refuge); other climbs include two AD routes via the eastern arête. From the summit a view west shows Pic du Midi d'Ossau beyond the great bulk of the Balaïtous.

The frontier ridge rises on the north side of Col de la Fache to a massive pile of rocks that rejoice in the name **Pène d'Aragon** (2951m), and the standard route to the summit of that pile follows

From the frontier ridge by the Grande Fache, the view south shows the Campo Plano lakes and Respomuso reservoir

the ridge without difficulty. The Petite Fache stands on a spur to the east of Pène d'Aragon, a spur which continues to **ⓑ Pic Arraillous** (2704m), whose *voie normale* (PD) attacks the mountain from the north, while two routes on the East Arête are graded PD+ and AD+. One of the finest climbs on the **Petite Fache** (2947m) is the rather delicate 280m North Face route dating from 1973 (Audoubert, Bouchet, J. & P. Ravier) and graded TD+, V+/A2, which runs up the centre of the face in an almost direct line.

From Pène d'Aragon the frontier crest kinks to the northwest and dips to Col d'Aragon (2808m) before rising to **⊗ Pic de Cambalès**, whose position is such that a splendid grandstand view is given of the Balaïtous to the northwest and Picos del Infierno in the south, while to the southeast Vignemale, Marboré and even the distant Maladeta crowd the horizon. The summit of Pic de Cambalès (2965m) may be gained in about 4hrs from the Wallon hut, the route leaving the path of the HRP among the Cambalès tarns and working a way to Col d'Aragon, from where the final ascent is made along the Spanish slopes. The same summit may be reached by a long ridge scramble from Col de la Fache, collecting Pène d'Aragon on the way.

While the frontier crest twists southwest from Pic de Cambalès to Pic de la Peyre then steeply down to Port de la Peyre-St-Martin, north of the summit a ridge drops to Col de Cambalès before rising to Peyregnets de Cambalès, where the retaining wall of peaks curves as a majestic amphitheatre within which the tarns, streams and pastures of the upper Vallée du Marcadau are held.

The opposite side of this amphitheatre wall carries the frontier ridge southeast from Grande Fache, with the 2765m **Pic Falisse** being the next point of focus. Col Falisse lies between the two, and it is via this col that the *voie normale* is made in 3hrs from Wallon. However, the **ⓑ** Northeast Pillar has a respectable 300m line graded D, IV+, which was first climbed in 1983 by Jean and Pierre Ravier with Paul Bouchet.

The **Pics de la Muga** are next, followed by the **Grand Pic de Péterneille** (2763m) at the northwestern end of the long Crête de Péterneille. Steeply below on the south side of the crest lie the Bramatuero lakes, Embalse de Bachimaña and the trail to Balneario de Panticosa, while the Picos del Infierno (Pics d'Enfer) rise as a backdrop; some magnificent walking terrain lies down there, as well as there being a cluster of 3000m peaks to tackle (see 1:10). Meanwhile, on the frontier ridge the Grand Pic de Péterneille has several routes in the PD–AD range, while an entertaining traverse of the *crête* involves crossing the **Pics Jumeaux**.

Just west of these last-named peaks a subsidiary ridge pushes north, acting as a divider between the upper reaches of the Marcadau and its tributary, the valley of the Gave d'Arratille, which opens opposite Refuge Wallon. The **Vallée d'Arratille** falls from a high and stony basin in which lie yet more tarns below the various Pics d'Arratille. The lower reaches of the glen are a mixture of grass bluffs,

low-growing shrubs and glacier-smoothed rocks – although there are no glaciers left among these mountains, their signature is everywhere to be seen. But from Lac d'Arratille upwards vegetation is sparse, for this is mostly a rugged landscape of bare rocks and screes. Yet the shoreline of Lac de la Badète, 100m above the Arratille tarn, is a botanist's delight.

Trekkers following the HRP travel through the Vallée d'Arratille and cross the 2528m Col d'Arratille in order to traverse the head of the Spanish Ara valley on the way to the Vignemale, on what is unquestionably one of the finest of all stages of this classic trek. That col could be used for an assortment of multi-day tours, as outlined below, but mention should first be made of a 4–5hr exploration of the Arratille glen suitable for good mountain walkers.

- For this ◖★ **exploratory tour of the Vallée d'Arratille** leave the Wallon refuge and take the HRP trail as far as the southern end of Lac d'Arratille among granite rocks, then exchange the main waymarked path (and granite for limestone) for a cairned route climbing to Lac de la Badète. Northwest of this tarn Col du Chapeau in a secondary ridge-spur is gained by grass slopes. A very fine viewpoint, the col is worth lingering on before plunging over diced rock and screes into the minor glen on the west side of the spur. This is the glen which is topped by the Crête de Péterneille and the Pics Jumeaux, and by which the *voies normale* on both the Pics Jumeaux and Pic de la Badète d'Arratille are made. (Brèche de la Badète in the ridge west of the latter peak offers a way over the frontier to the upper Bramatuero lake, and is used by Wallon-based climbers tackling the Dents des

Refuge Wallon, a large barrack-like hut near the head of the Vallée du Marcadau, gives access to a number of fine walks and easy climbs

183

Batanes.) Walkers, however, should descend through the Badète glen and rejoin the HRP trail for a return to Refuge Wallon.

Grand Pic d'Arratille (2900m) is the most southerly of the Marcadau peaks. From it the frontier ridge makes a sharp northwesterly angle as far as the slightly higher Pics Chabarrou, which stand at the very head of the Ara valley. The Grand Pic and neighbouring Petit Pic both have several medium-grade routes to their summits. The Grand Pic's *voie normale* tackles the mountain face-on from Lac de la Badète (PD), coming onto the ridge between the two peaks by way of a straight-forward chimney. The 🅑 North Face was climbed in wartime (1942) by Cornélius and Durand (D-, III), the NNW Spur (also D-) chooses a line midway between the previously mentioned routes, while the Northeast Arête tackled from Col d'Arratille is graded AD+.

Opportunities for 🌑 **multi-day walking tours using Col d'Arratille** as a key link include a two-day circuit beginning at the Wallon refuge, crossing the head of the Ara valley between the cols of Arratille and Mulets along the route of the HRP, and descending to Refuge des Oulettes de Gaube at the foot of the Vignemale's great North Face after about 6hrs. Next day wander down through the Vallée de Gaube to the Plateau du Clot above Pont d'Espagne, and from there return to Wallon. Another suggestion is to descend the Ara valley to San Nicolás de Bujaruelo, where there's a privately owned refuge, and next day return to France by way of the Port de Boucharo (Port de Gavarnie), where the HRP is then followed northward as far as Refuge de Bayssellance. The third and final stage carries the circuit over Hourquette d'Ossoue, down to Refuge des Oulettes de Gaube and by way of Col des Mulets and Col d'Arratille back to the Wallon hut.

•   The two suggestions above take walkers out of the 🌑★ Marcadau, but there's plenty to do within the valley itself. There are, for example, dozens of tarns and pools to visit in the valley's western extremity under Col de Cambalès; or, still with a watery theme, try the classic **Marcadau Lakes Circuit**. This magnificent walk of 4–5hrs could be tackled either clockwise or anti-clockwise, with the clockwise circuit having the edge. Initially the route follows the HRP northwest among pines, but on reaching a small level area the way divides. The lake circuit strikes off to the right, where a stream issues from an obvious corrie and climbs to a rocky, grassless basin containing Lac Nère. At the far end of this tarn the path climbs to Lac du Pourtet, above which the ragged Aiguilles du Pic Arrouy (Aiguilles de Piarrouy) tempt rock climbers with prospects of an exhilarating traverse (see below). The trail forks near the lake's outlet stream and a descent is then made to the Lacs de l'Embarrat, passing directly below the Aiguilles de Castet Abarca. From the lower and larger of the Embarrat tarns the path drops steeply to Pont du Cayan in the bed of the

Marcadau, where you then return to the Wallon refuge by the valley's main, well-trodden path.

Climbers could do worse than look to the Aiguilles du Pic Arrouy and those of neighbouring Castet Abarca for sport. An east–west traverse of the ❺ **Aiguilles du Pic Arrouy** from the 2604m Pourtet col to Pic du Pourtet (200m, D+, V+) has a good reputation, while the south–north traverse of the **Aiguilles de Castet Abarca** (D-, IV), first completed in 1945, is said to make an excellent introduction to such expeditions on mostly sound rock and with a spectacular outlook. Both routes are accessible from either the Wallon or Ilhéou refuge.

2:6 VALLÉE DE GAUBE

The next valley east of the Marcadau, which also drains into Val de Jeret, is the shorter and more narrow **VALLÉE DE GAUBE**, with the Vignemale at its head. Easily accessible from Pont d'Espagne, the lower part of the valley as far as Lac de Gaube is extremely popular with tourists, many of whom seldom stray far from the *hôtellerie* on the lake's north shore, and who prefer to make a brief *télésiège* ride there in order to avoid the modest climb from the road. Though dominating the view, the Vignemale massif is only partially visible from the lake, but the deeper one penetrates the valley, so more of the mountain is revealed and its stature grows.

Unlike the Marcadau, the Vallée de Gaube has a somewhat uncompromising nature; beyond the lake it becomes considerably rougher and more sombre, trading trees and shrubs for scattered boulders, waterfalls, gravel beds and patches of old snow. But the abrupt wall created by the Vignemale and its immediate neighbours at the head of the valley makes it one of the most dramatic and awe inspiring of all Pyrenean glens.

A walk of 2½–3hrs from Pont d'Espagne brings you to a little ◕ ★ glacial plain out of which the Vignemale soars in an imposing sweep of rock at the right-hand end of a group of North Faces. On the edge of this plain stands the CAF-owned Refuge des Oulettes de Gaube (2151m), perfectly situated as a base for activists drawn by the complex range of climbs which begin just a few minutes' walk away. Before looking at climbing prospects on the main peaks, however, it is worth considering what is available for the walker, trekker and scrambler elsewhere.

It has to be said that modest mountain walks are severely limited here. The valley is too rough, too steep-sided and too forbidding to offer much more than a there-and-back walk between Pont d'Espagne and the refuge. But enthusiasts with a little grit, who are undaunted by either steep trails or barely marked ways and who can tackle a little scrambling, will find plenty of exciting prospects to enjoy. On

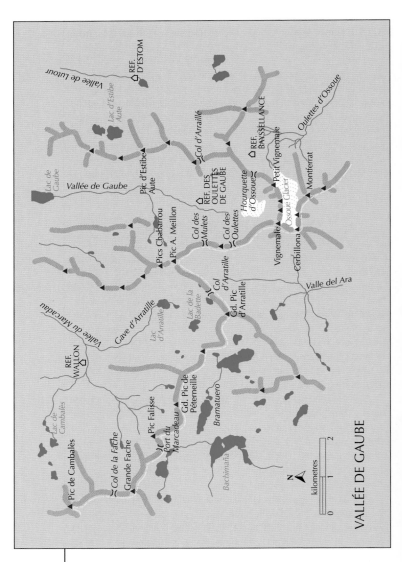

VALLÉE DE GAUBE

the west flank of the upper valley almost opposite the refuge, **Col des Mulets** (2591m) is crossed by the HRP. The path to it provides a very fine aspect of the Vignemale, as does the way to **Col des Oulettes** (2606m) further south; both cols give access to the Ara valley and the Spanish slopes of the Vignemale, while **Pic des Oulettes** (2760m), which stands between the two, teases with a steep but loose gully that gives out near the summit.

Trekkers planning a ● tour of both sides of the range could do worse than use either of the two cols (Mulets and Oulettes) to access the Ara, then descend through that delightful valley to Bujaruelo and return to France by way of the Port de Boucharo; or head west from Bujaruelo on a long route to Panticosa via the Collado de Tendeñera; or maybe continue down the Ara as far as the Ordesa canyon. All three options make rewarding expeditions.

Downvalley a little north of the refuge a ◐ sparsely marked trail slants up the western hillside, with a few cairns and zigzags leading the way to the outflow stream issuing from **Lac du Chabarrou**, about 250m above the Gave des Oulettes de Gaube. The continuing path fights among boulders, then cuts along the rock wall of the tarn's northern edge, but fades on gaining the western shore, where isard can often be seen in the shallow cirque that forms a backing to the lake. A partial trail rises to the **Brèche du Peyrot** (2650m), northwest of the lake, from where the Vignemale is seen to full dramatic effect. (In section 2:5, a circular route was suggested through the Vallon du Pouey Trénous which crossed this *brèche* in the opposite direction.)

West and southwest of Lac du Chabarrou rise the ⊗ **Pics Chabarrou** on the ridge separating the Vallées du Marcadau and de Gaube. The *voie normale* on the 2925m northern peak takes a mostly unmarked route from the lake, making first for the Brèche des Chabarrous (2821m) above a small tarn at 2422m. The southern peak (Chabarrou Sud, or Pic Alphonse Meillon) is just 5m higher than its northern neighbour and also has an ascent from Lac du Chabarrou as its *voie normale* (grade PD) by way of the clearly defined Brèche Entre-Les-Chabarrous. ❶ The South Pillar of Chabarrou Sud, however, has a more challenging line climbed in 1973 by Lechène and Coste (400m, D, IV/V).

Chabarrou Sud forms the apex of three ridges. Immediately to the south the mountain falls to the head of the Ara valley. The ridge system which runs southwest closes off the head of the Vallée d'Arratille, while that which strikes southeast and is crusted with the Aiguilles du Chabarrou forms part of the Vallée de Gaube's west wall. But the short northerly ridge which takes in Pic Nord and culminates in the Pouey Trénous summit leads to the headwall of the wonderfully wild Vallon du Pouey Trénous, a headwall which throws out its own enclosing ridges, broken with a *brèche* or two that could be linked by experienced mountain walkers with imagination and a penchant for rough country divorced from the crowds. But be warned, this is no place for an accident.

◐ The east flank of the valley has two major walking routes to consider which begin as one and the same from the refuge. The path slants southeastward, rising easily above the glacial plain and providing an excellent view into the fabled Couloir de Gaube – an obvious gully separating Pique Longue (the main Vignemale peak) from Piton Carré. The path is used as a GR10 *variante*, as well as by the HRP; is the link between Refuge des Oulettes de Gaube and Refuge de Bayssellance; and, since it crosses the bare saddle of Hourquette d'Ossoue, is also taken by all who ascend the Petit Vignemale by its *voie normale*. Not surprisingly it's a well-trodden trail. However, after climbing in tight zigzags the path forks some 250m above the refuge. The main trail swings round to the south, but the alternative climbs on eastward to gain Col d'Arraillé (2583m), the gateway to **Vallée de Lutour** and Refuge d'Estom. This valley is described in more detail below; suffice to say at this point that it's well worth a visit – not least by those who delight in making comparatively short circular tours, for a very fine two-day circuit can be achieved by using Col d'Arraillé to link the two valleys with an overnight spent at Refuge d'Estom. Another loop trip via the head of the Vallée de Lutour enables a return to be made to Oulettes de Gaube by way of Col de Labas and Refuge de Bayssellance.

The 800m face of the Vignemale, not climbed until the 1930s. The Couloir de Gaube is the obvious seam left of the North Face; then comes Piton Carré in the centre of this 1970s photograph. Pointe Chausenque is the domed summit with the left-slanting ridge.

The main GR10/HRP trail rises southward from the junction, with Petit Vignemale and Pointe Chausenque seen fully ahead. About 2¼hrs from the refuge Hourquette d'Ossoue is reached. This 2734m col looks down on Refuge de Bayssellance a short distance below. Beyond the hut the valley falls away, but the eye is led off to the Cirque de Gavarnie in the southeast, about 14km distant as the crow flies, while up the ridge to the right an uncomplicated walk of about an hour leads directly to the summit of the ⊗ **Petit Vignemale** (3032m), one of the easiest of the range's 3000m peaks.

The next summit along the ridge beyond Petit Vignemale is that of the 3204m ⊗ **Pointe Chausenque**, the highest Pyrenean summit entirely in France (the Franco-Spanish border runs across Pique Longue, making that the highest frontier summit). While the *voie normale* tackles the easy rocks that emerge from the Ossoue glacier (10mins from the glacier), an obvious extension along the ridge from

the Petit Vignemale is a recognised route graded AD-, III+ (1½hrs from Petit Vignemale). This is an interesting, airy and at times quite spectacular route, with the north side of the ridge plunging steeply to the Petit Vignemale's glacier. From Pointe Chausenque the descent is best made via the Ossoue glacier to Refuge de Bayssellance, but having dropped to the glacier it would be worth crossing the snow basin at its head to scramble up the final rock wall to the summit of the Vignemale itself.

The Vignemale

The Grand Vignemale, or Pique Longue (3298m), is not simply the highest frontier summit, but one of the finest and most dramatic of all Pyrenean mountains. It has the longest glacier, the greatest rock wall, one of the most celebrated ice climbs and, without question, the most fascinating history. Seen from the Vallée de Gaube the 800m high North Face captures the imagination. Topped by a prominent summit cone and outlined by the Arête de Gaube, it has an elegance of form rarely equalled. But Pique Longue is only the highest of four summits which constitute the valley's headwall. Studying these peaks face-on, from left to right they begin with Petit Vignemale, which dips to the Col des Glaciers then rises to Pointe Chausenque, with the leaning triangular buttress of the Aiguille des Glaciers standing slightly forward. This is followed by the pear-shaped Piton Carré, which is almost dwarfed by Pique Longue across the ice-choked Couloir de Gaube. The couloir creates a huge seam in the rock face, rising from the tiny Oulettes glacier to emerge, unseen from here, to an upper snow basin giving birth to the Ossoue glacier, which flows eastward into the Ossoue valley.

Leading away from the Vignemale six principal summits carry the frontier in a meandering line roughly south then southeast. Pique Longue is followed by: Pic du Clot de la Hount (3289m); Pic Cerbillona (3247m), with the 3051m secondary summit of Aiguille de Cerbillona jutting from a minor spur projecting towards the Ara; Pic Central (3235m); Montferrat (3219m); Grand Pic de Tapou (3150m); and Pic du Milieu (3130m). The frontier ridge linking each of these peaks up to, and including, Montferrat cradles the Ossoue glacier basin, with the projecting Crête du Montferrat forming the icefield's southern limit.

It was by way of the Ossoue glacier that the Vignemale's first recorded ascent was made on 8 October 1837 by two guides from Gèdre, Henri Cazaux and his brother-in-law Bernard Guillembet, whilst prospecting a route for a client. On the way they apparently fell into the Grande Crevasse when a snow bridge collapsed beneath them. Eventually escaping, they continued to the summit, but rather than face the glacier again they found an alternative descent route via one of the Cerbillona couloirs leading into the Ara valley. It was by this latter route that Cazaux guided the indomitable Miss Anne Lister from Halifax on the first tourist ascent the following August. Four days later Cazaux returned again to the Vignemale, this time as guide to the Prince de la Moskowa, whom he misled into believing that his was the first tourist ascent. When Anne Lister heard of this she threatened legal action and refused to pay Cazaux's fee until he signed a document stating the truth of the matter. Despite the fact that he did so, the prince still published a report in the local newspaper, followed by a more detailed account four years later, which made no reference at all to her ascent.

2: CIRQUES AND CANYONS

Cazaux and Guillembet's first ascent of the Vignemale was made just three years after the birth of Henry Russell (see 2:11), the eccentric mountaineer whose love affair with the mountain resulted in the creation of a number of caves there, several of which remain to this day, including Le Paradis just below the summit. It was Russell who made the first winter ascent in February 1869, describing the experience as: 'extremely fatiguing, as we walked in soft snow for sixteen hours'. Though Russell was the most fanatical and obsessive of climbers with regard to the Vignemale, it was left to others to create truly innovative routes on the limestone massif. None was more innovative than the classic ascent of the *Couloir de Gaube* in August 1889. Climbed without benefit of either crampons or ice axes, this route was many years in advance of its time, thanks to the ambitious Henri Brulle, with Bazillac and de Monts, and the guides Célestin Passet and François Bernard Salles. The inspiration and drive may have been Brulle's, but it was the skill of local man Passet, the foremost guide of his generation, that won the day. It took another 44 years before a second ascent was made.

Overlooking the North Face, the Arête de Gaube was claimed in 1908 by Jean d'Ussel, with Castagné, Courtade and Salles (again), but another 25 years were to pass before a line would be worked out on the North Face itself. This came on 8 August 1933 when Barrio and Bellocq claimed the 850m *Voie Classique* in just 4 hours without using pitons; the route long remained a much respected test-piece, but nowadays sees almost daily activity during the summer months. It received its first winter ascent from Bernard Clos and Marcel Jolly on 28 February 1949.

The Vignemale has attracted leading *Pyrénéistes* of every generation since the 1830s, and all the logical lines have been worked out. But that is not to suggest there is nothing left to achieve in the way of new routes, for today's leading-edge activists are still finding fresh challenges, while the classics of the past continue to win new admirers.

Couloirs overlooking the Vallée de Gaube often come into condition between December and May. For such routes ice axe, crampons and ice screws are needed. Crampons and/or skis are invariably required to reach the base of winter climbs, while for tackling summer rock routes a set of nuts, Friends and pitons should be carried.

When Robert Ollivier published his guide to this corner of the range in 1979 (*Pyrénées Centrales I,* see Cirques and Canyons summary box) he selected 15 routes on Pique Longue. Many others have been added to the mountain and its neighbouring peaks since then. The following is merely a small sample of what is available on the various North Faces.

ⓑ Petit Vignemale: The 300m *North Face Direct* has been described as 'serious and delicate' on account of the rather poor quality of the rock. Graded ED-; V+/6a+ it was won in 1958 by Couzy and Soubis, and the standard time for the climb these days is about 6hrs from the Oulettes refuge. To the right of the Direct a rather tight little gully gives a splendid 300m mixed route when in condition – this is the *Goulotte Lechêne* (Lechêne/Santoul, 1975; TD-, IV/4a, 70°); while the Northwest Arête and North Buttress are two classic lines that come under frequent attention. The first dates from 1890 (D-) and is another of Henri Brulle's routes, which he tackled with Célestin

The north face of the Vignemale rises abruptly at the head of the Vallée de Gaube

Passet and F.B. Salles a year after their joint success in the Couloir de Gaube. The other (the North Buttress, 360m, D-/IV+) was climbed by Cazenave, Cornélius, Paradis and Subot in August 1947. Although seldom in condition, a respected mixed route on the Northwest Face is *Tagada Tac Tic* (350m, TD, 65–75°), created in March 1998 by P. Bogino and J. Thinières.

Jean Arlaud, one of the great names of *Pyrénéisme* from the 1920s and 30s, made the first ascent of the **ⓑ Aiguille des Glaciers** in the company of Lescamela and Souriac in 1933. This was from the west, using a couloir which binds the aiguille to Pointe Chausenque (600m, D+, IV). When in condition the full couloir makes a first-class ice route, although one of the best but infrequently climbed lines on the aiguille proper is that achieved by Guy Chabanneau and Robert Ollivier on the Northwest Buttress in 1946, and now graded D (500m). Ten years earlier Ollivier climbed the 300m North Face

Three of the Vignemale's four summits. From left to right: Pointe Chausenque, Piton Carré and Pique Longue

(D-) with A. Pracherstofer, but the rock is of poor quality and this route is not often repeated.

Named for the man responsible for its first ascent in 1822, **Pointe Chausenque** has an easy *voie normale* from the south via the Ossoue glacier, and some challenging lines on the face which overlooks the Vallée de Gaube. The *North Face Direct* (700m, ED, V/A1/6a) is a long route of about 15hrs, first climbed over three days in 1961 by Bescos, Montaner and Vicente, and infrequently repeated today, unlike the classic Northwest Buttress. This popular climb (Boyrie/Simpson, 1945) is another lengthy line of 700m graded TD, while a more recent generation of activists put up *Mixed Emotions* in 1995 (Latorre/Vilarasau). Usually needing a bivouac, this last-named route is about 600m long with some difficult aid pitches from the start.

Between Pointe Chausenque and **Piton Carré** the *'Y' Couloir* branches left from the Couloir de Gaube and provides a magnificent climb when in condition. The original 600m line was climbed over two days in March 1965 by Jean and Pierre Ravier (TD+/V-/5+, 60–90°), but Serge Casteran and L. Petitjean worked out a variation in 1986 which has sections of vertical ice and rock steps of V+. The Ravier brothers were also responsible for the very fine North Face (with Jacques Teillard in 1954), which is graded TD, but when verglazed this becomes a mixed route of some seriousness. In summer the face can be damp and dangerous, with some rotten rock in the upper half.

The **Couloir de Gaube** has already been mentioned as having classic status. A mixed route of some 600m, it was originally climbed in summer, although it is now tackled at all times of the year, with the final few pitches involving IV+ moves on the right-hand wall from springtime onwards. In winter the exit onto the col is an elegant ice pitch.

This brings us to the impressive North Face of ⓑ★ **Pique Longue**, on which a number of lines have been worked out following the Barrio/Bellocq 1933 original. The quality of rock is not always good, although the setting is magnificent and one gains a distinct sense of being among 'big' mountains. In 1964 Jean and Pierre Ravier made one of their many inspired routes with Bernard Grenier when they climbed the *Dièdre Jaune* (ED) with 70 points of aid on questionable rock, the final 100m or so being vertical or overhanging – a 500m route that is now climbed mostly free at 6b+, with one section of A2/3, and first climbed solo during 7–9 March 1993 by Jerome Thinieres. The elegant *North Face Integrale* (TD+, V-), put up by F Golica and the Ravier brothers in July 1967, was the first success at taking a North Face route directly to the summit, rather than finishing on the Arête de Gaube. When Benoît Dandonneau, Christian Ravier and Rémi Thivel put up the difficult *Délinquants de l'Inutile* on 24 March 1994, they showed what could be achieved when there's a decent layer of ice holding the rock in place. This very hard mixed route is more than 800m in length (ED, IV+/6-/A3, 70–80°) and will take between 12–15hrs to climb depending on conditions. An earlier generation developed the *North Spur* (800m, ED-, V+/6a/6b+) in stages during 1965–6 when de Bellefon, Despiau, Mirabel, and S. and T. Sarthou pushed a line from the tiny Oulettes glacier to the Arête de Gaube, with a first complete ascent being achieved in 1967 by Carsou, Despiau and Lucqet. This has now attained classic status.

Dating from 1908 the ⓑ **Arête de Gaube** is of a different order to the big North Face climbs listed above, but it nevertheless follows a

Séracs at the snout of the Ossoue glacier

fine line of around 400m. Overlooking the Vignemale's North Face, this western arête (AD+) of the mountain may be gained as easily from the Ara valley and Clot de la Hount glacier as from the Oulettes refuge, and takes 4–5hrs in all.

As for the **❿ Pic du Clot de la Hount**, the classic route here is the 300m couloir which runs between Pique Longue and the Pic du Clot itself. Dating from 1879, this is another mixed climb of Henri Brulle's. On this occasion Brulle was sharing his rope with Bazillac, Bordenave and Sarettes. Graded D- (IV, 50°) it remains a popular outing today, while the nearby *Goulotte du Clot de la Hount*, first climbed in 1984, makes an interesting alternative (300m, D, III, 65–70°).

📖 *World Mountaineering* edited by Audrey Salkeld (Mitchell Beazley, 1998) has a review of major North Face routes on the Vignemale written by Catalan climber Araceli Segarra Roca, while the climbing guide *Rock Climbs in the Pyrenees* by Derek L. Walker (Cicerone Press, 1990) includes 10 routes on Pique Longue and its neighbours. For a larger selection of hard routes (in French), see *Passages Pyrénéens* by Rainier Munsch, Christian Ravier and Rémi Thivel (Editions du Pin à Crochets, 1999).

Flowing down the east flank of the Vignemale, the Ossoue glacier is the longest in the Pyrenees

The *voie normale* on ⊗ ★ **Pique Longue** is usually made from a base at Refuge de Bayssellance, since the 3hr ascent goes by way of the Ossoue glacier, followed by a short scramble up the summit rocks from the upper glacial basin. An alternative route goes by way of the Montferrat arête and is graded PD-. The Glacier d'Ossoue is also adopted as the standard descent route for most Vignemale climbs, but it should be noted that it is seriously crevassed and normal safety precautions should be taken.

2:7 VALLÉE DE LUTOUR

Flowing parallel to the Vallée de Gaube the more gentle **VALLÉE DE LUTOUR** rises south of La Raillère where waterfalls come crashing through the forested entrance. It's a splendid glen, broader and more wooded than its neighbour, and although it has no great rock peak to match the Vignemale the mountains at its head are no less shapely and attractive, while walking prospects are more varied than those to be found in the Gaube valley. The national park boundary runs along the Gave de Lutour and curves at its head to enclose the tarn-littered cirque of Estom Soubiran.

In the lower reaches a narrow road climbs out of the Val de Jeret and projects as far south as La Fruitière, a small hotel-restaurant with a few beds and a good reputation for evening meals. ◓★ Walkers without transport can enjoy a woodland path from La Raillère which

Adjacent to the Vallée de Gaube, the Vallée de Lutour is noted for its waterfalls

195

climbs above the Cascades de Lutour to join another trail that begins behind the thermal baths in Cauterets. This eventually meets the Gave de Lutour and follows the stream to La Fruitière before continuing upvalley by a series of natural steps to the privately owned Refuge d'Estom (1804m), standing on a bluff overlooking Lac d'Estom, about 1½–2hrs from La Fruitière. Though small, the refuge makes a comfortable, if simple, base for exploration of the valley. A basic hut nearby, equipped only with minimal facilities and often used by local shepherds, can accommodate 8–10 when the refuge is closed.

On the way to Refuge d'Estom a secondary path branches off from the main trail about 50mins beyond La Fruitière, and climbs more than 400m in zigzags up the eastern hillside to reach the very basic and unmanned shelter of Refuge Russell (1980m).

- Above Refuge Russell the noted viewpoint of ⊗ **Pic d'Ardiden** (2988m) makes a worthwhile day out for experienced mountain walkers or scramblers by way of the Pourtau des Agudes and the mountain's southwest ridge. Due to its considerable height gain the way is strenuous rather than difficult, but the final ridge consists of much loose and broken rock demanding care (3hrs from the refuge, 5–5½hrs from La Fruitière). Some 500m below and to the north of the summit the Lacs d'Ardiden are reached by a long walk from the Gave de Pau near Luz St-Saveur (see below), while south of Pic d'Ardiden the narrow **Crête d'Aubiste** leads to the 2949m Pic de Chanchou. An airy traverse of this crest is graded PD+, more on account of the poor rock than for any particular difficulty encountered; allow 2–3hrs from peak to peak and descend via Col de Culaus (2565m).

- ⊙**Col de Culaus** forms a saddle above a boulder field at the head of the Cirque des Culaus, southeast of Refuge Russell, and forms a link for experienced trekkers between the Vallée de Lutour and that of the Gave de Pau. On the east side of this saddle a cairned route picks a way down to an unnamed tarn, then to Lac Noir and the Cabane de Cestrède before dropping to the Granges de Bué, where the GR10 is met in the valley of the Gave de Cestrède about 1½hrs from the Pragnères power station.

- Southwest of the col, ⊗ **Pic de Cestrède** (2947m) is another summit accessible to strong mountain walkers and scramblers, with tremendous views to compensate for the labour involved in negotiating the boulder field leading to the col, the unstable rocks on the ridge, and a few exposed places where the ridge narrows considerably (3hrs from Refuge Russell, 5–5½hrs from La Fruitière).

In addition to those routes already mentioned, this eastern wall of the Vallée de Lutour contains a number of crusty summits and ridges of fairly unstable rock which, with due care, can be tackled to give long days without the crowds associated with some of the better-known peaks. There are also several rough cols which could be linked to create circuits and tours and the exploration of wild hanging valleys. But you'll need settled weather and an eye for the country, for there are few waymarks or cairns to guide you should mist or darkness descend when you're still far from a recognisable valley base.

The west flank of the valley contains two large tarns and a cluster of smaller pools in a scoop below the Crêtes d'Estibe Aute, some 700m above the valley floor. These ◒ **Lacs d'Estibe Aute** are accessed by a minor path rising southwestward from the main valley trail alongside the Ravin d'Estibe Tremouse, and gained about 3½hrs from La Fruitière. Southwest of the larger of the lakes **Pic d'Estibe Aute** (2816m) is the highest point on the Gaube–Lutour dividing ridge and the southern limit of the *crêtes*, whose *voie normale* is a PD route slanting from the lakes up to an obvious col on the ridge crest (2622m), then left along the ridge itself to the summit (5–6hrs from La Fruitière).

Most visitors to the Vallée de Lutour who are prepared to walk content themselves with a lunchtime stop at Refuge d'Estom or a picnic beside the lake before returning downvalley. That walk in itself is good enough reason to inspect the valley, for it's full of charm and with just enough of a pull to give a sense of achievement to those unused to the mountain environment. Views from the refuge are very pleasant indeed, with the Pics de la Sède and Labas channelling one's attention upvalley but giving little hint of the cirque that lies nearby.

◒★ The valley path divides just beyond the refuge above the lake's northwest shore. The upper trail quickly gains height, turns a spur of Pic de l'Estibet d'Estom and divides again. The main path here is the right-hand option that zigzags steeply then swings off towards

The privately owned Refuge d'Estom in the Vallée de Lutour

Col d'Arraillé on the way to Refuge des Oulettes de Gaube. The alternative trail, incomplete in its upper reaches, works a way south through the Vallon de Labas in order to gain **Col de Labas** (2719m) at its head. From the col the Vignemale suddenly appears – a very fine view – before the way descends to Refuge de Bayssellance.

In the rough granite cirque of ◐★ **Estom Soubiran** at the very head of the Vallée de Lutour lie more than a dozen tarns and small pools left behind by a long-vanished glacier. This is wild country, almost completely ringed by peaks and ridges that fall just short of the 3000m mark. In this high north-facing hollow snowbanks linger until mid-summer, and sometimes remain until the following winter. From a base at Refuge d'Estom several days could be spent exploring the varied facets of Estom Soubiran, going from tarn to tarn, crossing the walling crests and climbing those peaks that entice. On the south side of Pic d'Estom Soubiran the 2729m saddle of **Col des Gentianes** provides an excellent view of the Ossoue glacier plastered between Montferrat and the rising peaks of the Vignemale. The Bayssellance refuge and Hourquette d'Ossoue are also clearly seen, and a marked route leads down to the Gavarnie–Bayssellance path, which it joins below Russell's Bellevue caves.

Another crossing, but on the east side of the Estom Soubiran Cirque, is by way of ◐ **Col de Malh Arrouy** (Male-Rouge) at 2745m. This gives strong walkers a way into the valley of the Gave de Cestrède, which eventually drains into the Gave de Pau north of Gèdre. As an alternative option, one could cross the head of the Cestrède glen to locate Col de l'Oule by which Gavarnie can be reached through the valley of the Gave d'Aspé.

South of Col de Malh Arrouy the 2965m peak of ⊗ **Malh Arrouy** is the culmination of three ridge systems and a first-class viewpoint from which to study the Cirque de Gavarnie, Vignemale and the tarns immediately below. The *voie normale* here ignores all three ridges and instead attacks the mountain's west flank, where an obvious couloir leads almost directly to the summit (3–3½hrs from Refuge d'Estom). The ridge cutting southwest from the summit is the Crêtes d'Aspé, leading to **Soum d'Aspé** (2969m), which marks the PNP boundary. One of several routes here climbs from the lakes through a couloir to gain Col d'Aspé in the *crête*, then scrambles along the ridge to the right (3½–4hrs from Refuge d'Estom). This is another spectacular vantage point, with a 360° panorama to contemplate and the Vallée de Lutour spilling off to the north.

• • •

The D921 remains with the Gave de Pau at Pierrefitte-Nestalas and soon heads through a gorge before emerging to a pleasant, more open stretch of valley where a string of hamlets stand away from the road. About 12km from Pierrefitte, the once fashionable **LUZ-ST-SAUVEUR** is a small spa resort consisting of two parts facing one another across the river. The elegant thermal buildings of St-Saveur line the west bank, but the more attractive and older part is Luz, capital of a compact mountain canton, the Pays Toy, whose 12th-century church of St-André was fortified in the 14th century by the Hospitallers of St John of Jerusalem; it has an impressive Romanesque doorway, two square towers and a crenellated wall. The town is popular as a summer resort, and thanks to nearby Luz-Ardiden is considered a minor winter resort too. Luz has a Maison du Parc with displays detailing the natural history of the national park (PNP), and there's a useful tourist office (☎ 05 62 92 30 30) in the central square with a Bureau des Guides nearby. There are plenty of shops, restaurants and bars, and a Monday street market. There's a reasonable choice of hotels, a *gîte d'étape* and two campsites. And if you need an instant laxative, you could try bungee jumping from Pont Napoléon. The town is served by bus from Lourdes, and there are continuing bus services to Gavarnie and Barèges. To get to Cauterets take the bus north to Pierrefitte-Nestalas and change there.

- Although ◖ Luz-St-Sauveur is really too far out of the main mountain block to attract the serious walker, there are one or two outings that may be of interest. One of these begins in St-Saveur and initially heads south on a GR10 *variante* towards Gavarnie (although it's a *variante*, it is often the understandable choice of long-distance walkers in preference to the direct cross-country route from Cauterets). Before long an alternative path breaks off to Agnouède and continues in a long uphill slant to Cabane d'Estorous and eventually **Lac de Bastampe**, lying in a hollow at 2019m below Pic de Bastampe. A sharp 200m pull above this tarn brings the continuing path over a spur and as steeply down to a second tarn, **Lac de Litouése**. A small shelter has been built on the north shore and there's a cave below. Either return to Luz by the same path or descend by a series of minor trails through steep woodland.

- A second long walk from ◖ Luz-St-Sauveur takes the trekker southeast through the Vallée de l'Yse towards mountains that rim the granitic Néouvielle region. By crossing the narrow 2466m gap of Col de Pierrefitte east of Soum de Marraut, yet more hidden tarns are discovered in wild country north of Pic Long, where the unmanned **Cabane de Rabiet** (6hrs from Luz) offers little more than basic shelter. By skirting the tarns southeast of the *cabane* a continuing route leads to **Lac Tourrat**, out of which soars the North Face of Pic Long. This is country for the serious mountain trekker, with another scrambly route that crosses an extension of the Arête de Cap de Long at the Hourquette de Bugarret southeast of the tarns and descends to **Lac de Cap de Long**. Yet another option from Cabane de Rabiet crosses the col of the same name almost due north of the hut where the unmanned **Refuge Packe** recalls the great Victorian pioneer who wrote the first English guidebook to the range. From there one could work a way roughly northward on a reasonable trail to **Refuge de la Glère** and down to Barèges, or curve westward before reaching the Glère refuge and cut down through the Vallée du Bolou to pick up the GR10 for a return to Luz. These suggestions will demand at least two days of fairly rough trekking.

It is at Luz that the road to Barèges breaks away to the east, but before taking that diversion the guide briefly strays to **LUZ-ARDIDEN**, a small ski station set on the west slopes of the valley and reached by 12km of minor road from St-Saveur which passes above **SAZOS** (camping) and **GRUST** (gîte d'étape). The route of GR10 comes this way from Cauterets by way of **Col de Riou**, and one could follow that path across ski grounds to the col and continue north along the ridge to Pic de Viscos or take a trail south to the Soum des Aulhères as outlined in section 2:4 above. But perhaps better still is the opportunity to visit the **Lacs d'Ardiden**, which lie some way south of Luz-Ardiden and may be reached either by a path leading from GR10 where it follows the road for a short spell below Ardiden, or by way of a farm road heading for the Plateau de Bernazau and the hamlet of Aynis, where you join the alternative trail to the lakes. Whichever route is chosen the walk will be a rewarding one, taking you high above the valley to a cluster of half a dozen tarns lying 200m or so below the ridge dividing the Vallée de Lutour from that of the Gave de Pau. It will take around 3½–4hrs to reach the lakes, and another 2hrs or so for the return.

2:8 VALLÉE DE BASTAN

From Luz-St-Sauveur the D918 climbs alongside the Gave de Bastan towards Barèges and the Col du Tourmalet. In the 8km journey to Barèges the road gains 500m in altitude, passing through **ESTERRE**, bypassing **VIELLA** and **BETPOUEY** to the south, and below **VIEY** and **SERS**, which hang on the north side of the valley. Footpaths link the old villages of Viey and Sers with Barèges and provide very pleasant, though not dramatic, walks which reveal a traditional pattern of life that is only slowly changing.

GR10 also makes its way from Luz-St-Sauveur to Barèges, but does so in a manner which studiously avoids the road altogether, climbing the south flank of the valley through woodland and across open hillsides in a walk of about 4hrs. Linking paths from Viella and Betpouey climb steeply to join GR10 and provide opportunities to continue into the Bolou glen and visit such tarns as Lac du Pourtet, the Lacs de la Manche and Estelat, and those which lie below Refuge de la Glère. But these occupy country best explored from Barèges.

BARÈGES is little more than a one-street village astride the Tourmalet road – 'the only street which runs through the town

throws the houses on one side against the mountains, and on the other suspends them over the Gave' is how the pioneering Pyrenean explorer Ramond de Carbonnières described it more than 200 years ago in *Travels in the Pyrenees*. An old health resort, it became the site of a military hospital in the 18th century and later a military spa under Napoléon. At first glance it may not appear to have any great appeal, but first impressions can be misleading for it has much to commend it as a base for a walking or skiing holiday, and its charm soon grows. One or two UK companies specialising in mountain walking holidays have a long association with the resort, while a short distance upvalley there are five paragliding launch sites, with English-speaking instructors giving introductory flights. The tourist office (☎ 05 62 92 16 00 www.bareges.com) occupies a prime site in the centre of Barèges; and there is a number of modest hotels, a 45-place *gîte d'étape*, l'Oasis (☎ 05 62 92 69 47, e-mail: gite-oasis@wanadoo.fr), and a campsite situated a little below the village beside the road to Luz. Several lifts operate behind and just beyond the resort, but the ski station of Super Barèges, a short distance upvalley on the way to Col du Tourmalet, provides a link with La Mongie to give the largest area of piste skiing in the Pyrenees. Barèges is also a good place to practise snowshoeing.

In addition to several simple shelters and a couple of chalet-hotels by the lakes of Orédon and l'Oule on the route of GR10, two mountain refuges on the outer edge of the Néouvielle region are accessible from Barèges. **Refuge de la Glère** (90 places, manned June–Sept, ☎ 05 62 92 69 47) and the unmanned **Refuge Packe** (8 places, basic facilities only) – the latter gained about 5½hrs from Barèges (2–2½hrs from la Glère) – are located roughly south of the village, while **Refuge du Bastanet** (or Bastan; 20 places, manned June–Sept, ☎ 05 62 98 48

Lac de Bastan is just one of many lakes that give the Néouvielle region its charm

80) and **Refuge Campana de Cloutou** (25 places, manned June–Sept, ☎ 05 62 91 87 47) are found southeast of Col du Tourmalet.

• • •

Before covering walking and climbing opportunities in the vicinity of the Néouvielle reserve, the guide takes a brief look at what is accessible on the north side of the valley. For a start, a series of typically Pyrenean *granges* are linked by an easy path which may be gained from the Tournaboup parking area upvalley on the way to Super Bagnères – follow GR10 out of the village to avoid the road. If you follow this path westward a gentle traverse of the northern hillside brings you to a cross marked as **St Justin** (1277m) on IGN maps. This is situated on a spur of hillside at the entrance to a side-valley in which the Bastan stream rises. Views from the cross are very pleasant, especially downvalley, and a 45min stroll there from Barèges on a summer evening enables you to enjoy sunset views.

Various paths and a minor road from **Sers** project into the tributary glen, and one could wander towards its head to enjoy a taste of solitude and, as you climb higher, to gain more interesting distant views. The highest point on the western side of this glen is ⊗ **Soum de Nère** at 2394m. From the summit a huge panorama is won, overlooking the valleys of Bastan and Bolou and encompassing many of the Néouvielle peaks, while the Cirque de Gavarnie looks magnificent, and Monte Perdido rises above a shimmer of summer haze. A fairly steep walkers' route of about 3hrs from Sers leads to the crown of this modest peak, using footpaths nearly all the way.

- At the head of the glen, ⊗ **Soum Arrouy** (2488m) draws together three ridge systems which effectively divide the Bastan valley from the basin containing Lac d'Izabit, whose outlet stream flows down to Pierrefitte-Nestalas. The standard route of ascent begins in Barèges and mounts the wooded Montagne Fleurie on the north side of the valley, where, on gaining the lower Crête d'Erès Tiarrères, a path cuts left towards a small stone shelter. Beyond Cabane des Toucouets, the way makes for a couple of little tarns in the Cirque de Lagues below and to the east of Soum Arrouy. From here climb northwest to gain the mountain's east ridge, by which the summit is reached about 4–4½hrs from Barèges.

- ⊗ **Pène det Pouri** (or Pène Pourry; 2587m) is another summit which may be gained from the north side of Montagne Fleurie, making first for a col on the ridge running south from the peak. By this route Pène det Pouri can be scaled in 3½–4hrs from Barèges, while some 600m below on the north side of the mountain lies the ever popular Lac Bleu.

- ◗ The shortest and more usual way to reach this beautiful tarn, fairly trapped among the mountains below the long western ridge of Pic du Midi de Bigorre, is from the hamlet of Le Chiroulet in the Vallée de Lesponne, south of Bagnères de Bigorre. By this way **Lac Bleu** is reached at the end of a steep walk of about 2½hrs. But there are routes to it from Barèges, one of which descends from the summit of Pène det Pouri (care required). However, the easiest way for walkers based in the village goes up to the Turnaboup car park and slants northeast to the Cabanes d'Aoube, from where a waymarked trail climbs north to Lac d'Aouda (usually dry in summer) about 150m below Col d'Aoube (2369m). Once this col has been gained Lac Bleu is clearly seen to the west with a much smaller tarn before it, and is reached about 4½hrs from Barèges.

* ◓ Lac Bleu lies to the west of Pic du Midi de Bigorre, but **Lac d'Oncet** is caught in a steep-walled hollow immediately below and to the southwest of that mountain, in effect directly above Super Bagnères. Overlooking the lake from the west is **Pic d'Oncet**, whose north and east ridges help form the hollow, a circuit of which makes a good day out of about 5hrs. Begin at the Tournaboup car park and take a clear path heading northeast away from the Super Bagnères road after the third hairpin and eventually enter the Oncet glen, where the path heads north. On gaining the lake basin keep above the western shore and climb steeply to cross Col d'Oncet a little north of the peak. Now descend to the dried-up Lac d'Aouda and follow the Lac Bleu path mentioned above down to the Cabanes d'Aoube and back to Tournaboup.

'To toil up a mountain without a prospect of a view, is of course pure waste of labour,' wrote Charles Packe in the first edition of his *Guide to the Pyrenees* (1862), 'but if the sky be tolerably clear, no visitor to these parts should omit the ascent of the Pic du Midi de Bigorre.' Standing forward of the main chain, and largely isolated on most sides except the south where a crest (Belloc called it an isthmus) carries the Tourmalet road, ⊗ **Pic du Midi de Bigorre** (2872m) is one of the great Pyrenean vantage points, and has been recognised as such for well over 200 years. In 1787 the 32-year-old Ramond de Carbonnières, first of the true pioneers of mountain exploration in the Pyrenees, reached the summit and was inspired by what he saw. Exactly 100 years later an observatory was built there, and this has been followed by an 85m television transmitter mast and an Institute of World Physics building, all of which severely devalue the mountain's stature.

Although hordes of visitors flock there during the summer months, aided by motor vehicle on a toll road from the Col du Tourmalet, an ascent on foot from Barèges can be rewarding. (An annual fell-running competition records times of just over 2hrs for the route Barèges-Pic du Midi-Barèges!) Once again the Turnaboup parking area on the way to Super Barèges is the place to aim for if you plan to make the ascent, then you head through the Oncet glen towards Lac d'Oncet at 2254m. The path cuts up the eastern slope above the lake, rising to meet the toll road linking Col du Tourmalet with Pic du Midi's summit (allow 4–4½hrs for the ascent). Needless to say the panoramic view is extensive. Henry Russell said of it that mornings here 'must make the saints long to be on Earth!' Both Ramond de Carbonnières ('the chaos was unravelled') and Charles Packe spilled plenty of ink in expressing the extent of the view, while Hilaire Belloc was no less constrained when he wrote: 'from its summit you will get a better view of the eastern Pyrenees than from any other point reached with equal ease, and that you can see in one view, as you look southward, the Maladetta [*sic*] on your extreme left, the Pic du Midi d'Ossau on your extreme right, each about 30 to 40 miles away. It is also a point from which the sharp demarcation between the mountain and the plain, which characterises the northern slope of the Pyrenees, is very clear' (*The Pyrenees*, Methuen, 1909).

• • •

So much for the north side of the valley of Barèges, we will now look at prospects on the southern side, beginning with an ascent of the easy ⊗ **Pic d'Ayre**, which rises to an altitude of 2422m south of the resort. A track (then path) goes all the way, starting by the thermal baths and up through beechwoods to the Plateau de Lienz, then continuing by a series of long loops through more forest before tackling the final slopes to the summit, where another vast panoramic view is gained. The Néouvielle massif is particularly impressive from here.

Pic d'Ayre is flanked on its southwest side by the ◖ Vallée de Bolou, and on the east by the Vallée de la Glère. By linking these two glens an enjoyable **circuit of Pic d'Ayre** can be achieved.

A dirt road, built by hydro-engineers, projects through the Vallée de la Glère from Barèges as far as Refuge de la Glère (2103m), a large stone building on the edge of delightfully wild country speckled with tarns. To approach the refuge on foot takes about 3–3½hrs from Barèges, at first climbing through woodland to gain a restaurant, Chez Louisette, then across pastures to enter the valley proper – a valley that becomes more wild and austere the deeper you penetrate. Footpaths shortcut the road's hairpins as you gain height towards the head of the glen before reaching the hut overlooking the lake of the same name. La Glère is a little more upmarket than most Pyrenean refuges and is, in fact, almost of hotel standard with central heating, full restaurant service and showers. With such wild landscapes on its doorstep to explore, and with the opportunity to climb several Néouvielle peaks, it would be worth spending a few nights here.

2:9 IN AND AROUND THE NÉOUVIELLE RESERVE

Created in 1935 the Réserve Naturelle de Néouvielle continues the protected status of the Parc National des Pyrénées (PNP) into an enclave of lakes, pine forests and granite peaks southeast of the Col du Tourmalet. Road access is from the upper Vallée d'Aure (see 3:1) on the south side, but walkers' routes abound, not only within the *réserve* itself, but around the periphery too, which puts it within reach of walkers and climbers without transport. One of the best points

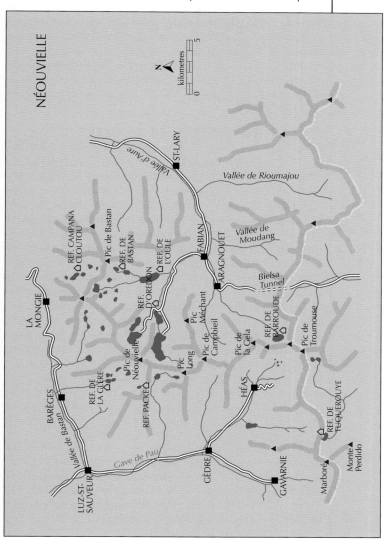

of entry is Pont de la Gaubie, east of Barèges on GR10; another approach enters from the north, from the Tourmalet road below the ski resort of La Mongie; yet another approach is from Vielle in the Vallée d'Aure to the east. A glance at the Carte de Randonnées map 4 shows these options and hints at the region's potential, but the exploration described below begins at Refuge de la Glère on the northwest edge of the Néouvielle *réserve*.

There are around two dozen tarns and pools lying among the rough granite slopes between the refuge and the main Néouvielle ridge system, and a tour of these lakes would take care of a good day's wandering. On this it would be possible to stray as far as another **Lac Bleu** (one of the so-called Lacs de Maniportet) at the foot of Turon de Néouvielle, or maybe cross the 2790m **Brèche de Chausenque** southeast of the refuge to reach Lacs d'Aubert and Aumar within the *réserve naturelle*. Or you could take a good trail heading south to Refuge Packe and drop to a seemingly secretive country beyond, where another group of tarns and granite peaks gives a wonderful sense of remoteness.

CLIMBS FROM REFUGE DE LA GLÈRE

A popular walkers' route from La Glère leads to the crown of the 3035m ⊗ **Turon de Néouvielle**, the first Pyrenean 3000m summit to be reached (by Reboul and the astronomer Vidal in 1787). The Turon forms the junction of three ridges above the Lacs de Maniportet, by which the standard ascent route makes its way, leading up to the mountain's northeastern ridge from where Pic Long provides just one focus of attention to the south. This is a 3hr route from the refuge, making the Turon one of the easiest of all the 3000m summits to climb. An alternative, and no more difficult, route keeps west of that previously described, and wanders alongside the Lacs d'Estelat before rising to Col de Coume Estrète on the mountain's Northwest Ridge. These are the *voies normale*, rewarding if undemanding, although in the early part of the summer it's possible you will need crampons and ice axe. However, these are far from being the only routes to tackle. From Refuge Packe, for example, the Hourquette de Bugarret in the Turon's southern ridge (leading to Pic Long) gives access to an ⑬ AD+ route, to the Southern Arête which has a TD alternative, and to a PD+ line just to the right of that above Lac de Cap de Long. The East Arête is graded AD, the East Face D-, while a route linking the Turon with Pic des Trois Conseillers along the Northeast Ridge is ungraded.

⊗ **Pic des Trois Conseillers** (3039m) is another non-technical summit, but one which also rewards walkers with scrambling skills based at Refuge de la Glère. Midway between this peak and Pic de Néouvielle, the Brèche de Néouvielle is a major feature of the ridge. Above it rises one of the Néouvielle summits at 3021m, whose West Face above the Lacs de Maniportet holds several 250m bolted sport routes in the range ED/TD+ established in the 1980s/90s.

Pic de Néouvielle (3091m), one of the most popular mountains in the area, is usually climbed from the east or northeast, but one particular route to be tackled from a base at Refuge de la Glère is the *Couloir Ouest*, best climbed as a winter or spring expedition. Graded D, the couloir is about 250m in length and was first climbed in 1969 by Paul Buchet with the Ravier twins. The summit boasts a very broad panoramic view which is said to stretch from Pic d'Anie in the west to the peaks of Andorra to the east, and includes Pic du Midi de Bigorre to the north and Monte Perdido (Mont Perdu) to the south.

In the dividing ridge north of Pic de Néouvielle the Brèche de Chausenque, mentioned above, effectively marks the southern limit of the **Crête d'Espade**. A number of hard modern routes have been established on the ⓑ West Face of both the Petit Pic d'Espade and the Grand Pic. On the former, climbs are 180m long with several graded TD+, while on the Grand Pic they are in the region of 200m with TD/ED grades. Some of the hardest of these have received winter ascents.

At the northern end of the Crête d'Espade rises the 2679m ⓑ **Pic de la Mourelle** whose ridge crest traverse makes a very fine outing; this is AD with individual passages of III+ and IV. It is usually tackled from Refuge de la Glère by first mounting the ridge at the Hourquette de Mounicot (1½hrs from the hut), and it forms part of a much longer expedition, the integral traverse of the long North Ridge of **Pic de Néouvielle**. This is a classic traditional route which involves plenty of climbing on mostly sound granite. The overall grade is AD, and the complete traverse usually takes around 7hrs from Hourquette de Mounicot to Pic de Néouvielle.

Turon de Néouvielle, Trois Conseillers and Pic de Néouvielle seen from the barrage at Lac de Cap de Long

★ INTO THE *RÉSERVE NATURELLE*

Beyond Hourquette de Mounicot the ridge pushes north all the way to the Vallée de Bastan and forms the divide between the Vallée de la Glère and another region of sparkling tarns, the **Vallée dets Coubous**, whose entrance lies 3km east of Barèges at Pont de la Gaubie. This is where the Tourmalet road makes a pronounced curve south, with a café and space for parking at the point where the GR10 crosses the road.

- ◐ The GR10 path cuts along the east flank of the valley and forks when crossing the stream at 1741m. The left-hand path (the continuing GR10) veers east to the lovely Vallée d'Aygues-Cluses, while the right-hand alternative sweeps up the southern hillside in numerous zigzags to gain the upper hanging valley containing a string of lakes. The path links a number of these before climbing more steeply to the bare 2498m Hourquette d'Aubert, across which lies the Réserve Naturelle de Néouvielle, with the much larger Lacs d'Aubert and Aumar seen below.

Whilst at the Hourquette d'Aubert it's worth mentioning that one of the *voies normale* on ⊗ **Pic de Néouvielle** tackles the ridge heading southwest from the saddle, passing below the Crête d'Espade to the foot of the Brèche de Chausenque, so named after the man who made the first ascent of the mountain in 1847. Continuing southwest the route gains the little Ramoun glacier northeast of Pic de Néouvielle and climbs to its highest point, where a line of cairns leads to a path heading directly for the summit.

- ◐★ In the lower Vallée dets Coubous where the path forks, the eastern alternative (GR10) rises in natural steps into the splendid valley of **Aygues-Cluses**, adorned with stunted pines, the stream tumbling over minor cascades as it twists through meadows. Heading upstream the way then opens to a broad and fairly shallow basin lively with marmots and containing yet more tarns. Above one of these is found the small, unmanned Cabane d'Aygues-Cluses (2150m), with bed spaces for about six, reached in 2hrs from Pont de la Gaubie.

- ◐ From here one has several options to consider for onward exploration. A little west of south, for example, **Col de Madaméte** carries GR10 over a ridge and into the Néouvielle *réserve* passing between Lacs d'Aumar and Aubert, joining the path from Hourquette d'Aubert mentioned above. This could be used to make a 6–7hr circular walk back to Pont de la Gaubie.

In the eastern ridge walling the basin above the Aygues-Cluses *cabane*, two passes flank Pic d'Aygues-Cluses, both of which give access to the fringe of the Néouvielle nature reserve. The more northerly of these, the bare saddle of **Hourquette Nère** (2465m), leads to another wonderland of tarns and more path options, one of which goes directly to the comfortable Refuge du Bastanet (2250m), where another trail heads north to Refuge de Campana de Cloutou (2220m) in 2hrs. Ignoring this option, a two-day circuit leading back to Barèges would continue after a night spent in the Bastanet refuge by following a trail south to Lac de l'Oule, and there take GR10 through the *réserve* heading roughly west to Lac d'Aumar. There you leave GR10 in favour of the major path crossing Hourquette d'Aubert into the Coubous glen mentioned above, which leads back to Pont de la Gaubie.

- The Cloutou and Bastanet refuges are both on the route of a ◐ ★ **north–south traverse of the Néouvielle region**. This 7hr crossing begins 3.5km below La Mongie on the eastern side of Col du Tourmalet, where the D918 road makes a sharp hairpin bend; parking is available here. From this point a good path rises to a minor col then swings southwest to reach the dammed Lac de Caderolle after 1½hrs or so, skirts the lake on its western side, then passes alongside the larger Lac de Gréziolles and, 3hrs from the road, comes to Refuge de Campana de Cloutou. Striking south the waymarked path (GR10C) climbs nearly 300m to reach the 2507m Col de Bastanet, where, if you have time and energy, a short diversion (1hr there and back) leads to the summit of Pic de Bastan, a superb viewpoint. About 40mins descent from the col brings you to Refuge du Bastanet (or Bastan), and the way continues from tarn to tarn until the large Lac de l'Oule is reached. At its southern end by the barrage stands the Chalet-Hotel de l'Oule, open mid-June to mid-September, and mid-December to April, with 26 places. From here descend to the road which snakes out of the Néouvielle *réserve* to Fabian in the Vallée d'Aure, where you may be able to hitch a ride out. Alternatively, follow GR10 from the lake heading east to Vielle-Aure, or west and northwest for another long day's walk to Barèges.

SELECTED CLIMBS
IN THE NÉOUVIELLE REGION

As mentioned above the only road into the Néouvielle region rises from Fabian in the Vallée d'Aure. South of Lac d'Orédon this road forks, with D929 cutting across the lower slopes of Pic Méchant and ending at the barrage at Lac de Cap de Long. Across the lake rise Pic de Néouvielle, Pic des Trois Conseillers and Turon de Néouvielle, while standing well back from the lake's southwestern end is the 3192m Pic Long, first climbed in 1856 by the Duc de Nemours, son of King Louis Phillippe, with his guide, Marc Sesquet.

Thanks to glacial shrinkage the *voie normale* on **Pic Long** is now graded AD+ (increased from a simple *facile*). The approach leads south of the lake into a broad valley known as the Montagne de Cap de Long, where a line of cairns directs the way around boulders and over several rock terraces, passing a small tarn and working up to a snout of moraine below the fast-receding Glacier de Pays Baché, draped against the mountain's East Face. Cross the glacier to the cleft of Hourquette du Pic Long, the lowest point in the ridge linking Pic Long with Pic Badet. There a steep 30m chimney is the key to reaching the *hourquette*, and depending on the condition and height of snow/ice against the rock, the initial moves can be a little tricky. Once the ridge has been gained turn towards the right, but shortly move left along a ledge onto the South Face, where an easy gully climbs directly to the summit.

Pic Long's 500m North Face, which rises from Lac Tourrat in an impressive sweep of rock with a shrinking ice midriff, looks out across a remote patch of country. To give an idea of its isolation, the nearest hut is the unmanned Cabane de Rabiet, and this lies 6hrs from Luz. However, it's possible to reach Lac Tourrat and the foot of the North Face in about 4hrs from the Cap de Long roadhead by crossing the 2614m Hourquette de Bugarret in Pic Long's northeast ridge (Arête de Cap de Long). The first, now classic, direct route up this truly appealing ❺ North Face (D, with one exposed passage of IV+) was achieved in 1933 by Roger Mailly and Robert Ollivier, while just to right of this original line the *Voie Candau-Cassayre* (TD-, IV+/V) dates from 1964.

Southeast of Pic Long, across the saddle of Hourquette de Cap de Long, stands the easy ⊗ **Pic de Campbieil** (3173m), which is generally reckoned, along with the Petit Vignemale, Pic du Taillon, and the nearby Turon de Néouvielle, to be one of the easiest 3000m summits in the Pyrenees. The Institut Géographique National unaccountably misplaces this mountain by transposing it with Pic Badet on its 1:25,000 maps. The reality is that Pic Badet is the 3160m peak whose ridge links it with Pic Long above that mountain's East Face, while Pic de Campbieil stands almost 2km away as the Pyrenean chough flies. The standard ascent route involves little more than a rough 5hr walk from Lac de Cap de Long. It ascends through the valley of Montagne de Cap de Long to the wide 2902m *hourquette* at its head, then bears left over rocks and boulders to Point 3157m, where the ridge makes a north–south turn. Head north along the left-hand side of this ridge as far as the summit of Pic de Campbieil. A direct descent of the East Face is described in the Ollivier guide, *Pyrénées Centrales II*. Graded PD, this descent is said to be 'without difficulty', and it drops into the flower-rich meadows of the Vallon de Badet opposite the Piau-Engaly ski grounds above Le Plan d'Aragnouet in about 2½hrs.

⊗ **Pic Méchant** (2944m) has an attractive, shapely profile, with a sharp, cone-like summit on a climbing ridge northeast of Pic de Campbieil. Standing directly above the Orédon–Cap de Long road, the approach from the north is very short, and the *voie normale* (PD-) makes a 3½–4hr ascent by way of the Vallon d'Estaragne and a *brèche* in the southwest ridge between the summit and Pic des Toudes. There are many other routes on this peak, ranging from *facile* to D+, with the 1100m *Couloir en Z* on the **🅑** South Face (Baudrimont/Viorrain, 1981) being a recommended winter special (AD, 50°), with access from Piau-Engaly.

• • •

Rejoining the Gave de Pau at Luz-St-Sauveur we journey south once more along D921 towards Gavarnie, a route described by George Sand as 'primeval chaos; it is hell itself'. Just outside Luz the valley is squeezed by the St-Saveur gorge, and another gloomy defile just beyond where the road then crosses a bridge and bypasses the hamlet of **SIA**, where the valley opens a little. Between here and **PRAGNÈRES** a campsite (Camping St-Bazerque) is found west of the road.

*   **◖** The hydro-electric power station at Pragnères (open to visitors) is said to be the most powerful in the Pyrenees, its turbines charged by waters from the Néouvielle massif, which are pumped underground from Lac de Cap de Long. Behind it a narrow road leaves the D921 and snakes eastward into the valley of the Gave de Barrada. A path also enters this valley and rises for about 5km to the **Cirque de Lis** (Cirque d'Erès Lits), where the way appears to be blocked by the looming cirque walls. Although it appears unlikely, there is a continuing route which climbs steeply just left of a stream draining through a gully – do not attempt to scale the gorge of the main Barrada stream. It's quite a strenuous route which soon strays across the stream and cuts round the end of a rock barrier, then moves northward on a traverse above this barrier and, across the stream, edges close to the Barrada gorge. Easing above the gorge you reach Lac de Rabiet and a choice of trails. One climbs left to cross Col de Pierrefitte (beyond which the Vallée de l'Yse flows out to Luz-St-Sauveur), another swings right to more lakes and the Hourquette de Bugarret (for the Néouvielle region), while a third option takes the path over Col de Rabiet north of the lake to gain the unmanned Refuge Packe (6–7hrs from Pragnères).

*   On the west side of the valley at Pragnères a **◖** GR10 *variante* offers a footpath route to Gavarnie by way of a tributary glen drained by the Gave de Cestrède. For much of the way through this valley the route is in woodland, but eventually you climb out of trees to cross a spur known as the Crête de Pouey Boucou, then slope down into another tributary glen, that of the Gave d'Aspé. Having crossed the Aspé stream the way turns the hillside and comes to an attractive thatched building, the *gîte d'étape* La Saugué (**☎** 05 62 92 48 73). From there a long hillside traverse provides enticing views of the Cirque de Gavarnie ahead, then, turning another spur, GR10 descends to the Vallée d'Ossoue which leads downhill to Gavarnie.

So much for the walker's alternative. The road from Pragnères remains east of the Gave de Pau (also known here as the Gave de Gavarnie), passes two more campsites and, 12km from Luz, reaches **GÈDRE**, overlooking a basin of meadows where the Gave de Héas emerges from its valley. Although Gavarnie is only another 9km along the road, Gèdre could be used as a low-key holiday base, but you'd need your own transport to make the most of it. The village is served by the Luz–Gavarnie bus and shaken by Gavarnie-bound traffic by day, but by early evening the road is quiet. It has a modest number of hotels and *pensions*, several campsites, restaurants and a tourist office (☎ 05 62 92 48 05) in the village centre. The prime reason for staying here is to explore the nearby cirques of Estaubé and Troumouse, both approached by way of the Vallée de Héas.

2:10 VALLÉE DE HÉAS

The main road climbs out of Gèdre with two tight hairpins, and after rounding the second of these a minor road, D922, cuts back to the left and twists into the Vallée de Héas heading southeast. Almost at once a tributary glen is seen across the valley. That glen is drained by the Gave de Campbieil, and at its head the 2596m Port de Campbieil carries a walker's route over the mountains south of the Néouvielle massif to Aragnouet and the Vallée d'Aure. There is just one point of access to the Vallon de Campbieil from the Héas road where a path cuts down to cross the stream at Pont de Peyregnet, but the main path into the glen leaves Gèdre on the north side of the Héas torrent, goes up to Gèdre-Dessus and follows a minor road until it crosses the Gave de Campbieil. It then climbs through woodland and forks. Both options lead to the Port de Campbieil in 4–5hrs from Gèdre – the right-hand trail via Lac de Bassia, the left-hand alternative going by way of the Granges de Campbieil – while a linking path which passes Cabane de Sausset provides an opportunity to make a pleasant circular tour.

In summer the Vallée de Héas is bright, attractive and ideal for walks of all standards, and a starting point for a range of multi-day trekking routes. There are climbs and ridge walks on the Cirque de Troumouse and frontier crossings into Spain through faults in the headwall of the Cirque de Estaubé. In winter there are cross-country ski tours to be enjoyed, while the valley makes a popular ice-climbing venue with numerous icefalls accessible from the road on the way to the Estaubé glen, and also near the Auberge le Maillet on the Héas–Troumouse toll road.

About 6km from Gèdre, and before reaching the Héas hamlet, a side-road forks right then twists uphill to the Gloriettes dam built at the mouth of the Estaubé valley. A good path adopted by the HRP edges the reservoir's western shore to provide a very fine view south to the walls of the **Cirque de Estaubé**, above which the upper reaches of Monte Perdido (Mont Perdu) can just be seen. When he came here in 1797 Ramond de Carbonnières did not realise that another valley lay between the cirque headwall and Monte Perdido, the mountain he was aiming for, and it was only when he reached the cleft of Brèche de Tuquerouye that he discovered how he'd been misled. But of the Estaubé valley Ramond wrote: 'In silence we contemplated its quiet solitudes... Vegetation flourishes up to the very foot of the rocky ridges... A little river with grassy banks flows peacefully over a stony bed, and afterwards, further on, it becomes a torrent.'

Beyond ◒ Lac des Gloriettes the valley opens to pastureland littered with boulders. The path remains on the right-hand side of the stream and forks near a footbridge. Ignoring the left branch the main trail slants up the hillside, and after gaining about 500m of height it forks once more. The right-hand path is the one used by trekkers on the HRP, and this continues to climb to the **Hourquette d'Alans** (2430m) on the walling ridge, beyond which lies a descent to Gavarnie. The left-hand trail rises a little further, then contours round the cirque wall until, below a prominent rock named the Borne de Tuquerouye, it divides yet again. The continuing contour path makes for the **Port Neuf de Pinède**, a 2466m col in the frontier ridge overlooking the Spanish Circo de Pineta, while the upper trail (not to be attempted by inexperienced walkers) climbs above the Borne to gain a gully by which a scrambly ascent leads to the **Brèche de Tuquerouye**. This dramatic breach in the cirque's rim contains the unmanned **Refuge de Tuquerouye** (2667m), the first CAF hut built in the Pyrenees. The outlook into Spain is tremendous, with the ice tiers of Monte Perdido's Northeast Face holding one's attention: 'It signified nothing that I had seen it a hundred times at a distance; it appeared to me more fantastic than ever' is how Ramond described his first close view of Perdido from the *brèche*. Steeply below lies the Lac Glacé, often half-frozen until mid-summer, while beyond the rocky wilderness of the Balcón de Pineta, the Valle de Pineta stretches into blue distances. 'I know of no point from which such a grand near mountain view may be obtained with so little exertion', wrote Packe in 1893. (It takes about 2½–3hrs to gain Hourquette d'Alans from the Gloriettes dam; 5hrs to Port Neuf de Pinède; 4½–5hrs to the Brèche de Tuquerouye under good conditions.)

The *brèche* is a classic way for climbers to approach Perdido from France, and trekkers experienced in wild mountain terrain could also use it as a means of crossing into Spain and descending to the Valle de Pineta, which lies some 1400m below (see 2:15). With sufficient time, energy and experience, a whole raft of expeditions could be enjoyed – cross-border circuits, extensive tours and climbs enough to last almost a whole summer.

Back in the Vallée de Héas the road soon reaches the hamlet after which it is named. At 1520m **HÉAS** is one of the highest permanently inhabited Pyrenean settlements, but it consists of little more than a few simple houses and a pilgrimage chapel, Notre-Dame de Héas, which was rebuilt after devastation by avalanche in 1915.

The chapel's interior is graced by stained-glass windows added in the 1930s depicting pastoral scenes of the mountains, and a visit is recommended. Accommodation may be found at La Chaumière (☎ 05 62 92 48 66 – camping space also available), the 10-place *gîte d'étape* Auberge de la Munia (☎ 05 62 92 48 39) and, some 4km above the hamlet on the toll road to the Cirque de Troumouse, at the Auberge le Maillet (☎ 05 62 92 48 97). Standing at an altitude of 1830m this last-named auberge is open from early June to the beginning of October, with accommodation for 35 in dormitories and bedrooms.

- ◐★ The Pyrenean High Route (HRP) passes through Héas ignoring the delights of the Cirque de Troumouse, the site which brings the vast majority of visitors here. Instead it climbs steeply out of the hamlet heading north then east through the Vallon de l'Aguila on the way to the surprise pass of **Hourquette de Héas** (2608m), reached by a narrow ledge cut out of the steep and thin Crête des Aguilous. The pass is reached in 3–3½hrs, and just before gaining it a splendid long westward view reveals the Vignemale far off, with the Ossoue glacier clearly visible. On the east side of the *crête* the HRP descends in zigzags, then swings round to the southeast and crosses another pass, the 2439m Hourquette de Chermentas, before coming to Lac de Barroude and the neat, 20-place, PNP-owned **Refuge de Barroude** (manned July to mid-Sept, ☎ 05 62 39 61 10), at the end of a fabulous day's trekking of about 6hrs from Héas.

- Just below the Hourquette de Héas, on the east side of the Crête des Aguilous, another ◐ path breaks away north to join the Port de Campbieil trail and the route to Aragnouet. By crossing the Port and descending westward it would be feasible to make a **2–3 day tour** beginning and ending in Gèdre. Alternatively, one could cross the Port, then work a way north over Hourquette de Cap de Long into the Néouvielle region.

- A fairly demanding ◐ **5-day trek** beginning in Héas and ending at Gavarnie could be achieved by taking the HRP trail outlined above as far as Refuge de Barroude, with a crossing into Spain next day by the Port de Barroude (2534m) and a descent of the Cirque de Barrosa and its valley as far as **Bielsa**. Next day wander up the easy Valle de Pineta, to be followed on the fourth stage by a gruelling ascent to the 2460m Collado de Añisclo into the head of the Añisclo canyon, then climb out again to find Refugio de Góriz (see 2:11). The final day's trekking passes through the fabled Brèche de Roland and descends to **Gavarnie**.

THE CIRQUE DE TROUMOUSE

Just outside Héas a toll is levied on all vehicles using the final stretch of road, which now climbs in a series of hairpins, passes Auberge le

Maillet and ends 3km later in a huge parking area at 2103m, where everything is dwarfed by the vastness of the **Cirque de Troumouse**. A stroll of 15mins northeast of the car park brings you onto a 2134m bluff topped by a statue of the Virgin which, being at an almost central point in the cirque, makes a superb viewpoint. Measuring 10km from end to end, this is the largest of all Pyrenean cirques, a striking amphitheatre, much of whose crest appears from below to be of almost uniform height, and whose basin pastures are full of wild flowers. Gazing south and working anti-clockwise the main summits are: Pène Blanque, Pic de la Munia, Pic de Troumouse, Pic Heid, Petit Pic Blanc and Pic de Gerbats. Unseen from here, the eastern side of the central wall forms part of the Cirque de Barroude, while the southeastern quarter curves as the Cirque de Barrosa in Spain. Within the basin formed by the cirque lie the ◑ **Lacs des Aires**, a collection of small tarns and pools accessible by an undemanding walk of 30mins from the car park. Walkers without transport are not restricted to using the road from Héas to get there, for a path leaves the road between the chapel and toll booth and makes for the Cabane des Aires below Pic de Gerbats, then swings south to reach the lakes (2hrs from Héas).

A more devious, but interesting, way of gaining the lakes is to take the HRP trail up the Vallon de l'Aguila (see above) as far as the Oratoire de la Ste-Famille near the Cabane de l'Aguila (1910m). This is reached in about 1hr from Héas. From there you can work a way south beneath a spur on a sloping terrace where a path edges round to Cabane des Aires, and at that point join the main trail to the tarns and the car park, or alternatively descend to Héas by the path which follows the Gave des Touyeres (5hrs for the round trip).

Pic de Gabiédou guards the western end of the vast Cirque de Troumouse

There's no shortage of climbs and scrambles to enjoy around the cirque, with summits accessible to walkers used to the mountain environment and some hard rock routes of interest too. In winter the cirque makes a destination for cross-country skiers.

⊗ **Pic de Gabiédou** and **Pic de Bounéu**, standing either side of Port de la Canau southwest of the car park, can be combined in a single outing by serious walkers with some scrambling experience. A line of cairns signals the path to the foot of a broad gully of scree and snow patches which leads in 1–1½hrs to Port de la Canau (2686m) on the frontier ridge. Views of the Valle de Pineta and Northeast Face of Monte Perdido are magnificent from here. To the east the summit of Pic de Bounéu (2726m) is gained in just 10mins, then you return to the col and climb the 2809m Pic de Gabiédou on the Spanish side of the crest – 20mins from Port de la Canau. As an alternative to returning by the same route, you could descend north, a little left of the ridge, to find a minor col which offers a way down through the scoop shown on the map as the Montagne du Grand Gabiédou.

The 2905m **Pène Blanque de Troumouse** boasts a classic North Face comparable to that of the Vignemale, with an original line (the *Voie Ravier*) dating from 1969. This ❶ TD route is about 500m long, while the nearby *North Face Direct*, graded ED-, took two days when it was first climbed by Despiau and de Boysson in 1970. Under prime winter conditions the same face contains a number of good mixed routes, several of which were worked out in the late 1990s, while the 350m couloir leading to the **Brèche de la Clé du Curé** (between Pène Blanque and Mont Arrouy) has a D-graded mixed route which steepens to 80°. As for **Mont Arrouy** (2888m) the classic line here is the

Despite its size, any real impression of height is lost from the floor of the Cirque de Troumouse at 2000m. Central to this view is Pic de la Munia (3133m)

450m *Dièdre Nord* (ED, V+), the creation of Despiau, de Boysson, Luquet and Cassou in 1972, and climbed on notoriously poor rock.

The highest Troumouse summit is the 3133m ⊗ **Pic de la Munia** on the frontier ridge. By its *voie normale* (PD) the summit is gained without undue difficulty in 3½hrs from the cirque car park, a steep gully (often snow-filled) being the key before a partial chimney is climbed that eventually takes the route onto the ridge at the 2853m Col de la Munia. The easiest route, graded F, tackles the mountain from the Cirque de Barrosa, while the North Face of the Pic, above a little glacier, has two routes which, when combined, give 700m of climbing that have an appeal in winter.

Standing proud of the headwall at the foot of Pic de Troumouse are two limestone monoliths known as the Two Sisters of Troumouse (**Les Deux Soeurs**). The taller of these reaches 2549m; the top of the other, more shapely tower is at 2538m. Both offer attractive if delicate climbing.

Pic Heid (3022m) stands on the wall which also borders the Cirque de Barroude between Pic de Troumouse and Petit Pic Blanc. While the summit is of little significance when making a traverse of the ridge crest, the ❺ 550m West Face contains an ED route of some note (Despiau/Fabbro, 1980).

On the northeast side of the cirque, Col de la Sède (2651m) provides an easy way onto the main ridge crest, and the ascent of ⊗ **Pic de la Gela** (2851m) on the neighbouring Cirque de Barroude suggests an interesting day out via the col. From Héas follow the HRP up into the Vallon de l'Aguila, then branch away from that main path at the Cabane des Aiguillous (2hrs) heading roughly southeast towards Col de la Gela, but then cut back southwestward to gain Col de la Sède in a little over 3hrs from Héas. The col is a first-class viewpoint from which to study the Cirque de Troumouse, with Monte Perdido beyond. Follow the easy ridge round to the southeast, but before reaching Pic de Gerbats veer left, descending a little then contouring east to Col de la Gela (2706m). Pic de la Gela is climbed easily from the col in 20mins or so, and the summit panorama is vast, which more than repays the 4hrs of effort to get there. By following the northwest ridge (the Crête des Aiguilous) to Hourquette de Héas, the HRP path can then be taken down through the Vallon de l'Aguila back to Héas (6½hrs total).

TRAVERSE OF THE CIRQUE HEADWALL

Perhaps the finest and most demanding non-technical expedition in the Cirque de Troumouse is the ❺ ★ traverse of the headwall from Port de la Canau in the south to Col de la Sède in the northeast (PD+). This tremendous long outing (11–12hrs) has abundant variety, exquisite views, enough exposure to keep you alert, and a few scrambling sections that could be dangerous in less than perfect conditions. In places the ridge is extremely narrow. Beginning at the Port de la Canau follow the ridge eastwards on the Spanish side, and in 30mins come to the Cheval Rouge (tackled *au cheval* as the name suggests), after which you traverse the Heche de Bounéu (2704m). On gaining a small col just before the Pène Blanque a path contours onto the south side of the Pène, then along a rake at the foot of smooth limestone slabs (watch for isard here) to a route leading onto the mountain's Spanish ridge, which is followed to the summit cairn at 2905m. The way continues along the ridge, over Mont Arrouy to Col de la Munia, which offers an escape route down to the car park if needed. From the col the *voie normale* is taken onto Pic de la Munia, which should be reached about 4–5hrs from Port de la Canau, representing the halfway point of the traverse in terms of time. The ridge crest now curves northward, with Pic de Serre Mourène bringing you up suddenly on its northeast side with a short and exposed descent pitch (grade IV; abseil peg *in situ*) leading to a col below Pic de Troumouse. Over this 3085m summit the rather scrambly traverse continues with Cirque de Troumouse to the left and the steep wall of the Cirque de Barroude to the right, the route eventually being led onto the west side of the ridge. Between Petit Pic Blanque and Pic de Garbats three giant couloirs of white limestone are crossed on thin isard tracks – the way is very exposed and great care is required. After the third of these is crossed the way leads back onto the ridge, which is now followed easily to Col de la Sède (2653m). From the col you can either descend by a cairned route into the cirque or cut northeast to a point below Col de la Géla then down through the Vallon de l'Aguila to Héas.

The Cirque de Gavarnie is without doubt the best-known feature of the Pyrenees, its walls offering some challenging winter routes

2.11 CIRQUE DE GAVARNIE

Beyond Gèdre the final 8km of the journey to Gavarnie along D921 provides a partial view into the glacier-carved hanging valley of the Gave d'Aspé to the right. From it the Cascade d'Arroudet dashes down to the Gave de Pau as the road goes through the Chaos de Coumély, said to have been created by the collapse of a mountain spur following an earthquake in the sixth century. It is from here that the Cirque de Gavarnie begins to announce itself with Pic du Marboré, Brèche de Roland and the Taillon coming into view. Soon after, with the Vallée d'Ossoue stretching off to the right, the D921 comes to an end on the outskirts of Gavarnie, where a statue of Henry Russell stands just above the road gazing west towards the Vignemale.

Henry Russell (1834–1909)

Born in Toulouse of an Irish father and French mother, Count Henry Patrick Marie Russell-Killough was the most enthusiastic and romantic of Pyrenean mountaineers, a man whose passion for the Vignemale in particular led to some curious acts of eccentricity. At the age of six he walked from Cauterets to the Lac de Gaube and caught a glimpse of the North Face, but it was only after his wanderlust had been sated with extensive travels around the world in his mid-20s that he climbed the mountain for the first time in 1861. From then until shortly before his death, Russell was to climb every Pyrenean summit of note, often by a new route and frequently solo, yet it was to the Vignemale that he would invariably return. He climbed it at least 33 times, and made the first winter ascent in 1869, but by 1880 he was looking for a way to spend more of his time upon the mountain itself. On 16 August that year he placed himself in a shallow grave on the summit and encouraged his two guides to cover him with scree, leaving just his head protruding. There he spent the night alone 'between the earth and the moon'.

Count Henry Russell (1834–1909)

This bizarre act inspired Russell to create a series of caves hacked from the walls of the Vignemale where he could stay in rather more comfort than the summit grave had provided. Workmen from Gèdre toiled up the Vallée d'Ossoue in all weathers laden with explosives, firewood and provisions and battled against the elements to satisfy his requirements. What they thought of it is not recorded, but the first cave, Villa Russell, was completed by the end of July 1882. Others followed, and the Grotte des Guides and Grotte des Dames were ready for occupation in 1885 and 1886 respectively. Villa Russell's door was painted red. Measuring 3m x 2.5m the cave was made snug, and Russell invited mountain friends to join him there. On one occasion the Comte de Monts erected a large tent on the glacier directly outside, where they dined on Bayonne ham and drank vintage claret. Persian carpets and silk cushions completed the décor, and Russell wore full evening dress – at an altitude of 3200m!

In 1889 Russell's peculiar attachment to the mountain was officially recognised by the *syndicat* of Barèges, which leased him the four summits of the Vignemale (without right to forbid access) for 99 years, for the sum of one franc a year. In obvious delight he wrote: 'It is certainly the highest estate in Europe and, despite its sterility, I would not change it for the finest in France.' But the Ossoue glacier began to stir, winter snow and ice blocked the grottoes, and when summer came the glacier had engulfed them. Russell was forced to create others, noting that nature 'allows her temples to be scaled but she does not tolerate them being mutilated and always avenges herself'. Grotte Bellevue and its two annexes were made at the lower elevation of 2378m, but aching for the greater solitude of the upper regions Russell carved a seventh and final grotto just 18m below the summit crown. Carpeted with straw, Le Paradis faced south and was dry, and it was there at the age of 60 that he celebrated the 'silver wedding' of his first ascent. Ten years later he made his final pilgrimage, paying homage to the Vignemale over a period of 17 days of isolated meditation there.

Souvenirs d'un Montagnard is Russell's literary legacy. The museum at Luchon has a section devoted to him, and the Musée Pyrénéen at Lourdes contains some of his original letters and photographs, while his statue at the entrance to Gavarnie gazes with longing at his very own mountain. See *The Man Who Married a Mountain* by Rosemary Bailey (Bantam Books, 2005).

GAVARNIE is without question the busiest village in the Pyrenees. Throughout the summer season it receives a huge influx of visitors who journey there by car, bus or coach simply to gaze on the spectacular cirque for which it is renowned. Few stay overnight, but as soon as vehicles arrive each morning the mule touts are active, cajoling young and old alike to rent a donkey, mule or pony for the 4km ride to the Hôtellerie du Cirque, where phenomenal close views are obtained of the towering walls and waterfalls.

Served daily by bus from Lourdes via Luz-St-Sauveur, the village itself is unbelievably tacky. Souvenir and postcard stands spill into the manure-spattered streets that are lined with snack bars and kiosks besieged by day-trippers. But in the evening, when the day's visitors have withdrawn and the streets cleared, Gavarnie's attraction is considerably enhanced. The tourist office is located within the Maison du Parc (☎ 05 62 92 49 10), where occasional guided walking tours are organised. Information on local walks is available here. Gavarnie has several shops, including a mini-supermarket. It has a post office at the village entrance, and although there's no bank, there is a cash dispenser by the tourist office. There are restaurants and bars, seven

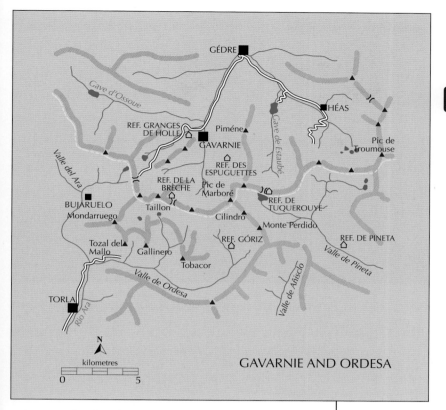

GAVARNIE AND ORDESA

rather pricey hotels, a few *chambres d'hôte*, a 45-place *gîte d'étape*, Le Gypaète (☎ 05 62 92 40 61), and a campsite (La Bergerie), located just south of the village on the east bank of the stream. The **CRS mountain rescue service** has its base almost opposite the campsite, while the main ski grounds are found in the Vallée des Espécières to the west, where the top lift rises to 2300m on Pic de Tentes.

Four manned refuges are accessible from Gavarnie: the CAF-owned **Les Granges de Holle**, situated just outside the village to the northwest (50 places, manned all year except Nov, ☎ 05 62 92 48 77); **Refuge de Bayssellance**, near the head of the Vallée d'Ossoue, conveniently placed for *voie normale* ascents of the Vignemale (70 places, manned mid-June to Sept, ☎ 05 62 92 40 25); **Refuge de la Brèche** (or des Sarradets), which is just below the Brèche de Roland (60 places, manned May–Sept, ☎ 06 83 38 13 24); and the PNP-owned **Refuge des Espuguettes**, on the eastern hillside on the path of the Pyrenean High Route (60 places, manned June–Sept, ☎ 05 62 92 40 63).

The glacier-scoured **Cirque de Gavarnie** is a truly majestic sight, a natural phenomenon that never fails to impress. Streaked with waterfalls and interrupted by two terraces of snow and ice, the rock bands that form the semi-circular wall rise abruptly for over 1300m to

Used by High Route trekkers, Refuge des Espuguettes is located on the eastern hillside above Gavarnie and provides a fine view of the cirque. The skyline gash shown in this picture is the Brèche de Roland

a group of 3000m summits on the frontier ridge. Looking south from Gavarnie and naming from left to right, these are: the Grand and Petit Pics d'Astazou (3071m and 3012m), Pic du Marboré (3248m) and the three Pics de la Cascade (3161m, 3095m and 3073m). In this eastern corner the Grande Cascade is a long and slender thread in summer, but in the spring thaw, when all the walls are running with snow-melt, it makes a powerful show. Next comes the undistinguished lump of the Tour du Marboré (3009m) and, to the west of that, the Casque de Marboré (3006m), which buttresses the profound U-shaped cleft of the Brèche de Roland – unseen from Gavarnie itself. Continuing the skyline westward the pyramidal Taillon (3144m) and neighbouring Pics de Gabiétous (3031m and 3034m) are part-concealed behind the Sarradets Ridge.

For choice panoramas of the cirque, the view from the ◗★ trail to Refuge des Espuguettes on the east side of the valley takes a lot of beating, but so too does the rounded summit of **Pic de Tentes** (2323m), easily reached by path from the road through the Vallée des Espécières, southwest of Gavarnie. Just above Gavarnie at the lower end of the ridge shared by Pic de Tentes, the 2101m **Pic Mourgat** is another not-to-be-missed viewpoint, served by a path rising from the ski station of Les Espécières (1hr). This provides the most extensive panorama of the Cirque de Gavarnie accessible to walkers, and is a truly dramatic vantage point.

Wildlife of the area is rich and varied: birds such as the eagle, lammergeier, chough, alpine swift, alpine accentor, black redstart and rock bunting may all be sighted. Moreover, the marmot's whistle is regularly heard in the meadows and isard are seen roaming the uninhabited upper glens. The range of walks and climbs is no less impressive.

- By far the most popular is that which is daily taken by the caravans of mules and ponies as far as the Hôtellerie du Cirque, an hour above the village. ● Should you be using Gavarnie as a base it would be worth tackling this walk either first thing in the morning before the crowds arrive or after they've departed on a summer's evening. If you're fortunate enough to be there with a full moon, don't miss it by moonlight. The broad trail is impossible to lose for it follows the Gave de Gavarnie upstream, and as you enter the national park it goes through the beautiful Plateau de la Prade, an area of cropped grass, streams and pines, beyond which the way climbs to the hotel. This is as far as most of the crowds go. The view of the **Grande Cascade** (which at 423m claims to be Europe's longest) is very fine, but the steep cirque walls can seem oppressive under a cloudy sky. By continuing to the base of those walls across increasingly rough ground carpeted with irises in summer, a more intimate impression is gained, but it would be a pity to return to Gavarnie by the same trail. A much better option is to take a marked path behind the *hôtellerie*. It enters forest and mostly contours along the eastern side of the valley to the lower Plateau de Pailla before dropping to the riverside path near the campsite.

- ●★ The other option for strong walkers at the Hôtellerie du Cirque is to ascend the **Échelle des Sarradets**, a very steep and challenging trail which climbs the western side of the cirque to the Refuge de la Brèche (2587m; 3hrs from the *hôtellerie*). This is a route not recommended for anyone troubled by vertigo. For a round-trip leave the refuge on the main path which cuts round the hillside to the Port de Boucharo, but break away just after crossing below the Taillon glacier and descend with care into the Vallée de Pouey Aspé. Curve northeast in this hanging valley and wander across the aptly named Plateau de Bellevue for a terrific view of the cirque. The path forks, but both branches eventually lead down to Gavarnie.

● Before tackling other walking and climbing options within the main body of the cirque, it is worth studying routes to east and west of Gavarnie. Mention has already been made of the HRP trail which climbs the eastern hillside and provides such marvellous views of the cirque from near Refuge des Espuguettes (2027m). This path continues to rise for another 400m to cross the ridge at **Hourquette d'Alans** (3¼hrs), by which both the Brèche de Tuquerouye and Vallée d'Estaubé are reached. Before gaining the pass, however, another path branches north to ascend the 2801m ⊗ **Piméné**, a popular vantage point for walkers (4–4½hrs from Gavarnie).

West of Gavarnie the Vallée d'Ossoue leads to Refuge de Bayssellance (2651m) and the ⊗★ **Vignemale**. The walk to the Bayssellance refuge is long (6–6½hrs) but not difficult, and may be

223

shortened by as much as 9km by driving as far as the Barrage d'Ossoue. It's an interesting approach, passing as it does Russell's Bellevue grottoes, but as the hut is almost 1300m higher than Gavarnie, the walk can be purgatory on a hot summer's day if you're weighed down with climbing gear. The refuge itself is an old yet atmospheric beehive-shaped building that is often heaving with climbers and trekkers in the high season. From it **Petit Vignemale** may be reached in about 1hr via the Hourquette d'Ossoue, and the **Grand Vignemale** (Pique Longue) in 3hrs by the Ossoue glacier *voie normale* (see 2:6 above). Trekkers could follow GR10 over Hourquette d'Ossoue and descend to the Vallée de Gaube, or cross into the Vallée de Lutour by either Col de Labas or Col des Gentianes, both of which are briefly described in the Vallée de Lutour section (2:7).

- Refuge de Bayssellance is visited by the Pyrenean High Route, which is usually tackled west to east, and visitors to Gavarnie who may have spent a night in the refuge could vary their return to the valley by following that route. On leaving the refuge the official HRP does not descend directly to Gavarnie but instead turns off the main Ossoue valley track on a devious trail leading to the **Port de Boucharo** at the head of the Vallée des Espécières, then on a clear path below the westernmost summits of the Gavarnie Cirque to Refuge de la Brèche. It then descends the Échelle des Sarradets to the floor of the cirque.

Refuge de Bayssellance, traditional base for tackling the Vignemale's voie normale, *is the highest manned hut in the Pyrenees*

- Another trail breaks away from the HRP after leaving the Barrage d'Ossoue, rising through the little Vallée de la Canau to the **Col de la Bernatoire** (2336m) on the frontier ridge. Below this

on the Spanish side lies the circular Lac de la Bernatoire, and the trail descends steeply from it to a track leading to **San Nicolás de Bujaruelo** in the valley of the Rio Ara (see 2:12).

- ◐ The easiest route to Bujaruelo from Gavarnie crosses the frontier at the 2270m **Port de Boucharo** (Puerto de Bujaruelo or Port de Gavarnie). A road over this pass was planned in Napoléon's time, but although one reached the frontier from the north several decades ago, happily the long-delayed crossing has again been halted on the Spanish side. An old mule track is followed instead down into the Ara valley.

These two crossings are interesting enough, but they cannot compare with the classic trekker's route which passes between the vertical portals of the **Brèche de Roland** (2807m), that prominent and much-loved cleft in the cirque's crest wall, which measures some 100m high by about 40m wide. Legend has it that on 15 August 778, the dying Roland, nephew of Charlemagne, sought to break his magical sword here lest it should fall into the hands of the Saracen invaders, and as he struck the rock so it shattered to reveal the *brèche*. Some sword! Some legend! Truth is, Roland died in battle at Roncesvalles far to the west, and the *brèche* was created when a section of the crest wall collapsed of 'natural causes'. The frontier ridge at this point is extremely thin, falling away on the Spanish side to a chaotic scene of rocks, boulders and scree, while the northern side is adorned by a small strip of glacier – an icy ramp between the Refuge de la Brèche and the *brèche* itself.

- ◐ Two ways of reaching the Refuge de la Brèche have already been mentioned above (from the floor of the cirque via the Échelle des Sarradets, and by the path leading round from Port de Boucharo), but there is a third route which is rather a fine one and well worth considering. It leaves Gavarnie by the church on a rising trail through west flank meadows onto the Plateau de Bellevue, curves into the **Vallée des Pouey Aspé**, but then crosses the Gave des Tourettes to climb in steep zigzags heading south. Eventually, under the Glacier du Taillon, the way joins the main Port de Boucharo trail, turns left to pass through a rocky area below Pic des Sarradets, and soon after comes to the refuge (3½hrs from Gavarnie).

Rock climbers are attracted to an assortment of routes on ⓑ **Pic des Sarradets** (2741m), which – being so conveniently accessible from the Refuge de la Brèche – serves as a popular training ground. Most of these lines are between 150m and 200m long, with several graded from AD to TD. The South Face backing the refuge enjoys plenty of activity, and on summer evenings numerous ropes are strung out across it.

From the Brèche de Roland a view across the cirque shows the bulk of Pic du Marboré

It only takes about 40mins to reach the Brèche de Roland from the refuge, but although the little glacier that leads to it is free of crevasses, there's potential danger, since it can be slippery either from bare ice or from a covering of slush late in the day, and it is easy to lose your footing and fall. Caution is advised. Once at the *brèche* the most popular ascent is that of the 3144m 🌂★ **Taillon** by an easy yet rewarding path which curves to the right along the Spanish slope, passes through the Fausse Brèche, guarded by the rock needle of the Doigt, and then rises along an uncomplicated ridge to the summit, whose outward views are among the best in this part of the range (about 1hr from the *brèche*).

On the east side of the *brèche*, the 🌂 **Casque** is another 3000m summit easily gained by walkers with a modicum of scrambling ability, as is the neighbouring **Tour du Marboré**. Farther to the east the massive **Pic du Marboré** is a little more demanding on account of the time needed for the ascent (3–3½hrs from the *brèche*), although the *voie normale* is only graded F+.

⑥★ GAVARNIE ROCK CLIMBS

Each of these peaks, and others of the cirque, have challenging lines on their north faces, approached either from the Refuge de la Brèche along one of the mid-wall terraces or from the base of the cirque proper. The 700m triangular North Face of the **Taillon** is one such. Climbed as long ago as 1895 by Henri Brulle and Célestin Passet, it had its first winter ascent (AD+, 55°) only in 1954. Nearby the Northwest Arête offers a pleasant climb of about 400m (AD), while the west wall of the Brèche de Roland gateway holds an entertaining 120m climb (the *Clos Buttress*) on the south side of

Pointe Bazillac, and another on the north of about 160m (*Dragon 64*: Durou/Sébie 1984; ED, A2/V+).

On the east side of the *brèche* the **Casque**'s North Face has a choice of short 100–150m lines on the upper wall reached directly from the *brèche* itself, while enjoying centre stage on the cirque headwall the **Tour du Marboré** has a classic North Face route (400m, TD+, V+) climbed by Claude Dufourmantelle and Jean Ravier over two days in September 1956. This highly respected original is now flanked by ED lines that are also well worth tackling. As for the 1200m **Mur de la Cascade**, which comprises all three tiers, this was climbed in its entirety in 1945 by Adagas and Malus. There are several alternatives, but the original 250m route on the base wall dates from 1887 (Bazillac, de Monts and Célestin Passet) and is now graded AD; the middle section known as the *Grand Dièdre* (200m, D) is a natural extension rising out of the first snow bank and slanting slightly left, while the upper wall (200m, D+, V) continues that line following a short traverse to the right.

Starting a little left of the Grande Cascade is the 1600m *Direct* on the **Pic du Marboré**, which includes the Arête Passet in its upper reaches. Completed in 1947 the overall grade is only D+, although it is a very long route of about 8–10hrs. Finally, in this brief selection of north-facing routes, mention should be made of the Northwest Arête of the **Petit Pic d'Astazou**, another splendid 500m itinerary (AD+) of Célestin Passet's dating from 1892, this time when guiding Brulle, Courtade and Roger d'Astorg. Lastly there's the *Couloir Swan* which divides the Petit Astazou from its higher twin. Impressive when seen from Gavarnie, the couloir is not unduly difficult, although its situation is dramatic. The easiest route by which the Pics d'Astazou may be climbed is via the Col d'Astazou in the southern ridge leading to Pic du Marboré (an ungraded *voie normale*).

❺ ★ Winter Climbing in the Cirque de Gavarnie

Though frequently threatened by avalanche the cirque offers some of the best winter climbing in the Pyrenees, with a number of serious routes being developed in the mid-1970s spearheaded by Dominique Julien and continued by activists from both sides of the border. *Voie de Mystiques* (Julien/Munsch, 220m, TD, 80°) set a standard in 1977, and was closely followed by the same pair with *Cascade des Banzayous* (300m, ED). During 7–9 March 1978 the spectacular *Voie de l'Overdose* was established on the summer line of the Grande Cascade (Julien/Boulanc/Casteran/Munsch, 450m, ED, 90°) – this was repeated only once before 1999, and was then soloed by Rémi Thivel. After *Overdose* came *Voie du Fluide Glacial* on the lower rock band in the centre of the cirque (Julien/Boulanc/Todas, 280m, ED), and in 1985 the big grade VI *Thanatos* was added to the list (Julien/Casteran, 230m, 80–90° with a 95° crux). This lies at the far right of the cirque and is not often in condition, while *Banzayous* tackles the lower tier just to the right of *Fluide Glacial*. In 1994 Frenchman Patrick Gabarrou and Ferran Latorre from Barcelona made the first complete and continuous direct winter ascent of the cirque over a three-day period in March, starting with Julien's *Banzayous*. Other complete ascents have followed, but there remains tremendous scope for more winter climbing here, especially on the water ice for which the cirque walls are well known, while some epic soloing continues to push standards ever higher.

Returning to the Refuge de la Brèche it is time to look at the district's much loved classic trekking route which crosses into Spain through the **Brèche de Roland** and forms a link with Refugio de Góriz, base for the ascent of Monte Perdido and others. The basic itinerary between huts takes 2½–3hrs and illustrates the contrasting nature of the two sides of the range more starkly than any other, for once you pass through the *brèche* you exchange the rich colours of France for a much more sombre landscape of bleached rocks and sandy grey screes of the foreground, reaching out to a middle-distance that hints of deep clefts, while the horizon fades across a maze of sierras.

- ◐★ The route to the Góriz refuge is uncomplicated, though in poor visibility difficulties could occur on the flat wastes of the Plana de San Ferlus. Once through the *brèche* you keep below the left-hand wall and pass to the south of the Grotte Casteret, discovered in 1926 by the French speleologist Norbert Casteret and so graphically described in his *Ten Years Under the Earth*. (It's possible to explore the initial, outer chamber without equipment, but you'll need crampons, headtorch and rope to reach the more spectacular lower chamber.) With the curious domed top of Pico del Descargador to the right, the way slopes down to the Plana de San Ferlus, whose streams drain into the Cotatuero Cirque. Keeping in a southeasterly direction you then rise to Cuello de Millaris (2467m), which is found north of the uninspiring Pico de Millaris. On the east side of this the trail passes below white limestone crags of the Faja Luenga and keeps along the north side of the Circo de Góriz before coming to **Refugio de Góriz**, otherwise known as Refugio Delgardo Ubeda or Refuge de Gaulis (2170m). The *refugio* is owned by the Federación Española de Montanismo (FEM), has dormitory places for 100 and is wardened throughout the year (☎ 974 34 12 01). It is extremely busy during the high summer season.

Prospects for continuing trekking routes deeper into Spain are enticing. The most obvious is to descend from the *refugio* into the **Ordesa canyon**, then return to Gavarnie by way of San Nicolás de Bujaruelo in the Ara valley and the Port de Boucharo, which leads back into France. This would make a splendid 3–4 day circuit. Another option is to remain above Ordesa and head southeast, cross Collado de Arrablo, then descend into the glorious **Añisclo canyon**. This is followed downstream as far as the Valle de Vió, which presents an opportunity to work a way northwest to gain the upper lip of the Valle de Ordesa, where there are several options. You could descend all the way into the depths of the Valle de Ordesa (a very steep and knee-jarring descent) and bear left for the Ara valley, San Nicolás de Bujaruelo and the way back to Gavarnie across Port de Boucharo as outlined above. Alternatively, break off halfway down the Ordesa wall and head southeast along the balcony path of the Faja de Pelay to return to the Góriz *refugio*. Yet another option is to enter the Añisclo canyon, but then climb out of its headwall at Collado de Añisclo and make an extremely steep descent into the **Valle de Pineta**, and there go to the head of the valley and cross back into France by way of the Brèche de Tuquerouye. These, and other options for exploring the Parque Nacional de Ordesa y Monte Perdido are dealt with in more detail below (see 2:13–15).

2:12 VALLE DEL ARA

Draining south from a tight little cirque whose headwall carries the frontier northwest of the Vignemale, the Spanish Valle del Ara forms a moat between the Panticosa–Tendeñera mountains and those of Ordesa, and provides a direct contrast to its neighbours on the French slope, where the vegetation, landform and the very atmosphere itself is different. Natural rock gardens spill over the margins of side-streams, and in summer the sun-dried grasses seethe with insect life as a herbal aromatic fragrance hangs in the air.

On breaking free of the Circo del Ara, the valley is an open sun-trap, its west wall cleft here and there by tributary glens that suggest walking routes over the mountains to Balneario de Panticosa. Below San Nicolás de Bujaruelo, however, it narrows to a twisting gorge that relaxes its grip only upon reaching the river's confluence with the Rio Arazas at the entrance to Ordesa's canyon. This confluence occurs a little north of **Torla**, the main base for tourist exploration of Ordesa, and it is here that the Valle del Ara becomes the Valle de Broto. Just 1km south of Torla the Ordesa road joins N260, the main east–west highway of Alto Aragón by which all motorised visitors to this exceedingly popular corner of the range make their approach. Westward the road journeys for 24km to Biescas and the Valle de Tena, while in the other direction N260 sweeps southeastward along-side the Rio Ara to Ainsa and the Rio Cinca.

A Monday to Saturday bus service runs in both directions all year round between Sabiñánigo and Ainsa, calling at Biescas, Torla and Broto. In the high season (mid-July to August) an additional bus plies the Sabiñánigo–Torla route daily except on Sundays.

Walkers or climbers arriving from the south will no doubt choose **TORLA**, if not as a base for exploration of the valley proper, then at least for stocking with provisions for the hills. It is easy to be dismissive of this rapidly expanding resort, now given up almost completely to cater to the tourist trade, which stands well above the west bank of the river. But there is still a romantic, medieval heart to the place, where narrow alleys climb between old stone buildings, and out of season its former charm is restored. On a practical level, Torla can supply most of the mountain activist's needs with its variety of shops, food stores, restaurants, a bank, post office and bars. There are several hotels, two *albergues* (the Lucien Bret, ☎ 974 48 62 21, and the smaller L'Atalaya, ☎ 974 48 60 22) and three campsites. But in August arrivals should expect every bed and tent pitch to be taken unless booked in advance. (For information try Torla *Turismo*, ☎ 974 22 98 04).

At the Puente de los Navarros a dirt road, or *pista*, turns into the Valle del Ara, initially running along the east bank of the river. This is the route of GR11, but when the road crosses to the west bank on the Puente de Santa Elena the path remains on the right-hand side. A little north of this bridge Camping Valle de Bujaruelo and its associated 30-place *refugio/gîte* (☎ 974 48 63 48) is found beside the track. Open from April to mid-October there's a restaurant, bar and useful shop on site, and the owner is ready to impart his enthusiasm for, and knowledge of, the local trails with his customers. Both the *pista* and the GR11 trail continue upvalley for a little under 3km to **SAN NICOLÁS DE BUJARUELO** (1338m) where there's another, rather basic, campsite (Camping San Nicolás) and a restored hospice, the Méson de San Nicolás de Bujaruelo, with 48 places and restaurant service, open from Easter to the end of September (☎ 974 48 64 12). Nearby stands the ruined 11th-century church after which the hamlet is named and a lovely old bridge spanning the Ara.

Bujaruelo is located on a bend in the river below the confluence with a stream which comes down from the ancient frontier crossing of the **Puerto de Bujaruelo** (known to the French as the Port de Boucharo or Port de Gavarnie). A mule track carries a route over that pass and down to Gavarnie on a road as the easiest crossing hereabouts. Another trail cuts off that mule track to cross the **Puerto Viejo** (or Col des Espécières) a little north of the Bujaruelo pass, after first visiting the Ibón de Lapazosa tarn, while a third option tackles the 2338m **Puerto de Bernatuara** north of San Nicolás.

- ◒ The Valle del Ara curves northwest above Bujaruelo – the dirt road and GR11 trail still on opposite sides of the river – but on coming to the concrete Puente Oncins the two unite. The former route of GR11, which heads **over the mountains to Panticosa**, crosses the river and makes a way westward up a hillside of woods and open meadows. Faint red–white waymarks may still be found, although another dirt road has made the old route virtually obsolete now as it snakes its way up to the 1605m Collado de Otal. Over the col lies the broad Valle de Otal, with the obvious

Collado de Tendeñera seen at the far end. The track goes as far as the Cabana-*refugio* de Otal (1642m; 1½hrs from Bujaruelo), which is useful for emergency shelter only, beyond which one would begin the climb proper to gain the pass. It's not a direct ascent, however, for the way tacks to and fro for another 2hrs or more above the *cabana* before the **Collado de Tendeñera** (2327m) is finally reached. The descent to Panticosa (see 1:10) on the west side of the pass is quite as long as the climb to it, with 8–9hrs needed for the cross-country trek from Bujaruelo.

Immediately north of Collado de Tendeñera rises **Pico Mallaruego** (2694m), a worthwhile diversion from the pass with the option of continuing along the ridge to the **Picos de Ferreras** (2614m and 2651m). It's feasible to return to the Rio Ara from here by way of the Valle de Ordiso.

Resuming upstream beyond the Puente Oncins along the east (true left) bank of the Rio Ara, the *pista* ends at the scruffy, unmanned Refugio de Ordiso. The river is spanned by another bridge here which carries a trail into the Valle de Ordiso, while the main GR11 continues ahead towards the Vignemale, which from this aspect bears no resemblance whatsoever to the graceful and impressive wall of rock that comprises its North Face seen from the Vallée de Gaube. Much of the frontier ridge is confused when studied from the valley bed, but since the west wall stands further back it is that which commands most attention.

A second unmanned *refugio* stands beside the GR11 trail at an altitude of some 1800m. This is the Refugio (or Cabaña) de Cerbillonar, with places for about half a dozen, and it's in rather better condition than the Ordiso hut. From a point a little west of here the ⊗ **ascent of the Vignemale** can be made in about 5hrs by the historic *Voie du Prince de la Moskowa*, by which the first tourist ascents were achieved in 1838. The route is somewhat laborious but not unduly difficult, and is graded AD-. It cuts up the hillside on the west bank of the Labaza stream to gain a small cirque, then turns to the left in order to climb a gully known as the Couloir de la Moskowa. Towards the head of this a 50m chimney gives onto the Cerbillona Ridge. Between the summits of Cerbillona and Pic Central the 3200m Col Lady Lyster leads out to the near-level upper basin of the Ossoue glacier, across which the final easy rocks take the route onto the summit of Pique Longue.

- About 7km or so beyond ◐ Puente Oncins at around 2050m the Barranco de Batanes spills from the west into the Ara. The GR11 crosses the Ara here and makes a 2hr ascent alongside the *barranco* rising to granite country on the way to **Cuello de Brazato** (2578m; 6hrs from Bujaruelo). Clusters of tarns lie on both sides of the pass: the tiny Ibónes de Batanes on the Ara slope; the larger Ibónes Alto de Brazato about 200m below on the Panticosa flank. **Balneario de Panticosa** is gained about 1½hrs from the pass (see 1:10).

- Another crossing to ◯ Balneario de Panticosa, used by a GR11 *variante*, tackles the higher 2637m **Collado de Letrero** northeast of the Brazato col and works its way just below the frontier ridge to the Bramatuero and Bachimaña lakes before dropping southward. Rather than make the descent to Balneario, an alternative option would be to break away at the western end of the lower Bramatuero lake, cross the Port du Marcadau on the frontier and take the easy route down to Refuge Wallon in the Marcadau valley (8–9hrs from Bujaruelo).

In its upper reaches the Rio Ara makes a divide between granite on the west and limestone on the east. At its very head converging ridges and spurs squeeze the valley into the tight little Circo del Ara. Pic Alphonse Meillon (or Chabarrou Sud) forms the lynchpin at the point where three ridges unite. Two nearby frontier crossings used by trekkers on the HRP are of great appeal: **Col d'Arratille** on the western ridge leads walkers into the Marcadau valley, while **Puerto de los Mulos** (Col des Mulets, 2591m) in the east ridge carries a route down to Refuge des Oulettes in the Vallée de Gaube below the Vignemale. The Marcadau option (via Col d'Arratille) is described in more detail in 2:5, while walks and climbs in the Vallée de Gaube are detailed in 2:6.

It will be obvious, then, that with such an assortment of walkers' passes in the high ridges either side of the Ara valley, the range of options available for creating multi-day circuits and wilderness treks is impressive. All one needs is sufficient time and energy to explore them all.

2:13 VALLE DE ORDESA

Matching the appeal of Gavarnie, which lies across the border to the north (see map, section 2:11), Ordesa is surely the best-known and most visited valley in the Spanish Pyrenees. And no wonder. Walled by awesome, multi-hued cliffs, the Rio Arazas has further deepened the canyon that was initially bulldozed by glaciers into a 1000m cleft southwest of Monte Perdido. Born on Perdido's slopes the river makes its way down to its confluence with the Ara in a succession of impressive waterfalls and cascades, while other waterfalls spray down the walls of tight horseshoe cirques on the north side of the canyon.

Ordesa is treated very much as the showcase of the *parque nacional*, which is hardly surprising since at its foundation in 1918 it was the valley alone which constituted the park. Seen from Monte

Perdido it looks as though it has been cut by a gigantic knife, and the sight made such an impression on Ramond de Carbonnières when he reached the summit in 1802 that he determined to make an exploration. Alfred Tonnelle marched through on his whirlwind journey of 1858, but it was Charles Packe whose visit in 1860 led to a wider publicity for the region.

The village of Torla and the cliffs of Mondarruego at the entrance to the Ordesa canyon

Having descended into the Circo de Soaso at the head of Ordesa, Packe and his companions discovered the river in full flood; one of the party fell in and lost his boots, which were retrieved only later after some effort. There followed a cold and uncomfortable night in a cave near the cascades of the Gradas de Soaso, but the discomfort was forgotten next morning. 'Truly grand is the walk down the valley', wrote Packe later in one of the early alpine journals, voicing sentiments that would be echoed by tens of thousands of visitors throughout the next century and a half.

> 'First we have a series of cascades... Then come the magnificent walls ... rising above the forest zone ... capped with snow. On the left bank of the stream the rocky wall is continuous, but on the right and grander side the precipices recede in deep ravines to the main chain, forming two huge amphitheatres, of which the sides are almost inaccessible – first that of Cotatoir [Cotatuero], and then that of Salarous [Carriata]. By a rift in the ledges of the last it is possible to mount to the snowfields of Excusana, and so to the Brèche de Roland.'

Thirty years later Packe was describing the lower valley again:

'On the south side ... the precipitous wall of rock ... is continuous for five or six miles ... while on the north side the mountains, which are the back of the Cirque of Gavarnie, present such a warm red colour as would make the delight of the photographer, and still more of the artist who could reproduce the sunlit tints. Alongside of the stream the willows mix their pale green with the darker tints of the box, and then come the dense forests... The beech and then the fir succeed each other in zones, and rising yet higher by 1,000 metres are the ruddy walls of rock, with their snow-capped summits.'

The first climbing practised here was by the ubiquitous hunters of isard and ibex, the most notable of whom was Edward North Buxton, whose book *Short Stalks* included a section devoted to Ordesa, but it was the visit by Lucien Briet in 1891 that was instrumental in having the canyon protected as a national park. This was achieved on 16 August 1918 when an area reaching along the Rio Arazas as far as the Gradas de Soaso, and amounting to 2066 hectares, was given special protection. In 1982 that protected area was greatly extended to include the complete Valle de Ordesa from its confluence with the Ara up to the frontier ridge where it becomes contiguous with the French Parc National des Pyrénées; it then spreads east to cover the Perdido massif, Circo de Pineta, Añisclo canyon and the gorges of Escuaín. The Parque Nacional de Ordesa y Monte Perdido is rightly considered to be one of the gems of the Pyrenees.

As mentioned in 2:12 above, **TORLA** serves as the main base for an exploration of the Ordesa canyon, since the nearest alternative accommodation is in the Refugio de Góriz (see 2:11) at 2170m on the slopes of Perdido above the Circo de Soaso. Camping is forbidden throughout the valley below the 2100m mark, which effectively means that the only place for a tent is around the Góriz hut – and then it's supposed to be taken down by day. In high summer the road into the canyon above Puente de los Navarros is closed to private vehicles, but a shuttle bus service operates between Torla and the former car park of Pradera de Ordesa at 1320m, where there's a bar-restaurant. A short distance up this road a secondary spur cuts off left to an interpretation centre housed in the former *parador* (open 9.00–14.00 and 15.00–18.00), where visitors can learn about the local geology, flora and fauna of the park through a number of well-presented displays and films.

Given sufficient time the best way into the valley from Torla is by a 6km walk along a *pista* which at first follows the east bank of the Ara. From the main road which bypasses the village a signed path beside Hostal Bellavista descends to the river and crosses on a hump-backed bridge where the Camino de Turieta goes alongside Camping

Rio Ara. When the way curves into the mouth of Valle de Ordesa with the huge cliffs of Mondarruego forming a wall to the north, GR11 joins the track, having come down from Bujaruelo. Although the walk is on *pista* throughout, for the majority of the way the only vehicles allowed to use it are those of the national park service, and these are few and far between. In summer the valley can be desperately hot, especially away from shade, and drinking water should be carried by all walkers. After about 2hrs from Torla the Camino de Turieta comes to the Puente de las Fuentes, on the far side of which spreads the large stony car park at Pradera de Ordesa, where most of the walks begin.

Seen from the outskirts of Torla, Mondarruego signals the entrance to the Valle de Ordesa

WALKS IN AND AROUND ORDESA

- ◐★ By far the most popular walk – for those prepared to stray beyond the first waterfall – heads upvalley on the north side of the river as far as the **Gradas de Soaso** cascades (1½hrs one way). It begins easily enough on a broad path, but this soon rises through woodland with several opportunities to divert to viewpoints overlooking the splendid waterfalls whose thunder can be heard for most of the climb. Eventually emerge from woodland and continue on more level ground with a short uphill stretch to the Gradas de Soaso.

- ◐ A longer route (6hrs) continues beyond the Gradas to the valley headwall in the **Circo de Soaso** on the standard trail to Refugio de Góriz. Instead of climbing the cirque wall, however, you cross the stream on the Puente de Soaso and return on the south side of the valley. Here a gently rising path soon levels among shrubs and dwarf pine trees to follow the natural ledge/

235

terrace of the **Faja de Pelay** along the 1900m contour, with amazing views looking down into the canyon and across to the great limestone cliffs on the far side. As you progress westward so the monstrous flake of Tozal del Mallo begins to dominate the scene. Shortly after passing a small shelter the *faja* comes to the **Senda de los Cazadores**, a steeply plunging path that returns you to the valley bed near the car park.

- ◔ A similar *faja* makes an exposed traverse of the east wall of the Circo de Cotatuero, whose entrance lies just beyond Pradera de Ordesa. For the first hour a path climbs through woodland into the narrowing cirque, then forks by a small wooden shelter. The right branch crosses a footbridge below a long feathery waterfall, then zigzags to gain a little more height before settling to the **Faja los Canarillos**, which cuts round the Fraucata face of Monte Arruebo. The situation is airy and views stupendous, but having rounded the south spur of the Cotatuero Cirque the path suddenly begins to descend through the woodland of Bosque de la Hayas, bringing you onto the Gradas trail and an easy walk back to the car park.

- ◔ The west side of the Circo de Cotatuero holds yet another *faja*, this one edging high above the valley on the slopes of Punta Gallinero to the Circo de Carriata. The **Faja de los Flores** offers a tremendous experience. It has even more exposure than the Canarillos and Pelay *fajas*, is gained by use of the iron rungs or pegs (*clavijas*) made by a Torla blacksmith in the 1880s for E.N. Buxton the ibex hunter, and makes its traverse at around the

2400m contour. It finally runs out in the Carriata Cirque, where an easily followed descent route leads to the road below the car park.

Other *fajas* offer yet more spectacular walks. There's the **Mondarruego** route from Carriata, which eases towards the Valle del Ara; the **Faja Racún**, which also links the cirques of Cotatuero and Carriata but at a lower level than the Flores route; and the **Fraucata** trail below Tobacor that escapes round by the Góriz *refugio*. And there are ways, too, of climbing out of both cirques and heading up to the frontier ridge. Each of these is reserved for experienced mountain trekkers with a good head for heights.

❻ ★ CLIMBING IN ORDESA

No climber could enter Ordesa without seeing at a glance a dozen opportunities for tackling quality routes in the most sublime of settings. 'Soon the fantastic walls and pinnacles ... begin to tower above you all glowing red' wrote one-time Alpine Club president, Claud Schuster, on his visit in 1913. 'If Arazas were in the Alps its peculiar and contrasted beauty of trees and rocks and the facilities for climbing would have made it a centre.' Well, it is now.

Since most of the major routes are either south or west facing, it's possible to climb here in all seasons. However, winter storms can be severe and long lasting, and special care should be exercised during periods of snow-melt. In summer and autumn plenty of water needs to be carried, especially on some of the longer routes. Climbing is on red or yellowish sandstone or limestone, and lines are vertical or nearly so, with some big overhangs. Quality technical moves are a feature, and the exposure can be awesome, but virtually all descents are straightforward.

The first wall to come in sight on approaching from the south is that of **Mondarruego**, the broad, multi-tiered cornerstone of the valley which looks so impressive from Torla. The summit is only 2755m, but it appears much higher than that. However, despite its distant appeal it attracts much less attention than Tozal del Mallo, Gallinero or Fraucata, although the 400m *Central Buttress* (TD, VI, A2) was climbed as long ago as 1964. On the first ascent the team of Escos, Falo, Mustienes and Vicente took a total of 23hrs, with two bivouacs on the face. Their route is not often repeated.

At the eastern end of the Mondarruego wall, and standing proud of the spur which forms the western limit of the Circo de Carriata (formerly known as the Circo de Salarous (or Salarons)), the **Tozal del Mallo** is the most spectacular individual rock feature in the Valle de Ordesa. Seen in profile it appears as a huge flat-topped, smooth-faced blade, whose appeal to climbers is obvious. Approach to the wall is by a direct path which leaves the road about 500m before the car park. The South Face looks directly onto the valley and has several lines and variations in the TD–ED range, varying in length from about 200m to 425m. One of the most respected of these is *Las Brujas*

On the eastern side of the Cotatuero cirque, the cliffs of La Fraucata hold several ED climbs of around 300m

(Rabada/Navarro/Dias, 1963), which initially tackles a crack system at the left-hand end of the wall, was originally climbed with about 100 pegs and is graded TD+ (V+, 6a, 6b). But the ultimate Tozal classic is the strenuous 300m *Voie Originale*, sometimes known as the *Ravier*, which was climbed over two days in April 1957 by Noël Blotti, Claude Dufourmantelle, Claude Jaccoux, Marcel Kahn and Jean Ravier, and is now treated as a popular test-piece. Taking a logical line on generally good rock (the crux chimney has become rather polished), this superb route was originally graded ED, but today goes at TD (V+, 6a).

Between the Carriata and Cotatuero cirques east of Tozal del Mallo are the cliffs of **Punta Gallinero**, whose vast wall known as El Libro Abierto has some impressive overhangs that loom over the Ordesa car park, and an east-facing section comprising El Tridente (the Trident), the Espolón Este (East Buttress) and La Pared de la Cascada (Cascade Wall) that guard the Cotatuero Cirque. The Navarro/Rabada duo created one of the finest routes here in 1961 on the East Buttress (TD+, 350m), but there's been plenty of activity in recent years that has seen a wealth of top-grade climbs from 150m to 500m in length being won.

On the east side of the Circo de Cotatuero the cliffs of **La Fraucata** receive less attention than their immediate neighbour, but nevertheless reward with some spectacular lines of around 300m in the ED range.

◐★ **Monte Perdido** (Mont Perdu to the French) towers at the head of the Valle de Ordesa. At 3355m it is the third highest summit in the Pyrenees, yet despite its bulk it is a singularly unimpressive mountain when viewed from the valley floor. To gain a better impression of its stature one should study it from either the Brèche de Tuquerouye on the frontier ridge to the north (see 2:10) or from the Balcón de Pineta, where the broken tiers of ice that adorn its Northeast Face give the mountain the character it deserves, and from where the more challenging routes lie (see 2:16). Having said that, the ascent of Perdido from Refugio de Góriz is one of the most popular non-technical routes on a big mountain this side of the frontier. Ice axe and crampons are useful most of the year, and the ascent normally demands about 3½–4hrs of effort. The route is adequately cairned up to the small Lago Helado at around 3000m, from where you then turn southeast to climb a steep slope and open couloir leading to a broad saddle, and the final snow ridge topped by the summit cross. The summit panorama is immense. The crags of Soum de Ramond immediately to the southeast plunge to the depths of the Valle de Pineta. To the south lies the great gash of the Añisclo canyon, with the Gargantas de Escuaín to the left of that. The upper reaches of Ordesa are clearly seen in the southwest, with a desert of limestone uplands between them and the frontier mountains. The Vignemale looks impressive to the northwest; the Posets massif is similarly appealing in the opposite direction.

If the *voie normale* on Perdido is one of the busiest routes in the Pyrenees, the *South Face*, first climbed by Jean and Pierre Ravier with M. and P. Jusnel in 1997, attracts only those in search of more secluded sport. The **ⓑ** Ravier route involves about 300m of climbing above the little Glacier de Ramond and is graded D+. The nearby **Soum de Ramond** (or Pico de Añisclo; 3254m) also has a D+ route of the Raviers on its Southeast Buttress dating from 1992, while **Punta de las Olas** (3002m), which overlooks the Añisclo canyon, has a modern TD route on its Southeast Buttress (passages of V+/6a) worked out by Christian Ravier and Philippe Barthez in 1997 and named by them *Les Marchands du Temple*.

North of Refugio de Góriz, midway between Perdido and Pic du Marboré, rises the lump of **ⓧ Cilindro de Marboré** (3328m), whose *voie normale* from this side is a 4hr ascent graded PD, which initially shares the Monte Perdido route as far as the tiny Lago Helado. From here a broad rocky couloir rises steeply west to a saddle. At the top of this couloir the way turns right, ascends a short chimney and comes onto the mountain's South Ridge which leads easily to the summit. More challenging routes on the North and Northeast Faces are climbed from the Balcón de Pineta (see 2:16).

MULTI-DAY TREKS OUT OF ORDESA

- **ⓢ** Several trek options are possible from Ordesa. The most obvious is the route of **GR11** which ascends through the valley to the Circo de Soaso and continues up to the Góriz *refugio*. After a night spent there the way then cuts southeast to the 2329m **Collado Arrablo**, where the trail forks. One option turns northeast along an easy grass ledge which later narrows round the slopes of Punta de las Olas, with a potentially dangerous section, and

Between the steep cliffs that wall it, Valle de Ordesa has some spectacular waterfalls

in 3hrs tops **Collado de Añisclo** overlooking the Valle de Pineta. The alternative, and easier, route descends into the head of the Añisclo canyon at Fon Blanca, then climbs out again to gain the same Collado de Añisclo for a severely steep descent into the **Valle de Pineta**, where the FAM's 73-bed **Refugio de Pineta** provides useful overnight accommodation. For *refugio* details and a description of the Valle de Pineta see 2:16.

- Less well known than GR11, the **GR15** (Sendero Prepirenaico) skirts to the south of Ordesa and follows the Ara downstream to Sarvisé, after which it turns east into the valley of the Barranco del Chate, eventually arriving at **FANLO** (1342m), perched high above the Valle de Vió. (From here it's feasible to return to Ordesa by one of two different routes, both of which give tremendous bird's-eye views into the canyon. Fanlo is also linked with Torla by a somewhat tortuous cross-country dirt road.) Although it boasts a tourist booth in summer, Fanlo has no accommodation, so it's necessary to descend another 5km to **NERÍN**, an atmospheric, 'lost-world' hamlet where you can stay in a dormitory at the Añisclo Albergue (☎ 974 48 90 10) or at the Pensión El Turista (☎ 974 48 90 16). In winter the Nerín/Fanlo region provides plenty of scope for cross-country skiing. Continuing eastward out of Nerín GR15 descends to the mouth of the **Añisclo canyon** (see 2:14) by way of the deserted Sercué, then goes on to explore the remote yet appealing country that lies between Añisclo and Escuaín.

- ◗★ To link the three canyons of the national park, walk up through Ordesa to the Refugio de Góriz, as outlined (above) for the GR11 route, and next day head southeast, still on GR11, across Collado Arrablo and work your way down to the head of the **Añisclo canyon** at Fon Blanca. Now descend through the canyon on a walk of great beauty as far as a small parking area at the confluence with the Rio Aso, just south of the chapel of San Urbéz. Here you join GR15 to cross first Añisclo's east wall and then the Rio Aires that flows parallel to it in order to reach **BESTUÉ**, in a charming setting high above the river. Here GR15 breaks north to Cuello Ratón, then east to **ESCUAÍN** overlooking the Gargantas de Escuaín. It's feasible to remain with GR15 almost as far as Tella (national park information office), then take the route of GR191 heading north across remote country to **BIELSA** at the mouth of the Valle de Pineta. And from there, if the idea of a multi-day circuit appeals, one could walk upvalley as far as the Refugio de Pineta and return to Ordesa by way of the GR11 route across Collado de Añisclo and Collado Arrablo. Such a circuit would require a minimum of 5–6 days using a variety of accommodation and some discreet wild camping – but what a trek that would make!

- Finally, for a challenging ◗ **high-level circuit** (for experienced mountain trekkers with some scrambling ability – ice axe and crampons advised) the following tour has much to commend it. Take a choice of trails from Ordesa to Refugio de Góriz, and on the second day follow the cairned route used on the ascent of Monte Perdido as far as Lago Helado. Leaving the Perdido route, now cross **Cuello del Cilindro** and descend with caution to the Balcón de Pineta and a much larger Lago Helado which lies below the **Brèche de Tuquerouye**. Cross the *brèche* (with its unmanned refuge) and descend into France – again with care – via the Estaubé flank on a route which then cuts round to cross **Hourquette d'Alans** and drops easily to Refuge des Espuguettes above Gavarnie. From here wander south to the Cirque de Gavarnie and climb by way of the Échelle des Sarradets to the

Refuge de la Brèche. A short ascent to the **Brèche de Roland** offers an easy return to Spain with a choice of descent routes to Ordesa. The easiest goes by way of the Góriz hut, but 'sporting' alternatives with considerable exposure tackle the steep walls of the Cotatuero and Carriata cirques.

2:14 VALLE DE AÑISCLO

Longer, more narrow and refreshingly less crowded than Ordesa, the Valle de Añisclo was only included as part of the *parque nacional* in 1982, in time to defeat a plan to dam the lower Rio Vellós (or Bellós) for hydro-electric purposes. Cutting south from the Collado de Añisclo on the edge of the Perdido massif this exquisite canyon is as wild as it is verdant, as beguiling as it is challenging, and few who make the effort to force a way through will fail to submit to its charms. Although Franz Schrader made a detailed exploration in the late 1870s, thanks to its difficult access the valley was largely ignored by tourists until comparatively recent times. But of the early pioneers Charles Packe is one who knew it well:

'Forcing its way through this rift in the mountains for twenty kilometres, the river at last issues near the village of Escalona. For two-thirds of the way the pedestrian may, with difficulty, descend, keeping the bottom of the gorge, but this for the last five kilometres is absolutely impracticable... For the first two hours our way lay through a virgin forest of box, yew, beech, and silver fir, many of them dead through age and prostrate upon the ground. In places the walls of rock so overhang the stream as all but to bar the passage; in others they recede in terraces, rising one above the other, and supporting on their ledges impossible fir-trees. Here and there for a few yards there is a more open turfy glade, but it is not grass but strawberry beds that carpet the soil, producing fruit and flavour only to be attained under a Spanish sun.'

Vehicular access is confined to the southern end of the canyon, where a narrow road has been created on shelves and galleries blasted from the towering rock walls of the Desfiladero de la Cambras between the lower end of the Valle de Vió and Puyarruego, a short distance west of Escalona in the Cinca's valley, the Valle de Bielsa. This road, incidentally, which breaks east of the main N260 at Sarvisé, makes for an interesting tour through the lonely, sparsely inhabited country that lies between the Ara and the Cinca, and for motorised activists needing to move east after spending time in Ordesa it provides a challenging drive; though paved it is badly potholed in places.

Much more narrow than the better-known Ordesa, the Añisclo canyon became included in the parque nacional *in 1982*

The nearest accommodation for visits to the lower Añisclo canyon is found at **NERÍN**, about 5km by road from the parking place near the Ermita de San Urbéz, but there's a well-appointed campsite, Camping Valle de Añisclo (open Easter–October), situated just below the village of **PUYARRUEGO**, and there are rooms in **ESCALONA**, where the road spills into the Valle de Bielsa. Escalona also has a national park information office, manned in summer. For an exploration of the upper canyon, Refugio de Góriz on the slopes of Perdido at the head of the Valle de Ordesa is the only available manned accommodation, although within the gorge there are simple shelters just north of Fon Blanca (Refugio de Cazadores) and, at 1780m above the left bank of the Rio Vellós, Refugio de San Vicenda, which has about eight bed spaces and an all-important spring nearby. Overnight camping is permitted adjacent to this *refugio*, and also at La Ripareta (1400m), near the confluence with the lateral gorge of the Barranco de la Pardina.

The majority of visitors to Añisclo come by road, park below San Urbéz, and explore a section of the canyon to the north. Initially there are paths on both sides of the river. The east bank trail first visits the cave-like shrine of the Ermita de San Urbéz, is then joined by the west bank path, and shortly after crosses to the left side of the canyon where it rises to meet the route of ◐★ GR15, which here climbs west to Sercué and Nerín. The canyon trail pushes on deeper into the Valle de Añisclo, for the most part shaded by trees. Of course, it's not an even trail, the demands of topography forcing the route up and down against the constricting wall above the river, but it's always an interesting route, and where it draws near the Vellós there are tempting green pools – although bathing is forbidden. After about 2½hrs or so from San Urbéz you come to the grassy area known as La Ripareta, a glorious site and often the limit for day-visitors to the canyon.

Here the Pardina tributary drains a much shorter canyon, through which it's possible to ascend west to Cuello Arenas, where there's a simple shelter and a high cross-country trail which journeys between Nerín and the Ordesa headwall. 'Ascending this [canyon],' wrote Packe in 1893, 'first through a tangled mass of box and raspberries, then through a wood of beech and fir, and further on over bare limestone rock, we emerged on an upland grassy plateau, which seemed fertile in many rare mountain plants.' There's an upper route here, the Faja de la Pardina, that skirts the Pardina canyon then curves north to the Barranco Capradizas, where one could descend back into the Valle de Añisclo near the Foradiello bridge. Alternatively a continuing trail remains on the upper lip of the Añisclo canyon, then veers northwest to Refugio de Góriz.

To continue upstream from La Ripareta as far as the Fon Blanca (or Fuen Blanca) cascades requires another 1½hrs, and from there to the Góriz hut you should allow a further 3hrs of fairly tough walking on the route of GR11.

This ascent of the canyon makes a wonderful day's trekking, but the route is perhaps better served in reverse, in descent from the

Góriz hut. As it is less physically demanding than the uphill route one has more time to linger, to study the canyon's individual features and to luxuriate in the cool freshness of vegetation enhanced by the river's spray. There are also temptations to divert from the main route and take you up onto the canyon's lip.

◑★ From Refugio de Góriz the route to the Valle de Añisclo takes a clear path gradually ascending southeastward to the easy, low-slung saddle of Collado Arrablo (Collado Superior de Góriz, 2329m), from where the canyon is first seen ahead. A grassy basin lies below, with the Barranco Arrablo (Barranco Fon Blanca) draining through it before tipping into its own minor gorge. A line of cairns directs the way for about 400m along the southwest edge of this gorge, then descends a broken line of cliffs to a grass terrace 50m below. More cairns lead down a series of terraces interrupted by bands of rock until you come at last to the Barranco Arrablo flowing through its gorge. The path crosses the stream, rises a little, then descends in steep zigzags on grit and scree to pass the Fon Blanca cascade, and reaches the bed of the upper Añisclo canyon among box trees near a small *cabaña* about 2½hrs from the Góriz hut. This is a beautiful site, where the infant Río Vellós tumbles down a natural stairway of rock steps into deep green pools, and the vegetation is both lush and fragrant.

The path forks. The left-hand option is that of GR11 climbing to Collado de Añisclo for the crossing to Valle de Pineta, while the right-hand trail eases into the canyon proper. At the Foradiello bridge, a little under 2km from Fon Blanca, the path to Refugio de San Vicenda breaks away up the eastern hillside, while the main canyon trail crosses the bridge and continues along the right bank to La Ripareta and, eventually, to the road below San Urbéz.

However, should you take the San Vicenda path two further options become possible at the *refugio*. A national park trail climbs to Cuello Viceto (2007m), with a short diversion to the summit of 2104m Tozal de San Vicenda, then heads southeast to the upper reaches of the **Gargantas de Escuaín**. An alternative easy trail swings north from Cuello Viceto to mount the **Montaña de Sensa** and the ridge crest which overlooks the Valle de Pineta. The second option from the San Vicenda hut continues south and southeast to Cuello de Plana Canal (1750m) and thence along a track to the small village of **BESTUÉ** at a roadhead above Puyarruego. But other trails break from this track: one (GR15) goes directly to **ESCUAÍN**; another leaves Bestué (also GR15) and descends once more to the canyon at the **Ermita de San Urbéz**.

2:15 VALLE DE TELLA

At the head of the Añisclo canyon, Collado de Añisclo effectively marks the southeast extent of the Perdido (or Las Tres Sorores) massif, while the continuing mountain ridge acts as the right-hand wall of the Valle de Pineta, and is known as the Sierra de las Tucas. On the southwest flank of this ridge the Montaña de Sensa is moulded round the headwall of the Circo de Gurrundué, a heart-shaped cirque that gives rise to the Rio Yaga. This is the river whose 12km journey through the Valle de Tella has carved the Gargantas (gorges) de Escuaín and, lower down, the Garganta de Miraval, and whose upper third is included in the Parque Nacional de Ordesa y Monte Perdido.

It's the least known sector of the national park, although canyoning enthusiasts discovered its delights and challenges some time ago. These are not restricted to the Rio Yaga, however, for other canyoning venues, such as that of the Barranco Consusa, are found among tributaries that join the main river downstream of Escuaín.

The Yaga drains into the Cinca at **HOSPITAL DE TELLA**, some 18km south of Bielsa. A little east of this small village a good, though minor, paved road climbs through Cortalaviña and forks about 2km later. The right-hand option twists up to **TELLA**, a seemingly remote community at 1395m huddled around a Romanesque church and a national park information office (open daily July–Oct). Nearby there's a prehistoric dolmen and a group of *ermitas* (shrines, or rural chapels), with views south across the Cinca to the massive Peña Montañesa. The left-branching road beyond Cortalaviña is unpaved, and pushes on for another 5km or so through empty country before coming to cliff-backed **REVILLA** (1220m), a lonely hamlet situated on the east bank of the Gargantas de Escuaín opposite Escuaín village, by which it is linked by footpath. Revilla is deserted in winter, although some of its houses have been renovated for summer use.

Walkers without transport have several options to access this remote country, none of which involves roadwork. ◓ Two trails leave Hospital de Tella: one strikes north along the west bank of the Garganta de Miraval (popular for white-water rafting) and makes for Revilla by way of **ESTARONILLO**; the other climbs to **CORTALAVIÑA**, then joins GR15 as far as Estaronillo before taking the previously mentioned route heading north. (The GR15 trail swings northwest at Estaronillo on its way to Escuaín on the west bank of the *gargantas*.) A third option for walkers is to follow GR19, the Sendero del Sobrarbe, out of **LA FORTUNADA**, 3km east of Hospital de Tella. This climbs direct to Tella, and a little north of the village GR15 is adopted for the continuing walk to Estaronillo, where you join the Revilla trail.

There is no accommodation to be had up here, although camping is possible outside the confines of the national park at **LAMIANA**, and there's a simple unmanned shelter, the Foratarruego, with 10 places, on the edge of the Gurrundué Cirque.

On the west bank of the *gargantas*, **ESCUAÍN** is reached by 15km of unpaved track accessed from the Añisclo road (HU631) about 1km west of Escalona. This passes **BELSIERRE** and **PUERTOLAS**, then forks. The left branch goes to Bestué, while the right-hand dirt road cuts along the wooded slopes of Castillo Mallor (Mayor) and ends at the crumbling hamlet of Escuaín (1215m). A noticeboard at the roadhead plots the hamlet's depopulation, a history that has been duplicated in many remote villages along the Spanish side of the Pyrenean chain, and especially here in Sobrarbe. In 1850 Escuaín had 138 inhabitants. By 1960 it was completely deserted, then in 1981 one person lived there alone, but by 1991 the population had risen to three. In the early summer of 2000 a solitary goatherder was in residence.

◗ Several walking options converge here, among them GR15 on its way from Bestué to Estaronillo and Tella. One possibility is to take a track which strikes northwest above the *gargantas* and in a little under 2hrs reaches the Puente de los Mallos in the upper Rio Yaga, where you can either continue up into the Circo de Gurrundué, visit the Foratarruego *refugio*, take an alternative path heading southeast to Revilla or return to Escuaín on a trail through the gorge itself. The same track leading to the Mallos bridge has a path breaking from it (at the Mallos fork) which goes to the Cuello Viceto in about 3hrs, from where one can join a good path descending into the Añisclo canyon by way of the San Vicenda *refugio*. Should you choose to take this option and descend the canyon to the road just below San Urbéz (see 2:14 above), 6–6½hrs should be allowed for the full walk from Escuaín.

◗ The Escuaín gorge trail begins in the hamlet itself and heads upstream along the west bank all the way, providing access to the main canyoning area – a delight of cascades, pools and water chutes. Wetsuits and ropes are a must for anyone taking part in this activity. The GR15 trail, however, descends steeply southeast of Escuaín, crosses the gorge and its confluence with the Barranco Consusa, and climbs up to Revilla, about 1½–2hrs from Escuaín. From there further explorations are possible.

Perhaps the best map to use is the 1:40,000 *Ordesa and Monte Perdido National Park* sheet published by Editorial Pirineo of Huesca, which is accompanied by a slim guidebook with English text.

2:16 VALLE DE PINETA

As we have seen, Monte Perdido is a dominating presence over virtually the whole national park area. It forms a natural headwall to the Valle de Ordesa, stands almost side-on to the Valle de Añisclo, and looms large with Soum de Ramond above the mysterious upper reaches of the Valle de Tella. As for the Valle de Pineta, the park's easternmost valley, this too is blocked by Perdido, the so-called 'lost mountain' whose slopes give birth to the Rio Cinca.

In truth it is only the uppermost reaches of this valley that belong to the *parque nacional*, but if grace of form and scenic beauty were the only criteria for inclusion, practically its whole 15km length as far as Bielsa would enjoy protection. It's a classic U-shaped, glacier-carved valley, whose bed is an exquisite blend of park-like meadows, lines of dappled trees, and a milky-blue river flanked on either side by abrupt limestone walls down which spray numerous cascades. The right-hand wall is that of the Sierra de las Tucas, uninterrupted by any tributary glen throughout its length, while the opposing flank of the Sierra de Espierba has the delightful hanging valley of Lalarri between it and the Circo de Pineta.

The Pineta Cirque supports the Balcón de Pineta, a stony wasteland of sun-bleached rocks and boulders and ancient moraines, the debris of Perdido's fast-disappearing glaciers, whose remnants hang in two tiers on the mountain's Northeast Face. The *balcón* pushes against the frontier crest, whose summits range between 2800m and 3200m, and in which the 2660m Brecha de Tucarroya (Brèche de Tuquerouye) offers a convenient scrambler's way across the mountains to France. Immediately below this cleft on the *balcón* side lies the Lago Helado de Marboré, its waters a vivid blue in mid-summer, but flecked with ice for some time after the spring thaw has cleared most of the surrounding snows. West of the lake, where the frontier ridge makes a sharp southward bend, the higher Cuello de Astazu (Col d'Astazou) is another cross-border option with an awesome view of the Cirque de Gavarnie as a reward.

At the valley's outflow stands the little township of **BIELSA**, just 13km from the road tunnel which pushes through the mountains to France. Thanks to this convenient road link Bielsa is on the must-visit list of cross-border day-trippers, but fortunately not all its commerce is cheap booze and tacky souvenirs, for parts of the town retain a refreshing indifference to this passing trade and cling to a more traditional mountain-based identity. A stronghold of the Republican cause during the Spanish Civil War, it finally fell in June 1938 to the Nationalists who left Bielsa in flames. The porticoed

Valle de Pineta stretches 15km from Monte Perdido to Bielsa

town hall, church and bridge are about all of the old township that remain from this unhappy era.

For the walker, climber or cross-country ski enthusiast with ambitions to explore the Valle de Pineta and its mountains, Bielsa can supply most needs. It has a national park/tourist information office (☎ 974 50 11 27) open in summer only, a few shops stocking provisions for the hills, and accommodation in the three-star Hotel Bielsa, Hotel Valle de Pineta and several *hostals*. Halfway along the valley there's a busy wardened campsite, Camping Pineta, with a small supermarket attached, and on the right bank of the Cinca near the roadhead is a low-priced, limited-facilities camping area with easy access to some of the valley's best walking. Between these two campsites the road passes just above the 73-bed **Refugio de Pineta**, run by the Federació Aragonesa de Montañismo, open all year with meals provision (☎ 974 50 12 03), while at the roadhead the luxury Parador Nacional de Monte Perdido offers its guests gourmet meals and marvellous views.

- ◗★ A short distance beyond the *parador* the Rio Lalarri spills down the northern hillside in a series of cascades. A jeep track (no private vehicles allowed) swings round the head of the valley from the parking area on the west bank of the Cinca, crosses the Rio Lalarri then loops up the hillside to enter the **Llanos de Lalarri** in a very pleasant pastoral valley worth exploring. Two paths that begin by the *parador* suggest steep alternatives to walking along this rough track, which is used by the GR11: one climbs alongside the cascades to join the track where it crosses beside a waterfall at about 1500m; the other is more demanding and

The hanging valley of Llanos de Lalarri is a major tributary of the Pineta

comes onto the same track but much higher. Having entered this tributary glen near a small shepherd's *cabaña* (1–1½hrs, depending on route taken), it's worth going up onto a nearby hillock, starred with gentians in springtime, that makes a magnificent vantage point from which to study Monte Perdido, the Circo de Pineta and the valley itself more than 300m below.

The Lalarri glen is a grassy hanging valley that runs parallel with the frontier ridge. A little over 2km beyond the shepherd's *cabaña* it makes a sharp right-hand curve to the headwall of the **Circo de la Munia**, whose basin contains two lakes, backed by the 3003m Pico Robiñera (Pic de la Louseras). This is splendid country, easily reached in about 3hrs from the *parador*, and with opportunities to continue either north with an undemanding ascent of **Pic de la Munia** (3133m) by way of the col of the same name in another 2hrs, or south to the Cuello de las Puertas, and northeast from there along the crest to the summit of **Pico Robiñera** (1½-2hrs from the lakes).

* ◓ The **GR11** stage which journeys between the Circo de Pineta and Parzán in the mouth of the Rio Real's valley breaks away from the Lalarri glen just beyond the *cabaña* and climbs to the Collado de Pietramula in another 2½hrs. By this route the upper reaches of the Rio Real can be gained by a zigzag descent, with a track on the left bank that carries the GR11 all the way down to **CHISAGÜÉS**, a small village which seems to hang from the steep slope, and then to **PARZÁN**, just off the main road. This is a walk of 5½hrs from the *parador*. Note that there is no certainty of accommodation in either Chisagüés or Parzán, and Bielsa lies another 3.5km to the south.

On the south side of the Valle de Pineta the GR11 has one of its toughest sections (for trekkers heading west), where it climbs out of the valley for nearly 1200m to reach **Collado de Añisclo** on a 9hr stage to Refugio de Góriz. The way is marked from both the Refugio de Pineta and the Ermita de la Virgen de Pineta (shown on the EA map as the Capella de Nuestra Señora de Pineta) near the *parador*. It's an uncompromisingly steep ascent that should not be attempted unless either the route is snow free, or ice axe and crampons are to be used. About 500m below the Añisclo col the route is joined by the **Faja de la Tormosa**, a scenic belvedere trail that runs along the mountainside at around the 1900m contour between the GR11 route and the Circo de Pineta – at the cirque end the way is signed by a bridge near the Cascada del Cinca.

The Cascada del Cinca is particularly impressive when boosted by snowmelt from the **Balcón de Pineta**, and is clearly seen from the valley floor as you approach the upper meadows. The stony jeep track mentioned above which loops round the headwall from the parking area on the west bank of the Cinca crosses just below the cascada, and a few paces beyond the bridge a path leaves the track for a steep climb to the *balcón*. The gradient and height gain is similar to that of the GR11 route to Collado de Añisclo, and it is also by this strenuous trail that the *faja* is reached. From valley to *balcón* takes 3–4hrs, and views down the length of the Valle de Pineta are tremendous, making it worth the climb for these alone. But Pineta views form only part of the *balcón's* appeal. By continuing across the wilderness of rocks and boulders towards the frontier ridge, the great Northeast Face of Monte Perdido grows in stature to the left. No wonder Ramond de Carbonnières was filled with awe when he first gazed on the scene from the ridge above in 1797: 'It signified nothing that I had seen it a hundred times at a distance; it appeared to me more fantastic than ever', he wrote. 'The Cylindre and Mont Perdu towering up into a stormy sky, and that rocky, naked, and rugged enclosure, from one of the battlements of which we were contemplating the most imposing and frightful scene in the Pyrenees; all and everything defied comparison.' Between Cilindro de Marboré (Le Cylindre) and Monte Perdido the 3074m saddle of the Cuello del Cilindro suggests a way of crossing the massif to Refugio de Góriz and the Valle de Ordesa; but note that ice axe and crampons are usually needed for this, as the ascent crosses glacier ice and a snowfield.

CLIMBS FROM THE VALLE DE PINETA

The main focus of attention is, understandably, **Monte Perdido** itself. While the *voie normale* from the Góriz hut is tackled by all and sundry, the face which looks out over the Balcón de Pineta is far more formidable. This Northeast Face provides the mountain with the stature it deserves, for it is hung with glacial tiers undercut by seracs and

Monte Perdido, northwest face, in the early 1970s – today the glacial tiers are shrinking fast

bands of rock, and is topped by a long ridge of bare limestone which directs the eye to the 3355m summit dome. A PD route climbs immediately to the right of the seracs that support the lower glacier, and by way of successive rock bands leads onto a snowfield below the Cuello del Cilindro. ❶ After crossing the col, the way then veers left up steep but non-technical slopes to the summit – about 3½hrs from the *balcón*. A more direct route up the nearby 900m North Face, now graded AD (4hrs), was put up in 1888 by Roger de Monts, Célestin Passet and François Bernard Salles when the glacier was much more extensive than it is today. Their route, now adopted as a winter or spring expedition, takes a line up the left-hand edge of the glacier to avoid the serac barriers and gives onto the East Ridge just below the summit, while in March 1993 Patrick Gabarrou and Paschal Girault created a variation, the *North Face Direct*, which confronts the seracs head-on and then climbs directly to the summit – a line best attempted between December and May.

Further round, between Perdido and Soum de Ramond, the ❶ *Esparrets Buttress* is clearly seen from the Valle de Pineta, a great upthrusting sweep of rock that from below blocks from view the icefields of the North Face. The Ravier brothers climbed the 800m of this in 1973, creating a D+ route (individual passages of IV+ and V) that is now also tackled in winter.

To the right of Perdido stands the **Cilindro de Marboré**, whose North and Northeast Faces hold some exacting lines of around 150–200m on their bare uppermost walls. ❶ On the first of these a TD+ (V/V+, A2) route, though only 150m long, takes about 7hrs to climb. This is another Ravier creation, climbed with Marcel Kahn in September 1964, while on the Northeast Face Bescos and Montaner pushed a TD line (IV+/V+) on quality rock in 1957.

2:17 VALLE DE BARROSA

North of Bielsa the main road rises towards the frontier mountains alongside the Rio Barrosa, passing the valley of the Rio Real on the left, then on the right the Valle de Urdiceto, which leads the GR11 and an HRP *variante* to the Posets massif. And finally, the highest valley in this section, that of the Barrosa itself, breaks into the western mountains just 3km short of the Bielsa tunnel.

There's a small amount of parking space at the entrance to this valley. There is neither village nor hamlet within its confines, only a cluster of stone buildings where the river breaks into the main Valle de Bielsa, from where a teasing view gives a hint of the glen's lonely charm. At its head rises the abrupt arc of the Circo de Barrosa, whose headwall, known here as the Sierra Morena, carries the frontier ridge, with Pic de la Munia, its highest point, being just one of several 3000m summits in this headwall. On the northern side of the frontier ridge the back-to-back cirques of Troumouse and Barroude counter-balance the little amphitheatres of La Munia and Pinarra, which flank that of Barrosa on either side.

◓ The Cirque de Barroude is accessible from here by way of the 2535m Puerto de Barrosa. This crossing is adopted by the HRP *variante*, a splendid day's trek that journeys the length of the Barrosa valley. By following this route upstream, first on a track, then on a mountain trail, the delights of the glen can be sampled without undue effort.

ACCESS, BASES, MAPS AND GUIDES

Access

Vallée du Gave de Pau N21 south from Lourdes. Main-line trains from Paris to Lourdes. By bus from Lourdes to Luz-St-Sauveur and Gavarnie.

Vallée d'Arrens D918 from Argelès-Gazost. Bus from Lourdes to Argelès Gazost and Arrens-Marsous.

Vallée de Cauterets D920 from Pierrefitte-Nestalas. SNCF bus direct from Lourdes to Cauterets.

Vallée de Bastan D918 from Luz-St-Sauveur to Barèges and Col du Tourmalet. By SNCF bus from Pierrefitte-Nestalas or Luz to Barèges.

Valle de Ordesa N260 from either Biescas or Ainsa with a short spur to Torla. By bus from Sabiñánigo or Ainsa to Torla.

Valle de Añisclo HU631, a minor road which breaks east of N260 at Sarvisé, and west of Valle de Bielsa at Escalona.

Valle de Pineta N640, 11km south of the Bielsa road tunnel. The nearest bus route in Spain ends at Ainsa, 33km to the south.

Valley Bases

Vallée du Gave de Pau Argelès-Gazost, Luz-St-Sauveur, Gédre, Gavarnie

Vallée d'Arrens Arrens-Marsous

Vallée de Cauterets Cauterets

Vallée de Bastan Barèges

Valle de Ordesa Torla

Valle de Pineta Bielsa

Huts

Several mountain huts, both staffed and unmanned, are found in the more popular upper valleys on the French side of the frontier, owned by the CAF or PNP authorities. There are only two wardened *refugios* on the Spanish slopes included in this chapter, Refugio de Góriz, above Ordesa, and Refugio de Pineta in the Valle de Pineta. Details are given in the text.

Maps

IGN Top 25: 1647 OT *Vignemale, Ossau, Arrens*, 1748 OT *Gavarnie*, and 1748 ET *Néouvielle, Vallée d'Aure*, 1:25,000

Carte de Randonnées 4 *Bigorre*, 1:50,000

Editorial Alpina *Vignemale Bujaruelo,* 1:30,000, and *Ordesa y Monte Perdido,* 1:40,000

Editorial Pirineo *Ordesa and Monte Perdido National Park* at 1:40,000

Walking and/or Trekking Guides

Walks and Climbs in the Pyrenees by Kev Reynolds (Cicerone Press, 5th edn, 2008)

100 Walks in the French Pyrenees by Terry Marsh (Hodder & Stoughton, 1992)

The GR10 Trail by Paul Lucia (Cicerone Press, 2003)

Through the Spanish Pyrenees: GR11 by Paul Lucia (Cicerone Press, 4th edn, 2008)

Trekking in the Pyrenees by Douglas Streatfeild-James (Trailblazer, 3rd edn, 2005)

The Pyrenean Haute Route by Ton Joosten (Cicerone Press, 2nd Edn, 2009)

Trekking in Spain by Marc Dubin (Lonely Planet, 1990)

Walking in Spain by Miles Roddis *et al* (Lonely Planet, 2nd edn, 1999)

Pyrenees West and *Pyrenees Central* by Arthur Battagel (West Col, 1988, 1989)

100 Randonnées dans les Hautes-Pyrénées by Georges Véron (Rando Editions, 1991)

Le Guide Rando – Vignemale-Balaïtous by Georges Véron (Rando Editions)

Le Guide Rando – Gavarnie-Luz by Michel Record (Rando Editions)

Le Guide Rando – Néouvielle by G. Caubet, J.F. Dutilh, J.P. Lafon (Rando Editions)

Les 50 Plus Belles Randonnées dans le Parc National des Pyrénées by Gérard Névery and Didier Castagnet (Rando Editions)

Climbing Guides

Rock Climbs in the Pyrenees by Derek L. Walker (Cicerone Press, 1990)

Passages Pyrénéens by Rainier Munsch, Christian Ravier and Rémi Thivel (Éditions du Pin à Crochets, 1999)

Pyrénées – Courses Mixtes, Neige et Glace by Francis Mousel (Éditions Franck Mercier, 1997)

Pyrénées Centrales I and II by Robert Ollivier (Ollivier/FFM, 1979)

Gavarnie Cascades de Glace by J. Paredes (Desnivel, 1995)

Pyrénées, Guide des 3000m by Luis Alejos (SUA Edizioak, 2003)

100 Sommets des Pyrénées by Georges Véron (Rando Editions, 2001)

See Also

Classic Walks in the Pyrenees by Kev Reynolds (Oxford Illustrated Press, 1991)

Long Distance Walks in the Pyrenees by Chris Townsend (Crowood Press, 1989)

Les Pyrénées – Les 100 Plus Belles Courses et Randonnées by Patrice de Bellefon (Editions Denoël, 1976)

Le Parc National des Pyrénées by Jean-François Labourie (Rando Editions)

Le Tour du Mont Perdu by Bernard Clos *et al* (Rando Editions)

Parcs Nationaux des Pyrénées by Bernard Clos (Éditions Jean-Marc de Faucompret/PNP, 1991)

CHAPTER 3: The Central Pyrenees

The Vallées d'Aure, Louron, Oô and Pique with their tributaries in France, and the high massifs of Posets and Maladeta in Spain

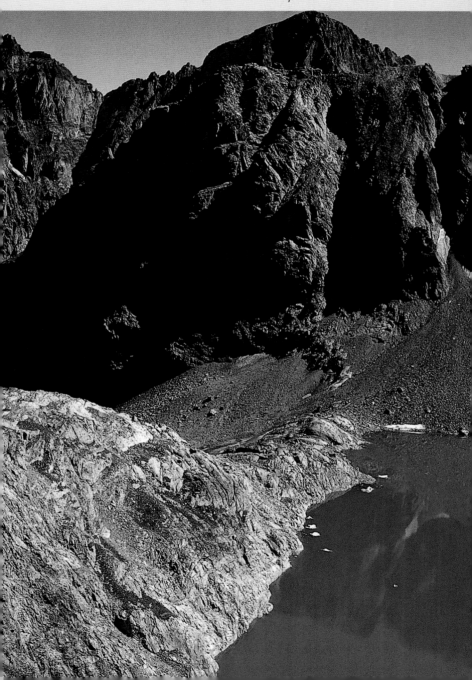

THE CENTRAL PYRENEES: CHAPTER SUMMARY

Location

In the very heart of the range where, on the northern side of the watershed, several high valleys drain into the Neste d'Aure, west of Col de Peyresourde, and, east of the col, to the Pique or Garonne in the Pays de Luchon. South of the watershed the major valleys are those of Gistaín and Benasque, flowing from the highest of all Pyrenean mountains.

★ Highlights

◎ WALKS
- in the Vallées du Louron (3:2) and Lys (3:4)
- in the vicinity of Lac d'Oô (3:3)
- from hut to hut in the Posets massif (3:5, 3:7, 3:8)
- in the Estós and Ésera valleys (3:8, 3:10)
- sections of the GR10, GR11 and HRP (3:1–3:10)

Ⓑ CLIMBS
- routes on assorted peaks in the Cirque d'Espingo (3:3)
- on and around Pico Posets (3:5, 3:7, 3:8)
- the Maladeta group (3:10)
- Pico de Aneto (3:10)
- Pico Forcanada (3:10)
- Tuc del Mig de la Tellada (3:10)

◉ SUMMITS FOR ALL
- Pico Posets (3:7)
- Pico de la Maladeta (3:10)
- Pico de Aneto (3:10)

Contents

CHAPTER 3
THE CENTRAL PYRENEES

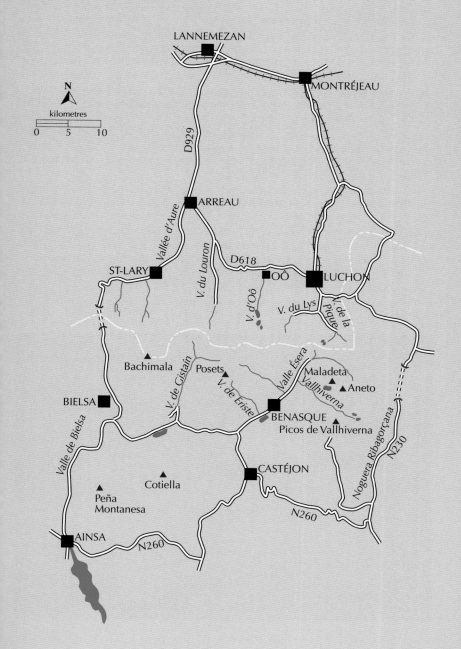

THE CENTRAL PYRENEES: INTRODUCTION

East of the Réserve Naturelle de Néouvielle all the more interesting and challenging mountains are either gathered astride of, or nudge close to, the international border. On the northern flank these are abrupt, rocky peaks that rise from largely bare, tarn-filled cirques, but the major summits on the Spanish side are found among big massifs wearing fast-shrinking glaciers, separated from the frontier crest by luxuriantly verdant valleys that flow parallel to that crest. There are more than 60 3000m peaks within this central region, including the two highest, Pico de Aneto (3414m) and Pico Posets (3375m), both of which project from extensive ridge systems that afford long expeditions of unquestionable appeal.

Granite dominates, yet outcrops of limestone also occur, and the Posets and Maladeta massifs reveal a mixture of both. But the valleys on both sides of the border are as memorable as the mountains. Among the meadows in late spring and early summer an abundance of alpine plants give credence to the Pyrenean epithet of Flower Garden of Europe, and the trails that work through these valleys and, in some cases, cross the passes that link one with another are among the most rewarding of all.

This central section of the High Pyrenees is surrounded by good roads. In France the Route des Pyrénées climbs out of the Vallée d'Aure at Arreau and crosses Col de Peyresourde to Luchon. In Spain the east–west N260 skirts the high mountains from Ainsa to the valley of the Noguera Ribagorçana, which forms the boundary between Aragón and Catalunya. At the western end the Bielsa road tunnel, which is open all year round, links both sides of the frontier, while at the eastern limit of this region the Viella tunnel at the head of the Noguera Ribagorçana provides access to the lower Vall d'Aran and France. On the French side of the mountains Bagnères de Luchon is the most important centre, while Benasque in the Spanish Valle del Ésera enjoys a perfect location on the edge of the Parque Natural Posets-Maladeta.

The Barroude lakes lie in a scoop below the walls of the Cirque de Barroude

3:1 VALLÉE D'AURE

Southeast of Tarbes the valley of the Neste d'Aure (*neste* is local dialect for 'river') spills out of the foothills at **LANNEMEZAN**, a small town near the junction of the main north–south D929 road and the east–west N117. It has a station on the important Pau–Tarbes–Toulouse railway line, and a useful bus service through the Vallée d'Aure as far as Aragnouet, just short of the Bielsa road tunnel. Lannemezan, then, is the key to a northerly approach. To obtain local information contact the Office du Tourisme on the Place de la République (☎ 05 62 98 08 31).

As far as Arreau, some 27km south of Lannemezan, the D929 passes along the eastern edge of the wooded foothill country of the Baronnies, a pear-shaped, damp and misty land, sparsely inhabited but strangely attractive without being scenically dramatic. **ARREAU** is the first place of any real importance, a pleasant slate-roofed, half-timbered little township at the confluence of the Neste d'Aure and Louron, and at the intersection of the D929 and Route des Pyrénées. Once the capital of the Pays de Quatre Vallées (those four valleys being the Aure, Magnoac, Neste and Barousse), Arreau has a fine medieval covered market place on the left bank of the Louron, and on the right bank the interesting Chapelle Saint-Exupère. In summer tourist information is found in the Château des Nestes (☎ 05 62 98 63 15), which also houses a **Pyrenean museum**. There are two hotels, the Angleterre and the more simple Hôtel de l'Arbizon, and three municipal campsites: one a little south of town; another, the Gentils at Pailhac, just 1km to the north (open April–Sept); and a third nearby, Camping Le Refuge, which is open all year.

Leaving Arreau, D929 continues south along the right bank of the river and soon passes through **CADÉAC**, where a curious rock arch squeezes the road. Bypassing **ANCIZAN**, which has a group of 16th-century houses that recall more prosperous times, the road crosses to the left bank and continues through cultivated land to **ST-LARY-SOULAN**.

In the 1950s St-Lary was developed as a ski resort, and now the pistes of **Pla d'Adet** and **Espiaube**, linked by gondola to the west of town, encroach right up to the boundary of the Réserve Naturelle de Néouvielle, where the highest lift reaches 2400m. (Pla d'Adet also has facilities for cross-country skiing.) In addition the town provides access for skiers to the extravagently modern resort of **Piau-Engaly**, 20km upvalley. In summer St-Lary has an agreeably bright and sunny appearance, but activists using it as a base for a walking or climbing holiday would be advised to have their own transport. As for accommodation, there are two local campsites, plenty of two- and three-star hotels, the one-star Hôtel Pons Le Dahu, and a 46-place *gîte d'étape*, Le Refuge (☎ 05 62 39 46 81), at the Pla d'Adet *téléphérique* station. The tourist office is situated at 37 rue Principale (☎ 05 62 39 50 81), and there's also a separate Maison du Parc with interesting displays and publications relating to the PNP. St-Lary has a number of shops catering to the outdoor enthusiast, a few restaurants, banks and a post office.

The nearby village Although there's no longer a *gîte d'étape* here, there are several *chambres d'hôte*, a two-star hotel on the road to St-Lary, and a tourist office in the heart of the village (☎ 05 62 39 56 90, www.vielleaure.com). Heading west the GR10 climbs onto a grassy spur leading to the Col de Portet and the Espiaube ski grounds on the edge of the Néouvielle *réserve* (6–7hrs from Vielle-Aure to Refuge de Bastan; see 2:9), while the eastbound route crosses the Vallée d'Aure and works its way up the eastern hillside through **AZET** (*gîte*), an attractive village with a fine view over the valley, then crosses the Col de Peyrefite before dropping into the Vallée du Louron in 3½hrs (see 3:2).

WALKS IN THE VALLÉE DE RIOUMAJOU

Beyond St-Lary the valley narrows to a gorge, and in a little less than 4km a minor road cuts back to the left and climbs into the small, huddled village of **TRAMEZAÏGUES**, which guards the entrance to the **Vallée de Rioumajou**. This is a glorious, heavily wooded tributary valley drained by a lovely mountain stream and protected as a *site classé*. A narrow paved road intrudes for 8km beyond Tramezaïgues to a small parking area and *aire du bivouac* near the *granges*, or barns, of Frédancon. Beyond that a track continues for another 4km as far as the ancient **Hospice de Rioumajou** at 1560m. In the 19th century Henry Russell described it as 'an execrable inn ... where I dine on milk soup'. There were no beds and he had to sleep in the hay. 'But what a marvellous place to spend a week in,' he continued,

Trekkers on a variante of the Pyrenean High Route descend to the Rioumajou

'if only there were an inn!' Although the hospice was renovated in the late 1980s/early 1990s, with plans to provide overnight accommodation for walkers and HRP trekkers, the scheme failed through a lack of electricity, so it is open only in summer for snacks and drinks, and closes each day at 6pm. Camping in the nearby meadows, however, appears to be tolerated, and is the only option for an overnight stay in the valley.

- Above and behind the hospice the frontier ridge curves in a deeply indented horseshoe of steep grass- and tree-covered slopes. Several walkers' passes breach the frontier ridge, and on the valley's eastern wall there are two 3000m summits, ⊗ **Pic de Lustou** (3023m) and **Pic de Batoua** (3034m), both of which may be reached without difficulty, the first in 4½–5hrs via Frédancon and the Col de Lustou northwest of the summit, the second by

A steep path climbs out of Rioumajou to the Port de Caouarère for a way into Spain

way of the 2526m Port de Cauarère in about 5hrs. The Posets massif looks tremendous from Pic de Batoua, while a ragged sea of peaks ranged ESE of Pic de Lustou makes this another exceptionally fine viewpoint.

The North Face of **❶ Pic de Batoua** contains a medium-grade winter climb (D with passages of 70°) of about 550m, which usually comes into condition between January and April.

- Southeast of the Hospice de Rioumajou, **◒ Port de Caouarère** is used by HRP trekkers on the stage leading to Refugio de Viadós at the base of the Posets massif (see 3:5). A remorseless 3hr climb among trees and shrubs, and up a final long slope of black scree and schist, brings you onto the pass, but the descent into the valley of the Cinqueta de la Pez (the upper Valle de Gistaín) and on to Viadós is a delight of grass-covered hillsides and alpenroses.

- South of the hospice the cirque projects into Spain at its deepest point on Pic d'Ourdissetou. Along the frontier ridge northwest of this peak lies the 2403m **◒ Port d'Ourdissetou**, by which trekkers can cross to **Lago Ordiceto** and the GR11. By bearing west along GR11 (a dirt road), Parzán or Bielsa could be reached within the day, while an HRP *variante* shared by the eastbound GR11 crosses the **Paso de los Caballos** (2326m) and in 6½–7hrs from Rioumajou reaches Viadós.

- On the western side of the Rioumajou Cirque the HRP climbs on steep slopes of crumbly schist and eventually gains the frontier crest at a vague pass below **◒ Pic de Lia**, where three ridges come together. The way then continues westward either on or just below the crest to reach Refuge de Barroude at the end of a very long and tough day's trekking.

- A somewhat less challenging, but no less rewarding, **◒** walk of about 4hrs in the lower Vallée de Rioumajou can be tackled about 2km from Tramezaïgues, where the road crosses to the east bank of the stream on Pont Tisné. Here a path zigzags up to the Cascade de Pichaleyt and continues climbing southeast along a line of cairns into the shallow valley of Hitte Longue above a *cabane*. At the head of this valley, below the Crête de Hitte Monte, the way crosses a spur and on the far side comes to the three **Lacs de Consaterre** (2349m), set close together in a grassy basin about 1100m above the valley.

WALKS IN THE VALLÉE DU MOUDANG

Beyond the Rioumajou turning the D929 continues through the narrows of the Vallée d'Aure, and in another 4km comes to the Pont de Moudang, with a campsite at the entrance to the **Vallée du Moudang**.

Shorter, though no less lovely than the Vallée de Rioumajou, Moudang is another charming wooded valley that opens to an attractive collection of shepherds' *cabanes*, the **Granges de Moudang** (1521m), a little over 5km from the main road. The broad track which pushes through the valley on the west bank of the stream is closed to unauthorised vehicles, but is worth walking along, for the upper valley is a delight of pastureland, streams and cascades.

From the huddled Granges de Moudang paths lead onto the frontier ridge

- At the *granges* (no accommodation), 1¾hrs from the valley entrance, the valley forks. The right branch cuts southwest and is drained by the Neste de Moudang; the left-hand option is that of the Neste de Chourrious, alongside which a ◐ path climbs to the 2495m **Port de Moudang** on the frontier ridge (2hrs from the *granges*). A route continues on the Spanish side of the pass descending southward into the valley of the Barranco de Trigoniero, which empties out into the Valle de Bielsa, roughly midway between the tunnel entrance and Parzán.

- Southwest of the *granges* the Neste du Moudang flows down through the Vallon de Héchempy. A ◐ path picks a way up this, keeping well above the stream's right bank, and divides below the frontier ridge. One option is to continue up to the **Port de Héchempy** (2450m, 2hrs), a little west of the pyramid of Pic de Marty Caberrou, to join the HRP along the ridge, while the alternative veers right and makes for the tiny **Lac de Héchempy** at 2305m (2½hrs). A third option is to turn left at Port de Héchempy and follow the route of the HRP round the north flank of Pic de Marty Caberrou as far as Port de Moudang, and then descend back to the Granges de Moudang through the steep valley of the Neste de Chourrious.

THE UPPER VALLÉE D'AURE

FABIAN sits at the confluence of the Neste d'Aragnouet and Neste de Couplan about 2km west of Pont de Moudang. It is here that D929 deserts the Vallée d'Aure and climbs north into a defile that winds up to the **Réserve Naturelle de Néouvielle**. The road was built for hydro-engineers at work harnessing the numerous lakes and streams of the area to produce electricity, but following the departure of the engineers an increasing number of tourists use this road to gain access to a wonderland of granite peaks, forests and lakes. In summer the road is open as far as Lac d'Orédon, and from there a *navette* operates a service deeper into the *réserve* as far as Lac d'Aubert. (For walks and climbs in the Néouvielle region, see 2:9.)

Beyond Fabian the Vallée d'Aure curves southwest, the road now being the D118, which climbs through **ARAGNOUET** (according to Packe the village is named after Aragónese migrants who settled here in the Middle Ages) before passing the restored 12th-century Chapelle des Templiers at **LE PLAN**, where the valley divides. To the south the main road sweeps up in a series of hairpins to gain the **Vallon de Saux** and the northern entrance to the Bielsa tunnel. The roadless valley ahead is the **Vallon de la Géla**, while that which forks right is the **Vallon de Badet**, where a secondary road climbs to the ski resort of Piau-Engaly.

PIAU-ENGALY claims to be the highest ski resort in the French Pyrenees, an ultra-modern, crescent-shaped development of apartment buildings at 1850m, with 21 lifts (the highest at 2500m) serving 37 pistes that appeal to both moderate and, with six black runs, experienced skiers. The resort enjoys an exceptional record for snowfall, and there's night skiing three times a week (for information, go to www.piau-engaly.com).

With the PNP boundary cautiously outlined to avoid the ski development, the **Vallon de Badet** curves south below Pic de Campbieil beyond Piau-Engaly, a valley carpeted with alpine flowers in the early summer when it's a relief to escape the bizarre out-of-place architecture and scarred pistes laid bare by a lack of snow. The Neste de Badet tumbles over a series of small cascades, marmots frolic in the meadows, and isard can often be spied on the hillsides. In the valley's upper basin at 2804m lies the tiny **Lac de Badet**, reached by a ◒ walk of about 1½hrs from Piau-Engaly. Nearby there's a simple unmanned hut. Above the lake, where the valley narrows under the summit of Pic de la Géla, cols in the ridge systems extending from that peak afford ways for walkers to cross into neighbouring valleys. To the east **Hourquette de Chermentas** (2439m) gives access to the Vallon de la Géla and Cirque de Barroude, while on the western side the 2608m **Hourquette de Héas** provides a way down to Héas, the Cirque de Troumouse and

Gèdre. These two cols are traversed by trekkers following the HRP and are described in 2:10.

- A third option for strong walkers is to cross ⬤**Port de Campbieil** in the ridge linking Pic de Campbieil with Pic des Aguillous (the latter now shown on maps as Soum des Salettes). The 2596m crossing of the valley's west wall leads to the twisting valley of the Campbieil stream, which flows roughly westward below spurs of Pic Long and its neighbours and eventually spills out at Gèdre in the Vallée du Gave de Pau. Should the idea of this long walk not appeal, the uncomplicated ascent of the 2976m ⬤ **Pic des Aguillous** from the pass rewards with a magnificent view of the cirques of Troumouse, Estaubé and Gavarnie, and with the distant Vignemale distinguished by its long glacial tongue. Monte Perdido is also seen to advantage from here. Allow 3½hrs from Piau-Engaly for this ascent.

More challenging routes can be found on the Pic des Aguillous, the first of these being on the ⬤ East Face (D), climbed in 1927 by Jean Arlaud and Gaston Fosset. Another was made on the imperfect rock of the Southeast Spur by Robert Ollivier when guiding a Mme Daudu in 1953. Reached by way of the Hourquette de Héas, this route is graded AD+ (III+), while a third alternative tackles the mountain from the south, above Héas. The *Voie Arruyer-Barrio-Ollivier* dates from 1936, is graded AD and involves about 900m of climbing.

The *voie normale* on **Pic de Campbieil** (3173m) from Lac de Cap de Long, described in 2:9, justifies its reputation as being one of the easiest routes on a 3000m peak. However, a more interesting and

Built by the PNP in 1974, Refuge de Barroude is a useful base for climbers and HRP trekkers

only slightly more difficult route, graded PD, ascends the Arête de Lentilla from Port de Campbieil in about 1½hrs, joining the *voie normale* shortly before the summit is gained.

WALKS AND CLIMBS IN THE CIRQUE DE BARROUDE

Above Le Plan d'Aragnouet, where the main road makes a tight hairpin to begin the final ascent to the Bielsa tunnel, a good path breaks away heading southwest to enter the **Vallon de la Géla**. Initially the path keeps to the true right bank of the Neste de la Géla, but after an hour crosses by a pair of simple *cabanes* to enter the national park, then climbs towards Pic de Gerbats, where it joins the trail of the HRP, swings left and comes down to the **Lacs** and **Refuge de Barroude** at 2373m. Built in 1974 by the PNP authorities and facing the impressive curve of the vast Barroude Wall, the tent-shaped refuge has 20 places (plus 10 in a seasonal annexe) and is staffed from July to mid-September (☎ 05 62 39 61 10). The setting is ideal. Grass-covered hillocks fold behind the refuge, separating the lakes that add much to the valley's appeal. A rising hump of shale to the south marks the Port de Barroude on the frontier ridge, the remnants of a dying glacier hug the lower slopes of Pic de Troumouse, while the banded limestone of the Muraille de Barroude itself spills an apron of scree towards the shoreline of the main lake.

Brief mention was made of this wall when describing the Vallée de Héas and Cirque de Troumouse in 2:10, but this major feature of the Cirque de Barroude deserves greater focus. As a venue for climbing the attraction is obvious. Backing the Cirque de Troumouse, the wall varies in height between 400m and 500m and is about 3.5km

Pic de Troumouse and the impressive Barroude Wall

long, reaching from Pic de Troumouse in the south to Pic de la Géla in the north. A number of fine lines were ticked off by the Ravier brothers in the 1950s and 60s, and these have since become local classics.

Working from south to north a sample of routes, of varying degrees of difficulty, begins with the logical crest-line ascent of **❶ Pic de Troumouse** (3085m), thought to have been taken during the mountain's first ascent in 1825. This PD *voie normale* starts at the Port de Barroude and follows the frontier ridge west as far as a *brèche*, then tackles the peak by way of a series of grooves, minor couloirs and a short chimney (II).

Then comes the Barroude Wall proper. Between Pic de Troumouse and Pic Heid, the unnamed **❷ Point 3028m** is gained by a 500m Ravier route dating from 1962 (ED-, V+/VI), while on **Petit Pic Blanc** (2957m) north of Pic Heid, Jean Ravier and his sister Lysette climbed the rather exposed *Central Buttress* (AD+, III/IV) in August 1957. Six years later came the 450m *Northeast Buttress* (J. & P. Ravier with Bernard Grenier), graded TD, with several passages of IV and one of V.

Pic de Gerbats (2904m) acts as a giant hinge where the Barroude Wall begins to angle NNE towards Pic de la Géla. On its East Face there's a meandering line created in 1952 by the Ravier twins with X Defos du Rau (AD, III), which comes onto the crest of the wall a little south of the summit. And finally, in this brief survey, the wall ends with **❸ Pic de la Géla**, whose classic line is the *Couloir de Barroude* (AD, with one passage of IV), first climbed in the summer of 1960 by Jean and Pierre Ravier with François Rouzaud, and repeated under winter conditions in December 1979 by the brothers from Bordeaux with Christian and François Ravier and Bernard Chaussade. As a winter climb it's best tackled between January and April, with a descent by way of the Hourquette de Chermentas.

- Although the abrupt wall may be beyond the ambitions of most mountain walkers, a group of minor summits that make worthy viewpoints on and around the frontier ridge southeast of the refuge can be collected without resorting to climbing techniques. First go up to the **◗ Port de Barroude** (2534m) in about 40mins to gain a spectacular view of the Cirque de Barroude, and south into the depths of the Circo de Barrosa where a *variante* of the HRP descends to the Valle de Bielsa. From the saddle follow the frontier round to the east, then cut along the Spanish flank to join a ridge-spur projecting southeast to the 2746m **Pico de Barrosa** (40mins from Port de Barroude). Return to the frontier ridge in 20mins, cross the unremarkable bald crown of **Soum de Barroude** (2674m) and continue north to **Pic de Port-Vieux** at 2723m in another 20mins. Either return along the frontier ridge to Port de Barroude and descend to the refuge in an hour, or descend the steep grass slopes of the Spanish side of Pic de Port-Vieux for about 200m, then make a northeasterly traverse to regain the ridge near Port Vieux (2378m). From there it's possible to descend either to the Vallon de la Géla or into Spain, where a path leads to the southern end of the Bielsa road tunnel.

TOWARDS THE FRONTIER

The last tributary to feed into the Vallée d'Aure comes down through the **Vallon de Saux**, which since the 1970s has been dominated by the 3km-long Bielsa tunnel. Before this was built a cross-border route went over the narrow, rock-guarded but easy Port de Bielsa (2429m) for an 8hr trek from Aragnouet to Bielsa, but that has long since fallen out of favour. Year-round traffic has rather devalued this short valley, although in winter it is known for a wealth of excellent middle-grade **icefalls** located towards the tunnel entrance.

On the east side of the road, about 1500m south of the customs post, a **ⓑ** group of three-pitch icefalls make a fine introduction. Higher up, **Pic de Garlitz** has routes of up to 300m in length, while close to the tunnel itself there are a number of short but demanding climbs. Thanks to their altitude and situation, conditions are often superb.

3:2 VALLÉE DU LOURON

ARREAU is now bypassed by the Route des Pyrénées which climbs above the town heading southeast to Col de Peyresourde. At first the road eases up the valley of the Neste du Louron between wooded slopes, and about 5km from Arreau comes to **BORDÈRES-LOURON**, where the Maison du tourisme de la Vallée du Louron is located (open summer only, Mon–Sat, ☎ 05 62 98 64 12). In another 4km, at the entrance to **AVAJAN**, the D618 begins to angle across the eastern hillside above the valley floor, while a minor road, D25, goes through Avajan, past its small lake and campsite and into an open basin dotted with villages, several of which are noted for their intricately painted Romanesque churches. (Contact the tourist office in Bordères-Louron for information about these churches and for details of access.)

A little over 3km south of Avajan a larger and extremely attractive lake used for a variety of water sports stretches across the valley floor. **GÉNOS** enjoys a privileged position on the northwest shore, its 15th-century church and ruins of a 13th-century castle standing on a nearby bluff. A path leads up to the ruins, where a pleasing view shows the valley stretching ahead to a backdrop of mountains, while a minor road twists southwest from the village to the modest ski station of **Val Louron**. With its highest lift only reaching 2100m, snow conditions are not dependable, but there are 20 downhill pistes and 15km of nordic (cross-country) trails.

Overlooking Lac de Génos-Loudenvielle from the east, the hamlet of **ARANVIELLE** has a *gîte d'étape*, the Auberge des Isclóts (☎ 05 62 99 66 21), with 24 places in dormitories and rooms. Just

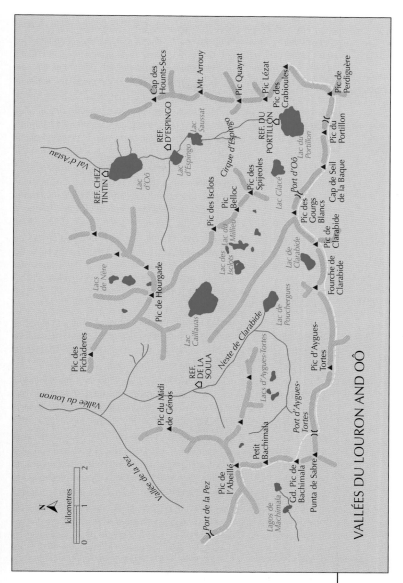

VALLÉES DU LOURON AND OÔ

beyond the lake's southern end, and reached by bus from Arreau, **LOUDENVIELLE** is the last of the Vallée du Louron's villages. A trim, pleasant little place on the route of GR10, in the past it made a reasonable base for a few days of a walking holiday. Sadly, there's no longer any accommodation to be had here, and the only facilities that remain are the campsite, a shop and an ATM. But modest walks abound in and on the walling slopes of the valley, and more challenging outings may be had among the mountains further south.

From the village a 40min walk along GR10 heading up the eastern hillside leads to **GERM**, another hamlet, where a busy 45-place *gîte*, the Centre de Montagne, has a swimming pool and restaurant (☎ 05 62 99 65 27) – booking recommended. From here GR10 veers south along a track, then cuts off on a footpath that contours for a while before rising to the 2131m **Couret d'Esquierry**, a col which marks the border between the *départements* of Hautes-Pyrénées and Haute-Garonne. On the east side of the ridge the path sweeps down among flowery hillsides to the Vallée d'Oô, where there's another *gîte d'étape* at the Granges d'Astau (see 3:3 below), about 4–4½hrs from Germ.

South of Loudenvielle the Vallée du Louron remains broad and flat-bottomed for a few more kilometres, with several traditional *granges* among the hay meadows. But after 6.5km the narrow road, which keeps to the east side of the stream, comes to a small car park at **Pont du Prat** (1229m) near the Tramezaygues power station, and it is this roadhead that marks the start of a number of expeditions.

Towering above the power station, the pointed Pic du Midi de Génos (2445m) separates the Vallée de la Pez from the Gorges du Clarabide. *Variantes* of the HRP traverse both these valleys. At the head of the Vallée de la Pez on the frontier ridge the 2451m **Port de la Pez** (3½hrs) suggests a long way over the mountains to either Plan de Gistaín or Viadós, while the southeast alternative offers a full day's trek (7½–8hrs) across the 2683m **Port d'Aygues-Tortes**, also to Viadós, and an equally long day's crossing of **Port de Clarabide** (2615m) to the Estós *refugio* beneath Pico Posets.

At the head of the deep Clarabide gorges stands the 60-place **Refuge de la Soula** at 1690m, reached in 2hrs from the roadhead. The refuge was built as part of the La Soula hydro-electricity scheme, and is open with a guardian from June to the end of September (☎ 06 16 85 68 66, www.refugelasoula.com). From it a ★ variety of outings can be made. One path continues alongside the Neste de Clarabide and curves up into the Aygues-Tortes valley under the frontier ridge, where a few small lakes lie in a rugged terrain. A cairned route leads out of this valley up to the Port d'Aygues-Tortes, southeast of Grand Pic de Bachimala (Pic Schrader), for the descent into Spain mentioned above. Another option on the way up to the Vallon d'Aygues-Tortes breaks away to the left by a small metal shelter and heads northeast to the lovely Lac de Pouchergues, then returns to the refuge.

- For a good but demanding ◓★ day-long (6½hr) **lake circuit**, take the path winding eastward from the refuge and climb up to the dammed Lac Caillauas, trapped in a huge basin below Pic de Hourgade at 2158m. This is reached about 1¼hrs from the hut. Continue rising southeast for another 40mins to find the smaller Lac des Isclots (2390m), noted for its little island, then pass to the right of Lac du Milieu. The right-hand ridge that projects from Pic des Gourgs Blancs, the Crête de Quartau, now has to be crossed, and this is achieved by way of the 2718m Col de Pouchergues, gained in a little over an hour from the Isclots tarn. Below to the south lies yet another lake, Lac de Clarabide, at the foot of a huge upward sweep of granite, the water often half-frozen well into summer. Descend towards the northern end of the lake in about 45mins, then swing northwest along sloping rock shelves until a grassy gully enables a descent to be made to the final lake of the walk, Lac de Pouchergues, from where a good path returns to Refuge de la Soula.

- Experienced trekkers, equipped with ice axe and, preferably, crampons too, could tackle the magnificent ◔ **crossing from Refuge de la Soula to Refuge d'Espingo** as adopted by a challenging HRP *variante*. This 7½hr stage crosses Col des Gourgs Blancs, a high (2877m) pass reached by way of a glacier on its west side, and with a steep and difficult descent on the east slope which should not be attempted in poor visibility. In good conditions the view of the Cirque d'Espingo from the col is tremendous.

CLIMBS FROM REFUGE DE LA SOULA

The **Grand Pic de Bachimala** (3174m) is the highest of a group of summits on the long north–south ridge that carries the international frontier southwest of the refuge. Also known as Pic Schrader, after the man who made its first ascent with Henri Passet in August 1878, it is generally considered to have one of the finest summit panoramas in the Pyrenees. On this summit the frontier briefly departs from the main ridge, which continues to Punta del Sabre (3136m) by flanking southeast to the Port d'Aygues-Tortes, while the East Ridge of **Punta del Sabre** is climbed by an interesting PD route which continues to the Bachimala in 2hrs from Port d'Aygues-Tortes. The Port is crossed by one of the *voies normale* which tackles the Grand Pic by way of the Southeast Face of Punta del Sabre, but an alternative *voie normale* ignores this approach and instead strikes northwest out of the Aygues-Tortes valley to gain the long northerly ridge of the massif at a point midway between Pic de l'Abeillé and the Petit Bachimala. The ridge is then followed south across the summit of **Petit Bachimala** to **Pointe Ledormeur** before topping out on the Grand Pic de Bachimala for a 5hr ascent from the hut.

Various other routes exist on the Grand Pic, including some that are mounted directly from the Spanish side of the frontier, either from a base at the Refugio de Viadós or from the unmanned Refugio de Tabernés in the Valle de Gistaín (the valley of the Cinqueta de la Pez – see 3:5). One of the best and longest expeditions tackles the 5km ridge between the Port de la Pez and Port d'Aygues-Tortes, the so-called ◑ **Crêtes du Bachimala** (PD), which collects eight 3000m summits and is a list-ticker's dream of a route.

Immediately north of the Lacs d'Aygues-Tortes rises **Pic Pétar** (2542m), the easternmost summit on a ridge extending out from Pic des Bacherets. This ridge in effect forms the north containing wall of the Vallon d'Aygues-Tortes, and provides a way of reaching Pic Pétar by angling northwest across its face to gain a saddle just west of the summit. From there the ridge is easily followed to the top.

The southern wall of the Vallon d'Aygues-Tortes, of course, carries the frontier. Of the several summits along the crest the 2873m ⊘ **Pic d'Aygues-Tortes** may be gained by a short F+ ridge-walk from Port d'Aygues-Cruces (2811m), which lies east of the peak and is easily gained from the *vallon*.

Further east along the frontier, where the crest thrusts forward, stands the elegant **Fourche de Clarabide** (2857m), an excellent viewpoint from which to study the Posets massif to the south, Pic de Hourgade to the north, the nearby Gourgs Blancs and more distant Maladeta in one direction, and Pic du Midi de Bigorre in the other. A PD- route ascends the mountain from Lac de Pouchergues and the Port de Clarabide, then via the frontier ridge, while a more serious route exists on the ❻ North Arête (D-, IV/A1), first climbed in 1949 by a large party which included Marcel Jolly. This route includes the crossing of the 2679m Aiguille de Clarabide.

Then come the **Pics de Clarabide**, above the cirque and *lac* of the same name. Of several routes here, the classic has to be the traverse of the ❻ **Arêtes de Clarabide** (PD+), first achieved solo in two expeditions (four years apart!) by Pierre Abadie, long-time climbing partner of Jean Arlaud. Abadie's route begins at the Port Superieur de Clarabide and ends with the Port de Gias, but in 1970 Jean, Pierre and Jacques Ravier, with J.-L. Anglade, created an AD-variation. Their route begins by tackling the East Pic directly from the north, and reverses the Abadie trend by heading southwest across the other summits and down to the Port Superieur for descent to the valley.

Commanding a junction of ridges, and flanked by Pointe Lourde-Rocheblave (3105m) and the 3065m Pic Jean Arlaud, the **Pic des Gourgs Blancs** (3129m) owes its name to the string of semi-frozen tarns that lie below to the northwest. The mountain received its first ascent in 1864 by the well-known team of Bazillac, de Monts, Russell and the great guide Célestin Passet. Their route, the *Voie Russell*, now graded PD, ascends past the tarns up to the Col des Gourgs Blancs, then flanks the mountain heading southwest to a couloir which leads up to the ridge west of Pointe Lourde-Rocheblave. Over this summit the way tackles some loose rocks (the cause of Jean Arlaud's death in 1938) before gaining the crown of Pic des Gourgs Blancs.

A recommended ❻ PD+ route here also attacks the mountain from Col des Gourgs Blancs but uses the North Ridge, broken by several couloirs that could confuse the ascent, since not all of them have easy exits. Care is required. Pic des Gourgs Blancs was first climbed by this ridge in August 1933 by Tony Cabuzet and Robert Ollivier.

Pic Jean Arlaud is usually climbed from either Refuge d'Espingo or Refuge du Portillon (see 3:3) via Port d'Oô, but the PD- *voie* *normale*, another Henry Russell/Célestin Passet route dating from 1852, approaches from the Col des Gourgs Blancs, so is worth the consideration of climbers based at Refuge de la Soula.

The foregoing routes provide merely a sample of climbs to be had from the La Soula refuge, but before leaving the head of the Vallée du Louron and moving east, mention should be made of the ⓑ South Face of **Pic de Hourgade**, which rises 800m above Lac Caillauas. In 1933 a party from Jean Arlaud's Groupe des Jeunes made the first ascent of this face, finding poor rock, but nevertheless they created a route which today is graded AD-, a climb of 3½–4hrs from the lake. Standing well back from the frontier crest, Hourgade's summit provides a tremendous grandstand from which to study a wealth of peaks spread out to the south. It's a great place on which to be inspired for a whole summer's climbing, and is a view that was first enjoyed by Henri Brulle and Célestin Passet in 1882.

FROM LOURON TO OÔ

As the D618 climbs above the Vallée du Louron and comes to the 1569m **Col de Peyresourde**, another road breaks away south to the ski resort of **PEYRAGUDES**, which has developed on either side of the Hautes-Pyrénées/Hautes-Garonne border crest. The resort is the result of twinning Peyresourde-Balestas on the Vallée du Louron flank with Les Agudes on the east side. There are 17 lifts and 40 ski runs (including three black and 12 red), and no less than 70 snow-making machines to make up for any shortage of natural powder. The top lift reaches 2400m, and the slopes which face northwest, north and east usually give reasonable conditions. In January each year a snowboarding competition takes place here, the Peyragudes Rider's Cup, and there's a variety of cross-country pistes too. (For information contact the Office de Tourisme, 31110 Les Agudes, ☎ 05 61 79 17 88.)

Descending now to the Vallée du Larboust and Bagnères de Luchon another minor road breaks away heading southwest to **GOUAUX-DE-LARBOUST** and Les Agudes, providing a very pleasant view over the Vallée d'Oô. Just beyond this turning, but still on D618, stands the first of the valley's three Romanesque churches, the 9th-century Chapelle St-Pé-de-la-Moraine, an interesting and historic place of worship largely built of Roman materials just outside the village of **TRITOUS**. Another 2km down the road brings you to **CAZEAUX-DE-LARBOUST**, whose church is decorated with a series of 15th-century frescoes, while that of the hillside village of **ST-AVENTIN**, some way further down towards Luchon, is the most famous of all – a 12th-century two-towered treasure worth spending time in. But of more interest to readers of this guide, at **CASTILLON-DE-LARBOUST**, between Cazeaux and St-Aventin, another road branching south leads into the lovely valley of the Neste d'Oô.

3:3 VALLÉE D'OÔ

The valley (see map, section 3:2) has been popular with visitors to Luchon for well over 200 years, thanks to the fame of the Lac d'Oô and its 273m-high waterfall, and no one should bother to go there for solitude in summer unless they're prepared to push on into the higher regions towards the frontier. Even then the peaks and two CAF huts that serve them are busy with local French climbers.

At first the valley is green and fertile and flanked by an ancient moraine. Ash and walnut trees add contrast to a scene of rugged back-drop mountains, and the slate-roofed village of **Oô** on a bend in the river offers accommodation at the Hotel-restaurant La Spijeoles. The road runs alongside the Neste d'Oô and ends 4km beyond the village at the **Granges d'Astau** (1139m), whose *gîte d'étape*, the Auberge d'Astau, has 16 places and is open from May to mid-October (☎ 05 61 79 35 63). There's a very busy bar-restaurant in an adjacent building and plenty of parking space nearby.

To the west, on the opposite side of the valley, a once-celebrated waterfall known as the Chevelure de la Madeleine marks the entrance to the **Val d'Esquierry**, which has long been noted for its abundant alpine flora. In fact the whole area surrounding Astau and the Lac d'Oô was so rich in plantlife that in the first (1862) edition of his *Guide to the Pyrenees* Charles Packe listed 117 different species, or sub-species, that he found there. So before moving south to focus on the higher mountains, it's worth noting the possibility of a full day's walk from Astau which climbs through the Val d'Esquierry, providing an opportunity to enjoy the rich plantlife along the way.

- ◓★ It takes about 2½hrs to ascend through the valley to the Couret (or Pas) d'Esquierry (2131m) at its head, following the route of the GR10 all the way. But on the west side of the ridge where that major route descends into the Val d'Aube, our walk trends south into a hanging valley (the Vallon de Nère) below the north side of Pic de Hourgade. Up there, in that hanging valley, are found the two **Lacs de Nère**. The first is reached about 45mins from the pass; the second, which lies at an altitude of about 2400m, is about 15mins further south. A third and much smaller tarn, the Lac Glacé de Nère, is trapped under the summit ridge at 2780m, but to reach this would require an additional hour's effort. Without climbing to this upper tarn you should allow about 6hrs for the round trip.

The South Face of ◉ **Pic de Hourgade** was mentioned as a climb (AD-) from Refuge de la Soula in section 3:2. However, the ungraded *voie normale* on this peak is made from the northwest, on the oppo-site side of the ridge (the Crête de Hourgade) that contains the Vallon de Nère, where yet another lake is found. This is Lac de Hourgade (2425m), reached in about 35mins from the Lacs Nère. Under normal conditions the ascent of Hourgade requires little more than 1½hrs of scrambling from the lake.

Back in the Vallée d'Oô it will be noted that the GR10 comes down through Val d'Esquierry from the Vallée du Louron, then heads south along the broad track from Astau, which climbs in another hour to **Lac d'Oô**. This path is walked by all and sundry, for the lake is one of the most celebrated sites in this corner of the Pyrenees. Packe described it as 'a deep dark basin of most cold clear water, fed by the ice streams from the mountains, and shut in on all sides except the north ... by precipitous rocks'. Not noted for colourful phrases, he was nonetheless moved to reflect that 'the most favourable time for appreciating this scene is on a fine summer's night, when the mountain tops gleam cold in the moonlight, and the twinkling stars are mirrored in the tremulous waters'.

It's possible to experience this night-time scene today, for above the northwest end of the lake, across the water from the cascade, on the site of a simple inn used as a base by Packe, Russell and other pioneers, stands the **Refuge Chez Tintin** (Refuge-Auberge du Lac), open from May to mid-October with 20 places (☎ 05 61 79 12 29).

The continuing path climbs above the eastern shore to gain the saddle of Col d'Espingo (1967m), where GR10 leaves the main path, doubles back to the left, then heads northeast to cross two cols on the way to Luchon. From the saddle **Refuge d'Espingo** is seen about 200m away to the right overlooking Lac d'Espingo, Val d'Arrouge and Pic de Hourgade. Owned by the CAF the hut can sleep 70 in its dormitories (20 in the winter room), and has a guardian from May to the end of October (☎ 05 61 79 20 01).

Refuge de Espingo is a perfect base for climbs on a variety of peaks

This, or Lac Saussat a little further south, is about as far as most day-trippers go, for the country ahead is quite clearly of another order. However, **Val d'Arrouge**, stretching west of Lac d'Espingo, can repay a visit. At its head the 2809m **Porte d'Arrouge** on the ridge south of Pic de Hourgade can be gained in 3hrs from the refuge, while another 30mins from the Porte leads to **Pic d'Arrouge** (2853m). There's one other summit easily attained from the Val d'Arrouge, **Pic de Leytarous** (2856m), climbed in about 3½hrs from the hut.

Further south, beyond Lac Saussat and above the Cirque d'Espingo, a host of abrupt granite peaks provide almost unlimited sport for climbers, while experienced mountain trekkers have a wonderland of lakes, ridge crests and high passes to enjoy. The following paragraphs offer a sample, using as a base either the Espingo hut or **Refuge du Portillon** (2560m), which was built 600m higher than, and almost 2hrs beyond, Espingo below the dammed Lac du Portillon. This refuge is also owned by the CAF, has 80 places and is manned from mid-June to mid-September (☎ 05 61 79 38 15).

TREKS AND CLIMBS FROM THE ESPINGO AND PORTILLON HUTS

Much of the path from Espingo to the Portillon refuge was paved with flat stone slabs in the 1930s during hydro work at the upper lake, so it is not a difficult route to follow, but the scenery grows increasingly wild the higher you go, with grey rock slabs and boulders stained here and there with lichens, and patches of snow and slender draperies of ice in shadowed corners. The trail passes alongside Lac Saussat and continues south, rising to an upper region before veering left towards Pic Quayrat, but an alternative path heads southwest under Pic des

Illustration from Packe's Guide to the Pyrenees (1862)

LAC DE PORTILLON D'OO

276

Spijeoles, making for Port d'Oô on the frontier crest above a hollow containing the jade-green Lac Glacé. Meanwhile, the Portillon trail rises below the west face of both Pics Quayrat and Lézat, scarred with gullies that fall to screes, while a bank of frontier peaks lined with remnant glaciers crowd the southern headwall.

Seil de la Baque and the frontier crest above Port d'Oô

Up here the frontier crest is breached in four places by high trekkers' passes. Naming from west to east, these are: **Port d'Oô** (2908m), **Portillon d'Oô** (2913m), **Col Supérieur de Litérole** (3049m) and the snow saddle of **Col Inférieur de Litérole** (2983m), which is adopted by a *variante* of the HRP. None of these passes is particularly difficult to reach from the French side, although there are often unstable rocks and screes to contend with, but each presents a long, and in places confusing, descent into Spain and should not be attempted by inexperienced trekkers. The first two lead down to the Valle de Estós, while the Litérole cols take routes east through the Valle de Remuñe to the Rio Ésera and the Maladeta massif.

West of the Refuge du Portillon and a little north of Port d'Oô, **Col des Gourgs Blancs** (see 3:2) provides a tough day's walk across the mountains to the Gourgs Blancs lakes, Lac Caillauas and Refuge de la Soula. But apart from these pass crossings, the non-climber is restricted in this high country to pottering around on bare glacial pavements, visiting Lac Glacé, making the ascent in about 1½hrs of the very fine viewpoint of the 2889m **Tusse de Montarqué** west of the Portillon hut, or going up to the easier summits that punctuate the frontier ridge. Among these ⊗ **Pic de Perdiguère** (3222m) will be high on the list, since it is not only the most elevated local summit, but counts as one of the highest of all the frontier peaks after the Vignemale and Pic du Marboré. The *voie normale* goes by way of the Portillon d'Oô in 2½–3hrs from the refuge.

The Portillon d'Oô also provides a short, moderate (30mins, PD) route to the summit of 3050m **Pic du Portillon d'Oô**, while this same peak has more difficult routes from the northeast (D+) and northwest (D-). Jean Arlaud, once again, was active here in 1934 with members of his Groupe des Jeunes and was responsible for creating the 250m *Voie Arlaud*.

From the Pic du Portillon the so-called **Crête du Portillon** runs west along the Franco-Spanish border to the **Pics du Seil de la Baque**. The traverse of this ridge is a semi-classic expedition dating from 1910 and is graded PD+ (III). But a **⑥** longer traverse in the opposite direction, starting with Pointe Lourde-Rocheblave and crossing Pic des Gourgs Blancs and Pic Jean Arlaud before reaching the Seil de la Baque and continuing to the Portillon d'Oô, makes an epic expedition some 3km long and graded AD-, which takes anything from 6–9hrs, depending on conditions. There are three summits to the Pics du Seil, the highest being the 3110m **Cap du Seil de la Baque**, whose first ascent was made in 1857 by Russell, Straefield and Firmin Barrau, who built a small cairn on the summit. The *voie normale* here is graded only F, approaching by way of the last vestige of the glacier which lies on the north slope, and after which the Cap takes its name (*seil* being the local dialect word for 'glacier').

At the western end of the frontier crest above the depression of the Port d'Oô (the Port is neither a distinctive cleft nor saddle) the 3065m **Pic Jean Arlaud**, formerly known as Pic du Port d'Oô, has a selection of PD routes that either begin at the Port itself or from the Col des Gourgs Blancs to the north, including the *voie normale* mentioned in 3:2.

Returning to the eastern end of the Franco-Spanish crest, a much more serious outing on a frontier peak above Refuge du Portillon is the TD- winter challenge of **⑥** *Goulotte Jean-Rémy* on the north-facing **Pic Royo**, whose 3121m summit is located midway between Pic de Perdiguère and Pic des Crabioules. This is a 200m mixed route put up in December 1994 by Pierre Satgé and André Vendoze, with passages of 70–80° and one of vertical water ice. The *Goulotte* would normally come into condition between December and February.

To the northeast the western **Pic des Crabioules** forms a cornerstone of the Portillon Cirque. There are, in fact, two summits of 3106m and 3116m which stand at either end of a narrow 50m ridge, the Northeast Face being the centre-piece of the Cirque des Crabioules at the head of the Vallée du Lys (see 3:4). Often climbed from Refuge du Maupas, the *voie normale* (the *Voie Mamy*), however, approaches from the Portillon refuge, goes up towards the Col Inférieur de Litérole, then slants left to the base of a couloir which leads without difficulty onto the summit (2½–3hrs from the hut).

From Pic des Crabioules a narrow ridge projects northwestward to separate the valleys of Oô and Lys. Crossing Pointe Mamy and Pointe Lacq, this ridge dips then climbs again over sudden little *gendarmes* and several minor tops before reaching **Pic Lézat** (3107m). Named after the geographer who made its first ascent in 1852, the western aspect of Pic Lézat contains several fine lines on granite of mixed quality. The **ⓑ★** *West Spur* (Cornelius/Grelier/Prada/Prunet, 1942; 350m, D, IV+/V) was chosen by Patrice de Bellefon as one of his 100 best routes, but the West Face is adorned with a variety of routes in assorted grades. The *Abadie-Arlaud Couloir* (D, with one passage of V) is a prime choice; the 300m *Grande Fissure Ouest* (AD+, IV/V) is another of Jean Arlaud's inspirations dating from 1933 that has become a modern winter classic. The Southwest Face above the Portillon refuge has several lines too, including the *SW Couloir* (the *Voie Comet*), located to the right of the West Spur and climbed in 1951 by F. and P. Comet, with Boy and Cazal (D, IV+/V+), and the PD+ *Couloir Schmidt* that emerges onto the Southwest Arête.

North of Pic Lézat, the **Lézat-Quayrat Crête**, although consisting of mediocre rock, is a 3hr traverse won by Henri Brulle and Célestin Passet in 1884. Tackled south–north this is graded PD+, but reckoned to be AD- in reverse. Midway along this ridge the 2905m **Brèche Quayrat-Lézat** is gained by an obvious couloir from the west (PD, III).

★Pic Quayrat (also known as the Grand Quayrat, 3060m) is a big granite pyramid climbed as long ago as 1788 by Reboul. With two summits and two faces of interest to climbers based at either Refuge d'Espingo or the Portillon hut, Quayrat is a prominent mountain with a powerful presence. The granite is generally good; the West Face is one of the major walls of the district and is crinkled with arêtes, while the smaller Southwest Face with its complex of chimneys also holds some challenging climbs. Understandably both faces continue to receive plenty of attention in winter as in summer; several routes have been made in the TD range, a few at ED, but many more with more modest grades.

The granite pyramid of Pic Quayrat (3060m), seen from the southwest

One example is the 500m *Couloir des Avalanches*, located at the left-hand end of the West Face. In summer, when snow-free, the couloir is graded PD. The rock is good, the route straightforward, and it emerges almost directly onto the summit. As a winter climb it is given an AD+ grade; a splendid route when in condition, but the couloir is aptly named and a misjudgement of conditions could have serious consequences.

Opposite Pic Quayrat, on the west side of the Cirque d'Espingo, **⑮ ★ Pic des Spijeoles** (3065m) is a serious rock climber's mountain boasting probably more routes than any other peak in the neighbourhood. Situated at the southeastern end of a wall of mountains that effectively separates the Gourgs Blancs valley from that of Espingo, the summit forms the apex of four tapering ridges whose outline makes a crooked letter X, thus creating several faces. The north side falls to the Val d'Arrouge, the west flank tips down to the lakes and pools of the Gourgs Blancs, the south side commands a view of the Port d'Oô, while the East Face consists of one of the major Pyrenean walls.

The ungraded *voie normale* on Pic des Spijeoles takes around 3½–4hrs from Refuge d'Espingo, and only a little less from the Portillon hut. If starting from Espingo, the paved footpath that leads to the Refuge du Portillon is taken as far as a bridge which carries the path across to the east bank of a stream high above Lac Saussat. About 20m before the bridge a cairn marks the point where you leave the path and then climb towards the frontier ridge, passing below the Spijeoles East Face and Southeast Arête. From the foot of this arête you head west to locate a chimney on the South Face. This, and a second chimney above it, form the route to the summit.

Though generally shorter than those on Pic Quayrat, more than a dozen quality climbs have been created on the East Face of Pic des Spijeoles, a big block of granite about 300m–350m high and outlined by the Northeast and Southeast arêtes. A distinguishing feature is the *Grand Dièdre* that splits the upper face left of the summit. It was first attempted by M. Parant, solo, in August 1946; climbed less than three weeks later by Céréza and Malus; and almost exactly a year after that, on 13 September 1947, the *Grand Dièdre* received its *intégrale* ascent from Beauchamp, Boy, F. and P. Comet, and J. Couzy. However, the first winter ascent of the *Grand Dièdre* had to wait until January 1964, when Philippe Sol and Claude Valleau spent two days on the face. The route is 300m long (350m to the summit) and graded D (IV+/V) in summer. As a winter route it goes at TD (50–70°). A little to the right of this, Dutoit and Rouzeau established a 350m *diretissima* (D-, IV/V) in the summer of 1966, but most of the major routes on this face are graded either TD or ED.

Before leaving Pic des Spijeoles and the Vallée d'Oô it is perhaps worth mentioning the hour-long traverse of the northwest arête which leads to ⊗ **Pic Belloc**, the neighbouring 3008m summit named after Emile Belloc (1841– 1914), one-time honorary president of the Central

Pyrenean section of the CAF. This route, graded PD-, makes an interesting extension to an ascent of Spijeoles, and is often tackled by list-tickers collecting the 3000m summits.

3:4 VALLÉE DE LA PIQUE

Continuing the descent from Col de Peyresourde, the D618 Route des Pyrénées passes the Vallée d'Oô's entrance at Castillon de Larboust, goes through St-Aventin and soon enters the Vallée de la Pique at **BAGNÈRES DE LUCHON**, sophisticated spa town, railhead, and one-time mountaineering centre, located almost precisely in the heart of the Pyrenees midway between the Atlantic and the Mediterranean.

This is how Packe described the town's appeal in 1862:

'Of all the watering places in the Pyrenees, Bagnères de Luchon is the one possessing most attractions, fully equalling Bagnères de Bigorre in the comforts and appliances of Parisian life, and far surpassing it in grandeur and beauty of the surrounding scenery. The tourist, although pressed for time, must make Luchon his headquarters for at least 10 days, a period which, with fine weather, may suffice for some of the principal excursions; but in a stay of 6 weeks he will not tire of it, and will not have seen all.'

Luchon has been described as the Chamonix of the Pyrenees, an unfortunate comparison which raises unfulfilled expectation in the first-time visitor. One Victorian traveller was not impressed, describing it as 'Chamonix without Mont Blanc … a place where guides are *rarae aves* and ice axes almost unknown.'

Almost a century and a half later Luchon retains Packe's intimated air of sophistication and gentility, especially at the upper end of the long central avenue of lime trees, the **Allées d'Etigny**, where the fancy villas and spa buildings face neat gardens replete with statues. Everyday life in the town is mostly centred around the Allées, where plenty of shops are situated. This is where you'll find bars and restaurants, the post office, banks and cash dispensers, the tourist office at number 18 (☎ 05 61 79 21 21) and, next door, the Bureau des Guides (☎ 05 61 79 69 38), from which a programme of walks, climbs and ski expeditions is offered, and climbing courses arranged. There's no shortage of ungraded and two- and three-star hotel accommodation, but the nearest *gîte d'étape*, the Skioura lies 3km further south on the way to Superbagnères along D125. This has 40 places and is open all year (☎ 05 61 79 60 59). In addition there are plenty of campsites, three of which are located side by side at the southern end of town.

The **railway station**, which also serves as the main bus stop, is on the northern outskirts of Luchon. An infrequent train service runs downvalley to Montréjeau on the Tarbes–Toulouse main line, from which connections with Paris are made. A limited number of trains run direct to Toulouse.

From personal experience it rains a lot in Luchon. The lush forests of the Pique valley would substantiate that claim too, so a visit to the local **Museé du Pays de Luchon** (also in the Allées d'Etigny) has value if you're left kicking your heels for an hour or two, if only to study the very fine three-dimensional relief model of the local mountains on display there. Made to a scale of 1:10,000 by Lézat in 1854, it was recommended by Packe and still has the ability to stir plans for the days ahead among new arrivals in town.

Packe wrote:

'The main charms of the place are its scenery, its delicious climate, and the many and beautiful excursions which are so easily made from this spot. The excursions ... may be made on foot, on horseback, by chaise à porteurs, and some few in carriages... To all the ordinary points of interest there is a well-marked track, quite practicable for horses, and this constitutes one of the principal drawbacks to the enjoyment of this exquisite scenery; for a noisy cavalcade of frivolous Frenchmen, who come galloping down the road, cracking their whips and hallooing, ill harmonises with the solitude and grandeur of the mountains.' (*Guide to Pyrenees*, Longman, Green, 1862)

Today there are few horses, but there's no shortage of motor traffic funnelling south through the narrows of the Vallée de la Pique, which 'ill harmonises with the solitude and grandeur of the mountains' as much as, or more than, the annoyances faced by Packe. Straying from the roadhead in the main summer season, the marked paths and tracks are very busy too, although it is possible here, as well as practically everywhere else in these mountains, to find solitude if that is what you seek.

In winter skiers gather on the local hilltop resort of **SUPERBAGNÈRES**, which at around 1800m is not really high enough to hold onto decent snow for long, although snow-making equipment is on hand. The highest skiing is at the 2260m Secteur du Céciré, where there's one black run and several long reds. (The chairlifts here also operate in summer.) Superbagnères has 15 lifts in all and runs to suit most abilities. The resort is reached by *télécabine* from Luchon or by 17km of twisting road served by ski-bus during the winter season.

While the main D618 crosses the Pique a little south of the Allées d'Etigny, then heads east towards the low Col du Portillon on the Franco-Spanish border, the D125 pushes deeper into the Vallée de la Pique below Superbagnères and forks 5km from town. The route to the Hospice de France takes the left branch, while the right-hand option is the road for Superbagnères and the Vallée du Lys.

Luchon Guides in the 19th Century

By the mid-19th century Luchon was enjoying its dual role as spa resort and centre for the cautiously adventurous tourist, as well as attracting serious mountaineers. With the Maladeta just across the border to the south and no shortage of outings close by the local guides, dressed in a pretence of 'traditional' Pyrenean costume, found employment for themselves that ranged from accompanying the well-heeled but physically delicate to such tourist hot-spots as Lac d'Oô and the Hospice de France to more demanding explorations on glacier peaks in nearby Spain. By and large this diversity of excursions did little to further the cause of real mountaineering, for a comfortable living could easily be made by conducting tourists to certain viewpoints they could reach perfectly well on their own, and many passed as guides without ever facing the hazards or hardships of untrod peaks.

In 1862 Packe saw things differently. 'If the tourist is sufficiently hale and hearty to trust to his own feet,' he wrote from experience, 'there is scarcely an excursion from Luchon, with the exception of the Maladetta [sic], requiring other guide than a good local map and compass; and the interest of pioneering one's own way will be found not a little to increase the pleasure.'

Addressing his fellow mountaineers, he continued: 'Of guides there are more than enough at Luchon, and among them some serviceable fellows, with a really good knowledge of the mountains, though seldom beyond their own district.' He then found it necessary to put forward the names of a few 'who will not grumble at being asked to use their own legs and carry your knapsack'. Among those whom he recommended were the brothers Pierre and Firmin Barrau, and Jean and Pierre Redonnet, said to be 'specially qualified guides des sommets, and not only may be trusted as pioneers over the mountains, but, when the day's work is done, will be found cheerful companions and useful aids in preparing the bivouac al monte'.

Both the Barrau and Redonnet families had been successful in guiding first ascents of the highest summits on the Spanish side of the frontier. In 1787 Pierre Barrau (an ancestor of Packe's guides) had accompanied Ramond de Carbonnieres to the Maladeta massif, was with Parrot on the first ascent of Pico de la Maladeta on 29 September 1817, but lost his life seven years later when, at the age of 68, he fell into a crevasse on the Maladeta glacier whilst acting as guide to Blavier and de Billy (who became first president of the CAF). Barrau's body, incidentally, emerged from the glacier 117 years later. The second generation Pierre, along with Pierre Redonnet, guided the first two ascents of Pico Posets in 1856, while Firmin Barrau made a new route on the same mountain in 1873 with Packe and Russell, and new routes on Aneto (Nethou) and the Maladeta with Russell three years later. The fame of Pierre Redonnet, a one-time isard hunter, had been assured long before his Posets climbs, for he had been partly responsible for finding the route to the summit of Aneto whilst guiding Franqueville and Tchihatcheff on their pioneering first ascent of 1842.

In Luchon the charge for ordinary excursions was fixed by a published tariff, but it was not uncommon for local guides to ignore this and attempt to overcharge their clients. 'Most of the guides', warned Packe, 'have been spoilt by having their own way, and are very apt to assume the position of master rather than servant; but when with an Englishman, especially when they find he is not a novice among the mountains, they are soon brought into their proper place.'

In the 1860s the usual charge for a guide employed to lead a standard excursion was five, or sometimes six, francs per day, plus the same amount for each horse. But for ascents or mountain tours not mentioned in the tariff, special arrangements had to be made beforehand and a price agreed. For climbs on the Maladeta massif, Packe advised that: '30 francs per guide is the established charge; and for any mountain excursion where the guide is required to sleep *sub Jove*, 10 francs a day seems to be required as remuneration, exclusive of provisions. For a course extending over more than 4 days, I should consider 8 francs per day quite as much as ought to be given.'

The Lys is the first of the Pique's major tributaries, its proper name being the Bat de Lys, a corruption of the Gascon *lis*, by which it gains the term 'Valley of avalanches'. It's an attractive valley of meadows, a few scattered houses and barns, tree-lined streams and cascades that stripe the steep walls. Easing southward the valley opens as a green, pastoral basin, and the road ends after 6km by a restaurant at the base of the Cirque du Lys. Just ahead the Cascade d'Enfer crashes through a defile. To the left of that *téléphérique* and pipeline of the EDF Portillon hydro-electricity works (Centrale du Portillon) scar the mountainside. 'Above this, and on either side [of the Cascade d'Enfer], rise the gloomy fir forests, tier upon tier, higher and higher, till lost in the clouds,' said Packe. 'High above all, through a break in the sky, gleam the white glaciers of the Crabioules. They seem so far raised above the solid earth that it takes some moments to be convinced it is not an illusion.'

WALKS AND CLIMBS IN THE VALLÉE DU LYS

- The roadhead marks the start of several walking and trekking routes. One climbs the western hillside to a ◐ **2272m col** crossed by GR10 from the Vallée d'Oô. This col lies just below the Sommet de la Coume de Bourg and close enough to the easy Pic de Céciré to be visited by walkers out for the day from Superbagnères, wandering along the continuing path of GR10.

- Southeast of the roadhead, or rather from a little way north of it, a bridge over the Lys takes a path up through mixed woodland and into the narrow valley of Houradade. Here the trail breaks into a number of options. One climbs to the Crête de la Serre des Cabales, crosses the Col de Pinata into the head of another steeply falling valley under Pic de Sacroux, then crosses Col de Sacroux into the ◐ ★ **Cirque de la Glère**. From the cirque a way climbs south over the ridge into the Valle del Ésera at the foot of the Maladeta massif; another descends northward into the Vallée de la Pique; while a third twists northeast to the Hospice de France, which it reaches about 7hrs from the Vallée du Lys.

Trail junction signpost in the Vallée du Lys

- Another option on the Houradade trail southeast of the Cirque du Lys roadhead, and a major route at that, is the ●★ path numbered 41 on signposts which swings right at a marked junction and angles across a steep hillside clothed in birch, pine, bilberry and masses of alpenroses. The way leads towards the EDF pipeline, cableway, and a beehive-shaped hut at Prat-Long, then climbs quite steeply to gain the CAF-owned **Refuge du Maupas** (2450m), standing below a small tarn about 3½–4hrs from the roadhead. The refuge is manned from the middle of June to mid-September and has 35 places (☎ 05 61 79 16 07).

- To the east and southeast, but unseen from here, a string of high lakes lie in hollows scooped out by glaciers that have all but disappeared: the ● **Lacs du Port Vieil, Célinda, Charles, Bleu** and, on a lower level, **Lac Vert**, all of which may be visited on paths that exploit long views out to the foothills and beyond.

- On the frontier ridge, which kinks northward to pass above Lacs du Port Vieil and Célinda, the 2754m ⊗ **Pic d'Estauas** makes a tremendous viewpoint from which to study both the Cirque du Lys and the Maladeta massif. The *voie normale* ascent from Refuge du Maupas climbs from Lac Célinda to a *brèche* in the ridge north of the peak, then tackles the ridge heading south to the summit in 3½–4hrs from the hut.

Above and to the south of the refuge, Pic du Maupas (3109m) stands astride the frontier ridge. Its northern arête leads to the minor 2900m summit of Tusse de Maupas, from which a spur descends towards the

285

hut, effectively dividing the upper cirque in two. The eastern side of the spur is where the lakes are found; the western side is the wild-looking Cirque des Crabioules, beyond whose west wall the Cirque d'Espingo rises above the Vallée d'Oô (see 3:3). First climbed in 1825 by the military surveyors Peytier and Hossard, best known for their ascent of the Balaïtous, **Pic du Maupas** is a prominent viewpoint with numerous routes in grades ranging from PD to TD. The *voie normale* is little more than an easy 2hr scramble along the east flank of the dividing spur, while another goes over the Tusse de Maupas, then along the arête to a col, where it moves onto the east flank to join the previously mentioned route. ⓑ The North Face, however, is noted for its TD rock climbs which contain one or two artificial passages: the classic *Voie Céréza*, dating from 1948 (Barrère/Céréza), is a 200m meandering route with several pitches of IV and one of V (A2/A3). The West Face has an AD route (Barrué/Leclère, 1934) and one graded D (IV/V) via the northwest chimney, while the West Arête makes a pleasant PD ascent first climbed in 1905 by the brothers Cadier. The East Arête, reached by way of the Col du Boum, is rated AD-. Col de Boum is also the key to reaching the South and Southeast faces for climbers based at the Maupas refuge. On the 300m granite wall of the South Face, which overlooks the Valle de Remuñe, Jean Arlaud, with Escudier and Pérès, created the original route in 1931, a D- climb involving two pitches of IV. A more direct route on the same face is graded D+ (V), while the nearby Southeast Face has a choice of routes of around 200m in the D to TD+ range.

About 1km east of Pic de Maupas along the frontier ridge, the 3006m ⓑ **Pic de Boum** holds at least two AD climbs of about 150m, while a traverse of the Maupas–Boum crest makes an excellent AD-outing on good rock.

West of Refuge du Maupas, across the Cirque des Crabioules, **Pic Quayrat** (see 3:3) offers some rewarding expeditions, though not as long or numerous as those on its West Face and needing somewhere in the region of 2½–3hrs to reach from the hut. Yet again Arlaud and his companions were active here in 1928 with a Southeast Face climb on poor rock (PD+). The ENE Spur is a different proposition, a ⓑ 400m climb on firm granite, graded AD and with one exposed pitch of IV.

The nearby **Pic Lézat** is another attraction, its East Face holding several interesting medium-grade lines, while the easy *voie normale* is a 4–5hr ascent dismissed as *facile*. To the left (southeast) of Lézat the North Face of the **Crabioules** massif was systematically worked on throughout the 20th century, and now holds numerous lines of 350m–400m on rock of variable quality. ⓑ Climbs are in the range AD to TD+, with one of the most respected being the 300m *Voie Couzy* on the Northeast Face of the Pic Oriental des Crabioules (TD+, IV/V, A2), climbed by Jean Couzy and Lucien Georges in 1948. Couzy was an influential figure in post-war French climbing circles, making numerous difficult ascents in the Alps, taking part in the renowned Annapurna expedition of 1950, and making the first ascent of both Chomo Lonzo and Makalu. He was killed by stonefall on the Southwest Face of the Crête des Bergers in 1958.

WALKS AND CLIMBS
FROM THE HOSPICE DE FRANCE

Eleven kilometres from Luchon a large car park at the roadhead in the upper Vallée de la Pique gives an indication of its popularity. Nearby the ancient **Hospice de France** (1385m), a one-time staging post for mule-trains trading across the frontier, dates from the 14th century, when it was established by the Knights of St John. At the time of writing, the building is due to be renovated and the site developed. And not before time. For decades it was mostly abandoned and left to crumble into decay, yet in 1896 it had been described as 'a fair-sized inn, quite plain in structure, but well catered and admirably served' (Harold Spender, *Through the High Pyrenees*, A.D. Innes, 1898). In the 1960s it was described as 'an inn with five bedrooms, a dining-room which contains a stuffed Pyrenean bear, an out-of-doors café and some large St Bernard dogs. It certainly has atmosphere' (J.M. Scott, *From Sea to Ocean*, Geoffrey Bles, 1969). If you don't mind the crowds, the site would make a useful base for a few days of a walking holiday, for it lies at a junction of routes in rough pastureland, with woodland above and below, and a view up a narrow sub-valley towards the frontier mountains. It has been understandably popular with Luchon visitors for centuries, as Spender observed: 'altogether there is, on a bright summer day in the season, a perpetual flow of humanity – an unceasing running to and fro, with harnessing of horses, and bridling of mules, as the obedient, melancholy-eyed tourists are hurried through their day's work.'

The classic view of the Maladeta massif from the Port de Venasque

- By far the best-known walk from here leads across the Pique and up to the 2444m ◗ **Port de Venasque** in order to gain a direct view over the depths of the Ésera to the Maladeta massif. Under snow-free summer conditions the route is steep but uncomplicated on an old mule trail, but in winter and spring the way is threatened by avalanche. About 2–2½hrs from the hospice you come to a stony basin containing a group of lakes known as the Boums du Port. Next to the largest of these stands the tiny **Refuge de Venasque** at 2249m. Despite its modest size (15 places, but 30 with tent annexe) the hut has a guardian from the beginning of June to the end of September (☎ 05 61 79 26 46). No more than 30mins above it to the south the narrow cleft of the Port de Venasque is gained. Out of the shadows and into the sunshine of Spain you emerge to a wide view of the Valle del Ésera, its upper reaches to the left where the double-pronged Forcanada looks impressive, while directly ahead across the valley stretches the Maladeta massif, the last of its once powerful glaciers draped across the north-facing slopes. From here the rocky Cresta de los Portillones can be clearly seen dividing the Maladeta glacier on the right from that of Aneto to the left. Above this left-hand glacier the summit of the Pyrenees rises as an innocent-looking peak, while below the Portillones arête you should be able to make out the Renclusa refuge, base for climbs on the massif. If you're headed that way, allow another 2½hrs by a good path.

Rising above the Port de Venasque, Pic de la Mine rewards with scrambles along the frontier crest

The Port de Venasque consists of a rocky breach in the north wall of the Ésera's valley, and is guarded on the east by Pic de la Mine and to the west by the slightly higher ◗ **Pic de Sauvegarde** (2738m). An

easy route zigzags up the south flank of Sauvegarde from the pass in about 45mins, using a path created in the 1860s as a result of Archdeacon Hardwick's death whilst descending the steep rocks after an ascent with Packe in 1859. Experienced scramblers could reach the crown of Sauvegarde directly from the pass, following the ridge all the way to the summit, while an ascent of the 2708m **Pic de la Mine** uses one of several gullies to gain the ridge a little west of the top. However, a 🅑 longer and more interesting route carrying a PD grade climbs the east (frontier) ridge all the way from the Pas de l'Escalette. The summit of Pic de la Mine is broad, flat and featureless, unlike that of the Sauvegarde, but both give much more extensive views than the Port de Venasque, and are therefore worth tackling.

- Rather than return to the Hospice de France by reversing the path of ascent, a worthwhile 🌑 **6–7hr circuit** can be made by descending briefly from the Port de Venasque towards the Ésera, then cutting left on a reasonable path which crosses the grassy 2477m saddle of **Puerto de la Picada**. Over this descend eastwards, then cross back into France at the **Pas de l'Escalette** (shown as Coth de Lunfern on the latest EA map), but remain just below the frontier ridge on a path which leads to the **Pas de la Montjoie** (2069m). Now follow the path into the Vallée de la Frèche and down to the Pique at the Hospice de France.

- From the Refuge de Venasque it's possible to cross the ridge on the far western side of the lakes at the 2421m Col de la Montagnette (½hr from the hut), which gives access to another high basin containing the 🌑 **Lac de la Montagnette**. A rough scramble up to Port Viell on the frontier ridge south of this lake gives a view of the Maladeta to match that from the better-known Port de Venasque.

The east side of the narrow valley in which the Refuge de Venasque is found is walled by the **Crête de la Pique**, which runs south from the 2394m Pic de la Pique to Col de la Frèche. 🅑 A traverse of this crest gives an AD outing, while the West Face boasts an exposed 500m mixed winter climb, the *Voie Frénésie Chevaleresque*, won in March 1996 by Pierre Satgé and Sébastien Thomas. This is graded TD+ (V+, 75–90°). Above Col de la Frèche the Northeast Arête of Pic de la Mine is graced by three *gendarmes*: the Petit Corbeau, Bec du Corbeau and the **Aiguille Morin**, named after the noted alpinist Jean Morin, who made the first ascent (with Giroix and Gysin) in 1923. The ascent of this aiguille from the west results in an exposed AD+ climb (one pitch of grade IV) on rather poor rock. Meanwhile, facing Pic de la Pique from across the valley, **Pic Penjat** (2113m) provides winter sport in the 330m East Couloir (AD-, 45–50°).

Southeast of the Hospice de France a broad path goes through woodland at the entrance to the **Vallée de la Frèche**. Ten minutes later, and still within the woods, it divides. One path continues ahead into the rough pastures of the valley, which curves south between Pic de la Pique and Pic de la Montjoie. Near the head of this valley the trail twists up to the small Étang (or Lac) de la Frèche under the frontier ridge. The other woodland path flanks left, then loops up the hillside to gain a grassy shelf, the Plateau de Rioumingaou, which supports great drifts of narcissi in spring. A crossing path is met up here. By forking left one could either make a return to the Hospice de France or remain above the valley as far as Col de Barèges, then descend through forest to Luchon.

• The right-hand trail goes to the Pas de la Montjoie (described below), while another continues up the hillside a little south of east, crosses the frontier to a basin containing one or two small pools, and concludes with an easy ascent of ⊗ **Pic de l'Entécade** (Tuc dera Entecada, 2272m) in about 3hrs from the Hospice de France. This modest peak commands a long view of mountains that stretch from Pic du Midi de Bigorre to Pic de Montcalm and the mysterious country of Ariège, and also makes a first-rate grandstand from which to study the Maladeta massif to the south-west and the Vall d'Aran stretching off to the east. It's possible to descend to the lower reaches of the Vall d'Aran (see 4:7) at Las Bordas (Es Bòrdes) by way of a trail which crosses a 2013m saddle southwest of Pic de l'Entécade.

• The right-hand path that was met on the Plateau de Rioumingaou makes a pleasant ◒ walk, with several options occurring as you advance along it. It rises without making any undue demands and gains the frontier, marked by a stone, at the 2069m **Pas de la Montjoie**. One path breaks off at the pass and descends into the Vall del Joeu, otherwise known as the Vall de l'Artiga de Lin, which drains into the Vall d'Aran at Las Bordas. The main path, however, does not cross the pass but instead swings to the right and works its way south just below the crest heading for the **Pas de l'Escalette**, also on the frontier close to the point where the Franco-Spanish border makes a 90° turn.

• ◒ Once across the pass one could either bear right (west) for the Puerto de la Picada, Valle del Ésera and/or Port de Venasque (as outlined in reverse above), or turn left and descend alongside the Barranco de Pomero to the unmanned Refugi dera Artiga de Lin beside a dirt road in the **Plan dera Artiga**. A short way down this road, which leads eventually to Las Bordas, you come to the resurgence of the Joeu, one of the sources of the Garonne whose origins lie in the Aneto glacier (see 3:10).

3:5 VALLE DE GISTAÍN

South of the Vallée d'Aure's Vallon de Saux tributary, the Bielsa road tunnel ejects its traffic into the glaring light of Spain and the long valley which divides the limestone massifs of the west from the largely granite and schistose mountains at the heart of the range. This dividing valley is initially drained by the Barrancos Pinara and Barrosa, but is soon strengthened by the Cinca, coming from valleys described in Chapter 2. The present chapter, however, describes those valleys that drain from the eastern mountains, and in particular the big Posets massif, which supports the second highest summit of the Pyrenees.

The first of these is the short but steep valley of the **Barranco de Trigoniero**, which has a fall of more than 1200m from its upper lake to its confluence with the Rio Barrosa, a distance of only 5km. A simple unmanned *cabane* with 6–8 places, the so-called Refugio de Trigoniero, stands at about 1990m, but apart from that there's no other shelter in this valley. Two border crossings are possible at its head. The first is by way of the 2495m Puerto de Trigoniero (known in France as the Port de Moudang), which leads down to the Granges de Moudang on the northern side; the second tackles the frontier ridge east of Lago Ibonet at the 2588m Puerto de la Plana o Castet (or Port d'Arrouère) above the Hospice de Rioumajou (see 3:1).

Two kilometres further south of the Trigoniero, and shortly before reaching Parzán, a stony road (*pista*) breaks off to the east to enter the narrow, gorge-like **Valle de Ordiceto** (Urdiceto), with a sign at the entrance giving 11km to Lago de Ordiceto. Both the GR11 and a *variante* of the Pyrenean High Route (HRP) follow this *pista* all the way to the valley head at the Pas de los Caballos en route to Viadós below Pico Posets. Twice the length of the Trigoniero valley, Ordiceto bears the scars of the hydro-engineer. About 15mins above the Caballos pass at 2369m, Lago Ordiceto has been dammed. The *pista* was created to service the dam's construction, and power lines now trace a way through the valley. Despite the unsightly dam and stark terrain, decent views can be had from the lakeside, and it is these that motorised Spanish picnic parties come for.

* Without traffic the walk upvalley is not at all unpleasant; there are occasional footpath shortcuts, and it takes about 3hrs or so to gain the Pas de los Caballos from the valley entrance. This is not a frontier pass, although the Franco-Spanish border ridge is only 500m to the north. There is, however, a border crossing nearby, at the **Puerto (or Port) de Ordiceto**, which leads into the delightful Vallée de Rioumajou (see 3:1), should such a route appeal. But for GR11 and HRP trekkers, ◔ Viadós is the day's goal, and once over the **Pas de los Caballos** there's the relief of neither traffic nor dirt road, with a trail working its way eastward through meadows that make perfect campsites, then descending to the Valle de Gistaín (the valley of the Rio Cinqueta), 2hrs from the pass. But having at

last gained this valley another *pista* directs the now uncomplicated onward route to the summer grazing hamlet of Viadós, reached in 5½–6hrs from the mouth of the Valle de Ordiceto.

The next valley of consequence met on the way south along the Cinca, and the main one dealt with in this section, is the **Valle de Gistaín** (also known as the Valle de Gistau (or Chistau)), entered at the hamlet of **SALINAS DE SIN**, some 20km from the Bielsa tunnel. For accommodation Salinas has only a single hotel, the Méson de Salinas, but there's a useful summer-only tourist office (☎ 974 50 40 89) dispensing information about the surrounding area, and if you have a tent there's a campsite 5km upvalley on the south bank of the Rio Cinqueta (Camping Los Vives).

There is no public transport in the Valle de Gistaín, so those without a vehicle are left with the option of trying to hitch a lift or walk. It is more than 12km from Salinas to Plan, and another 6km to Gistaín along the road. Although the valley is very attractive, with graceful poplars growing alongside the river, road walking cannot be recommended since there are several tunnels in which it could be dangerous to meet an oncoming vehicle. However, there are preferred walking routes on both north and south flanks of the valley: GR19 goes along the northern hillsides, while GR15 on the south side can be joined at Saravillo.

The HU641 road into the Valle de Gistaín is paved and of good quality, broad at first but becoming more narrow soon after. Six kilometres from Salinas de Sin, and shortly after passing the campsite, a secondary road cuts right for **SARAVILLO** (950m), built at the mouth of the Vall de la Guerva just 1km above the main valley road. Accommodation may be found here at the Casa Cazcarrea. The GR15 passes through Saravillo heading west then south to La Fortunada in the Valle de Bielsa, and east to Plan by way of the popular Ibón de Plan, and passing on the way the unmanned Refugio Ibón (16 places). Both destinations are no more than 2hrs distant from Saravillo, and both make pleasant walks in their own right. But anyone choosing to stay here may well be attracted to some of the neighbouring mountains. For example, looming over the village from the southwest the 2246m ⊗ **Punta Llerga** can be climbed without difficulty via the Collado de Santa Isabel (reached by *pista*) in 2–2½hrs, while the same col gives access to the higher ⊗ **Movison Grande** (2593m) which rises southeast of the village. But the highest summit of the neighbourhood is that of ⊗ **Cotiella**, at 2912m the loftiest by far. By its north ridge it is linked with **Pico de Espouy**, from which other ridge-spurs project to enclose the Valle Lenes on the west and the Circo de Armeña to the east. The ascent from the Collado de Santa Isabel takes about 5hrs, and the landscape which unfolds from the summit is one that has immense appeal.

Challenging winter routes, as well as exposed rock climbs and easy *voies normale*, can be enjoyed on the ⓑ Cotiella massif. Grouped fairly close together around the cirque that encloses the Ibón de Plan, the central couloir on the Northeast Face of 2684m **Peña de la Una** offers 350m at AD; the *Grande Diagonale* on **Pico de Espouy** is a classic PD+ route dating from 1955; the Northeast Couloir on **Peña els Litase** (2618m) gives 500m of climbing at D+; while on the east side of the cirque the 500m Northeast Spur of **Peña de las Once** is a spectacular mixed route from 1991 that goes at D+ (IV+/V; 60°).

Just beyond the Saravillo turning another road breaks away, this time to the left, crossing the Rio Cinqueta and climbing to **SIN** and **SERVETO**, two modest villages on the north side of the Valle de Gistaín at 1218m and 1306m respectively. Trekkers pass through following the route of GR19, and there's potential for climbing on the crags of the Peña de Sin and Peña de Arties on the other side of the Barranco Campimeu. An *albergue/gîte,* Albergue de Sin, in the first of these villages offers dormitory accommodation and rooms with a total of 68 places, and is open thoughout the year (☎ 974 50 61 12). From the roadhead at Serveto a path leads to Plan, the valley's tourist centre.

The valley road passes through a series of tunnels and beneath overhangs before crossing to the north bank of the Cinqueta, then running alongside a dammed lake and lovely meadows that lead directly to **PLAN** at a junction of valleys. This huddled village has a few shops, a bar-restaurant, a bank and a mountain guides office (Guis de la Bal de Chistau, ☎ 974 50 61 78), but only one hotel, the one-star Mediodia. Plan has a tourist information kiosk and a rash of new buildings on the edge of the crowded original village.

- One of the best walking options from here is the 2½–3hr trek to the ◐ **Ibón de Plan**, nestling in a cirque at 1913m and backed by screes and contorted rock strata. The route to it follows the GR15 south of the river on paths and tracks that climb steeply through a narrow valley. From the southeastern end of the lake a continuing path veers east on an easy 400m climb to Collado del Ibón (2345m), a saddle between the Llosat peaks and Punta Baja. Across the col the path forks, with the right-hand option skirting round to **Refugio Armeña** (25 places, sometimes manned, ☎ 974 31 10 20) and down to the little Armeña lake. From here it would be feasible to continue as far as **BARBARUENS**, a hamlet nestling high above the lower Ésera valley and linked with Plan by a cross-country *pista*.

The road forks on the edge of Plan. The right branch crosses the Rio Cinqueta and, unpaved, journeys for some 25km across country via the 1905m Collado de Sahun, and then down to **CHÍA** in the Ésera valley some way upstream of the Barbaruens turn-off. The left branch, however, continues as a paved road curving north and bypassing **SAN JUAN DE PLAN** in another 1km (accommodation at the 22-place Albergue El Molin Viejo, ☎ 974 50 62 44) before making a sharp hairpin and snaking up the hillside to **GISTAÍN** (Chistén), a closely built, traditional mountain village with plenty of character and a splendid outlook over the valley which lies some 300m below. Both GR19 and a GR11 *variante* pass through, with trekkers having limited opportunities to restock with food at the two local shops; but overnight accommodation is provided at the Fonda Casa Elvira.

Where the road makes its first hairpin to Gistaín above San Juan de Plan, a dirt road ahead pushes deeper into the Valle de Gistaín along the west bank of the Rio Cinqueta. After another 1.5km the *pista* crosses to the east bank and later recrosses to the west side again before being joined by GR11 at La Sargueta, a short distance from Es Plans, where there's a 20-place unmanned *refugio*, and a campsite, Camping El Forcallo, open in the high summer season only. On coming to the confluence of the Cinqueta de la Pez (which flows from the north) and that of the Añes Cruces, the *pista* swings to the right and soon comes to the summer grazing hamlet of **VIADÓS** at 1760m.

With its collection of old stone barns spaced across the hillside and a wonderful view of the extensive West Face of the Posets massif, Viadós is the perfect base from which to spend a few days exploring. Overlooking the hamlet from a knoll at 1810m, the privately owned and atmospheric **Refugio de Viadós** is open and staffed by Joaquín Cazcarra and his family at Easter and weekends until mid-June, then permanently until the end of September. It has 70 places and an ever-open winter annexe with 6 places (☎ 974 50 61 63). However, since the creation of the Parque Natural Posets-Maladeta, camping is no longer allowed here, even though Viadós lies just outside the park's boundary.

Viadós is a pastoral settlement of barns and old stone houses occupied only in summer

Before looking at the walking and climbing potential from Viadós, it's worth noting that the nearby valley of the Cinqueta de

la Pez, which pushes north to the frontier peaks, has the unmanned 30-place Refugio de Tabernés at 1740m above the east bank of the stream, about 2.5km from Viadós. From it a trekker's trail follows the stream upvalley as far as the 2451m **Puerto (Port) de la Pez**, and over that pass the trail descends to the Vallée du Louron (see 3:2). Another route which passes through the Cinqueta de la Pez is the HRP *variante* which crosses the **Puerto (Port) de Caouarère** (2526m) above the Vallée de Rioumajou (3:1), while the Tabernés *refugio* is conveniently placed for a visit to the **Lagos de Bachimala**, which lie directly below the Northwest Face of the Grand Pic de Bachimala.

WALKS, TREKS AND CLIMBS FROM VIADÓS

The following selection of walks and climbs disregards routes on Pico Posets. These are covered in the box in 3:7, where all sides of the mountain and its satellite peaks come under scrutiny.

- For an introductory view of the Posets massif and a layout of the valley systems below, the easy 2½hr ascent of the 2600m ◒ **Señal de Viadós** northeast of the *refugio* is highly recommended. Though not much more than a big hill, the Señal makes a very fine grandstand. The route to it via the Collado de Señal de Viadós forms the lower section of an ascent of the Punta del Sabre and Grand Pic de Bachimala (5–5½hrs).

- East of Punta del Sabre on the frontier ridge, the 2683m ◒ **Puerto Superior de Aigües Tortes** (Port d'Aygues-Tortes) is crossed by an HRP *variante*, but could be worth visiting as a day out from Viadós or as a way of border-hopping on the way to Refuge de la Soula (see 3:2). The way to it heads upvalley from Viadós on the clear GR11 trail through meadows for a little over an hour, until you come to the Plan d'Añes Cruces and the confluence of the Barranco de Añes Cruces and a stream coming from the frontier mountains. While GR11 veers right to climb to the Puerto de Gistain, the Aigües Tortes route strikes up the hillside ahead, then slants northwest to the pass, which is gained about 3hrs from Viadós.

- West of Viadós, on the far side of the Valle de Gistaín, the East Couloir of 2478m ◓ **El Montó** is a 600m PD route (the couloir is 500m long) recommended as a winter climb (45°, grade II/III) when it comes into condition, which is usually from January to April.

- When gazing southeast from Viadós the **Valle de Millares** appears to cut into the southern end of the Posets massif. Headed by a ridge that supports the various summits of the Picos de Bagüeñola (or Picos de Eriste), the valley is a mix of meadows, pine trees, rocks, screes and lakes. In its upper reaches it offers a stark contrast to the more gentle, pastoral nature of the country around Viadós, but in that contrast lies much of its appeal. A ⊜ 6½–7hr circular tour of the valley and its lakes is one way to experience that contrast. A wooden footbridge carries a path across the Añes Cruces stream below the *refugio*. Thereafter a trail strikes up the left-hand (eastern) side of the Barranco de la Ribereta and, as height is gained, makes a number of zigzags towards a prominent rocky crown. Here the way veers right and, leaving an alternative route to the Collado de Eriste heading left, crosses the stream to reach the first of the lakes. **Ibón (or Lago) d'es Millares** (2353m, 2½hrs) has a small dam at its northern end, as has the second lake, **Ibón d'es Leners** (2508m) a little further west, reached in another 30mins. Continuing westward, a cairned route leads up and over a dividing ridge crest, then down to the **Lago de Luceros** (2430m) and **Lago de la Solana** (2320m), the latter hemmed in between screes and pine trees. The return to Viadós now works down through the Solana valley keeping roughly north, with views into the valley of the Cinqueta de la Pez blocked by the frontier mountains.

- The highest point on the Bagüeñola ridge is found above and SSE of Ibón d'es Leners. ⊗ **Bagüeñola Central** (3053m) is also known as the Grand Eriste,   the culminating point of four ridges. First climbed in 1878 by Henry Russell and Firmin Barrau, there are several approaches to it, none of which is particularly difficult. A *voie normale* from the Valle de Millares tackles the mountain from the Leners lake and is graded PD. From the southern end of the lake climb towards the upper end of the northwest ridge aiming for a point just before it joins the summit. A short couloir here is often choked with snow or ice, so use of an ice axe is advised. Allow 5–5½hrs from Viadós (2hrs from the lake).

- Immediately south of Bagüeñola Central, **Bagüeñola Sur** (3045m, Eristé Sud) is partially concealed from some routes of approach by the more prominent Pico de Sein. The summit panorama, however, is largely uninterrupted, and was enjoyed by Henry Russell, who made the first ascent, solo, in 1878. Russell had tackled the mountain from the Pleta de la Vall on the east side of the ridge, but in 1930 Jean Arlaud led a ⓑ traverse of the crest from Bagüeñola Central to Bagüeñola Sur, an ungraded but enjoyable route on near-perfect rock (one pitch of III and a 20m rappel) which takes about 1hr from summit to summit.

- The ridge crest at the head of the Valle de Millares is broken by two passes that provide ways for trekkers to cross to the south side of the Posets massif, both being useful if you're considering a complete traverse of the massif, wish to explore another section of it, or have ambitions to climb some of the bristling slabs and aiguilles that adorn the Valle de Llardaneta. Early in the season, or following a particularly harsh spring, ice axe and crampons could be useful to tackle either of these passes. ◐★ **Collado de Eriste** (2860m) lies between Diente Royo and La Forqueta, is gained in about 3–3½hrs from Viadós, and gives access to Lago Llardaneta and Refugio Angel Orús (2100m). This is reached in 5hrs from Viadós, or more easily from Eriste in the Ésera valley in 3½hrs. Walking and climbing options from this hut, as well as hut details, are discussed in 3:7.

- The second pass is that of the ◐ **Collado de Millares** (2831m), above the lake of the same name. The way to it is guided by cairns (3½hrs), and on the southeast side of the ridge you descend into the wild Bagüeña Cirque, in which there are several lakes dotted around. Given time one could spend hours or even days here, wandering from lake to lake and crossing a variety of cols into neighbouring valleys. To gain access to the Angel Orús *refugio* bear east from the upper Bagüeño lake, cross the 2842m Brecha de Llantia and descend with care into the Valle de Forcau to find the hut, some 6–7hrs from Viadós.

- Guarding the Collado de Millares from the southwest, ⊗ **Bagüeñola Norte** (3025m) is also known as Pic Beraldi after Henri Beraldi, Pyrenean activist and bibliographer who died in 1931. First climbed from the southeast by Louis le Bondidier and J.M. Sansuc in 1905, the shortest route of approach is through the Valle de Millares. An uncomplicated scramble up the northeast ridge should take no more than about an hour from Collado de Millares (4½hrs from Viadós).

- As the most northerly of the four 3000m summits along the crest overlooking the Millares valley, ⊗ **La Forqueta** (Pic des Tourets, 3007m) has the shortest approach of all and is accessible by a very easy 30min ascent (the *voie normale*) from Collado de Eriste. Le Bondidier and Sansuc made the first ascent the day before their climb on Bagüeñola Norte mentioned above. The summit panorama is magnificent, with the Maladeta in one direction, Monte Perdido in another, and a splendid overview of the inner recesses of the Posets massif. A ❶ **traverse of the crest** from La Forqueta to Bagüeñola Norte, over the summit of Punta Millares and crossing Collado de Millares on the way, makes a worthwhile extension. Graded AD (with one pitch of IV), the traverse from summit to summit takes about 3hrs.

- Trekkers self-sufficient with tent and supplies for a couple of days could make a fine ◐ **multi-day tour** by crossing **Collado de Millares** into the Bagüeña Cirque, then, after visiting the southern group of lakes, crossing a 2512m col on the ridge south of the Ibón de Pardines. This **Collado de Bocs** lies midway between Tosal de Bocs and Tuca de Cambra. On the south side of the ridge descend for about 200m, then flank west above the Barbarisa valley to join a path which then heads south to the **Collado de Sahun** on the *pista* that runs from Plan to the Ésera valley. Follow this down to **Plan**, then return upvalley to Viadós to complete the circuit.

• The short stage which takes GR11 and High Route trekkers from ◑★ **Viadós to Refugio de Estós** is an undemanding yet rewarding walk of about 4½hrs, and is highly recommended. A clear path heads upvalley beyond the *granges* and through meadows on the west side of the Cinqueta d'Añes Cruces, and in a little over an hour leads to the Plan d'Añes Cruces. The trail to the Puerto de Aigües Tortes goes up towards the head of the valley and the frontier mountains, while the Estós path veers right (east) and climbs to the broad saddle of the **Puerto de Gistaín**, whose altitude is variously quoted as 2524m, 2560m, 2577m, 2592m and 2603m. From the saddle the Maladeta massif is seen in the distance, but the Posets just to the south is hidden. For a broader view a 45min diversion north to an insignificant bald summit is worth considering, given sufficient time and energy. But to continue to the Estós *refugio* descend on the eastern side, first skirting right of the infant Barranco de Estós, then crossing to the left bank near its confluence with the Clarabide stream and taking the trail directly to the popular three-storey **Refugio de Estós** at 1835m. (A description of the Valle de Estós and a selection of walks, treks and climbs there is found at 3:8, as are hut details.)

3:6 VALLE DEL ÉSERA

Beyond **SALINAS DE SIN**, in the valley of the Rio Cinca, the main road continues south, passing **ESCALONA** and the turning for Añisclo, with the impressive lump of the Peña Montañesa on the left. It then comes to **AINSA**, an attractive old town commanding a major crossroads – west along the Ara to Broto and Torla (for Ordesa); east to the Ésera, Benasque and the Parque Natural Posets-Maladeta. The spendid **Plaza Mayor**, with its mellow stone arcades and balconies, is one of the best things in the old part of Ainsa; the Romanesque church of **Santa Maria** is another reason for stopping for a while. Most of the accommodation, and facilities such as shops, restaurants and banks, are centred on the less appealing and busy new town, however, below the original hilltop quarter. For hotel details contact the tourist office (☎ 974 50 05 12), which is open only in summer. The nearest campsite lies about 1km to the east.

Taking N260 eastward a good view towards the frontier is gained as you cross the Cinca before the mountains become veiled by intervening foothills on the climb to the Collado de Forado (1020m). It's a total of 32km across this pass from Ainsa to **CAMPO** in the valley of the Río Ésera on a pleasant if undramatic route. The Ésera is one of the major rivers of the Central Pyrenees. Rising among glaciers on the north slope of the Maladeta, the river initially flows west, then south to pass between the two highest massifs, and continues through all the sierras of the pre-Pyrenees down to the badlands of the Ebro basin.

From Campo to Castejón de Sos the road follows the river upstream, crossing and recrossing several times through a series of limestone gorges. About 12km from Campo a minor offshoot branches west for **BARBARUENS** at the foot of the Cotiella massif. From this roadhead hamlet at 1128m, a track then path leads up to the **Refugio Armeña** (1840m, 25 places, sometimes manned, ☎ 974 31 10 20) in the Circo de Armeña. From here the ascent of **Cotiella** can be made in 2–2½hrs, or there's a very fine trek to tackle which crosses Collado del Ibón and descends to Plan in the Valle de Gistaín (see 3:5).

The N260 continues upstream, and just after a turning to **CHIA** (with its 25km *pista* link with the Valle de Gistaín by way of the 1989m Collado de Sahún), the road forks at a junction of valleys. N260 swings east across the river to **CASTEJÓN DE SOS** and Coll de Fades, while the C139 pushes on alongside the Ésera towards its source among the highest mountains of all. From here the valley is also known as the Valle de Benasque, after its highest and most important township.

The road crosses to the east bank of the river, then returns to the west side just before a minor access road breaks left to **SAHÚN**, a quietly attractive village with uncrowded trails leading from it. For accommodation here try the Hostal Casa Lacreu, which has a good reputation.

WALKING FROM SAHÚN

Backing the village, the Sierra de Cambra forms the southeast rim of a large amphitheatre containing more than a dozen post-glacial lakes and pools that drain into the Valle de Aigüeta, which in turn feeds into the Valle de Eriste that has its outflow 3km beyond Sahún. The main headwall of this cirque is the Bagüeñola (Eriste) crest (see 3:5), while the southwest flank of that crest walls the upper Valle de Sahún (Valle de Barbarisa), in which there are also several lakes. These two valleys, now drawn into the Parque Natural Posets-Maladeta enclave, are the major attractions for walkers and trekkers based in this part of the Ésera.

- The most direct route into the **Valle de Sahún** in order to visit the 🌑**Ibóns de Barbarisa** begins on the edge of the village. Initially heading southwest, the trail then curves right along the north flank of the valley above the Aigüeta de Llisat, and eventually comes to the unmanned Cabaña de Barbarisa on the borders of the Parque Natural. The hut stands at the head of a track which comes from the Collado de Sahún, and this offers the shortest route to the Barbarisa lakes for walkers with their own transport. Above here the way heads roughly north into the narrowing valley where the string of lakes are located (about 4hrs from Sahún). From the lakes it would be possible to make the ascent of **Pico Bagüeña** (2946m) in another 2½hrs or to cross the east wall of this upper valley via the 2538m Collado de la Ribereta into the Bagüeñola Cirque, which would then enable a long circular trek to be completed through the Valle de Aigüeta.

• The **Valle de Aigüeta** is reached from Sahún by first wandering north along the slip road leading to the Sanctuario de la Guayén, where a trail breaks away rising northeast round the slopes of the Sierra de Cambra, then west into the Aigüeta's valley. The deeper you go into the valley so its appeal increases. A few shepherds' *cabanes* are the only man-made features. On natural shelves and in hollows under ragged peaks the lakes and pools add a lustre to the scene. Here again a number of cols provide opportunities to cross from one valley to another, and there's no shortage of summits to aim for, all of which are mostly deserted, by contrast with the better known massifs further north.

The Parque Natural Posets-Maladeta

Designated a protected area in June 1994, the *parque natural* was a belated acknowledgement of the need to bring special environmental safeguards to the two highest massifs in the Pyrenees which stand either side of the Valle del Ésera. Until the 1970s the upper valley above Benasque remained a near-pristine region. Then a *pista* was bulldozed through flower meadows to a point just below and north of the Renclusa *refugio*, and at the same time a major highway of international standards was built along the west bank of the Ésera as far as the valley's right-angled curve near the old Hospital de Benasque. The intention was to push the highway through the mountains to France, while the *pista* encouraged a motorised invasion of a lost wilderness. As Fernando Barrientos Fernandez wrote many years ago: 'Urban motorised man has no responsible conservationist regard for nature.' And so it proved. Vehicular access resulted in an eruption of insensitive wild camping, with all the sorry consequences that that entails. Litter and human waste quickly devalued the once magnificent and unspoilt meadowlands of the upper Ésera below the Maladeta massif, while the paved highway remains to this day a dead-end, a symbol of misguided political ambition that failed to realise EU funding.

The creation of the 33,267 hectare Parque Natural Posets-Maladeta now restricts both access by private vehicle between 10 July and 31 August, and wild camping at all times within the park's limits. But alongside restrictions such as these, upgrading to park status has also brought about a rash of signposting and waymarking of trails previously unknown here – a form of taming that tends to detract from the pristine nature of the region that once made it so special, and to which it ought surely be returned.

The *parque natural's* boundary runs along the Franco-Spanish frontier from Pic de Cauarère (Culfreda), which overlooks the Cinqueta de la Pez at the head of the Valle de Gistaín, as far east as Pic de Pessó, close to the point where the frontier makes a sharp northerly bend above the upper Ésera. It then stretches southeast almost as far as the Noguera Ribagorçana to enclose not only the upper Ésera above the Baños de Benasque, but also the Valle de Salenques and the Vallhiverna, lying south of the Maladeta. West of the Ésera all of the Posets massif is protected, including the Valle de Estós, much of the Eriste and upper Sahún valleys, and all of the Cinqueta de Añes Cruces above Viadós.

Wildlife within the park is typically representative of the Pyrenees as a whole, with small herds of isard and numerous marmots being the most obvious. But there are also weasel, sable and hare, the fire salamander and hundreds of lizards. Capercaillie inhabit the more inaccessible forests and hibernate in deep snow burrows in winter. Butterflies are abundant, especially in the summer-damp Plan d'Estan. One of the rarest is the skipper butterfly (*Pyrus andromedae*), restricted in the Pyrenees to only three sites, one of which is the Ésera, where it flies above 2000m and keeps near watercourses. Wild flowers add much to the park's appeal, and every habitat from valley floor to the upper ridge crests repays the attention of both trained botanist and layman alike.

Most of the protected area lies well above the 1500m contour. Not only does it include all the high summits of the Maladeta and Posets massifs, but 13 small glaciers and more than 100 post-glacial tarns. It's a magnificent series of landscapes, among the best of the Pyrenean chain. But they're vulnerable and environmentally sensitive landscapes under increasing pressure and in need of protection.

For further information the *parque natural's* Visitor Centre in Benasque opens daily from 15 July to 15 September (10am–2pm and 4–8pm), but at weekends only during the rest of the year (☎ 974 55 20 66).

3:7 VALLE DE ERISTE

After the turning for Sahún, the way continues north for a further 3km to **ERISTE**, a village sadly overshadowed by an ugly electricity works, while the Ésera close by has been dammed to create a small lake, the Embalse de Llinsoles, which is host to a modest water sports centre. Three one-star *hostales* on the main road and the Casa Roy in the old village provide accommodation. But rather than as a place to stay, Eriste's main interest lies in the valley cutting behind the village. At first seemingly insignificant, the Valle de Eriste (Ball de Grist on the EA map) projects into the very heart of the Posets massif, thus providing an almost unlimited range of walks, climbs and cross-country treks. One manned *refugio*, about 3½hrs walk from Eriste or 1½hrs from the parking place at Puente de Espiantosa, serves as the base for most activities. **Refugio Angel Orús** (2100m) has 98 places, and is manned throughout the year (☎ 974 34 40 44). The unmanned Refugio Clot de Chil, which for several years provided alternative simple accommodation east of

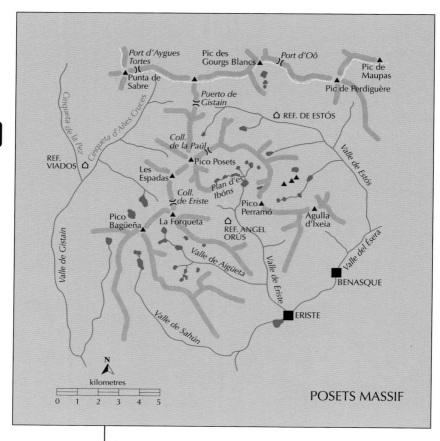

Port d'Aygues
Tortes

Pic des
Gourgs Blancs

Port d'Oô

Punta de
Sabre

Pic de
Maupas

Pic de Perdiguère

Puerto de
Gistain

REF. DE ESTÓS

Coll.
de la Paúl

Pico Posets

Valle de Estós

REF.
VIADOS

Cinqueta de la Pez

Cinqueta d'Añes Cruces

Les
Espadas

Plan d'es
Ibóns

Coll.
de Eriste

Pico
Perramó

Agulla
d'Ixeia

Pico
Bagüeña

La Forqueta

REF. ANGEL
ORÚS

Valle de Gistain

Valle de Aigüeta

Valle de Eriste

Valle del Ésera

BENASQUE

Valle de Sahún

ERISTE

N

kilometres

0 1 2 3 4 5

POSETS MASSIF

the Espiantosa bridge, has been destroyed by avalanche. There are,
however, a few other small *cabañas* in the upper valley with minimal
facilities that can be utilised for overnight shelter, in which case note
that you'd need to carry food and cooking equipment.

WALKS AND CLIMBS IN THE VALLE DE ERISTE

• A minor road heads up into the Valle de Eriste on the east bank
  of the stream, while a ☉ path takes the west bank through a
  ravine behind the village. Before long the path forks, with one
  side branching left into the Valle de Aigüeta to join the trail from
  Sahún going up to the Bagüeña Cirque mentioned above (3:6),
  while the main path continues ahead to the arched Puente de
  Tramarrius. Crossing the bridge to the east bank the dirt road
  is now joined and followed to its head at the concrete Puente
  de Espiantosa (1505m, 2hrs). Off to the left the Cascada de
  Espiantosa bursts down the western hillside. Now on the west
  bank again a good clear path winds among trees and shrubs close
  to the stream, then swings left at the Pleta de les Riberes, where

Approached through the Valle de Eriste, Refugio Angel Orús sits amid a wild landscape. It has been rebuilt and enlarged since this photograph was taken

there's a domed *cabaña* and a sign for the hut. From here the way climbs steeply to **Refugio Angel Orús**.

For those using the hut as a base there's plenty of exploring to be done. Above and beyond the *refugio* the landscape is wild and uncompromising. Steep little aiguilles and slab walls rise out of slopes of boulders, scant grass and screes, while a score or more lakes and pools lie in the upper valley, some of which are semi-frozen well into the summer.

- Northeast of the Angel Orús *refugio* the ◗ Plan d'es Ibóns (Valle de los Ibóns) holds a clutch of these tarns and pools in a plateau of rock below the Batisielles crest. To reach these make your way to the unmanned Cabaña de Llardaneta north of the hut, and

303

from there head northeast among boulders to a point from which you can see the Ibóns de las Alforches. Keep left of these and, working north, pass a string of pools on the steady rise to the **Plan d'es Ibóns** (3hrs).

- In the same upper reaches of the Valle de Eriste, ESE of Ibón de las Alforches, the ⬤**Collado de la Piana** (2702m) offers a walker's way of reaching either the Valle de Batisielles or Valle de Perramó, both of which drain into the Estós. The pass is gained from the Alforches lake outflow stream in 1–1½hrs, with a few cairns to add reassurance. About 20m below the saddle on the western side another lake is reached; at 2681m Ibón de la Plana can be partly frozen well into summer. From the pass two descent options may be considered. The left-hand route is cairned and leads northeast below the Agullas de Perramó to the Batisielles lakes, while the right-hand alternative goes round the south side of the Agullas (aiguilles) to the Perramó lakes. Both routes eventually disgorge into the Valle de Estós after a long day's trekking of 6–7hrs or so. A discreet overnight camp in the Batisielles glen is probably the best solution.

- Other exit routes include the crossing of ⬤ **Collado de Eriste** (1½–2hrs) WNW of the Angel Orús *refugio*, followed by a descent through the Valle de Millares to Viadós. This route was outlined in the opposite direction in 3:5, and as was noted there the col is used as a means of gaining the 3007m summit of **La Forqueta** in 30mins.

- Immediately above and to the west of the *refugio* the 2786m **Forcau Baixo** (Aiguille du Fourcau) is a prominent rock peak at the eastern end of a spur enclosing the little Valle del Forcau. While there are some difficult routes on the east arête, the *voie normale* on the South Face is an ungraded scramble first achieved by Henri Brulle and his party in 1913. Seventeen years later Jean Arlaud made a ⬤ north–south traverse of the aiguille, a route now graded AD.

- On the east side of the Valle de Eriste, and accessible from the Espiantosa bridge, the ⬤ **Ixea/Xinebro** (Igea/Cinebro) group of aiguilles forms a three-legged ridge system on which Henri Brulle did the lion's share of pioneering work in the years 1911–14. Routes are in the medium grades, and summit views particularly rewarding.

Pico Posets

Overlooking the valleys of Gistaín, Eriste and Estós, the granite and schistose Posets massif is a large sprawling fortress of ridges which, if we discount the Bagüeñola group south of Collado de Eriste, contains no less than 14 3000m summits. The central point is the 3375m Pico Posets (Pico Llardana), the second highest peak in the Pyrenees, below which on three sides the last glacial remnants shrivel with the effects of global warming. Apart from the view of its formidable West Face seen from Viadós (3:5), the mountain is not particularly attractive, appearing from many angles as an untidy, shapeless mass of high rocky cirques and stony basins spattered with tarns.

The little-known H. Halkett made the first ascent on 6 August 1856 with Pierre Barrau and Pierre Redonnet as his guides. Although no record of their route has been discovered, it is thought that from a camp in the Valle de Estós they approached by way of the Batisielles lakes, crossed the col at the head of this side-valley and then tackled the mountain from the east up the Posets glacier. When Packe made the third ascent in 1861 with the Barrau brothers he made a variation of the original route, but when he returned with Firmin Barrau two years later he pioneered the route later taken as the *voie normale* (but mostly ignored today because of stonefall danger) through the Coma (or Vallon) de la Paúl. On Packe's visit a steep little glacier filled the bed of this narrow valley, but this has almost completely disappeared now.

At the head of the Coma de la Paúl, the old Packe route crosses a 3062m col and moves onto the Glaciar de Posets. From here you get onto the mountain's East Face. Though not difficult to climb, a narrow gully above the glacier is threatened by stonefall, and this gives onto the North Ridge, where a short scramble leads to the summit.

A climber approaches Collado de la Paúl for an ascent of Pico Posets

The summit of Pico Posets enjoys the reputation of the finest panorama in the Pyrenees. On the other hand, though the extent of the view is immense, it can be a little disappointing, for in its vastness it is not easy to apportion scale. Here is Packe's description:

'I can confidently say that there is no spot in the Pyrenees that will compete with the Pic des Posets for a comprehensive view of all the higher summits, and their relative position in the chain. The Pic de Nethou, the loftiest point of the Maladetta [sic], is placed rather too much to the east; but from the spot on which we were now standing the central and highest peaks were spread out before us, as on a map. Pre-eminent in the west were the giant forms of Mont Perdu and the Vignemale, and beyond these the Pics du Midi d'Ossau, Baletous, Gers, and Gabisos. Then came the Neouvielle, conspicuous in the north-west, with the Pic du Midi de Bigorre seen over its shoulder. Full in front was a glorious view of abrupt mountains and snowy cols, from the Clarabide to the Perdiguère, and beyond this rose the menacing peak of the Sauvegarde... To the right of this were the well-known Ports of Venasque and Picade, and then came the ponderous mass of the Maladetta, with its crowning point, the silver Pic de Nethou, marking 10° north of east. Looking southward the eye rested on the successive ranges of the barren mountains of Arragon; and beyond these in the distant south-west, I fancied I could recognise the blue outline of the Sierra de Moncayo.' (*Peaks, Passes and Glaciers, vol. 2, 1862*)

The main backbone ridge of the massif runs roughly north to south as far as Pico Posets, then slants southwest to Las Espadas before resuming its southward trend. A secondary arête branches northeast from Posets to Pico de Bardamina and beyond to enclose the Valle de Bardamina on the north. Another veers southeast and east, with yet another going south and east away from the Espadas crest. Each of these, and their individual summits and faces, provides ample scope for climbs of varying lengths and standards of difficulty.

Seen from Viadós the West Face is almost intimidating in scale. Although it has no major rock wall or ice feature, an initial study shows a confusion of gullies and spurs. The classic route here is the ❻★ *Couloir Jean Arlaud* at the head of the Llardana glacier. When it was originally climbed in 1927 the glacier was more pronounced than it is now, and these days it makes a much more valid mixed winter climb than a summer route. The route is 350m long and graded AD, with an average angle of 50°, but with two short ice steps of 60°. Arlaud was one of the main activists in the Posets arena during the inter-war years, and it was he who made the *West Face* route direct to the summit in 1935. This is graded PD, but the rock on the final pitches is mediocre to poor. However, the *voie normale* from a Viadós base is both varied and easy, and best tackled early in the season when ice axe and crampons will be needed. Discovered in 1875 by Henry Russell and Firmin Barrau, this cuts right across the face, then tackles a slope which brings the route onto the ridge north of the summit.

From the Valle de Eriste the original east flank *voie normale* from the vicinity of the Refugio Angel Orús went up into the Valle des Ibóns, then climbed to the Glaciar de Posets to join the standard route up the broken gully leading to the North Ridge. Once again Jean Arlaud has left behind a ⓑ semi-classic PD route via the *Triangle* created at the junction of the East and Southeast arêtes, while a variation of this climbs the *South Arête* known as the Espalda de Posets. This variation (ungraded) is now the most popular route of ascent.

The Coma de la Paúl drains northward into the Rio Estós, and on the way up this valley the *North Face* is seen to the right, above the little Glaciar de la Paúl. Yet again it was Jean Arlaud who made the first ascent of this face in 1927, now graded AD-, while on the ⓑ *North Arête* a PD+ route (Carrive/Ledormeur, 1921) makes a logical ascent from the Puerto de Gistaín. Another route worth considering from a base in the Estós valley climbs the *SE Arête* after crossing Collado de la Paúl. This is gained by way of an obvious gully rising above the south side of the Posets glacier. Graded AD-, it was first climbed in 1955 by André Armengaud and J. Guilbaud. But one of the most rewarding expeditions is the ⓑ east–west traverse of Posets from Estós to Viadós. Taking about 8hrs in all, the ascent is usually made via the Coma de la Paúl and East Face *voie normale*, while the descent reverses the standard Russell/Barrau route from Viadós. A splendid day's outing which carries an overall grade of PD+.

BENASQUE

Not more than 4km north of Eriste in the Valle del Ésera lies **BENASQUE**, arguably the most important, and certainly the most optimistically developed, centre for mountain-based activities in

The broken SE Arête of Pico Posets

the Spanish Pyrenees. The old quarter lies at the heart of the place, and its narrow cobbled alleys, 13th-century church, medieval tower and thick-walled stone houses retain the atmosphere of a traditional mountain community. Around it a bustling development grows apace, but this expansion is partly limited by the ring road which curves round to bypass it to the east. A place of history, Benasque was the seat of the Counts of Ribagorça and summer home of the Aragónese nobility, their 17th- and 18th-century houses still bearing worn escutcheons over the doorways. Modern Benasque has spread out from the old village without detracting from it, and is now well established as a pleasant small town with good amenities.

Benasque has plenty of two- and three-star hotels, as well as more simple budget accommodation. There are restaurants, bars and food shops, as well as stores that specialise in outdoor gear, with others stocking maps and guides to the neighbouring mountains. The town has banks and ATMs, a laundrette and three campsites upvalley. The tourist office is the place to visit first to gather current information with regard to facilities. Open daily 9am–2pm and 5–8pm (☎ 974 55 12 89), the **Turismo** is located at the southeast corner of the old town and stocks a variety of leaflets and details of local walks. For information regarding the *parque natural*, the **Centro de Visitante** (Visitor Centre) lies about 500m south of town, just off the Carretera de Anciles. The **Compañia de Guias Valle de Benasque** (☎ 974 55 13 36) is the local guiding company, which organizes walks, climbs and trekking expeditions in the locality.

Reached by bus from Barbastro, and with taxi services and a shuttle bus operating upvalley, Benasque can accommodate the needs of both visitors reliant on public transport and those with their own vehicle. Since access by private vehicle into the *parque natural* is restricted during the high summer season (10 July – 31 August) the shuttle bus to La Besurta in the upper Ésera valley on the north side of the Maladeta is a worthwhile consideration.

Heading upvalley away from Benasque the road keeps to the east side of the Rio Ésera, while a path follows the west bank. After 2km a side-road cuts back to the right and climbs for another 4km to the ski resort of **CERLER** at 1540m (for information, ☎ 974 55 10 12). The village is said to be the highest in Aragón, but with assorted lifts it's possible to ski from 2700m on the slopes of El Gallinero (a mountain that was climbed by Dr Friedrich Parrot in 1817 during his epic traverse of the Pyrenees). Cerler boasts around 30 runs, two of which are black rated. Most of the facilities are closed in summer, but some accommodation remains open. From here it's possible to make the ascent of several summits of the Sierra Negra which overlook the village from the east. Of these **Cap de les Roques Trencades** (2756m) can be gained in about 4–4½hrs, while **Pic de Castanesa** (2859m) is climbed via the Col de Basibé in 3½–4hrs or from the north via Collado de Castanesa in 4hrs. Summit views of the south side of the Maladeta massif are said to be very fine.

Continuing alongside the Ésera beyond the Cerler turning, the road curves left to cross the river between Camping Aneto and Camping Ixeia above the old hump-backed Puente de Cubera. Just across the river a stony track turns left to Camping Chuise located at the uninspiring entrance to the Valle de Estós.

3:8 VALLE DE ESTÓS

Rimmed to the north by the frontier ridge, and traversed by GR11 and High Route trekkers, the Estós valley is one of the most attractive in the Spanish High Pyrenees. Curving round the northeast flank of

The Valle de Estós

the Posets massif it also serves as the main approach route for climbers drawn to the second highest Pyrenean summit. Until the *parque natural* was established, the delightful streamside meadows made the most idyllic of wild campsites, but camping is now officially forbidden here. However, the three-storey **Refugio de Estós** can sleep 180 and is open throughout the year (☎ 974 55 14 83). Despite its size it is often completely full in the high season, so advanced booking is advised.

The entrance to the Valle de Estós is obscured by a short and rocky defile breached by a track that pushes north into the valley proper, sometimes among trees, often through open pastures, at first along the east bank, then on the west. Views ahead are charming, and the true value of the valley is soon realised. The way passes the unmanned Cabaña de Santa Ana (1540m, 15 spaces), continues upstream and crosses below the Valle de Batisielles before veering right to reach the Cabaña del Turmo at 1730m. It was here that the pioneers used to make their base before tackling ascents of the Posets. 'The Cabane de Turmes', wrote Packe in an article that appeared in an early *Peaks, Passes and Glaciers*, 'is a very convenient station, as there is an abundant supply of firewood close at hand.'

But contrast that statement with the advice given in his *Guide to the Pyrenees*:

> 'The Cabane de Turmes is a rude stone cabane on the right bank of the stream, but the weather must be very bad indeed before you are driven to take shelter in such a smoke-grimed, filthy den; and ... most will prefer to make their resting-place to the lee of one of the boulder stones here scattered about.'

No longer an overnight option, smoke-grimed or not, the *cabaña* sits at a junction of trails leading on to the Estós *refugio*. One route crosses the stream and veers left to work upvalley heading northwest, while the alternative waymarked path remains on the south bank, as it is now, before crossing at the next bridge and joining the original approach route to the hut, which is seen perched on a bluff high above the stream at 1890m, about 4hrs from Benasque.

In addition to the standard ascent of Pico Posets, which begins at the hut and is outlined in 3:7, the valley holds plenty of alternative excursion possibilities, the following being a small selection.

WALKS AND CLIMBS FROM REFUGIO DE ESTÓS

- ◓ As all routes to the frontier ridge are steep and mostly confusing, the majority of sites of interest lie on the south flank of the valley. The first site is the **Valle de Batisielles**, a delightful region of pools, streams and stands of pine some way downvalley from the *refugio*. The entrance is gained by a trail that leads up to a damp and lightly wooded meadow graced by a small tarn, the Ibónet Pequeño de Batisielles, which has a small, vandalised hut set on its northwest shore (1½hrs). Heading west from the

The tributary glen of Valle de Perramó attracts both climbers and walkers

hut a cairned trail rises to the larger, but no less charming, Ibón Gran de Batisielles at 2222m. Other tarns lie higher up the valley under the north side of the Agullas (aiguilles) de Perramó, and a whole day could be spent just wandering from one lake to the next before returning to the Estós *refugio*.

- On the south and northeast sides of the Agullas de Perramó another collection of a dozen or so lakes and pools adds more than a sparkle to an already attractive scene. From the hut on the shore of Ibón Pequeño de Batisielles a ⬤ path cuts south then rises a little west of south for nearly 200m to gain the two Escarpinosa tarns. The onward route to Ibón Perramó and the Tartera lake under the Agullas is fussed among alpenroses and bold granite slabs, but the wild landscape of the **Valle de Perramó** is magnificent. The southern skyline consists of the Tucas d'Ixeia and a long ridge that runs round to the Batisielles peaks, broken by one or two cols that give access to the Valle de Eriste on the far side.

- A full day's ⬤ **circuit of the Perramó and Batisielles valleys**, linking many of these lakes, could be achieved by crossing from one valley head to the next under the Collado de la Piana. Allow at least 8hrs for this circuit.

- The ⬤★ **Agullas de Perramó** form a major attraction for rock climbers. The northern flank which overlooks the Valle de Batisielles holds several decent routes in the AD–TD range, mostly put up by Spanish climbers, although once again it was Jean Arlaud and his companions who created a grade D traverse of the needles in 1934. On the south (Valle de Perramó) side some D grade climbs exist, while facing these across the valley the ⬤ **Tucas d'Ixeia** (or Igea) extend the range of climbs in this corner of the massif with some moderate routes on the North Face and Northwest Arête.

- At the head of the Batisielles/Perramó valley, the 2904m ⬤ **Pico Perramó** makes an excellent belvedere from which to study a large part of the southern Posets massif. The standard ascent is ungraded. The way leads through the Valle de Perramó, and from the Tartera lake climbs northwest to the Collado de la Piana (2702m) about 4½–5hrs from the Estós *refugio*. This col lies north of the peak, and the final ascent is made without major difficulty along the ridge in about 30mins.

- The next tributary valley to the north of the Batisielles is the **Valle de Montidiego**, whose stream flows down to the Rio Estós a little below the Cabaña del Turmo. This is shorter and steeper than the previous valley, and has its own lake caught in a cirque at about 2527m between the peak of Montidiego and Batisielles Norte (2803m). ⬤ The lake is reached in about 3hrs from the *refugio*. Beyond the headwall crest above the Ibón de Montidiego lies the granite and tarn plateau of the Plan d'es Ibóns (see 3:7), while the Collado de Montidiego northwest of the lake not only gives access to the Bardamina glen but also provides a way to the summit of **Montidiego** (2764m), climbed in 1914 by Henri Brulle and his son Roger, who found a large cairn on the summit. From here they made a traverse of the ridge crest as far as Batisielles Norte, a route now graded PD.

- A minor sub-valley lying to the west of Montidiego provides one of several approaches to Pico Posets, this one pioneered by Henry Russell in 1864. The **Valle de Bardamina** flows into the Estós below Pico de Bardamina and is graced by the Ibón (or Lago) de Bardamina at about 2350m. This lake is reached in about 1½hrs from the Estós *refugio*, while a saddle above and to the southwest gives access to the Coma de la Paúl to join the standard route to Posets. Southeast of the lake three little aiguilles provide modest sport in the PD range, but to the south the valley is enclosed by the Cresta de Bardamina, a long granite ridge spreading west from the Breche de Bardamina to the Collado de la Paúl. A 5hr ascent of **ⓑ Pico de Bardamina** (3079m) can be made from the Brecha de Bardamina, while the complete traverse of the crest, first made by Henri and Roger Brulle, gives an ongoing series of panoramas that reveal most of the south side of the Posets massif.

- Each of the above-mentioned routes can be achieved from a base in the Valle de Estós, while a **◒★ multi-day tour of the Posets massif** is recommended for anyone who enjoys trekking across wild country. The first stage is spent heading west from the Estós hut, crossing the Puerto de Gistain and following the Cinqueta d'Añes Cruces downvalley below the West Face of Posets to Refugio de Viadós. Next day ascend through the Valle de Millares opposite Viadós, cross the Collado de Eriste to the wild country at the head of the Eriste valley on the south side of the highest Posets peaks, and descend to Refugio Angel Orús. This route is briefly described in 3:5 above. On the third day either descend to Eriste and Benasque in the Valle del Ésera, or traverse across the southern slopes of the massif to the 2702m Collado de la Piana and head down through the Batisielles or Perramó glens to the **Valle de Estós** and return to its *refugio* (a long day's crossing mentioned in 3:7).

FROM ESTÓS TO VALLHIVERNA

Beyond the Estós turning the valley of the Rio Ésera seduces further north, the metalled road keeping to the left side of the river while GR11 advances on the east bank, the two soon coming to the Embalse de Paso Nuevo. At the northern end of the reservoir a track slants away from the road and crosses the river to the Plan de Senarta, a shrub-dotted pasture where wild camping is permitted. Above this to the southeast lies the Vallhiverna (Ball de Ballibierna).

3:9 THE VALLHIVERNA

Cutting along the lesser-known southern side of the Maladeta massif, the Vallhiverna offers an alternative approach to the high mountains, as well as providing opportunities to explore yet more remote lake regions and make the ascent of several peaks of around 3000m on the south side of the valley, and the highest of them all on the valley's north flank. A very pleasant valley, especially in its upper reaches, the Vallhiverna has been included within the *parque natural*, so wild camping is forbidden. There is, however, a small hut about 1½hrs walk from Plan de Senarta, the Cabaña-refugio del Quillón, with about six spaces, and an hour further upvalley is the unmanned Refugio de Pescadores (also known as the Refugio Forestal del Puente de Coronas) at 1990m near the Puente de Coronas. This hut has space for about 14, but is often very busy at weekends.

A dirt road climbs into the valley from Plan de Senarta (the track is closed to vehicles between 8am and 8pm during the high summer season), and it is this which carries GR11 on its eastbound journey to the Anglos lakes, where there's another small unmanned hut, and on into the valley of the Noguera Ribagorçana.

Aneto seen from the Cresta de los Portillones – a 19th-century impression

When the track ends GR11 continues through the meadows of the Pleta de Llosás and rises towards the head of the valley, where it passes alongside the two Ibóns de Vallhiverna and, 3hrs from the *refugio*, tops the 2710m **Collado de Vallhiverna**. This is one of several crossing points in the valley's headwall, another being Collado des Isards north of Cap de Llausat. Yet more tarns lie on the eastern side of the ridge, and walkers making a base for a few days at the Pescadores *refugio* could do worse than spend time exploring here, while those with their own transport could approach these eastern lakes from the village of Aneto in the Ribagorçana's valley by a *pista* that twists up to a parking area by a dam at the southeast end of Estany de Llausat.

Southeast of the *refugio* the **Picos de Vallhiverna** are the highest summits on that side of the valley, the twisted strata revealing wavelike bucklings of their formation. There are three main summits over 3000m: Tuca de Vallhiverna at 3056m, Vallhiverna East (3030m) and the 3051m Tuca de les Culebras. The altitudes of these summits, as in many other parts of the range, have been redefined in recent years, the main peak having lost as much as 9m in the most recent survey. Packe, Barnes and Firmin Barrau were the first to climb here in 1865 and, typical of the man to whom flowers were as important as summits, Packe named one of the peaks Pic Papaver after the alpine poppy which he found growing there. More recently the Northwest Face of the highest peak has gained the attention of climbers in winter. In December 1993 Jordi Agusti and Miguel Roca created *Arcadia*, a 500m D+ route mostly up a series of gullies of 45–60°, but with one section of 70°. The ski ascent of Tuca de Vallhiverna is also a possibility.

- **The ascent of Pico de Aneto** from a base at the Pescadores *refugio*, whilst not having the popularity of the standard route from the Renclusa (see box 'Maladeta Massif', 3:10), provides a certain novelty, and more or less follows the line taken during the first ascent on 20 July 1842. Graded only *facile*, it's a longish route of 5–6hrs, with a height gain of more than 1400m. Above the *refugio* a trail climbs alongside the Barranco de Coronas as far as a small tarn, then among boulders and a clutter of rocks to a gully giving out to a second tarn. Above this lie yet more lakes at over 2700m under Aneto's western ramparts. Tucked high up in the cirque, partially enclosed by the Cresta de Cregüeña and Cresta de Llosás, a small glacier invites access to the Collado de Coronas, on whose northern side the standard route is joined for the final climb to the summit. This route offers a magnificent ski descent in winter, while on the West Face of Aneto the 300m medium-grade snow route of the **❻** *Estasen Couloir* (PD+) makes a good introduction to winter climbing here in the heart of the range when the chance of stonefall, which threatens the route in summer, is reduced by a glaze of ice. The couloir was first climbed as long ago as 1930 by Luis Estasen and José Rovira.

On the east side of the Cresta de Llosás, uncomplicated ascents are made of **Pico de Tempestades** (3296m), **Pico Margalida** (3244m) and the 3205m **Pico de Russell** on the long ridge wall that extends southeast of Aneto. The first of these was climbed initially by Henry Russell, who also made the first ascent of the peak that now carries his name, although both Pico de Russell and Margalida were climbed from the Llosás Cirque in 1905 by Louis Le Bondidier who, incidentally, named Pico Margalida after his wife.

VALLHIVERNA TO UPPER ÉSERA

Continuing upvalley through the Plan de Senarta on the east side of the Rio Ésera, the track comes to the Plan de Campamento, where a cairned path on the right strikes up the wooded hillside for a steep walk leading to the teardrop-shaped **Lago (or Ibón) de Cregüeña**, nearly 1200m above the valley. Said to be the third largest in the Pyrenees, Cregüeña lies in a deep and rocky cirque rimmed by some of the highest peaks of the Maladeta massif. Challenging onward routes from the lakeside take sure-footed trekkers with scrambling experience over Collado Cregüeña in the southeast rim to the Coronas valley above the Vallhiverna, or north into the upper reaches of the Ésera via Collado Cordier and Collado de Alba. These, however, are options that should not be attempted by general walkers, while scramblers have a choice of routes to consider. One of these tackles the west flank of **Pico de la Maladeta** (PD), and another makes the ascent of **Pico le Bondidier** (3146m) directly from the lakeside.

A short distance beyond the start of the Cregüeña path, at the far end of the Plan de Campamento, the track, or dirt road, enters the Parque Natural Posets-Maladeta, whose boundary has thus far merely edged the valley. It is here that a spur breaks away from the metalled road following the west bank of the river in order to bring traffic to the rather gloomy-looking old spa building of the Baños de Benasque, which stands on the eastern hillside with a commanding view of the Ésera and the Lliterola tributary on the far side.

Above this the valley narrows and begins to curve into its upper reaches, where the infant Rio Ésera flows, in places underground, parallel to the frontier crest.

3:10 THE UPPER ÉSERA

On the bend of the valley, on a slight rise on the left bank of the river, stands the renovated Hospital de Benasque (or Llanos del Hospital, ☎ 974 55 20 12), one-time pilgrims' hospice, but described by Packe in 1862 as 'a wretched douane station [where] all travellers are subjected to an interrogation'. He went on to say that 'refreshment, and even a bed, may be here procured, but both the fare and lodging are anything but desirable'. For decades the building stood empty and derelict, but in the mid-1990s it was transformed into an all-year centre for mountain activities with three-tier accommodation (*hostal*, *refugio* and *albergue* standard), a restaurant and bar. In winter cross-country skiing is practised here along the valley as far as La Besurta, where the dirt road ends.

The valley's metalled road comes to an abrupt end on the true right bank of the Ésera almost directly opposite the Hospital at about 1820m. Near the roadhead a path cuts up among trees to climb into the **Valle de Remuñe**, which rises to the west. A few small lakes lie in this hanging valley under Pico de Remuñe, while another is found just below Pic de Maupas.

• But by far the most popular lakes visited by walkers in this part of the Ésera are the three **Ibónes de Gorgutes** north of the Hospital immediately below the frontier ridge. ◗★ The path leading to these begins at the very end of the metalled road and climbs steeply, initially among shrubs and dwarf pine, then later over an open hillside, curving east towards the two smallest lakes, then up and round a rocky dome to locate the upper lake, about 1½hrs from the roadhead. The 2364m saddle of the Puerto de la Glera, a walker's pass leading across the border to the Cirque de la Glère and the Vallée de la Pique, is just 20mins above the lake. From the saddle a pleasant scramble (PD-) along the ridge heading northwest leads to the summit of ⊗ **Pico Sacroux** (2676m), which, thanks to its position at an apex of ridges set slightly back from the main watershed crest, enjoys one of the finest panoramic views in this part of the Pyrenees.

East of the Hospital de Benasque the Ésera acquires its most attractive face, with a series of open meadowlands rising in pine-topped steps to the Plan dels Aigualluts below the glaciers of Pico de Aneto. The first of these steps is known as the Plan d'Están ('plain of the lake'). Were you to visit in the height of summer, you may find one or two small pools shown on the map as the Ibones de Plan d'Están, but no real lake. Yet in springtime there's often a substantial sheet of water lying across at least half the valley's width, which gives the area not only its name but a charm that is all the more welcome for its temporary nature. By the end of June the lake has virtually disappeared.

At this point the valley forms a green moat between the Maladeta massif and a line of modest peaks that carry the Franco-Spanish border as a flanking wall to the north, the opposing sides of the valley offering a striking contrast one to the other. The Maladeta is a clearly defined massif adorned with a few small glaciers, the frontier crest a string of crags atop a long grass-covered hillside. In that ridge-crest almost immediately above the Plan d'Están lies the cleft of the well-known Portillón de Benás (Port de Venasque – see 3:4), the easiest and most practical of the three border crossings accessible from the

The lake in the Plan d'Están has usually disappeared by early summer

Upper Ésera. The others are the Puerto de la Glera and the Puerto de la Picada/Pas de l'Escalette.

The shuttle bus service which operates in summer from above Benasque terminates its journey at La Besurta, where there's a *kiosko* serving snacks and drinks in the main season, and it is just beyond here, where the track runs out, that the 40mins walk begins that leads to the Renclusa, base for climbs on Aneto and other summits of the Maladeta massif.

The large, barn-like **Refugio de la Renclusa** has recently been enlarged and can now accommodate 110. Owned by the Centre Excursioniste de Catalogne (CEC), it is staffed at Christmas, Easter, spring weekends, and daily from July to September (☎ 974 55 21 06). The *refugio* stands not far from the overhanging rock which made a cave-like shelter for the pioneers. Known also as Le Rencluse, this shelter served as a rough bivouac for several generations of climbers until a small hut was built nearby in 1916, where the amiable Madame Sayo from Benasque took care of the needs of visiting mountaineers.

The Maladeta Massif

When Ramond de Carbonnières came here in 1787 he was impressed by what he described as 'a very majestic summit ... covered with eternal snows [and] surrounded with large bands of ice'. Of course, much has happened in the two centuries since that was written, for the large bands of ice have shrunk considerably and very little eternal snow remains. It might also be argued that Ramond's idea of a majestic summit barely fits the Maladeta of which he was writing, although that's a subjective view, and one might suspect that this early pioneer was excited more by the overall appearance of the massif than any individual peak, of which it has several.

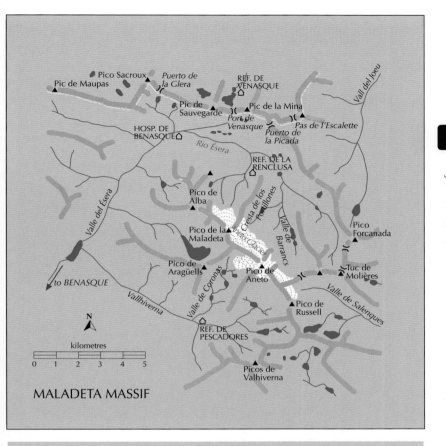

MALADETA MASSIF

'The situation, the volume, the height and ices of this mountain, made a very lively impression upon me,' he wrote. The sheer bulk of the massif *is* impressive. From Pico de Alba at its northwestern end to the subsidiary tops of Pico de Russell in the southeast, there are no less than 36 3000m summits, and nowhere in that 7km crest does the ridge fall below the magical 3000m mark. Several high lateral ridges project either side of the main crest, the easternmost of these thrusting out from Pico Margalida to Pic de les Salenques (2992m), which in turn connects with another 3000er, Tuc de Molières (or Mulleres), to enclose the Valleta de la Escaleta an upper extension of the Valle del Ésera.

Ramond's attempt to climb one of the Maladeta's summits is thought to have ended at the Collado de Alba, but 30 years later, in September 1817, Dr Friedrich Parrot arrived at the base of the mountain during his epic trans-Pyrenean trek, having collected Pierre Barrau in Luchon as his guide. After spending a night in the crude shelter of the Rencluse, they studied the Maladeta glacier, which was found to be heavily crevassed and lightly covered with snow, and perversely (for ropes were seldom used in those days on Pyrenean glaciers) they chose to ascend it by different

The Maladeta massif, from the northwest

routes. Parrot took a direct line, found a snow bridge over the bergschrund, but was then stopped by a difficult rock wall. 'The rocky mass', he wrote, 'constituted an impossible obstacle to an isolated individual', so he made a traverse to rejoin Barrau below the Collado de la Rimaya. From there it was simply a matter of finding the easiest route up the final rocks which guard the 3308m summit of Pico de la Maladeta.

The Maladeta affords a magnificent view over much of the massif northwest of Pico de Aneto, and from his vantage point Parrot made the discovery that the elegant peak seen across the eastern glacier was, in fact, unquestionably the higher summit. This was later confirmed by Reboul who computed its height at 3404m.

In 1842 Aneto received its first ascent from a French count, Albert de Franqueville, and a Russian imperial officer, Platon de Tchihatcheff, with their guides. Although beginning at the Rencluse they crossed into the Vallhiverna and attacked the mountain from the south, via the Valle and Collado de Coronas, from where they mounted the final slopes to the summit. Four days later Tchihatcheff made a second ascent, but this time by the much more direct route from the Rencluse across the Aneto glacier, which has since been adopted as the *voie normale*.

Today this ⊗ ★ popular ascent (graded PD) is achieved by hundreds of visitors each summer in 5–5½hrs from the *refugio*. At first the long Portillone crest which effectively divides the massif must be climbed, and this is usually crossed at the Portillón Superior, an obvious gap in the ridge with a gully on the eastern side by which to gain the Aneto glacier. Depending on conditions, one either crosses the glacier direct to the Collado de Coronas or skirts round the base of the Portillone to then make a traverse below the main ridge (beware bergschrunds) to join the standard route at the Coronas col. On any crossing of the glacier, rope, ice axe and crampons should be used, for there are many crevasses. Above Collado de Coronas a steep snow dome leads to the rocky crest of the Puente de Mahoma (Pont de Mohammed), which culminates on the summit. Unless glazed with ice, as it can be early in the season, the Puente de Mahoma barely warrants mention, but it's interesting to read what Packe had to say about it in the 19th century:

> 'This is an arête about 60 yards in length, composed of huge fragments of granite piled one upon the other, in a manner to present anything but a secure footing; and below this, on either side, there is a precipice, – that to the right hand extending down to the lake and gorge of Malibierne, – and the pebbles that your foot dislodges on the left fall down many hundred feet of sheer descent, and are lost in the gaping crevasses of the Nethou glacier. This bit is the most trying to the nerves of the whole expedition; and as you bestride this narrow ledge, crossing it on hands and feet, with the clouds floating around you, you feel verily suspended in mid air.' (*Guide to the Pyrenees*, 1862)

If Aneto's *voie normale* attracts large numbers in summer, it also makes a very fine ski ascent in winter and spring, while a route which combines the southeast ridge (Cresta de Tempestades) and the Cresta de Salenques provides climbing of an altogether different nature. First achieved in its entirety in 1934 by Robert Ollivier and Herbert Wild, this **ⓑ** AD+ route (rock pitches of III and IV-) begins at the 2807m Coll de Salenques, which heads the narrow Barrancs valley above the Plan dels Aigualluts and climbs along the ridge to Pico Margalida to join the Tempestades crest, which is then traced northwestward to Aneto. The north side of this crest consists of a steep rock wall giving both winter and summer climbs of up to about 350m, approached via the Tempestades glacier. Here on the Northeast Face a **ⓑ** nine-pitch route, *Gran Blau* (V/5+, 90°), was climbed in the winter of 1995 by Joan Jovier and Eduard Requeña.

There are many other routes and variations on Aneto, including 1Jean Arlaud≈'s *North Face* (AD), accessed by way of the Barrancs glacier, which finishes up a couloir on the Puente de Mahoma. This and other variations are described in the (admittedly outdated) Ollivier guide *Posets-Maladeta*, which is translated into French from the original Spanish version of André Armengaud and Agustín Jolis.

Pico de la Maladeta, being much closer to the *refugio*, offers three routes of about 4hrs each, only one of which treads glacier ice. This is the route chosen by Parrot on the first ascent in 1817 (PD). It ascends the short Maladeta glacier to a gully leading to the Collado de la Rimaya, which lies between Pico de la Rimaya (the first of the Maladeta's western peaks) and Maladeta itself, then climbs southeast to the summit. The second route works a way along the Portillone ridge (PD+, II) which terminates at the summit; and the third and easiest descends the ⊗ ★ east side of the Portillón Superior, skirts the base of the ridge aiming towards Collado Maldito, then tackles one of several short gullies that give onto the ridge south of the summit, where firm granite invites an easy way to the top.

Two or three other routes approach from the Cregüeña Cirque, while by far the most interesting is that which makes a traverse of the West Ridge from Pico de Alba – a very fine outing, mostly on good coarse granite and with a 'big mountain' feel about it, graded AD with one passage of IV.

It is the ridges of the massif, rather than the summits, that hold most appeal, and a traverse of the main central ridge which runs between Collado Maldito and Aneto is an obvious attraction. If taken in a high-level traverse from Pico de la Maladeta all the way to Aneto, this becomes a very full-day's route of about 7hrs, summit to summit, and is graded PD+. Taken one step further, a **ⓑ** full traverse of the massif from Pico de Alba to the Coll de les Salenques is perhaps the finest expedition of its kind in the Pyrenees. Anyone tempted by this should wait for good weather, carry food and plenty of water, and prepare for at least one bivouac.

On the summit ridge of Pico de Aneto, with the Cresta de los Portillones, dividing the Aneto and Maladeta glaciers, in the distance

WALKS AND CLIMBS IN THE UPPER ÉSERA VALLEY

In addition to those climbs alluded to in the box 'Maladeta Massif' (above), there are many other outings of interest to consider whilst in the upper valley.

- The 3107m **⊗ Pico de Alba** is one worth mentioning. Located at the far northwestern end of the Maladeta massif, the *voie normale* provides an uncomplicated scramble (3½hrs from the Renclusa) after passing through an attractively rugged corner of the mountains moulded by a long-departed glacier. The summit view is rewarding. To the west stretches the **ⓑ ★** Cresta de Alba, known for its 15 *gendarmes*. Graded D, and with several rock pitches of III and IV, the traverse of this ridge is reckoned to take between 5 and 7hrs, and was first completed in 1930 by Arlaud, Barrué and Escudier.

- North of Pico de Alba, to which it is joined by another ridge, stands the 2847m **ⓑ Tuca Blanca de Paderna**. An ascent via this southern arête is graded AD, while the peak's northern ridge linking it with the smaller **Tuqueta Blanca** has a short but interesting PD+ route climbed by Jean Arlaud and his companions three days before they tackled the Cresta de Alba mentioned above.

- On the north side of the valley the frontier ridge is noted for the easy ascent of ⊗ **Pic de Sauvegarde**, which is shown as Tuca de Salbaguardia on the latest EA map. A good path zigzags up to the summit from the **Portillón de Benás** (Port de Venasque – see 3:4), and a superb panoramic view of the Maladeta massif makes the walk worthwhile. A more demanding scramble can be made east of the Portillón cleft to gain the crown of **Pico de la Mina**. At 2708m this is just 30m lower than Sauvegarde, but is visited much less often than its neighbour.

The Portillón de Benás is one of the best-known frontier crossings in the Pyrenees and was used for centuries by muleteers, traders, brigands and armies travelling between Benasque and Luchon long before the present-day procession of trippers, trekkers and climbers came to it with an air of breathless expectation. Arrival at the rocky cleft does not disappoint, whichever way you approach it, for the two sides are totally different from one another. If coming from France, the appearance of the Maladeta across the green moat of the Ésera is a revelation. If leaving Spain, the sudden drama of the cliff-banked Boums du Port is no less exciting.

- The path to the Port which rises from the Ésera is well marked and obvious, and it could be used in a ◐ **circular walk** linking several other passes, as outlined under the Vallée de la Pique section (3:4). There it is described as beginning at the Hospice de France. It could, of course, just as easily begin in the Valle del Ésera.

From La Besurta below the Renclusa *refugio*, a low-level path continues upvalley to the **Plan dels Aigualluts**, a broad, flat and grassy plain dissected by streams draining from the Valleta de la Escaleta, the Barrancs valley and Aneto's glacier. A small metal bivouac hut, the so-called Cabana dels Aigualluts (8 places – emergency use only) stands on a bluff at the entrance to the Plan just above the cascade that pours the collected streams into the celebrated pit of Forau dels Aigualluts (known to the French as the Trou du Toro). This pit, or rock-walled hollow, has no obvious outlet, although until the summer of 1931 it was assumed that the Ésera itself in its several resurgences downvalley was the beneficiary of all that water. The speleologist Norbert Casteret was not so sure, and was busy studying the hydrology of the valley when he learned that a Spanish power project was planned to divert the waters of the Forau for a large electricity plant to be built in the Valle del Ésera. 'I was sure that the building of the plant would have irreparable consequences in the upper valley', wrote Casteret in *Ten Years Under the Earth* (Dent, 1940), which tells

Aneto's glacier drains into the Plan dels Aigualluts in the upper Ésera valley

how he was determined to prove his theory that the Forau's outflow was not into the Ésera, but on the northern side of the mountains.

On 19 July 1931 Casteret, his wife, mother, two friends and a Spanish muleteer arrived at the head of the valley with six barrels of fluorescein, a powerful colouring agent. The contents of these barrels were tipped into the hollow, and early the following morning the party separated to watch the various resurgences along the valley. Casteret himself crossed the ridge at the 2236m Col du Toro (Còth deth Hòro on the EA map) and descended into the Vall del Joeu (Vall de l'Artiga de Lin – see 4:7). On coming to the Goueil de Joeu he discovered that the stream pouring from it was a vivid green, thereby proving that the glaciers on the highest mountain in the Spanish Pyrenees give birth to the Garonne, the river that waters the vineyards of Bordeaux.

At the southern end of the Plan dels Aigualluts the narrow Barrancs valley, fjord-like at mid-section where lies the long Estany de Barrancs, rises to the ridge linking Pico Margalida, near the southern end of the Maladeta massif, with Pic de les Salenques and the Molières crest. Midway along this ridge the **Coll de les Salenques** provides a way into the Valle de Salenques, which falls ultimately to the valley of the Noguera Ribagorçana. A partially cairned trekker's route descends to that valley through some fine wild country.

INTO THE VALLETA DE LA ESCALETA

At the southeastern corner of the Aigualluts water-meadows a path rises alongside a stream to enter the **Valleta de la Escaleta**, at the head of which rises the double-pronged Pico Forcanada. The path approaches a cascade, rises above it, mounts a rocky bluff and edges a minor gorge to reach the first of several small tarns. Working deeper

into the glen the landscape grows more rugged, with rocks, boulders and post-glacial slabs. The right-hand (western) ridge-line is formed by a spur pushing forward from Pic de les Salenques. This is mostly glacial pavement, whose crevices are gradually being adopted by plants tolerant of the high and somewhat spartan environment. The eastern ridge is more pronounced, and links Tuc de Molières (Tuc de Mulleres) with the Forcanada and Pico Pomero, while a high but modest crest runs round from Tuc de Molières to Pic de les Salenques.

At 2807m Coll de Salenques lies at the head of the Barrancs valley

Below and a little west of Pico Pomero the easy pass of **Coll de Toro** (2236m) leads to a lake and a view down to the Pla de l'Artiga. A steep route descends to that meadowland, from where a reasonable path then climbs northwest through the Pomero valley for a return to the Ésera via the Puerto de la Picada, close to the international border.

Midway between Tuc de Molières and the Forcanada lies another pass, this one known as the **Coll d'Alfred** (2844m), which was named after the young French poet Alfred Tonnelle who made the first ascent of the Forcanada in August 1858, and is used today by climbers approaching the mountain from the Ésera.

The rock of **Pico Forcanada** (2881m) is notoriously loose, although the *voie normale* via Coll d'Alfred provides an interesting scramble graded PD (1hr from the Coll). Summit views are impressive, for the Maladeta massif focuses one's attention to the west, while to the east stretches the Vall d'Aran and a vast sea of mountains folding one after another into the muddled distances of the Pays de Couserans. The north side of the mountain falls steeply into a cirque at the head of the Vall del Joeu, and it is here that the ❶ 400m Northwest Couloir makes a fine winter route of PD+, while the East Arête holds an AD line climbed in 1927 by Abadie, Frossard and

The view northwest from Coll d'Alfred shows the Maladeta massif beyond an expanse of glacial pavement

Arlaud. The East Face is noted for its *Voie Billon* dating from 1961 (Billon, Frieux, Roynes, AD+). This is also climbed in winter, while the NNW Arête was put up by members of Arlaud's Groupe des Jeunes in the summer of 1927.

FROM THE VALLETA DE LA ESCALETA TO THE NOGUERA RIBAGORÇANA

★ The Pyrenean High Route makes its highest ridge crossing just north of Tuc de Molières at around 2900m, where a steep descent leads to a very rough and rocky terrain as the mountainside tumbles in crags to the tarns and pools of the upper Vall de Molières. The south-flanking wall of this valley is of particular interest to climbers, because roughly halfway along it rises the popular winter playground of ★ **Tuc del Mig de la Tellada** (2791m), on whose steep North and Northwest faces some first-class ice routes up to grade TD+ have been created in the couloirs. Some of these routes are as much as 500m long and boast a few spectacular near-vertical pitches. On a bluff above the north shore of the lowest of the Molières lakes, 500m or so below the ridge crossing, stands an orange-painted metal bivouac hut, Refugi de Molières, with about 12 places, which could be useful in an emergency. Below this, cairns guide the way in a wide left-hand loop to avoid a series of rock bands, then more easily down to the valley floor, where a path follows the stream as it cascades to a lower level. As height is lost, so the valley takes on a new appearance, losing its rugged upper face as the way descends to trees and meadows, and then opens to the valley of the Noguera Ribagorçana near the ugly concrete tube that signals the entrance to the Viella road tunnel.

ACCESS, BASES, MAPS AND GUIDES

Access

Vallée d'Aure D929 south from Lannemezan. Main-line trains from Tarbes or Toulouse to Lannemezan. By bus from there through the valley to Aragnouet.

Vallée du Louron D618 (Route des Pyrénées) from Arreau to Avajan, then minor road D25 south into the valley. There are buses from Arreau to Loudenvielle.

Vallée d'Oô D618 (Route des Pyrénées: Col de Peyresourde-Luchon) passes the entrance.

Vallée de la Pique Main-line trains from Toulouse to Bagnères de Luchon via Montréjeau. Minor road D125 runs from Luchon to the Hospice de France passing the entrance to the Vallée du Lys.

Valle de Gistaín Entrance to the valley is at Salinas de Sin, 20km south of the Bielsa road tunnel. There is no public transport in the valley.

Valle del Ésera Turn off N260 at Castejón de Sos and head north on C139. Bus services from Huesca and Barbastro to Benasque.

Valle de Eriste There is no road into the valley. See details for Valle del Ésera to access Eriste at the valley entrance.

Valle de Estós No road access into the valley, but there's limited parking at the entrance.

Vallhiverna Vehicle access to dirt road in the valley banned 8am–8pm. Possible taxi to the entrance from Benasque along C139.

Upper Ésera Access to the parque natural by private vehicle is subect to restrictions during the period 19 July – 31 August, but a shuttle bus service operates in high summer from the El Vado car park, about 12km north of Benasque, to La Besurta.

Valley Bases

Vallée d'Aure Arreau, St-Lary-Soulan

Vallée du Louron Arreau, Loudenvielle

Vallée d'Oô Oô, Granges d'Astau

Vallee de la Pique Bagnères de Luchon

Valle de Gistaín Plan, San Juan de Plan, Gistaín, Viadós

Valle del Ésera Sahún, Benasque

Valle de Eriste Eriste

Valle de Estós Benasque

Vallhiverna Benasque

Upper Ésera Benasque, Hospital de Benasque

Huts

There are manned huts in all the main mountain areas covered by this chapter, except on the south side of the Maladeta massif, as well as a few simple unmanned emergency shelters with only the most basic of facilities.

Maps

IGN Top 25: 1748ET *Néouvielle, Vallée d'Aure*, 1847OT *St-Bertrand-de-Comminges*, and 1848OT *Bagnéres de Luchon, Lac d'Oô* at 1:25,000

Carte de Randonnées 5 *Luchon* 1:50,000

Editorial Alpina: *Bachimala* (*Valles de Gistaín, Bielsa, Barrosa*), *Cotiella* (*Peña Montañesa etc*), *Posets, Maladeta Aneto, El Turbón* and *La Ribagorça* all at 1:25,000

Walking and/or Trekking Guides

Walks and Climbs in the Pyrenees by Kev Reynolds (Cicerone Press, 5th edn, 2008)

The GR10 Trail by Paul Lucia (Cicerone Press, 2003)

Through the Spanish Pyrenees: GR11 by Paul Lucia (Cicerone Press, 4th edn, 2008)

Trekking in the Pyrenees by Douglas Streatfeild-James (Trailblazer, 3rd edn, 2005)

The Pyrenean Haute Route by Ton Joosten (Cicerone Press, 2nd edn, 2009)

Trekking in Spain by Marc Dubin (Lonely Planet, 1990)

Walking in Spain by Miles Roddis *et al* (Lonely Planet, 2nd edn, 1999)

Pyrenees Central by Arthur Battagel (West Col, 1989)

Le Guide Rando – Luchon by Georges Véron (Rando Editions)

50 Randonnées – Aure, Louron, Luchonnais by Louis Audoubert (Éditions Milan)

Climbing Guides

Pyrénées Centrales III by A Armengaud etc (Robert Ollivier)

Posets-Maladeta by André Armengaud and Agustin Jolis
(Robert Ollivier – French edition of the CEC guide)

Pyrénées – Courses Mixtes, Neige et Glace by Francis Mousel
(Éditions Franck Mercier, 1997)

Pyrénées, Guide des 3000m by Luis Alejos (SUA Edizioak, 2003)

100 Sommets des Pyrénées by Georges Véron (Rando Editions, 2001)

See Also

Classic Walks in the Pyrenees by Kev Reynolds (Oxford Illustrated Press, 1989)

Long Distance Walks in the Pyrenees by Chris Townsend (Crowood Press, 1991)

Les Pyrénées – Les 100 Plus Belles Courses et Randonnées by Patrice de Bellefon (Editions Denoël, 1976)

CHAPTER 4: Enchanted Mountains

*Remote valleys of the Pays de Couserans district of Ariège in France, with the Vall d'Aran,
valleys of the Parc Nacional d'Aigües Tortes i Estany de Sant Maurici, and tributaries
of the Noguera Pallaresa in Spain*

ENCHANTED MOUNTAINS: CHAPTER SUMMARY

Location

East of the Maladeta massif as far as the Andorran rim. On the northern side of the border a succession of valleys drain out to the Garonne through the Pays de Couserans in Ariège. On the Spanish flank the main valleys are those that feed the Noguera Ribagorçana on the west, and Noguera Pallaresa below the Port de la Bonaigua.

★ Highlights

◔ WALKS

- a selection of routes at the head of the Vallée du Biros (4:2)
- to the Cirque de Cagateille (4:5)
- to various lakes and cascades in the mountains above Aulus-les-Bains (4:6)
- in tributaries of Vall d'Aran (4:7)
- anywhere in the Aigües Tortes national park (4:8–4:11)
- at the head of Vall Fosca (4:10)
- in the upper reaches of Vall Ferrera (4:14)
- sections of GR10, GR11 and the HRP (4:1–4:14)

● CLIMBS

- various routes on Mont Valier (4:2)
- North Face of Tuc de la Contesa in Vall de Conangles (4:8)
- long ridge routes in the Besiberri massif (4:9)
- Els Encantats and Agulles d'Amitges above Espot (4:11)

◉ SUMMITS FOR ALL

- Mont Valier (voie normale) (4:2)
- Pic de Montcalm (4:14)
- Montardo d'Aran (4:8)
- Pica d'Estats (4:14)

Contents

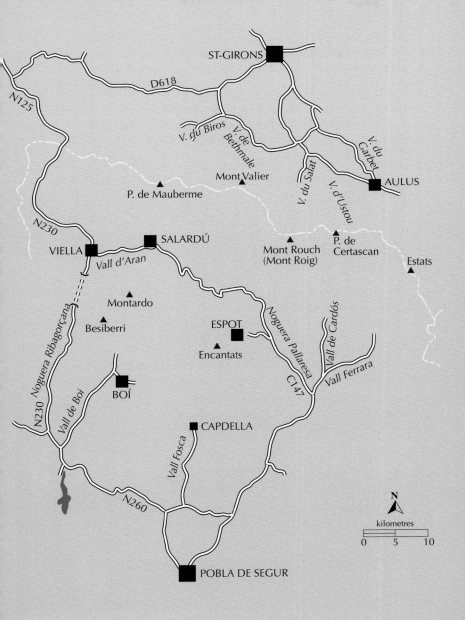

ENCHANTED MOUNTAINS: INTRODUCTION

The Vall d'Aran lies roughly central to this region of ragged peaks, lakes and forests. Although it belongs politically to Spain, the valley is geographically French, since it's located on the northern side of the watershed. The international frontier runs along mountains several kilometres to the north, and the French valleys that drain the border country are among the most remote and economically deprived in all France.

Once penetrated the Ariège landscape rewards with some surprisingly attractive terrain. The high country emerges from a sea of forested foothills to reveal a secluded upland where only a comparative handful of trails seek ways across ribs and spurs that project from rarely visited summits. It's a damp, green, but mist-wreathed country. Abandoned mines and ungrazed pastures speak of its isolation, for habitation is scarce, and communities boasting anything more useful than a foodstore, simple hotel or *gîte d'étape* are few and far between and generally situated a long way from mountains of interest. Public transport is infrequent or non-existent, and the narrow winding roads provide little more than a tortuous link from one side of the region to the other. The only cross-border route for vehicles lies at the western end, where N125 south of Montréjeau follows the Garonne upstream into the Vall d'Aran.

Although north of the border the country has considerable appeal for those who appreciate solitude, it is the Spanish side of the region that wins most plaudits. The Parc Nacional d'Aigües Tortes i Estany de Sant Maurici is the prime attraction. It is roughly bordered on the north by the Vall d'Aran, to the west by the Noguera Ribagorçana, to the east by the Noguera Pallaresa, and to the south by the upper reaches of the Valls de Boí and Fosca. This is a splendid lake-dazzled country of both granite and limestone mountains, where walks of quality abound and entertaining climbs can be found on many of its scattered peaks. Despite their appeal most of these are of modest height, but along the western edge of the national park the Besiberri group boasts six 3000m summits, while a seventh rises a little farther to the east above the Cavallers lake.

East of the Noguera Pallaresa the Valls de Cardós and Ferrera push deep into the mountains, similar in their remote appeal to neighbouring valleys across the border. Vall Ferrera gives access to the most easterly of Pyrenean 3000m mountains; a group of four main peaks and two secondary summits, most notably Pica d'Estats and Pic de Montcalm – the first actually astride the frontier, the second a short step away in France.

Collado de l'Estany de Mar makes a belvedere from which to study the granite plateau dominated by Estany Tort de Rius to the northwest

4:1 THE PAYS DE COUSERANS

Major road systems splay out of Toulouse heading for Ariège and the Pyrenean foothills, among them N117 which follows the Garonne upstream. About 60km from Toulouse D117 breaks away heading south and southeast to **ST-GIRONS**, a pleasantly situated market town that serves as capital of the Couserans district in the administrative *département* of Ariège. Built at a confluence of three rivers – the Baup, the Lez and the Salat – about 45km west of Foix, St-Girons holds the key to access to the remote country up towards the frontier, with infrequent bus services feeding into, or towards, the empty heart of the region. The Maison de Couserans on Place Alphonse-Sentein houses the Office du Tourisme (☎ 05 61 96 26 60), and a handful of modest hotels provide accommodation. About 2km to the southeast there's a campsite at the Centre de Loisirs du Parc de Paletès, with 50 dormitory places.

Should you find yourself marooned here for a day or two, the little stone-walled hilltop township of **ST-LIZIER** is worth a visit. Just 2km from St-Girons, this impressive cluster of red-roofed buildings, turreted 14th-century bishop's palace and a wonderful **cathedral** with an octagonal tower and marble-pillared Romanesque cloisters will take care of at least half a day whilst waiting for transport into the mountains.

In summer buses (not Sundays) leave St-Girons heading for small towns or villages that have access to valleys of interest to outdoor activists: Les Bordes at the mouth of Vallée de Bethmale (with the Vallée du Riberot nearby), Sentein in the Vallée du Biros, Seix (and/or Pont de la Taule) for the Upper Salat and Vallée d'Ustou, and Aulus-les-Bains near the head of the Vallée du Garbet.

The road out of St-Girons which leads to Les-Bordes and Sentein is the D618. Heading southwest it follows the Lez river through a few small villages, and then forks at **ANDRESSEIN**, about 12km from St-Girons. The continuing route for the Vallées de Bethmale and Biros here becomes the D4, while D618 branches right (west) into the Vallée de la Ballongue on the way to the Col de Portet d'Aspet and Luchon.

COL DE PORTET D'ASPET is at a modest 1069m. A café-restaurant (Chalet des Pyrénées) stands on the south side of the road, and there's parking space to the north. The northern hillside rises to the limestone Crête de Cornudère, which provides good views over the green Ariège foothills and up to summits that trace the frontier ridge.

WALKS FROM COL DE PORTET D'ASPET

One of the region's multi-day walking tours, the Tour de Cagire Burat, crosses the road heading south, and other walking routes of varying lengths can be joined here too.

- From the parking area on the north side of the road a ◐ 4hr circular walk begins where a path sets off left of a forest track. At first aiming northeast, it soon cuts west then northwest through woods before rising to a 1478m saddle between Tuc de la Casse and Tuc de Haurades. Here you bear right along the ridge, crossing the summits of Tuc de Haurades and Cap des Tèches, north of which lie the celebrated *gouffres* (potholes) of la Henne-Morte and Coume Ouarnède. The **Crête de Cornudère** continues, dips to the Pas de l'Ane and rises again to Tuc de Tucol, the high point of the circuit at 1579m. Leave the ridge and traverse eastward to a *cabane*, then gain the Sommet de Cornudère (1561m) about 30mins from Tuc de Tucol. The circuit then descends southward to pick up the forest track seen at the start of the walk, and follows it back to the Col de Portet d'Aspet.

• Another possibility worth considering from the col is the easy ascent of ⊗ **Le Puech**, a 1669m summit south of the road, from which more fine views of the Ariège mountains can be studied, in particular Mont Valier to the southeast and the distant Maladeta massif to the SSW. Allow 3–3½hrs for the round-trip via Col de la Bène.

• • •

Returning towards Audressein, D618 describes a few hairpins, passes through the village of Portet d'Aspet and descends further to **ST LARY**, where a minor road (D304) breaks off to the south alongside the Bouigane river. The valley cut by this river divides about 2km from St Lary, the two upper stems being separated by a wooded spur pushed north from the 2210m ⊗ **Pic de la Calabasse**. A forest road penetrates the southwest valley stem, with parking space at 1130m about 8km from St Lary. From here the ascent of Pic de la Calabasse can be made in 3½hrs, the first 1½hrs of which simply follow the continuing forest track as far as the Col de l'Herbe Soulette, marked by a large concrete cross. The summit is gained by way of an uncomplicated ridge-walk, and the panorama is far-reaching. ❶ The Northwest Face of this same mountain boasts a 300m grade PD route that makes a fine winter climb.

4:2 VALLÉE DU BIROS

South of Audressein D4 passes through **CASTILLON-EN-COUSERANS**, an old village with a weekly market overlooked by the fortified 12th-century Chapelle-St-Pierre, which stands on a wooded bluff on the site of a one-time fortress of the Counts of Comminges. The village houses the local district Office de Tourisme in the now defunct railway station (☎ 05 61 96 72 64).

At **LES BORDES-SUR-LEZ**, the next village along the valley, interest is centred on the oldest bridge in the 18 valleys of the Pays de Couserans and the 12th-century Romanesque church of Ourjout,

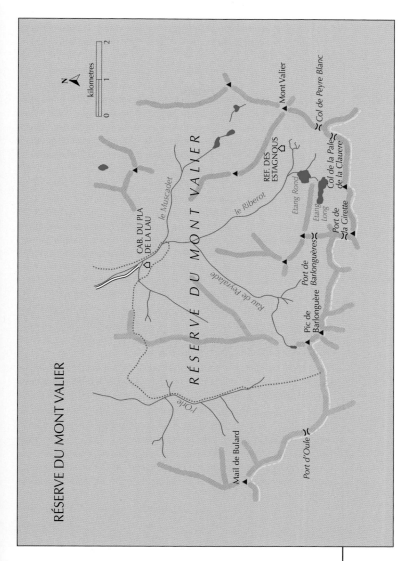

RÉSERVE DU MONT VALIER

RÉSERVE DU MONT VALIER

Mont Valier
Col de Peyre Blanc
Col de la Palle
de la Clauere
REF. DES
ESTAGNOUS
Etang Rond
Etang
long
Port de
la Cirette
Port de
Barlonguères
CAB. DU PLA
DE LA LAU
le Muscadet
le Riberot
Rau de Peyralade
Pic de
Barlonguère
l'Orle
Mail de Bulard
Port d'Oule

kilometres

near where the road to Port de la Core and Seix breaks off into the Vallée de Bethmale.

Ignoring for now this side-road, continue along the inviting Vallée du Biros for another 2km to the opening of the Riberot tributary on the left. Signed Ayer and Riberot, a narrow paved road turns into this valley and after 6km becomes a good quality track, which ends after another 2km at a terraced parking area complete with picnic tables, toilet block and a large information board showing a variety of walking possibilities, most of which are routed within the 9000 hectare Réserve du Mont Valier – the oldest in the Pyrenees. The path of GR10 crosses the valley at this point where the unmanned, concrete-built Cabane du Pla de la Lau (927m) provides basic shelter for eight trekkers.

Apart from walks along the waymarked GR10, a trio of small lakes below the North Face of Mont Valier may be reached by the ● **Circuit du Trois Lacs**. Two other lakes, the **Etangs Rond and Long**, are approached from the path to Refuge des Estagnous west of the mountain. Using the Estagnous hut for an overnight base (see below for details), these last-named lakes may be visited as part of a longer walk which crosses Port de Barlonguère and descends through the Peyralade valley back to the car park. Alternatively, there's a ● grade D *via ferrata* on rocks above the lake. **Col de la Pale de la Clauere** (2522m) on the frontier ridge above Etang Long is also accessible from Pla de la Lau in 6hrs, while the ascent of the 2802m **Pic de Barlonguère**, astride the frontier west of Mont Valier, may be made in about 4½–5hrs when approached through the Peyralade valley. Between Pic de Barlonguère and Mont Valier, where the frontier ridge makes a brief north–south kink, **Port de la Girette** (2442m) provides a cross-border route to Montgarri in the upper reaches of the Noguera Pallaresa in Spain. Although not marked on the 1:50,000 Carte de Randonnées, this col is sometimes adopted by trekkers as a High Route *variante*.

CLIMBS ON MONT VALIER

Three and a half hours from Pla de la Lau by a path heading southeast beyond the Cascade de Nerech leads you to **Refuge des Estagnous** (2246m), base for climbs on Mont Valier which rises to the east. The refuge has places for 76 and is staffed continuously from June to mid-October (plus weekends, weather permitting, from May to mid-November, ☎ 05 61 96 76 22). From here the ⊗★ *voie normale* ascent of **Mont Valier** (2838m) takes 1½–2hrs. The standard route follows an obvious path southeast up to the 2643m Col de Faustin, then northeast without difficulty to the summit, located about 1km north of the frontier ridge.

Seen from as far away as Toulouse, the elegant Mont Valier was once considered to be the highest Pyrenean mountain, and according to legend was climbed by the first Bishop of Couserans, St Valier, in the fifth century. What is certain is that in 1672 a white stone cross was placed on the top on the orders of B. de Marmiesse, Bishop of St-Lizier. The summit panorama is justifiably celebrated as one of the best and most extensive in this corner of the Pyrenees.

From the foothills Mont Valier appears as a graceful pyramid, but the 800m East Face presents a very different aspect, and is divided from the Southeast Face by a profound rib. Both of these faces, which are best reached not from the Vallée du Riberot but via the long Estours valley (see 4:4), have a number of routes in the D–TD range, including the ● 900m Bellefon/Viorrain route on the *SE Spur* (D+, IV/ IV+, 60°) put up over two days in January 1983, as well as the *Faustin*

Couloir (AD, IV), which is also treated as a winter climb. The ★ *Voie du Trou Noir* on the great East Face is one of the classics. Climbed over a two-day period in September 1971 by a rope of four led by Louis Audoubert, it's graded TD- with pitches of IV+ and V, and is celebrated as one of Patrice de Bellefon's *100 Plus Belles Courses*.

The 🅑 North Face, which overlooks three small tarns, is reached from the Estagnous refuge by crossing the Col de Pouech to the north. The original on this face is graded TD and was first climbed in winter in January 1970.

THE UPPER VALLEY

Back in the main Vallée du Biros, southwest of the Riberot valley's entrance, a secondary road climbs 200m up the northern hillside to the hamlet of **BALACET** (909m), which is on the route of the 3–4 day Tour du Biros (see below) and outlined in red on the 1:50,000 Couserans–Cap d'Aran map. Following this route for an hour up the hillside leads

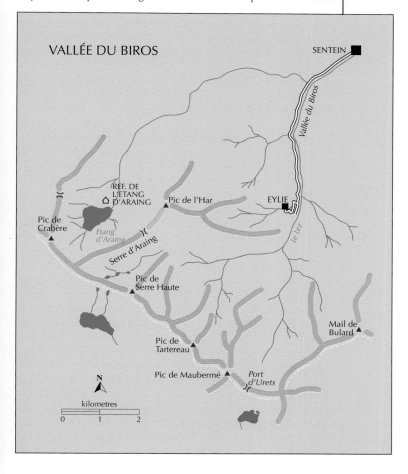

to Col de l'Arraing (1350m). The Tour du Biros then heads west across the flank of Pic de l'Arraing, but the easy ridge that runs between that summit and ◐ **Pic de Sérau** (1720m) by way of Pic de Moussau provides an entertaining walk along a belvedere from which to study the layout of the Vallée du Biros and its walling mountains to the south, and the Vallée de la Ballongue to the north. Allow 2hrs to reach Pic de Sérau from Col de l'Arraing.

The bus from St-Girons terminates in **SENTEIN**, the main village in the upper Vallée du Biros and the last place to stock up with supplies for the mountains. This modest thermal spa has an interesting 14th-century church flanked by two towers that were once part of a fortified curtain wall. There's a tourist office (☎ 05 61 96 10 90), PTT and foodstore, and accommodation is found in the hotel, Le Crabère. Sentein also has a municipal campsite, La Grange, while 2km back along the valley, there's a 24-place *gîte d'étape* in **BONAC**, Le Relais Montagnard (open all year, ☎ 05 61 04 97 57).

Although devoid of public transport, the road continues beyond Sentein, where the valley narrows and curves southward. The tarmac eventually ends after another 6km at the small two-part village of **EYLIE**, a one-time mining settlement semi-enclosed by the Cirque du Lez.

Writing about his exploration of the nearby Grotte de la Cigalère in 1932, Norbert Casteret described the head of the Vallée du Biros in his celebrated memoir, *Ten Years Under the Earth (Dent, 1940)*:

> 'Its walls are abrupt and covered with frozen snow; cliffs striped with waterfalls drop from five thousand five hundred feet to the forest zone, and so to the bottom of the valley, where the torrent of Lez unites all the streams of the cirque.'

Casteret's explorations revealed what he called 'a palace of crystal,' but this has since been sadly ransacked. The *grotte*, incidentally, interconnects with the Gouffre Martel, one of the world's deepest potholes, also discovered by Casteret.

Despite its modest size and general lack of facilities, the upper part of Eylie hamlet, **EYLIE D'EN HAUT**, boasts a 20-bed *gîte d'étape* (open all year, ☎ 05 61 96 14 00), which is usefully placed, since not only do the GR10 and Tour du Biros pass through, but a variety of other ◐★ walks and modest ascents can be made from a base here.

About 4hrs west of Eylie across the ridge of Serre d'Araing on the route of GR10, **Étang d'Eraing** lies in a deep basin below Pic de Crabère and the frontier ridge. This mountain lake is a popular excursion, especially as it has a CAF refuge on its north shore providing an opportunity for overnight accommodation. **Refuge de l'Étang d'Araing** stands almost 1000m higher than Eylie at 1950m; it has 53 places and is fully manned from mid-June to the end of September (☎ 05 61 96 73 73). From it – or indeed from Eylie itself – several ascents of a non-technical nature can be made: **Pic de Crabère** (2629m) and **Pic de Serre Haute** (2713m) on the frontier ridge overlooking the Vall d'Aran, and **Pic de l'Har** (2424m) to the east of the refuge. Although Pic de Crabère can be summited by an undemanding route from the refuge, the ⓑ 300m *NorthEast Couloir* is a very different proposition. A noted winter route, it is graded AD, with one 20m section of 60°.

Standing at the very head of the valley on the frontier ridge, **Pic de Maubermé** (2880m) is the highest mountain in the Pays de Couserans, claiming an extensive summit view which includes Pic du Midi de Bigorre and Pic Long far to the west, the nearer Posets and Maladeta massifs, and the Encantats to the south. The *voie normale* ascent route is long (9hrs there and back) but uncomplicated, while on its northwest flank the ⓑ Couloir de Tartereau gives 1300m of climbing at AD-. This route is becoming a favourite among locals in search of winter sport.

Northeast of Pic de Maubermé, 2750m, **Mail de Bulard** also carries the frontier ridge, and pushes forward a spur to the north which effectively divides the upper Vallée du Biros from the shorter Vallée de l'Orle. GR10 crosses that ridge-spur at Col de l'Arech (2hrs from Eylie), from where a 2½hr ascent of Mail de Brulard can be made. Allow about 7½–8 hrs for the round trip. This mountain also overlooks the Vallée de l'Orle where the *Cabane de Grauillès* provides basic shelter for about eight, and is used by climbers tackling the ⓑ 500m NorthEast Face (D+, III/IV) which, as a winter route, has been compared to the North Face of the Taillon above Gavarnie.

Before leaving this brief intrusion into the head of the Vallée de l'Orle, mention ought to be made of **Pic des Cingles** on the frontier ridge above Port de l'Orle. The ⓑ banded North Face of this 2582m mountain has an AD+ route of about 630m chosen by Francis Mousel as one of his recommended 'courses mixtes, neige et glace' (see 'Climbing guides' in Summary box below).

At the northern end of the ridge-spur projecting from Mail de Bulard, the modest ⊗ **Pic de Courbayran** (1759m) is sufficiently detached from the frontier ridge's alignment that its isolated position makes it an exceptionally fine viewpoint. All the major summits of the Pays de Couserans are spread in a line to the south, east and west, and the ease by which the Pic is reached makes it worth seeking out. Whether starting from the Vallée du Biros (a little under 2km north of Eylie d'un Bas) or at Luentein in the neighbouring Vallée de l'Orle, Col des Cassaings is the point to make for on the ridge. From the col a path heads north, just below the main crest on the west flank, skirts the crown of Tuc de la Ruère and gains the unmarked summit of Pic de Coubayran in about 1½hrs.

THE TOUR DU BIROS

This 3- to 4-day walking tour is traced in red on the 1:50,000 Carte de Randonnées sheet of the region, and is included in the topoguide

6 Grandes Randonnées en Ariège. Being a circuit it can be joined at any one of a number of locations, but here it's described from **EYLIE**.

- ◖★ The first stage is relatively short, since it follows the route of GR10 westward to Refuge de l'Étang d'Araing, about 4hrs away, but then GR10 is left behind as the tour goes roughly northeast among beechwoods to **LE PLAYRAS**, where there's a *gîte d'étape* (☎ 05 61 96 77 14). Out of Le Playras the way continues over a series of cols and across the flank of Pics de Serau, Moussau and Arraing before dropping to the valley floor near **BONAC** and another *gîte d'étape* with 24 places (☎ 05 61 66 75 57). Thereafter the Tour du Biros turns along its eastern stage, the first section of which journeys south along the mid-height wooded east flank of the Vallée de l'Orle. Eventually rejoining GR10, the trek then descends into the valley and climbs out again heading west to Col de l'Arech before swooping down to the Vallée du Biros and Eylie, where the circuit began.

4:3 VALLÉE DE BETHMALE

At **LES BORDES-SUR-LEZ** the D17 Route des Pyrénées enters the broad, open Vallée de Bethmale, climbs southeastward to the Port de la Core, and continues over that pass for another 10km to Seix. The valley is noted for its beauty, its folklore, the distinctive costumes traditionally worn by its inhabitants, and for the sparsity of its population. In 1990, for example, the village of Bethmale (or Arrien-en-Bethmale) contained only 96 inhabitants, and it's said that the valley as a whole numbers no more than 300 now. The few tightly clustered hamlets are either semi-deserted or their houses have been taken over for holiday homes, while the hillsides are pocked with old stone barns as a reminder of the pastoral nature of lost generations, for these would once have housed families from the valley during the summer transhumance. Only **AYET** is of interest to outdoor activists looking for somewhere to use as a base, for it has a 12-place *gîte d'étape* open throughout the year (☎ 05 61 96 81 71).

- West of Port de la Core near the head of the valley, and reached by a ◖ walk of only a few minutes, the shallow green **Étang (or Lac) de Bethmale** is an exquisite site and a popular destination for both trippers and anglers. Visited by walkers on the GR10, the lake is circled by beech trees and has a basic shelter on its eastern shore.

- A second small post-glacial lake worth a visit from the ◖ upper Vallée de Bethmale is the **Étang d'Ayes**. This too is on the route of GR10 and can be reached by following a forest track west of

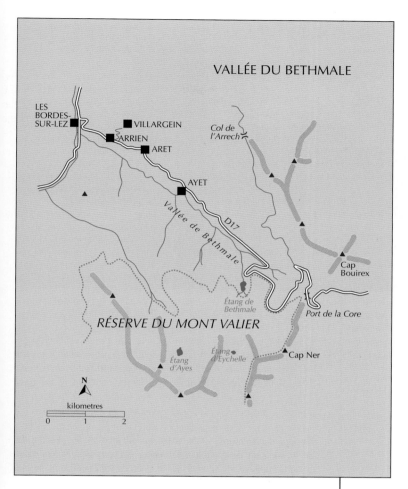

VALLÉE DU BETHMALE

LES BORDES-SUR-LEZ
VILLARGEIN
ARRIEN
ARET
AYET
Col de l'Arrech

Vallée de Bethmale
D17

Cap Bouirex

Étang de Bethmale
Port de la Core

RÉSERVE DU MONT VALIER

Étang d'Ayes
Étang d'Eychelle
Cap Ner

N

kilometres
0   1   2

4:3 VALLÉE DE BETHMALE

Étang de Bethmale as far as a parking area, then continuing along the former GR10 (the route of which now takes a higher path) for about 2–2½hrs. To make a circular tour of around 5–6hrs, return to Étang de Bethmale by sticking to the current path of the GR10 via Col d'Auédole (1730m).

- Remaining with GR10, a walk of little more than an hour from the lake leads to the **Port de la Core** (1395m), which has a few kilometres of *ski de fond* trails in winter (ski information, ☎ 05 61 96 52 90). Along the ridge to the south the summits of **Tuc d'Eychelle** (2315m, 2½hrs) and **Tuc de Quer Ner** (2389m, 3½hrs) are worth a diversion, while a return to the road pass could be varied by heading west from the latter peak, then north into a basin draining down to a tiny lake, Étang d'Eychelle. Northwest of the lake a path continues as far as GR10, then immediately

Étang de Bethmale is one of the most popular sites in the Bethmale valley

breaks away east to return to Port de la Core, making a circuit of about 7hrs in all.

- A much shorter walk from Port de la Core, and one that comes highly recommended on account of its 360° panorama, leads to the 1873m **Cap de Bouirex**, which lies northeast of the pass and is set far enough away from the frontier crest to have an almost unbroken view of Mont Valier and its neighbours.

- Finally, a rather full day's walking **tour of the Vallée de Bethmale** can be created by linking some of the valley's old farming trails in a circuit of 6–7hrs. From **ARET**, 30mins below Ayet, a path climbs east along the north-flanking hillside visiting a succession of old *granges* on the way to **Col de l'Arrech**. This is crossed by a *piste forestière* which links Castillon-en-Couserans with the Port de la Core. Now heading southeast, a path is taken between the ridge crest and the forest track all the way to the **Port de la Core**, where GR10 is joined (3½hrs). Descend along GR10 to the Lac de Bethmale, and continue from there down to Ayet.

4:4 THE UPPER VALLÉE DU SALAT

Out of St-Girons the most direct route to gain the upper valley of the Salat is the D618 which accompanies the river heading southeast, passing on the left the entrance to the luxuriant valley of the Nert, and continuing beyond **LACOURT** into the Gorges de Ribaouto as far

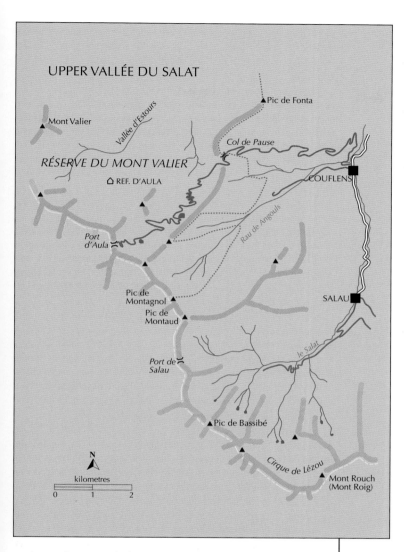

UPPER VALLÉE DU SALAT

▲ Pic de Fonta

Mont Valier

Vallée d'Estours

Col de Pause

RÉSERVE DU MONT VALIER

⌂ REF. D'AULA

COUFLENS

Rau de Angouls

Port
d'Aula

Pic de
Montagnol

SALAU

Pic de
Montaud

Port de
Salau

le Salat

▲ Pic de Bassibé

N

kilometres

0   1   2

Cirque de Lézou

▲ Mont Rouch
(Mont Roig)

as the confluence with the Arac. Here the road divides. D618 now leaves the Salat on a winding course through the foothills below the Massif de l'Arize to Massat, ancient capital of the Couserans, while D3 turns south to **SOUEIX, OUST** (at the mouth of the Vallée du Garbet) and **SEIX**, where the cross-country route from Les Bordes via the Bethmale valley and Port de la Core enters from the west.

SEIX is an old market town and the obvious place from which to begin an exploration of the upper valley. Overlooked by a crumbling 16th-century château, in summer tourist information with route guides, maps and timetables for sale is housed on Place de l'Allée (☎ 05 61 96 00 01). There are two hotels, a campsite, Le Haut Salat (open throughout the year) and several useful shops apart from food outlets, cafés, bank (infrequent opening) and a post office. A 15-place *gîte d'étape* is found 3km to the southwest in **AUNAC** on the route of GR10 (☎ 05 61 66 82 15).

The road south out of Seix continues alongside the Salat with a determination to stick close to the river through wooded narrows almost as far as its source. At the hamlet of **COUFLENS DE BETMAJOU**, a little under 3km from Seix, the **Vallée d'Estours** slices into the foothills of Mont Valier to the southwest. It's an attractive wooded valley, at first with a minor metalled road running into it, but this soon becomes a stony track that eventually gives way to a footpath. GR10 comes this way, working upstream to the unmanned Refuge d'Aula at 1550m in the cirque immediately to the east of Mont Valier. Permanently open, the refuge can house about 10 in two rooms.

Using the refuge as a base, climbs on the East and Southeast faces of Mont Valier (see 4:2) become accessible by a very short approach. Walkers, trekkers and scramblers can also find outings to suit in the head of the Estours valley. Southeast of the hut, for example, ◖**Étang d'Areau** is reached by a walk of less than 1½hrs along the route of GR10. **Port d'Aula** on the frontier ridge is easily gained too, by a combination of GR10 and a road that has fallen into disrepair, and from there one could either descend to the Noguera Pallaresa in Spain, trace the frontier to the right (on the Spanish flank) and use that as a means of climbing Mont Valier, or trek southeast across high Spanish pastures to Port de Salau, where you re-enter France and descend into the head of the Vallée du Salat. Both these last two options are for experienced mountain trekkers only, and adopt sections of the HRP or one or other of its *variantes*.

Between Port d'Aula and Port de Salau, the ⊗ 2496m **Pic de Montaud** stands astride the frontier ridge just outside the Réserve du Mont Valier. This can be approached from the north and climbed along the frontier crest in 30mins from the Portanech d'Aurénère (2331m) – a col midway between Montaud and Pic de Montagnol.

Another secondary peak, but a splendid belvedere, ⊗ **Pic de Fonta** (1934m), is located northeast of Col de Pause and can be reached from there by an uncomplicated route in a little under 2hrs. As for GR10, this long-distance trek crosses an unnamed col above and to the southeast of the Aula refuge, descends to Étang d'Areau, then more or less follows a minor road over the 1527m **Col de Pause** and down broom-golden hillsides to **Couflens** in the upper Salat valley.

SALAU AND THE BORDER COUNTRY

Beyond Couflens de Betmajou the road twists round to **PONT DE LA TAULE**, gateway to the Vallée d'Ustou and a cross-country route to Aulus-les-Bains (see 4:5) – accommodation may be found here at the one-star Auberge des deux Rivières. The Salat route continues south through the wooded wedge-like valley for another 5km to **COUFLENS**. The village has no facilities, but there's a basic campsite just outside to the west (Camping Les Bouriès) and a *gîte d'étape* 30mins walk uphill to the east along the GR10. The Gîte-Ferme de Rouze can accommodate 15 in its dormitories (☎ 05 61 66 95 45), with home-made cheese and excellent views among its attractions.

Another 5km alongside the river brings the road to **SALAU**, once a haunt of smugglers, the highest of the Salat villages buried deep within the heart of Ariège. In the early1960s there were plans to drive a trans-Pyrenean tunnel through the mountains here, but that seems to have been forgotten – or perhaps those plans were overtaken when the road out of Couflens was built over Col de Pause and up to the frontier at the Port d'Aula, but which being unmet from the Spanish side is now breaking up for lack of maintenance under the onslaught of a hostile climate.

The valley divides into two stems, with Salau standing at the confluence of the rivers Salat and Cougnets that drain them. In the autumn of 1937 these rivers flooded, sweeping through the village and destroying many houses. But Salau has since come back to life and in the summer can be used as a base from which to explore the high country beyond. Accommodation may be found in the Auberge des Myrtilles and the 15-place Gîte La Fourque (☎ 05 61 66 96 74).

⊘ **Mont Rouch** (or Mont Roig) is the dominant mountain hereabouts. At 2858m it's the highest frontier summit between Pic de Maubermé and the 3000m Estats massif, and one that looks out over some of the least-inhabited country in all the Pyrenees, Spanish as well as French. Two HRP *variantes* skirt round it: one to the north, the other to the south, but those who make the effort to reach its summit will be rewarded, on the proverbial clear day, by a striking panoramic view that clearly illustrates the difference between the two sides of the watershed. A narrow road continues out of Salau into the southwest, Salat, stem of the valley. At the first hairpin a path, adopted by the HRP, breaks off for the Port de Salau, while the route to Mont Rouch continues on the road. About 1km beyond the path junction a sign announces limited access for vehicles. Those making for Mont Rouch will carry on to the very fine Lézou waterfall and a series of hairpin bends before climbing into the Cirque du Lézou, which drains the northwest flank of the mountain. High in the cirque the ascent route veers left in order to gain the Crête du Laquet, which is then followed round to the summit (6hrs from Salau).

The route to **Port de Salau**, as mentioned above, cuts away from the road at its first hairpin out of the village and angles up the forested hillside, heading roughly west before breaking out across more open country. On the way to the pass there's an unmanned hut, the Cabane du Pouill, at 1550m, with places for about a dozen, and just below the frontier crest is shelter for eight in a simple refuge.

• The southeastern stem of the valley carries the ◐ continuing HRP on a difficult stage that crosses the **Col de Crusous** (2217m) heading east. For the first 4km the route follows a road built to service France's only tungsten mine, opened in the 1960s but now closed down. Thereafter the HRP follows paths and tracks for a total of about 3½hrs from Salau to reach the col, which lies north of the frontier ridge. Standing on that ridge to the south ⊗ **Pic de la Montagnoule** (2623m) is gained in another hour, and once again the summit enjoys an immense view, with a cluster of lakes on the Spanish side lending a sparkle to the landscape. (Allow 3–3½hrs to descend back to Salau.)

4:5 VALLÉE D'USTOU

Wider and much more pastoral in nature than the Salat, the Vallée d'Ustou is another of the gems of Pays de Couserans. Drained by the Alet, the valley is traversed by the D8, on which public buses journey between Pont de la Taule and Aulus-les-Bains via Col de la Trape, while a secondary road breaks away to the south to provide access to the upper valley, of primary interest to walkers, trekkers and climbers.

The Vallée d'Ustou angles southeastward out of the Salat at **PONT DE LA TAULE**, with mottled stone barns lining the valley and, from a distance, creating an impression of freckles on the hillsides. After about 6km the road enters **LE TREIN D'USTOU**. Though little more than a village, Le Trein is the valley's largest community, and its hotel, L'Auberge des Ormeaux, is one of the few places in which to stay. Beyond the village D8 begins the climb to Col de la Trape, while the upper valley entices to the south with D38 curving into it, passing through **Bielle**, then **ST-LIZIER** (or St-Lizier-d'Ustou, to give its full title). Visited by trekkers following GR10, this one-street village has a municipal campsite, a shop, café and swimming pool. A little further south, on the east bank of the stream, **BIDOUS** has a 20-place *gîte d'étape*, L'Escolan (☎ 05 61 96 58 72) that has been converted from the village school.

The green and gentle countryside grows more attractive as you progress further south with good mountain views ahead, and at the small hamlet of **STILLOM** (not marked on the 1:50,000 map), where the valley forks, a sign directs the way for the Cirque de Cagateille across the stream to the left. (The right branch of the valley is the one to take for a crossing of Port de Marterat, described below.) The left-hand road continues for another 4km through what is now the valley of the Cors, and ends at a small parking area at 1000m altitude, complete with picnic tables and toilet block.

Local publicity heralds the **Cirque de Cagateille** as the second major Pyrenean amphitheatre after Gavarnie. It is, indeed, impressive, but there are many other cirques that could claim as much. Comparisons, though, are invidious; the Cirque de Cagateille is a site of great beauty and the walk to it one to enjoy. ◗★ From the car park trailhead it will only take 45mins to reach its base, and less

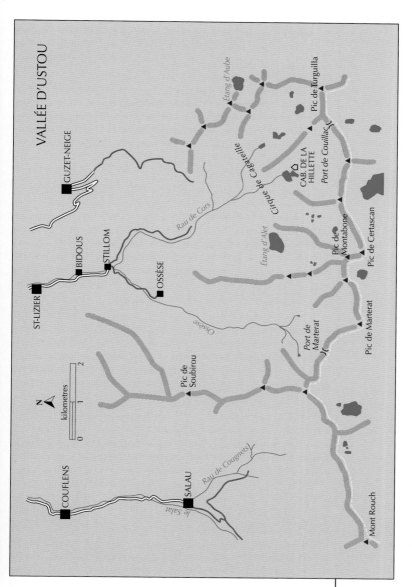

Map labels:
GUZET-NEIGE
ST-LIZIER
BIDOUS
STILLOM
OSSÈSE
COUFLENS
SALAU
Rau de Cors
Ossèse
le Salat
Rau de Cougnets
Etang d'Aube
Etang de Cabatelle
Cirque de Cabatelle
Etang d'Alet
CAB. DE LA HILLETTE
Pic de Turguilla
Port de Couillac
Port de Couillac
Pic de Montabone
Pic de Certascan
Pic de Marterat
Port de Marterat
Pic de Soubirou
Mont Rouch
N
kilometres
0   1   2

than that to gain a splendid view of it. The path is well trodden and easy to follow, leading through broadleaved woodlands and crossing streams before emerging (in 30mins) to a direct view of the cirque ahead, its walls – on which hardy trees cling at an impressive angle – streaming with cascades in springtime. The mountains whose linking ridges head the cirque are shapely but little known other than by the *cognoscenti*: the Pics de Montabone, Certascan and Couillac, and Pointe de Rabassère.

- Rough grassland dotted with trees and shrubs carpets the floor of the cirque, and a ◐★ path climbs out of this a little left of centre, passing close to cascades and with fine grandstand views downvalley. There's another band of woodland, and above that (2½hrs from the trailhead) the path gains **Étang de la Hillette**, a glacial tarn lodged in the upper cirque at 1797m, with the stone-built Cabane de la Hillette providing basic shelter for about four people on its east bank. (A *variante* of the HRP comes this way.) By following the HRP southwest from here, strong, fit and experienced trekkers could make a very full day's circular walk by going to a point below the Port de Marterat, then descending into the sub-valley cut by the Ossèse stream, which is the southwest tributary of the Vallée d'Ustou, and at Stillom turning back up through the Cors valley to regain the trailhead car park.

Other walks options that continue from Étang de la Hillette include: (in clear conditions only) a border crossing at the 2416m **Port de Couillac** (in another 1¾hrs), dropping on the Spanish side to a glorious lake-studded region; the ascent of **Pointe de Rabassère** in 30mins from the pass or the ascent of **Pic de Couillac** in 40mins; or head northwest to **Étang d'Alet** (larger and more circular than Hillette), from where it's possible to descend directly to the trailhead for another fine round-trip on reasonable paths all the way. (The upward path to Étang d'Alet from the trailhead car park takes 2½–3hrs.) Another option from the Hillette lake involves the ascent of the granitic **Pic de Montabone** (2788m) on the frontier ridge north of the higher Pic de Certascan. Between Hillette and the peak lie several small pools or 'lakelets' – the Étangs de Montabone – and these are visited on the way to the summit, which is surmounted by an aluminium cross and reached in about 3hrs. Lastly, the *voie normale* on 2840m **Pic de Certascan** itself is tackled from the Hillette Cirque and is achieved in a similar time to the Pic de Montabone route.

Before leaving the upper reaches of the Vallée d'Ustou, it's worth pointing out that the southwestern stem, that of the Ossèse stream briefly alluded to above, has its own appeal. The valley road that divided at Stillom continues into this right-hand branch as far as **OSSÈSE** hamlet, where a path heads upvalley on the east bank of the stream, and after 3½hrs of effort comes onto the 2217m **Port de Marterat** overlooking more lakes on the Spanish flank. Descent on the south side of the ridge leads to the picturesque hamlet of **NOARRE** in a back-of-beyond country far from any sizeable town or village, but visited by the omnipresent HRP in one of its many *variante* guises.

Southeast of Port de Marterat, ⊗ **Pic de Marterat** (2662m) may be climbed in another 1½hrs by crossing onto the Spanish slope and traversing left under the crest as far as the mountain's west ridge, where this is followed without difficulty to the summit.

VIA COL DE LA TRAPE
TO THE VALLÉE DU GARBET

Returning to Le Trein d'Ustou, the D8 road rises only slightly to **SÉRAC** before it makes a series of hairpins on the way to Col de la Trape. Shortly before reaching the col, however, an alternative road (D68) cuts off to the right and snakes along the hillside to the ski resort of **GUZET-NEIGE**. Architecturally this purpose-built resort would win no prizes for elegance, but the setting is fine and views of the frontier peaks are worth the diversion to see. Since the uppermost lift is at only about 2050m, snow conditions can be pretty unreliable, so the 61 snow cannons are an important stand-by. Served by ski-bus from Aulus-les-Bains, Guzet-Neige has 21 mechanical lifts and 40km of pistes, with 10 green runs, 8 blue, 10 red and 6 black (for information, ☎ 05 61 96 00 11).

A track extends beyond the metalled road above Guzet-Neige, winds round to Col d'Escots and ends in the so-called Cirque de Gérat. From here a cairned and waymarked route crosses the Crête de Séron, curves round to the little tear-drop shaped Étang de la Piède and continues into what has been called a *vallée enchantée* – a narrow scooped trench whose waters (those of the ruisseau de Turguilla) drain into the Cors below the Cirque de Cagateille. Headed by the 2527m Pic de Turguilla, the valley contains two larger lakes, the Étangs de l'Astoue and Réglisse. These ◉ **Étangs de Turguilla** and the ascent of **Pic de Turguilla** make interesting outings to suit experienced mountain walkers and scramblers.

Col de la Trape (1111m) takes the road out of the environs of the Vallée d'Ustou. The D8 then twists down to a wooded basin near the head of the Vallée du Garbet, in which lies Aulus-les-Bains, one of the best centres for a walking holiday in all the Ariège.

4:6 VALLÉE DU GARBET

The most direct route to Aulus-les-Bains from St-Girons turns out of the Vallée du Salat at **OUST**. An insignificant village built across the mouth of the Garbet, it has a couple of campsites and conventional hotel accommodation in the Hostellerie de la Poste. It is here that D32 claims the true right bank of the Garbet river and remains with it all the way to Aulus, a distance of about 16km. Several small hamlets, as well as the village of **ERCÉ** and a number of chapels and wayside shrines, line the bed of the densely forested valley, and it's difficult to gain any real impression of the country ahead until almost the last minute. **AULUS-LES-BAINS** comes as a welcome surprise with its hint, little more than that, of promising uplands not far away, accessed by three upper valleys.

In truth, Aulus is a rather sad, run-down, semi-neglected spa, whose situation is everything. Discovered by the Romans, the spa

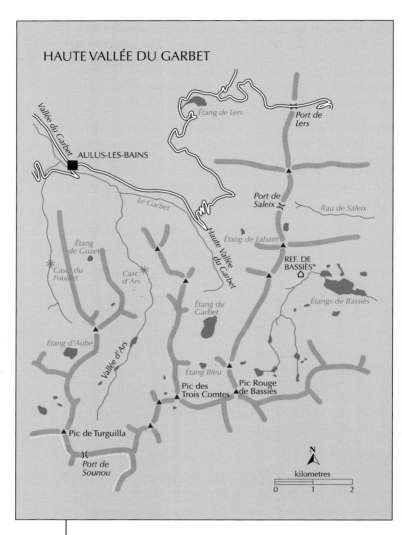

enjoyed a revival in the mid-19th century during the heyday of 'the cure'. Some 150 years later the healing waters still attract – but only just, and today the typically ornate thermal baths draw a predictable, if uncertain, clientele. Meanwhile Aulus enjoys a growing reputation as a walking centre. There are two *gîtes d'étape*, the long-established Le Presbytère (☎ 05 61 96 02 21), the more recent addition, La Goulue (☎ 05 61 66 53 01) and a few hotels.. There's a pleasant woodland campsite open throughout the year, an all-important foodstore and a well-equipped tourist office (☎ 05 61 96 01 79) with helpful staff eager to dispense both advice and literature.

The GR10 calls in at Aulus at the end of the stage which, for most trekkers, begins at the *gîte* in Rouze above Couflens in the Vallée du

Salat, and next day heads southeast across the mountains to the tiny hamlet of Mounicou in the valley of Vicdessos. Following this route in either direction provides good exercise in a pleasant landscape for walkers based for a few days at Aulus, but there are plenty of other options to consider too, some of which adopt sections of that long-distance path.

- Of the three feeder valleys above Aulus, the most westerly is the Fouillet in which a ◯ link path for GR10 meets that major trans-Pyrenean route near the **Cascade du Fouillet**, but adventurous walkers could continue further up this least-visited of the three tributaries to visit the **Étang d'Aube**, trapped in a remote basin almost at the head of the valley.

- The central tributary is the longest and the best known, its stream – the Ars – draining down from a frontier cirque of granite peaks headed by the Pics de Turguilla and Rouge. The fame of this valley rests on the justifiably popular ◯★ **Cascade d'Ars**, which bursts through woodland in three successive falls. The path leading to it is the most frequented in the hills above Aulus-les-Bains, and not without good reason. In truth there are two paths out of the town that come together some way below the cascade. The first of these begins on the south side of the D8 as it leaves Aulus bound for the Col de Agnes; a sign beside the road indicates the way to Prabis, with GR10 waymarks as an additional guide. The other route leaves the road at its first hairpin above Aulus on the way to Col de la Trape, where a sign proclaims 'Chemin de Cascade d'Ars'. Both paths climb through beechwoods for about

Above Aulus-les-Bains the Cascade d'Ars bursts through woodland in the Vallée d'Ars

1½–1¾hrs to reach the foot of the cascade, best seen in the spring when snowmelt from the higher mountains provides a tumultuous roar of water and a heady cloud of spray damping vegetation all around. At its most powerful the falls plunge in a single cataract of more than 100m, but the classic vision is of three cascades; the first a single fall from a rocky lip, the second a band of wide tresses, and the third as a final cascade among the trees.

• Between the Cascade d'Ars and Cascade du Fouillet lies the **Étang de Guzet**, a clear pool lying on the route of GR10 at 1459m. By following the path of GR10 a recommended ◐★ **circular walk** can be achieved which links the Cascade d'Ars, Étang de Guzet and Cascade du Fouillet in a tour of 5–5½hrs.

• Above its magnificent cascade, the upper reaches of the **Vallée d'Ars** contain a string of small lakes, some of which appear to be merely broader stretches of the stream, except for one, the Étang du Turon d'Ars, which lies a little above and to the west of the valley bed. Each of these lakes – the Étangs de Cabanas, des Truites, Hille and Hille de la Lauze – ◐ may be reached by a cairned route extending beyond the GR10. (Allow 5½hrs for a there-and-back walk.) Above the highest of the lakes snow patches often lie throughout the summer, but experienced mountain walkers could continue over these to reach the 2371m **Port de Sounou** on the frontier ridge.

• The third and most easterly of the upper Garbet's valleys is a classic example of glacier-carving. The **Haute Vallée du Garbet** is noted for the lovely **Étang du Garbet** (1683m), the destination of many a visitor to Aulus-les-Bains. However, there's another much smaller lake which lies just to the south of this, but 300m higher in the secluded upper cirque. The glacier that scoured out this cirque has long since disappeared, but signs of its work are clearly read; dwarfed by the looming Pic Rouge de Bassiès to the southeast, and Pic des Trois Comtes to the southwest, **Étang Bleu**, being glacier-blue under a summer sky, is well named. ◐★ The way into the valley begins at the first hairpin on the road to Col d'Agnes, about 5km from Aulus, where there's an enticing view and a small parking place marked as Agnesserre. For the first part of the walk the path is a good one, taking about 1½hrs to reach Étang du Garbet. But the hour-long climb from there to Étang Bleu is more serious, and caution is advised when tackling steep snow patches or when these are melting. Experienced scramblers may be tempted by ◉ **Pic des Trois Comtes** (2620m), the ascent of which will take another 2hrs from Étang Bleu by its *voie normale*, an unmarked route under the crest linking the peak with Pic de la Lesse.

★ On its way out of Aulus-les-Bains heading for Mounicou, GR10 crosses the mountain rim that effectively contains the head of the Vallée du Garbet at Port de Saleix, a little south of east above the town. The way then curves roughly south then southeast and drops into a charming hidden valley graced by the Étangs de Bassiès. Above the uppermost of these lakes, and near the head of this valley in the Pla de la Fount, stands the well-appointed **Refuge de Bassiès** (50 places, manned from the end of May to the end of Sept, ☎ 05 61 64 89 98). By following GR10 all the way from Aulus the refuge is reached in something like 4hrs, but walkers with their own transport can shorten this by 1¾hrs by joining the path where it crosses the D8 at a point marked as Coumebière, a little over 7km from Aulus on the way to Col d'Agnes.

The Bassiès valley in Ariège is graced by several fine lakes

• At first meandering across pastures mattressed with bilberries, the path soon forks, with one branching south in order to visit the tiny **Étang de Labant**. Before returning to the GR10 it's worth looking at this alternative route, for not only does it visit the lake, but a continuation goes up onto the ridge some way south of Port de Saleix. The ridge is gained at an unnamed col (altitude 1944m) midway between Pic de Cabanatous and Pic des Planes, and from it the *voie normale* ascent of ⊗ **Pic Rouge de Bassiès** can be made by following the crest-line on its east flank heading south. The granite 2676m Pic Rouge is named with good reason, and from the summit a tremendous view is gained of the 3000m Estats-Montcalm group to the south and the beautiful Bassiès lakes far below to the northeast.

At 1794m the Port de Saleix is an important link for GR10 trekkers on the way to the Bassiès cirque

- The route to Bassiès from the Plateau de Coumebière climbs eastward after the Étang de Labont fork, gaining height in generous loops to gain the **Port de Saleix** (1794m) in a little over an hour from the road, and there one enjoys a sudden view directly down the Saleix glen towards unseen Vicdessos. The five-day ◯ **Tour du Massif des Trois Seigneurs** sweeps down that valley, while another path heads off to the left for an uncomplicated walk to the 2088m crown of **Pic de Girentes**. The ◯★ Bassiès path turns abruptly to the right and for about 15mins mounts the steep but easy ridge leading to Mont Garias, then breaks away at a small cairn in order to descend to Étang d'Alate. A clutter of rocks is negotiated with the aid of cairns, a grass saddle reached, and a first view won of the glorious lake-spangled Bassiès valley below, with its rocky headwall topped by Pic Rouge de Bassiès. The path now angles down to the grassland and divides once more: straight ahead to the **Étangs de Bassiès**, Mounicou and the valley of Vicdessos; the right branch for the refuge. Beside this last-named trail there stands a small *orris* – a low, stone-walled shepherd's shelter roofed with turf and bilberry shrubs – and, just beyond it, the Refuge de Bassiès.

In addition to the main lakes spread below the refuge, another collection can be found lying in a rock-strewn landscape at the very head of the valley below Pic Rouge de Bassiès, and so delightful is the hut's location that two or three days could easily be spent there, drifting from tarn to tarn or simply absorbing the peaceful atmosphere of one more exquisite corner of the Ariège heartland.

PORT DE LERS

It's 15km by road from Aulus-les-Bains to the Port de Lers via Col d'Agnes – 15 winding kilometres through a charming landscape, with wide-ranging views of crusted rocky peaks to the south, and endless green foothills filling every space to the north. Between Col d'Agnes and the Port de Lers the D8 enters a moorland-like basin containing yet another lake, Étang de Lers, with a bar-restaurant beside the road just above the lake. Nearby the road divides. The left-hand option twists down to the north, heading for Massat and back to St-Girons, leaving the main route to continue up to **Port de Lers** at a modest 1517m where, in winter, there's an *éspace nordic*. Footpaths entice to north and south. An obvious goal is the ⊘ 2199m **Pic des Trois Seigneurs** northeast of the road pass, while **Pic de Girentes** to the south is much nearer, lower and easier to reach.

Port de Lers and the crest of hills it crosses mark the outer limits of the Pays de Couserans. Ahead to the east lies the valley of Vicdessos, in the ancient feudal county of Pays de Foix, whose mountainous region forms part of the Haute-Ariège to be visited in Chapter 5.

4:7 VALL D'ARAN

On the western side of Col de Portet d'Aspet the D618 runs down to the valley of the Garonne by way of **Juzet d'Izaut** and the Col des Ares, while an alternative road, breaking away from D618 a short distance below the Portet d'Aspet, crosses Col de Mente on its way to **ST-BÉAT**, also on the Garonne and known in the Middle Ages as the 'key to France'. The Romans quarried marble just outside this huddled village which is wedged in a narrow defile, and it was marble from St-Béat that was used for many of the statues and fountains in the gardens of far-away Versailles, and also in the construction of the bridge which spans the river in the heart of the village. Other than that, this grey-roofed community is unremarkable in appearance, its situation somewhat gloomy. It is, however, as much a gateway to Spain as it is the key to France, for by following the Garonne upstream, through **ARLOS** and **FOS**, the valley kinks south and southwest and then crosses the international border in a forbidding gorge bridged by the Pont du Roi.

Unlike most other frontier road crossings in the High Pyrenees, such as the Cols du Somport and Pourtalet, and even that of the Bielsa tunnel, there's no obvious difference here between France and Spain. Indeed, none should be expected. This is still the same valley, after all – the same valley, same river, and still on the same northern side of the watershed. This international boundary is purely political and historically anomalous, as arbitrary as a line drawn in the sand.

Journeying south through this wooded trench, parallel with Luchon's valley just across the hills to the west, one passes through

LES and **BOSOST**, where another road climbs out of the valley to the **Col du Portillon** and the realigned French border, which here runs north–south, and across which a short and easy descent leads to Luchon. Instead of taking this diversion, remain in the bed of the Garonne's valley, the Vall d'Aran (the 'valley of all valleys') as it makes a long gradual curve flanked by campsites and then bypasses **LAS BORDAS** (Es Bòrdes in the Aranése language) at the confluence with the Joeu.

The **Vall del Joeu**, also known as the Vall de l'Artiga de Lin, is a narrow wooded tributary in which the Garonne finds resurgence from its subterranean journey that began in the Forau dels Aigualluts, and whose upper reaches lie beneath the Pico Forcanada (see 3:10). ◓ There's good walking to be had in that upper valley, and an unguarded 20-place hut, Refugio dera Artiga de Lin, stands at the point where it divides in the Plan dera Artiga. One route climbs a little north of west alongside the Canaleta de Pomero as far as the frontier ridge overlooking the Vallée de la Frèche (see 3:4), and then curves west in order to reach the Upper Ésera. Another, a steep route swept by avalanche in late spring, climbs southwest to Coll de Toro and the Valleta de la Escaleta; while a third option explores the little hanging valley under the Forcanada's North Face. By careful study of the map, trekkers with ambition and imagination could create one or two interesting circuits, linking some of the most appealing of Pyrenean valleys and cols, by using the Plan dera Artiga as a springboard.

On reaching **VIELLA** (Vielha), 28km from the French border, the Spanishness of Vall d'Aran is well established, although this is mostly apparent in its buildings. As the valley capital, with an appearance resembling parts of urban Andorra, Viella attempts to cash in on day-trippers from France who stop here in search of a bargain, though probably few, if any, exist. This is no tax-free haven, yet the streets are crowded with mottled stone-built boutiques, restaurants, super-markets and shops selling ski gear. Buses arrive from as far away as Barcelona and Lerida (Lleida), and in winter the town sparkles with aprés-ski chic – the ski slopes of **La Tuca** overlook Viella from the south. There's plenty of accommodation, with in excess of 20 hotels and *pensions*, but not much incentive for the active walker, trekker or climber to linger when mountains and valleys are calling. Perhaps, with dirt roads or *caminos* grinding up hillsides to north, south and west, the mountain biker may be tempted by Viella, but Vall d'Aran has more to offer than this. For those who do stay, the tourist office is located near the main church square at Sarriulèra 5 (☎ 973 64 01 10).

The Vall d'Aran

Though politically Spanish, the Vall d'Aran is hydrographically and geographically French, a curious anomaly that has its foundation in the Treaty of the Pyrenees. An oft-told, but presumably apocryphal, story suggests that when diplomats were arguing the course of the frontier, the representative from Spain said: 'The Vall d'Aran you naturally regard as Spanish?', to which his French counterpart, not wishing to admit his ignorance of the valley's position, replied, 'Of course'. But no matter how the decision was reached, the fact is that a line was drawn not, as one might expect, through the Port de la Bonaigua, but at the valley's narrowest point where it is bridged by the Pont du Roi about 50km from the actual watershed. Since snowfall usually closes the Bonaigua pass throughout the winter, the Vall d'Aran was effectively cut off from the rest of Spain for several months at a time until, that is, the Viella road tunnel was opened after the Second World War. Such isolation enabled the unique language of Aranése to flourish, and today many local signs give Aranése spellings as opposed to Castilian Spanish or Catalan.

Vall d'Aran and its tributary valleys cover an area of just 620km^2. A predominantly green and fertile landscape, there are no major peaks to attract climbers, although the Maladeta can be seen from the upper valley, and several worthwhile peaks of more modest altitude are within reach on the southern borders. It's the valleys that offer the primary appeal, yet the former romance of Vall d'Aran has been jeopardised by high-tension power cables and their pylons, and by the downhill ski industry, which although it has been a boon to the local economy has had a far less agreeable visual impact. On the other hand, each part of the valley contains some wonderful Romanesque churches and centuries-old houses with dates carved in their lintels – and it's true that traditional architectural styles are mirrored by many recent developments, although the once-compact villages are now spilling into former pastures in a rash of new holiday homes. The hay meadow of today could quite possibly be tomorrow's construction site. Vall d'Aran is changing fast. In 1909 Hilaire Belloc could claim that in Viella, 'You are quite cut off, you will hear no news.' But in the decades since that was written the Vall d'Aran, like much else in the Pyrenees, has been transformed.

The road forks in Viella. N230 takes the right branch rising to the south, and 7km later plunges into the road tunnel that emerges in another 6km at the head of the valley of the Noguera Ribagorçana, by which access is gained into the western edge of the Aigües Tortes national park. This, however, will be left for later exploration (see 4:8).

Remaining within the Vall d'Aran the C142 road heads east through **ESCUNHAU** and **CASARILH**, bypasses **GARÒS**, and in another 3km comes to **ARTIES**, with its fascinating fortified church of Santa María. The village has a small tourist office (☎ 973 64 16 61), half a dozen hotels, rated one- to four-star, a couple of *pensions*, and the only official campsite in the valley above Viella – the Yerla d'Arties, with its own pool.

To the south a tributary valley, the **Valarties**, projects towards a granite rim of mountains that marks the outer peripheral zone of the Aigües Tortes national park. A feeder route of both GR11 and the HRP heads that way, at first along a metalled road for about 5km, then on 3km of driveable track, followed by an uphill walk among pine trees to reach the Refugi de la Restanca (for details see 4:8), built on the east side of the dammed Restanca lake at 2010m, while its predecessor falls into decay on the opposite bank. All the country to the south, east and west, is worth exploring – an enticing landscape of glittering tarns and grey granite peaklets traversed by long-distance paths (more fully described in 4:8).

The Valarties forks at Pont de Ressec. The southeast stem is used by a *variante* of GR11 linking the Restanca and Colomers huts by way of the Coll de Ribereta, and the head of this particular tributary contains a couple of small cirques and a collection of lakes. The **Estanys de Ribereta** are certainly worth a visit, while experienced trekkers could climb above these and use the Port de Caldes southwest of the upper lake to gain access to the Aigües Tortes national park.

Vall d'Aran, meanwhile, has other tributaries to discover, and as you journey further upstream towards the Port de la Bonaigua, so the whole area in spring becomes a botanical treasure-trove. With the departing snows, meadows explode with a riot of flowers – several species of narcissi, the horned pansy and alpine pasque flower among them. Then, as summer warms the air, a number of fairly uncommon butterflies appear, adding interest to days in the mountains.

SALARDÚ has more to offer the outdoor enthusiast than Viella, by which it is linked by a bus service. Located at a junction of valleys at an altitude of 1268m, it's probably the best and most logical base, as well as having an attractive group of original and semi-traditional buildings at its centre, a 13th-century Romanesque church, and views of the distant Maladeta massif, its snowy crown hovering like a cloud in the west. For accommodation there's a youth hostel, the Auberja Era Garona with 190 beds (☎ 973 64 52 71), but to stay you need to be a member of a hostels organisation affiliated to the

In the upper Vall d'Aran, Salardú makes a useful base for a range of mountain activities

IYHF. There are two *refugis* – the CEC's Xalet-Refugi Juli Santaló (80 places ☎ 973 64 50 16) and Refugi Rosta (☎ 973 64 53 08), with 50 places and an atmospheric bar. Apart from these the village has about a dozen hotels and pensions, a few restaurants, supermarket, a bank and a cash dispenser, and a tourist office/kiosk situated near the supermarket by the turning for Bagergue.

A short distance to the east, just beyond **TREDÒS** and set at the foot of the 2480m Cap de Baqueira, the purpose-built ski resort of **BAQUEIRA-BERET** claims to be the largest winter sports centre in the Spanish Pyrenees, and its impact on the upper Vall d'Aran has been considerable. Facing west, the resort opened in 1964 and has since grown into a major development, with around 6000 beds and a ski area of 77km served by a system of 23 lifts. Of the 47 pistes, 4 are green runs, 19 blue, 20 red and 4 black. There's also a 7km cross-country piste (for information, ☎ 973 64 44 55 or visit www. baqueira.es). The Mirador, El Bosc and Bonaigua chairlifts also operate in summer, but the once pristine nature of this upper region has been sorely compromised, and anyone in search of the real Pyrenees will need to look elsewhere.

South of Salardú or, to be precise, south of Tredòs, the **Vall d'Aiguamotx** is one of the Vall d'Aran's flower gardens, and there are periods in springtime when from a distance it's hard to tell the difference between retreating snowfields and meadows of densely growing narcissi. In summer these same meadows are grazed by cattle and horses, while those that flank the Aiguamotx stream attract Spanish picnic parties. About 8km along a paved road stands an expensive hotel-restaurant on the site of the Banhs de Tredòs. For decades the thermal springs steamed unattended and mostly ignored outside the crumbling spa building. When Robin Fedden came through the valley on his way to climb the Gran Tuc de Colomers in the 1950s, he described how by 'forcing a door we found, in a reek of sulphur, bathing-rooms long-deserted, and fragment of a linen towel worked in red gothic script with a coronet and the initials A.B.' (*The Enchanted Mountains*).

Just beyond the hotel the paving ends but the road continues as a dirt track pushing deeper into the valley and climbing, as is the way of Pyrenean valleys, from one step to another until at last, about 4km from the hotel, a path breaks away for a short, steep climb to a dammed lake, beside which stands the **Refugi de Colomers** at 2125m. Enlarged in 2006, the *refugi* is owned by the FEEC and is manned in the late winter/spring and from mid-June to late September, with 60 places (☎ 973 64 05 92 or 973 25 30 08). A rather squalid alternative hut, offering basic shelter only, stands about 50m away.

WALKS AND CLIMBS
FROM REFUGI DE COLOMERS

The lake is the Estany Major de Colomers, just one of literally dozens of mountain tarns scattered within the exquisite **Circ de Colomers**.

The Circ de Colomers lies in the peripheral zone on the northern side of the Aigües Tortes national park

There's much to see and to do here, including hut-to-hut tours to make that lead into the wonderland of granite and water that lies beyond the confines of the *circ* in the Aigües Tortes national park (see 4:9). Climbers and scramblers have a variety of peaks to work on, including the 2932m **Gran Tuc de Colomers** that crowns the *circ* SSE of the *refugi* – a 4hr ascent by its *voie normale*.

- One of the nicest day-walks to be made using the Colomers hut as a base is a ⬒★ 5hr **tour of the lakes** which lie within the *circ*. The preferred direction for this circular tour is counter-clockwise, starting along the route of GR11's waymarks heading briefly upstream beside the Gargantera as far as a path division marked by a metal pole. Ignoring both path options turn southwest (red–yellow waymarks) and soon cross the outflow stream from Estany Mort, then rise from tarn to tarn towards the curving walls of the *circ* until you reach the upper Estany deth Port de Colomers at about 2420m. Here you veer left (southeast) towards Tuc de Podo, cross its southern shoulder to the eastern side of the circ and descend to Estany deth Cap de Colomers and Estany Ratera, after which the circuit turns north. More lakes are visited on the way to the lovely Estany Obago, where the GR11 is joined for the return to Refugi de Colomers.

- Having achieved this fine walk you might want to head off across one of any number of passes to visit other huts. To the west, across **Port de Caldes** and Port de Güellicrestada, ⬒★ Refugi de la Restanca is a good day's trek along the route of both GR11 and the HRP.

- Port de Caldes could also be used as a way of accessing Refugi Ventosa i Calvell (details in 4:9), set within the national park among yet more charming mountain lakes. However, the ◓★ best way to reach this hut from Colomers is to head up through the Circ de Colomers along part of the route of the lake circuit described above, then cut away to cross **Port de Colomers** in the western ridge system, followed by a descent towards Estany Negre – a great cross-country trek of about 4hrs described more fully as part of the Travessani circuit in 4:9.

- Probably the best-known hut destination from the Colomers *refugi* is that of Refugi d'Amitges in the national park above Espot to the southeast. This is reached by using the easy ◓**Port de Ratera** in an inspiring and not overly long walk of 3½–4hrs, following the GR11 for much of the way, while in the next valley to the east of Colomers stands Refugi de Saboredo. ◓A connecting hut-to-hut route of less than 3hrs also climbs to Port de Ratera before diverting into the **Circ de Saboredo** (see below). There are, in fact, two Ports de Ratera about 10mins apart. The first (Port de Ratera de Colomers) is higher than the second (Port de Ratera d'Espot), and in the middle a sign indicates the way to the Saboredo *refugi* – about 45mins away.

THE CIRC DE SABOREDO

The **Circ de Saboredo** is approached from the Vall d'Aran by way of a broad track beginning at Tredòs – allow about 4–4½hrs for the walk from Salardú to the *refugi*. The track keeps company with the Riu de Ruda all the way, at first running through pastures that lie parallel with, but below, the Bonaigua road, then curving south where it eventually gives way to footpath as the mountains start to crowd in. On the west side of the valley, on the slopes of the Serra de Sendrosa, two small lakes lie about 300m above the river, and these are visited much less frequently than those that adorn the *circ*.

Built at around 2310m by the FEEC, **Refugi de Saboredo** has places for just 21 and is manned in spring and from mid-June to September (☎ 973 25 30 15). Rugged granite peaks form a horseshoe to the south, and as in so many regions of the Pyrenees, more than a dozen lakes and pools form a major landscape feature. A tour of the main Saboredo lakes is an obvious excursion, but there are also several summits to aim for, as well as passes to cross into neighbouring valleys. Southeast of the *refugi*, for example, the containing ridge can be crossed at Coll de Gerber, a 2587m pass above Lac Glacat, in order to visit **Vall de Gerber** and the Refugi Mataró, a small unmanned hut (see 4:12 for details). From this simple *refugi* descend northeast from one exquisite alpenrose- and rock-rimmed lake to another, dropping steeply here, less so there, on a path that leads either to the upper reaches of Vall d'Àneu, below the Port de la Bonaigua, or to the road pass itself for eventual return to Salardú. Such a route makes a very pleasant two-day trek full of contrasts.

THE BORDER COUNTRY

On the northern side of Vall d'Aran, the **Arriu Unhòla valley** (sometimes referred to as the Yñola), which cuts into the sierras behind Salardú, gives a full day's there-and-back trek, on a *camino* for at least half the way, to a collection of lakes near its head. The largest of these, the **Estanh Long de Liat**, is at 2130m, but an alternative option is to visit the higher **Estanh de Montoliu** (3½hrs from Salardú), which lies under the frontier ridge southeast of Pic de Maubermé at 2350m. Less than 200m above this lake it's possible to cross into France by way of the **Port d'Urets** and continue down to the *gîte d'étape* at Eylie d'en Haut in the Vallée du Biros (see 4:2).

The **ascent of Pic de Maubermé** is made possible from the Montoliu lake by one of two routes. The first, graded PD, leads up to Port d'Urets then cuts along the Spanish flank just below the actual ridge, which is then gained by a short gully; the crest is followed more or less to a rock face under the actual summit. Another gully on the right of the rock face overcomes any undue difficulty (1½hrs from the Port d'Urets). The ⊗ second route, slightly easier than that from Port d'Urets, taking 2hrs from the lake and graded PD-, tackles the South Face from the depression of Còth (Col) de Maubermé in a spur descending from the peak. The rock is generally poor, and caution is advised, but the summit view, as mentioned above, is extensive and worth the effort involved in getting there.

THE ALTA VALL NOGUERA PALLARESA

East of the Unhòla valley, and also accessible from Salardú, the Noguera Pallaresa rises in the lovely open meadows of the Pla de Beret above Baqueira. Instead of spilling into the Vall d'Aran, however, the river flows northeast to Montgarri before curving east then south in a long arcing curve to create an effective divide between the jagged mountain groups of the Aigües Tortes and the highlands of Pallars Sobirà. The HRP, or at least, one of its *variantes*, wanders this way for about 4hrs to the 12th-century Santuari de Montgarri, where there's a convenient *refugi*.

The **Alta Vall Noguera Pallaresa** is a pleasant grassy swathe, broad and open in places, narrow and wooded elsewhere. To reach it from Salardú entails walking at first along the Bagergue road for about 400m, where an obvious path cuts away to the right, mounts the hillside and comes onto the Bagergue–Baqueira track. Turning the southern spur of the Serra de Comalada you enter the broad flat meadows of the **Pla de Beret**, a pastoral scene of considerable charm – as long as you avoid looking towards the Baqueira ski slopes, that is. To the north frontier mountains rim the horizon, while in the southeast the valley wall contains, unseen from below, a number of lakes and opportunities for long mountain days for experienced trekkers. A little-used HRP *variante* crosses the highest part of that wall over the Marimanya massif and descends past more lakes to the attractive little hamlet of **ALÓS DE ISIL** after about 9hrs.

The Pla de Beret, meanwhile, marks the true birthplace of the Noguera Pallaresa. Tiny pools and trickling streams sift through cattle-grazed meadows to be boosted by other streams draining the eastern hills. It's an idyllic spot, but if you're committed to the 16km walk from Salardú to Montgarri, time spent here will no doubt be restricted. It's possible to drive all the way to Montgarri, but the walk can be very pleasant despite the motorable track, and one can swing along without constant reference to the map and enjoy the valley for itself.

Dating from 1117 the **Santuari de Montgarri** stands on the north bank of the Noguera Pallaresa among a few ruins where the valley curves eastward below the frontier crest. Here, at about 1657m, the **Refugi Amics de Montgarri** provides a welcome service for trekkers in summer and cross-country skiers in winter. With 50 places the *refugi* is open from mid-May to mid-October and from December to April (☎ 973 64 50 64).

For mountain trekkers Montgarri stands, if not precisely at a crossroads, certainly at a major junction of routes with a number of possible border crossings comparatively nearby, as well as a continuation of the track which keeps company with the river for many more pleasant kilometres. Of the border crossings the 2318m **Port d'Orla** is found to the northwest and is reached through the tributary valley of the Arriu deth Horcath, while the 2344m **Port de l'Esca** (Trauc de Lesca) is located almost immediately north of Montgarri hamlet. One of the Pyrenean High Route *variantes* opts for the 2442m **Port de la Girette** as a means of accessing Refuge des Estagnous (see 4:2) on the slopes of Mont Valier in 6–6½hrs, but this French hut can also be gained by crossing the frontier at **Col de la Pala**, which is 100m higher than the Girette pass.

The HRP is well served with options in this valley, for ◖ another *variante* of this, the ultimate in tough mountain treks, crosses the international frontier at the **Port de Salau** (2087m), then descends to Salau, highest of the villages in the Vallée du Salat (see 4:4), about 7hrs from Montgarri.

These upper reaches of the Noguera Pallaresa east of Montgarri make for pleasant though not dramatic walking. Vegetation is abundant and varied, with soft fruit such as wild raspberries and strawberries growing beside the track; there are occasional granaries and a few low ruins, and the river – now growing in size and strength – makes an easy companion.

Some 12km or so from Montgarri the **Bonabé *ski de fond* centre** has accommodation in the **Refugi El Fornat**. With 40 places the *refugi* is open both summer and winter (☎ 973 62 65 22 – via Casa Sastrés in Isil), providing another useful overnight facility for HRP trekkers and for nordic skiers, who have around 25km of marked trails to explore or can have guided snowshoe walks arranged (www.web.caos.es/bonabe, e-mail: bonabe@tresnet.com).

At the Palanca de Pine there begins a classic, tough, yet magnificent cross-country stage of the HRP, which makes a high traverse of ridge-spurs extending from Mont Roig (Mont Rouch) and eventually descends to the upper Vall de Cardós (see 4:13). But before being drawn into this wildly enchanting region, we ought to continue along the Noguera Pallaresa a little further.

It's 17km from Montgarri to **ALÓS DE ISIL**, where the paved road begins, and another 3km beyond that where the next accommodation is found by the river at **ISIL** in the 19th-century **Refugi Casa Sastrés** (45 places, ☎ 973 62 65 22). A little south of the village stands the Romanesque church of St Joan, and beyond that the valley soon curves southeastward, sloping down to **ESTERRI D'ÀNEU** (see 4:12) and the junction with the road from the Port de la Bonaigua, the pass which marks the upper limits of the Vall d'Aran.

4:8 VALL NOGUERA RIBAGORÇANA

Estany Tort de Rius, set in a bewitching landscape of water and rock

Returning to Viella below Salardú the main road forks, with N230 rising southward to the 6km road tunnel that was largely responsible for restoring new life to the Vall d'Aran. At its southern end lies the valley of the Noguera Ribagorçana, which acts as a dividing moat between the Maladeta region on the west and the Besiberri range on the east. Near the tunnel's exit/entrance, on the site of a one-time hospice, stands the **Refugi Sant Nicolau** (also known as Boca Sud) on

the route of both GR11 and the HRP. The *refugi* is manned virtually throughout the year and has 40 places (☎ 973 69 70 52), but is useful more as a transit hostel than an expedition base except, perhaps, for climbers drawn by prospects of choice routes in the neighbouring Vall de Conangles where, among others, there's icefall climbing with lines of up to 300m in a good winter.

The **Vall de Conangles** carries GR11 and the Pyrenean High Route east of the tunnel and into the buffer zone of the Parc Nacional d'Aigües Tortes. The valley itself is flanked by the ⓑ 450m North Face of the **Tuc de Contessa** (2760m), on which a number of hard winter routes have been created with overall grades of IV+/6. The West Face has three couloirs that offer PD/AD routes of as much as 1000m, and since these frequently come into condition they have a certain appeal for local Spanish activists. In summer the ⊗ *voie normale* offers an uncomplicated ascent of about 3–3½hrs from the Sant Nicolau *refugi*.

At the head of the valley, east of Tuc de Contessa, stands **Tossal (Tuc) dels Estanyets** (2887m), which has a ⓑ 300m north-facing couloir providing fairly uncomplicated snow and ice climbing, but with a section of grade V rock in the middle, and an 80° finish. ⊗ **Tuc de Conangles** to the north of this, across the Coll (Coth) de Conangles, provides a pleasant and easy ascent in summer, with wonderful views (similar to those gained from Estanyets) over the idyllic lake region on the eastern side.

The **Port de Rius**, whose altitude is variously recorded as 2315m, 2344m or even 2355m, provides an easy way out of the upper Vall de Conangles and into the national park's peripheral zone, and is used by trekkers following both GR11 and the Pyrenean High Route. The two part company half an hour later, however, at the eastern end of Estany de Rius. GR11 takes an easy, direct route to the Restanca *refugi* along the right flank of the upper Valarties (in 2hrs), while the ◗★ HRP curves away to the southeast into a bewitching landscape of water and rock, where the **Estany Tort de Rius** lies in a granite plateau rimmed with attractive peaklets and with the more substantial Besiberri massif rising in the south.

In addition to the Estany Tort de Rius with its little islets, there's another smaller lake and numerous pools scattered in a haphazard manner between grey–white boulders and slabs, cushions of moss and patches of grass. The altitude of the main lake is around 2350m, and most of the peaks that surround the plateau are 2500–2800m high, so the scale is anything but intimidating – this is country that deserves a reverential approach by all who wander through. Collado de l'Estany de Mar, a depression in the southeast ridge line, carries the HRP onward, but it also makes a tremendous belvedere from which to study the wonderland below and, in the opposite direction, the blocking wall of the Serra de Tumeneia that plunges to the next lake, Estany de Mar.

Trapped in a steep-sided well that eases at its northeastern end, **Estany de Mar** is magnetically attractive. With an island of rock in

Estany de Mar and the peak of Montardo d'Aran

the middle of the lake, a fine view to the distinctive Montardo ahead and the more forbidding Besiberri Nord behind, the way down to the eastern shoreline maintains interest throughout. At the far end the path descends to yet another lake, this one being the dammed Estany de la Restanca, with the **Refugi de la Restanca** beside it, reached after a walk of about 8hrs from the Sant Nicolau *refugi*. The hut can sleep 80, and is fully manned from mid-June to late September (☎ 608 03 65 59, www.rotativo.com/restanca/).

The Restanca lake is by a junction of major routes at 2010m. The well-marked GR11 comes from the west and leaves heading north down the Valarties. The HRP (and a GR11 *variante*) heads southeast, while (as we have seen) the route to Estanys de Mar and Tort de Rius rises to the southwest. The *refugi*, then, is very much a trekker's hut, but it would also repay a visit by walkers from the Vall d'Aran who could use it as a base from which to make a circuit of the upper lakes or an uncomplicated ascent of Montardo (Montardo d'Aran), the 2830m peak which rises east of the hut and enjoys a much-lauded panorama from its crown. Seen from the Valarties it also has an elegant pyramid shape which captures the imagination and ensures that it is one of the most popular mountains in this corner of the range.

ROUTES FROM REFUGI DE LA RESTANCA

- First, a suggested ◗★ **circuit of the upper lakes**, a walker's route of about 5½–6hrs. From the hut take the clear path signed 'Llac de Mar', which rises southwest to a grassy bowl then zigzags up again to Estany de Mar. The cairned route picks its way along the eastern shoreline, and at the far end swings right to climb to the Collado de l'Estany de Mar (3hrs). With the lakeland plateau spread below, descend easily to the right-hand shore of Estany Tort de Rius. Continue beyond the lake as far as Estany de Rius and a path junction. Here take the right branch to follow the waymarked GR11 on its eastbound course alongside the Barranc de Rius back to the Restanca refugi.

- For the 3hr ⊗★ **ascent of Montardo** follow the continuing HRP/ GR11 path which climbs southeast to the Estany de Cap de Port, with the cliffs of Pic de Monges looming ahead. Pass along the north shore of the lake, and climb again among boulders and rocks to gain the Port de Güellicrestada (Coll de Crestada: 2475m) about 1½hrs from the hut. On the east side of the pass bear left to a path which rises steadily, then zigzags up a rocky gully to a false summit, crosses a saddle and continues up to the true summit.

The country south and east of the Güellicrestada pass, a large portion of which lies within the boundaries of the Aigües Tortes national park, is described in 4:9, as is the continuing GR11/HRP route to Refugi de Colomers.

VALL DE BESIBERRI

Less than 3km south of the Viella tunnel, a second tributary valley drains out of the eastern mountains and into the Noguera Ribagorçana. This is the **Vall de Besiberri**, which as its name suggests is headed by the Besiberri massif, a tremendous wall of granite, best viewed from the east, containing six 3000m summits whose long connecting ridge, aligned roughly north–south, carries the western boundary of the Parc Nacional d'Aigües Tortes.

The valley measures a little under 5km from its confluence with the Ribagorçana at 1500m to the headwall at over 3000m. Within it lie two lakes, the Estany de Besiberri and a much smaller tarn lodged at 2173m, Estanyet de Besiberri de Dalt. A number of seldom-visited passes suggest ways over the valley's containing walls, and scramblers looking for sport on the main summits can take their pick. The ascent of 3030m **Besiberri Sud** is one of the highlights from here.

In the summer of 1866 Charles Packe entered the valley and made what was almost certainly the first crossing of the Besiberri ridge, together with the first ascent of Besiberri Sud and another unspecified peak, with Sir Edward Dashwood. At the time this was very much unknown country to mountaineers, and even the local shepherds and isard hunters, though knowing 'every nook and corner of their own gorge, and the mountains immediately hemming it in', were completely ignorant as to what lay beyond. Even to discover the names of individual peaks or other features was to invite confusion. According to Packe, the Besiberri chain was simply referred to as Pic de Montarto – although in truth this is not even connected to the same ridge, but stands almost isolated above the Restanca lake overlooking the Vall d'Aran. Despite (or perhaps because of) this, Packe's description of the mountains and the account of his traverse, though frustratingly bereft of actual detail of his ascent, make interesting reading in spite of the formal language and guidebook writer's commitment to timings. The following quotation, from the *Bulletin de la Société Ramond* of 1867, begins in the Ribagorçana valley which Packe reached after a two-day storm-bound crossing of the mountains from Luchon.

'Up the right bank of this [tributary] stream, a path, only practicable on foot, leads in 1 hour 10 minutes to the small lake Becibére, at the foot of the Pic de Montarto [Besiberri]… The mountains around, though very rugged and abrupt, are not too difficult, being entirely of granite. On them izards seem to be pretty plentiful, as also ptarmigan.

'It is difficult without a map to give an idea of a country; and the [Besiberri] is a mountain of a rather irregular form… On three sides of the mountain, the north, east, and west, there are vast snow slopes; in many places overlying blue ice, and amounting to actual glacier. The northern and southern ridges … as well as the medial connecting one, are very nearly of equal height: from each of them rise jagged peaks of from 2900 to 3000 metres, five of which contend so nearly for preeminence, that it is impossible without most careful, and simultaneous barometric measurement to determine to which it must be adjudged.

'From the Lac Becibére to reach the baths of Caldas, requires about 8 hours. Following up the stream eastward, about 4 hours places you on the top of the crête de [Besiberri]. The way is steep, but not dangerous. On attaining the crête, I was astonished at the size of the snowfields spread before us on the eastern side. A glissade, uninterrupted I should think for a thousand metres [this must mean feet], brought us down to a diminutive lake; whence the way down the gorge is easy. At the bottom of the gorge, the torrent falls into the main stream… On reaching this stream cross over to the left bank; 30 minutes from here, bearing south, brings you to a very pretty piece of water, the Lac de Caballeros [now the dammed Estany de Cavallers]. After skirting this, the path at the south end of the lake crosses to the right bank of the stream; and thence 45 minutes of gradual descent to the baths at Caldas.'

RIBAGORÇANA TO VALL DE BOÍ
The Ribagorçana continues to flow south below the Vall de Besiberri, with the main road skirting the Embalse de Senet and passing

between the villages of Senet and Aneto, from the latter of which the Pyrenees' highest summit takes its name. From Senet it's possible to make a traverse of the eastern mountains to gain access to the Vall de Boí, for a *camino* makes a laboured ascent to the 2075m Port de Gelada, from where a trail sweeps round the left-hand side of a coombe, crosses a ridge-spur that contains it, and then drops to Erill la Vall. But apart from this crossing, and the west bank tributaries coming from the Maladeta region already referred to in 3:10, there's little to delay the walker or climber in this part of the Ribagorçana's valley. However, once the river has turned towards El Pont de Suert and meets the Noguera de Tor coming from the northeast, you should leave the N230 in favour of the L500 road to Caldes de Boí.

4:9 VALL DE BOÍ

Once a day in summer buses journey north from El Pont de Suert to Caldes de Boí through the valley of the Noguera de Tor, bringing public transport within reach of the Aigües Tortes national park. The lower valley has its attractions, it's true, but unless you're especially interested in Romanesque churches (of which there are some true gems) it is the upper valley beyond Caldes, whose secrets are hidden behind a huge concrete dam wall, that will repay anyone who loves wild mountain scenery. Equally appealing is the tributary of the Vall de Sant Nicolau – a honeypot, but with plenty of charm – which is among the most accessible in all the national park.

It's 20km to Caldes de Boí. On the way you pass two campsites before reaching **BARRUERA**, which has a few hotels, the valley's main tourist office (☎ 973 69 40 00) and a busy campsite. But the village is suited more for passing visitors than for those looking for a mountain base, so it's better to continue upvalley. About 4km beyond Barruera a side-road breaks away to the right and climbs for 1km to **BOÍ**.

Although situated too far from the most interesting areas of the national park to be of use to non-motorised visitors, Boí has a reasonable supply of accommodation, with several one- and two-star *hostals* and *pensiós*, a few restaurants, supermarket, a bank with an ATM and a national park information office, the **Casa del Parc National** (☎ 973 69 61 89), located near the village square. This is the place to buy a ticket for one of the official jeep-taxis that ferry visitors to the park entrance in the Vall de Sant Nicolau, so those who do make a base here can at least enjoy day-trips into one section of the park.

The side-road into Boí continues through and twists up the hillside to **TAÜLL**, a once-peaceful village with a medieval air that is in danger of being swamped by a modern development that seeks to cash in on the Boí-Taüll ski resort at the roadhead. What remains of significance in Taüll, though, are the two magnificent Romanesque churches with their notable belfries: Sant Climent de Taüll beside the road, and the parish church of Santa Maria right in the crowded heart of the village. Accommodation here is in two- and three-star *hostals* and *pensiós*, as at Boí, but there are several lower-priced rooms to be had in a variety of *casas*, and a campsite on the hillside below Sant Climent.

About 10 lonely kilometres on from Taüll, through a landscape of vast, moorland-like mountains, the road ends in the Pla de Vaques, site of the **BOÍ-TAÜLL ski station**. From it a view northwest shows the Besiberri massif, an abrupt and welcome contrast to the immediate terrain with its complex of lifts and tows. At 2020m Boí-Taüll claims to be the highest ski resort in the Pyrenees, with its top lift at 2750m. Should this be insufficient for skiable snow in some seasons, the resort is equipped with 121 snow cannons. Of the 41 runs, 19 are red and 8 black (information from Pla de l'Ermita de Taüll, 25528 Vall de Boí, Lleida, Spain, ☎ 973 69 60 44, e-mail: boi@boitaullresort.es, website: www.boitaullresort.es).

VALL DE SANT NICOLAU

The **Vall de Sant Nicolau** lies just 1km beyond the Boí turning, its narrow wooded entrance effectively concealing any real hint of what lies ahead. This is one of the most popular valleys in the national park, and there are car parks to accommodate visitors, as the only vehicles allowed beyond the control booth are the special 4WD jeep-taxis that convey passengers about 5km inside the park's boundary to Aigüestortes, leaving a walk of a little over an hour to the *refugi* at Estany Llong. Trail information is posted at the park entrance and at the roadhead, with suggestions for several day-walks given.

The valley is noted for its fine scenery, its streams, waterfalls, its water-meadows and lakes, but then practically the whole Aigües Tortes region has these features in abundance – the name actually means 'twisted waters' in the Catalan language. What promotes the Vall de Sant Nicolau more than the inner valleys is its accessibility. There's nothing like vehicular access, albeit in a 4WD taxi, to encourage the honeypot effect.

Just inside the park boundary lies Estany de la Llebreta, and a short distance beyond this the Barranc de Serrader flows down the northern hillside from the lake of the same name. A trail follows this stream up to the lake, and it is from there that the uncomplicated ascent is made of ⊗ **Pala Alta de Serrader**, at 2982m one of the park's highest summits.

An overnight base at **Refugi d'Estany Llong** (1985m) gives an opportunity to explore the valley's upper levels at a more leisurely pace than would be allowed if a return downvalley were planned by taxi. As the only hut owned by the park authority, the *refugi* can officially accommodate 36 in its dormitories, and is fully manned from June to mid-October – reservations are essential (☎ 973 29 95 45 or 629 37 46 52). There's a simple, unmanned hut with room for about eight nearby, **Refugi Centraleta**.

High in the valley's south-eastern recesses above the hut lie a number of lakes and pools – the **Estanys Negre**, **Gavatxos**, **Perdut**, **Cometes Amitges**, the **Gran Dellui** and **Pletiu de Dellui** to name just a few – and a ⬭ linking circular walk that visits most or, indeed, all of them makes a worthwhile outing.

On the north side of the valley yet more lakes invite inspection: **Estany de Contraix** (or Contraig) is cupped in a steep-walled cirque, while **Estanys Redó** and **Bergús** lie in that angle formed by the Serra de Crabes and the ridge running east of the ⬭ **Gran Tuc de Colomers**. The ascent of the Gran Tuc (2933m) is made by way of these lakes in just 2½hrs from the *refugi*. But this is just one of a number of undemanding ascents that can be achieved from a base at Estany Llong. Others include the **Creu de Colomers** and **Tuc de Contraix** in the same ridge as that containing the Gran Tuc, while the valley's south wall has such peaks as **Subenuix, Pic de Dellui** and **Pic Neriolo** to name just three, each of which will reward with views over a huge complex of lakes and shapely jutting mountains.

Of a very different nature, the ❶ **Agulles de Dellui** south of the *refugi* have a choice of winter climbs with the *Isards Couloir* (AD-) on the north side of the group, the mixed 240m *Hilo Gris* on the slab-face of the West Peak, and *Linea Maginot* (III/3+), which attacks the prominent crack in the face leading to the East Summit.

Cross-country walks abound, with treks across the containing ridges to yet more lake-spattered landscapes. One uses the **Collado de Dellui** (2520m) above the lakes of the same name, and descends southeast to Refugi Colomina (see 4:10). Another, a more demanding route, crosses the **Coll de Contraix** (2770m) with a tricky descent to Refugi Ventosa i Calvell, but the most obvious, and certainly the most well used, is that which makes a ⬭ complete traverse of the park by way of the 2429m **Portarró d'Espot** at the head of Vall de Sant Nicolau, descending on the far side to Estany de Sant Maurici and Espot (4:11). This easy walk follows a GR11 *variante* all the way and takes just 3½–4hrs from Estany Llong to Espot.

CALDES DE BOÍ AND BEYOND

Beyond the Sant Nicolau turning the main valley road – and the bus from El Pont de Suert – continues for almost 3km to the spa buildings of **CALDES DE BOÍ**, which stand complete with fountains, neat lawns and expensive accommodation across the stream to the left. After this the road deteriorates on the way to the huge Cavallers dam. A manned control booth marks the boundary of the national park's peripheral zone, beyond which the road grinds on for another 3km or so up the 'tumbled detritus below the snout of an ancient glacier, [where] time had rooted pines and alders in crevices, had covered boulders with moss and couched them with grass' (Robin Fedden, *The Enchanted Mountains*). With a final twist or two at the end the road runs out at the dam where, out of the main summer season, parking is permitted for private vehicles. This marks the Vall de Boí roadhead, the springboard

Approach to the Besiberri massif from the Riu Malo grassland

of access to the Riu Malo pastures and, beyond them, a wonderland of lakes, peaks and passes which, in many respects, is quite the finest region within the Aigües Tortes national park.

A much-trodden path heads along the eastern side of the lake at the base of the lofty Punta Alta, tracing the national park boundary into the meadows at the far end where several streams come together, most of which have their birth among lakes or remote mountain pools. The main path continues across the grassy plain before veering northeast and rising to an upper level where the CEC's Refugi Ventosa i Calvell makes a convenient base for a host of walks and climbs, while high above the Riu Malo grassland to the west stands the Besiberri massif with its celebrated ridge connecting a row of 3000m summits.

The Besiberri Massif

Decades after the highest Pyrenean summits had been claimed, the Besiberri massif remained a *terra incognita*, for it was not until 1866 that it drew the attention of mountaineers when Packe and Dashwood made the first ascent of **Besiberri Sud** (see 4:8). It's difficult to understand why it should have taken so long to attract attention, although Henry Russell alluded to a possible reason when, writing about the illogicality of fashion in mountaineering, commented: 'One imagines that between the Maladeta and Perpignan the Pyrenees become second-class mountains, as in the Basque country.'

Clearly this is not so, for as Packe pointed out:

'Many a tourist returning from the Port de Venasque must have lingered on the col de Monjoyo to take a last look … on the tumultuous and billowy forms of the mountains of Catalonia. Beautiful and purple-tinted as they appear in the evening light; not a trace of verdure can be seen upon those stony ridges, for the narrow vallies lie deep concealed and far between. One lofty, and not very distant dome-shaped peak is conspicuous among the rest, with its large snow-field, seen over the Port de Viella… The Luchon guides for the most part do not appear to know its name. Many of them designate it as the Mont Blanc.'

That large snowfield has all but disappeared today, but even without it the granitic Besiberri massif can be appreciated as a backdrop of formidable proportions, and an obvious attraction to climbers.

The main spine of the massif extends for roughly 2km along a north–south alignment between Besiberri Nord and Punta Lequeutre. It's a consistently high crest which contains no less than six 3000m summits, the highest being the 3033m **Pic Comaloforno** near the southern end. A PD route of 4–5hrs from Caldes de Boí tackles the mountain from the lake-studded southwest slopes, then by way of a gully that emerges on the ridge just north of the summit. But it could also be climbed from the Vall de Besiberri (see 4:8) using much the same route as Packe's original leading to Besiberri Sud.

The most southerly of the massif's 3000ers is **Punta Passet** (3001m), named in honour of the great Gavarnie guide Célestin Passet, who climbed here in 1882 with

Henri Brulle and Jean Bazillac. On 25 July of that year they made the first ascent of Pic Comaloforno.

North of Besiberri Sud the two peaks of **Besiberri del Mig** (3001m and 3003m) remained unclimbed until 1926, when Jean Arlaud led a rope of five members of his Groupe des Jeunes along the first ever ⓑ ★ 374374 traverse of the ridge – a route now graded AD- with individual pitches of III/III+. This traverse makes an exceptionally fine winter expedition.

As for **Besiberri Nord** (3014m), this was climbed in August 1899 by the guide J.-A. Sansuc, with Nils de Barck and the brothers Henri and Marcel Spont. This 'severe pyramid' defines a junction of ridges. A little west of north a crest continues to the Pics del Collado, from where other arêtes splay out to wall the lake country of Estanys Tort de Rius and de Mar (see 4:8). Sansuc was also active on this northwest arête in 1905, making the first ascent with Louis Le Bondidier and H. Decause. But northeast of Besiberri Nord the splendid crest of the Serra de Tumeneia is enlivened by Punta Harlé and the Pa de Sucre, both of which have significance when viewed from the east. Between Besiberri Nord and Punta Harlé, the ridge descends to a cleft in which a small bivouac hut has been anchored. **Refugi de Besiberri** could sleep about 10 in an emergency. Having only basic facilities this hut, the highest in the Pyrenees, is reached in 4–4½hrs from the Cavallers dam, and the PD *voie normale* on Besiberri Nord climbs a broad crack system in the ridge wall about 100m to the left. At the top of the crack the route eases onto terraces, above which easy slabs lead to the exposed summit crest. From here, as from the whole ridge, the view is far-reaching and magnificent – a tremendous grandstand from which to study the complex landscapes spreading all around.

At 2826m the bivouac hut of Refugi de Besiberri is the highest in the Pyrenees, anchored just below the northeast ridge of Besiberri Nord

From the Riu Malo pastures at the northern end of the dammed Cavallers lake, the main path loops up the northeast slope, pocked with grey granite slabs and boulders, to gain an upper level described by Robin Fedden in *The Enchanted Mountains*, the most evocative book yet written about climbing in the Pyrenees:

> 'As though cupped in two vast hands, an ample saucer rested below a crescent of snow-mottled peaks. To one side rose the Aiguilles de Travesany with their dramatic sky-line; to the other rose the Pic del Mig and the Beciberri; facing us at a dignified distance was the shapely Montarto. Here was the prototype of all gentle upland valleys. The saucer held a series of lakes, revealed progressively as we walked. They were separated by rock-shapes, smooth as basking hippopotami, and by intimate useless pastures.'

Refugi Ventosa i Calvell is set in this landscape above Estany Negre. Not surprisingly, given its location and the number and diverse range of outings available, it's a very popular hut. With 80 places and a guardian in residence from mid-June to October, reservations are essential during the high season (☎ 973 29 70 90).

WALKS AND CLIMBS
FROM REFUGI VENTOSA I CALVELL

The major interest for climbers and scramblers will almost inevitably be centred on routes among the Besiberri massif, as briefly outlined in the box (above). The PD *voie normale* on 🌐 **Besiberri Nord** is an obvious attraction, taking about 5–6hrs. Fit climbers could then continue

Estany Negre, in the wild setting near Refugi Ventosa i Calvell

Serra de Tumaneia continues the Besiberri ridge to the northeast

south along the ridge, collecting other summits, but a bivouac is likely to be needed if all the 3000m tops are to be included.

Both ⬤ **Punta Harlé** (2887m) and **Pa de Sucre** (2863m) on the crest of the Serra de Tumeneia can be climbed from the *refugi* by way of a col that separates the two peaks, while the 2781m **Tumeneia Nord** is reached by a different col just southwest of a secondary summit. That col, incidentally, could be used by experienced wild-country trekkers/scramblers to make a tough crossing to the Restanca hut.

South of Ventosa i Calvell, ⬤ **Punta Alta** (3014m) is the only 3000er in the national park unconnected with the Besiberri massif. This, the highest peak of the Comalesbienes, is usually climbed from just south of the Cavallers dam, where the route follows the Barranc de Comalesbienes to the lakes in which the stream rises, and from there tackles the mountain from the southeast. But it can also be climbed from Ventosa i Calvell via a circuitous route.

To the southeast the 2894m ⬙ **Creu de Colomers** on the ridge walling the Vall de Sant Nicolau makes a pleasing ascent by its *voie normale* in about 2½hrs.

The crocodiles' teeth of the ⬤ **Agulles de Travessani** soar above the *refugi* to the northeast, making an appealing sight and a clear attraction to climbers with assorted routes on offer. Best of all is an end-to-end traverse of the serrated ridge on trusty granite.

Easier, in fact little more than an uphill walk, is the ⬙★ **Montardo d'Aran**, already suggested as an outing from Refugi de la Restanca (4:8). This exceedingly popular 2830m outlook over Vall d'Aran can be gained without difficulty by a cairned route accurately marked on the Editorial Alpina map (which is not always the case) in 2½hrs.

As for day-long walks in the vicinity of the hut, the choice is only limited by the amount of time one has available. A glance at the map is sufficient to conjure numerous options. Perhaps the best is a ⬤★ 7–8hr **circuit of the Agulles de Travessani**. This wonderful long day's walk, with its ever-changing views, is one of the finest expeditions of its kind in the Pyrenees. At first weaving north between lakes, the tour then follows the route of both GR11 and the HRP east across Port de Caldes and down to the Estany Major de Colomers. From here you turn south, climbing in the Circ de Colomers among more lakes and pools, before turning west, eventually zigzagging up a stony depression to gain the Port de Colomers at 2591m. The view from here is magnificent, for you gaze west across a huge drop to the distant Besiberri wall. Cairns and occasional signs of a path lead down a series of natural steps containing yet more pools, with Estany Negre lying near the foot of the slope and the *refugi* just above it.

Three other wardened mountain huts are accessible within a day's walk of Ventosa i Calvell: the **Refugis de la Restanca** (in 3½hrs), **de Colomers** (in 3hrs) and **Estany Llong** (in 6½–7hrs) by way of the Coll de Contraix. This last-named route should only be attempted by experienced trekkers, and in the early part of the summer an ice axe could be useful. Since both Restanca (in 4:8) and Estany Llong (above) have been dealt with in some detail, it's time to give attention to Refugi de Colomers, from where an onward route can be made into the Sant Maurici section of the national park.

As mentioned in the outline of the Travessani circuit (above), both GR11 and the Pyrenean High Route traverse the valley head above Ventosa i Calvell on a linking route between the Restanca and Colomers refugis. This route climbs southeast from Restanca to the

Agulles de Travessani, an attractive, compact group above the Ventosa i Calvell refugi

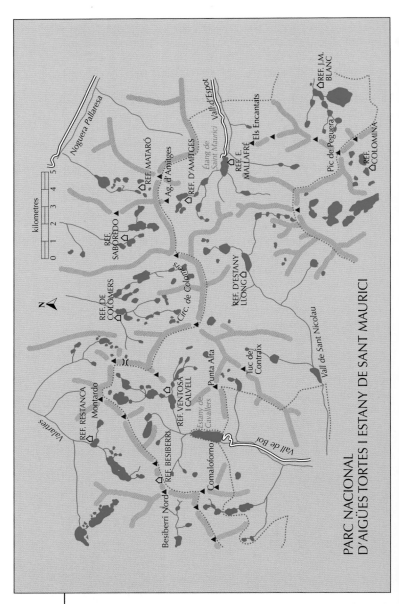

PARC NACIONAL
D'AIGÜES TORTES I ESTANY DE SANT MAURICI

Port de Güellicrestada and then offers a choice. One route descends to the east side of Estany de Monges (as a link with Ventosa i Calvell) and skirts the outflow of Estany de Mengades. But the reworked and waymarked GR11 keeps above the first of these lakes heading ESE to a minor ridge, then descends to pass between two lakes – Estanys de Mengades and del Port de Caldes. The way then slants up a boulder-land to the Port de Caldes, which offers a way over the east walling

ridge of the valley and into the Circ de Colomers. Looking south and southwest from the approach to Port de Caldes is revealing, for the chaotically serene landscape (if that's not a contradiction in terms) is set before you in all its untamed, rock-littered splendour. Glistening tarns and scraggy grass interrupt a foreground of granite, while the Pa de Sucre, Punta Harlé and the long Besiberri wall outline the south-west horizon, and it is on the approach to the Port de Caldes that the path from Ventosa i Calvell joins this traverse route.

From the grassland between the Ports de Güellicrestada and Caldes, the Besiberri massif forms a long wall to the southwest

At 2550m **Port de Caldes** is an easy grass saddle in the Travessani ridge which carries the national park boundary, here running north–south. On its eastern side the descent bypasses a small tarn, then follows the Gargantera stream down to the dammed Estany Major and the small **Refugi de Colomers**, reached about 1¼hrs from the pass. Mentioned above in 4:7, when it was visited from the Vall d'Aiguamotx in the upper Vall d'Aran, the Colomers *refugi* offers a variety of walks and climbs, and can be used as a link in a hut-to-hut tour of the region. The best option here is a crossing, next day, of the Serra de Saboredo at the uncomplicated **Port de Ratera**, followed

Parc Nacional d'Aigües Tortes i Estany de Sant Maurici

After he visited the site of a hydro-electric project centred on the lakes above Espot in the 1950s, General Franco ordered the establishment of the national park which came to be known as the Aigües Tortes i Estany de Sant Maurici. This, the second national park in the Spanish Pyrenees, was inaugurated in October 1955, ironically coinciding with a rash of hydro-schemes that directly contravened the rules laid down by the International Union for the Conservation of Nature and Natural Resources.

At first the park was largely concentrated west and southwest of Espot (the region noted for the Estany de Sant Maurici) in an area often referred to as the Sierra de los Encantados, but also spilling into the Vall de Sant Nicolau to include the charming water-meadows, streams and cascades of Aigüestortes. Twice since its conception the boundaries have been extended – first in 1986, then in 1996 – to reach as far west as the Besiberri chain and northwest as far as Montardo d'Aran, so the park now covers a total area of 14,119 hectares, with an additional 27,000 hectare peripheral zone. Within it there are over 60 lakes and dozens of pools, and seven granite peaks of more than 3000m.

Access is unrestricted for walkers, trekkers, climbers and cross-country skiers, but all private vehicles are banned (apart from those belonging to locals with special permits). Wild camping is forbidden except in the peripheral zone (officially a permit should be obtained from the nearest village), and overnight stays are limited to the five *refugis* that are wardened during the summer season: Ventosa i Calvell, Estany Llong, Amitges, Ernest Mallafré and J.M. Blanc.

The twin Encantats are the best-known and most distinctive peaks within the Aigües Tortes national park

National park information offices are located in Boí (☎ 973 69 61 89) and Espot (☎ 973 62 40 36), while the park administration is based at Parc Nacional d'Aigües Tortes i Estany de Sant Maurici, Camp de Mart 35, 25004 Lleida (☎ 973 24 66 50). Further information may be obtained on www.catalunya. net/aiguestortes, while Editorial Everest publishes a useful guide to the region: *El Parque Nacional de Aigüestortes y Lago San Mauricio.*

by descent to either Refugi d'Amitges or the village of **Espot** in the national park's eastern sector. This crossing is outlined in 4:7.

4:10 VALL FOSCA

Pushing up to the southern border of the national park between Vall de Boí and the Noguera Pallaresa, Vall Fosca is both narrow and sparsely populated; and but for a major hydro-electric scheme that has transformed its upper regions it would have retained an air of almost medieval isolation. As it is, the valley is probably the least known of all those that give access to the park, and this is one of its benefits.

Vall Fosca lies north of La Pobla de Segur, by which it is connected by an infrequent bus service as far as Capdella, the northernmost village. The N260, a Spanish equivalent of the Route des Pyrénées running along the foothills in the central part of the range, joins the Pobla road at **SENTERADA**. A little northeast of this a minor road branches north into Vall Fosca itself, drained by the Riu Flamisell. It's 19km from Senterada to Capdella. At first the valley is gentle and flanked by soft wooded hills, but as you progress towards its head it grows more rugged and mountainous. The few hamlets appear to have nothing for the modern visitor, some being lodged on seemingly inaccessible heights way above the valley bed.

CAPDELLA is a village in two parts, neither of which has either shops or restaurants. The bus goes as far as the lower section, dominated by a power plant. On the hillside nearly 2km above it stands the original village, the houses crowded below a stumpy little church. There's not much choice of accommodation beyond the Hostal Leo (☎ 973 66 31 57) and Hostal Monseny (☎ 973 66 30 79), otherwise it's a 4½hr trek to the nearest *refugi*.

Being largely above the treeline, the upper valley beyond Capdella is more open, with near-level pastures in its bed. It's an attractive region bordered by mountains whose individual features are too remote to be fully revealed. Here the road skirts the eastern side of the pastures, then crosses the river and angles up the western hillside to gain a large dam at the southern end of the **Embalse de Sallente**. To walk this far from Capdella takes at least 2hrs, while those with their own transport can park on the eastern side of the causeway at about 1790m. At the far end of the reservoir a works cableway has been adapted for visitor use, rising more than 350m to the vicinity of Estany Gento, but by taking the cableway you miss out an hour or so of interesting walking. It is interesting because, ◗ after making a sharp ascent on a zigzag path above the dam, you come to the line of a pre-First World War tramway, used to service a complex of hydro-works. Following this miniature tram-line, the way leads through a series of tunnels before reaching Estany Gento and the upper station of the *teleféric*.

Estany Gento is just one of more than a dozen lakes that have been harnessed to the Sallente hydro-scheme. These, plus a number of smaller lakes, lie trapped in a wild landscape of grey–green granite and scant patches of grass on the south side of the main national park boundary, but contained within the park's peripheral zone. Various trails, some well defined, others less so, weave routes among these lakes and tease over spurs and ridges into neighbouring regions.

There's only one *refugi* on this side of the national park's mountain rim, but it's easily accessible from the Sallente dam either by taking the *teleféric* or by walking to Estany Gento and then following a good path for a little over 45mins. Beyond the *telefèric* station the path is rough at first, but it then improves and is almost paved in places. As you climb into increasingly wild country another section of tramline is reached, but this is soon traded for a waymarked trail that crosses a broad rocky shoulder with the **Refugi Colomina** seen ahead. Owned by the Federació d'Entitats Excursionistes de Catalunya (FEEC), the *refugi* is a timber chalet-style building standing on a bluff on the south bank of the dammed Estany Colomina, with the horseshoe cliffs of the Circ de Saburó beyond and a fine view to the south over folding sierras. With places for 40, the hut is manned in the spring and from mid-June to mid-September (☎ 973 25 20 00).

Using the *refugi* as an overnight base, several summits are accessible to walkers and scramblers. To the east, for example, **Pic de Pala Pedregosa** (2889m) rewards an ascent of less than 2hrs with an excellent panoramic view, as does **Pic de Mainera** (2905m) along the ridge to the north. **Pic de Peguera**, at 2982m the highest in this section of the mountains, can be gained by way of the Coll de Peguera in about 2hrs. Almost due north of the Colomina hut the 2902m **Pic dels Vidals** (Pic d'Estany de Mar) and its neighbour to the west, **Pic d'Estany Tort** (2886m), can be linked in the same expedition, while to the northwest of the *refugi*, on the national park boundary above Estanys Tort and Neriola, **Pic Neriola** (2857m) is climbed along its southern ridge from a col used by walkers to gain the Aigüestortes area of the Vall de Sant Nicolau.

Approached from Vall Fosca, Refugi Colomina stands near the southern rim of the national park

- Trekkers could make a ◯4–5hr **tour of the lakes** by taking a path round the west side of both the Estanys Colomina and de Mar, then veering away from the Saburó lake, bearing NNW guided

by cairns up to a string of six small tarns below Pic dels Vidals, and on over a minor col in its southern ridge. On the far side in a stony plateau lie more lakes, the Estanys Vidals d'Amunt, linked with much smaller pools and reached after about 1¾hrs. Above these to the north you could cross a second col, the 2780m Collado de Carboners, and descend northwest to the Estanys Morto and Castiesso under the looming crest of Pic de Subenuix. From these you curve south to the dammed Cubiesso lake, then continue to pass between Estany Neriola and the largest of them all, Estany Tort, a long arthritic finger of water at 2291m. At the southeastern end of this final lake you come across one of the old works tramways and rejoin the path used on the approach to Refugi Colomina from Estany Gento.

The Colomina *refugi* is often used as a convenient overnight stage in a hut-to-hut tour of the Aigües Tortes national park, for three huts within the park proper are accessible to trekkers. The first of these is the national park's own Refugi d'Estany Llong near the head of the Vall de Sant Nicolau (4:9), and the way to reach it uses either **Collado dels Gavatxos**, southwest of Pic de Subenuix, or the easy **Collado de Dellui** west of Estany Cubiesso.

• The second hut is Refugi Ernest Mallafré (see 4:11) situated at the foot of the celebrated twin Encantats peaks above Espot. ◖ A full day is required to make the traverse from Colomina via the steep **Coll de Peguera** (2726m) in the ridge west of the peak of the same name, followed by a descent through the long and lovely Monastero valley, but it's a delightful and rewarding trek amid fascinating mountain scenery throughout.

• The final route leads to the ever-popular Refugi J.M. Blanc, which is normally accessed from Espot (see 4:11). ◖ The most direct way to it from the Colomina refugi is a 3½–4hr trek along a GR11 *variante* by way of the 2670m **Collado de Saburó** in the ridge linking Tuc de Saburó with Pic Mainera, one of the retaining ridges of the Circ de Saburó northeast of the refugi. The route is waymarked, and on the park side of the col there are yet more lakes to skirt before reaching J.M. Blanc on the edge of the glorious Estany Tort de Peguera – a fabulous setting for a refugi. Espot, the village at the eastern gateway to the national park, lies another 1½hrs or so beyond the hut.

4:11 VALL D'ESPOT

High in the valley of the Noguera Pallaresa on the way to the Port de la Bonaigua and the Vall d'Aran, a side-road cuts west from the

C147 highway, twisting steeply up the hillside before running along to **ESPOT**, at 1321m the most important village/resort on the eastern side of the Aigües Tortes national park. It's 7km from the main highway to Espot, and there's no public transport leading to it, but jeep-taxis occasionally meet the bus which runs between La Pobla de Segur and the Vall d'Aran, so all may not be lost for the heavily laden non-motorised visitor in search of a lift.

Despite finding itself drawn into the superficial world of tourism through ease of access into the nearby national park, Espot remains defiantly bucolic. There may be hotels, bars and restaurants, a bank, two supermarkets, campsites, a swimming pool and a national park information centre, the **Casa del Parc Nacional** (☎ 973 62 40 36), but the cobbled streets and little side-alleys have about them the smell of animal husbandry and haymaking, and for many villagers the old ways of the past have yet to be submerged by the fluctuations of tourist economy.

Among the places to stay, there's the long-established Hotel Saurat, a large white building in the village centre, Hotel Roya, the Residència Felip and several *casas de pagès* (the local equivalent of b&b/*chambres d'hôte*). Downvalley, just below the road, Camping La Mola also has a few apartments to rent. The campsite has a useful shop, café and bar, and is open from June to the end of September, while two other smaller campsites are located a little closer to the village, the Sol i Neu and Solau.

From the middle of the village a secondary road twists up the southern slope to the ski station of **SUPER ESPOT**, or Espot Esqui, as it's also known. Dating from 1968, skiing here is rather low key, for the northeast-facing slopes are wooded, the highest lift is at 2500m, and the 31 pistes give 5 black runs, 11 red, 11 blue and 4 green (for information, ☎ 934 14 19 26, e-mail: espotestacio@espoesqui.com, website: www.espotesqui.com).

The prime attraction, of course, is the plethora of lakes and jaunty granite peaks that lie within the national park, for Espot has gained a reputation as a base from which to tackle a range of walks and climbs among a sublime landscape. The starting point for some of the best-known routes is the dammed lake of Sant Maurici, about 7km to the west at the end of a tarmac road. Access by private vehicle is banned, but a jeep-taxi service operates from the village. Otherwise it's a walk of around 2hrs along the GR11. When full, and viewed from carefully chosen sites, the **Estany de Sant Maurici** takes on a serene appearance, especially with the twin Encantats peaks mirrored in the water. But often one finds the water level depressingly low, with dead trees gesticulating from black exposed mudbanks. Then it's a sorry mess, and an insult to its pretence as a jewel in the crown of the national park.

On the south side of the lake, about 15mins walk from the road-head at the foot of the Encantats, **Refugi Ernest Mallafré** is a small 36-place hut owned by the FEEC and manned from mid-June to the end of September (☎ 973 25 01 18).

In Pyrenean mythology the Gran and Petit Encantat (Sierra de los Encantados, or Montagnes Enchantées) are erring shepherds turned to stone. They also happen to be among the most appealing of mountains, an obvious attraction to climbers thanks to their prominent position and dolomitic stature. The lower and more northerly of the two, the **Ⓑ** ★ 2738m **Petit Encantat**, is a climber's peak, and the Central Gully which divides the twins offers an overall AD route amounting to 600m of climbing, with the broken rocks and slabs of the gully graded PD as far as the cleft of the Enforcadura, followed by a more sustained effort to the summit. There's also a ★ 500m winter climb (*Voie Cerdà-Pokorsky*, TD) on the Northwest Face, and another TD route on the North Face, the 700m *Estasen Couloir*.

As for the **Gran Encantat** (2747m), this was first climbed in 1901 by de Negrin, Romeu, Ciffre and the Gavarnie guide François Bernard Salles. Here the same Central Gully provides an enjoyable scramble as far as the Enforcadura, followed by a more exposed, but not difficult climb to the top. This route is graded no higher than PD, the same as the Monastero Gully route on the Southwest Face, while on the **Ⓑ** Northwest Face, the *Voie des Gardes* is a 500m grade D route often tackled as a winter climb.

Heading upstream alongside the Riu Monastero to a string of small lakes and pools, a path leads into a cirque crowned by the 2982m **Pic de Peguera**, which makes a popular ascent via the easy Coll de Monastero (in 3hrs from Sant Maurici), or by way of the Coll de Peguera (3½–4hrs, PD) in its western ridge, then across the south summit. If using the Coll de Monastero route, **Pic de Monastero** (2878m) above to the northeast can also be claimed.

Refugi d'Amitges, with the Encantats peaks as a backdrop

Both Pic de Peguera and Pic de Monastero can as easily be climbed from a base at the **Refugi Josep Maria Blanc**, the magnificently situated CEC hut perched on the east bank of Estany Tort de Peguera at 2350m, about 3–3½hrs walk from Espot. With places for 40, the *refugi* is usually manned from mid-June to mid-September (☎ 973 25 01 08). From here Pic de Peguera forms the main attraction for scramblers, although the headwall rimming the cirque south of the hut appears to contain a number of short rock problems that could be worth an examination. In that headwall **Pic Mainera**, overlooking the Colomina lake country, is accessible in about 3hrs. Of an entirely different nature, the modest ⊗ 2689m **Pala Sudorn** southeast of the J.M. Blanc hut requires little more than a steep walk, and from the summit one gains one of those extraordinary contrasting views of which the Pyrenees has many. In one direction rock peaks and mirror lakes are the norm, in the other gentle rolling hills and forests merge their subtle forms and textures. The ski slopes of Super Espot lie to the east, while a more rugged and much more satisfying landscape fills the view west and southwest.

By crossing the cirque headwall at the **Collado de Saburó**, Refugi Colomina can be reached in 4hrs or so (see 4:10), and strong trekkers could then return to the J.M. Blanc hut by way of **Coll de Peguera** and **Coll de Monastero**, thereby creating a rewarding circuit.

- A walking ◗★ **tour of the Encantats** which links the J.M. Blanc and Ernest Mallafré *refugis* makes a very fine walk if spread over two days. It could be tackled in either direction, but for preference try the clockwise circuit, beginning in Espot and making first for the J.M. Blanc hut. Jeep-taxis use a track from the village, but there's an enjoyable footpath route which breaks off from the road to Super Espot and follows the Riu de Peguera virtually all the way. After exploring the country above the hut, spend a night at the *refugi*, and next day cross the **Coll de Monastero** in the western ridge and descend on the other side to the Monastero valley, down which you then wander as far as the Mallafré hut and Estany de Sant Maurici. From there follow the route of GR11 back to Espot.

West of the Sant Maurici lake a much-used track leads across the **Portarró d'Espot** (2429m) to the Refugi d'Estany Llong in the Vall de Sant Nicolau, which is, of course, within the Aigüestortes sector of the national park (see 4:9). Measuring about 15km between driveable sections (Sant Maurici to Aigüestortes), the track is an upgraded mule-path adopted as a GR11 *variante*. Although it serves as a direct route from one side of the park to the other, it's not the nicest walk hereabouts, despite the very pleasant scenery. On either side of the pass, however, there are summits to reach by uncomplicated ways, and routes that continue from them that suggest more interesting outings.

Between Estany de Sant Maurici and the Portarró d'Espot, a tributary valley knuckles into the southern mountains, drained by the

The Agulles d'Amitges offer a number of fairly short rock climbs in a wild setting

Barranco de Subenuix. A path heads into this valley and continues to the cirque that encloses it. At 2949m **Pic Subenuix** marks the highest point on the ridge that separates the Sant Maurici and Sant Nicolau valleys, and there are two possible routes to that summit, neither of which are particularly difficult. When conditions allow, Pic Subenuix is sometimes climbed on ski by way of a col in the cirque headwall between Subenuix and Pic Morto.

From the roadhead at Sant Maurici a driveable track used by jeep-taxis angles up the northern hillside on the way to **Refugi d'Amitges** (2380m), a comfortable CEC hut with 66 places about 1½hrs walk from the lake. The hut is usually manned from June to mid-September (☎ 973 25 01 09, www.amitges.com), and from it one gains a fine view of Els Encantats to the southeast, while above to the north soar the equally impressive **Agulles d'Amitges**.

These twin pinnacles make obvious targets for rock climbers. The more southerly peak, which is slightly lower than its counterpart, has a number of ⓑ ★ fairly exposed routes varying from D to TD on its

Spanish climbers in action on the Agulles d'Amitges

South Face, but the ⊗ northeast summit (2665m) is gained by a delightful scramble rated PD, which takes only 1½hrs from the *refugi*. This route tackles a gully that seams the western face and climbs to a minor col, from which a final pitch up a broad crack emerges onto the summit block.

The Agulles d'Amitges are separated from the Saboredo watershed ridge by a rough terrain of rocks and boulders, but in its very wildness lies much of its appeal. Pools and small lakes add a sheen to the landscape, and in the western half of this rugged cirque, under the Port de Ratera d'Espot – used as a GR11 link with the Colomers *refugi* – the Estany del Port de Ratera heads the Ratera valley which carries GR11 down to Sant Maurici.

Hut to Hut in the Aigües Tortes National Park

A splendid six-stage tour in and around the national park rim can be created using the various manned *refugis* for overnight accommodation. Most of the stages are fairly short, thus allowing time to explore valley systems along the way or to divert to a nearby summit. The route suggested is not an officially adopted tour, and is open to refinement and variation. Hut details, as well as more precise route information for some of the stages, will be found elsewhere in this chapter. Note that if attempted in the early weeks of the summer, an ice axe could be useful for crossing the higher passes.

Day 1: From **ESPOT** follow GR11 upvalley to Estany de Sant Maurici, then take the track as far as **REFUGI D'AMITGES**.

Day 2: Cut across country to Estany del Port de Ratera and over the col above it on the path of GR11 again, then descend on the far side to **REFUGI DE COLOMERS**. This short and easy stage allows plenty of time to enjoy the lake-jewelled Colomers *circ*.

Day 3: Heading west along the path of both the HRP and GR11, cross Port de Caldes and, remaining high, divert away from the main course of the tour to make the ascent of Montardo d'Aran (4:9) before descending south to **REFUGI VENTOSA I CALVELL**.

Day 4: On this stage the tour crosses the 2770m Coll de Contraix into the Vall de Sant Nicolau, with an overnight spent in the national park's **REFUGI D'ESTANY LLONG**.

Day 5: Going from lake to lake the way climbs into the Vall de Sant Nicolau's south-eastern corner to cross Collado dels Gavatxos. On the south side of the col descend to Estany Tort, then take a good path up to **REFUGI COLOMINA** described in 4:10.

Day 6: On this final stage cross Collado de Saburó and descend via the J.M. Blanc *refugi* to **ESPOT**, thereby completing a fine circuit of the national park.

4:12 VALL D'ÀNEU

Above the Espot turning, as far north as the Port de la Bonaigua, the valley of the Noguera Pallaresa is known as the Vall d'Àneu, inhabited by a string of three villages whose names are identified with that of the valley itself: **LA GUINGUETA D'ÀNEU** at the northern end of a reservoir; **ESTERRI D'ÀNEU** where the road forks (left for the Bonaigua pass and Vall d'Aran, straight ahead to Isil and the long track leading to Montgarri); and the highest of all **VALÈNCIA D'ÀNEU**, beyond which the road curves west towards the pass.

Trekkers following GR11 out of the Aigües Tortes national park have to cross Vall d'Aneu to continue eastward. To achieve this waymarks lead down the right bank of the Riu Escrita below Espot, but later emerge onto the valley road by Camping La Mola. From here a roadwalk heading roughly north takes the route as far as **JOU**, a resurrected village (no facilities other than a water fountain) looking across the Vall d'Àneu. It is here that a clearly marked footpath breaks away to descend to the Noguera Pallaresa and **LA GUINGUETA**, the lower of the villages gathered alongside the road at around 945m. Though small, the hamlet boasts two large campsites (both with bar-restaurants) and several other accommodation choices.

The GR11 crosses the valley here, and soon begins a 450m climb to the almost completely abandoned hamlet of **DORVE** (Dorbe), which has a convenient water supply in the square. Another 350m above the hamlet the poorly maintained route, which is not always easy to follow despite waymarks, reaches the Collado de la Serra, and climbs on from there to gain Coll de Calvo (2207m) on the ridge dividing Vall d'Àneu from the valley of the Ribera d'Estaon. An alternative path goes up the slope to the left to gain the north summit of Calvo (Cauvo, 2290m), and from this elevated point the ragged peaks of the national park are seen ranging across the western horizon, while the little-known country that crowds the upper valleys to the northeast signals with its own undeniable attraction.

ESTERRI D'ÀNEU (948m) lies 4km upvalley beyond La Guingueta. By far the largest community in the Vall d'Àneu, the old village has been overshadowed by resort-style development. The nearest campsite is located 1km downstream, while the village itself has at least 10 places for an overnight stay. Offering good value, Fonda Agustí has a reputation for generous-sized meals, while the two-star Esterri Park Hotel represents a more expensive type of accommodation (for tourist information, ☎ 973 62 60 05).

Since the Port de la Bonaigua is closed in winter (late November to May), Esterri is the valley's uppermost village served year-round by the bus from La Pobla de Segur. It is here, in the middle of the village, that the main C147 road curves sharply to the left on its way to the pass, while a more narrow road stays close to the Noguera Pallaresa, crosses to the east bank just outside the village near the confluence with the Riu de la Bonaigua, and after twisting round **ISAVARRE** enters the **Alta Vall Noguera Pallaresa**, which is also referred to here as the **Vall d'Isil** after the village of the same name (see 4:7).

Another road crosses the Noguera Pallaresa on the eastern edge of Esterri and swings round a mountain spur into the pastoral tributary valley of the Riu d'Unarre, in which there's a group of huddled hamlets. When the road ends a *pista* grinds on upstream as far as the **Planell de Sartari** at almost 2000m – the last few kilometres only really suitable for 4WD vehicles. From the Planell a footpath climbs on to a high region of lakes guarded by Pic de Mitjana and Pedres Picades. First of the lakes is the dammed Estany de la Gola, but above that to the north lies **Estany Calverante** and a wonderfully remote region traversed by a *variante* of the Pyrenean High Route. This is country to repay a visit by self-sufficient trekkers – but choose settled conditions, for when the mists are down, it can be a testing place.

Apart from the two options mentioned above, the main road breaks away from Esterri and writhes uphill to **VALÈNCIA D'ÀNEU** (1143m), a typical Catalan-style group of mottled stone buildings, as yet untouched by developers with an eye to expansion, offering a choice of at least five places in which to stay.

There may be no higher villages on the way to Port de la Bonaigua, but the road passes one or two other accommodation opportunities on its long rise west, guided by high-tension cables and their grotesque pylons. About 3km short of the pass, a path cuts back to the left, heading southeast to gain entry to the **Vall de Gerber**, a delightful though relatively short valley inside the national park's peripheral zone, with a collection of lakes and a small *refugi* in the cirque at its head. Owned by the CEC, **Refugi Mataró** (2460m) is a simple unguarded metal hut with about 16 places, set beside a tiny lake (see 4:7). ◗ From here linking routes cross the 2582m Coll de Gerber in the western ridge in order to visit the Circ de Saboredo and its manned *refugi*, and heading south via Coll d'Amitges (2740m) on the national park boundary, followed by a steep descent to Refugi d'Amitges and, eventually, Espot. And finally, southeast of the Mataró hut, a third pass, Collado de Bassiero, gives access to another collection of tarns that drain into the **Vall de Cabanes**. This little tributary valley flows north to join the Vall d'Àneu about 16km above Esterri, so an excellent day-long partial circuit could be achieved by linking this valley with the Vall de Gerber.

4:13 VALL DE CARDÓS

The bus from La Pobla de Segur to the Vall d'Aran sets passengers down in **LLAVORSI**, an uninspiring village at the confluence of the Noguera Pallaresa and Noguera de Lladorre, several kilometres south of the Espot turning. At the entrance to Vall de Cardós (the valley of the Noguera de Lladorre) a huge electricity substation glowers within the valley confines, while alongside the C147 road a string of bars, restaurants and *hostals* cater largely to an enthusiastic tourist trade centred on water sports. The Noguera Pallaresa is the major river for rafting and canoeing in the Spanish Pyrenees, especially the stretch below Llavorsi, and the village has more than its share of adventure outfitters to exploit the river's reputation. But lying between the Noguera Pallaresa and Andorra, Vall de Cardós and its neighbour Vall Ferrera are very much mountain-based, and those who have a preference for 'back-of-beyond' country should find satisfaction by penetrating to their uppermost regions. Getting there is not easy, though, unless you have your own transport. Buses do not stray into these quarters, and the most interesting places often require effort and commitment to discover.

The lower Vall de Cardós is narrow and almost gorge-like in places, but beyond the Vall Ferrera turning, 4km from Llavorsi, it begins to open out on the way to **RIBERA DE CARDÓS**, where the valley forks. Although nothing out of the ordinary, Ribera is a quietly attractive village, about 9km from Llavorsi. In addition to two campsites, there are at least three accommodation choices: Hostal Sol i Neu, the Cardós and the two-star Cal Quet.

The main Vall de Cardós, with the Riu la Noguera de Lladorre flowing through it, lies north of Ribera, but the short northwest branch of the valley, drained by the Ribera d'Estaon, narrows again, and after the tarmac runs out travel is limited to old farm tracks and footpaths. About 6km upstream from Ribera de Cardós, the hamlet of **ESTAON** stands on the west slope of the valley at 1240m. Visited by GR11 trekkers following a steep descent of almost 1000m from Coll de Calvo (see 4:12), this lovely little group of buildings has been rescued from near abandonment by city folk resurrecting the houses as holiday homes.

About an hour's walk upstream beyond Estaon, GR11 turns away a couple of minutes or so after passing the old farm buildings known as the Bordes de Nibrós, and works up the eastern hillside in order to cross the dividing ridge, on the far side of which lies Tavascan (Tabescan) in the main Vall de Cardós. The trans-Pyrenean GR11 avoids a direct descent into the valley, and instead angles down along old tracks and footpaths to reach the village, which is built where the valley forks again some 11km from Ribera de Cardós.

The standard route to Tavascan and the northernmost limits of the Pallars Sobirà district follows the road through Vall de Cardós, crossing and recrossing the Riu la Noguera de Lladorre that drifts through meadows, and a short distance upstream of Ribera passes through **AINET DE CARDÓS** (bars, restaurants and a campsite), then below the medieval-looking hamlet of **LLADROS**. Modestly attractive **LLADORRE** clusters on the river's east bank and is visited on a signed circular walk from Tavascan, which links a few tiny hamlets and old barns in a half-day walk. About 3km beyond Lladorre you come at last to **TAVASCAN** (1120m) which, though small and insignificant in appearance, has pretensions as a resort, thanks to the as yet low-key development of the **Pleta del Prat ski station**, 11km to the northwest.

Tavascan's single main street, which acts as a façade to the original village, is lined with hotels, bars, restaurants and two shops. Cheapest accommodation is the *casa* attached to Bar-restaurant Feliu. Then there are the hotels: the Llacs de Cardós and three-star Estany Blaus sharing the same management, and the cheaper Hotel Marxant (marxant@autovia.com) often used by GR11 trekkers. The local campsite, though by no means the nearest to Tavascan, is Camping Bordes de Graus, which is located 5km away beside the Riu de Tavascan northwest of the village and is open from April to October.

As for **Pleta del Prat**, this is reached by a narrow road that swings left immediately beyond Tavascan's electricity substation. Before reaching the campsite and a small dammed lake, the road becomes a poor track that serves the tiny hamlet of Cuanca, then twists uphill for a few more kilometres to arrive at the ski station's only chairlift, built at 1725m. Nearby stands the **Refugi la Pleta del Prat** which, when open, has 60 places and all services (☎ 973 62 30 79). Initially planned as a nordic ski centre, in 1998 Pleta del Prat began to expand for downhill skiing. The present maximum altitude is 2250m and there are only five pistes, but snowshoe routes are possible, and the chairlift is open in summer to provide access for walkers. (For information contact: Casal de la Vila, 25577 Tavascan, ☎ 973 62 30 89, e-mail: lapleta@cambrescat.es).

The GR11 ignores both the upper stems of Vall de Cardós above Tavascan, and instead heads away from the high mountains and works up the hillside in a southeasterly direction. After a couple of hours walkers enter the peaceful village of **BOLDÍS SOBIRÀ**. Much of the way from here to the Coll de Tudela follows a *pista*, and from the pass views are splendid. On the eastern side of the ridge the way-marked route descends to **Àreu** in the **Vall Ferrera** (see 4:14).

THE RIU DE LAVASCAN

Both valley sections above Tavascan have their upper reaches nudging against the frontier with France. Like so many districts of the Pyrenees, lakes are an important feature of these uplands, and in past decades hydro-engineers forged routes to them and harnessed some of their power. But as Robin Fedden remarked of a neighbouring district in *The Enchanted Mountains*: 'When the landscape has been scarred, the surgeons leave. Vegetation does its work. These valleys are not ruined.' Though he may have been writing about valleys now included within the national park, the same can be said about these upper reaches of Pallars Sobirà, where walking routes entice into some of the most secluded corners of all.

The northwest branch above Tavascan, drained by the Riu de Lavascan, is sub-divided by short tributary glens worth the effort to explore. Not all the paths marked on Editorial Alpina maps exist on the ground, however, and even when they do, some demand a fair degree of concentration for the trekker to remain on course. Tough though some of these routes may be, the country they explore has a sense of being wonderfully untamed and rewarding.

The HRP *variante* described earlier as coming from Salardú via Montgarri (4:7) makes a high traverse of this wonderland of long ridge-spurs and intimate cirques in which there are to be found any number of idyllic wild campsites, while by the side of Estany de la Gallina at 2280m there's a simple unmanned bivouac hut. **Refugi Enric Pujol** (otherwise known as Refugi Mont-Roig) is owned by the FEEC, is permanently open and can sleep about 12. Given settled weather, experienced scramblers and trekkers could enjoy many days of activity based on a lonely camp in one of these cirques, for there are numerous little lakes to discover, cols to cross, ridges to scramble on and summits to gain. The highest of these is the 2858m **Mont Roig**, which carries the frontier crest northwest of the Pujol *refugi* and whose altitude, like so many Pyrenean summits, is open to dispute. And it's not only altitude measurements that give rise to speculation here, for the maps on occasion confuse the names and even the position of some of the cols, while, as mentioned earlier, the existence of the odd path drawn on certain sheets appears in reality to be no more than the product of a rich imagination. Although such inconsistency can easily create problems and some frustration, there is something rather heartwarming in the knowledge that in 21st-century Europe it is still possible to be hopelessly lost when relying on the latest cartography.

From Mont Roig the frontier trends northeastward as far as Pic de Montarenyo (Pic de la Montagnoule to the French), throwing out a spur or two to the south to contain minor cirques before cutting back to the southeast. Caught in the upper reaches of two of these cirques lie the Estanys de Mariola and del Port, the two separated by the lump of Turo del Estany Xic. These lakes are accessible from a *pista* that ends at the Pleta Palomera north of **NOARRE** (1593m), a remote hamlet visited by a *variante* of the HRP.

At the end of an epic 10-hour trek from Palanca de Pine in the Alta Vall Noguera Pallaresa, the HRP descends to the Tavascan campsite at Bordes de Graus. An alternative option avoids descending this far, however, and instead goes through Noarre. Since there are no facilities in this hamlet, and it's a good 4hrs or so before one could reach accommodation other than that in Tavascan, trekkers would need to think out their staging of this part of the route well in advance. The high-route alternative leaves Noarre by heading northeast into the little glen behind it, and then crossing Coll de Certascan at 2615m. On the east side of the col, lying right up against – but 300m below – the frontier crest, Estany de Certascan is the largest, deepest and most impressive of the many lakes in these uplands, with the **Refugi de Certascan** sited at its southern end at 2240m. The hut is owned by the FEEC, and has 40 places and a guardian from mid-June to mid-September (☎ 973 62 32 30, e-mail: certascan@teleline.es).

A popular ascent from this *refugi* is the uncomplicated *voie normale* on ◔ **Pic de Certascan** (2853m) by way of Coll de Certascan in about 2hrs, but there are also some fine day-walks to be had too. ◑ A tour of the Romedo lakes east of the *refugi* is just one suggestion, for which about 5hrs is needed. Meanwhile the HRP either crosses into France at the 2481m Port de l'Artiga above Estany de Romedo, then descends to Mounicou in Haute-Ariège, or takes a winding trail, waymarked by the *refugi's* guardian, down to the charming Planell de Boavi near the head of the Vall de Cardós.

NOGUERA DE LLADORRE HEADWATERS

The northeast stem of the Vall de Cardós above Tavascan is a little longer than its counterpart, and the *pista* that accompanies the Riu la Noguera de Lladorre through it reveals an increasingly tranquil landscape, a valley of meadows, woodlands and barns, with minor streams and cascades spilling from the hillsides. Private vehicles are allowed only as far as a barrier, 6km from Tavascan, which leaves a 30min walk to the **Planell de Boavi** at 1460m. Once popular with motorised Spanish picnic parties and overnighters, sadly the glorious tree-lined meadows became littered and degraded, and these have only been saved at the eleventh hour by being declared a protected zone with vehicular access denied. It's a sorry acknowledgement that those with the easiest and most convenient means of carrying out their rubbish, are often the ones who leave most behind them. On the way to the Planell another track winds up the western hillside, from which a path climbs to the Estany de Naorte and continues to Refugi de Certascan.

North of Boavi, but unseen from the parkland-like meadows, the Romedo lakes lie 600m or more above the valley bed, while to the east the Riu de Broate drains from yet another lake, near which stands the small, unmanned **Refugi de Broate** at 2200m (18 places, permanently open). From here the ascent of **Pic de Sotllo** (3072m) via its north ridge requires less than 2hrs of effort.

●★ Trekkers following the HRP on a very pleasant stage that ends in the Vall Ferrera, turn away from the Broate stream a short way beyond Boavi, and head south alongside the Ribera de Sallente en route for a crossing of **Coll de Sallente** at 2485m. This col is an easy saddle in the southwest boundary ridge of the Circ de Baborte. Contained within the cirque are several small pools that feed down into the larger Estany Baborte. On a knoll above its north shore stands an inauspicious-looking metal bivouac hut, **Refugi de Baborte** at 2438m. More comfortable than it looks, the official capacity of this hut is 16, but half that number would be about right. Yet since it is reached in less than 4hrs from the Planell de Boavi, most trekkers would consider moving on to the Vall Ferrera *refugi* at the foot of Pica d'Estats, another 2–2½hrs away. For details of this hut, and suggestions for making the most of the upper reaches of Vall Ferrera, see 4:14 below.

Estany Baborte, southwest of Pica d'Estats, is visited by trekkers following the High Route

4:14 VALL FERRERA

The Riu la Noguera de Vall Ferrera is the last of the rivers of Pallars Sobirà before Andorra's mountain rim is reached. Most of its feeder streams are short and therefore fairly modest, with the exception of the Noguera de Tor, which drains its own individual valley whose head butts directly against Andorra's western limits. At first, on entering Vall Ferrera from its confluence with Vall de Cardós just 4km from Llavorsi, the narrow wooded confines are gorge-like and gloomy, but by the time you reach **ARAÓS** the hillsides are less oppressive and allow some sunshine through. Mostly, though, the lower Vall Ferrera

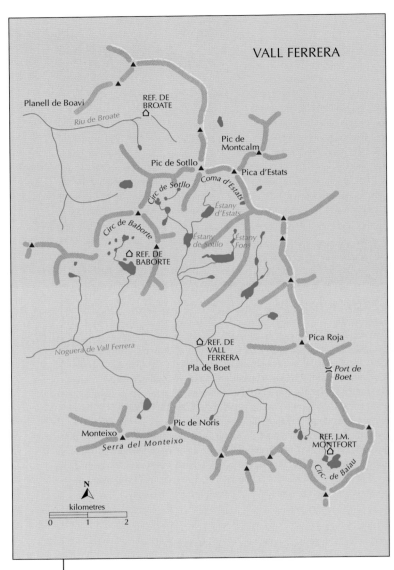

VALL FERRERA

Planell de Boavi

REF. DE
BROATE

Riu de Broate

Pic de
Montcalm

Pic de Sotllo

Circ de Sotllo

Coma d'Estats

Pica d'Estats

Éstany
d'Estats

Circ de Baborte

Éstany
de Sotllo

Éstany
Fons

REF. DE
BABORTE

REF. DE
VALL
FERRERA

Pica Roja

Noguera de Vall Ferrera

Pla de Boet

Port de
Boet

Pic de Noris

Monteixo

REF. J.M.
MONTFORT

Serra del Monteixo

Circ. de Baiau

N

kilometres

0   1   2

is a narrow swathe whose forest cover is broken here and there by
parcels of meadowland.

AINET DE BESAN, just 2km upstream of Araós, is a two-part village with the older, traditional quarter on the left of the road, and
an estate of modern bungalows standing out like the proverbial sore
thumb on the right, but ahead the mountains, when seen, take on a
rugged appearance. **ALINS** (1068m), 13km from Llavorsi, is the valley's largest village and the only one with a reasonable choice of
accommodation, among which there's the two-star Hotel Salòria,

Hostal Montaña and Casa Xicot. The village also has a bar-restaurant, a shop and a campsite, Camping Vall Ferrera. Just beyond Alins the valley forks, with the Riu la Noguera de Tor coming from the northeast, its only settlement being **TOR**, 12km away below the Port de Cabús at 1649m.

The last village in the Vall Ferrera is **ÀREU** (1219m), which lies just 5km beyond Alins. This small, seemingly remote settlement is an important staging post for trekkers following the GR11, and it also serves as a convenient midway halt on the approach to Refugi de Vall Ferrera, another 3hrs walk away. Although accommodation is limited to just one hotel, the two-star Hostal Vall Ferrera, Àreu has at least half a dozen *casas de pagès*, among them Casa Besolí, Casa Curona and Casa Gallardó. There's also a restaurant and a foodstore, and a campsite with swimming pool and bar. Camping Pica d'Estats is open from mid-June to mid-September.

The Estats massif rises abruptly from the Sotllo valley

The tarmac runs out at Àreu, but a rough track, or *pista*, continues to push upvalley, first on the right bank, then on the true left bank of the river. Badly rutted and waterlogged at times, the *pista* is more suited to 4WD vehicles, but it leads through pleasant mixed forest of birch and fir trees. In places waymarks direct the GR11 onto sections of path that shortcut the track on the way to the Pla de la Selva, and again between Pla de la Selva and the point beyond which the track is officially closed to private vehicles, about 10km from Àreu – this is within a few minutes of the signed path leading to the *refugi*.

A footbridge spans the river, then the path goes up a slope beside the Barranc d'Areste before crossing by a cascade just below **Refugi de Vall Ferrera** at 1940m. Opened in 1935, renovated in 1980 and again more recently, this small FEEC hut has places for 30 and is usually manned from May to late September (☎ 973 62 07 54 or 973 62 43 78). Above to the north rises **Pica d'Estats** (3143m), the most easterly 3000m summit in the Pyrenees. Naturally enough this is the main focus of attention for visitors to the *refugi*. The ascent, though quite long, is not difficult, and it's perfectly feasible for practised scramblers to add several other high tops to the day's expedition.

⏾★ ASCENT OF PICA D'ESTATS

Pica d'Estats, most easterly of the Pyrenean 3000m peaks, and contender for the title of most cluttered summit

The path of ascent begins at the hut, twisting up the slope for about 15mins before veering left into the charming Sotllo valley. The way goes up through the valley from one level to the next, marked by lateral moraines from a long-vanished glacier. Over the third of these lies Estany de Sotllo at 2352m, but higher still, cupped within the cirque of the Coma d'Estats, lies Estany d'Estats. More than 400m above this to

the north the pass of Port de Sotllo is clearly visible, guarded on its left by Pic de Sotllo (3072m) and on its right by Pica d'Estats.

The way to the pass is on scree and, quite often, on patches of snow that lie well into the summer. Once there either scramble up the right-hand ridge (experienced scramblers only) or descend briefly on the northern side, then traverse right over rocks and snow to gain a point midway between the peaks of Estats and Montcalm. From the 2978m Coll de Riufret bear right over the secondary summit of Punta NE (3131m) to the crown of Pica d'Estats (5hrs from the *refugi*). This, the highest Catalan summit, is one of the most cluttered in all the Pyrenees, but the panorama is magnificent.

Pica d'Estats is on the frontier ridge, but its bald, unattractive, but almost better-known neighbour ⊗ **Pic de Montcalm** (3077m) stands wholly in France and is reached by an easy walk of just 30mins from Estats. (For the ascent of this mountain from the north, see 5:1.)

Rather than descend by the same route, a traverse of the southeast ridge of Pica d'Estats gives an opportunity to collect two more 3000m tops (Punta SE at 3115m and Pt 3004m – Rodó de Canalbona) before cutting down to Estany d'Estats, where you rejoin the path back to the *refugi*. This traverse is graded PD+ and caution is required because of unstable rocks – the use of helmet and rope is advised.

An alternative descent, in effect a south–north traverse of the mountain, is possible by descending northward below Port de Sotllo, partly on glacier, partly on rocks, then steeply down to **Refuge du Pinet** (about 2–2½hrs from the col). From the refuge (details under 5:1) a clear path continues into the Vicdessos valley, where there's a *gîte d'étape* at Mounicou on the route of GR10 (allow 7½hrs for this crossing).

THE CIRC DE BABORTE

Even were Pica d'Estats and its neighbours of no great appeal, the Sotllo glen would still be worth visiting by walkers, as would the **Circ de Baborte** southwest of the Coma d'Estats. To gain entry to this cirque, leave Estany de Sotllo by heading west alongside its feeder stream, then up towards the Circ de Sotllo before breaking away southwestward to gain the Coll de Baborte (2618m). At the col you'll find a sign directing the onward route to the **Refugi de Baborte**, which stands atop a knoll overlooking the lake of the same name. The way to it is guided by cairns, and is reached in about 40mins from the col (4–4½hrs from the *refugi*). But should you be tempted to spend a night there, and there are good enough reasons to do so, be warned that the hut is unmanned and you'll need to be self-sufficient. The cirque has some idyllic wild camping sites too.

◖ This route could be turned into a 7hr circular walk by returning to the Refugi de Vall Ferrera along the HRP. This descends from the southern end of Estany de Baborte as far as a flat hillside shelf on which stands the Cabane de Basello overlooking the Vall Ferrera. From here to the Vall Ferrera *refugi* the path is adequately waymarked.

PLA DE BOET AND BEYOND

A few minutes' walk from the footbridge spanning the Noguera below the *refugi* leads to the pastures of **Pla de Boet**, an idyllic wild campsite of use not only to walkers and scramblers seeking a degree of solitude, but to backpackers tackling the Pyrenean High Route, for the HRP crosses out of Spain at the easy Port de Boet less than 2hrs away. Once over the pass, the HRP descends to cross the head of the Vicdessos valley which forms a narrow, finger-like enclave of France, on the far side of which the Port de Rat carries the route into Andorra.

From a camp in the Pla de Boet the ascent of **Pica Roja** (2902m) on the frontier ridge takes only 45mins or so from the Port de Boet, while the individual lump of ⊘ **Monteixo** (2905m) across the pastures to the southwest requires a little more time and effort, although this summit can still be reached in about 3½hrs. As it stands well away from the major peaks of the area, Monteixo makes a splendid viewpoint from which to study the district. It would also be possible to follow the crest of the Serra del Monteixo roughly eastward over several minor tops to obtain an unfolding, ever-changing perspective of those mountains that wall the Vall Ferrera to the north, and also of Andorra's rocky outline that makes a dramatic contrast to the Baiau grasslands below.

Southeast of the Pla de Boet, the headwaters of the Noguera de Vall Ferrera gather in the open pasturelands of the Pla de Baiau. Above these, partly cradled by the crags of the **Circ de Baiau**, lie a few lakes and pools, and perched upon a rocky promontory overlooking the largest and highest of these is an unmanned metal bivouac hut at 2517m. Reached in 2–2½hrs from Pla de Boet, **Refugi Josep Maria Montfort** is another FEEC hut, with places for 12. Andorra's highest mountains gather near or along the cirque rim, and the GR11 has been routed across this ridge above the hut at the Portella de Baiau (2757m), on which snow can remain until July or even later and cause problems for the unwary – especially on the Andorran side.

The Sotllo valley and its tarns below the Estats massif

ACCESS, BASES, MAPS AND GUIDES

Access

Pays de Couserans N117 southwest of Toulouse, then D117 to St-Girons, from which minor roads splay into the inner valleys. By train from Toulouse to Foix, then bus to St-Girons.

Vallée du Biros Take D6 out of St-Girons to Audressein, then D4 to Eylie. There's a bus service from St-Girons as far as Sentein.

Vallée de Bethmale The valley is traversed by D17 which strikes southeast from Les Bordes-sur-Lez on D4. The nearest public transport serves Les Bordes from St-Girons.

Vallée du Salat D618 southeast of St-Girons, then D3 south as far as Salau. Seix is as far as the bus runs from St-Girons.

Vallée d'Ustou Southeast of Couflens, the valley is traversed by D8 and served by bus from St-Girons.

Vallée du Garbet D32 southeast of Oust. A bus service from St-Girons feeds Aulus-les-Bains.

Vall d'Aran By road from France access is via N125, which becomes N230 at the Spanish border. From Spain access is via N230 along the Noguera Ribagorçana and through the Viella tunnel, or through the valley of the Noguera Pallaresa (C147) and across the Port de la Bonaigua (closed in winter). Buses from La Pobla de Segur (via the Bonaigua) and Lleida (Viella tunnel).

Vall Noguera Ribagorçana N230 from Lleida via Pont de Suert. Buses from Lleida and Viella.

Vall de Boí The CL500 road breaks away from N230 northwest of El Pont de Suert. The valley is served by bus from Pont de Suert as far as Caldes de Boí.

Vall Fosca By minor road heading north from N260 outside Senterada. Infrequent bus service between La Pobla de Segur and Capdella.

Vall d'Espot By minor road (LV5004) west of the C147 through the Noguera Pallaresa. The nearest public transport is the Pobla de Segur–Vall d'Aran bus which passes the valley entrance, 7km from Espot.

Vall d'Àneu The C147 along the Noguera Pallaresa serves this valley, as does the bus from La Pobla de Segur to Viella (terminates in Esterri in winter).

Vall de Cardós Via a minor road cutting northeast from Llavorsi on the C147. No public transport in the valley – nearest bus (Pobla de Segur–Vall d'Aran) goes through Llavorsi.

Vall Ferrera By minor road out of Vall de Cardós. Nearest public transport at Llavorsi – see Vall de Cardós above.

Valley Bases

Pays de Couserans St-Girons

Vallée du Biros Sentein, Eylie d'En Haut

Vallée de Bethmale Ayet

Vallée du Salat Seix

Vallée d'Ustou Le Trein d'Ustou, Bidous

Vallée du Garbet Aulus-les-Bains

Vall d'Aran Salardú

Vall Noguera Ribagorçana None

Vall de Boí Boí

Vall Fosca Capdella

Vall d'Espot Espot

Vall d'Àneu La Guingueta, Esterri d'Àneu

Vall de Cardós Tavascan

Vall Ferrera Àreu

Huts

Most of the valley regions covered by this chapter are well equipped with manned huts. There are also several unguarded bivouac huts. Details are given within the main text.

Maps

IGN Top 25: 1947OT Aspet, *Pic de Mauberme*, 2047OT *St-Girons, Couserans*, 2048OT *Aulus-les-Bains, Montvalier*, 2047ET *Massat, Pic des Trois Seigneurs*, 2148OT *Vicdessos, Pics d'Estats et de Montcalm* at 1:25,000

Cartes de Randonnées: *5 Luchon, 6 Couserans-Cap d'Aran, 7 Haute-Ariège Andorre* at 1:50,000

Editorial Alpina: *Val d'Aran* 1:40,000, *La Ribagorça* 1:25,000, *Pont de Suert* 1:40,000, *Vall de Boí* 1:25,000, *Montsent de Pallars* 1:25,000, *Sant Maurici* 1:25,000, *Montgarri Mont Valier* 1:25,000, *Pica d'Estats* 1:40,000

Walking and/or Trekking Guides

Walks and Climbs in the Pyrenees by Kev Reynolds (Cicerone Press, 5th edn, 2008)

The GR10 Trail by Paul Lucia (Cicerone Press, 2003)

Through the Spanish Pyrenees: GR11 by Paul Lucia (Cicerone Press, 4th edn, 2008)

Trekking in the Pyrenees by Douglas Streatfeild-James (Trailblazer, 3rd edn, 2005)

The Pyrenean Haute Route by Ton Joosten (Cicerone Press, 2nd end, 2009)

Trekking in Spain by Marc Dubin (Lonely Planet, 1990)

Walking in Spain by Miles Roddis et al (Lonely Planet, 2nd edn, 1999)

Pyrenees Central by Arthur Battagel (West Col, 1989)

Randonnées dans les Pyrénées Ariègeoises by Georges Véron and Michel Grassaud (Rando Editions)

Le Guide Rando – Couserans by Georges Véron (Rando Editions)

Le Guide Rando – Haute Ariège by Georges Véron and Michel Grassaud (Rando Editions)

Rando Poche – Aigüestortes (Rando Editions)

Randonnées à Raquettes dans les Pyrénées by Alban Boyer (Rando Editions)

Climbing Guides

Pyrénées – Courses Mixtes, Neige et Glace by Francis Mousel (Éditions Franck Mercier, 1997)

Pyrénées, Guide des 3000m by Luis Alejos (SUA Edizioak, 2003)

See Also

Classic Walks in the Pyrenees by Kev Reynolds (Oxford Illustrated Press, 1989)

Long Distance Walks in the Pyrenees by Chris Townsend (Crowood Press, 1991)

Les Pyrénées – Les 100 Plus Belles Courses et Randonnées by Patrice de Bellefon (Editions Denoël, 1976)

The Enchanted Mountains by Robin Fedden (John Murray, 1962/Ernest Press, 2000)

CHAPTER 5: ANDORRA AND THE EASTERN HIGH PYRENEES

The independent state of Andorra, the neighbouring valleys of Haute-Ariège and mountains that border the Cerdagne as far east as Mont-Louis

ANDORRA AND THE EASTERN HIGH PYRENEES: CHAPTER SUMMARY

Location

From the Port de Lers on the French side of the border, stretching as far east as the Capcir. All the valleys of mountain-locked Andorra are included, as well as the Cerdagne, and the Spanish side of the Puigmal in the valley sanctuary of Núria.

★ Highlights

◖ WALKS

- in the Vallée d'Orlu (5:4)
- almost anywhere in the Carlit region (5:5)
- Queralbs to Núria (5:7)
- sections of GR10, GR11 and the HRP (5:1–5:7)

◑ CLIMBS

- South and Southeast faces of Dent d'Orlu (5:4)
- winter climbs in the Vignole–Valletes group near Col de Puymorens (5:5)
- assorted routes in the Sierra del Cadí (box, 5:7)

◔ SUMMITS FOR ALL

- Pic de Montcalm (5:1)
- Pic de Coma Pedrosa (5:3)
- Pic Carlit (5:5)
- Puigmal (5:6)
- Pedraforca (box, 5:7)

Contents

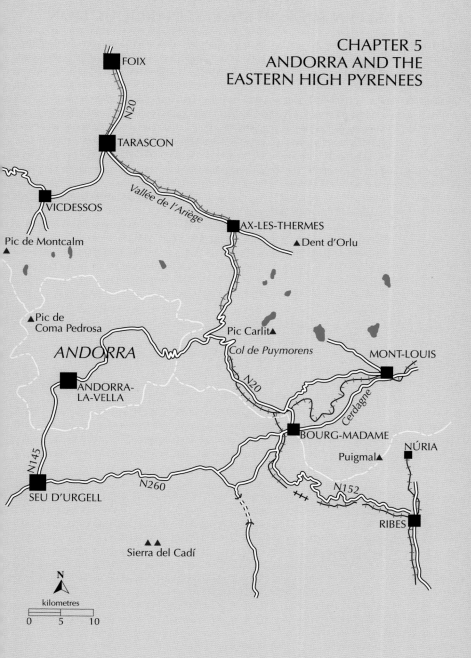

■ FOIX

N20

■ TARASCON

■ VICDESSOS

Vallée de l'Ariège

■ AX-LES-THERMES

▲ Dent d'Orlu

▲ Pic de Montcalm

▲ Pic de
Coma Pedrosa

ANDORRA

Pic Carlit▲

Col de Puymorens

■ MONT-LOUIS

N20

■ ANDORRA-
LA-VELLA

Cerdagne

■ BOURG-MADAME

NÚRIA ■

Puigmal▲

N145

N260

■ SEU D'URGELL

N152

RIBES ■

▲▲
Sierra del Cadí

N

kilometres
0   5   10

ANDORRA AND THE
EASTERN HIGH PYRENEES: INTRODUCTION

East of Port de Lers, the Pays de Foix slices into the high country that shoulders the Andorran border, and, in common with the Pays de Couserans further west, proves the Haute-Ariège to be a region of complex, rugged terrain in which the wooded and steep-walled valleys are topped by little-known mountains – in many places a testing landscape to explore for all but the most experienced of wild-country trekkers. The Ariège valley carries the main road link with Andorra, for south of Ax-les-Thermes the N20 makes its laborious climb to either Col de Puymorens or Pas de la Casa. The Pas de la Casa route serves Andorra, while the 1920m Col de Puymorens gives access to the broad, flat-bottomed Cerdagne, a plateau-like valley shared unequally with Spain. Flanked on the north by the granite peaks of the Carlit massif, and on the south by the large rolling Puigmal mountains, the Cerdagne claims to be the sunniest region in all France. Perhaps of more relevance in the context of this guide, however, is the fact that the Carlit is the most easterly alpine massif, and it effectively marks the true outer limit of the High Pyrenees.

Autonomous, peak-rimmed Andorra, with an area of little more than 450km² and a number of inner valleys draining into the Valira del Orient, forms the hub of this chapter. From its connecting road with France via Pas de la Casa over the Port d'Envalira at more than 2400m to where it spills into Spain some 40km later at around 850m, Andorra is both protected and dwarfed by mountains. The romantic image of this tiny former co-principality has long been buried beneath cheek-by-jowl duty-free hypermarkets, and its mountains laced with cableways for the ski trade, yet still there remain a few fairly unspoilt villages and hidden regions at the head of remote valley systems where solitude may be found. It is there that the real Andorra retains its magic.

Apart from the Sierra del Cadí, which stands well back from the main watershed crest and is not strictly part of the Pyrenean range, the Spanish end of the High Pyrenees is represented by a series of rounded summits overlooking the Cerdagne and culminating in the 2910m Puigmal, southeast of Andorra.

There are no 3000m summits here, but that is not to suggest a lack of climbing interest nor of landscape appeal. Granite dominates, but gneiss and limestone are also found, and as with other regions covered by this book, scores of mountain lakes add their own character to each and every district, while certain valleys feeding into the Cerdagne are among the most botanically rich of the whole range.

In the Circ dels Pessons, a wonderland of tarns, peaks and alpine flowers

5:1 VALLÉE DU VICDESSOS

With its conspicuous triple-turreted skyline, **FOIX** is said to be the smallest capital of any *département* in France. Historic, attractive and well preserved, it makes an agreeable foothill base from which to launch expeditions into the high country to the south, and stands a little way north of the terminal point of the long-vanished glacier that fashioned the surrounding landscape some 10,000 years ago. (For tourist information visit rue Théophile-Delcasse or ☎ 05 61 65 12 12. Regional information can be gathered by e-mail at: tourisme.ariege. pyrenees@wanadoo.fr, website: www.ariegepyrenees.com.)

Ariège, the *département* over which the town reigns, is named for the river that flows right through it and whose valley forms the main communications link with the rest of the region. Easily accessible by both road and rail from Toulouse, Foix is the terminus for bus services that feed west to St-Girons in the Pays de Couserans (see 4:1) and east to Quillan in the Pays de Sault. But for access to valleys that push deeper into the mountains it's necessary to travel further south along the Ariège to such towns as Tarascon and Ax-les-Thermes.

Sixteen kilometres upstream of Foix, **TARASCON-SUR-ARIÈGE** spills across a basin-like widening of the valley where the Corbière and Vicdessos rivers drain from the western hills. The first of these comes out of a valley topped by the Pic des Trois Seigneurs on the ridge beyond which lies the Pays de Couserans. At the head of this **Vallée de la Corbière** two small lakes (Étangs Long and Bleu) can be reached by a pleasant ◐ walk of just under 2hrs from a parking area at the end of a minor road, D523, which extends 8km west of Surba. A third lake, Étang d'Artats, is the destination of a slightly longer walk from Gourbit on the south flank of the valley. But north of Surba, where the D618 begins to climb out of the Corbière valley's entrance en route to the Col de Port, Massat and St-Girons, the village of **BÉDEILHAC** stands below one of the great decorated caves for which the region is justly famous. It's the prehistoric wall paintings, engravings of animals and a huge stalagmite (120m in circumference) that make the **Grotte de Bédeilhac** such an interesting place to visit, yet no matter how impressive this is, it's a mere sideshow by comparison with the **Grotte de Niaux**, which flanks the east side of the Vallée du Vicdessos about 3km southwest of Tarascon.

After being led by torchlight for almost 800m through chambers and passageways you come to the Salon Noir, the centre-piece of Niaux, whose glacier-smoothed walls were decorated nearly 11,000 years ago by palaeolithic artists using manganese oxides to depict an amazing collection of animals – outlines mostly of bison and horses, but with a few ibex and a solitary deer. What is on public show forms just one section of a 4km series of galleries, and in order to preserve these ancient artforms, visitor numbers are strictly regulated and admission allowed only to guided parties (for reservations, ☎ 05 61 05 88 37).

VALLÉE DE LA SIGUER

The Vallée du Vicdessos, a U-shaped trench typical of its glacial origins, pushes deeply into the mountains beyond the caves, and is served by public bus between Tarascon and Auzat near Vicdessos. About 5km upstream of Niaux village past the ruined Miglos château, a secondary road, D24, breaks away to the south into the **Vallée de la Siguer**. The road leads to a dead-end at Bouychet (928m), and from there a good  path climbs through forest on the right bank of the Escales stream to gain the Jasse de Brouquenat, a footbridge and a trail junction. The right-hand trail breaks off to cross the stream on the way to the lengthy **Étang de Gnioure**, which lies at an altitude of 1832m (3hrs from the roadhead). Given sufficient time and energy, the walk could be extended for another 2hrs or so in order to visit **Étang du Rouch** (2549m) in a rocky cirque below Pic du Port on the Franco-Andorran frontier ridge. There's also a cluster of tiny lakes northeast of this, and separated from it by a minor col, that could be included for added interest.

Near the head of the Vallée du Vicdessos, a knot of peaks gather to form the borders of France, Spain and Andorra

West of the ridge that walls Étang de Gnioure lies the Vallon d'Arties, but to the east yet more lakes are accessible on foot from the Bouychet roadhead. **Étangs de Peyregrand** (1897m) and **des Roudouneilles des Vaches** (2127m) can be combined in a circular walk of 6–6½hrs, while **Étang Blaou** at 2335m in another rocky cirque under the frontier ridge takes about 5hrs to reach. Above this upper lake the 2396m **Port de Siguer** was used as an escape route by many French nationals during the Second World War. On the south side of the pass a path leads to **El Serrat** in Andorra's Valira del Nord.

VICDESSOS AND BEYOND

Back in the Vallée du Vicdessos another 6km along the D8 beyond the Siguer turning brings you to **VICDESSOS** itself. This modest village nestles at a confluence of rivers whose opening provides the community with a greater sense of space and light than almost anywhere else hereabouts, for the valley is largely hemmed in by misty, damp forests that turn it into a sunless trench in winter. For accommodation Vicdessos has a simple hotel, the Hivert, one or two *chambres d'hôte* and a large campsite. There are also a few shops, a restaurant, a bank with ATM, parapente school and a tourist office

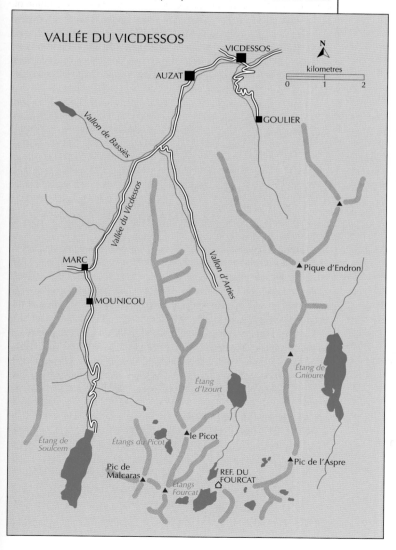

that's open in summer only (☎ 05 61 64 87 53). Vicdessos is also the contact address for the Association Départemental Pyrénéenne des Accompagnateurs en Montagne de l'Ariège (1 route de la Prade, 09220 Vicdessos, ☎ 05 61 64 83 96).

Behind the village D18 climbs through the narrow valley of the Suc heading northwest to the Port de Lers and Aulus-les-Bains (see 4:6), but on the south side of Vicdessos another road snakes tightly uphill to **GOULIER** (two *gîtes d'étape* on the route of GR10) and, above that, to the tiny ski station of **GOULIER-ENDRON**, otherwise known as Goulier-Neige at 1490m. Almost 1000m above the ski station, the ⊗ 2472m **Pique d'Endron** is reckoned to be one of the finest viewpoints in Haute-Ariège, and the ascent takes a little under 2½hrs to achieve by way of its easy northeast arête rising from Pic du Sarrasi.

A short distance upstream beyond Vicdessos the little industrial township of **AUZAT** lacks the simple charm of its neighbour, but there's accommodation to be had in the Hôtel Denjean-La Bonne Auberge, and like Vicdessos it also has a campsite, a few shops and a restaurant. This is as far as the bus travels from Tarascon, so visitors without transport will face a longish walk to the roadhead from here. Trekkers following GR10 take a high route that snakes along the southern hillside to locate the *gîte d'étape* at Mounicou, and on the way (assuming, that is, they're walking against the trend by going west) make a diversion into the Vallon d'Arties which cuts into the mountains roughly south of Auzat.

A minor road projects into the **Vallon d'Arties** as far as the Pradières electricity station where there's a small parking area, and from there a popular ◑ 1½hr walk along GR10 leads to the lovely blue **Étang d'Izourt** (1647m), where a number of abandoned buildings stand forlorn near the dam at its northern end. Southeast of this lake, ⊗ **Pic de l'Aspre** – the high point on the east ridge, which makes a very fine belvedere at 2744m – can be climbed in a little over 1½hrs by an interesting route through the hanging valley of the Petsiguer stream. After a ◑ walk of another 2½–3hrs upvalley beyond the Izouart lake on a steep, well-marked and cairned path, you come to the two **Étangs Fourcat** at around 2445m. Up here, in what seems to be the very heart of the mountain world, stands the highest manned refuge in Ariège. Owned by the CAF, **Refuge du Fourcat** has 44 places and is manned from July to mid-September (☎ 05 61 65 43 15).

WALKS AND CLIMBS FROM REFUGE DU FOURCAT

Using the hut as a base a range of walks and climbs can be tackled, for the horseshoe of peaks that curl above and around the lakes, and the hidden country that lies beyond, have no shortage of options to consider. But summer comes late to these high, north-facing cirques, and snow tends to hang in shadowed corners for much of the time, so caution is advised when planning routes up here – especially early in the season.

- Most tempting of the options available must be the ascent of ⬡ **Pic de Tristagne** (Pic de Tristaina), the 2878m frontier peak rising from the southern end of the upper lake, which can be gained in about 3hrs. **Pic de l'Étang Fourcat** is another temptation. This 2859m peak stands to the west of Tristagne, while 2865m **Pic de Malcaras** rises on the west side of Étang Fourcat.

- A ⬤ **circular tour** could be made by following a small section of the HRP which passes this way. En route to its crossing of the frontier ridge into Andorra, the HRP visits the Étang de la Goueille (30mins from the hut) in an often snowbound valley east of the refuge. It is here that the circular walk leaves the route of the HRP, turning north over grass to an easy rocky barrier, beyond which the way descends to the Petsiguer lakes below Pic de l'Aspre. Near the foot of the hanging valley either join a GR10 *variante* heading back to the Étang Fourcat refuge, or continue to the main path at Étang d'Izourt and then return by this in order to complete a tour of about 5hrs.

- And of course the ⬤ **HRP** could be followed in either direction to vary the return to the Vallée du Vicdessos, but note that the way is not always easy to find, and you'll need good visibility and navigational skills to avoid trouble. The shortest and most obvious option involves crossing the west walling ridge above the lower Fourcat lake and descending NNW to pass the Étangs du Picot, then slanting across a steep hillside to a collection of low stone shelters, the Orris de Tignalbu. Below these the way becomes a little easier until a good path leads directly down to the valley road near **Mounicou**, and its simple *gîte*. Given fair conditions this route should be feasible in about 5hrs.

- A ⬤ **two-day return to the Vicdessos valley** from Refuge du Fourcat, adopting sections of the Pyrenean High Route (for wild campers only, since there's no accommodation along the way), involves crossing into Andorra by the 2601m **Port de l'Albeille** in the ridge southeast of Pic de Tristagne. The way to the pass is steep and invariably snow-patched even in August, but it makes an interesting and enjoyable crossing, and on the south side leads directly down scree and boulder slopes to the lovely Tristaina lakes in a cirque at the head of the Valira del Nord. South of these lakes is one of Andorra's main ski grounds, but the worst of the landscape degradation can be avoided on the way to Port de Rat (2540m), which carries a major *variante* of the HRP back into France near the head of the Soulcem valley. This valley drains down to Mounicou and thereby provides a direct return to the Vallée du Vicdessos.

THE UPPER VICDESSOS VALLEY

The Vallée du Vicdessos takes a more southerly trend upstream of Auzat, and a short distance beyond the mouth of the Vallon d'Arties, where the D108 makes its first hairpin, a tributary stream flashes through the woods on the right. ● A feeder path for the GR10 breaks off from the hairpin, rises to a junction with the main GR10, then follows this on a long climb into the spectacularly beautiful **Vallon de Bassiès**, a glacier-carved, lake-dazzling valley walled by granite mountains. To the west of the largest of the lakes stands the comfortable manned **Refuge de Bassiès** in an utterly delightful situation at 1650m (see 4:6). After spending a night here, a return to Vicdessos could be made by taking the continuing GR10 north to Port de Saleix (1794m), but instead of crossing this turn right away from GR10 and descend through the Saleix glen along a path adopted by the Tour du Massif des Trois Seigneurs (marked as such on the local Carte de Randonnées) which leads into the Suc valley above Vicdessos.

Nine kilometres upstream from Vicdessos the valley forks again at the small hamlet of **MARC**, dominated by the church of St-Antoine de Montcalm – an unbelievably large place of worship in comparison to the parish it serves – where the road makes a sharp crossing of the river. Visited by GR10 trekkers, Marc has neither shop nor café, but an 18-place *gîte d'étape* (☎ 05 61 64 88 54) and two *chambres d'hôte*. Otherwise the last accommodation in the Vallée du Vicdessos is to be had at tiny **MOUNICOU** (16-place *gîte d'étape*, ☎ 05 61 64 87 66) just 1km above Marc at 1087m, or at Refuge du Pinet high above the western stem of the valley on the slopes of Pic de Montcalm.

Turning out of the main valley at Marc, a minor road pushes west into a tributary valley noted for the Cascades de l'Artigue. When the road ends, a path waymarked with yellow paint continues upvalley alongside the stream before climbing through the Bois de Fontanal in a southwesterly direction to reach the **Refuge du Pinet** after about 2½–3hrs. Enjoying a splendid view across the Artigues valley from its position close to the Étang du Pinet at 2242m, the refuge is owned by the CAF, has 50 places, and is permanently manned from June to the end of September, and at weekends in May and October (☎ 05 61 64 80 81). Until this hut was built in the early 1990s, any ascent of Pic de Montcalm from the north involved a very long approach, but provision of the Pinet refuge has considerably reduced the ascent time, and the *voie normale* starting here now takes about 2½hrs.

ASCENT OF PIC DE MONTCALM (3077m)

The easternmost 3000m summit in the French Pyrenees was climbed by Coraboeuf and Testu in the course of their cartographic survey of 1827, and the large cairn which they built to aid their survey remains to this day. Although the mountain is singularly unappealing when viewed from its frontier-straddling neighbour, Pica d'Estats, it presents a much more respectable profile when seen from the north. Montcalm has no major rock or ice climbs, but it has at least four routes of ascent to suit climbers of moderate ability at grades of no more than PD. The standard ascent from the south has already been described in 4:14 from a base at the Vall Ferrera *refugi*, but that leaves three different routes of approach on the French slopes. When attempted in the early weeks of the summer season, an ice axe and rope should be taken on each of these.

- ⊗★ The first route climbs directly from the Pinet hut, rising on the east side of a steep, snow-filled, ravine-like valley. Gaining a point overlooking the Étang d'Estats, the way curves sharply to the left (southeast) to reach the smaller Étang de Montcalm at 2557m, a little under an hour from the hut. Glacier-smoothed rocks waymarked with yellow circles continue the route above the lake, climbing south for another 350m or so as far as a minor col (Coll de Riufret, 2978m) between Estats and Montcalm. From here the way bears left to ascend the final slope for about 30mins, so to reach the summit of Pic de Montcalm (3hrs).

- East of the Pinet refuge lies the **Subra valley**, in which the standard ascent was made before the hut was built. This route, thought to have been pioneered by Chausenque in 1829, is graded PD and is much longer than the ascent from Pinet unless, that is, a high camp or bivouac is taken the night before the climb in order to shorten the approach from the valley (5½–6hrs from the Artigue road). A track rises nearly 500m out of the valley, then a way-marked path continues along the right bank of the stream to the Pla Subra (1590m) with its ruined stone huts. Nearby a rock bears the message that it's another 3½hrs to Montcalm. Heading south-west now the torrent is crossed, then the slope steepens to gain an enclosed little valley known as the Tables de Montcalm, from which the route turns to the south towards a gully. This is climbed without difficulty (given good conditions) to about 2760m, where the mountain's north ridge is then followed to the summit.

- The third ascent route begins at the southern end of the dammed Étang de Soulcem, about 8km beyond Mounicou, and tackles Ⓑ Pic de Montcalm by way of the **Riufret Couloir** – the route by which the mountain's first ascent was made. As well as ice axe and rope, crampons may well be useful here. To access this couloir necessitates cutting along the lake's southwest shore before the climb begins. Keeping to the right of a stream, about 2½hrs from the start you pass above the little Étang de Riufret 750m above the lake. The route now veers northwest across the face of Montcalm towards Coll de Riufret, and once this has been gained you bear right to the summit. Allow 4–5hrs for the ascent from Étang de Soulcem, and descend either via Refuge du Pinet (2½–3hrs) to make a traverse of the mountain or by the Riufret couloir in another 3–4hrs.

• • •

At the southern end of the Étang de Soulcem the final upper reaches of the Vallée du Vicdessos are bounded on the west by Spanish frontier mountains, and on the east by a ridge which carries the border with Andorra. On the western slopes lie several lakes, and a handful of walkers' passes suggest ways over the ridge into the head of the Vall Ferrera (4:14). There are passes into Andorra too, and trekkers with imagination, a tent and provisions for a few days could happily wander from pass to pass, valley to valley and from one country to another following a whim. This is mountain country full of charm. It's in no way threatening or severe, although navigational skills will be needed to avoid straying from any planned route, no matter how or by whom that route is devised. Walkers should consult the maps to formulate ideas, but retain a degree of scepticism in regard to their accuracy.

• As for specific ideas, a ◖ **tour of the western lakes** would give a reasonably energetic 6hr circular walk, conditions being favourable. From the Soulcem reservoir the tour begins by heading southwest up the left bank of the Ruisseau de la Gardelle to where five lakes of varying size are caught in a cirque guarded by Pointe de Roumazet and Pic Sud de Canalbonne. These Étangs de la Gardelle are reached in a little under 2hrs from the start, and from them a sporadic line of cairns guides the way across a ridge-spur to the southeast in order to gain access to the Étangs de Roumazet and de la Soucarrane, the latter about 1½hrs from the Gardelle Cirque. Above the Soucarrane lake to the southwest the Port de Boet (or Bouet) suggests a straightforward crossing into Spain following a section of the HRP, but to continue with this circular walk, you need to descend steeply on the left of the lake's drainage stream into the bed of the Vallée du Vicdessos, and then head downvalley to the Étang de Soulcem.

Of the walling summits, several of these are within reach of wild country trekkers, and among them ⊘ **Pic Sud de Canalbonne** (2849m) on the frontier crest above the Étangs de la Gardelle is high on the list. Reputed to have a *panorama superbe* from the summit, the top is gained in about 1½hrs from the upper lake. **Pic de la Rouge** is another worth considering. This rises some way to the south of Canalbonne and is most easily climbed from the Port de Boet. Known to the Spanish as Pica Roja (see 4:14), this 2902m frontier summit may be traversed as far as Port de Roumazet on the north ridge, with a return to the upper Vallée du Vicdessos made by following the Roumazet stream most of the way.

On the east side of the valley above Étang de Soulcem, **Pic de Malcarras** and **Pic de l'Étang Fourcat** can both be climbed without too much difficulty in about 3hrs from the Orris de Carla, but to traverse the linking ridge from one to the other needs the security of a rope.

At the very head of the valley the 2914m ⊗ **Pic de Medecourbe** is where the borders of France, Spain and Andorra come together. Marked by a metal pole, this is yet another summit with an outstanding view that includes a vast sea of peaks that challenges one's map-reading skills to name the highlights. The snow-crowned Maladeta is one of the easiest to identify, beyond and above the long green ribbon of the Vall Ferrera which lies immediately to the west. To the south stands Andorra's highest peak, Pic de Coma Pedrosa, with the Vall d'Arinsal draining out to the southeast, while to the north the Soulcem carves its great wedge-like trench through the mountains. To the east of Medecourbe a secondary summit, Pic de Rocofred, stands between the main summit and Port Dret (Port des Bareytes), the latter defended by rocks. This is the way of ascent – beside the stream which begins just below the pass, up towards the pass, then heading west below the frontier crest, over Pic de Rocofred and on to the summit of Pic de Medecourbe (4hrs). Instead of retracing the route of ascent back into the valley, descend a little to the south-west, then contour along the Spanish flank to gain the 2740m Port de Medecourbe, from where you then cut down into the hollow containing Étang de Medecourbe. Once there a cairned route leads down into the valley. (For an ascent from the southeast, see 5:3.)

5:2 HAUTE VALLÉE DE L'ARIÈGE

Three kilometres southeast of Tarascon-sur-Ariège a huge network of subterranean passages and chambers near the little spa of **USSAT-LES-BAINS** is noted for its stalagmite formations, the vast central chamber known as the Cathedral, and for the variety of inscriptions and graffiti etched into the cave walls that identify a succession of uses and users down the centuries. So extensive are the **Grottes de Lombrives** that it would take several days to do them justice, but guided tours are available daily during July and August, and less frequently at other times (for information, ☎ 05 61 05 98 40).

At **LES CABANNES** the Ariège broadens a little where it is joined by the **Vallée d'Aston** coming from the south. At the head of this tributary the Massif de l'Aston rises against the Andorran border, and a narrow road (D520) seeks it out, passing through Aston and continuing among wooded narrows for 10km to the Étang de Riete. Above and to the east of this reservoir, and unseen from the valley, the **Plateau de Bielle** is one of the main cross-country ski regions of the French Pyrenees, with some 55km of pistes, reached by a some-what tortuous road from Les Cabannes.

At the southern end of the Riete reservoir, the road surface dete-riorates as it climbs southeastward for a little over 6km as far as the

Étang de Fontargente near the head of the Vallée d'Aston, just below the Franco-Andorran border

Barrage de Laparan at 1550m. A 5-minute walk beyond the barrage leads to a signed path rising on the left among trees, which then follows the Rieutort stream towards its head. There, just below the Col de Terre Negre at 2185m, stands the **Refuge du Rulhe**, a modern 50-place hut manned permanently from June to the end of September, and at weekends in October and November when booked (☎ 05 61 65 65 01 or 06 09 90 44 66). Now adopted as an overnight stage by trekkers tackling the GR10 on the way to Mérens-les-Vals, Refuge du Rulhe also makes a good base from which to explore the rugged high country along the Andorran border, where once again a number of lakes add lustre to the landscape. Meanwhile **Pic de Rulhe** (2783m) southeast of the hut rewards with a magical summit view.

Walkers with their own transport could also visit some of these upper lakes starting from the Pla de Laspeyre (1706m) at the end of a track which extends from the barrage roadhead (50mins walk). From here the **Étangs de Fontargente** can be reached in a little over an hour, the **Étang de l'Estagnol** by an alternative route that climbs through a natural flower garden in 1½hrs, and the **Étang de Joclar** in another hour or so beyond that – a rugged region of rock, lake and cascade.

🔵 Above the Fontargente lakes the Franco-Andorran border may be crossed at the 2262m **Port de Fontargente**, followed by an easy descent through the lovely Vall d'Incles to **Soldeu**. And above the Étang de Joclar another crossing is possible at the **Collada de Juclar** (2442m), with descent not only to the Vall d'Incles but eastward by way of the linking **Col de l'Albe**, which gives access to yet more lakes at the head of the Mourguillou valley. This eventually spills into the upper Ariège at Mérens-les-Vals.

The next place of importance in the Vallée de l'Ariège is **AX-LES-THERMES**, a small town about 15km upstream of Les Cabannes, built at the confluence of the Ariège, Oriège and Lauze rivers. Ax has developed not only around its reputation as a thermal spa but also as something of a modest winter ski resort, and is the last community of any size on the way to Andorra. The town has a good selection of food shops and stockists of maps and guidebooks. There's a helpful Bureau des Guides et Accompagnateurs (☎ 05 61 64 31 51) with a tourist office next door (☎ 05 61 64 60 60, e-mail: vallees.ax@wana-doo.fr, website: www.vallees-ax.com). Having a station on the main Toulouse–Barcelona railway line, and all major services and facilities, Ax makes a useful temporary base in which to stock up with provisions for the hills. Accommodation is plentiful, and there's a year-round municipal campsite on the banks of the Ariège a little way downstream from the railway station.

The local ski grounds are centred on the Plateau du Saquet above **AX-BONASCRE**, reached by the winding D820 which climbs above the town to the southwest. With some 55km of pistes and a top lift above le Saquet at 2305m, skiers can enjoy fine views of the Dent d'Orlu to the east, as well as Andorran frontier peaks to the south and southwest.

Tour des Montagnes d'Ax

Outlined on sheet number 8 of the Carte de Randonnées series, the Tour des Montagnes d'Ax is a multi-day walking circuit of the country surrounding Ax-les-Thermes. Depending on which variation is used and where the stages are broken, the tour will take between four and six days, and is actively promoted locally. Sleeping bag, provisions for at least two days and cooking equipment will need to be carried.

Day 1: Leaving **AX-LES-THERMES** the tour heads downvalley, at first on the right, then on the left bank of the Ariège, as far as le Castelet. Here the way climbs out of the valley through forest, emerging at a simple *cabane* at 1695m, shown as **MOUSCADOU** on the map.

Day 2: The path continues to climb, gaining a ridge crest that rises towards the south. At Col de Beil (2247m) it would be possible to divert from the tour in order to spend a night at the manned Refuge du Rulhe, otherwise the route descends to the northeast on the former path of the GR10 as far as another simple shelter, **PRAT REDOUN**, at 1795m.

Day 3: A steepish climb of more than 400m takes the onward route to the Couillade de Combeille on the uppermost edge of the Saquet ski slopes before descending on long sweeps to **MÉRENS-LES-VALS** in the upper Ariège valley, where there's a *gîte d'étape* used by GR10 trekkers.

Day 4: This stage follows GR10 all the way to the modern **REFUGE DES BÉSINES** (2104m) on the edge of the Carlit massif, crossing on the way the 2333m Porteille des Bésines.

Day 5: The penultimate stage is the shortest of all, leading into the Réserve Nationale d'Orlu by way of the 2470m Col de Coume d'Agnel (Coll de Coma d'Anyell), where you leave the GR10 and gain a fine view of Pic Carlit and the Étang de Lanoux. Turning northeast another ridge is crossed, followed by a descent alongside several small lakes to reach **REFUGE D'EN BEYS**.

Day 6: There are two options for this final stage. The easiest is to wander downvalley away from the Carlit region on a well-used path, descending to the Vallée d'Orlu roadhead and thence to Ax. The other, a longer and more demanding stage, crosses the ridge west of Refuge d'En Beys at the Couillade d'En Beys (2365m), then picks a way down into a hanging valley dominated by the dammed Étang de Naguille. From the northern end of the reservoir, a path descends through forest to the Oriège river, which is then followed downstream to **AX-LES-THERMES** and the end of the tour.

Of the three rivers that come together in Ax, the Lauze is the smallest, draining as it does a folding of hills to the east. Next is the Oriège, a mountain river that springs from the outer edges of the Carlit massif and cuts through the Vallée d'Orlu southeast of Ax-les-Thermes. This valley, the nature reserve caught within it, and the mountains that wall it are visited in 5:4. But for now, continue towards the head of the Ariège, here turning to the south and cutting through wooded narrows of the Gorges des Mérens, with the road and river side by side, while the railway is carried by a series of bridges to arrive at **MÉRENS-LES-VALS**.

Mérens stands astride the main road at a confluence of three rivers, an unpretentious village built after the original Mérens-d'en-Haut was destroyed by Spanish mercenaries in October 1811 during the Franco-Spanish Napoleonic war. The GR10 crosses the Ariège here, and there's a 38-place *gîte d'étape* with a good reputation in the upper, eastern, part of the village (☎ 05 61 64 32 50). Mérens has a small shop and a post office, a railway station and a campsite about 1km to the south, Camping Ville de Bau.

◗★ On the east flank of the Ariège GR10 (and the Tour des Montagnes d'Ax) climbs through the narrow **Vallée du Nabre** and, in its upper reaches, kinks to the right, works through a boulder-field overlooked by a soaring fang of granite belonging to Pic de l'Estagnas, and comes onto the Porteille des Bésines. Below the pass on its southern side stands the **Refuge des Bésines** at 2104m. This modern, well-appointed hut is owned by the Ariège section of the CAF, has 56 places and is permanently manned from June to the end of September, during school holidays in winter and spring, and at weekends when booked in advance (☎ 05 61 05 22 44). Below the refuge there's a lake, and a path used by a *variante* of the HRP which cuts across the western hillside on the way to L'Hospitalet, while GR10 continues to the northeast on the climb over Col de Coume d'Agnel and into the Carlit massif.

West of Mérens-les-Vals, the ◗ **Vallée du Mourguillou** carries the GR10 out of (or into) the Massif de l'Aston. Walkers seeking ways of accessing the Franco-Andorran frontier mountains have a choice of routes to look at from this valley, a popular place with day-visitors and picnic parties since an unmade road noses into it. To make the most of some of these routes it would be advisable to carry a tent or bivvy gear, and food for a night out. The waymarked GR10 begins to climb out of the valley at the Jasse de Mourguillou, but a little further upstream the Étang de Comte entices. Towards the head of the valley a scrambly ascent through a ravine brings you up to the Étangs de Couart and de l'Albe right under the frontier ridge. Ahead the 2539m **Col de l'Albe** carries a path into Andorra's Vall d'Incles, while the nearby **Collada de Joclar** teases an alternative route back into France and on to the Refuge du Rulhe – as mentioned above. Another option would be to work a way southeast from the Étang de Couart to the Pédourres lake, then bear southwest to cross Porteille du Sisca into the **Cirque de Sisca** with its lake and collection of tiny pools, before descending alongside its drainage stream all the way to l'Hospitalet.

A Victorian traveller described **L'HOSPITALET-PRÈS-L'ANDORRE** as a 'dour little hamlet'. More than 100 years later it has barely outgrown that description. Situated 10km south of Mérens and almost 500m higher, l'Hospitalet is where the trans-Pyrenean railway disappears into the tunnel which emerges on the other side of the Col de Puymorens. Since Andorra has no railway of its own, the main reason for the existence of this village appears to be as a temporary halt for travellers, for it transfers visitors from the Toulouse–Barcelona line into and out of Andorra by way of the twice-daily buses that grind over the Port d'Envalira to the southwest. However, the HRP, or one of its *variantes*, comes through after leaving Andorra on the way to the Carlit region, so the presence of both road and railway provides a useful means of escaping the mountains in the event of bad weather. Should you find yourself trapped in l'Hospitalet waiting for a train or bus out, there are bar-restaurants but no shops, and for accommodation there are two one-star hotels, a campsite, and a *gîte d'étape* open throughout the year except November, with 40 places in dorms and bedrooms (☎ 05 61 05 23 14, e-mail: gitedetape.lhospitalet@libertysurf.fr, website: www.vallees-ax.com).

To all intents and purposes this is virtually the head of the Haute Vallée de l'Ariège, for above l'Hospitalet the road splits. The Col de Puymorens route, whose toll tunnel opened in 1994, carries traffic across the mountain divide along the edge of the Carlit massif and into the Cerdagne, while the N22 alternative goes through increasingly bleak country to the ski station of Pas de la Casa and Andorra. Both the Carlit region and the Cerdagne are described later in this chapter, as is the Vallée d'Orlu southeast of Ax-les-Thermes. Meanwhile we take the high road to Andorra.

5:3 ANDORRA

Unless it's covered with snow, the frontier resort of **PAS DE LA CASA** is not exactly a welcoming sight – grim, character-free buildings and a clutter of ski tows in a desolate landscape on the French slope of the Envalira at 2150m. It is, however, a major ski attraction with a fair guarantee of decent snow, and, being linked with Grau Roig on the other side of the pass, has a total of 33 lifts, the highest being 2640m, serving nearly 100km of pistes (for snow information, ☎ 862 515 www.pasdelacasa.ad). Two hundred and fifty metres above Pas de la Casa, and 4km of hairpins later, you crest the Port d'Envalira at 2408m, and all of Andorra lies below.

Having neither railway nor airport, the only way to travel through Andorra (other than walking) is by road, and this can be a frustratingly slow business, for in both the high summer and winter

Overlooking the Juclar lakes from the frontier ridge, Pic d'Escobes (2799m) is known as the Matterhorn of Andorra

seasons nose-to-tail traffic is funnelled through the main Valira del Orient with no possibility of escape except into a dead-end side-valley. Until 1931 there was no vehicular access with France, and the greatest difficulty for the traveller was faced when laden mules were met on the narrow Andorran 'footway'. But the world has changed since then, and this tiny independent state has been almost completely transformed by the effects of tourism and hydro-electric power, by haphazard and insensitive development, including the mushrooming of high-rise buildings, and the scarring of mountain-sides on behalf of the downhill ski industry.

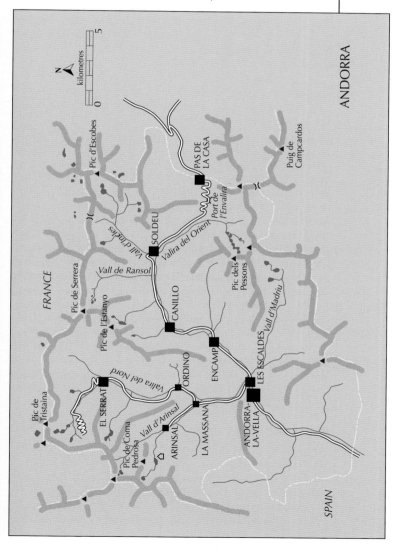

The Valira del Orient focuses the majority of the state's commerce into the capital, Andorra-la-Vella, and adjacent Les Escaldes-Engordany – the two merged into one duty-free metropolitan shopping mall situated less than 10km from the Spanish border. It's impossible to avoid unless you leave the road behind, don boots and rucksack, and stick to the high country where the best of Andorra is still to be found.

With a handful of road-free valleys, 54 peaks over 2000m and almost 60 mountain lakes of considerable charm, the best of Andorra is still worth exploring. There is good walking, scrambling and modest climbing to be found here, and in recent years there appears to have been a determination to improve some of the paths and way-marks. A number of *via ferrata* protected routes have been developed on select rock walls and a few relatively short bolted sport routes established. (For information contact the Andorran Mountaineering Federation, ☎ 867 444, fax: 867 467.)

Pic de Coma Pedrosa, the highest peak, stands close to the Spanish border above Arinsal, with Andorra's only manned *refugio* built conveniently nearby. Elsewhere, 24 unmanned huts of varying size and comfort provide shelter for the outdoor activist. Discreet wild camping can be enjoyed in some remote high cirques, while official sites are located near a few of the villages. Trekkers working along the mountain chain on the route of the HRP make a brief sortie across the top of Andorra, and two major GR routes pass through the country: the Spanish coast-to-coast GR11 and the GR7, which starts in the Vosges in northern France and enters Andorra by its southeastern corner. A fourth multi-day trek makes a near-circuit of Andorra. This is the GRP1, one end of which is located near La Massana north of Andorra-la-Vella, the other being at Juberri, the southernmost hamlet situated a little east of the road exit into Spain. On or close to this GRP1 there are some 14 *refugis*, which enable trekkers to dispense with camping equipment, although food for several days would need to be carried.

The 1:50,000 Carte de Randonnées sheet 7 (*Haute-Ariège Andorre*) covers most of the main walking and trekking options, although the accuracy of some of the routes marked is not all that it might be. Official Andorran maps are produced by Edicions M.I. Govern at a variety of scales, none of which manages to keep up to date with developments, urban or rural. No less than 19 sheets cover the country at a scale of 1:10,000, but the most commonly used are the 1:50,000 or 1:25,000 sheets, both titled *Andorra* and available locally.

THE CIRC DELS PESSONS

Wriggling down from the Envalira, under which there's now a road tunnel, the upper reaches of the Valira del Orient are seen to the left, and 400m or so below the pass a road breaks away to the south into that upper valley where the ski station of **GRAU ROIG** is set in a roadhead basin. Leaving the buildings and ski machinery behind, it's worth wandering up into the **Circ dels Pessons** (Cercle de Pessons) that lies to the southwest. Cradled by a horseshoe of peaks, the cirque

is a charming corner of shrubs and rocks and more than a dozen little lakes and pools, not all of which are indicated on the maps. One of the highest of its walling peaks is ⊗ **Pic dels Pessons**, whose altitude is variously quoted as 2818m, 2858m or even 2865m, and the direct ascent by way of a path heading southwest from the northern end of the first lake near a small restaurant is a straightforward outing of about 2hrs. Turn this into a circuit of the upper lakes, and an enjoyable 5hr walk leads back to the Grau Roig car park. Other summits worth visiting are those of **Alt del Cubil** (2833m) and **Pic de Montmalús**, which at 2827m looms over the uppermost lakes.

A short walk from the Grau Roig ski station leads into the unspoilt Circ dels Pessons

The GR7 comes this way, having crossed by a circuitous route from France over the Portella Blanca d'Andorra (2517m) southeast of Grau Roig. The Portella, which gets its name from a whiteish rock on the crest, makes an obvious choice for a day out, especially if you combine it with the ascent of **Pic Nègre d'Envalira** (2825m) to the north – this peak attracts climbers in winter, where the ⊗ West Face has a 50–60° snow couloir. As for GR7, having made the descent from the Portella, it turns into the Circ dels Pessons and continues over the Crestes de Gargantillar to yet more lakes under the headwall of the Vall d'Madriu, where the large, unmanned Refugi de l'Illa is located (see section on Vall d'Madriu below).

VALL D'INCLES

The first place of any consequence as you come down the road from the Port d'Envalira is **SOLDEU**, a village of resort hotels and bars built of local stone which makes a useful base for a walking holiday. Thanks to a regular bus link with the capital, visitors without transport are able to reach most of Andorra's valleys from Soldeu.

The south side of the Valira del Orient is equipped with ski tows and lifts that access 80km of pistes based on the Tossa de la Llosada, but just around the corner below the village lies the charming, and as yet unspoiled Vall d'Incles, one of the most seductively tranquil valleys within Andorra's ring of peaks, in which a sea of narcissi makes a breathtaking sight in the springtime. A narrow road eases through the pastures for 3km as far as a modest campsite (open mid-June to mid-September) near the confluence of two streams, less than an hour's walk from the main road. The northern stream is the Riu de la Manegor, the eastern the Riu de Juclar. The HRP comes this way, and heading east progresses upstream a short distance before dividing. One route breaks away to the southeast, making across the mountains for the Port d'Envalira, while a *variante* follows the stream to its source at the **Éstanys de Juclar**, walled by peaks and tucked below Pic d'Escobes (or Ascobes), the 'Matterhorn of Andorra', on whose ● West Face there's good climbing to be had. Just above the first lake you'll find the **Refugi de Juclar** at 2310m, unmanned but with places for about 30. The High Route *variante* climbs on to the Franco-Andorran border to gain the **Collada de Juclar**, from which a gently rising traverse path leads east to Col de l'Albe before starting the descent to L'Hospitalet. ● The Juclar col could be used either as a way of reaching the Refuge du Rulhe in Haute-Ariège, or of making a 6hr circular walk to include the Fontargente lakes southwest of the refuge (see 5:2) and then returning to the Vall d'Incles via the 2262m **Port de Fontargente** (Port d'Incles is the Andorran name). It is this last-named pass that lies in the headwall above the Riu del Manegor, the valley's northern stem.

The large, but unmanned Refugi de Juclar is a convenient base for a number of climbs and scrambles on neighbouring frontier peaks

The main ⬤ HRP path that bears southeast a short way upstream of Camping d'Incles offers a pleasant if steepish walk to the *refugi* and **Estanys de Siscaró**, but if this is extended as far as **Port Dret** (2564m) in company with the HRP, walkers based at Soldeu could then descend west to the village to make an entertaining circuit of 5hrs or so.

Estany de Siscaró, one of many lakes accessible from the Vall d'Incles

Meanwhile, northwest of Camping d'Incles another option is to visit **Estany de Cabana Sorda** with a small unmanned *refugi* on the way. The lake lies below the 2755m Pic de la Portaneille (also known as Pic de la Coma Varilles) and, like the Juclar lakes, is tucked against the steep frontier ridge. One of the HRP *variante* routes takes in the summit of Pic de la Portaneille and continues more or less on the frontier ridge across the head of the next valley to the west, the Vall de Ransol. This is a very fine route, but it should be attempted only by experienced wild-country trekkers and in good conditions. A lower version of this crossing uses a saddle a little northeast of the Clot Sord on the ridge-spur separating the two valleys, but this option misses the far-reaching views gained from the frontier mountains.

VALL DE RANSOL

The hotels of **EL TARTER** are clustered just west of the Vall d'Incles entrance, but the older neighbouring hamlets of **RANSOL,** on one side of the Riu de la Coma, and **ELS PLANS**, on the other, stand just above the main road and virtually guard the mouth of the Vall de Ransol that stretches north between wooded slopes towards the frontier mountains. A narrow road cuts into the valley for a few kilometres, but ends just short of the broadening cirque that closes it. Lodged on a shelf of the cirque at 2218m, the **Refugi Coms de Jan** on the route of the HRP has room for about 10 trekkers. Behind it the cirque walls stream with cascades, while to the west more small lakes can be visited, and the frontier summit of ⊘ **Pic de la Serrera** (2912m) can be climbed without difficulty in 30mins from the Col de la Mine (Collada dels Meners), which carries the HRP into the Valira del Nord.

EL TARTER TO ANDORRA-LA-VELLA

Descending beyond the Vall de Ransol on the main highway through the Valira del Orient, a knuckle tributary is soon detected creasing the northern hillsides. This is the short **Vall del Riu** which is blocked some way south of the French border. Yet again there are lakes lodged high in this valley at well above 2500m, and a path giving access to them leaves Els Plans and, keeping well above the stream, works along the east flank of the valley where another unmanned *refugi* is reached in 1–1½hrs. **Cabane de la Vall del Riu** provides shelter for about 10 people at an altitude of 2180m. Beyond it the path curves round the head of the valley rising steadily, and about 1½hrs from the hut comes to the largest of the lakes, overshadowed by the 2915m Pic de l'Estanyo, third highest Andorran summit, which looks down on El Serrat in the neighbouring Valira del Nord.

Beyond Vall del Riu **CANILLO** enjoys a pleasant location and is worth considering as a base for a few days. The tourist office and most of the hotels are gathered around the main through road, and a campsite can be found on the south bank of the river (for tourist information, ☎ 751 090, www.vdc.ad). The ⓘ flanking rock walls nearby hold four *via ferrata* routes, while east of the village and beside the main road near the Vall del Riu's entrance an artificial climbing wall has been created in the form of a towering pinnacle, known locally as the Agulla de Canillo.

Behind Canillo another short but steep valley, the **Vall de Montaup**, intrudes into the hillsides, and it would be possible to use this as a means of accessing the Valira del Nord across the 2539m **Coll d'Arènes**. From this col one could follow the narrow and somewhat jagged ridge northeast to the summit of **Pic de l'Estanyo** in just 1hr to enjoy a notable panorama. This route, however, is really best suited to experienced scramblers.

On the way down the Valira del Orient a bird's-eye view is gained of **ENCAMP**, the last sizeable village before reaching the ribbon development of the capital. Trekkers on GR11 come through Encamp after crossing the road pass of Coll d'Ordino, and by reversing that way-marked trail yet another cross-country route can be made across the dividing ridge to the Valira del Nord. While GR11's onward journey heads south past the Engolasters lake to find a way into the Vall d'Madriu, a narrow road on the east side of the valley makes a serpentine route up the hillside into the little valley of the Riu dels Cortals, from which **Alt del Griu** (2874m), a neighbour of Pic dels Pessons, can be climbed in about 3hrs. ◗ From the Bordes del Castellar on the same road, a splendid trekker's route heads south to the little unmanned **Refugi de les Agols** (in 1½hrs), then crosses the granite crest of Gargantillar at about 2664m before flanking eastward into a cirque containing a dozen or more lakes and pools, among them the large Estany de l'Ille at the head of the Vall d'Madriu (4½hr one way).

Six kilometres below Encamp, the valley is dominated by a concentration of shops, hotels, restaurants, discos and high-rises that comprise **LES ESCALDES-ENGORDANY** and the adjacent capital, **ANDORRA-LA-VELLA**. The tourist office situated on c/Doctor Vilanova (☎ 820 214) is worth an early visit for information on just about every aspect of interest involving the principality including, of course, accommodation lists and bus timetables. If you need to replace any outdoor equipment, Andorra-la-Vella also has plenty of sports shops with near-unbeatable prices.

VALL D'MADRIU

Southeast of Les Escaldes the Vall d'Madriu is a steep and narrow road-free valley of immense charm which runs below the Spanish border. Flanked by 2500m mountains and traversed by both GR7 and GR11, the wooded lower regions give out towards its head where the tarn-filled **Gargantillar Cirque** (4hrs from Les Escaldes) adds colour and character to what is already a truly delightful valley. Three unmanned *refugis* (**Fontverd** with 15–20 places; **Riu dels Orris** with just 6 places set in the Pla de l'Ingla; and **Refugi de l'Illa** with spaces for about 60 by its eponymous lake) provide simple accommodation, and there are plenty of decent wilderness campsites too. The valley headwall backs the Circ dels Pessons (see above), while the 2550m Collado de l'Illa (or Coll de Vall Civera) just southeast of the Illa hut carries GR11 across the mountains into the Spanish Civera valley.

Meanwhile, a short distance into Vall d'Madriu from Les Escaldes, a side-valley cuts off to the south where the Riu de Perafita drains yet another scattering of small lakes and pools under the Port de Perafita. **Refugis de Perafita** (6–10 places) and **de Claror** (15–20 places) are both on the route of the round-Andorra GRP1, and could be linked to make a circular walk.

VALIRA DEL NORD

After the Valira del Orient this is the longest of Andorra's valleys and, lying just north of the capital, it has seen plenty of tourist development. At **LA MASSANA**, 7km from Les Escaldes, the valley forks. The left branch is the Vall d'Arinsal, which leads to the popular ski resort of Arinsal, while the right fork to Ordino and El Serrat is the Valira del Nord. After 3km the right-hand road reaches **ORDINO** with its network of little streets and a few 17th-century houses crowded by more recent developments. The village has a sports centre equipped with a climbing wall, and the tourist office is at c/Nou vial (☎ 737 080, e-mail: ito@andorra.ad, website: www.andorra.ad/comuns/ordino/index.html).

The farther one travels beyond Ordino, the easier it is to recapture some of the 'old' Andorra in its fields and barns and groups of mottled stone houses. There's a botanical richness to be found too, and as you advance towards the head of the valley walking opportunities become more evident. GR11 crosses the valley at **ARANS**, and 2km up the road at **LLORTS** (1430m) another path heads northwest on the true left bank of the Riu de l'Angonella, whose little valley is closed by a cirque comprising three peaks, one of which, **Pic de les Fonts** (2748m), is climbed without difficulty from a group of lakes which lie below it on the northern side.

EL SERRAT, 17km from Les Escaldes, is the highest of the Valira del Nord's villages, with several hotels standing beside the road and a choice of valleys to explore. The main valley slants northwest, but northeast and east of the village trekking routes lead up to high passes. The northeasterly route serves **Refugi de Rialp** (6–10 places) and the **Port de Siguer** on the Franco-Andorran border, beyond which a long descent eventually spills into the Vallée de Vicdessos (see 5:1). ◖ The eastern route, however, which is used by the HRP, remains within Andorra's borders, first visiting the 30-place **Refugi Borda de Sorteny** (1980m), then rising to the Col de la Mine (Collada dels Meners) and the Vall de Ransol. It would also be feasible to make the ascent of Pic de l'Estanyo from the Sorteny hut, or at least to visit a small lake cupped below its west face.

As for the upper reaches of the Valira del Nord beyond El Serrat, the road climbs northwest to the ski station of **Ordino-Arcalís**, where a dozen tows and lifts mount the north-facing slopes of Pic d'Arcalís. The highest lift reaches 2620m, and most of the 26km of pistes enjoy superb views. The road actually projects beyond the ski station, curving into a high pastoral basin below the Port de Rat as part of a projected link with the Vallée de Vicdessos, now decades old and incomplete. The HRP also uses the **Port de Rat** (2540m) to enter Andorra on the stage which usually begins below the Estats-Montcalm massif.

To escape the clutter of ski machinery and the cleverly engineered road, a popular ◖ walk takes a path up to the three **Tristaina lakes** in Andorra's northwest corner. With the ridge carrying the French border arcing north and west, the path climbs alongside streams and waterfalls before topping a crest with the first lake lying below (about 1hr from the ski station ticket booths). The other two are easily reached by a path which angles up the hillside from one to another. The largest of the lakes is lodged below the steep flanks of **Pic de l'Étang Fourcat** and **Pic de Tristaina**, both of which are noted for the extent of their summit panoramas. The first of these is climbed from the south along the frontier ridge to a secondary summit above the lake at 2820m, followed by a short stretch of ridge heading northwest to gain the main summit at 2859m. As for Pic de Tristaina (2878m), the standard route curves to the right above the upper Tristaina lake on the HRP towards Port de l'Albeille, but soon strikes off across the face of the mountain to gain the summit by a scramble in a little over 1½hrs from the first lake.

*The Tristaina
cirque, in Andorra's
northwest corner*

VALL D'ARINSAL

High mountains rising out of woodland enclose the upper reaches of
the Vall d'Arinsal, a much shorter stem than that of the main Valira
del Nord into which it drains. Near the head of the valley on its western side, but not quite against the Spanish border, stands Andorra's
highest summit, Pic de Coma Pedrosa. To the north of that Pic de
Medecourbe gathers three frontiers, while the ridge that runs east to
Pic del Pla de l'Estany dips to the Port Dret, a link with the upper
Vallée de Vicdessos in France.

    GR11 enters Andorra from the head of Spain's Vall Ferrera (see
4:14) just west of Coma Pedrosa, and makes a brief visit to the Vall
d'Arinsal before climbing out again at the Coll de las Cases east of
Arinsal village. Passing through Arinsal after experiencing so recently
the uninhabited delights of the Vall Ferrera uplands is bound to come
as something of a culture shock.

By road one approaches of course from Andorra-la-Vella, after which there can be few surprises left. Four kilometres from La Massana where the Valira del Nord forks, you reach **ARINSAL**, transformed in recent years from a slumbering huddle of old houses by an explosion of building development. Now a canyon of high-rise apartment blocks and hotels challenge the walling mountains and gather the ski crowds in winter. A dozen or so lifts adorn the slopes of Pic Alt de la Capa just west of town, serving 21 pistes, with a maximum altitude of 2560m (for information, ☎ 737 020, e-mail: emap@andornet.ad, website: www.arinsal.ad). South of Alt de la Capa the neighbouring resort of **PAL** has most of its pistes on wooded slopes facing north (www.pal.ad), although, as they are lower than Arinsal's, snow cannons are often called upon as a back-up. A road snakes above Pal and curves round the western flank of Alt de la Capa to gain the Spanish border at the 2328m Port de Cabús (closed in winter) above the Vall de Tor tributary of the Vall Ferrera.

In order to experience the best of the Vall d'Arinsal it's necessary to push north upvalley beyond Arinsal village, following waymarks of the GR11 that eventually curve left and climb into a valley drained by a stream that has its source in a high basin under Coma Pedrosa. About an hour's walk from Arinsal and a little short of that basin, not far from the Éstany de les Truites, stands Andorra's only manned refuge, the 60-bed **Refugi de Coma Pedrosa** (2260m), which is guarded from June to September (☎ 327 955 or 835 093). Across the valley to the north rises the featureless south face of Andorra's highest mountain.

From the *refugi* the **ascent of** **Pic de Coma Pedrosa** (2946m) is a major attraction, and there are two ways to achieve this. The first strikes across the marshy valley below the hut to find a grassy gully that

High in the Vall d'Arinsal, on the way to Refugi de Coma Pedrosa

leads up to a shoulder. Once there gain the mountain's southeast ridge and turn right along it to reach the summit, crowned by a large cairn (2½–3hrs). The alternative, and probably more popular, route heads upstream into the upper basin northwest of the *refugi* on the continuing GR11 to reach the Éstany Negre at 2629m. The final approach to this lake is through a rocky defile at the lower end of Coma Pedrosa's southwest ridge. Immediately before the tarn is reached leave the GR11 which continues up to the frontier crest at Port de Baiau, and turn right to climb the ridge all the way to the summit (4–4½hrs).

At the head of Vall d'Arinsal the ascent of **Pic de Medecourbe** makes another popular outing from a base at Arinsal. Already described from the north (see 5:1) this southern approach tackles the mountain by way of the frontier ridge overlooking the Vall Ferrera, and takes about 4hrs from the Vall d'Arinsal roadhead. A waymarked route continues beyond the road on the east flank of the valley until shortly before reaching the basic **Refugi del Pla d'Éstany** at 2030m. With one route breaking away to the right to attack Pic Pla de l'Éstany, the Medecourbe route continues ahead before sweeping left and climbing to the Éstanys Forcats that lie just below the frontier ridge at 2629m. From the western end of the larger of the two lakes climb northwest for another 100m to gain the ridge at the Collada dels Estanys Forcats, which provides a way into the Circ de Baiau (see 4:14). The final scramble heading north above the col leads to the summit.

Andorra's Frontier Ridge

Perhaps the ultimate outdoor challenge for climbers and scramblers in Andorra is the complete **circuit of the frontier peaks**. With a reputation for being of a similar grade to the Cuillin ridge, it has the additional *frisson* of being about six times as long as the classic Skye route. The overall distance measures around 160km, and somewhere in the region of 15,000m of ascent will be made. Depending on fitness and experience of the party, and conditions prevailing at the time, the circuit will take about 12 days to complete. A rope is an essential item of equipment on this route, and camping or bivvy gear will need to be carried. However, to keep loads as light as possible, it would be advisable to make a series of food caches in advance.

The circuit is best tackled in an anti-clockwise direction, starting at Port Negre southeast of Andorra-la-Vella and working eastward above Vall d'Madriu on the first stage. In places the ridge is loose and precipitous and demands great caution, although often firm granite gives exhilarating climbing. There are numerous exposed places, but there are also a few broad and easy sections on which to relax. Several times bristling *gendarmes* interrupt the route, but while these naturally call for climbing skills to overcome, steep slopes of innocent-looking grass can be lethal, especially when dampened by overnight dew or soaked by rain. Beware of sudden storms.

The most difficult sections of the circuit are found on the Cresta de Varilles approach to the Pic de la Portaneille and on the gendarme-splintered Cresta del Forcats south of Pic de Medecourbe neighbouring the Coma Pedrosa. Whilst there are

The Cercle de Coma Pedrosa

probably no pitches harder than VS, the length of the route and the need to carry fairly heavy loads combine to make it an expedition to take seriously and plan with care.

An article by T.A.H. Peacocke describing the circuit of Andorra, but in a clockwise direction, was published in Vol. 83 of *The Alpine Journal* (1978).

5:4 VALLÉE D'ORLU

This pleasant wooded valley, lying southeast of Ax-les-Thermes and drained by the Oriège, has lots of appeal for outdoor activists, with numerous opportunities for walkers, and the famed granite tooth of the Dent d'Orlu attracts technical climbers to its South and Southeast faces. The valley can also be used as a convenient means of accessing the Carlit massif, albeit by a long trek broken by an overnight spent either in Orlu village or at the refuge in the valley's upper regions. Being a dead-end, the Vallée d'Orlu is not bothered by through-traffic; only those who have business there will take the trouble to seek it out.

At the southern end of Ax-les-Thermes a minor road breaks away from the N20 and soon draws alongside the Lac (or Étang) d'Orgeix, goes through stone-built **ORGEIX** which straddles the road, and continues for another 2km to reach **ORLU**, a popular walking centre with a *gîte d'étape*, the Relais Montagnard which has 34 places (☎ 05 61 64 61 88), and a large municipal campsite nearby that is open throughout the year.

On the north side of the valley above the village a path snakes back and forth on the climb to **Col de l'Osque** in about 1hr, and continues on the far side of the ridge to descend through the Bois de la Bassugue in order to reach the village of **Ascou** (3hrs) high above Ax-les-Thermes. This walk forms a section of the longer Tour de la Vallée d'Ax – not to be confused with the Tour des Montagnes d'Ax outlined in the box in 5:2.

On the south side of the Oriège, across the river from Orlu, a ◐ path twists up through woodland to gain entrance to the narrow **Vallée d'Orgeix**, which tapers towards its head where the **Lac d'Aygue Longue** lies beneath the Col de la Barade at 2076m. A road also climbs into this tributary from Orgeix, but advances only about a third of the way towards its head. From the roadhead a popular 2hr walk leads to the lake (4hrs from Orlu), while above and to the east of it **Pic de l'Homme** (2464m) is easily reached by way of Col de la Barade in about 1hr. An ◐★ extended walk from the col could be made to include three more lakes (Étangs Tort, Déroun and Naguille) in the valley northeast of Pic de l'Homme, and this would require fully 8hrs, Orlu to Orlu.

Beyond Orlu the valley road extends to the Forges d'Orlu and a power station at 912m (9km from Ax), where a 3hr walk to the **Étang de Naguile** heads across the Oriège and skirts the boundary of the Réserve Nationale d'Orlu. Just beyond the Forges, where a secondary branch road continues upvalley, the 2220m **Dent d'Orlu** (officially known as the Pic de Brasseil) is screened from view by trees. As one of the major test-pieces of the eastern High Pyrenees, it has attracted leading climbers since the first routes were created on the ❶★ South and Southeast faces in 1964. A variety of hard routes of up to 1000m have been made on these walls in the years since, practically all graded TD or higher. Nonetheless, as is true of so many Pyrenean summits, a non-technical ascent is feasible, in this case from the more gentle north slope, where a path rises without difficulty and in about 2hrs from the Col de Pailhères road.

The narrow road that continues for 3km beyond the Forges d'Orlu ends at a woodland picnic area on the edge of the Réserve Nationale. This is as far as visiting motorists are allowed to drive. There's a public toilet block and a large information board giving details of a range of walks, and a track which crosses the river at the Pont de Caralp (1180m) then pushes further upstream. Beyond this bridge the upper part of the valley is known as the Vallée d'en Gaudu, and it is here that the approach is made to the Refuge d'En Beys and various other walks destinations. One of these is the little ◐ **Étang de Baxouillade**, which lies in a cirque under the Roc Blanc east of the Pont de Caralp and is reached in about 2½hrs by a path used by a GR7 *variante*.

The main focus of attention in this part of the valley, however, has to be the stone-built **Refuge d'En Beys** and the many lakes scattered beyond it. Standing at 1954m and overlooking the largest of the Étangs d'En Beys, the refuge is reached in about 3hrs from the roadhead. It has places for 50, and is manned from the middle of May until the end of

September (☎ 05 61 64 24 24). Beyond it the valley is rumpled with the vegetated remains of glacial debris, but it's a splendid bit of country for all that, and with a choice of passes to cross in order to extend one's explorations. West of the hut, for example, the ◑★ **Couillade d'En Beys** (crossed by the Tour des Montagnes d'Ax) gives access to the Peyrisses lakes with a continuation down to the Naguille reservoir and, eventually, to the valley bed at the Forges d'Orlu – 5hrs or so from the refuge. Then there's the **Portella d'Orlu** at the head of the valley from which one overlooks the splendid Étang de Lanoux and Pic Carlit, and the **Coll de la Grave** south of the refuge which leads into a different section of the Carlit massif. And lastly, for experienced wild-country trekkers only, southeast of Refuge d'En Beys the **Portella Gran** (Grande Porteille d'Espagne), reached by way of a rocky basin and a steep gully scramble with few signs of a trail despite one being suggested by the map, looks across to the Puig Peric (Pic Peric) and down into yet another granitic cirque liberally spattered with tarns.

Réserve Nationale d'Orlu

The boundary line of the 4000 hectare Réserve Nationale d'Orlu follows the high crest that walls the upper valley of the Oriège southeast of the Dent d'Orlu and descends to the eastern half of the tributary valley containing the Naguille reservoir above and to the south of the Forges d'Orlu. Established in 1981 as a wildlife reserve, roe deer inhabit the forests, while a number of marmot colonies have taken over former pasturelands and the rough boulder country near the head of the valley. Golden eagles and lammergeiers are also listed, but it is the local isard population that has benefited most from protection afforded by the reserve. There are now estimated to be more than 1000 isard roaming the uplands, although in winter they regularly descend to lower levels where food sources are more readily available in the undergrowth. Although this Pyrenean chamois is prized elsewhere by hunters, it enjoys complete protection here, ranging throughout the valley from around 900m to the seemingly barren upper reaches at 2500m, and may sometimes be seen in herds of a dozen or more. In summer its coat is a gingery-gold in colour, darkening to a dull brown with patches of white in winter. Although not especially timid within the reserve, if surprised the isard makes an asthmatic warning snort before bounding away with impressive agility.

5:5 THE CARLIT MASSIF

Southeast of the Vallée d'Orlu the high, lake-jewelled plateau of the Carlit massif is characterised by either granite or schistose peaks and ridges that, while being mostly accessible and relatively undemanding in ascent, are nonetheless truly alpine in nature – they are, in fact, the last of the High Pyrenees.

Stand on the 2921m summit of Pic Carlit and you become aware that this is, to all intents and purposes, the final mountain of substance,

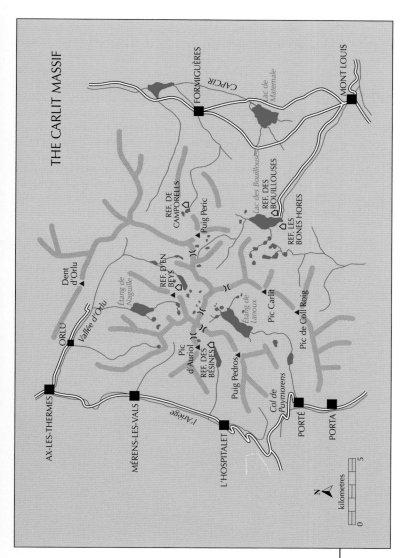

THE CARLIT MASSIF

FORMIGUÈRES

CAPCIR

MONT LOUIS

Lac de
Matemale

Lac des Bouillouses

REF. DE
CAMPORELLS

Puig Peric

REF. DES
BOUILLOUSES

REF. LES
BONES HORES

Dent
d'Orlu

REF. D'EN
BEYS

Étang de
Naguille

Pic Carlit

Pic de Coll Roig

ORLU

Vallée d'Orlu

Étang de
Lanoux

AX-LES-THERMES

Pic
d'Auriol

REF. DES
BÉSINES

Puig Pedros

Col de
Puymorens

MÉRENS-LES-VALS

l'Ariège

PORTÉ

PORTA

L'HOSPITALET

N

kilometres

0   5

for Pic du Canigou's singular appeal in the Eastern Pyrenees is not evident from here, and there are no other peaks nearby to challenge Carlit's supremacy. The middle view, east of Lac des Bouillouses, is a sea of forests that cradle the sedimentary plateau of the Capcir, birthplace of the Aude river and an excellent terrain for cross-country skiing. Beyond that the mountains are more like hills – big hills, it's true, many of which top 2000m, but hills for all that, if appearances are anything to go by. This is not meant to be taken as a dismissive statement, for there's some wonderful country to explore on foot, but it lies geographically outside the scope of this guide.

To the south stretches the Cerdagne, basin of a one-time glacial lake and now the only broad, flat-bottomed valley in all the Pyrenees. On the far side of that stands the Puigmal, almost as high as Pic Carlit but presenting an altogether different face. However, the western limit of the Carlit massif is drawn by the Vallée du Carol spilling down from the Col de Puymorens and backed by thrusting peaks that contain Andorra. All beyond that wall is undeniably High Pyrenean in scale, character and appeal.

In winter the slopes west of the 1920m Col de Puymorens are given over to skiing, but the rim of rough granite peaks that form a backing to some of the pistes as they edge round towards the Andorran border contain several quality routes for the winter climbing specialist too. Best approached from the car park at the Col, the first of these is on ❻★ **Pic des Valletes** (2814m), whose *Grand Dièdre* and *Couloir de la Virgule* both provide respectable TD climbs of 300m and 250m respectively; the first giving 70° ice with passages of IV and V+, the second 70–80° with a crux pitch of V+/A1. In the same crest as these, the 2727m **Pointe de la Vignole** has a wonderful craggy outline and a 220m D+ climb in the *NW Couloir*, while just to the right of this, the *Couloir du Tunnel* gives 220m of grade IV, with 70° ice. Then, immediately to the west, **Pic Oriental de Font Nègre**, the 2788m junior of the two Font Nègre peaks that effectively continue the watershed wall, has a splendid 300m mixed route in the *Couloir Nord* first climbed in 1983 by Daniel Gillereau and Guy Lesthivent (TD+, V+/A1, 70–80° but steepening to 90°). These are perhaps the best known among many worthwhile lines that have become popular in recent years among Catalan climbers.

Étang de Font-Vive lies near the head of the Vallée de Lanous on the edge of the Carlit massif

The ski grounds of Col de Puymorens are made accessible from the growing resort village of **PORTÉ-PUYMORENS**, whose original cluster of houses stands away from the main road below the pass, guarding the entrance to the Vallée de Lanous, one of the main valleys of approach to the Carlit massif. A scrum of hotel building appears to be under way nearby, presumably to service the ski trade, but meanwhile Porté, as it's more generally known, is a pleasant, unassuming place once the ski season is over, with accommodation for outdoor types in the very heart of the old village at the Auberge Cajole (☎ 04 68 04 85 47, e-mail: nathalie.komaroff@wanadoo.fr). There's also a campsite, La Riviere, that enjoys a view along the Vallée de Lanous, in which there are not only herds of isard to be found, but a large number of mouflon too. Reintroduced to the Pyrenees in 1957, the local mouflon population in this corner of the Carlit massif is said to have grown to more than 1000.

Being gently graded, as well as open in places and sheltered in others, the **Vallée de Lanous** is popular with cross-country skiers in winter and with walkers in summer, when it's bright with broom and silver birch. An anglers' lake lies in the bed of the valley about 3km from Porté, and another, the Étang de Font-Vive, is found at a higher level. Beyond the first of these an electricity works cableway (the *télépherique du Passet*) rises overhead on its way to the dammed Étang de Lanoux, which at 2500m long is the largest lake in the French Pyrenees. A narrow lane goes as far as the cableway building, while the GR7 path makes a steady rising traverse of the north flanking hillside in order to reach Étang de Lanoux, lying below Pic Carlit, in 2½–3hrs. The ascent of the mountain (see below) is easily made from here, but before tackling this, it's worth mentioning that a very pleasant ◖ 4–5hr **circuit of the Vallée de Lanous** can be made by taking the minor road from Porté to the *télépherique*, followed by a climbing path to the Font-Vive lake, then heading east before curving back downvalley below the Serra de Bac d'Ortella as far as Porté once more. Porté is also an obvious place from which to begin a west-to-east traverse of the Carlit massif or to embark upon the three-day Tour du Carlit.

◖★ Tour du Carlit

Being a circular walk with three main points of access, the tour could be started in Porté-Puymorens, Porta or one of the refuges by Lac des Bouillouses which is linked by road with Mont-Louis in the Cerdagne, The route is outlined in red on the Carte de Randonnées sheet number 8 and is usually tackled in a counter-clockwise direction.

Day 1: From Porté one could either take a path heading south high above the Vallée du Carol or use the GR7 to descend directly to the modest village of Porta on the original route of the Tour. If using the Porta route, you must then climb eastward through steep forest to join the first-mentioned path coming from Porté, which now rises straight up the hillside to gain the Coll de l'Homme Mort at 2300m. Once over the pass descend to **BÉNA**, a small hamlet with a delightful 40-place *gîte d'étape* (☎ 04 68 04 81 64).

Day 2: Out of Béna the route heads east on a track leading to two more hamlets, then crosses the insignificant Coll de Juell to the village of Dorres, one of the jewels of the Cerdagne. Shortly after leaving Dorres the way strikes north, first above, then in, the Vallée d'Angoustrine edging below the so-called Désert du Carlit on the approach to the **LAC DES BOUILLOUSES**, where there's a chalet-refuge run by the CAF, a larger refuge and a privately owned *auberge*.

Day 3: This is by far the best stage of the walk for it crosses the Carlit region from east to west by way of the 2426m Porteille de la Grave below the Puig (or Pic) de la Grave northwest of Bouillouses. The western slopes of the pass overlook the Étang de Lanoux, where the path of GR7 is met once more, to be followed all the way back to **PORTÉ** along the north flank of the Vallée de Lanous.

The Carlit region makes a favourable destination for a few days of a walking holiday. The fact that GR7, GR10 and the Pyrenean High Route all work their separate (and in places, combined) ways through would indicate that waymarks are more than adequate and paths clearly defined. However, there are less-travelled corners worth seeking out, as well as a number of modest summits to visit.

- Above and to the west of Étang de Lanoux, for example, ⊗ **Pic Pedros** acts as a boundary stone between the *départements* of Ariège and Pyrénées Orientales. The 2842m summit creates yet another fine belvedere, and is easily gained from the Lanoux dam in about 2hrs, with the route making first for a point at about 2615m on the mountain's eastern arête.

- Southeast of Étang de Lanoux the schistose summit of ⊗★ **Pic Carlit** is also climbed without difficulty in a little under 2hrs. A walker's peak claimed by trekkers on the HRP, it is thought that Henry Russell made the first ascent in 1864. From the vandalised shelter of Refuge de la Guimbarde on a bluff at the southern end of the lake, the mountain looks imposing. Packe described it as a 'sharp pyramid' and 'the monarch of the Eastern Pyrenees' but by the *voie normale* it makes no undue demands, in fact it consists of little more than a steeply twisting path up a Y-shaped gully to a small col on the ridge leading to the summit. Yet for all its ease Pic Carlit is a very satisfying grandstand from which to study the surrounding country, and a traverse of the mountain that incorporates a descent to Lac des Bouillouses in the east makes a worthwhile expedition. Pic Carlit falls abruptly on three sides, but the initial descent on the eastern flank is cairned and well used, leading to a spiky, shattered rib, then onto a path easing down to a miniature garden-like landscape of streams and pools and larger

*Pic Carlit rises
above Étang de
Lanoux*

lakes, divided by clumps of dwarf pine and alpenrose, low-growing sprays of juniper and mattresses of heather – an immensely
attractive and popular area.

Once the Lac des Bouillouses has been reached, there's a surprising
choice of accommodation to be had. A short way below the dam at
the lake's southern end stands the CAF's **Refuge des Bouillouses** (☎
04 68 04 20 76). With 45 places, the refuge is manned from June to
the end of September, and from the end of December to the beginning of May. Behind it stands the smaller **Auberge du Carlit** (☎ 04
68 04 22 23), while on the western side of the dam there's the largest
of all the buildings, the massive **Refuge les Bones Hores** (☎ 04 68
04 24 22), which has both dormitory accommodation and bedrooms.
   Lac des Bouillouses gathers several long-distance routes: GR10,
the HRP, Tour du Carlit and the neighbouring 3–4 day Tour du

The spiky rib used on the descent of Pic Carlit's east flank

Capcir. And thanks to the road providing ease of access from Mont-Louis in the Cerdagne, the place is often heaving with day-visitors in summer and at weekends. Whilst perhaps the majority will stray no farther than the nearest cluster of lakes, a number will inevitably head west to make the ascent of Pic Carlit in 2½–3hrs.

A close second in popularity of ascent from here is ⊗ **Puig (Pic) Peric** to the north. Climbed in about 3½hrs via a col in its east ridge, this conical grey-brown mountain of 2810m appears from the lake to stand alone save for the smaller Petit Peric, its neighbour to the east. However, it has a link by its north ridge to Pic de la Portella Gran and Pic de Mortiers, both unseen from Bouillouses, while the cirque formed by this north ridge, together with the east ridge leading to the Petit Pic contains the charming Camporells lakes – also popular with walkers.

- ◗ The walk to these lakes begins by following the GR10 path north through woods that line the west side of Lac des Bouillouses. On reaching the wide, grassy Têt valley at the lake's far end, the Camporells route then departs from GR10 and veers right to find the Balmette *cabane* before turning north across easy terrain that forms the outer edge of the Carlit massif. Beside the eastern-most Camporells lake at 2240m stands the 25-place **Refuge de Camporells**, which is manned from June to the end of September (☎ 04 68 04 49 86) and is more easily reached from the head of a chair lift (in operation during summer) above Formiguères, a major Capcir cross-country ski resort.

A little southwest of Lac des Bouillouses stretches the Désert du Carlit. Travelling here in 1896 on his way to climb Pic Carlit, Harold

Spender, a distinguished journalist and early member of the Alpine Club, described this region as 'a vast treeless waste, covered with scanty grass and scattered with masses of stones of every size, ranging from gigantic granite blocks to small fragments'. He went on to say: 'No words can describe the melancholy solitude and forlorn destitution of those vast denuded Pyrenean deserts [which] lie on that higher plateau which in Switzerland is draped with glorious pine-woods' (*Through the High Pyrenees*, A.D. Innes, 1898).

Pic Carlit's near-neighbours to the southwest, overlooking the Désert du Carlit, are the two ⊗ **Pics de Coll Roig**, one at 2804m, the other measuring 2833m. These peaks, which stand either side of the Coll Roig, effectively extend their granite ridge away from Pic Carlit to form the south wall of the Vallée de Lanous, and it is from Étang de Font-Vive near the head of that valley that the ascent is usually made in about 4hrs. But the Pics de Coll Roig can also be climbed from the west using Porta as a base. From here the ascent begins by going up to the Coll de l'Homme Mort (see Day 2 of the Tour du Carlit in the box above), then heading northeast to gain the 2536m Portella de Bac d'Ortella, where the mountain's southwest arête is joined. This is then traced to the first and higher summit (Pic Occidental de Coll Roig) and is reached in some 5hrs from Porta. The lower summit, Pic Oriental, is easily gained in another 20mins or so, and a traverse could then be achieved by returning to Coll Roig between the two peaks, descending into the Vallée de Lanous, and walking downvalley to Porté-Puymorens.

5:6 THE CERDAGNE

The N20 descends below Porté-Puymorens towards the Cerdagne and shortly passes around the edge of **PORTA**, a small village of stone-built houses, narrow alleys, a squat church, hotel and a *gîte d'étape*. Of particular interest to trekkers, La Pastorale has 28 places and meals on offer (☎ 04 68 04 83 92, e-mail: enoff@wanadoo.fr). It is here that the GR7 crosses the Vallée du Carol and enters the **Vallée du Campcardos**, at the head of which the 2517m **Portella Blanca d'Envalira**, meeting place of the borders of France, Spain and Andorra, provides a trekker's route into Andorra by way of the Circ dels Pessons (see 5:3) and another into the head of Spain's Vall de la Llosa. The Portella is an old smuggler's pass where Andorran tobacco was transported, often at night, before heavy lorries grinding over the Envalira transformed the life of the *contrabandière*.

On the eastern side of the Andorran border at the head of the Campcardos valley lies a small group of lakes, the Éstanys des Passaderes, cradled among high pastures on the flank of Pic Nègre d'Envalira and just below the Coll des Isards, which presents a way over the northern ridge to Pas de la Casa not far from where the Ariège rises.

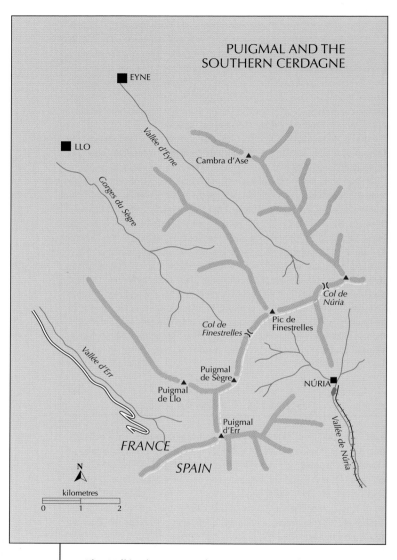

PUIGMAL AND THE SOUTHERN CERDAGNE

The Vallée du Campcardos is France's southernmost tributary hereabouts, for the border with Spain runs along the crest of the valley's south wall, whose highest point is the ⊗ **Puig de Campcardos** (Puig Pedros, 2905m), third highest summit east of Andorra after Pic Carlit and the Puigmal. A non-technical ascent of this mountain is made in 3–3½hrs from Porta, while some interesting rock routes exist on the nearby Pic de Peiraforca.

Beyond the entrance to the Vallée du Campcardos, the road descends past the Tours de Carol, two ruined towers built on a great lump of rock in order to defend the Cerdagne against the attentions of the Counts of Foix. Below these the valley becomes less severe as it begins to open out on the approach to **LATOUR-DE-CAROL** and **ENVEITG**. Between the two is sited the Gare Internationale, where the Toulouse–Barcelona railway line enters Spain. It is here too that the narrow-gauge **Train Jaune** (known affectionately as 'the little yellow train') begins its 2½hr, 62km journey through the Cerdagne to Villefranche-de-Conflent. Decorated in the Catalan colours of red and yellow, this predominantly single-track tourist railway, which began life as an important local service over a century ago, negotiates the Têt gorges east of Mont-Louis with some spectacular viaducts, tunnels and bridges.

The Franco-Spanish border kinks here, the road and railway both making a sharp northerly twist where the road divides. While N20 corrects itself again to swing round to the south, D618 breaks away to the north in order to skirt the foothills of the Carlit massif. This road takes the sunny, south-facing side of the Cerdagne known locally as La Soulane, which boasts the sunshine record for all France.

At **ANGOUSTRINE** there's a *gîte d'étape* with 20 places, Cal Xandera (☎ 04 68 04 61 67), on the route of the Tour du Carlit which cuts into the valley stretching north behind the village on the way to Lac des Bouillouses. The D618 twists out of the village and comes to the **Chaos de Targasonne**, a deposit of granite boulders dumped by Quarternary glaciers. Just beyond this a fine view south and east shows the long line of mountains across the valley stretching from the Puigmal to the Canigou, while the more distant and ragged peaks of the Sierra del Cadí appear beyond the main chain.

In his 1909 book, Hilaire Belloc says that the Cerdagne is best approached from the west, where the view is of

Hilaire Belloc described the Cerdagne as being 'broad as a small English county might be'

'a whole country side as broad as a small English county might be, full of fields, and large enough to take abreast a whole series of market towns… This picture is framed in two great lines of hills roughly parallel to each other, and the effect when one comes upon it out of the last of the narrow valleys, may be compared to the effect upon a child's mind when he first sees the sea.' (*The Pyrenees*, Methuen, 1909)

Close to **ODEILLO** stands the huge concave mirror of the now obsolete Four Solaire, a solar reflector consisting of 9500 individual mirrors angled to concentrate the sun's rays into a central area of just 80cm, where temperatures exceeding 3500°C have been achieved. Odeillo itself has a *gîte d'étape* with 33 dormitory places, open from June to November (☎ 04 68 30 25 48, e-mail: gite.cariolettes@wanadoo. fr), and a station on the Train Jaune line. **FONT-ROMEU** is next, a purpose-built resort built around a 14th-century shrine, backed by pinewoods and with a panoramic view across the Cerdagne (for tourist information, ☎ 04 68 30 68 30). Despite a range of accommodation and facilities, the town has little to hold the walker or climber, although the HRP passes through on an easy stage from Lac des Bouillouses to Eyne. But Font-Romeu comes alive in winter as a ski resort in common with nearby **PYRÉNÉES 2000**, the architecturally hideous winter sports resort of Superbolquère. The two resorts share around 50km of pistes and more than 400 snow cannons as a back-up in the event of poor natural snow cover, and the various lift systems are mostly focused on the 2204m Roc de la Calme.

Below Bolquère the GR10 crosses the valley at the 1581m **Col de la Perche**. This marks the Cerdagne watershed, for while all rivers in this section of the Pyrenees eventually find their way to the Mediterranean, streams west of this modest road pass feed into the Riu Segre, which flows southwest to join the Ebro, while east of Col de la Perche the Têt drains northeast through deep gorges to Perpignan. The gorges begin near **MONT-LOUIS**, the austere little garrison town fortified in 1679 by Vauban, which acts not only as the eastern gateway to the Cerdagne, but also to the Carlit massif by way of a narrow road which rises through forest to Lac des Bouillouses (described in 5:5).

THE CERDAGNE'S SOUTH FLANK

The south side of the Cerdagne (l'Ombrée – the 'shady side') is distinguished by a series of pleasant little villages built at the mouth of tributary valleys flowing from the green, rolling Puigmal range. When approaching from the Vallée du Carol in the north, the N20 runs initially alongside the Franco-Spanish border which separates French **BOURG-MADAME** from Spanish **PUIGCERDÀ** by a strip of less than 2km. A little to the east of these the nondescript Spanish enclave of **LLIVIA** is the result of a curious throwback to the 1659 Treaty of the Pyrenees, but scenically this end of the Cerdagne has little to excite the imagination. The Carlit massif on the north side of the valley is confused by intervening hills, and the southern heights are severely foreshortened. But by travelling just a short distance from Bourg-Madame on N116, you come to a sign indicating the village of **ERR** just off to the right, where the landscape suddenly becomes more interesting.

At the head of the Vallée d'Err stands the 2910m frontier summit of the Puigmal (or Puigmal d'Err to be correct) which, despite being the second highest in the Eastern Pyrenees, happens to be one of the easiest of all to reach. A small 17-place *gîte d'étape* (☎ 04 68 04 74 20) in the village caters for walkers and trekkers passing through and serves as a base for a few days' exploration of the neighbourhood.

- Towards the head of the valley a low-key ski station has a top lift at more than 2500m on the Pic de Duraneu, and a road runs up the valley to service it. This road considerably shortens the approach for walkers intending to scale the ◌★ **Puigmal**, reducing the time to reach the summit from the roadhead to about 2¾hrs. (If you are without transport, it might be worth splashing out on a taxi ride as far as this roadhead.) Rather than return by the same route, you could make a ◯ 5hr circuit by descending north along the frontier ridge to a 2760m col, then ascending the **Petit Puigmal de Sègre** (2810m), which serves as a cornerstone for both the Vallée d'Err and the Vallée du Sègre. Here you abandon the main frontier crest and turn left to gain the summit of the 2767m **Puigmal de Llo** on the ridge between the Err and Sègre valleys. From this minor top descend its southwest spur for about 150m, then turn left (southeast) into a little valley draining down into the main Err tributary in order to get back to the roadhead.

The nearest station on the Train Jaune railway line is at **SAILLAGOUSE,** which along with nearby **LLO** gives access to the Gorges du Sègre. On the edge of Saillagouse there are two campsites, while the Hôtel Planes is situated within the village itself on the place de Cerdagne. There's also a youth hostel here (☎ 04 68 04 71 69), while the much smaller village of Llo, which is noted for its fine Romanesque church and a ruined watchtower standing above it, has accommodation in a 20-place *gîte d'étape* (☎ 04 68 04 19 68).

- The gloomily dramatic **Gorges du Sègre** cut into the mountains immediately behind Llo, and even when their walls eventually slacken their grip the valley remains a deep V-shaped shaft. A forest track has been engineered through the ravine but is closed to unauthorised vehicles after about 3½km. After another 3km the track reaches the simple **Refuge de la Culasse**, and from there a ◯ path strikes up the headwall hillside aiming for the Col de Finestrelles, which overlooks the splendid amphitheatre of Núria. Instead of descending into Spain, go along the frontier crest heading south to gain the **Puigmal de Sègre** (2843m), about 45mins from the col.

The last of these southern valleys to drain into the Cerdagne is the **Vallée d'Eyne**, long recognised for its botanical riches and for the importance of the Col de Núria at its head as a major route of bird migration. Most of the valley is now protected as a *réserve naturelle*. Just below its entrance **EYNE** makes an attractive village base for a few days of a walking or botanical holiday, with a two-star hotel, Le Roc Blanc, and a 16-place *gîte d'étape* (☎ 04 68 04 06 96) providing accommodation. The Pyrenean High Route marches through the valley and climbs to the 2670m **Col de Núria** by a path that has become a popular section of a multi-day walk for commercial groups that cross into Spain at the col and spend the next night in the great basin of Núria (see 5:7). The **Cambra d'Ase** (Cambre d'Aze, 2711m) on the east side of the valley, a little over 4km from Eyne, is usually ascended in less than 3hrs from the ski station of Eyne 2600. Looking out to Mont-Louis, the North Face of Cambra d'Ase has a couple of spurs which hold rock climbs of some interest, as well as one or two gullies that, when in condition, provide some entertaining ice routes of around 200–250m. The classic route here is the ❻ *Couloir Vermicelle*, a 280m winter climb (grade PD) created in 1962 by the talented rope of Anglada, Guillamon, Pons and Riera. Farther along the same crest as that which supports Cambra d'Ase, the ❻ 2850m **Tour d'Eyne** is also worth a winter visit for the *Couloir Nord*, which gives a 250m climb graded AD-.

➲ A Tour of the Cerdagne

This basic four-day itinerary could be extended by spending extra days exploring the country around Núria and Lac des Bouillouses in order to create a full and active holiday.

Day 1: From **ERR** ascend the Puigmal d'Err as described above, and then continue north along the frontier crest over the Petit Puigmal and on to the Puigmal de Sègre. The ridge continues a little east of north and drops to the Col de Finestrelles (2604m), at which point bear right and descend southeastward, losing about 650m, to reach **NÚRIA** in its large open basin dominated by a complex of buildings around the Santuario (see 5:7).

Day 2: Return to France and the Cerdagne by way of the Col de Núria, which is due north of the Santuario. From the col a well-used path descends through the Vallée d'Eyne to **EYNE**.

Day 3: Cross the Cerdagne by way of the Col de la Perche where you meet the GR10, then follow this up the north flank of the valley as far as the **LAC DES BOUILLOUSES** on the eastern edge of the Carlit massif. Accommodation details are given in 5:5.

Day 4: To complete the Tour of the Cerdagne, leave Lac des Bouillouses heading south and southwest, walking down through the Angoustrine valley to Angoustrine, Villeneuve-des-Escaldes, Ur and **BOURG-MADAME**, which has a station on the Train Jaune railway line.

5:7 VALL DE NÚRIA

Travelling east through the broad Sègre valley along N260 south of Andorra, the impressive wall of the Sierra del Cadí is seen standing well back to the right, parallel to the Pyrenean chain but not part of it. On arrival at Puigcerdà at the western end of the Cerdagne another road, N152, runs off at a right angle, heading south alongside the Barcelona railway line then climbing among broom-covered hillsides to the 1800m Collada de Toses on the edge of the Puigmal range in a district known as the Pirineu de Gerona. It's a splendid journey.

Over the pass the road makes a long contour before embarking on an erratic descent to the deep valley of the Rigard and passing through **PLANOLES**, a pleasant small town with a 170-bed youth hostel, Albergue Pere Figuera (☎ 972 73 61 77), and a campsite a little higher on the route of GR11. Trekkers following GR11 arrive in Planoles after a very long stage from Puigcerdà, and after spending a night there set off to cross a spur projecting from Puig de Dorria on the way to Queralbs and the Vall de Núria.

Seven kilometres from Planoles N152 enters **RIBES DE FRESER**, where the Rigard joins the Riu Freser. This unexceptional workaday town (altitude 912m) serves as the southern gateway to the beautiful Vall de Núria. Although one would not automatically choose to stay in Ribes, there's plenty of accommodation should you run out of time to go elsewhere, in which case the tourist office by the church on Plaça de l'Ajuntament will advise on availability. Ribes is not only well served by the Barcelona–Puigcerdà line, but is also the terminus of the rack-and-pinion **Cremallera** railway, a Spanish equivalent of the Train Jaune which runs through the Cerdagne on the other side

The Cremallera works its way into the Núria gorge above Queralbs

of the mountains. Unless you're prepared to walk all the way, the Cremallera is the only means of reaching Núria at the head of the valley, although a narrow road pushes upstream for another 7km to Queralbs (1220m), where an intermediate station is located.

Trim, attractive and well cared for, **QUERALBS** is a neatly restored stone-built village that appears to hang from the steep hillside near the entrance to the Núria gorge. Visited by the GR11, the village has *hostal* accommodation, bars, restaurants and shops, and some exquisite rugged country on its doorstep.

Núria lies 700m higher and 6½km north of Queralbs, a 20min journey by the Cremallera or ●★ 2½hrs along the GR11. The path, at first among broom and fragrant box shrubs, accompanies the railway for part of the route – sometimes beside it, sometimes above and occasionally below it. And the walk is a delight all the way. Not long after leaving Queralbs the valley forks and there's a direct view northeast into the **Gorges del Freser**, at the head of which stand the twin peaks of the Gra de Fajol, where some fine ice climbs have been made in recent years.

Immediately beyond the entrance to the Freser gorge, GR11 enters the **Gorges de Núria**, a dramatic section of towering walls and steep slopes plunging to the river. The path angles down and crosses to the east side by the arched Pont del Cremat, then zigzags to regain height. Working through the gorge the scenery is constantly changing but always dramatic, with overhanging cliffs, shallow caves, exposed drops and waterfalls cascading down the opposite wall. Near the head of the gorge the path eases to river level and crosses again by a suspension bridge directly beneath the railway. Then it's up a slope among alpenrose, juniper and pine to gain a grassy shoulder with a sudden view into an extraordinary open basin with a man-made lake below, meadows beyond and grass slopes rising to big hills that

The Núria gorge

carry the border with France. But most of all, one's attention is caught by a vast three-sided complex of barrack-like buildings at 1967m, hideously out of place in what Paul Lucia, in his guide to the GR11, rightly describes as 'the middle of nowhere'.

This is the **Santuario de Núria**, founded in the 11th century but now absorbed within a block that comprises hotel, restaurant, ski centre, church and tourist office (for information, ☎ 972 73 20 20, www.valldenuria.com). The Cremallera station is just to the right of the complex, and there's a 130-place youth hostel, Albergue Pic de l'Aliga (☎ 972 73 00 48), built impressively at the top of the ski centre's cable car – not as shown on the Carte de Randonnées. A camping area is found northwest of the Santuario, with a nearby café, toilet and shower block.

The crescent of hills which forms a backdrop rises to over 2800m, but because they're grass-covered, and the valley floor is reasonably high anyway, the individual tops give no impression of great height. Were these bare of grass and ragged like those of the Carlit massif, they would appear far more impressive, like real mountains.

The highest summit of the crescent is the 2910m **Puigmal d'Err**, unseen from the basin floor as it stands back to the southwest and is lost behind a pushy forward slope. From it the frontier crest curves gently round in a graceful clockwise arc that dips here and there to walkers' passes that suggest ways over to the Cerdagne (see 5:6). There's the **Col de Finestrelles** (2684m), by which you could cross to Err, Llo or Saillagouse; **Col de Núria** (2670m), from which you can join the HRP for descent into the Vallée d'Eyne; or you could perhaps follow GR11 up to the 2645m **Collado de Noufonts**, where you then remain high to work a way eastward to Pic de la Vaca before cutting away from the frontier crest in order to reach the Refugio de Ull de Ter. But that would lead beyond the geographical limits of this book, away from the High Pyrenees and across the declining hills of eastern Catalonia to the Mediterranean.

Núria, a sanctuary in every sense of the word, below the Puigmal crest

Sierra del Cadí

Viewed from a distance of 10km on the Seu d'Urgell to Puigcerdà road, the north flank of the Sierra del Cadí gives the appearance of being a vast blank wall of limestone. Extending west to east for around 20km between Cap de la Fesa and Coll de Tancalaporta, these mountains form the western half of the Parc Natural Cadí-Moixeró, a wonderfully undeveloped reserve inaugurated in 1983 and now containing Spain's largest herd of isard. Separate from the main range, the Sierra del Cadí is one of the many pre-Pyrenean massifs which, though being considerably lower than major summits of the High Pyrenees, nonetheless have an appeal all their own. A number of paths and tracks either run along the foot of the massif or cross from one side to the other to invite exploration, and two *refugis* provide accommodation. On the north side **Refugi de Prat d'Aguilo** (also known as Refugi César Augus Torras) stands at 2037m below the Pas dels Gosolans, has room for 36 and is manned in summer (☎ 973 25 01 35), while south of the Cadí block **Refugi Lluís Estasén** (1640m) is used as a base for the ascent of the ever-popular **Pedraforca** (2497m). Named after the climber who pioneered hard routes on Pedraforca's North Face in the 1920s, the Estasén hut is a large one with room for 100 and, like the Prat d'Aguilo, has showers and meals provision (☎ 608 31 53 12). It is open throughout the year. Both *refugis* are owned by the FEEC. There's also simple mattress accommodation available in a barn near the hamlet of Estana, southwest of Martinet – apply at the Fonda di Cai Basté (☎ 973 51 53 45).

Despite the modest altitude and proximity to the Mediterranean, the Sierra del Cadí receives a surprising amount of snow, and when consolidated (usually from January to April) gives good climbing in the gullies, or *canals*, that streak the north-facing walls. The central part of the massif, which includes the highest summit, Puig de la Canal Baridana (2648m), receives the most attention from climbers in summer and in winter, thanks to comparative ease of access from Estana, which in turn is reached by road from Martinet on the N260. Most routes are 300–400m high and lie in the middle grades, although some lines are as much as 500m and graded a very respectable TD. *Escalades al Parque Natural del Cadí* by Jaume Matas is the local Catalan-language guide, and a route book is kept at the Cai Basté bar-restaurant in Estana. See also *Pyrénées – Courses Mixtes, Neige et Glace* by Francis Mousel.

The distinctive twin-peaked Pedraforca is linked to the Cadí by a short ridge-spur and is best approached from the road south of the Túnel del Cadí, where a side-road leads for about 16km to Saldes, a small village at the foot of the mountain and a good place from which to explore the south side of the massif. The Lluis Estasén *refugi* is an hour's walk from the village, although a partly paved road extends to a car park and the Mirador de Gresolet, within a 15min approach to the hut.

Whilst the majority of ascents of Pedraforca are made by walkers and trekkers, the formidable 800m north wall which soars above the hut has a number of lines for climbers in the middle grades, as well as the classic Anglada/Guillamon route on the North Buttress which is 600m high and graded TD+ (V+/A2) (see *Les Pyrénées, les 100 Plus Belles Courses et Randonnées* by Patrice de Bellefon and *Escalades al Parque del Cadi* by Jaume Matas).

Maps to use are the Editorial Alpina *Serra del Cadí/Pedraforca* at 1:25,000, with accompanying brief guide, and *Cerdanya* at 1:50,000

ACCESS, BASES, MAPS AND GUIDES

Access

Vallée du Vicdessos N20 from Toulouse south through Foix to Tarascon-sur-Ariège, then southwest along D8. Trains from Foix to Tarascon, and bus to Vicdessos and Auzat.

Haute Vallée de l'Ariège A continuation of N20 south of Tarascon to L'Hospitalet-Près-l'Andorre. The whole valley is served by the Toulouse–Latour-de-Carol–Barcelona railway.

Andorra N22 from l'Hospitalet to Pas de la Casa, then CG2 as far as Andorra-la-Vella, and CG1 from there to the Spanish border. Approaching from Spain N145 leads from La Seu d'Urgell to the Andorran border. Daily bus services from l'Hospitalet, Barcelona and La Seu d'Urgell to Andorra-la-Vella. Domestic bus services within Andorra journey between the capital and Arinsal, El Serrat, Encamp, Soldeu and Pas de la Casa. The nearest airport is at Toulouse, from which a twice-daily minibus service connects with Andorra – reservations essential (e-mail: novatel@andorrabybus.com).

Vallée d'Orlu D22 southeast of Ax-les-Thermes. No access by public transport.

The Carlit Massif From the west via N20 south of Col de Puymorens; trains to Porté-Puymorens and Latour de Carol; bus from Andorra-la-Vella to Porté. From the south via D618 Ur to Mont-Louis; Train Jaune stations at Odeillo, Boquère and Mont-Louis.

The Cerdagne D618 Ur to Mont-Louis for the northern slope, N116 between Bourg-Madame and Mont-Louis for the south and central Cerdagne. The Train Jaune (Latour de Carol to Villefranche-de-Conflent) travels through the valley serving many villages.

Vall de Núria N152 Puigcerdà–Ripoll road as far as Ribes de Freser, then minor road north to Queralbs. The Barcelona–Latour de Carol railway has a station at Ribes de Freser, and from there by way of the Cremallera railway to Núria via Queralbs.

Valley Bases

Vallée du Vicdessos Vicdessos, Auzat

Haute Vallée de l'Ariège Ax-les-Thermes, Mérens-les-Vals

Andorra Soldeu, Canillo, Encamp, Ordino, El Serrat, Arinsal

Vallée d'Orlu Orlu

The Carlit Massif Porté-Puymorens

The Cerdagne Saillagouse, Eyne

Vall de Núria Queralbs, Núria

Huts

Most of the mountain regions covered by this chapter are equipped with huts, although many are unmanned. Andorra only has one manned refugi, but 24 others offering varying degrees of comfort.

Maps

IGN Top 25: 2148OT *Vicdessos, Pics d'Estats et de Montcalm*, 2148ET *Ax-les-Thermes*, 2249OT *Bourg-Madame, Col de Puymorens, Pic Carlit*, 2249ET *Font Romeu, Capcir*, 2250ET *Bourg-Madame, Mont-Louis, Col de la Perche* at 1:25,000

Cartes de Randonnées: *7 Haute-Ariège Andorre, 8 Cerdagne-Capcir* at 1:50,000

M.I. Govern *Andorra* at 1:50,000 and 1:25,000

Editorial Alpina: *Cerdanya* at 1:50,000 *Serra del Cadí/Pedraforca* at 1:25,000

Walking and/or Trekking Guides

Walks and Climbs in the Pyrenees by Kev Reynolds
(Cicerone Press, 5th edn, 2008)

The GR10 Trail by Paul Lucia (Cicerone Press, 2003)

Through the Spanish Pyrenees: GR11 by Paul Lucia
(Cicerone Press, 4th edn, 2008)

The Pyrenean Haute Route by Ton Joosten (Cicerone Press, 2nd edn, 2009)

Trekking in the Pyrenees by Douglas Streatfeild-James
(Trailblazer, 3rd edn, 2005)

The Mountains of Andorra by Alf Robertson and Jane Meadowcroft (Cicerone Press, 2005)

Guia Montanera: Andorra by Figuera and Brosel (Sua Edizoak, Bilbao, 1998)

Walking in Spain by Miles Roddis et al (Lonely Planet, 2nd edn, 1999)

Pyrenees East by Arthur Battagel (West Col)

Andorra and the Serra del Cadí by Jacqueline Oglesby (Inghams)

Randonnées dans les Pyrénées Ariègeoises by Georges Véron and Michel Grassaud
(Rando Editions)

Randonnées dans les Pyrénées Orientales by Georges Véron
(Rando Editions)

Balades en Raquettes dans les Pyrénées – Cerdagne, Capcir, Haut Conflent by Ronald
Berger (Rando Editions)

Le Guide Rando – Haute-Ariège by Georges Véron and Michell Grassaud (Rando Editions)

Le Guide Rando – Cerdagne et Capcir by Georges Véron (Rando Editions)

Climbing Guides

Pyrénées – Courses Mixtes, Neige et Glace by Francis Mousel
(Éditions Franck Mercier, 1997)

Escalade en Haute Vallée de l'Ariège by Thierry and Colette Pouxviel

Escalades al Parque del Cadi by Jaume Matas

Itineraris pel Pirineu Andorra: Ascensions i Escalades by Joan Prat (Viladomat Esports, 1991)

Escalada a Andorra by Carlo Ferrari (Federacion Andorran de Muntabyismo, 2001)

See Also

Classic Walks in the Pyrenees by Kev Reynolds
(Oxford Illustrated Press, 1989)

Long Distance Walks in the Pyrenees by Chris Townsend
(Crowood Press, 1991)

Les Pyrénées – Les 100 Plus Belles Courses et Randonnées by Patrice de Bellefon (Editions Denoël, 1976)

Rough Guide to the Pyrenees by Marc Dubin
(Rough Guides, 4th edn, 2001)

100 Sommets des Pyrénées by Georges Véron (Rando Editions, 2001)

APPENDIX A
A PYRENEAN GLOSSARY

Abri — basic shelter, suitable for bivouac

Agua/aigue/aygue — water, a stream

Aiguille/agulle — pinnacle, slender mountain peak

Arres — fissured limestone rocks

Arribet/arrieu/aigüeta — small stream

Arrouy/rouyo/royo — red

Arroyo — a stream

Artiga/artigue — pasture or forest clearing

Barranc/barranco — a gorge or ravine

Bat/bal — valley

Barrage — dam

Bieilh/vielh — old

Blanque/blanca — white

Borde/borda — a stable, barn or sheepfold

Boum — a small deep lake

Brèche — narrow rocky pass or gap

Cabane/cabaña — shepherd's hut

Caillaou/calhaù — isolated rock

Caillaouas — rubble or scree

Cami — drover's track

Campana — pointed rock

Cap — prominent point on a ridge

Caperan — individual rock tower

Cirque/circ — mountain amphitheatre

Clot — a depression or mountain basin

Col/cuelo — a pass or saddle

Collade — a broad or easy pass

Coma/coume — a bare slope

Corral — animal enclosure

Cortal — shepherd's hut

Desfiladero/garganta — gorge

Embalse — reservoir

Estang/étang/estany — mountain lake

Estibe/estive — summer pasture

Faja — natural limestone terrace

Font/fount/fuente — a spring or source of a river

Forat/fourat — a deep hole, cave or chasm

Forc/fourc/fourcat — a fork or separation

Gave — mountain river

Gorg/gourg — a deep mountain lake

Grange/granja — barn

Grau — a pass

Güell — a resurgence

Hont/hount — see font

Hourquette — steep pass

Ibón — small mountain lake

Jasse — mountain pasture

Lago/lac — lake

Laquette/laqueta — small lake

Mal/mail — ancient term for rocks

Marcadau/marcat — market place

Mas/masia — a farm

Neste — mountain river

Noguera — river

Orri — simple shelter of stone, often turf-roofed

Oule/oulette — mountain basin

Parador — Spanish state-owned hotel

Pas/passet/passe — a narrow or difficult section

Passerelle/passarella — suspension bridge

Peña/peyre — steep cliff or prominent outcrop

Pic/puig — peak

Pista — dirt road or track

Pla/plan — a plain or level ground

Port/porteille/puerto — a long-used pass

Prat/pradère/prado — meadowland

Punta/pujol/pouey — a high point or rock pinnacle

Quebe — rock shelter

Raillère/ralhère — scree chute

Ribera — river valley

Rio/riu — river

Salhèt — river bank

Salto — waterfall or cascade

Seil/seilh — glacier

Senda — footpath

Serra/sierra — mountain massif

Serre/serrat — a long or jagged ridge

Soula/solana/soulane — south-facing slope

Soum — a secondary, or rounded, summit

Tartera — scree slope

Tozal/tuc/tuqua — steep cliff

Trou — a deep hole or gulph

Turon — a secondary summit

Val/valle/vallée/vallon — valley

Veinat — district or neighbourbood

APPENDIX B
INDEX OF PYRENEAN VALLEYS – WEST TO EAST

APPENDIX C
INDEX OF MAPS

INDEX

INDEX

LISTING OF CICERONE GUIDES

EUROPEAN CYCLING
Cycle Touring in France
Cycle Touring in Ireland
Cycle Touring in Spain
Cycle Touring in Switzerland
Cycling in the French Alps
Cycling the Canal du Midi
Cycling the River Loire
The Danube Cycleway
The Grand Traverse of the Massif Central
The Way of St James

AFRICA
Climbing in the Moroccan Anti-Atlas
Kilimanjaro: A Complete Trekker's Guide
Trekking in the Atlas Mountains
Walking in the Drakensberg

ALPS – CROSS-BORDER ROUTES
100 Hut Walks in the Alps
Across the Eastern Alps: E5
Alpine Points of View
Alpine Ski Mountaineering
 1 Western Alps
 2 Central and Eastern Alps
Chamonix to Zermatt
Snowshoeing
Tour of Mont Blanc
Tour of Monte Rosa
Tour of the Matterhorn
Walking in the Alps
Walks and Treks in the Maritime Alps

PYRENEES AND FRANCE/SPAIN CROSS-BORDER ROUTES
Rock Climbs In The Pyrenees
The GR10 Trail
The Mountains of Andorra
The Pyrenean Haute Route
The Pyrenees
The Way of St James
 France
 Spain
Through the Spanish Pyrenees: GR11
Walks and Climbs in the Pyrenees

AUSTRIA
Klettersteig – Scrambles in the Northern Limestone Alps
Trekking in Austria's Hohe Tauern
Trekking in the Stubai Alps
Trekking in the Zillertal Alps
Walking in Austria

EASTERN EUROPE
The High Tatras
The Mountains of Romania
Walking in Bulgaria's National Parks
Walking in Hungary

FRANCE
Ecrins National Park
GR20: Corsica
Mont Blanc Walks
The Cathar Way
The GR5 Trail
The Robert Louis Stevenson Trail
Tour of the Oisans: The GR54
Tour of the Queyras
Tour of the Vanoise

Trekking in the Vosges and Jura
Vanoise Ski Touring
Walking in Provence
Walking in the Cathar Region
Walking in the Cevennes
Walking in the Dordogne
Walking in the Haute Savoie
 North & South
Walking in the Languedoc
Walking in the Tarentaise and Beaufortain Alps
Walking on Corsica
Walking the French Gorges
Walks in Volcano Country

GERMANY
Germany's Romantic Road
King Ludwig Way
Walking in the Bavarian Alps
Walking in the Harz Mountains
Walking in the Salzkammergut
Walking the River Rhine Trail

HIMALAYA
Annapurna: A Trekker's Guide
Bhutan
Everest: A Trekker's Guide
Garhwal and Kumaon: A Trekker's and Visitor's Guide
Kangchenjunga: A Trekker's Guide
Langtang with Gosainkund and Helambu: A Trekker's Guide
Manaslu: A Trekker's Guide
The Mount Kailash Trek

IRELAND
Irish Coastal Walks
The Irish Coast to Coast Walk
The Mountains of Ireland

ITALY
Central Apennines of Italy
Gran Paradiso
Italian Rock
Italy's Sibillini National Park
Shorter Walks in the Dolomites
Through the Italian Alps
Trekking in the Apennines
Treks in the Dolomites
Via Ferratas of the Italian Dolomites Vols 1 & 2
Walking in Sicily
Walking in the Central Italian Alps
Walking in the Dolomites
Walking in Tuscany
Walking on the Amalfi Coast

MEDITERRANEAN
Jordan – Walks, Treks, Caves, Climbs and Canyons
The Ala Dag
The High Mountains of Crete
The Mountains of Greece
Treks and Climbs in Wadi Rum, Jordan
Walking in Malta
Western Crete

NORTH AMERICA
British Columbia
The Grand Canyon
The John Muir Trail
The Pacific Crest Trail

SOUTH AMERICA
Aconcagua and the Southern Andes
Torres del Paine

SCANDINAVIA
Trekking in Greenland
Walking in Norway

SLOVENIA, CROATIA AND MONTENEGRO
The Julian Alps of Slovenia
The Mountains of Montenegro
Trekking in Slovenia
Walking in Croatia

SPAIN AND PORTUGAL
Costa Blanca Walks
 1 West
 2 East
Mountain Walking in Southern Catalunya
The Mountains of Central Spain
Trekking through Mallorca
Via de la Plata
Walking in Madeira
Walking in Mallorca
Walking in the Algarve
Walking in the Canary Islands
 2 East
Walking in the Cordillera Cantabrica
Walking in the Sierra Nevada
Walking on La Gomera and El Hierro
Walking on La Palma
Walking the GR7 in Andalucia
Walks and Climbs in the Picos de Europa

SWITZERLAND
Alpine Pass Route
Central Switzerland
The Bernese Alps
Tour of the Jungfrau Region
Walking in the Valais
Walking in Ticino
Walks in the Engadine

TECHNIQUES
Indoor Climbing
Map and Compass
Mountain Weather
Moveable Feasts
Outdoor Photography
Rock Climbing
Snow and Ice Techniques
Sport Climbing
The Book of the Bivvy
The Hillwalker's Guide to Mountaineering
The Hillwalker's Manual

MINI GUIDES
Avalanche!
Navigating with a GPS
Navigation
Pocket First Aid and Wilderness Medicine
Snow

For full and up-to-date information on our ever-expanding list of guides, visit our website:
www.cicerone.co.uk.

Cicerone's mission is to inform and inspire by providing the best guides to exploring the world

Since its foundation 40 years ago, Cicerone has specialised in publishing guidebooks and has built a reputation for quality and reliability. It now publishes nearly 300 guides to the major destinations for outdoor enthusiasts, including Europe, UK and the rest of the world.

Written by leading and committed specialists, Cicerone guides are recognised as the most authoritative. They are full of information, maps and illustrations so that the user can plan and complete a successful and safe trip or expedition – be it a long face climb, a walk over Lakeland fells, an alpine cycling tour, a Himalayan trek or a ramble in the countryside.

With a thorough introduction to assist planning, clear diagrams, maps and colour photographs to illustrate the terrain and route, and accurate and detailed text, Cicerone guides are designed for ease of use and access to the information.

If the facts on the ground change, or there is any aspect of a guide that you think we can improve, we are always delighted to hear from you.

Cicerone Press
2 Police Square Milnthorpe Cumbria LA7 7PY
Tel: 015395 62069 Fax: 015395 63417
info@cicerone.co.uk www.cicerone.co.uk